ISBN 978-1-330-51524-2
PIBN 10072341

Forgotten Books is a registered trademark of FB &c Ltd.
Copyright © 2018 FB &c Ltd.
FB &c Ltd, Dalton House, 60 Windsor Avenue, London, SW19 2RR.
Company number 08720141. Registered in England and Wales.

For support please visit www.forgottenbooks.com

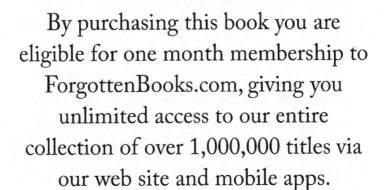

THEOLOGICAL TRANSLATION LIBRARY

VOL. XIX

HARNACK'S THE MISSION AND EXPANSION OF CHRISTIANITY IN THE FIRST THREE CENTURIES

VOL. I

THE
MISSION AND EXPANSION
OF CHRISTIANITY IN THE
FIRST THREE CENTURIES

BY

ADOLF HARNACK

PROFESSOR OF CHURCH HISTORY IN THE UNIVERSITY OF BERLIN, AND
MEMBER OF THE ROYAL PRUSSIAN ACADEMY

Translated and edited by

JAMES MOFFATT, B.D., D.D. (St Andrews)

SECOND, ENLARGED AND REVISED EDITION

VOL. I

WILLIAMS AND NORGATE

14 HENRIETTA STREET, COVENT GARDEN, LONDON
NEW YORK: G. P. PUTNAM'S SONS
1908

TRANSLATOR'S PREFACE

DR HARNACK opened the course of lectures which have been translated in this library under the title *What is Christianity?* with a reference to John Stuart Mill. The present work might also be introduced by a sentence from the same English thinker. In the second chapter of his essay upon "Liberty," he has occasion to speak with admiration and regret of the Emperor Marcus Aurelius, confessing that his persecution of the Christians seems "one of the most tragical facts in all history." "It is a bitter thought," he adds, "how different a thing the Christianity of the world might have been, if the Christian faith had been adopted as the religion of the empire under the auspices of Marcus Aurelius instead of those of Constantine." Aurelius represents the apex of paganism during the first three centuries of our era. Chronologically, too, he stands almost equidistant between Christ and Constantine. But there were reasons why the adjustment of the empire to Christianity could not come earlier than the first quarter of the fourth century, and it is Dr Harnack's task in the present work to outline these reasons in so far as they are connected with the extension and expansion of Christianity itself. How did the new religion come to win official recognition from the state in A.D. 325? Why then? Why not till then? Such is the problem set to the historian of the Christian propaganda by the ante-Nicene period. He has to explain how and why and where, within less than three centuries, an Oriental religious movement which was originally a mere ripple on a single wave of dissent in the wide sea of paganism, rose into a breaker which swept before it the vested interests, prejudices, traditions, and authority of the most powerful social and political organization that the world hitherto had known. The main causes and courses of this transition, with all that it involves of the inner life and worship of the religion, form Dr Harnack's topic in these pages.

In editing the book for an English audience I have slightly enlarged the index and added a list of New Testament passages referred to. Wherever a German or French book cited by the author has appeared in an English dress, the corresponding reference has been subjoined. Also, in deference to certain suggestions received by the publishers, I have added, wherever it has been advisable to do so, English versions of the Greek and Latin passages which form so valuable and characteristic a feature of Dr Harnack's historical discussions. It is hoped that the work may be thus rendered more intelligible and inviting than ever to that wider audience whose interest in early Christianity is allied to little or no Greek and Latin.

The first edition of this translation was issued in 1904–1905, and the first volume is now out of print. Meanwhile, Dr Harnack published, in 1906, a new edition of the original in two volumes, which has been so thoroughly revised and enlarged that, with its additions and omissions, it forms practically a new work. His own preface to the second edition gives no adequate idea of the care and skill with which nearly every page has been gone over in order to fill up any gaps and bring the work up to date. The present version has been made directly from this edition. I have taken the opportunity of correcting some misprints which crept into the first edition of my translation, and it is hoped that English readers will now be able to find easy access to this standard history in its final form.

PREFACE TO THE FIRST GERMAN EDITION

No monograph has yet been devoted to the mission and spread of the Christian religion during the first three centuries of our era. For the earliest period of church history we have sketches of the historical development of dogma and of the relation of the church to the state—the latter including Neumann's excellent volume. But the missionary history has always been neglected, possibly because writers have been discouraged by the difficulty of bringing the material to the surface and getting it arranged, or by the still more formidable difficulties of collecting and sifting the geographical data and statistics. The following pages are a first attempt, and for it I bespeak a kindly judgment. My successors, of whom there will be no lack, will be able to improve upon it.

I have one or two preliminary remarks to make, by way of explanation.

The primitive history of the church's missions lies buried in legend; or rather, it has been replaced by a history (which is strongly marked by tendency) of what is alleged to have happened in the course of a few decades throughout every country on the face of the earth. The composition of this history has gone on for more than a thousand years. The formation of legends in connection with the apostolic mission, which commenced as early as the first century, was still thriving in the Middle Ages; it thrives, in fact, down to the present day. But the worthless character of this history is now recognised on all sides, and in the present work I have hardly touched upon it, since I have steadily presupposed the results gained by the critical investigation of the sources. Whatever item from the apocryphal Acts, the local and provincial legends of the church, the episcopal lists, and the Acts of the martyrs, has *not* been inserted or noticed in these pages, has been deliberately omitted as useless. On the other hand, I have aimed at exhaustiveness in the treatment of reliable material. It is only the Acts and traditions of the martyrs that present any real difficulty, and from such sources this or that city may probably fall to be added to my lists. Still, the number of such addenda must be very small. Inscriptions, unfortunately, almost entirely fail us. Dated Christian inscriptions from the pre-Constantine age are rare, and only in the case of a few groups can we be sure that an undated inscription belongs to the third and not to the fourth century. Besides, the Christian origin of a very numerous class is merely a matter of conjecture, which cannot at present be established.

As the apostolic age of the church, in its entire sweep, falls within the purview of the history of Christian missions, some detailed account of this period might be looked for in these pages. No such account, however, will be found. For such a discussion one may turn to numerous works upon the subject, notably to that of Weizsäcker. After his labours, I had no intention of once more depicting Paul the missionary; I have simply confined myself to the general characteristics of the period. What is set down here must serve as its own justification. It appeared to me not unsuitable, under the circumstances, to attempt to do some justice to the problems in a series of longitudinal sections; thereby I hoped to avoid repetitions, and, above all, to bring out the main currents and forces of the Christian religion coherently and clearly. The separate chapters have been compiled in such a way that each may be read by itself; but this has not impaired the unity of the whole work, I hope.

The basis chosen for this account of the early history of Christian missions is no broader than my own general knowledge of history and of religion—which is quite slender. My book contains no information upon the history of Greek or Roman religion; it has no light to throw on primitive myths and later cults, or on matters of law and of administration. On such topics other scholars are better informed than I am. For many years it has been my sole endeavour to remove the barriers between us, to learn from my colleagues whatever is indispensable to a correct appreciation of such phenomena as they appear inside the province of church history, and to avoid presenting derived material as the product of original research.

With regard to ancient geography and statistics, I have noticed in detail, as the pages of my book will indicate, all relevant investigations. Unfortunately, works on the statistics of ancient population present results which are so contradictory as to be useless ; and at the last I almost omitted the whole of these materials in despair. All that I have actually retained is a scanty residue of reliable statistics in the opening chapter of Book I. and in the concluding paragraphs. In identifying towns and localities I have followed the maps in the *Corpus Inscriptionum Latinarum*, the small maps in the fifth volume of Mommsen's Roman History, Kiepert's *Formae orbis antiqui* (so far as these have appeared), and some other geographical guides ; no place which I have failed to find in these authorities has been inserted in my pages without some note or comment, the only exception being a few suburban villages. I had originally intended to furnish the book with maps, but as I went on I had reluctantly to abandon this idea. Maps, I was obliged to admit, would give a misleading impression of the actual situation. For one thing, the materials at our disposal for the various provinces up to 325 A.D. are too unequal, and little would be gained by merely marking the towns in which Christians can be shown to have existed previous to Constantine ; nor could I venture to indicate the density of the Christian population by means of colours. Maps cannot be drawn for any period earlier than the fourth century, and it is only by aid of these fourth-century maps that the previous course of the history can be viewed in retrospect.—The demarcation of the provinces, and the alterations which took place in their boundaries, formed a subject into which I had hardly any occasion to enter. Some account of the history of church-organization could not be entirely omitted, but questions of organization have only been introduced where they were unavoidable. My aim, as a rule, has been to be as brief as possible, to keep strictly within the limits of my subject, and never to repeat answers to any settled questions, either for the sake of completeness or of convenience to my readers. The history of the expansion of Christianity within the separate provinces has merely been sketched in outline. Anyone who desires further details must, of course, excavate with Ramsay in Phrygia and the French *savants* in Africa, or plunge with Duchesne into the ancient episcopal lists, although for the first three hundred years the results all over this field are naturally meagre.

The literary sources available for the history of primitive Christian missions are fragmentary. But how extensive they are, compared to the extant sources at our disposal for investigating the history of any other religion within the Roman empire! They not only render it feasible for us to attempt a sketch of the mission and expansion of Christianity which shall be coherent and complete in all its essential features, but also permit us to understand the reasons why this religion triumphed in the Roman empire, and how the triumph was achieved. At the same time, a whole series of queries remains unanswered, including those very questions that immediately occur to the mind of anyone who looks attentively into the history of Christian missions.

Several of my earlier studies in the history of Christian missions have been incorporated in the present volume, in an expanded and improved form. These I have noted as they occur.

I must cordially thank my honoured friend Professor Imelmann for the keen interest he has taken in these pages as they passed through the press.

A. HARNACK.

BERLIN, *Sept.* 4, 1902.

PREFACE TO THE SECOND GERMAN EDITION

THE second edition is about ten sheets larger than the first, six of these extra sheets falling within Book IV. The number of fresh places where I have been able to verify the existence of Christianity prior to Constantine is infinitesimally small; my critics have not been able to increase the list. But I have tried to put more colour into the description of the spread of the religion throughout the various provinces, and also to incorporate several out-of-the-way passages. Several new sections have been added; the excursus on the "Alleged Council of Antioch," at the close of the first book, has been omitted as superfluous, however, though not as erroneous. After my disclaimer in the preface to the first edition, some may be surprised to find that maps are now added. What determined me to take this step was the number of requests for them, based invariably on the opinion that the majority of readers cannot form any idea of the diffusion of Christianity unless they have maps, while the ordinary maps of the ancient world require detailed study in order to be of any use for this special purpose. Consequently, I have overcome my scruples and drawn the eleven maps which are appended to the second volume. I attach most importance to the attempt which I have made in the second map. It was a venture, but it sums up all the results of my work, and without it the following maps would be misleading, since they all depend more or less upon incidental information about the period.

The index I have worked over again myself.

A. H.

BERLIN, *Dec.* 1, 1905.

TABLE OF CONTENTS

BOOK I

INTRODUCTORY

BOOK II

MISSION-PREACHING IN WORD AND DEED

xiv CONTENTS

BOOK III

THE MISSIONARIES: THE METHODS OF THE MISSION AND THE COUNTER-MOVEMENTS

The
Mission and Expansion of Christianity in the First Three Centuries

———•———

BOOK I

INTRODUCTORY

CHAPTER I

JUDAISM: ITS DIFFUSION AND LIMITS

To nascent Christianity the synagogues in the Diaspora meant more than the *fontes persecutionum* of Tertullian's complaint; they also formed the most important presupposition for the rise and growth of Christian communities throughout the empire. The network of the synagogues furnished the Christian propaganda with centres and courses for its development, and in this way the mission of the new religion, which was undertaken in the name of the God of Abraham and Moses, found a sphere already prepared for itself.

Surveys of the spread of Judaism at the opening of our period have been often made, most recently and with especial care by Schürer (*Geschichte des jüdischen Volkes*, Bd. III.[(3)] pp. 1–38; Eng. trans., II. ii. 220 f.). Here we are concerned with the following points:

(1) There were Jews in most of the Roman provinces, at any rate in all those which touched or adjoined the Mediterranean, to say nothing of the Black Sea; eastward also, beyond Syria, they were thickly massed in Mesopotamia, Babylonia, and Media.[1]

---

[1] The conversion of the royal family of Adiabene (on the Tigris, at the frontier of the Roman Empire and of Parthia) to Judaism, during the reign of Claudius,

(2) Their numbers were greatest in Syria,[1] next to that in Egypt (in all the nomes as far as Upper Egypt),[2] Rome, and the provinces of Asia Minor.[3] The extent to which they had

is a fact of special moment in the history of the spread of Judaism, and Josephus gives it due prominence. A striking parallel, a century and a half later, is afforded by the conversion of the royal house of Edessa to Christianity. Renan (*Les Apôtres*, ch. xiv.) is not wrong when he remarks, in his own way, that "the royal family of Adiabene belongs to the history of Christianity." He does not mean to say, with Orosius (vii. 6) and Moses of Chorene (ii. 35), that they actually became Christians, but simply that "in embracing Judaism, they obeyed a sentiment which was destined to bring over the entire pagan world to Christianity." A further and striking parallel to the efforts of Queen Helena of Adiabene (cp. Jos., *Antiq.*, xx. 2 f.; *B.J.*, v. 2-4, v. 6. 1, vi. 6. 3) is to be found in the charitable activity of Constantine's mother, Queen Helena, in Jerusalem. Possibly the latter took the Jewish queen as her model, for Helena of Adiabene's philanthropy was still remembered in Jerusalem and by Jews in general (cp. Eus., *H.E.*, ii. 12, and the Talmudic tradition).—Comprehensive evidence for the spread of Judaism throughout the empire lies in Philo (*Legat.* 36 and *Flacc.* 7), Acts (ii. 9 f.), and Josephus (*Bell.*, ii. 16. 4, vii. 3. 3; *Apion*, ii. 39). The statement of Josephus (οὐκ ἔστιν ἐπὶ τῆς οἰκουμένης δῆμος ὃ μὴ μοῖραν ἡμετέραν ἔχων : "there is no people in the world which does not contain some part of us") had been anticipated more than two centuries earlier by a Jewish Sibylline oracle (*Sib. orac.*, iii. 271 πᾶσα δὲ γαῖα σέθεν πλήρης καὶ πᾶσα θάλασσα : "every land and sea is filled with thee "). By 139-138 B.C. a decree for the protection of Jews had been issued by the Roman Senate to the kings of Egypt, Syria, Pergamum, Cappadocia and Parthia, as well as to Sampsamê (Amisus?), Sparta, Sicyon (in the Peloponnese), Delos, Samos, the town of Gortyna, Caria and Myndus, Halicarnassus and Cnidus, Cos and Rhodes, the province of Lycia together with Phaselis, Pamphilia with Sidê, the Phœnician town Aradus, Cyrene and Cyprus. By the time of Sulla, Strabo had written thus (according to Josephus, *Antiq.*, xiv. 7. 2): εἰς πᾶσαν πόλιν ἤδη παρελήλυθει, καὶ τόπον οὐκ ἔστι ῥᾳδίως εὑρεῖν τῆς οἰκουμένης ὃς οὐ παραδέδεκται τοῦτο τὸ φῦλον μηδ᾽ ἐπικρατεῖται ὑπ᾽ αὐτοῦ ("They have now got into every city, and it is hard to find a spot on earth which has not admitted this tribe and come under their control "). For the intensive spread of Judaism, Seneca's testimony (cited by Augustine, *De Civit. Dei*, vi. 11) is particularly instructive : cum interim usque eo sceleratissimae gentis consuetudo valuit, ut per omnes iam terras recepta sit ; victi victoribus leges dederunt ("Meantime the customs of this most accursed race have prevailed to such an extent that they are everywhere received. The conquered have imposed their laws on the conquerors"). Justin declares that "there are nations in which not one of your race [*i.e.* of the Jews] can be found" (ἔστι τὰ ἔθνη ἐν οἷς οὐδέπω οὐδεὶς ὑμῶν τοῦ γένους ᾤκησεν, *Dial.* 117), but the following claim that there were Christians in *every* nation shows that his statement is due to tendency.

[1] The large number of Jews in Antioch is particularly striking.

[2] For the diffusion of Jews in S. Arabia, cp. Philostorgius's important evidence (*H.E.*, iii. 4). The local population, he avers, οὐκ ὀλίγον πλῆθος Ἰουδαίων ἀναπέφυρται.

[3] Philo, *Legat.* 33: Ἰουδαῖοι καθ᾽ ἑκάστην πόλιν εἰσὶ παμπληθεῖς Ἀσίας τε καὶ Συρίας ("The Jews abound in every city of Asia and Syria "). The word "every"

made their way into all the local conditions is made particularly clear by the evidence bearing on the sphere last named, where, as on the north coast of the Black Sea, Judaism also played some part in the blending of religions (e.g., the cult of "The most high God," and of the God called "Sabbatistes"). The same holds true of Syria, though the evidence here is not taken so plainly from direct testimony, but drawn indirectly from the historical presuppositions of Christian gnosticism.[1] In Africa, along the coast-line, from the proconsular province to Mauretania, Jews were numerous.[2] At Lyons, in the time of Irenæus,[3] they do not seem to have abounded; but in southern Gaul, as later sources indicate, their numbers cannot have been small, whilst in Spain, as is obvious from the resolutions of the synod of Elvira (c. 300 A.D.), they were both populous and powerful. Finally, we may assume that in Italy—apart from Rome and Southern Italy, where they were widely spread—they

---

(ἐκάστην) is confirmed by a number of special testimonies, e.g. for Cilicia by Epiphanius (Hær., xxx. 11), who says of the "apostle" sent by the Jewish patriarch to collect the Jewish taxes in Cilicia: ὃς ἀνελθὼν ἐκεῖσε ἀπὸ ἑκάστης πόλεως τῆς Κιλικίας τὰ ἐπιδέκατα κτλ εἰσέπραττεν ("On his arrival there he proceeded to lift the tithes, etc., from every city in Cilicia"). On the spread of Judaism in Phrygia and the adjoining provinces (even into the districts of the interior), see Ramsay's two great Works, The Cities and Bishoprics of Phrygia, and The Historical Geography of Asia Minor, along with his essay in the Expositor (January 1902) on "The Jews in the Græco-Asiatic Cities." Wherever any con. siderable number of inscriptions are found in these regions, some of them are always Jewish. The rôle played by the Jewish element in Pisidian Antioch is shown by Acts xiii.; see especially verses 44 and 50 (οἱ Ἰουδαῖοι παρώτρυναν τὰς σεβομένας γυναῖκας τὰς εὐσχήμονας καὶ τοὺς πρώτους τῆς πόλεως). And the significance of the Jewish element in Smyrna comes out conspicuously in the martyrdom of Polycarp and of Pionius; on the day of a Jewish festival the appearance of the streets was quite changed. "The diffusion and importance of the Jews in Asia Minor are attested among other things by the attempt made during the reign of Augustus, by the Ionian cities, apparently after joint counsel, to compel their Jewish fellow-townsmen to abandon their faith or else to assume the full burdens of citizenship" (Mommsen, Röm. Gesch., v. pp. 489 f., Eng. trans. Provinces, ii. 163).

[1] Cp. also the remarks of Epiphanius (Hær., lxxx. 1) upon the cult of Παντοκράτωρ.

[2] See Monceaux, "les colonies juives dans l'Afrique romaine" (Rev. des Études juives, 1902); and Leclerq, L'Afrique chrétienne (1904), I. pp. 36 f. We have evidence for Jewish communities at Carthage, Naro, Hadrumetum, Utica, Hippo, Simittu, Volubilis, Cirta, Auzia, Sitifis, Cæsarea, Tipasa, and Oea, etc.

[3] To all appearance, therefore, he knew no Jewish Christians at first hand.

were not exactly numerous under the early empire, although even in Upper Italy at that period individual synagogues were in existence. This feature was due to the history of Italian civilization, and it is corroborated by the fact that, beyond Rome and Southern Italy, early Jewish inscriptions are scanty and uncertain. "The Jews were the first to exemplify that kind of patriotism which the Parsees, the Armenians, and to some extent the modern Greeks were to display in later ages, viz. a patriotism of extraordinary warmth, but not attached to any one locality, a patriotism of traders who wandered up and down the world and everywhere hailed each other as brethren, a patriotism which aimed at forming not great, compact states but small, autonomous communities under the ægis of other states."[1]

(3) The exact number of Jews in the Diaspora can only be calculated roughly. Our information with regard to figures is as follows. Speaking of the Jews in Babylonia, Josephus declares there were "not a few myriads," or "innumerable myriads" in that region.[2] At Damascus, during the great war, he narrates (*Bell. Jud.*, ii. 20. 2) how ten thousand Jews were massacred; elsewhere in the same book (vii. 8. 7) he writes "eighteen thousand." Of the five civic quarters of Alexandria, two were called "the Jewish" (according to Philo, *In Flacc.* 8), since they were mainly inhabited by Jews; in the other quarters Jews were also to be met with, and Philo (*In Flacc.* 6) reckons their total number in Egypt (as far as the borders of Ethiopia) to have been at least 100 myriads (=a million). In the time of Sulla the Jews of Cyrene, according to Strabo (cited by Josephus, *Antiq.*, xiv. 7. 2), formed one of the four classes into which the population was divided, the others being citizens, peasants, and resident aliens. During the great rebellion in Trajan's reign they are said to have slaughtered 220,000 un-believers in Cyrene (*Dio Cassius*, lxviii. 32), in revenge for which "many myriads" of their own number were put to death by Marcus Turbo (Euseb., *H.E.*, iv. 2). The Jewish revolt spread also to Cyprus, where 240,000 Gentiles are said to have

[1] Renan, *Les Apôtres* (ch. xvi.).
[2] *Antiq.*, xv. 3. 1, xi. 5. 2. According to *Antiq.*, xii. 3. 4, Antiochus the Great deported 2000 families of Babylonian Jews to Phrygia and Lydia.

been murdered by them.[1]   As for the number of Jews in Rome, we have these two statements : first, that in B.C. 4 a Jewish embassy from Palestine to the metropolis was joined by 8000 local Jews (Joseph., *Antiq.*, xvii. 2. 1; *Bell.*, ii. 6. 1); and secondly, that in 19 A.D., when Tiberius banished the whole Jewish community from Rome, 4000 able-bodied Jews were deported to Sardinia.   The latter statement merits especial attention, as it is handed down by Tacitus as well as Josephus.[2] After the fall of Sejanus, when Tiberius revoked the edict (Philo, *Legat.* 24), the Jews at once made up their former numbers in Rome (*Dio Cassius*, lx. 6, πλεονάσαντες αὖθις); the movement for their expulsion reappeared under Claudius in 49 A.D., but the enforcement of the order looked to be so risky that it was presently withdrawn and limited to a prohibition of religious gatherings.[3]   In Rome the Jews dwelt chiefly in

[1] Dio Cassius (*loc. cit.*).   The same author declares (lxix. 14) that 580,000 Jews perished in Palestine during the rebellion of Barcochba.

[2] There is a discrepancy between them.   Whilst Josephus (*Antiq.*, xviii. 3. 5) mentions only Jews, Tacitus (*Annal.*, ii. 85) writes : "Actum et de sacris Aegyptiis Judaicisque pellendis factumque patrum consultum, ut quattuor milia libertini generis ea superstitione infecta, quis idonea aetas, in insulam Sardiniam veherentur, coercendis illic latrociniis et, si ob gravitatem caeli interissent, vile damnum ; ceteri cederent Italia, nisi certam ante diem profanos ritus exuissent" ("Measures were also adopted for the extermination of Egyptian and Jewish rites, and the Senate passed a decree that four thousand freedmen, able-bodied, who were tainted with that superstition, should be deported to the island of Sardinia to put a check upon the local brigands.   Should the climate kill them 'twould be no great loss!   As for the rest, they were to leave Italy unless they abjured their profane rites by a given day ").   The expulsion is also described by Suetonius (*Tiber.* 36): "Externas caeremonias, Aegyptios Judaicosque ritus compescuit, coactis qui superstitione ea tenebantur religiosas vestes cum instrumento omni comburere.   Judaeorum juventutem per speciem sacramenti in provincias gravioris caeli distribuit, reliquos gentis eiusdem vel similia sectantes urbe summovit, sub poena perpetuae servitutis nisi obtemperassent" ("Foreign religions, including the rites of Egyptians and Jews, he suppressed, forcing those who practised that superstition to burn their sacred vestments and all their utensils.   He scattered the Jewish youth in provinces of an unhealthy climate, on the pretext of military service, whilst the rest of that race or of those who shared their practices were expelled from Rome, the penalty for disobedience being penal servitude for life ").

[3] The sources here are contradictory.   Acts (xviii. 2), Suetonius (*Claud.* 25), and Orosius (vii. 6. 15)—the last named appealing by mistake to Josephus, who says nothing about the incident—all speak of a formal (and enforced) edict of expulsion, but Dio Cassius (lx. 6) writes: τούς τε 'Ιουδαίους πλεονάσαντας αὖθις, ὥστε χαλεπῶς ἂν ἄνευ ταραχῆς ὑπὸ τοῦ ὄχλου σφῶν τῆς πόλεως εἰρχθῆναι, οὐκ ἐξήλασε μέν, τῷ δὲ δὴ πατρίῳ βίῳ χρωμένους ἐκέλευσε μὴ συναθροίζεσθαι ("As

Trastevere; but as Jewish churchyards have been discovered in various parts of the city, they were also to be met with in other quarters as well.

A glance at these numerical statements shows [1] that only two possess any significance. The first is Philo's, that the Egyptian Jews amounted to quite a million. Philo's comparatively precise mode of expression (οὐκ ἀποδέουσι μυριάδων ἑκατὸν οἱ τὴν Ἀλεξάνδρειαν καὶ τὴν χώραν Ἰουδαῖοι κατοικοῦντες ἀπὸ τοῦ πρὸς Λιβύην καταβαθμοῦ μέχρι τῶν ὁρίων Αἰθιοπίας: "The Jews resident in Alexandria and in the country from the descent to Libya back to the bounds of Ethiopia, do not fall short of a million"), taken together with the fact that registers for the purpose of taxation were accurately kept in Egypt, renders it probable that we have here to do with no fanciful number. Nor does the figure itself appear too high, when we consider that it includes the whole Jewish population of Alexandria. As the entire population of Egypt (under Vespasian) amounted to seven or eight millions, the Jews thus turn out to have formed a seventh or an eighth of the whole (somewhere about thirteen per cent.).[2] Syria is the only province of the empire where we

---

the Jews had once more multiplied, so that it would have been difficult to remove them without a popular riot, he did not expel them, but simply prohibited any gatherings of those who held to their ancestral customs"). We have no business, in my opinion, to use Dio Cassius in order to set aside two such excellent witnesses as Luke and Suetonius Nor is it a satisfactory expedient to suppose, with Schürer (III. p. 32; cp. Eng. trans., II. ii. 237), that the government simply intended to expel the Jews. The edict must have been actually issued, although it was presently replaced by a prohibition of meetings, after the Jews had given a guarantee of good behaviour.

[1] I omit a series of figures given elsewhere by Josephus; they are not of the slightest use.

[2] See Mommsen, Röm. Gesch., v. p. 578 [Eng. trans., "Provinces of the Roman Empire," ii. p. 258], and Pietschmann in Pauly-Wissowa's Encyklop., i., col. 990 f. Beloch (Die Bevölkerung der griechisch-römischen Welt, pp. 258 f.) questions the reckoning of Josephus (Bell., ii. 16. 4) that the population of Egypt under Nero amounted to seven and a half millions. He will not allow more than about five, though he adduces no conclusive argument against Josephus. Still, as he also holds it an exaggeration to say, with Philo, that the Jews in Egypt were a million strong, he is not opposed to the hypothesis that Judaism in Egypt amounted to about 13 per cent. of the total population. Beloch reckons the population of Alexandria (including slaves) at about half a million. Of these, 200,000 would be Jews, as the Alexandrian Jews numbered about two-fifths of the whole.

must assume a higher percentage of Jews among the population;[1] in all the other provinces their numbers were smaller.

The second passage of importance is the statement that Tiberius deported four thousand able-bodied Jews to Sardinia—Jews, be it noted, not (as Tacitus declares) Egyptians and Jews, for the distinct evidence of Josephus on this point is corroborated by that of Suetonius (see above), who, after speaking at first of Jews and Egyptians, adds, by way of closer definition, "Judaeorum juventatem per speciem sacramenti in provincias gravioris caeli distribuit." Four thousand able-bodied men answers to a total of at least ten thousand human beings,[2] and something like this represented the size of the contemporary Jewish community at Rome. Now, of course, this reckoning agrees but poorly with the other piece of information, viz., that twenty-three years earlier a Palestinian deputation had its ranks swelled by 8000 Roman Jews. Either Josephus has inserted the total number of Jews in this passage, or he is guilty of serious exaggeration. The most reliable estimate of the Roman population under Augustus (in B.C. 5) gives 320,000 male plebeians over ten years of age. As women were notoriously in a minority at Rome, this number represents about 600,000 inhabitants (excluding slaves),[3] so that about 10,000 Jews[4] would be equivalent to about one-sixtieth of the population.[5] Tiberius could still risk the strong measure of expelling them; but when

[1] Josephus, *Bell.*, vii. 3. 3: (Τὸ Ἰουδαίων γένος πολὺ μὲν κατὰ πᾶσαν τὴν οἰκουμένην παρέσπαρται τοῖς ἐπιχωρίοις, πλεῖστον δὲ τῇ Συρίᾳ: "The Jewish race is thickly spread over the world among its inhabitants, but specially in Syria"). Beloch (pp. 242 f., 507) estimates the population of Syria under Augustus at about six millions, under Nero at about seven, whilst the free inhabitants of Antioch under Augustus numbered close on 300,000. As the percentage of Jews in Syria (and especially in Antioch) was larger than in Egypt (about 13 per cent.), certainly over a million Jews must be assumed for Syria under Nero.

[2] Taking for granted, as in the case of any immigrant population, that the number of men is very considerably larger than that of women, I allow 2000 boys and old men to 4000 able-bodied men, and assume about 4000 females.

[3] See Beloch, pp. 292 f. His figure, 500,000, seems to me rather low.

[4] Renan (*L'Antéchrist*, ch. i.) is inclined to estimate the number of the Roman Jews, including women and children, at from twenty to thirty thousand.

[5] The total number, including foreigners and slaves, would amount to something between 800,000 and 900,000 (according to Beloch, 800,000 at the outside).

Claudius tried to repeat the experiment thirty years later, he was unable to carry it out.

We can hardly suppose that the Jewish community at Rome continued to show any considerable increase after the great rebellions and wars under Vespasian, Titus, Trajan, and Hadrian, since the decimation of the Jews in many provinces of the empire must have re-acted upon the Jewish community in the capital. Details on this point, however, are awanting.

If the Jews in Egypt amounted to about a million, those in Syria were still more numerous. Allowing about 700,000 Jews to Palestine—and at this moment between 600,000 and 650,000 people live there ; see Baedeker's *Palestine*, 1900, p. lvii.—we are within the mark at all events when we reckon the Jews in the remaining districts of the empire (*i.e.*, in Asia Minor, Greece, Cyrene, Rome, Italy, Gaul, Spain, etc.) at about one million and a half. In this way a grand total of about four or four and a half million Jews is reached. Now, it is an extremely surprising thing, a thing that seems at first to throw doubt upon any estimate whatsoever of the population, to say that while (according to Beloch) the population of the whole Roman empire under Augustus is reported to have amounted to nearly fifty-four millions, the Jews in the empire at that period must be reckoned at not less than four or four and a half millions. Even if one raises Beloch's figure to sixty millions, how can the Jews have represented seven per cent. of the total population ? Either our calculation is wrong—and mistakes are almost inevitable in a matter like this—or the propaganda of Judaism was extremely successful in the provinces ; for it is utterly impossible to explain the large total of Jews in the Diaspora by the mere fact of the fertility of Jewish families. We must assume, I imagine, that a very large number of pagans, and in particular of kindred Semites of the lower class, trooped over to the religion of Yahweh [1]—for the Jews of the Diaspora were genuine Jews only to a certain extent. Now if Judaism was actually so

---

[1] After the edict of Pius, which forbade in the most stringent terms the circumcision of any who had not been born in Judaism (cp. also the previous edict of Hadrian), regular secessions must have either ceased altogether or occurred extremely seldom ; cp. Orig., *c. Cels.*, II. xiii.

vigorous throughout the empire as to embrace about seven per cent. of the total population under Augustus,[1] one begins to realize its great influence and social importance. And in order to comprehend the propaganda and diffusion of Christianity, it is quite essential to understand that the religion under whose "shadow" it made its way out into the world, not merely contained elements of vital significance but had expanded till it embraced a considerable proportion of the world's population.

Our survey would not be complete if we did not glance, however briefly, at the nature of the Jewish propaganda in the empire,[2] for some part, at least, of her missionary zeal was inherited by Christianity from Judaism. As I shall have to refer to this Jewish mission wherever any means employed in the Christian propaganda are taken over from Judaism, I shall confine myself in the meantime to some general observations.

It is surprising that a religion which raised so stout a wall of partition between itself and all other religions, and which in practice and prospects alike was bound up so closely with its nation, should have possessed a missionary impulse[3] of such vigour and attained so large a measure of success. This is not ultimately to be explained by any craving for power or ambition; it is a proof[4] that *Judaism, as a religion, was already blossoming out by some inward transformation* and becoming a cross between a national religion and a world-religion (confession of faith and a church). Proudly the Jew felt that he had something to say and bring to the world, which concerned all men, viz., *The one and only spiritual God, creator of heaven and earth,*

---

[1] In modern Germany the Jews number a little over one per cent. of the population; in Austro-Hungary, four and two-thirds per cent.

[2] Compare, on this point, Schürer's description, *op. cit.*, III.(3), pp. 102 f. [Eng. trans., II. ii. 126 f.].

[3] The duty and the hopefulness of missions are brought out in the earliest Jewish Sibylline books. Almost the whole of the literature of Alexandrian Judaism has an apologetic bent and the instinct of propaganda.

[4] Cp. Bousset's *Die Religion des Judentums im neutest. Zeitalter* (1903), especially the sections on "The Theologians, the Church and the Laity, Women, Confession (Faith and Dogma), the Synagogue as an Institute of Salvation" (pp. 139-184), and the large section devoted to "The Faith of the Individual and Theology." If a popular religion passes into a confession of faith and a church, individual faith with all its reach and strain also comes into view together with the church. For the propaganda of Judaism in the pagan world, cp. pp. 77 f.

with his holy moral law. It was owing to the consciousness of this (Rom. ii. 19 f.) that he felt missions to be a duty. *The Jewish propaganda throughout the empire was primarily the proclamation of the one and only God, of his moral law, and of his judgment;* to this everything else became secondary. The object in many cases might be pure proselytism (Matt. xxiii. 15), but Judaism was quite in earnest in overthrowing dumb idols and inducing pagans to recognize their creator and judge, for in this the honour of the God of Israel was concerned.

It is in this light that one must judge a phenomenon which is misunderstood so long as we explain it by means of specious analogies—I mean, the different degrees and phases of proselytism. In other religions, variations of this kind usually proceed from an endeavour to render the *moral* precepts imposed by the religion somewhat easier for the proselyte. In Judaism this tendency never prevailed, at least never outright. On the contrary, the *moral* demand remained unlowered. *As the recognition of God was considered the cardinal point,* Judaism was in a position to depreciate the claims of the cultus and of ceremonies, and the different kinds of Jewish proselytism were almost entirely due to the different degrees in which the ceremonial precepts of the Law were observed. The fine generosity of such an attitude was, of course, facilitated by the fact that a man who let even his little finger be grasped by this religion, thereby became a Jew.[1] Again, strictly speaking, even a born Jew was only a proselyte so soon as he left the soil of Palestine, since thereby he parted with the sacrificial system; besides, he was unable in a foreign country to fulfil, or at least to fulfil satisfactorily, many other precepts of the Law.[2] For generations there had been a gradual neutralising of the sacrificial system proceeding apace within the inner life of Judaism—even among the Pharisees; and this coincided with an historical situation which obliged by far the greater number of the adherents of the religion to live amid conditions which had made them

[1] If he did not, his son did.

[2] Circumcision, of course, was always a troublesome wall of partition. Born Jews, as a rule, laid the greatest stress upon it, while pagans submitted to the operation with extreme reluctance.

strangers for a long period to the sacrificial system. In this way they were also rendered accessible on every side of their spiritual nature to foreign cults and philosophies, and thus there originated Persian and Græco-Jewish religious alloys, several of whose phenomena threatened even the monotheistic belief. The destruction of the temple by the Romans really destroyed nothing ; it may be viewed as an incident organic to the history of Jewish religion. When pious people held God's ways at that crisis were incomprehensible, they were but deluding themselves.

For a long while the popular opinion throughout the empire was that the Jews worshipped God without images, and that they had no temple. Now, although both of these "atheistic" features might appear to the rude populace even more offensive and despicable than circumcision, Sabbath observance, the prohibition of swine's flesh, etc., nevertheless they made a deep impression upon wide circles of educated people.[1] Thanks to these traits, together with its monotheism—for which the age was beginning to be ripe[2]—Judaism seemed as if it were elevated to the rank of *philosophy*, and inasmuch as it still continued to be a religion, it exhibited a type of mental and spiritual life which was superior to anything of the kind.[3] At bottom, there was nothing artificial in a Philo or in a Josephus exhibiting Judaism as the *philosophic* religion, for this kind of apologetic corresponded to the actual situation in which they found themselves[4] ; it was as the revealed and also the philo-

---

[1] This rigid exclusiveness in a religion naturally repelled the majority and excited frank resentment ; it was somewhat of a paradox, and cannot fail to have been felt as obdurately inhuman as well as insolent. Anti-Semitism can be plainly traced within the Roman empire from 100 B.C. onwards ; in the first century A.D. it steadily increased, discharging itself in outbursts of fearful persecution.

[2] It was ripe also for the idea of an individual recompense in the future life, as an outcome of the heightened valuation of individual morality in this life, and for the idea of a judgment passed on the individual thereafter.

[3] *E.g.*, especially to the idealistic schools of popular philosophy. Cp. Wendland, *Philo und die stoisch-kynische Diatribe* (1895).

[4] Cp. Friedländer's *Geschichte der jüdischen Apologetik als Vorgeschichte des Christentums*, 1903. On the heights of its apologetic, the Jewish religion represented itself as the idealist philosophy based on revelation (the sacred book), *i.e.*, materially as ideological rationalism, and formally as supra-rationalism ; it was the "most satisfying" form of religion, retaining a vitality, a precision, and a certainty

sophic religion, equipped with "the oldest book in the world," that Judaism developed her great propaganda.[1] The account given by Josephus (*Bell.*, vii. 3. 3) of the situation at Antioch, viz., that "the Jews continued to attract a large number of the Greeks to their services, making them in a sense part of themselves"—this holds true of the Jewish mission in general.[2] The adhesion of Greeks and Romans to Judaism ranged over the entire gamut of possible degrees, from the superstitious adoption of certain rites up to complete identification. "God-fearing" pagans constituted the majority; proselytes (*i.e.*, people who were actually Jews, obliged to keep the whole Law), there is no doubt, were comparatively few in number.[3] Immersion was more indispensable than even circumcision as a condition of entrance.[4]

While all this was of the utmost importance for the Christian mission which came afterwards, at least equal moment attaches to one vital omission in the Jewish missionary preaching : viz., that no Gentile, in the first generation at least, could become a

in its conception of God such as no cognate form of religious philosophy could preserve, while at the same time the overwhelming number and the definite character of its "prophecies" quelled every doubt.

[1] "As a philosophical religion Judaism may have attracted one or two cultured individuals, but it was as a religious and social community with a life of its own that it won the masses." So Axenfeld, on p. 15 of his study (mentioned below on p. 16). Yet even as a religious fellowship with a life of its own, Judaism made a philosophic impression—and that upon the uneducated as well as upon the educated. I agree with Axenfeld, however, that the Jewish propaganda owed its success not to the literary activity of individual Hellenistic Jews, but to the assimilating power of the communities with their religious life, their strict maintenance of convictions, their recognition of their own interests and their satisfaction of a national pride, as evidenced in their demand for proselytes to glorify Jehovah.

[2] The keenness of Jewish propaganda throughout the empire during the first century—"the age in which the Christian preaching began its course is the age in which the Jewish propaganda reached the acme of its efforts"—is also clear from the introduction of the Jewish week and Sabbath throughout the empire ; cp. Schürer, "Die siebentägige Woche im Gebrauch der christlichen Kirche der ersten Jahrhunderte" (*Zeits. f. die neut. Wiss.*, 1905, 40 f.). Many pagans celebrated the Sabbath, just as Jews to-day observe Sunday.

[3] *See* Eus., *H.E.*, i. 7, for the extent to which proselytes became fused among those who were Jews by birth.

[4] It must not be forgotten that even in the Diaspora there was exclusiveness and fanaticism. The first persecution of Christians was set afoot by synagogues of the Diaspora in Jerusalem ; Saul was a fanatic Jew of the Diaspora.

real son of Abraham.   His rank before God remained inferior. ⌣.
Thus it also remained very doubtful how far any proselyte—to ⁀ᵗ
say nothing of the " God-fearing "—had a share in the glorious
promises of the future.   The religion which repairs this omis-.
sion will drive Judaism from the field.[1]   When it proclaims this ᐟ
message in its fulness, that the last will be first, that freedom ꭇᷜ
from the Law is the normal and higher life, and that the
observance of the Law, even at its best, is a thing to be
tolerated and no more, it will win thousands where the previous
missionary preaching won but hundreds.[2]   Yet the propaganda ✓
of Judaism did not succeed simply by its high inward worth ;
the profession of Judaism also conferred great social and political advantages upon its adherents.   Comparei Schürer's sketch
(*op. cit.*, III.[3] pp. 56–90 ; Eng. trans., II. i . 243 f.) of the

---

[1] I know of no reliable inquiries into the decline and fall of Jewish missions in
the empire after the second destruction of the temple.   It seems to me unquestionable that Judaism henceforth slackened her tie with Hellenism, in order to drop it
altogether as time went on, and that the literature of Hellenistic Judaism suddenly
became very slender, destined ere long to disappear entirely.   But whether we are
to see in all this merely the inner stiffening of Judaism, or other causes to boot
(*e.g.*, the growing rivalry of Christianity), is a question which I do not venture to
decide.   On the repudiation of Hellenism by Palestinian Judaism even prior to the
first destruction of the temple, see below (P. 16).

[2] A notable parallel from history to the preaching of Paul in its relation to
Jewish preaching, is to be found in Luther's declaration, that the truly perfect man
was not a monk, but a Christian living in his daily calling.   Luther also explained that the last (those engaged in daily business) were the first.—The above
sketch has been contradicted by Friedländer (in Dr. Bloch's *Oesterr. Wochenschrift, Zentralorgan f. d. ges. Interessen des Judentums*, 1902, Nos. 49 f.),
who asserts that proselytes ranked entirely the same as full-blooded Jews.   But
Friedländer himself confines this liberal attitude towards proselytes to the
Judaism of the Greek Diaspora ; he refers it to the influence of Hellenism, and
supports it simply by Philo (and John the Baptist).   Note also that Philo usually
holds Jewish pride of birth to be vain, if a man is wicked ; in that case, a Jew is
far inferior to a man of pagan birth.   With this limitation of Friedländer's, no
objection can be taken to the thesis in question.   I myself go still further ; for
there is no doubt that even before the rise of Christianity the Jews of the Diaspora
allegorised the ceremonial Law, and that this paved the way for the Gentile church's
freedom from the Law.   Only, the question is (i.) whether the strict Judaism of
Palestine, in its obscure origins, was really affected by these softening tendencies,
(ii.) whether it did not exercise an increasingly strong influence upon Judaism
even in the Diaspora, and (iii.) whether the Judaism of the Diaspora actually
renounced all the privileges of its birth.   On the two latter points, I should
answer in the negative (even with regard to Philo); on the first, however, my
reply would be in the affirmative.

internal organization of Jewish communities in the Diaspora, of their civil position, and of their civic "isopolity,"[1] and it will be seen how advantageous it was to belong to a Jewish community within the Roman empire. No doubt there were circumstances under which a Jew had to endure ridicule and disdain, but this injustice was compensated by the ample privileges enjoyed by those who adhered to this *religio licita.* If in addition one possessed the freedom of a city (which it was not difficult to procure) or even Roman citizenship, one occupied a more secure and favourable position than the majority of one's fellow-citizens. No wonder, then, that Christians threatened to apostatize to Judaism during a persecution,[2] or that separation from the synagogues had also serious economic consequences for Jews who had become Christians.[3]

One thing further. All religions which made their way into the empire along the channels of intercourse and trade were primarily religions of the city, and remained such for a considerable period. It cannot be said that Judaism in the Diaspora was entirely a city-religion; indeed the reverse holds true of one or two large provinces. Yet in the main it continued to be a city-religion, and we hear little about Jews who were settled on the land.

So long as the temple stood, and contributions were paid in to it, this formed a link between the Jews of the Diaspora and

---

[1] The Jewish communities in the Diaspora also formed small states inside the state or city: one has only to recollect the civil jurisdiction which they exercised, even to the extent of criminal procedure. As late as the third century we possess, with reference to Palestine, Origen's account (*Ep. ad Afric.*, xiv.) of the power of the Ethnarch (or patriarch), which was so great "that he differed in no whit from royalty"; "legal proceedings also took place privately as enjoined by the Law, and several people were condemned to death, not in open court and yet with the cognizance of the authorities." Similar occurrences would take place in the Diaspora. The age of Hadrian and Pius did bring about a terrible retrograde movement; but afterwards, part of the lost ground was again recovered.

[2] Proofs of this are not forthcoming, however, in any number.

[3] Owing to their religious and national characteristics, as well as to the fact that they enjoyed legal recognition throughout the empire, the Jews stood out conspicuously from amongst all the other nations included in the Roman state. This comes out most forcibly in the fact that they were even entitled "The Second race." We shall afterwards show that Christians were called the Third race, since Jews already ranked thus as the Second.

Palestine.[1] Afterwards, a rabbinical board took the place of
the priestly college at Jerusalem, which understood how still
to raise and use these contributions. The board was presided
over by the patriarch, and the contributions were gathered by
"apostles" whom he sent out.[2]   They appear also to have
had additional duties to perform (on which see below).

To the Jewish mission which preceded it, the Christian
mission was indebted, in the first place, for a field tilled all
over the empire; in the second place, for religious communities
already formed everywhere in the towns; thirdly, for what
Axenfeld calls "the help of materials" furnished by the preliminary knowledge of the Old Testament, in addition to catechetical and liturgical materials which could be employed without much alteration; fourthly, for the habit of regular worship
and a control of private life; fifthly, for an impressive apologetic
on behalf of monotheism, historical teleology, and ethics; and
finally, for the feeling that self-diffusion was a duty. The
amount of this debt is so large, that one might venture to claim
the Christian mission as a continuation of the Jewish propaganda. "Judaism," said Renan, "was robbed of its due reward
by a generation of fanatics, and it was prevented from gathering
in the harvest which it had prepared."

The extent to which Judaism was prepared for the gospel
may also be judged by means of the syncretism into which it
had developed. The development was along no mere side-issues.
The transformation of a national into a universal religion may
take place in two ways: either by the national religion being
reduced to great central principles, or by its assimilation of a
wealth of new elements from other religions. Both processes
developed simultaneously in Judaism.[3] But the former is the

---

[1] Messengers and letters also passed, which kept the tie between Jerusalem and
the Jewish church of the Gentiles fresh and close. A good example occurs at the
close of Acts.

[2] On the patriarch, see Schürer, III.[(3)], pp. 77 f. [Eng. trans., II. ii. 270].
From Vopisc. *Saturn.* 8 we know that the patriarch himself went also in person
to the Diaspora, so far as Egypt is concerned. On the "apostles," see Book III.
ch. i. (2).

[3] For "syncretism," see espec. an. the last chapter in Bousset's volume (pp.
448–493). Syncretism melted each   he older elements within the religion of

more important of the two, as a preparation for Christianity. This is to be deduced especially from that great scene preserved for us by Mark xii. 28–34—in its simplicity of spirit, the greatest memorial we possess of the history of religion at the epoch of its vital change.[1] " A scribe asked Jesus, What is the first of all the commandments ? Jesus replied, The first is : Hear, O Israel, the Lord our God is one God, and thou shalt love the Lord thy God with all thy heart, and all thy soul, and all thy mind, and all thy strength. The second is : Thou shalt love thy neighbour as thyself. There is no commandment greater than these. And the scribe said to him, True, O teacher ; thou hast rightly said that he is one, and that beside him there is none else, and that to love him with all the heart, and all the understanding and all the strength, and to love one's neighbour as oneself, is far above all holocausts and sacrifices. And when Jesus saw that he answered intelligently, he said : Thou art not far from the kingdom of God."

With regard to the attitude of Palestinian Judaism towards the mission-idea (*i.e.*, universalism and the duty of systematic propaganda), the state of matters during the age of Christ and the apostles is such as to permit pleadings upon both sides of the question.[2] Previous to that age, there had been two periods which were essentially opposite in tendency. The older, resting upon the second Isaiah, gave vivid expression, even within Palestine itself, to the universalism of the Jewish religion as well as to a religious ethic which rose almost to the pitch of humanitarianism. This is represented in a number of the psalms, in the book of Jonah, and in the Wisdom-literature. The pious are fully conscious that Yahweh rules over the nation and over all mankind, that he is the God of each individual, and that he requires nothing but reverence. Hence their hope for the

Judaism, and introduced a wealth of entirely new elements. But nothing decomposed the claim that Judaism was the true religion, or the conviction that in " Moses" all truth lay.

[1] The nearest approach to it is to be found in the missionary speech put into Paul's mouth on the hill of Mars.

[2] Cp. Bertholet, *Die Stellung der Israeliten und Juden zu den Fremden* (1890) ; Schürer, III.[(3)], pp. 125 f.) ; Bousset, *op. cit.*, 82 ual Axenfeld, "Die judische Propaganda als Vorläuferin der urchristlichen Mi.at C. ^n the *Missionswiss. Studien* (Festschrift für Warneck), 1904, pp. 1–80 Sec.

ultimate conversion of all the heathen. They will have kings
and people alike to bow before Yahweh and to praise him.
Their desire is that Yahweh's name be known everywhere
among the heathen, and his glory (in the sense of conversion to
him) spread far and wide. With the age of the Maccabees,
however, an opposite tendency set in. Apocalyptic was keener
upon the downfall of the heathen than upon their conversion,
and the exclusive tendencies of Judaism again assert themselves,
in the struggle to preserve the distinctive characteristics of the
nation. "One of the most important results which flowed from
the outrageous policy of Antiochus was that it discredited for
all time to come the idea of a Judaism free from any limitation
whatsoever, and that it either made pro-Hellenism, in the sense
of Jason and Alcimus, impossible for Palestine and the Diaspora
alike, or else exposed it to sharp correction whenever it should
raise its head" (Axenfeld, p. 28).. Now, in the age of Christ
and the apostles, these two waves, the progressive and the
nationalist, are beating each other back. Pharisaism itself
appears to be torn in twain. In some psalms and manuals,
as well as in the 13th Blessing of the Schmone Esre, universalism still breaks out. "Hillel, the most famous representative
of Jewish Biblical learning, was accustomed, with his pupils,
to pay special attention to the propaganda of religion. 'Love
men and draw them to the Law' is one of his traditional maxims"
(Pirke Aboth, 1. 12). Gamaliel, Paul's teacher, is also to be
ranked among the propagandists. It was not impossible, however, to be both exclusive and in favour of the propaganda, for the
conditions of the mission were sharpened into the demand that
the entire Law should be kept. If I mistake not, Jesus was primarily at issue with this kind of Pharisaism in Jerusalem. Now
the keener became the opposition within Palestine to the foreign
dominion, and the nearer the great catastrophe came, the more
strenuous grew the reaction against all that was foreign, as well
as the idea that whatever was un-Jewish would perish in the
judgment. Not long before the destruction of Jerusalem, in
all probability, the controversy between the schools of Hillel
and Shammai ended in a complete victory for the latter.
Shammai was not indeed an opponent of the mission in prin-

ciple, but he subjected it to the most rigorous conditions.   The eighteen rules which were laid down included, among other things, the prohibition against learning Greek, and that against accepting presents from pagans for the temple.   Intercourse with pagans was confined within the strictest of regulations, and had to be given up as a whole.   This opened the way for the Judaism of the Talmud and the Mishna.   The Judaism of the Diaspora followed the same course of development, though not till some time afterwards.[1]

[1] Axenfeld remarks very truly (pp. 8 f.) that " the history of the Jewish propaganda is to be explained by the constant strain between the demand that the heathen should be included and the dread which this excited.   The Judaism which felt the impulse of propaganda resembled an invading host, whose offensive movements are continually being hampered by considerations arising from the need of keeping in close touch with their basis of operations."   But it seems to me an artificial and theological reflection, when the same scholar lays supreme weight on the fact that the Jewish propaganda had no "consciousness of a vocation," and that, in contrast to the Christian mission, it simply proclaimed its God zealously from the consciousness of an innate religious pre-eminence, devoid of humility and obedience.   I have tried in vain to find an atom of truth in this thesis, with its resultant defence of the historicity of Matthew xxviii. 19.   It is of course admitted on all hands that Christian missionary zeal was bound subsequently to be intensified by the belief that Jesus had directly enjoined it.

CHAPTER II

It is only in a series of headings, as it were, that I would summarize the external conditions which either made it possible for Christianity to spread rapidly and widely during the imperial age, or actually promoted its advance. One of the most important has been mentioned in the previous chapter, viz., the spread of Judaism, which anticipated and prepared the way for that of Christianity. Besides this, the following considerations [1] are especially to be noted :—

(1) The *Hellenizing* of the East and (in part also) of the West, which had gone on steadily since Alexander the Great : or, *the comparative unity of language and ideas* which this Hellenizing had produced. Not until the close of the second century A.D. does this Hellenizing process appear to have exhausted itself, [2]

---

[1] The number of works at our disposal for such a survey is legion. One of the most recent is Gruppe's *Kulturgeschichte der römischen Kaiserzeit* (2 vols., 1903, 1904).

[2] I know no investigations as to the precise period when the advance of Hellenism, more particularly of the Greek language, subsided and ceased at Rome and throughout the West. From my limited knowledge of the subject, I should incline to make the close of the second century the limit. Marcus Aurelius still wrote his confessions in Greek, but no indication of a similar kind can be discovered later. In the West, Greek was checked by the deterioration of culture as well as by the circumstances of the situation : the tidal wave grows shallower as it spreads. During the third century Rome began to shed off Greek, and in the course of the fourth century she became once more a purely Latin city. So too with the Western provinces as far as they had assimilated the Greek element ; so with Southern Italy and Gaul even, though the process took longer in these regions. During the second century people could still make themselves understood apparently by means of Greek, in any of the larger Western cities ; by the third century, a stranger who did not know Latin was sometimes in difficulties, though not often ; by the fourth, no traveller in the West could dispense with Latin any longer, and it was only in Southern Gaul and Lower Italy that Greek sufficed.

while in the fourth century, when the seat of empire was shifted to the East, the movement acquired a still further impetus in several important directions. As Christianity allied itself very quickly though incompletely to the speech and spirit of Hellenism, it was in a position to avail itself of a great deal in the success of the latter. In return it furthered the advance of Hellenism and put a check to its retreat.

(2) *The world-empire of Rome and the political unity* which it secured for the nations bordering on the Mediterranean; the comparative unity secured by this world-state for the methods and conditions of outward existence, and also the comparative stability of social life. Throughout many provinces of the East, people felt the emperor really stood for peace, after all the dreadful storms and wars; they hailed his law as a shelter and a safeguard.[1] Furthermore, the earthly monarchy of the world was a fact which at once favoured the conception of the heavenly monarchy and conditioned the origin of *a catholic or universal church.*

(3) The exceptional facilities, growth, and security of *international traffic* :[2] the admirable roads; the blending of different nationalities;[3] the interchange of wares and of ideas; the

---

[1] After Melito, Origen (*c. Celsum*, II. xxx.) correctly estimated the significance of this for the Christian propaganda. "In the days of Jesus, righteousness arose and fulness of peace; it began with his birth. God prepared the nations for his teaching, by causing the Roman emperor to rule over all the world; there was no longer to be a plurality of kingdoms, else would the nations have been strangers to one another, and so the apostles would have found it harder to carry out the task laid on them by Jesus, when he said, 'Go and teach all nations.' It is well known that the birth of Jesus took place in the reign of Augustus, who fused and federated the numerous peoples upon earth into a single empire. A plurality of kingdoms would have been an obstacle to the spread of the doctrine of Jesus throughout all the world, not merely for the reasons already mentioned, but also because the nations would in that event have been obliged to go to war in defence of their native lands. . . . . How, then, could this doctrine of peace, which does not even permit vengeance upon an enemy, have prevailed throughout the world, had not the circumstances of the world passed everywhere into a milder phase at the advent of Jesus?"

[2] Cp. Stephan in Raumer's *Histor. Taschenbuch* (1868), pp. 1 f., and Zahn's *Weltverkehr und Kirche während der drei ersten Jahrhunderte* (1877). That one Phrygian merchant voyaged to Rome (according to the inscription on a tomb) no fewer than seventy-two times in the course of his life, is itself a fact which must never be lost sight of.

[3] It is surprising to notice this blending of nationalities, whenever any inscrip-

personal intercourse; the ubiquitous merchant and soldier—one may add, the ubiquitous professor, who was to be encountered from Antioch to Cadiz, from Alexandria to Bordeaux. The church thus found the way paved for expansion: the means were prepared; and the population of the large towns was as heterogeneous and devoid of a past as could be desired.

(4) The practical and theoretical conviction of *the essential unity of mankind*, and of human rights and duties, which was produced, or at any rate intensfied, by the fact of the "orbis Romanus" on the one side and the development of philosophy upon the other, and confirmed by the truly enlightened system of Roman jurisprudence, particularly between Nerva and Alexander Severus. On all essential questions the church had no reason to oppose, but rather to assent to, Roman law, that grandest and most durable product of the empire.[1]

(5) *The decomposition of ancient society into a democracy*: the gradual equalizing of the "cives Romani" and the provincials, of the Greeks and the barbarians; the comparative equalizing of classes in society; the elevation of the slave-class—in short, a soil prepared for the growth of new formations by the decomposition of the old.

(6) *The religious policy of Rome*, which furthered the interchange of religions by its toleration, hardly presenting any obstacles to their natural increase or transformation or decay, (although it would not stand any practical expression of contempt for the ceremonial of the State-religion.) The liberty guaranteed

tion bears a considerable number of names (soldiers, pages, martyrs, etc.), and at the same time mentions their origin.

[1] At this point (in order to illustrate these four paragraphs) Renan's well-known summary may be cited (*Les Apôtres*, ch. xvi.): "The unity of the empire was the essential presupposition of any comprehensive proselytizing movement which should transcend the limits of nationality. In the fourth century the empire realised this: it became Christian; it perceived that Christianity was the religion which it had matured involuntarily; it recognized in Christianity the religion whose limits were the same as its own, the religion which was identified with itself and capable of infusing new life into its being. The church, for her part, became thoroughly Roman, and to this day has remained a survival of the old Roman empire. Had anyone told Paul that Claudius was his main coadjutor, had anyone told Claudius that this Jew, starting from Antioch, was preparing the ground for the most enduring part of the imperial system, both Paul and Claudius would have been mightily astonished. Nevertheless both sayings would have been true."

by Rome's religious policy on all other points was an ample compensation for the rough check imposed on the spread of Christianity by her vindication of the State-religion.

(7) *The existence of associations*, as well as of *municipal and provincial organizations.* In several respects the former had prepared the soil for the reception of Christianity, whilst in some cases they probably served as a shelter for it. The latter actually suggested the most important forms of organization in the church, and thus saved her the onerous task of first devising such forms and then requiring to commend them.

(8) *The irruption of the Syrian and Persian religions* into the empire, dating especially from the reign of Antoninus Pius. These had certain traits in common with Christianity, and although the spread of the church was at first handicapped by them, any such loss was amply made up for by the new religious cravings which they stirred within the minds of men—cravings which could not finally be satisfied apart from Christianity.

(9) *The decline of the exact sciences*, a phenomenon due to the democratic tendency of society and the simultaneous popularizing of knowledge, as well as to other unknown causes: also *the rising vogue of a mystical philosophy of religion with a craving for some form of revelation and a thirst for miracle.*

All these outward conditions (of which the two latter might have been previously included among the inward) brought about a great revolution in the whole of human existence under the empire, a revolution which must have been highly conducive to the spread of the Christian religion. The narrow world had become a wide world; the rent world had become a unity; the barbarian world had become Greek and Roman: *one* empire, *one* universal language, *one* civilization, a *common* development towards monotheism, and a *common yearning* for saviours![1]

---

[1] As Uhlhorn remarks very truly (*Die christliche Liebesthätigkeit in der alten Kirche*, 1882, p. 37; Eng. trans. pp. 40-42): "From the time of the emperors onwards a new influence made itself felt, and unless we notice this influence, we cannot understand the first centuries of the early Christian church, we cannot understand its rapid extension and its relatively rapid triumph. . . . . Had the stream of new life issuing from Christ encountered ancient life when the latter was still unbroken, it would have recoiled impotent from the shock. But ancient life had by this time begun to break up; its solid foundations had begun to weaken; and, besides, the Christian stream fell in with a previous and cognate

current of Jewish opinion.   In the Roman empire there had already appeared a universalism foreign to the ancient world.   Nationalities had been effaced.   The idea of universal humanity had disengaged itself from that of nationality.   The Stoics had passed the word that all men were equal, and had spoken of brotherhood as well as of the duties of man towards man.   Hitherto despised, the lower classes had asserted their position.   The treatment of slaves became milder. If Cato had compared them to cattle, Pliny sees in them his 'serving friends.' The position of the artizan improved, and freedmen worked their way up, for the guilds provided them not simply with a centre of social life, but also with the means of bettering their social position.   Women, hitherto without any legal rights, received such in increasing numbers.   Children were looked after.   The distribution of grain, originally a political institution and nothing more, became a sort of poor-relief system, and we meet with a growing number of generous deeds, gifts, and endowments, which already exhibit a more humane spirit," etc.

CHAPTER III

IN subsequent sections of this book we shall notice a series of the more important inner conditions which determined the universal spread of the Christian religion. It was by preaching to the poor, the burdened, and the outcast, by the preaching and practice of love, that Christianity turned the stony, sterile world into a fruitful field for the church. Where no other religion could sow and reap, this religion was enabled to scatter its seed and to secure a harvest.

The condition, however, which determined more than anything else the propaganda of the religion, lay in the general religious situation during the imperial age. It is impossible to attempt here to depict that situation, and unluckily we cannot refer to any standard work which does justice to such a colossal undertaking, despite the admirable studies and sketches (such as those of Tzschirner, Friedländer, Boissier, Réville, and Wissowa)[1] which we possess. This being so, we must content ourselves with throwing out a few hints along two main lines.

(1) In spite of the inner evolution of polytheism towards monotheism, the relations between Christianity and paganism simply meant the opposition of monotheism and polytheism— of polytheism, too, in the first instance, as political religion (the imperial cultus). Here Christianity and paganism were absolutely opposed. The former burned what the latter adored, and the latter burned Christians as guilty of high treason.

---

[1] Add the sketch of the history of Greek religion by Wilamowitz-Moellendorff (*Jahrb. des Freien deutschen Hochstifts*, 1904).

Christian apologists and martyrs were perfectly right in often ignoring every other topic when they opened their lips, and in reducing everything to this simple alternative.

Judaism shared with Christianity this attitude towards poly-theism. But then, Judaism was a *national* religion; hence its monotheism was widely tolerated simply because it was largely unintelligible. Furthermore, it usually evaded any conflict with the State-authorities, and it did not make martyrdom obligatory. That a man had to become a Jew in order to be a monotheist, was utterly absurd: it degraded the creator of heaven and earth to the level of a national god. Besides, if he was a national god, he was not the only one. No doubt, up and down the empire there were whispers about the atheism of the Jews, thanks to their lack of images; but the charge was never levelled in real earnest—or rather, opinion was in such a state of oscillation that the usual political result obtained: *in dubio pro reo.*

It was otherwise with Christianity. Here the polytheists could have no hesitation: deprived of any basis in a nation or a State, destitute alike of images and temples, Christianity was simple atheism. The contrast between polytheism and mono-theism was in this field clear and keen. From the second century onwards, the conflict between these two forms of religion was waged by Christianity and not by Judaism. The former was aggressive, while as a rule the latter had really ceased to fight at all—it devoted itself to capturing proselytes.

From the very outset it was no hopeless struggle. When Christianity came upon the scene, the polytheism of the State-religion was not yet eradicated, indeed, nor was it eradicated for some time to come;[1] but there were ample forces at hand which were already compassing its ruin. It had survived the critical epoch during which the republic had changed into a dual control and a monarchy; but as for the fresh swarm of religions which were invading and displacing it, polytheism could no more exorcise them with the magic wand of the imperial cultus than it could dissolve them under the rays of a protean cultus of the sun, which sought to bring everything

---

[1] Successful attempts to revive it were not awanting; see under (2) in this section.

within its sweep. Nevertheless polytheism would still have been destined to a long career, had it not been attacked secretly or openly by the forces of general knowledge, philosophy, and ethics; had it not also been saddled with arrears of mythology which excited ridicule and resentment. Statesmen, poets, and philosophers might disregard all this, since each of these groups devised some method of preserving their continuity with the past. But once the common people realized it, or were made to realize it, the conclusion they drew in such cases was ruthless. The onset against deities feathered and scaly, deities adulterous and infested with vice, and on the other hand against idols of wood and stone, formed the most impressive and effective factor in Christian preaching for wide circles, circles which in all ranks of society down to the lowest classes (where indeed they were most numerous) had, owing to experience and circumstances, reached a point at which the burning denunciations of the abomination of idolatry could not fail to arrest them and bring them over to monotheism. The very position of polytheism as the State-religion was in favour of the Christian propaganda. Religion faced religion; but whilst the one was new and living, the other was old—that is, with the exception of the imperial cultus, in which once more it gathered up its forces. No one could tell exactly what had come over it. Was it merely equivalent to what was lawful in politics? Or did it represent the vast, complicated mass of *religiones licitae* throughout the empire? Who could say?

(2) This, however, is to touch on merely one side of the matter. The religious situation in the imperial age, with the tendencies it cherished and the formations it produced—all this was complicated in the extreme. Weighty as were the simple antitheses of " monotheism *versus* polytheism " and " strict morality *versus* laxity and vice," these cannot be taken as a complete summary of the whole position. The posture of affairs throughout the empire is no more adequately described by the term " polytheism," than is Christianity, as it was then preached, by the bare term " monotheism." It was not a case of vice and virtue simply facing one another. Here, in fact, we must enter into some detail and definition.

Anyone who considers that the domination of the inner life over external empiricism and politics is an illusion and perversion, must date the disintegration of the ancient world from Socrates and Plato. Here the two tempers stand apart! On the other hand, anyone who regards this domination as the supreme advance of man, is not obliged to accompany its development down as far as Neo-Platonism. He will not, indeed, be unaware that, even to the last, in the time of Augustine, genuine advances were made along this line, but he will allow that they were gained at great expense—too great expense. This erroneous development began when introspection commenced to despise and neglect its correlative in natural science, and to woo mysticism, theurgy, astrology, or magic. For more than a century previous to the Christian era, this had been going on. At the threshold of the transition stands Posidonius, like a second Janus. Looking in one direction, he favours a rational idealism; but, in another, he combines this with irrational and mystic elements. The sad thing is that these elements had to be devised and employed in order to express new emotional values which his rational idealism could not manage to guarantee, because it lay spell-bound and impotent in intellectualism. Language itself declined to fix the value of anything which was not intellectual by nature. Hence the Ὑπερνοητόν emerged, a conception which continued to attract and appropriate whatever was mythical and preposterous, allowing it to pass in unchallenged. Myth now ceased to be a mere symbol. It became the organic means of expression for those higher needs of sentiment and religion whose real nature was a closed book to thinkers of the day. On this line of development, Posidonius was followed by Philo.

The inevitable result of all this was a relapse to lower levels; but it was a relapse which, as usual, bore all the signs of an innovation. The signs pointed to life, but the innovation was ominous. For, while the older mythology had been either naïve or political, dwelling in the world of ceremony, the new mythology became a confession: it was philosophical, or pseudo-philosophical, and to this it owed its sway over the mind, beguiling the human spirit until it gradually succeeded in destroying the sense of reality and in crippling the proper functions of all the senses within man. His eyes grew dim, his ears could hear no longer. At the same time, these untoward effects were accompanied by a revival and resuscitation of the religious feeling—as a result of the philosophical development. This took place about the close of the first century. Ere long it permeated all classes in society, and it appears to have increased with every decade subsequently to the middle of the second century. This came out in two ways, on the principle of that dual development in which a religious upheaval always manifests itself. The first was a series of not unsuccessful attempts to revivify and inculcate the old religions, by carefully observing traditional customs, and by restoring the sites of the oracles and the places of worship. Such attempts, however, were partly superficial and artificial. They offered no strong or clear expression for the new religious cravings of the age. And Christianity held entirely aloof from all this restoration of religion. They came into contact merely to collide—this pair of alien magnitudes; neither understood the other, and each was driven to compass the extermination of its rival (see above).

The second way in which the resuscitation of religion came about, however, was far more potent. Ever since Alexander the Great and his successors, ever since Augustus in a later age, the nations upon whose development the advance of humanity depended had been living under new auspices. The great revolution in the external conditions of their existence has been already emphasized; but corresponding to this, and partly in consequence of it, a revolution took place in the inner world of religion, which was due in some degree to the blending of religions, but pre-eminently to the progress of culture and to man's experience inward and outward. No period can be specified at which this blending process commenced among the nations lying between Egypt and the Euphrates, the Tigris, or Persia;[1] for, so far as we are in a position to trace back their history, their religions were, like themselves, exposed to con-

---

[1] It is still a moot point of controversy whether India had any share in this, and if so to what extent; some connection with India, however, does seem probable.

stant interchange, whilst their religious theories were a matter
of give and take.   But now the Greek world fell to be added,
with all the store of knowledge and ideas which it had gained
by dint of ardent, willing toil, a world lying open to any
contribution from the East, and in its turn subjecting every
element of Eastern origin to the test of its own lore and
speculation.

The results already produced by the interchange of *Oriental*
religions, including that of Israel, were technically termed, a
century ago, " the Oriental philosophy of religion," a term which
denoted the broad complex of ritual and theory connected with
the respective cults, their religious ideas, and also scientific
speculations such as those of astronomy or of any other branch
of knowledge which was elevated into the province of religion.
All this was as indefinite as the title which was meant to comprehend it, nor even at present have we made any great progress
in this field of research.[1]   Still, we have a more definite grasp
of the complex itself; and—although it seems paradoxical to
say so—this is a result which we owe chiefly to Christian
gnosticism.   Nowhere else are these vague and various conceptions worked out for us so clearly and coherently.

In what follows I shall attempt to bring out the salient features
of this " Orientalism."   Naturally it was no rigid entity.   At
every facet it presented elements and ideas of the most varied
hue.   The general characteristic was this, that people still
retained or renewed their belief in sections of the traditional
mythology presented in realistic form.   To these they did attach
ideas.   It is not possible, as a rule, to ascertain in every case
at what point and to what extent such ideas overflowed and
overpowered the realistic element in any given symbol—a fact
which makes our knowledge of " Orientalism " look extremely defective ; for what is the use of fixing down a piece of mythology
to some definite period and circle, if we cannot be sure of its
exact value ?   Was it held literally ?   Was it transformed into
an idea ?   Was it taken metaphorically ?   Was it the creed of
unenlightened piety ?   Was it merely ornamental ?   And what

---

[1] The origin of the separate elements, in particular, is frequently obscure—
whether Indian, Persian, Babylonian, Egyptian, Asiatic, etc.

was its meaning? Theological or cosmological? Ethical or historical? Did it embody some event in the remote past, or something still in existence, or something only to be realized in the future? Or did these various meanings and values flow in and out of one another? And was the myth in question felt to be some sacred, undefined magnitude, something that could unite with every conceivable coefficient, serving as the starting-point for any interpretation whatsoever that one chose to put before the world? This last question is to be answered, I think, in the affirmative, nor must we forget that in one and the same circle the most diverse coefficients were simultaneously attached to any piece of mythology.

Further, we must not lose sight of the varied origin of the myths. The earliest spring from the primitive view of nature, in which the clouds were in conflict with the light and the night devoured the sun, whilst thunderstorms were the most awful revelation of the deity. Or they arose from the dream-world of the soul, from that separation of soul and body suggested by the dream, and from the cult of the human soul. The next stratum may have arisen out of ancient historical reminiscences, fantastically exaggerated and elevated into something supernatural. Then came the precipitate of primitive attempts at "science" which had gone no further, viz., observations of heaven and earth, leading to the knowledge of certain regular sequences, which were bound up with religious conceptions. All this the soul of man informed with life, endowing it with the powers of human consciousness. It was upon this stratum that the great Oriental religions rose, as we know them in history, with their special mythologies and ritual theories. Then came another stratum, namely, religion in its abstract development and alliance with a robust philosophic culture. One half of it was apologetic, and the other critical. Yet even there myths still took shape. Finally, the last stratum was laid down, viz., the glaciation of ancient imaginative fancies and religions produced by a new conception of the universe, which the circumstances and experience of mankind had set in motion. Under the pressure of this, all existing materials were fused together, elements that lay far apart were solidified into a unity, and all previous constructions were shattered, while the surface of the movement was covered by broken fragments thrown out in a broad moraine, in which the débris of all earlier strata were to be found. This is the meaning of "syncretism." Viewed from a distance, it looks like a unity, though the unity seems heterogeneous. The forces which have shaped it do not meet the eye. What one really sees is the ancient element in its composition ; the new lies buried under all that catches the eye upon the surface.

This new element consisted in the political and social experience, and in speculations of the inner life. It would appear that even before the period of its contact with the Greek spirit, "Orientalism" had reached this stage; but one of the most unfortunate gaps in our knowledge of the history of religion is our inability to determine to what extent "Orientalism" had developed on its own lines, independent of this Greek spirit. We must be content to ascertain what actually took place, viz., the rise of new ideas and emotions which meet us on the soil of Hellenism—that Hellenism which, with its philosophy of a matured Platonism and its development of the ancient mysteries, coalesced with Orientalism.[1] These new features [2] are somewhat as follows :—

(1) There is *the sharp division between the soul* (or *spirit*) *and the body* : the more or less exclusive importance attached to the spirit, and the notion that the spirit comes from some other, upper world and is either possessed or capable of life eternal: also the individualism involved in all this.

(2) There is *the sharp division between God and the world*, with

---

[1] The convergence of these lines of development in the various nations of antiquity during the age of Hellenism is among the best-established facts of history. Contemporary ideas of a cognate or similar nature were not simply the result of mutual interaction, but also of an independent development along parallel lines. This makes it difficult, and indeed impossible in many cases, to decide on which branch any given growth sprang up. The similarity of the development on parallel lines embraced not only the ideas, but frequently their very method of expression and the form under which they were conceived. The bounds of human fancy in this province are narrower than is commonly supposed.

[2] Cp. further the essay of Loofs on "The Crisis of Christianity in the Second Century" (*Deutsch-evang. Blätter*, 1904, Heft 7), which depicts the problem occasioned by the meeting of Christianity and syncretism. Also, the penetrating remarks of Wernle in his *Anfängen unserer Religion* (2nd cd., 1904 ; Eng. trans., *The Beginnings of Christianity*, in this library).

the subversion of the naïve idea that they formed a homo-
geneous unity.

(3) In consequence of these distinctions we have *the sublimation of the Godhead*, " via negationis et eminentiae." The Godhead now becomes for the first time incomprehensible and in-
describable ; yet it is also great and good. Furthermore, it is
the basis of all things ; but the ultimate basis, which is simply
posited yet cannot be actually grasped.

(4) As a further result of these distinctions and of the exclusive importance attached to the spirit, we have *the depreciation of the world*, the contention that it were better never to
have existed, that it was the result of a blunder, and that it was
a prison or at best a penitentiary for the spirit.

(5) There is the conviction that *the connection with the flesh*
(" that soiled robe ") *depreciated and stained the spirit* ; in fact,
that the latter would inevitably be ruined unless the connection were broken or its influence counteracted.

(6) There is *the yearning for redemption,* as a redemption
from the world, the flesh, mortality, and *death*.

(7) There is the conviction that all redemption is redemption
to life eternal, and that it is dependent on *knowledge and expiation* : that only the soul that knows (knows itself, the Godhead, and the nature and value of being) and is pure (*i.e.*, purged
from sin) can be saved.

(8) There is *the certainty that the redemption of the soul as a
return to God is effected through a series of stages*, just as the
soul once upon a time departed from God by stages, till it ended
in the present vale of tears. All instruction upon redemption
is therefore instruction upon " the return and road" to God.
The consummation of redemption is simply a graduated ascent.

(9) There is the belief (naturally a wavering belief) that *the
anticipated redemption or redeemer was already present*, needing
only to be sought out : present, that is, either in some ancient
creed which simply required to be placed in a proper light,
or in one of the mysteries which had only to be made more
generally accessible, or in some personality whose power and
commands had to be followed, or even in the spirit, if only it
would turn inward on itself.

(10) There is the conviction that whilst knowledge is indispensable to *all the media of redemption*, it cannot be adequate; on the contrary, they *must ultimately furnish and transmit an actual power divine*. It is the "initiation" (the mystery or sacrament) which is combined with the impartation of knowledge, by which alone the spirit is subdued, by which it is actually redeemed and delivered from the bondage of mortality and sin by means of mystic rapture.

(11) There is the prevalent, indeed the fundamental opinion that *knowledge of the universe, religion, and the strict management of the individual's conduct*, must form a compact unity; they must constitute an independent unity, which has nothing whatever to do with the State, society, the family, or one's daily calling, and must therefore maintain an attitude of *negation* (*i.e.*, in the sense of *asceticism*) towards all these spheres.

The soul, God, knowledge, expiation, asceticism, redemption, eternal life, with *individualism* and with *humanity* substituted for nationality—these were the sublime thoughts which were living and operative, partly as the precipitate of deep inward and outward movements, partly as the outcome of great souls and their toil, partly as one result of the sublimation of all cults which took place during the imperial age. Wherever vital religion existed, it was in this circle of thought and experience that it drew breath. The actual number of those who lived within the circle is a matter of no moment. "All men have not faith." And the history of religion, so far as it is really a history of vital religion, runs always in a very narrow groove.

The remarkable thing is the number of different guises in which such thoughts were circulating. Like all religious accounts of the universe which aim at reconciling monistic and dualistic theories, they required a large apparatus for their intrinsic needs; but the tendency was to elaborate this still further, partly in order to provide accommodation for whatever might be time-honoured or of any service, partly because isolated details had an appearance of weakness which made people hope to achieve their end by dint of accumulation. Owing to the heterogeneous character of their apparatus, these syncretistic formations seem often to be totally incongruous. But this is a superficial estimate. A glance at their motives and aims reveals the presence of a unity, and indeed of a simplicity, which is truly remarkable. The final motives, in fact, are simple and powerful, inasmuch as they have sprung from simple but powerful experiences of the inner life, and it was due to them that the development of religion advanced, so far as any such advance took place apart from Christianity.

Christianity had to settle with this "syncretism" or final form of Hellenism. But we can see at once how inadequate it would be to describe the contrast between Christianity and "paganism" simply as the contrast between monotheism and polytheism. No doubt, any form of syncretism was perfectly capable of blending with polytheism; the one even demanded and could not but *intensify* the other. To explain the origin of the world and also to describe the soul's "return," the "apparatus" of the system required æons, intermediate beings, semi-gods, and deliverers; the highest deity was not the highest or most perfect, if it stood by itself. Yet all this way of thinking was monotheistic at bottom; it elevated the highest God to the position of primal God, high above all gods, linking the soul to this primal God and to him alone (not to any subordinate deities).[1] Polytheism was relegated to a lower level

---

[1] The difference between the Christian God and the God of syncretistic Hellenism is put by the pagan (Porphyry) in *Macarius Magnes*, iv. 20, with admirable lucidity: τὸ μέντοι περὶ τῆς μοναρχίας τοῦ μόνου θεοῦ καὶ τῆς πολυαρχίας τῶν σεβομένων θεῶν διαρρήδην ζητήσωμεν, ὧν οὐκ οἶδας οὐδὲ τῆς μοναρχίας τὸν λόγον ἀφηγήσασθαι. Μονάρχης γάρ ἐστιν οὐχ ὁ μόνος ὤν ἀλλ' ὁ μόνος ἄρχων· ἄρχει δ' ὁμοφύλων δηλαδὴ καὶ ὁμοίων, οἷον Ἁδριανὸς ὁ βασιλεὺς μονάρχης γέγονεν, οὐχ ὅτι μόνος ἦν οὐδ' ὅτι βοῶν καὶ προβάτων ἦρχεν, ὧν ἄρχουσι ποιμένες ἢ βουκόλοι, ἀλλ' ὅτι ἀνθρώπων ἐβασίλευσε τῶν ὁμογενῶν τὴν αὐτὴν φύσιν ἐχόντων· ὡσαύτως θεὸς οὐκ ἂν μονάρχης κυρίως ἐκλήθη, εἰ μὴ θεῶν ἦρχε. τοῦτο γὰρ ἔπρεπε τῷ θείῳ μεγέθει καὶ τῷ οὐρανίῳ καὶ πολλῷ ἀξιώματι ("Let us, however, proceed to inquire explicitly about the monarchy of the one God alone and the joint-rule of those deities who are worshipped, but of whom, as of divine monarchy, you cannot give any account. A monarch is not one who is alone but one who rules alone, ruling subjects of kindred nature like himself—such as the emperor Hadrian, for example, who was a monarch not because he stood alone or because he ruled sheep and cattle, which are commanded by shepherds and herdsmen, *but because he was king over human beings whose nature was like his own.* Even so, it would not have been accurate to term God a monarch, if he did not rule over gods. For such a position befitted the dignity of God and the high honour of heaven"). Here the contrast between

from the supremacy which once it had enjoyed. Further, as soon as Christianity itself began to be reflective, it took an interest in this "syncretism," borrowing ideas from it, and using them, in fact, to promote its own development. Christianity was not originally syncretistic itself, for Jesus Christ did not belong to this circle of ideas, and it was his disciples who were responsible for the primitive shaping of Christianity. But whenever Christianity came to formulate ideas of God, Jesus, sin, redemption, and life, it drew upon the materials acquired in the general process of religious evolution, availing itself of all the forms which these had taken.

Christian preaching thus found itself confronted with the old polytheism at its height in the imperial cultus, and with this syncretism which represented the final stage of Hellenism. These constituted the inner conditions under which the young religion carried on its mission. From its opposition to polytheism it drew that power of antithesis and exclusiveness which is a force at once needed and intensified by any independent religion. In syncretism, again, i.e., in all that as a rule deserved the title of "religion" in contemporary life, it possessed unconsciously a secret ally. All it had to do with syncretism was to cleanse and simplify—and complicate—it.

the Christian and the Greek monarchianism is clearly defined. Only, it should be added that many philosophic Christians (even in the second century) did not share this severely monotheistic idea of God; in fact, as early as the first century we come across modifications of it. Tertullian (in *adv. Prax.* iii.), even in recapitulating the view of God which passed for orthodox at that period, comes dangerously near to Porphyry in the remark: "Nullam dico dominationem ita unius esse, ita singularem, ita monarchiam, ut non etiam per alias proximas personas administretur, quas ipsa prospexerit officiales sibi" ("No dominion, I hold, belongs to any one person in such a way, or is in such a sense singular, or in such a sense a monarchy, as not also to be administered through other persons who are closely related to it, and with whom it has provided itself as its officials"). The school of Origen went still further in their reception of syncretistic monotheism, and the movement was not checked until the Nicene creed came with its irrational doctrine of the Trinity, causing the Logos and the Spirit to be conceived as persons within the Godhead. But although the pagan monarchical idea was routed on this field, it had already entrenched itself in the doctrine of angels. The latter, as indeed Porphyry (iv. 20) observed, is thoroughly Hellenic, since it let in polytheism through a back-door. In iv. 23 Porphyry tries to show Christians that as their scriptures taught a plurality of gods, they consequently contained the conception of God's monarchy which the Greeks taught. He refers to Exod. xxii. 28, Jerem. vii. 6, Deut. xii. 30, Josh. xxiv. 14, 1 Cor. viii. 5.

CHAPTER IV

IT is impossible to answer the question of Jesus' relation to the universal mission, without a critical study of the evangelic records. The gospels were written in an age when the mission was already in full swing, and they consequently refer it to direct injunction of Jesus. But they enable us, for all that, to recognise the actual state of matters.

Jesus addressed his gospel—his message of God's imminent kingdom and of judgment, of God's fatherly providence, of repentance, holiness, and love—to his fellow-countrymen. He preached only to Jews. Not a syllable shows that he detached this message from its national soil, or set aside the traditional religion as of no value. Upon the contrary, his preaching could be taken as the most powerful corroboration of that religion. He did not attach himself to any of the numerous "liberal" or syncretistic Jewish conventicles or schools. He did not accept their ideas. Rather he took his stand upon the soil of Jewish rights, i.e., of the piety maintained by Pharisaism. But he showed that while the Pharisees preserved what was good in religion, they were perverting it none the less, and that the perversion amounted to the most heinous of sins. Jesus waged war against the selfish, self-righteous temper in which many of the Pharisees fulfilled and practised their piety—a temper, at bottom, both loveless and godless. This protest already involved a break with the national religion, for the Pharisaic position passed for that of the nation; indeed, it represented the national religion. But Jesus went further. He traversed the claim that the descendants of Abraham, in virtue of their descent, were sure of salvation, and based the idea of divine sonship exclusively upon repentance, humility, faith, and love. In so doing, he disentangled religion from its national setting. Men, not Jews, were to be its adherents. Then, as it became plainer than ever that the Jewish people as a whole, and through their representatives, were spurning his message, he announced with increasing emphasis that a judgment was coming upon "the children of the kingdom," and prophesied, as his forerunner had done already, that the table of his Father would not lack for guests, but that a crowd would pour in, morning, noon, and night, from the highways and the hedges. Finally, he predicted the rejection of the nation and the overthrow of the temple, but these were not to involve the downfall of his work; on the contrary, he saw in them, as in his own passion, the condition of his work's completion.

Such is the "universalism" of the preaching of Jesus. No other kind of universalism can be proved for him, and consequently he cannot have given any command upon the mission to the wide world. The gospels contain such a command, but it is easy to show that it is neither genuine nor a part of the primitive tradition. It would introduce an entirely strange feature into the preaching of Jesus, and at the same time render many of his genuine sayings unintelligible or empty. One might even argue that the universal mission was an inevitable issue of the religion and spirit of Jesus, and that its origin, not only apart from any direct word of Jesus, but in verbal contradiction to several of his sayings, is really a stronger testimony to the method, the strength, and the spirit of his preaching than if it were the outcome of a deliberate command. By the fruit we know the tree; but we must not look for the fruit in the root. With regard to the way in which he worked and gathered disciples, the distinctiveness of his person and his preaching comes out very clearly. He sought to found no sect or school. He laid down no rules for outward adhesion to himself. His aim was to bring men to God and to prepare them for God's kingdom. He chose disciples, indeed, giving them special instruction and a share in his work; but even here there were no regulations. There were an inner circle of three, an outer circle of twelve, and beyond that a few dozen men and women who accompanied him. In addition to that, he had intimate friends who remained in their homes and at their work. Wherever he went, he wakened or found children of God throughout the country. No rule or regulation bound them together. They simply sought and shared the supreme boon which came home to each and all, viz., the kingdom of their Father and of the individual soul. In the practice of this kind of mission Jesus has had but one follower, and he did not arise till a thousand years afterwards. He was St Francis of Assisi.

If we leave out of account the words put by our first evangelist into the lips of the risen Jesus (Matt. xxviii. 19 f.), with the similar expressions which occur in the unauthentic appendix to the second gospel (Mark xvi. 15, 20), and if we further set aside the story of the wise men from the East, as well as one or two Old Testament quotations which our first evangelist has woven into his tale (cp. Matt. iv. 13 f., xii. 18), we must admit that Mark and Matthew have almost consistently withstood the temptation to introduce the Gentile mission into the words and deeds of Jesus. Jesus called sinners to himself, ate with tax-gatherers, attacked the Pharisees and their legal observance, made everything turn upon mercy and justice, and predicted the downfall of the temple—such is the universalism of Mark and Matthew. The very choice and com-mission of the twelve is described without any mention of a mission to the world (Mark iii. 13 f., vi. 7 f., and Matt. x. 1 f.). In fact, Matthew expressly limits their mission to Palestine. "Go not on the road of the Gentiles, and enter no city of the Samaritans; rather go to the lost sheep of the house of Israel" (Matt. x. 5, 6). And so in x. 23: "Ye shall not have covered the cities of Israel, before the Son of man comes."[1] The story of the Syro-Phœnician

[1] This verse precludes the hypothesis that the speech of Jesus referred merely to a provisional mission. If the saying is genuine, the Gentile mission cannot have lain within the horizon of Jesus.—There is no need to take the ἡγεμόνες and βασιλεῖς of Matt. x. 18, Mark xiii. 9 as pagans, and Matthew's addition (omitted by Mark) of καὶ τοῖς ἔθνεσιν to the words εἰς μαρτύριον αὐτοῖς can hardly be understood except as a supplement in the sense of xxviii. 19 f. Though Mark (vi. 7 f.; cp. Luke ix. 1 f.) omits the limitation of the mission to Palestine and the Jewish people, he does not venture to assign the mission any universal scope. "Mark never says it in so many words, nor does he lay any stress upon it; but it is self-evident that he regards the mission of Jesus as confined to the Jews" (Well-hausen on Mark vii 29).

woman is almost of greater significance. Neither evangelist leaves
it open to question that this incident represented *an exceptional case
for Jesus*;[1] and the exception proves the rule.

In Mark this section on the Syro-Phœnician woman is the only
passage where the missionary efforts of Jesus appear positively
restricted to the Jewish people in Palestine. Matthew, however,
contains not merely the address on the disciples' mission, but a
further saying (xix. 28), to the effect that the twelve are one day
to judge the twelve tribes of Israel. No word here of the Gentile
mission.[2]

Only twice does Mark make Jesus allude to the gospel being
preached in future throughout the world: in the eschatological
address (xiii. 10, "The gospel must first be preached to all the
nations," *i.e.*, before the end arrives), and in the story of the
anointing at Bethany (xiv. 9), where we read: "Wherever this
gospel shall be preached throughout the whole world, what this
woman hath done shall be also told, in memory of her." The
former passage puts into the life of Jesus an historical theo-
logoumenon, which is hardly original. The latter excites strong
suspicion, not with regard to what precedes it, but in connection
with the saying of Jesus in verses 8–9. It is a *hysteron proteron*,
and moreover the solemn assurance is striking. Some obscure
controversy must underlie the words—a controversy which turned
upon the preceding scene not only when it happened, but at a
still later date. Was it ever suspected?[3]

---

[1] According to Matthew (xv. 24), Jesus distinctly says, "I was sent only to the
lost sheep of the house of Israel." The πρῶτον of Mark vii. 27 is not to be pressed,
as it is by many editors.

[2] Here we may also include the saying: "Pray that your flight occur not on the
Sabbath" (Matt. xxiv. 20). Note further that the parable of the two sons (Matt.
xxi. 28 f.) does *not* refer to Jews and Gentiles. The labourers in the vineyard
(Matt. xx. 1 f.) are not to be taken as Gentiles—not, at any rate, as the evangelist
tells the story. Nor are Gentiles to be thought of even in xxii. 9.

[3] I leave out of account the section on the Wicked husbandmen, as it says nothing
about the Gentile mission either in Mark's version (xii. 1 f.), or in Matthew's
(xxi. 33 f.). The words of Matt. xxi. 43 ("God's kingdom shall be given to a
nation bringing forth the fruits thereof") do not refer to the Gentiles; it is the
"nation" as opposed to the official Israel. Mark *on purpose* speaks merely of
"others," to whom the vineyard is to be given. "On purpose," I say, for we
may see from this very allegory, which can hardly have been spoken by Jesus
himself (see Jülicher's *Gleichnissreden*, ii. pp. 405 f., though I would not commit
myself on the point), how determined Mark was to keep the Gentile mission apart
from the gospel, and how consistently Matthew retains the setting of the latter
within the Jewish nation. The parable invited the evangelists to represent Jesus
making some allusion to the Gentile mission, but both of them resisted the invita-

These two sayings are also given in Matthew [1] (xxiv. 14, xxvi. 13), who preserves a further saying which has the Gentile world in view, yet whose prophetic manner arouses no suspicion of its authenticity. In viii. 11 we read: "I tell you, many shall come from east and west, and sit down with Abraham and Isaac and Jacob in the kingdom of heaven, but the sons of the kingdom shall be cast out." Why should not Jesus have said this? Even among the words of John the Baptist (iii. 9) do we not read: "Think not to say to your-selves, we have Abraham as our father; for I tell you, God is able to raise up children for Abraham out of these stones"?

We conclude, then, that both evangelists refrain from inserting any allusion to the Gentile mission into the framework of the public preaching of Jesus, apart from the eschatological address and the somewhat venturesome expression which occurs in the story of the anointing at Bethany. But while Matthew delimits the activity of Jesus positively and precisely, Mark adopts what we may term a neutral position, though for all that he does not suppress the story of the Syro-Phœnician woman.

All this throws into more brilliant relief than ever the words of the risen Jesus in Matt. xxviii. 19 f. Matthew must have been fully conscious of the disparity between these words and the earlier words of Jesus; nay, more, he must have deliberately chosen to give expression to that disparity.[2] At the time when

tion (see further, Luke xx. 9 f.). Wellhausen (on Matt. xxi. 43) also observes: "By the phrase 'another nation' we may understand that Jewish, not simply Gentile, Christians were so meant; for ἔθνος is characterised ethically, not nation-ally."

[1] We may disregard the sayings in v. 13-14 ("Ye are the salt of the earth," "Ye are the light of the world"), as well as the fact that in Mark alone (xi. 17) πᾶσι τοῖς ἔθνεσιν (a citation from Isa. lvi. 7) is added to the words: "My house shall be a house of prayer." The addition "emphasizes not the universality of the house of prayer, but simply the idea of the house of prayer" (Wellhausen).

[2] Unless xxviii. 19 f. is a later addition to the gospel. It is impossible to be certain on this point. There is a certain subtlety, of which one would fain believe the evangelist was incapable, in keeping his Gentile Christian readers, as it were, upon the rack with sayings which confined the gospel to Israel, just in order to let them off in the closing paragraph. Nor are the former sayings presented in such a way as to suggest that they were afterwards to be taken back. On the other hand, we must observe that the first evangelist opens with the story of the wise men from the East (though even this section admits of a strictly Jewish Christian interpretation), that he includes viii. 11, that he shows his interest in the people who sat in darkness (iv. 13 f.), that he describes Jesus (xii. 21) as One in whose name the Gentiles trust, that he contemplates the preaching of the gospel to all the Gentiles in the eschatological speech and in the story of the anointing at Bethany, and that no positive proofs can be adduced for regarding xxviii. 19 f. as

our gospels were written, a Lord and Saviour who had confined his preaching to the Jewish people without even issuing a single command to prosecute the universal mission, was an utter impossibility. If no such command had been issued before his death, it must have been imparted by him as the glorified One.

The conclusion, therefore, must be that Jesus never issued such a command at all, but that this version of his life was due to the historical developments of a later age, the words being appropriately put into the mouth of the risen Lord. Paul, too, knew nothing of such a general command.[1]

Luke's standpoint, as a reporter of the words of Jesus, does not differ from that of the two previous evangelists, a fact which is perhaps most significant of all. He has delicately coloured the introductory history with universalism,[2] while at the close, like Matthew, he makes the risen Jesus issue the command to preach the gospel to all nations.[3] But in his treatment of the intervening material he follows Mark; that is, he preserves no sayings which expressly confine the activity of Jesus to the Jewish nation,[4] but, on the other hand, he gives neither word nor incident which describes that activity as universal,[5]

an interpolation. It is advisable, then, to credit the writer with a remarkable historical sense, which made him adhere almost invariably to the traditional framework of Christ's preaching, in order to break it open at the very close of his work. Mark's method of procedure was more simple : he excluded the missionary question altogether ; at least that is the only explanation of his attitude.

[1] It is impossible and quite useless to argue with those who see nothing but an inadmissible bias in the refusal to accept traditions about Jesus eating and drinking and instructing his disciples after death.

[2] Cp. i. 32 ("Son of the Highest"), ii. 10, 11 ("joy to all people," "Saviour"), ii. 14 ("gloria in excelsis"), ii. 32 ("a light to lighten the Gentiles"), and also (iii. 23 f.) the genealogy of Jesus traced back to Adam.

[3] xxiv. 47, also Acts i. 8 : "Ye shall be my witnesses both in Jerusalem and in all Judæa and in Samaria, and to the uttermost part of the earth."

[4] An indirect allusion to the limitation of his mission might be found in xxii. 30 = Matt. xix. 28 (cp. p. 41), but this meaning need not be read into it.

[5] All sorts of unconvincing attempts have been made to drag this in ; e.g., at Peter's take of fish (v. 1 f.), at the Samaritan stories (x. 33 f., xvii. 16), and at the parable of the prodigal son (xv. 11 f. ; cp. Jülicher's *Gleichn.*, ii. pp. 333 f.). Even the stories of the despatch of the apostles (vi. 13 f.) and the remarkable commission of the seventy (x. 1 f.) do not by any means represent the Gentile mission. It is by a harmless *hysteron proteron* that the twelve are now and then described by Luke as "the apostles." The programme of the speech at Nazareth (iv. 26-27) is here of primary importance, but even in it the universalism of Jesus does not seem to rise above that of the prophets. With regard to xxi. 24 = Mark xiii. 10 = Matt. xxiv. 14, we may say that Luke was quite the most careful of all those who

and at no point does he deliberately correct the existing tradition.[1]

In this connection the fourth gospel need not be considered at all. After the Gentile mission, which had been undertaken with such ample results during the first two Christian generations, the fourth gospel expands the horizon of Christ's preaching and even of John the Baptist's; corresponding to this, it makes the Jews a reprobate people from the very outset, despite the historical remark in iv. 22. Even setting aside the prologue, we at once come upon (i. 29) the words put into the mouth of the Baptist, "Behold the Lamb of God which taketh away the sin *of the world*." And, as a whole, the gospel is saturated with statements of a directly universalistic character. Jesus is *the Saviour of the world*, and God so loved *the world* that he sent him. We may add passages like those upon the "other sheep" and the *one* flock (x. 16). But the most significant thing of all is that this gospel makes Greeks ask after Jesus (xii. 20 f.), the latter furnishing a formal explanation of the reasons why he could not satisfy the Greeks as yet. He must first of all die. It is as the exalted One that he will first succeed in drawing *all* men to himself. We can feel here the pressure of a serious problem.

It would be misleading to introduce here any sketch of the preaching of Jesus, or even of its essential principles,[2] for it never became the missionary preaching of the later period even to the Jews. It was the *basis* of that preaching, for the gospels were written down in order to serve as a means of evangelization; but the mission preaching was occupied with the messiahship of Jesus, his speedy return, and his establishment of God's kingdom (if Jews were to be met), or with the unity of God, creation, the Son of God, and judgment (if Gentiles were to be reached). Alongside of this the words of Jesus of course exercised a silent and effective mission of their own, whilst the historical picture furnished by the gospels,

attempted with fine feeling to reproduce the prophet's style. He never mentions the necessity of the gospel being preached throughout all the world before the end arrives, but writes: ἄχρι οὗ πληρωθῶσιν καιροὶ ἐθνῶν ("till the times of the Gentiles be fulfilled"). As for the Samaritan stories, it does not seem as if Luke here had any ulterior tendency of an historical and religious character in his mind, such as is evident in John iv.

[1] The story of the Syro-Phœnician woman, which stands between the two stories of miraculous feeding in Mark and Matthew, was probably quite unknown to Luke. Its omission was not deliberate. If he knew it, his omission would have to be regarded as a conscious correction of the earlier tradition.

[2] Cp. my lectures on *What is Christianity?*

together with faith in the exalted Christ, exerted a powerful influence over catechumens and believers.

Rightly and wisely, people no longer noticed the local and temporal traits either in this historical sketch or in these sayings. They found there a vital love of God and men, which may be described as implicit universalism; a discounting of everything external (position, personality, sex, outward worship, etc.), which made irresistibly for inwardness of character; and a protest against the entire doctrines of "the ancients," which gradually rendered antiquity valueless.[1] One of the greatest revolutions in the history of religion was initiated in this way—initiated and effected, moreover, without any revolution! All that Jesus Christ promulgated was the overthrow of the temple, and the judgment impending upon the nation and its leaders. He shattered Judaism, and brought out the kernel of the religion of Israel. Thereby—*i.e.*, by his preaching of God as the Father, *and by his own death*—he founded the universal religion, which at the same time was the religion of the Son.

[1] On "The Attitude of Jesus towards the Old Testament," see the conclusive tractate by E. Klostermann (1904) under this title. No one who grasps this attitude upon the part of Jesus will make unhistorical assertions upon the "World-mission."

CHAPTER V

THE TRANSITION FROM THE JEWISH TO THE
GENTILE MISSION

"Christi mors potentior erat quam vita." The death of
Christ was more effective than his life ; it failed to shatter faith
in him as one sent by God, and hence the conviction of his
resurrection arose. He was still the Messiah, his disciples held
—for there was no alternative now between this and the rejection of his claims. As Messiah, he could not be held of death.
He must be alive ; he must soon return in glory. The disciples
became chosen members of his kingdom, witnesses and—apostles.
They testified not only to his preaching and his death, but to
his resurrection, for they had seen him and received his spirit.
They became new men. A current of divine life seized them,
and a new fire was burning in their hearts. Fear, doubt,
cowardice—all this was swept away. The duty and the right
of preaching this Jesus of Nazareth as the Christ pressed upon
them with irresistible power. How could they keep silence when
they knew that the new age of the world was come, and that God
had already begun the redemption of his people ? An old tradition (Acts i.–ii.) relates that the preaching of the disciples began
in Jerusalem on the fifty-first day after the crucifixion. We have
no reason to doubt so definite a statement. They must have
returned from Galilee to Jerusalem and gathered together there
—a change which suggests that they wished to work openly, in
the very midst of the Jewish community. They remained there for
some years [1]—for a period of twelve years indeed, according to

[1] We may perhaps assume that they wished to be on the very spot when the
Lord returned and the heavenly Jerusalem descended. It is remarkable how
Galilee falls into the background : we hear nothing about it.

one early account[1] ignored by the book of Acts (cp., however,
xii. 17)—they would undertake mission tours in the vicinity;
the choice of James, who did not belong to the twelve, as president of the church at Jerusalem,[2] tells in favour of this conclusion, whilst the evidence for it lies in Acts, and above all in
1 Cor. ix. 5.

The gospel was at first preached to the Jews exclusively.
The church of Jerusalem was founded ; presently churches in
Judæa (1 Thess. ii. 14, αἱ ἐκκλησίαι τοῦ θεοῦ αἱ οὖσαι ἐν τῇ
Ἰουδαίᾳ; Gal. i. 22, ἤμην ἀγνοούμενος τῷ προσώπῳ ταῖς ἐκκλησίαις
τῆς Ἰουδαίας ταῖς ἐν Χριστῷ), Galilee, Samaria (Acts i. 8, viii.
1 f, ix. 31, xv. 3), and on the sea-coast (Acts ix. 32 f.) followed.[3]
The initial relationship of these churches to Judaism is not
quite clear.   As a matter of fact, so far from being clear,
it is full of inconsistencies.   On the one hand, the narrative
of Acts (see iii. f.), which describes the Jerusalem church as

---

[1] This early account (in the preaching of Peter, cited by Clem., *Strom.*, vi. 5.
43) is of course untrustworthy ; it pretends to know a word spoken by the Lord
to his disciples, which ran thus : "After twelve years, go out into the world,
lest any should say, we have not heard" (μετὰ ιβ' ἔτη ἐξέλθετε εἰς τὸν κόσμον, μή
τις εἴπη· οὐκ ἠκούσαμεν).   But although the basis of the statement is apologetic
and untrue, it may be right about the twelve years, for in the *Acta Petri cum
Simone*, 5, and in Apollonius (in Eus., *H.E.*, v. 18. 14), the word (here also a
word of the Lord) runs that the apostles were to remain for twelve years at
Jerusalem, without any mention of the exodus εἰς τὸν κόσμον.   Here, too, the
"word of the Lord" lacks all support, but surely the fact of the disciples remaining for twelve years in Jerusalem can hardly have been invented.   Twelve
(or eleven) years after the resurrection is a period which is also fixed by other
sources (see von Dobschütz in *Texte u. Unters.*, XI. i. p. 53 f.); indeed it
underlies the later calculation of the year when Peter died (30 + 12 + 25 = 67 A.D.).
The statement of the pseudo-Clementine Recognitions (i. 43, ix. 29), that the
apostles remained seven years in Jerusalem, stands by itself.

[2] Acts assumes that during the opening years the apostles superintended the
church in Jerusalem ; all of a sudden (xii. 17) James appears as the president.

[3] The parallel mission of Simon Magus in Samaria may be mentioned here in
passing.   It had important results locally, but it failed in its attempt to turn the
Christian movement to account.   The details are for the most part obscure; it is
clear, however, that Simon held himself to be a religious founder (copying Jesus
in this ?), and that subsequently a Hellenistic theosophy or gnosis was associated
with his religion.   Christians treated the movement from the very outset with
unabated abhorrence.   There must have been, at some early period, a time when
the movement proved a real temptation for the early church : to what extent,
however, we cannot tell.   Did Simon contemplate any fusion? (Acts viii. and
later sources).

exposed to spasmodic persecutions almost from the start, is
corroborated by the evidence of Paul (1 Thess. ii. 14, ὅτι τὰ
αὐτά ἐπάθετε καὶ ὑμεῖς ὑπὸ τῶν ἰδίων συμφυλετῶν, καθὼς καὶ
αὐτοὶ [*i.e.* the churches in Judæa] ὑπὸ τῶν Ἰουδαίων), so that
it seems untenable to hold with some Jewish scholars that originally, and indeed for whole decades, peace reigned between the
Christians and the Jews.[1] On the other hand, it is certain that
peace and toleration also prevailed, that the churches remained
unmolested for a considerable length of time (Acts ix. 31,
ἡ ἐκκλησία καθ' ὅλης τῆς Ἰουδαίας καὶ Γαλιλαίας καὶ Σαμαρίας
εἶχεν εἰρήνην), and that several Christians were highly thought
of by their Jewish brethren.[2] By their strict observance of the
law and their devoted attachment to the temple,[3] they fulfilled
a Jew's *principal* duty, and since it was in the future that they
expected Jesus as their Messiah—his first advent having been
no more than a preliminary step—this feature might be overlooked, as an idiosyncrasy, by those who were inclined to think
well of them for their strict observance of the law.[4] At least

---

[1] Cp. Joël's *Blicke in die Religionsgeschichte* (Part II., 1883). The course
of events in the Palestinian mission may be made out from Matt. x. 17 f. :
παραδώσουσιν ὑμᾶς εἰς συνέδρια καὶ ἐν ταῖς συναγωγαῖς αὐτῶν μαστιγώσουσιν ὑμᾶς
. . . . παραδώσει δὲ ἀδελφὸς ἀδελφὸν εἰς θάνατον καὶ πατὴρ τέκνον καὶ ἐπαναστή-
σονται τέκνα ἐπὶ γονεῖς καὶ θανατώσουσιν αὐτούς . . . . ὅταν δὲ διώκωσιν ὑμᾶς ἐν
τῇ πόλει ταύτῃ, φεύγετε εἰς τὴν ἑτέραν.

[2] Hegesippus (in Eus., *H.E.*, ii. 22) relates this of James. No doubt his
account is far from lucid, but the repute of James among the Jews may be safely
inferred from it.

[3] Cp. Acts xxi. 20, where the Christians of Jerusalem address Paul thus :
θεωρεῖς, ἀδελφέ, πόσαι μυριάδες εἰσὶν ἐν τοῖς Ἰουδαίοις τῶν πεπιστευκότων, καὶ
πάντες ζηλωταὶ τοῦ νόμου ὑπάρχουσιν. This passage at once elucidates and confirms the main point of Hegesippus' account of James. From one very ancient
tradition (in a prologue to Mark's gospel, *c.* 200 A.D.), that when Mark became a
Christian he cut off his thumbs in order to escape serving as a priest, we may
infer that many a Christian Jew of the priestly class in Jerusalem still continued to
discharge priestly functions in those primitive days.

[4] As Weizsäcker justly remarks (*Apost. Zeitalter* (2), p. 38 ; Eng. trans., i. 46 f.) :
"The primitive Christians held fast to the faith and polity of their nation. They
had no desire to be renegades, nor was it possible to regard them as such. Even
if they did not maintain the whole cultus, this did not endanger their allegiance,
for Judaism tolerated not merely great latitude in doctrinal views, but also a
partial observance of the cultus—as is sufficiently proved by the contemporary
case of the Essenes. The Christians did not lay themselves open to the charge of
violating the law. They assumed no aggressive attitude. That they appeared
before the local courts as well as before the Sanhedrim, the supreme national

this is the only way in which we can picture to ourselves the state of matters. The more zealous of their Jewish compatriots can have had really nothing but praise for the general Christian hope of the Messiah's sure and speedy advent. Doubtless it was in their view a grievous error for Christians to believe that they already knew the person of the future Messiah. But the crucifixion seemed to have torn up this belief by the roots, so that every zealous Jew could anticipate the speedy collapse of " the offence," while the Messianic ardour would survive. As for the Jewish authorities, they could afford to watch the progress of events, contenting themselves with a general surveillance. Meantime, however, the whole movement was confined to the lower classes.[1]

council, tallies with the fact that, on the whole, they remained Jews. It is in itself quite conceivable (cp. Matt. x. 17) that . . . . individual Christians should have been prosecuted, but discharged on the score of insufficient evidence, or that this discharge was accompanied by some punishment. . . . The whole position of Jewish Christians within the Jewish commonwealth precludes the idea that they made a practice of establishing a special synagogue for themselves on Jewish soil, or avowedly formed congregations beside the existing synagogues. As the synagogue was a regular institution of the Jewish community, such a course of action would have been equivalent to a complete desertion of all national associations and obligations whatsoever, and would therefore have resembled a revolt. The only question is, whether the existence of synagogues for foreigners in Jerusalem gave them a pretext for setting up an independent one there. It is our Acts that mentions this in a passage which is beyond suspicion ; it speaks (vi. 9) about the synagogue of the Libertini, Cyrenians, Alexandrians, and those from Cilicia and Asia who disputed with Stephen. It is not quite clear whether we are to think here of a single synagogue embracing all these people, or of several—and if so, how many. The second alternative is favoured by this consideration, that the foreigners who, according to this account, assembled in meeting-places of their own throughout Jerusalem, proceeded on the basis of their nationality. In that case one might conjecture that the Christians, as natives of Galilee (Acts i. 11, ii. 7), took up a similar position. Yet it cannot be proved that the name was applied to them. From Acts xxiv. 5 we must assume that they were known rather by the name of ' Nazarenes,' and as this title probably described the origin, not of the body, but of its founder, its character was different. . . . . But even if the Christians had, like the Libertini, formed a synagogue of Galileans in Jerusalem, this would not throw much light upon the organization of their society, for we know nothing at all about the aims or regulations under which the various nationalities organized themselves into separate synagogues. And in regard to the question as a whole, we must not overlook the fact that in our sources the term synagogue is never applied to Christians."

[1] Cp. what is said of Gamaliel, Acts v. 34 f. For the lower classes, see John vii. 48, 49: μή τις ἐκ τῶν ἀρχόντων ἐπίστευσεν εἰς αὐτὸν ἢ ἐκ τῶν Φαρισαίων;

But no sooner did the Gentile mission, with its lack of restrictions (from the Jewish point of view) or laxity of restrictions, become an open fact, than this period of toleration, or of spasmodic and not very violent reactions on the part of Judaism, had to cease. Severe reprisals followed. Yet the Gentile mission at first drove a wedge into the little company of Christians themselves; it prompted those who disapproved of it to retire closer to their non-Christian brethren. The apostle Paul had to complain of and to contend with a double opposition. He was persecuted by Jewish Christians who were zealous for the law, no less than by the Jews (so 1 Thess. ii. 15 f., ἐκδιώξαντες ἡμᾶς . . . . κωλύοντες ἡμᾶς τοῖς ἔθνεσιν λαλῆσαι, ἵνα σωθῶσιν); the latter had really nothing whatever to do with the Gentile mission, but evidently they did not by any means look on with folded arms.

It is not quite clear how the Gentile mission arose. Certainly Paul was not the first missionary to the Gentiles.[1] But *a priori* considerations and the details of the evidence alike may justify us in concluding that while the transition to the Gentile mission was gradual, it was carried out with irresistible energy. Here, too, the whole ground had been prepared already, by the inner condition of Judaism, *i.e.*, by the process of decomposition within Judaism which made for universalism, as well as by the graduated system of the proselytes. To this we have already alluded in the first chapter.

ἀλλὰ ὁ ὄχλος οὗτος ὁ μὴ γινώσκων τὸν νόμον ἐπάρατοί εἰσιν. Yet Acts (vi. 7) brings out the fact that priests (a great crowd of them—πολὺς ὄχλος—it is alleged), no less than Pharisees (xv. 5), also joined the movement.

[1] Paul never claims in his letters to have been absolutely the pioneer of the Gentile mission. Had it been so, he certainly would not have failed to mention it. Gal. i. 16 merely says that the apostle understood already that his conversion meant a commission to the Gentiles; it does not say that this commission was something entirely new. Nor need it be concluded that Paul started on this Gentile mission *immediately*; the object of the revelation of God's Son (ἵνα εὐαγγελίζωμαι αὐτὸν ἐν τοῖς ἔθνεσιν) may have been only disclosed to him by degrees. All we are to understand is that after his conversion he needed no further conflict of the inner man in order to undertake the Gentile mission. Nevertheless, it is certain that Paul remains *the* Gentile missionary. It was he who really established the duty and the right of Gentile missions; it was he who raised the movement out of its tentative beginnings into a mission that embraced all the world.

According to Acts vi. 7 f.,[1] the primitive Christian community ın Jerusalem was composed of two elements, one consisting of Palestinian Hebrews, and the other of Jews from the dispersion ('Ελληνισταί).[2] A cleavage occurred between both at an early stage, which led to the appointment of seven guardians of the poor, belonging to the second of these groups and bearing Greek names. Within this group of men, whom we may consider on the whole to have been fairly enlightened, i.e., less strict than others in literal observance of the law,[3] Stephen rose to special prominence. The charge brought against him before the Sanhedrim was to the effect that he went on uttering blasphemous language against "the holy place" and the law, by affirming that Jesus was to destroy the temple and alter the customs ✓ enjoined by Moses. This charge Acts describes as false; but, as the speech of Stephen proves, it was well founded so far as it went, the falsehood consisting merely in the conscious purpose

[1] To the author of Acts, the transition from the Jewish to the Gentile mission, with the consequent rejection of Judaism, was a fact of the utmost importance; indeed one may say that he made the description of this transition the main object of his book. This is proved by the framework of the first fifteen chapters, and by the conclusion of the work in xxviii. 23-28 (verses 30-31 being a postscript). After quoting from Isa. vi. 9, 10—a prophecy which cancels Judaism, and which the author sees to be now fulfilled—he proceeds to make Paul address the Jews as follows: γνωστὸν οὖν ἔστω ὑμῖν ὅτι τοῖς ἔθνεσιν ἀπεστάλη τοῦτο τὸ σωτήριον τοῦ θεοῦ· αὐτοὶ καὶ ἀκούσονται. This is to affirm, as explicitly as possible, that the gospel has been given, not to Jews, but to the nations at large.—The above account of the work of the Gentile mission rests upon Acts, in so far as I consider its statements trustworthy. The author was a Paulinist, but he found much simpler grounds for Christian universalism than did Paul; or rather, he needed no grounds for it at all—the gospel being in itself universal—although he does not ignore the fact that at the outset it was preached to none but Jews, and that the Gentile mission was long in developing. The internal divisions of Christianity, moreover, are scarcely noticed.

[2] Acts vi. 5 (Νικόλαον προσήλυτον) shows that there were also Christians in Jerusalem who had been previously proselytes. The addition of 'Αντιοχέα betrays the author's special interest in this city.

[3] See Weizsäcker, Apost. Zeitalter [(2)], pp. 51 f.; Eng. trans., i. 62 f. Naturally they were "good" Jews, otherwise they would never have settled at Jerusalem; but we may assume that these synagogues of the Libertini (Romans), the Cyrenians, the Alexandrians, the Cilicians and Asiatics (Acts vi. 9), embraced Hellenistic Jews as well, who had mitigated the Jewish religion with their Hellenistic culture. Upon the other hand, they also included exclusive fanatics, who were responsible for the first outburst against Christianity. Palestinian Judaism (i.e., the Sanhedrim) sided with them. The earliest Christian persecution thus appears as a quarrel and cleavage among the Diaspora Jews at Jerusalem.

attributed to the words in question. Stephen did not attack
the temple and the law in order to dispute their divine origin,
but he did affirm the limited period of these institutions. In
this way he did set himself in opposition to the popular Judaism
of his time, but hardly in opposition to all that was Jewish. It
is beyond doubt that within Judaism itself, especially throughout the Diaspora, tendencies were already abroad by which the
temple-cultus,[1] and primarily its element of bloody sacrifices,
was regarded as unessential and even of doubtful validity.
Besides, it is equally certain that in many a Jewish circle, for
external and internal reasons, the outward observance of the
law was not considered of any great value; it was more or less
eclipsed by the moral law. Consequently it is quite conceivable,
historically and psychologically, that a Jew of the Diaspora who
had been won over to Christianity should associate the supreme
and exclusive moral considerations urged by the new faith [2] with
the feelings he had already learned to cherish, viz., that the
temple and the ceremonial law were relatively useless; it is also
conceivable that he should draw the natural inference—Jesus the
Messiah will abolish the temple-cultus and alter the ceremonial
law. Observe the future tense. Acts seems here to give an
extremely literal report. Stephen did not urge any changes—
these were to be effected by Jesus, when he returned as Messiah.
All Stephen did was to announce them by way of prophecy,
thus implying that the existing arrangements were valueless.
He did not urge the Gentile mission; but by his words and
death he helped to set it up.

When Stephen was stoned, he died, like Huss, for a cause
whose issues he probably did not foresee. It is not surprising
that he was stoned, for orthodox Judaism could least afford to
tolerate this kind of believer in Jesus. His adherents were also

---

[1] Particularly when it had been profaned over and over again by a secularized
priesthood.

[2] At this point it may be also recalled that Jesus himself foretold the overthrow
of the temple. With Weizsäcker (*op. cit.*, p. 53 ; Eng. trans., i. 65) I consider
that saying of our Lord is genuine. It became the starting-point of an inner
development in his disciples which finally led up to the Gentile mission. Cp.
Wellhausen's commentary on the synoptic gospels for a discussion of the saying's
significance.

persecuted—the grave peril of the little company of Christians being thus revealed in a flash. All except the apostles (Acts viii. 1) had to leave Jerusalem. Evidently the latter had not yet declared themselves as a body on the side of Stephen in the matter of his indictment.[1] The scattered Christians went abroad throughout Judæa and Samaria; *nolens volens* they acted as missionaries, *i.e.*, as apostles (Acts viii. 4). The most important of them was Philip, the guardian of the poor, who preached in Samaria and along the sea-board; there is a long account of how he convinced and baptized an Ethiopian officer, a eunuch (Acts viii. 26 f.). This is perfectly intelligible. The man was not a Jew. He belonged to the "God-fearing class" ($\phi o \beta o \acute{v} \mu \epsilon \nu o \varsigma \ \tau \grave{o} \nu \ \theta \epsilon \acute{o} \nu$). Besides, even if he had been circumcised, he could not have become a Jew. Thus, when this semi-proselyte, this eunuch, was brought into the Christian church, it meant that one stout barrier had fallen.

Still, a single case is not decisive, and even the second case of this kind, that of Peter baptizing the "God-fearing" ($\phi o \beta o \acute{v} \mu \epsilon \nu o \varsigma$) Cornelius at Cæsarea, cannot have had at that early period the palmary importance which the author of Acts attaches to it.[2]

[1] This seems to me an extremely important fact, which at the same time corroborates the historical accuracy of Acts at this point. Evidently the Christians at this period were persecuted with certain exceptions; none were disturbed whose devotion to the temple and the law was unimpeachable, and these still included Peter and the rest of the apostles. Acts makes it perfectly plain that it was only at a later, though not much later, period that Peter took his first step outside strict Judaism. Weizsäcker's reading of the incident is different (*op. cit.*, pp. 60 f.; Eng. trans., i. 75). He holds that the first step was taken at this period; but otherwise he is right in saying that "it is obvious that nothing was so likely to create and strengthen this conviction (viz., that the future, the salvation to be obtained in the kingdom itself, could no longer rest upon the obligations of the law) as Pharisaic attacks prompted by the view that faith in Jesus and his kingdom was prejudicial to the inviolable duration of the law, and to belief in its power of securing salvation. The persecution, therefore, liberated the Christian faith; it was the means by which it came to know itself. And in this sense it was not without its fruits in the primitive church."

[2] At least the importance did not lie in the direction in which the author of Acts looked to find it. Still, the case was one of great moment in this sense, that it forced Peter to side at last with that theory and practice which had hitherto (see the note above) been followed by none save the friends of Stephen (excluding the primitive apostles). The conversion of the Cæsarean officer led Peter, and with Peter a section of the church at Jerusalem, considerably further. It must be admitted, however, that the whole passage makes one suspect its

So long as it was a question of proselytes, even of proselytes in the widest sense of the term, there was always one standpoint from which the strictest Jewish Christian himself could reconcile his mind to their admission : he could regard the proselytes thus admitted as adherents of the Christian community in the *wider* sense of the term, *i.e.*, as proselytes still.[1]

The next step, a much more decisive one, was taken at Antioch, again upon the initiative of the scattered adherents of Stephen (Acts xi. 19 f.), who had reached Phœnicia, Cyprus, and Antioch on their missionary wanderings. The majority of them confined themselves strictly to the Jewish mission. But some, who were natives of Cyprus and Crete,[1] preached also to

historical character. Luke has treated it with a circumstantial detail which we miss elsewhere in his work ; he was persuaded that it marked the great turning-point of the mission.

[1] No names are given in the second passage, but afterwards (xiii. 1) Barnabas the Cypriote, Simeon Niger, Lucius of Cyrene, Manaen, and Saul are mentioned as prophets and teachers at Antioch. As Barnabas and Saul did not reach Antioch until after the founding of the church (cp. xi. 22 f.), we may probably re-cognize in the other three persons the founders of the church, and consequently the first missionaries to the heathen. But *Barnabas must be mentioned first of all among the originators of the Gentile mission.* He must have reached the broader outlook independently, as indeed is plain from Paul's relations with him. A Cypriote Levite, he belonged from the very beginning to the church of Jerusalem (perhaps he was a follower of Jesus: cp. Clem., *Strom.*, II. 20 ; Eus., *H.E.*, i. 12 ; Clem. Rom. *Hom.*, i. 9), in which an act of voluntary sacrifice won for him a high position (Acts iv. 36 f.). He certainly acted as an intermediary between Paul and the primitive apostles, so long as such services were necessary (Acts ix. 27), just as he went between Jerusalem and Antioch (Acts xi. 22 f.). On what is called the " first mission-tour " of Paul, he was almost the leading figure (Acts xiii.–xiv.). But his devotion to the Gentile mission seems to have affected his early prestige at Jerusalem ; he was suspected, and, like Paul, he had to justify his conduct (Acts xv., Gal. ii.). In the trying situation which ensued at Antioch, he fell under Peter's influence and failed to stand the test (so Paul says, at least, in Gal. ii. 13, but what would have been "hypocrisy" to Paul need not have been so in the case of Barnabas). His co-operation with Paul in mission-work now ceases (Acts also makes them separate owing to a misunderstanding ; but, on this view, xv. 36 f., they disagreed upon the question of Mark as a coadjutor). Barnabas goes with Mark to Cyprus. When Paul wrote 1 Corinthians and Galatians, Barnabas was still active as a missionary, and his name was familiar to the Corinthians (cp. 1 Cor. ix. 6). That Paul narrates to the Galatians with such exact chron-ology the "hypocrisy" of Barnabas, shows how the apostle could not forget the crisis when the Gentile mission was at stake, but it does not imply that Paul still felt himself at variance with Barnabas. The narrative simply mentions him in order to bring out sharply the magnitude of the disaster occasioned by Peter's pusillanimous conduct. The carefully chosen expression (καὶ Βαρνάβας συναπήχθη)

the Greeks[1] in Antioch with excellent results. *They were the first missionaries to the heathen;* they founded the first Gentile church, that of Antioch. In this work they were joined by Barnabas and Paul (Acts xi. 23 f.), who soon became the real leading spirits in the movement.[2]

The converted Greeks in Antioch, Syria, and Cilicia (to which Barnabas and Paul presently extended their mission), during this initial period were by no means drawn wholly from those who had been "God-fearing" ($\phi o \beta o \acute{v} \mu \epsilon v o \iota$) already, although this may have been the origin of a large number.[3] At any rate a church was founded at Antioch which consisted for the most part of uncircumcised persons, *and which now undertook the mission to the Gentiles* (Acts xiii. 1 f.). For this church the

shows that he was carried away half irresolutely. 1 Cor. i. 9 proves that Paul still recognized him as an apostle of Christ, and spoke of him as such in the churches (cp. also Col. iv. 10, which indicates clearly that Barnabas was also known to the Asiatic Christians as an important figure). But a hearty relationship between the two cannot have been ever restored, in spite of the great experiences they had shared for so long. Paul's silence in his epistles and the silence of Acts (after ch. xv.) are eloquent on this point. In the matter of the Gentile mission, however, Barnabas must be ranked next to Paul ; in fact we may suspect, as the very sources permit us to do, that the services of Barnabas as a peace-maker amid the troubles and suspicions of the mother-church at Jerusalem were much more important than even the extant narratives disclose. Perhaps we have a writing of Barnabas — not the so-called "Epistle of Barnabas," but the Epistle to the Hebrews. The external evidence for his authorship is not weak, but it is not adequate, and the internal evidence tells against him. Did he go from Cyprus to work at Alexandria, as the pseudo-Clementine *Homilies* make out (i.-ii.)?

[1] So Acts x. 20, reading Ἕλληνες, not Ἑλληνίσται. It is not surprising that the Gentile Christian mission began in Antioch. It was only in the international, levelling society of a great city that such a movement could originate, or rather propagate itself, so far as it was not hampered by any new restriction in the sphere of principle. Most probably those early missionaries were not so hampered. It is very remarkable that there is no word of any opposition between Jewish and Gentile Christians at Antioch. The local Jewish Christians, scattered and cosmopolitan as they were, must have joined the new community of Christians, who were free from the law, without more ado. It was the Jerusalem church which first introduced dissension at Antioch (cp. Acts xv. 1, Gal. ii. 11-13).

[2] All allusions to Antioch, direct or indirect, in the book of Acts are specially noticeable, for the tradition that Luke was a physician of Antioch deserves credence. In ch. vi., and in what immediately follows, there is a distinct line of reference to Antioch.

[3] Cp. Havet, *Le Christianisme*, vol. iv. p. 102 : "Je ne sais s'il y est entré, du vivant de Paul, un seul païen, je veux dire un homme qui ne connût pas déjà, avant d'y entrer, le judaïsme et la Bible." This is no doubt an exaggeration, but substantially it is accurate.

designation of Χριστιανοί ("Christians," Acts xi. 26) came into vogue, a name coined by their heathen opponents. This title is itself a proof that the new community in Antioch stood out in bold relief from Judaism.[1]

The Gentile Christian churches of Syria and Cilicia did not observe the law, yet they were conscious of being the people of God in the fullest sense of the term, and were mindful to keep in touch with the mother church of Jerusalem, as well as to be recognized by her.[2] The majority of these cosmopolitan converts were quite content with the assurance that God had already moved the prophets to proclaim the uselessness of sacrifice,[3] so that all the ceremonial part of the law was to be allegorically interpreted and understood in some moral sense.[4] This was also the view originally held by the other Gentile Christian communities which, like that of Rome, were founded by unknown missionaries.

The apostle Paul, however, could not settle his position towards the law with such simplicity. For him no part of the law had been depreciated in value by any noiseless, disintegrating influence of time or circumstances; on the contrary, the law remained valid and operative in all its provisions. It could not be abrogated save by him who had ordained it—i.e., by God himself. Nor could even God abolish it save by affirming at the same time its rights—i.e., he must abolish it just by providing for its fulfilment. And this was what actually took place. By the death and resurrection of Jesus Christ, God's Son, upon the cross, the law was at once fulfilled and abolished. Whether all this reflection and speculation was secondary and

---

[1] Details on the name of "Christian" in Book III. The theological vocabulary of Gentile Christianity, so far as it needed one, must also have arisen in Antioch.

[2] Cp. the narrative of Acts xi. 29 f., xii. 25, regarding a collection which the recently founded church at Antioch sent to Jerusalem during the famine under Claudius. This was the famine in which Queen Helena of Adiabene gave much generous aid to the poor Jews of Jerusalem.

[3] With regard to the sacrificial system, the right of abandoning the literal meaning had been clearly made out, as that system had already become antiquated and depreciated in the eyes of large sections of people. The rest of the law followed as a matter of course.

[4] The post-apostolic literature shows with particular clearness that this was the popular view taken by the Gentile Christians; so that it must have maintained its vogue, despite the wide and powerful divergences of Paul's own teaching.

derivative (resulting from the possession of the Spirit and the new life which the apostle felt within himself), or primary (resulting from the assurance that his sins were forgiven), or whether these two sources coalesced, is a question which need not occupy us here. The point is, that Paul was convinced that the death and resurrection of Christ had inaugurated the new age. "The future is already present, the Spirit reigns." Hereby he firmly and unhesitatingly recognized the gospel to be the new *level of religion*, just as he also felt himself to be a new creature. The new religious level was the level of the Spirit and regeneration, of grace and faith, of peace and liberty; below and behind it lay *everything old*, including all the earlier revelations of God, since these were religions pertaining to the state of sin. This it was which enabled Paul, Jew and Pharisee as he was, to venture upon the great conception with which he laid the basis of any sound philosophy of religion and of the whole science of comparative religion, viz., the collocation of the "natural" knowledge of God possessed by man (*i.e.*, all that had developed in man under the sway of conscience) with the law of the chosen people (Rom. I f.). Both, Paul held, were revelations of God, though in different ways and of different values; both represented what had been hitherto the supreme possession of mankind. Yet both had proved inadequate; they had aggravated sin, and had ended in death.

Now *a new religion was in force*. This meant that the Gentile mission was not a possibility but a duty, whilst freedom from the law was not a concession but the distinctive and blissful form which the gospel assumed for men. Its essence consisted in the fact that it was not law in any sense of the term, but grace and a free gift. The Christian who had been born a Jew might have himself circumcised and keep the law—which would imply that he considered the Jewish nation had still some valid part to play [1] in the world-wide plan of God. But even so, there was nothing in the law to secure the bliss of

---

[1] However, as Christians of Jewish birth had, in Paul's view, to live and eat side by side with Gentile Christians, the observance of the law was broken down at one very vital point. It was only Paul's belief in the nearness of the advent that may have prevented him from reflecting further on this problem.

the Jewish Christian; and as for the Gentile Christian, he was not allowed either to practise circumcision or to keep the law. In his case, such conduct would have meant that Christ had died in vain.

Thus it was that Paul preached the crucified Christ to the Gentiles, and not only established the principle of the Gentile mission, but made it a reality. The work of his predecessors, when measured by his convictions, was loose and questionable; it seemed to reach the same end as he did, but it was not entirely just to the law or to the gospel. Paul wrecked the religion of Israel on the cross of Christ, in the very endeavour to comprehend it with a greater reverence and stricter obedience than his predecessors. The day of Israel, he declared, had now expired. He honoured the Jewish Christian community at Jerusalem, the source of so much antagonism to himself, with a respect which is almost inconceivable; but he made it perfectly clear that "the times of the Gentiles" had arrived, and that if any Jewish Christian churches did not unite with the Gentile Christian churches to form the *one* "church of God," they forfeited by this exclusiveness their very right to existence. Paul's conception of religion and of religious history was extremely simple, if one looks at its kernel, for it was based upon one fact. It cannot be reduced to a brief formula without being distorted into a platitude. It is never vital except in the shape of a paradox. In place of the particular forms of expression which Paul introduced, and by means of which he made the conception valid and secure for himself, it was possible that others might arise, as was the case in the very next generation with the author of Hebrews and with the anonymous genius who composed the Johannine writings. From that time onwards many other teachers came forward to find fresh bases for the Pauline gospel (*e.g.*, Marcion and Clement of Alexandria, to name a couple of very different writers from the second century). But what they transformed was not the fruit and kernel of Paulinism. Essentially they were quite at one with the apostle. For it is the great prerogative of the historian in a later age to be able to recognise an essential unity where argument and proofs are widely different.

Historically, Paul the Pharisee dethroned the people and the

religion of Israel;[1] he tore the gospel from its Jewish soil and [
rooted it in the soil of humanity.[2] No wonder that the full
reaction of Judaism against the gospel now commenced—a reaction on the part of Jews and Jewish Christians alike. The
hostility of the Jews appears on every page of Acts, from chap.
xii. onwards, and it can be traced by the aid even of the
evangelic narratives,[3] whose sources go back to the period
preceding A.D. 65. The Jews now sought to extirpate the
Palestinian churches and to silence the Christian missionaries.
They hampered every step of Paul's work among the Gentiles;
they cursed Christians and Christ in their synagogues; they
stirred up the masses and the authorities in every country
against him; systematically and officially they scattered broad-
cast horrible charges against the Christians, which played an
important part (ὑμεῖς τῆς κατὰ τοῦ δικαίου καὶ ἡμῶν τῶν ἀπ' ἐκείνου
κακῆς προλήψεως αἴτιοι) in the persecutions as early as the
reign of Trajan; they started calumnies against Jesus;[4] they

_98-117 p. ii._

[1] Little wonder that Jews of a later day declared he was a pagan in disguise:
cp. Epiph. _Hær._, xxx. 16: καὶ τοῦ Παύλου κατηγοροῦντες οὐκ αἰσχύνονται
ἐπιπλάστοις τισὶ τῆς τῶν ψευδαποστόλων αὐτῶν κακουργίας καὶ πλάνης λόγοις
πεποιημένοις. Ταρσέα μὲν αὐτόν, ὡς αὐτὸς ὁμολογεῖ καὶ οὐκ ἀρνεῖται, λέγοντες ἐξ
Ἑλλήνων δὲ αὐτὸν ὑποτίθενται, λαβόντες τὴν προφάσιν ἐκ τοῦ τόπου διὰ τὸ
φιλάληθες ὑπ' αὐτοῦ ῥηθέν, ὅτι, Ταρσεύς εἰμι, οὐκ ἀσήμου πόλεως πολίτης. εἶτα
φάσκουσιν αὐτὸν εἶναι Ἕλληνα καὶ Ἑλληνίδος μητρὸς καὶ Ἕλληνος πατρὸς παῖδα,
ἀναβεβηκέναι δὲ εἰς Ἱεροσόλυμα καὶ χρόνον ἐκεῖ μεμενηκέναι ἐπιτεθυμηκέναι δὲ
θυγατέρα τοῦ ἱερέως πρὸς γάμον ἀγαγέσθαι καὶ τούτου ἕνεκα προσήλυτον γενέσθαι
καὶ περιτμηθῆναι, εἶτα μὴ λαβόντα τὴν κόρην ὠργίσθαι καὶ κατὰ περιτομῆς
γεγραφέναι καὶ κατὰ σαββάτου καὶ νομοθεσίας ("Nor are they ashamed to accuse
Paul with false charges concocted by the villainy and fraud of these false apostles.
While a native of Tarsus (as he himself frankly admits) they avow that he was
born of Greek parentage, taking as their pretext for this assertion the passage in
which Paul's love of truth leads him to declare, 'I am of Tarsus, a citizen of no
mean city.' Whereupon they allege that he was the son of a Greek father and a
Greek mother; that he went up to Jerusalem, where he resided for some time;
that he resolved to marry the daughter of the high priest, and consequently became
a proselyte and got circumcised; and that on failing to win the girl, he vented his
anger in writing against circumcision and the sabbath and the Mosaic legislation").

[2] No one has stated the issues of this transplanting more sublimely than Luke
in his narrative of the birth of Jesus (Luke ii.), especially in the words which he
puts into the mouth of the angel and the angels. _see addenda_.

[3] Cp. the speeches of Jesus when he sent out the disciples on their missions,
and also the great eschatological discourse in the synoptic gospels.

[4] Justin (_Dial._ xvii.; cp. cviii., cxvii.), after making out that the Jews were
responsible for the calumnies against the Christians, observes that the Jewish

provided heathen opponents of Christianity with literary am-
munition; unless the evidence is misleading, they instigated
the Neronic outburst against the Christians; and as a rule,
whenever bloody persecutions are afoot in later days, the Jews
are either in the background or the foreground (the synagogues
being dubbed by Tertullian "fontes persecutionum"). By a
sort of instinct they felt that Gentile Christianity, though
apparently it was no concern of theirs, was their peculiar foe.
This course of action on the part of the Jews was inevitable.
They merely accelerated a process which implied the complete

authorities in Jerusalem despatched ἄνδρας ἐκλεκτοὺς ἀπὸ Ἰερουσαλὴμ εἰς πᾶσαν
τὴν γῆν, λέγοντας αἵρεσιν ἄθεον Χριστιανῶν πεφηνέναι, καταλέγοντας ταῦτα, ἅπερ
καθ' ἡμῶν οἱ ἀγνοοῦντες ἡμᾶς πάντες λέγουσιν, ὥστε οὐ μόνον ἑαυτοῖς ἀδικίας αἴτιοι
ὑπάρχετε, ἀλλὰ καὶ τοῖς ἄλλοις ἅπασιν ἁπλῶς ἀνθρώποις ("Chosen men from
Jerusalem into every land, declaring that a *godless* sect of Christians had appeared,
and uttering everything that those who are ignorant of us say unanimously against
us. So that you are the cause not only of your own unrighteousness, but also of
that of all other men"). Cp. cxvii. : τοῦ υἱοῦ τοῦ θεοῦ ὄνομα βεβηλωθῆναι κατὰ
πᾶσαν τὴν γῆν καὶ βλασφημεῖσθαι οἱ ἀρχιερεῖς τοῦ λαοῦ ὑμῶν καὶ διδάσκαλοι
εἰργάσαντο ("The name of the Son of God have the chief priests of your nation
and your teachers caused to be profaned throughout all the earth and to be
blasphemed"). Also cviii. : ἄνδρας χειροτονήσαντες ἐκλεκτοὺς εἰς πᾶσαν τὴν
οἰκουμένην ἐπέμψατε, κηρύσσοντας ὅτι αἵρεσις τις ἄθεος καὶ ἄνομος ἐγήγερται ἀπὸ
Ἰησοῦ τινος Γαλιλαίου πλάνου, ὃν σταυρωσάντων ἡμῶν οἱ μαθηταὶ αὐτοῦ ἀπὸ τοῦ
μνήματος νυκτὸς . . . . πλανῶσι τοὺς ἀνθρώπους λέγοντες ἐγηγέρθαι αὐτὸν ἐκ
νεκρῶν καὶ εἰς οὐρανὸν ἀνεληλυθέναι, κατειπόντες δεδιδαχέναι καὶ ταῦτα ἅπερ κατὰ
τῶν ὁμολογούντων Χριστὸν καὶ διδάσκαλον καὶ υἱὸν θεοῦ εἶναι παντὶ γένει ἀνθρώπων
ἄθεα καὶ ἄνομα καὶ ἀνόσια λέγετε ("You have sent chosen and *appointed* men into all
the World to proclaim that 'a godless and laWless sect has arisen from a certain Jesus,
a Galilean impostor, Whom we crucified ; his disciples, hoWever, stole him by
night from the tomb . . . . and now deceive people by asserting that he rose
from the dead and ascended into heaven.' You accuse him of having taught the
godless, laWless, and unholy doctrines which you bring forWard against those who
acknoWledge him to be Christ, a teacher from God, and the Son of God"). For
the cursing of Christians in the synagogues, cp. *Dial.* xvi. (also the words οὐκ
ἐξουσίας ἔχετε αὐτόχειρες γενέσθαι ἡμῶν διὰ τοὺς νῦν ἐπικρατοῦντας, ὁσάκις δὲ ἂν
ἐδύνητε, καὶ τοῦτο ἐπράξατε = "You have no poWer of yourselves to lay hands on
us, thanks to your overlords [*i.e.*, the Romans], but you have done so Whenever
you could "), xlvii., xciii., xcv.-xcvi., cviii., cxvii., cxxxvii., Where Justin declares
that the rulers of the synagogue arranged for the cursing of Christians μετὰ τὴν
προσευχὴν (after prayers) during the course of public Worship (the pagan proselytes
of Judaism being even more hostile to Christians than the JeWs themselves, cxxii.) ;
Jerome on Isa. lii. 2 ; Epiph., *Hær.*, xxix. 9 ; *Apol.*, I. x., xxxi. (JeWish
Christians fearfully persecuted by JeWs during the Barcochba war) ; Tert.,
ad Nat., I. xiv. : et credidit vulgus Judaeo ; quod enim aliud genus seminarium
est infamiae nostrae ? ("The croWd believed the Jew. In What other set of
people lies the seedplot of calumny against us ?") ; *adv. Marc.*, iii. 23 ; *adv.*

liberation of the new religion from the old, and which prevented Judaism from solving the problem which she had already faced, the problem of her metamorphosis into a religion for the world. In this sense there was something satisfactory about the Jewish opposition. It helped both religions to make the mutual breach complete, whilst it also deepened in the minds of Gentile Christians—at a time when. this still needed to be deepened— the assurance that their religion did represent a new creation, and that they were no mere class of people admitted into some lower rank, but were themselves the new People of God, who had succeeded to the old.[1]

Jud., xiii. : ab illis enim incepit infamia ("They started the calumny"); *Scorp.* x.: synagogae Judaeorum fontes persecutionum ; *Iren.* IV. xxi. 3 : ecclesia insidias et persecutiones a Judaeis patitur ; IV. xxviii. 3 : Judaei interfectores domini . . . . apostolos interficientes et persequentes ecclesiam. Origen repeatedly testifies to the fact that the Jews were the originators of the calumnies against Christians ; cp. passages like *Hom.* I. on Ps. xxxvi. (t. 12, p. 54, ed. Lomm.): etiam nunc Judaei non moventur adversus gentiles, adversus eos, qui idola colunt et deum blasphemant, et illos non oderunt nec indignantur adversus eos; adversus Christiano vero insatiabili odio feruntur ("The Jews even now are not angry at the heathen who Worship idols and blaspheme God ; they do not hate them, but they attack Christians with insatiable hatred "; cp. also p. 155). By far the most important notice is that preserved by Eusebius (on Isa. xviii. 1 f.), although its source is unfortunately unknown—at any rate it did not come from Justin. It runs as follows : εὕρομεν ἐν τοῖς τῶν παλαιῶν συγγράμμασιν, ὡς οἱ τὴν Ἰερουσαλὴμ οἰκοῦντες τοῦ τῶν Ἰουδαίων ἔθνους ἱερεῖς καὶ πρεσβύτεροι γράμματα διαχαράξαντες εἰς πάντα διεπέμψαντο τὰ ἔθνη τοῖς ἀπανταχοῦ Ἰουδαίοις διαβάλλοντες τὴν Χριστοῦ διδασκαλίαν ὡς αἵρεσιν καινὴν καὶ ἀλλοτρίαν τοῦ θεοῦ, παρήγγελλόν τε δι᾽ ἐπιστολῶν μὴ παραδέξασθαι αὐτήν . . . . οἵ τε ἀπόστολοι αὐτῶν ἐπιστολὰς βιβλίνας κομιζόμενοι . . . . ἀπανταχοῦ γῆς διέτρεχον, τὸν περὶ τοῦ σωτῆρος ἡμῶν ἐνδιαβάλλοντες λόγον. ἀποστόλους δὲ εἰσέτι καὶ νῦν ἔθος ἐστὶν Ἰουδαίοις ὀνομάζειν τοὺς ἐγκύκλια γράμματα παρὰ τῶν ἀρχόντων αὐτῶν ἐπικομιζομένους ("In the Writings of the ancients we find that the priests and elders of the Jewish people resident at Jerusalem drew up and despatched written instructions for the Jews throughout every country, slandering the doctrine of Christ as a newfangled heresy which was alien to God, and charging them by means of letters not to accept it. . . . . Their *apostles* also, conveying *formal letters* . . . . swarmed everywhere on earth, calumniating the gospel of our Saviour. And even at the present day it is still the custom of the Jews to give the name of 'apostle' to those who convey encyclical epistles from their rulers "). According to this passage Paul would be an "apostle" before he became an apostle, and the question might be raised whether the former capacity did not contribute in some way to the feeling he had, on becoming a Christian, that he was thereby called immediately to be an apostle of Christ.

[1] In this connection one must also note the Christian use of ἔθνη ("gentes," "Gentiles"). In the Old Testament the ἔθνη are opposed to the people of Israel

But the Jewish Christians also entered the arena. They issued from Jerusalem a demand that the church at Antioch should be circumcised, and the result of this demand was the so-called apostolic council. We possess two accounts of this (Gal. ii. and Acts xv.). Each leaves much to be desired, and it is hardly possible to harmonize them both. Paul's account is not so much written down as flung down pell-mell; such is the vigour with which it seeks to emphasize the final result, that its abrupt sentences render the various intermediate stages either invisible or indistinct. The other account, unless we are deceived, has thrown the ultimate issue of the council into utter confusion by the irrelevant introduction of what transpired at a later period. Even for other reasons, this account excites suspicion. Still we can see plainly that Peter, John, and James recognized the work of Paul, that they gave him no injunctions as to his missionary labours, and that they chose still to confine themselves to the Jewish mission. Paul did not at once succeed in uniting Jewish and Gentile Christians in a single fellowship of life and worship; it was merely the principle of this fellowship that gained the day, and even this principle—an agreement which in itself was naturally unstable and shortlived—could be ignored by wide circles of Jewish Christians. Nevertheless much ground had been won. The stipulation itself ensured that, as did even more the developments to which it led. The

(which was also reckoned, as was natural under the circumstances, among the "peoples"), so that it was quite easy for a Jew to describe other *religions* by simply saying that they were religions of the ἔθνη. Consequently ἔθνη had acquired among the Jews, long before the Christian era, a sense which roughly coincided with that of our word "pagans" or "heathen." Paul was therefore unable to allow any Christian of non-Jewish extraction to be still ranked among the ἔθνη, nor would it seem that Paul was alone in this contention. Such a convert once belonged to the ἔθνη, but not now (cp., *e.g.*, I Cor. xii. 2: οἴδατε ὅτι ὅτε ἔθνη ἦτε πρός τὰ εἴδωλα . . . . ἤγεσθε, "ye know that when ye *were* Gentiles, ye were led away to idols"); now he belongs to the *true* Israel, or to the new People. It is plain that while this did not originally imply an actual change of nationality, it must have stimulated the cosmopolitan feeling among Christians, as well as the consciousness that even politically they occupied a distinctive position, when they were thus contrasted with all the ἔθνη on the one hand, and on the other were thought of as the new People of the World, who repudiated all connection with the Jews. We need hardly add that Christians were still described as members of the ἔθνη, in cases where the relationship caused no misunderstanding, and where it was purely a question of non-Jewish descent.

Jewish Christians split up.   How they could still continue to
hold together (in Jerusalem and elsewhere) for years to come,
is an insoluble riddle.   One section persisted in doing everything / c
they could to persecute Paul and his work with ardent enmity: (
to crush him was their aim.   In this they certainly were actuated
by some honest convictions, which Paul was naturally incapable
of understanding.   To the very last, indeed, he made concessions
to these " zealots for the law " within the boundaries of Palestine ;
but outside Palestine he repudiated them so soon as they tried
to win over Gentiles to their own form of Christianity. / The
other section, including Peter and probably the rest of the
primitive apostles, commenced before long to advance beyond
the agreement, though in a somewhat hesitating and tentative
fashion: outside Palestine they began to hold intercourse with
the Gentile Christians, and to lead the Jewish Christians also
in this direction.   These tentative endeavours culminated in a
new agreement, which now made a real fellowship possible for
both parties.   The condition was that the Gentile Christians
were to abstain from flesh offered to idols, from tasting blood
and things strangled, and from fornication.   Henceforth Peter,
probably with one or two others of the primitive apostles, took
part in the Gentile mission.   The last barrier had collapsed.[1]
If we marvel at the greatness of Paul, we should not marvel less
at the primitive apostles, who for the gospel's sake entered on a
career which the Lord and Master, with whom they had eaten
and drunk, had never taught them.

By adopting an intercourse with Gentile Christians, this
Jewish Christianity did away with itself, and in the second
period of his labours Peter ceased to be a " Jewish Christian."[2]

---

[1] We may conjecture that originally there were also Jewish Christian communities in the Diaspora (not simply a Jewish Christian set inside Gentile Christian
communities), and that they were not confined even to the provinces bordering on
Palestine.   But in Asia Minor, or wherever else such Jewish Christian communities
existed, they must have been absorbed at a relatively early period by the Gentile
Christian or Pauline communities.   The communities of Smyrna and Philadelphia
about 93 A.D. (cp. Rev. ii.–iii.) seem to have been composed mainly of converted
Jews, but they are leagued with an association of the other communities, just as if
they were Gentile Christians.

[2] Cp. Pseudo-Clem., *Hom.*, XI. xvi. : ἐὰν ὁ ἀλλόφυλος τὸν νόμος πράξῃ,
Ἰουδαῖός ἐστιν, μὴ πράξας δὲ Ἰουδαῖος Ἕλλην ("If one of other nation observe

He became a Greek. Still, two Jewish Christian parties continued to exist. One of these held by the agreement of the
apostolic council; it gave the Gentile Christians its blessing,
but held aloof from them in actual life. The other persisted in
fighting the Gentile Church as a false church. Neither party
counts in the subsequent history of the church, owing to their
numerical weakness. According to Justin (*Apol.*, I. liii.), who
must have known the facts, Jesus was rejected by the Jewish
nation "with few exceptions" (πλὴν ὀλίγων τινῶν). In the
Diaspora, apart from Syria and Egypt, Jewish Christians were
hardly to be met with ;[1] there the Gentile Christians felt them-

the law, he is a Jew: the Jew who does not observe it is a Greek"). His
labours in the mission-field must have brought him to the side of Paul (cp. *Clem.
Rom.*, v.), else his repute in the Gentile Christian church would be inexplicable ;
but we have no detailed information on this point. Incidentally we hear of him
being at Antioch (Gal. ii.). It is also likely, to judge from First Corinthians, that
on his travels he reached Corinth shortly after the local church had been founded,
but it is by a mere chance that we learn this. After Acts xii. Luke loses all
interest in Peter's missionary efforts ; why, we cannot quite make out. But if he
laboured among Jewish Christians in a broad spirit, and yet did not emancipate
them outright from the customs of Judaism, we can understand how the Gentile
Christian tradition took no particular interest in his movements. Still, there must
have been one epoch in his life when he consented heart and soul to the principles
of Gentile Christianity ; and it may be conjectured that this took place as early as
the time of his residence at Corinth, not at the subsequent period of his sojourn in
Rome. (He stayed for some months at Rome, before he was crucified. This we
learn from an ancient piece of evidence which has been strangely overlooked.
Porphyry, in Macarius Magnes (iii. 22), writes : "Peter is narrated to have been
crucified, after pasturing the lambs for several months" (ἱστορεῖται μηδ᾽ ὀλίγους
μῆνας βοσκήσας τὰ προβάτια ὁ Πέτρος ἐσταυρῶσθαι). This passage must refer to
his residence at Rome, and its testimony is all the more weighty, as Porphyry
himself lived for a long while in Rome and had close dealings with the local
Christianity. If the pagan cited in Macarius was not Porphyry himself, then he
has reproduced him.) At the same time it must be understood that we are not in
a position to explain how Peter came to be ranked first of all alongside of Paul
(as in Clement and Ignatius) and then above him. The fact that our First Peter in
the New Testament was attributed to him involves difficulties which are scarcely
fewer than those occasioned by the hypothesis that he actually wrote the epistle.

[1] Individual efforts of propaganda were not, however, awanting. Such include
the origins of the pseudo-Clementine literature, Symmachus and his literary efforts
towards the close of the second century, and also that Elkesaite Alcibiades of
Apamea in Syria, who went to Rome and is mentioned by Hippolytus in the
Philosophumena. The syncretism of gnostic Jewish Christianity, to which all these
phenomena belong, entitled it to expect a better hearing in the pagan world than
the stricter form of the Christian faith. But it would lead us too far afield from
our present purpose to go into details.

selves supreme, in fact they were almost masters of the field.[1]
This did not last, however, beyond 180 A.D., when the Catholic
church put Jewish Christians upon her roll of heretics.   They
were thus paid back in their own coin by Gentile Christianity;
the heretics turned their former judges into heretics.

Before long the relations of Jewish Christians to their kins-
men the Jews also took a turn for the worse—that is, so far as
actual relations existed between them at all.   It was the destruction of Jerusalem and the temple which seems to have provoked
the final crisis, and led to a complete breach between the two
parties.[2]   No Christian, even supposing he were a simple Jewish
Christian, could view the catastrophe which befell the Jewish
state, with its capital and sanctuary, as anything else than the
just punishment of the nation for having crucified the Messiah.
Strictly speaking, he ceased from that moment to be a Jew ; for
a Jew who accepted the downfall of his state and temple as a
divine dispensation, thereby committed national suicide.   Undoubtedly the catastrophe decimated the exclusive Jewish
Christianity of Palestine and drove a considerable number either
back into Judaism or forward into the Catholic church.   Yet
how illogical human feelings can be, when they are linked to a
powerful tradition !   There were Jewish Christians still, who
remained after the fall of Jerusalem just where they had stood
before ; evidently they bewailed the fall of the temple, and yet
they saw in its fall a merited punishment.   Did they, we ask,
or did they not, venture to desire the rebuilding of the temple ?
We can easily understand how such people proved a double
offence to their fellow-countrymen, the genuine Jews.   Indeed
they were always falling between two fires, for the Jews persecuted them with bitter hatred,[3] while the Gentile church

---

[1] The turn of affairs is seen in Justin's *Dial.* xlvii.   Gentile Christians for a long
while ceased to lay down any fresh conditions, but they deliberated whether *they*
could recognize Jewish Christians as Christian brethren, and if so, to what extent.
They acted in this matter with considerable rigour.

[2] We do not know when Jewish Christians broke off, or were forced to break
off, from all connection with the synagogues ; we can only conjecture that if such
connections lasted till about 70 A.D., they ceased then.

[3] Epiphanius (xxix. 9): οὐ μόνον οἱ τῶν Ἰουδαίων παῖδες πρὸς τούτους κέκτηνται
μῖσος, ἀλλὰ ἀνιστάμενοι ἕωθεν καὶ μέσης ἡμέρας καὶ περὶ τὴν ἑσπέραν, τρὶς τῆς
ἡμέρας, ὅτε εὐχὰς ἐπιτελοῦσιν ἐν ταῖς αὐτῶν συναγωγαῖς ἐπαρῶνται αὐτοῖς καὶ

censured them as heretics—*i.e.*, as non-Christians. They are dubbed indifferently by Jerome, who knew them personally,[1] " semi-Judaei " and " semi-Christiani." And Jerome was right. They were really "semis"; they were " half "this or that, although they followed the course of life which Jesus had himself observed. Crushed by the letter of Jesus, they died a lingering death. \

There is hardly any fact which deserves to be turned over and thought over so much as this, that the religion of Jesus has never been able to root itself in Jewish or even Semitic soil.[2] Certainly there must have been, and certainly there must be still, some element in this religion which is allied to the greater freedom of the Greek spirit. In one sense Christianity has really remained Greek down to the present day. The forms it acquired on Greek soil have been modified, but they have never been laid aside within the church at large, not even within Protestantism itself. And what an ordeal this religion underwent in the tender days of its childhood! " Get thee out of thy country and from thy kindred unto a land that I will show thee, and I will make of thee a great nation." Islam rose in Arabia and has remained upon the whole an Arabic religion; the strength of its youth was also the strength of its manhood. Christianity, almost immediately after it arose, was dislodged from the nation to which it belonged; and thus from the very outset it was forced to learn how to distinguish between the kernel and the husk.[3]

Paul is only responsible in part for the sharp anti-Judaism

ἀναθεματίζουσι φάσκοντες ὅτι· 'Επικαταράσαι ὁ θεὸς τοὺς Ναζωραίους. καὶ γὰρ τούτοις περισσότερον ἐνέχουσι, διὰ τὸ ἀπὸ 'Ιουδαίων αὐτοὺς ὄντας 'Ιησοῦν κηρύσσειν εἶναι Χριστόν, ὅπερ ἐστὶν ἐναντίον πρὸς τοὺς ἔτι 'Ιουδαίους τοὺς Χριστὸν μὴ δεξαμένους ("Not merely are they visited With hatred at the hands of JeWish children, but rising at daWn, at noon, and eventide, When they perform their orisons in their synagogues, the JeWs curse them and anathematize them, crying ' God curse the Nazarenes!' For, indeed, they are assailed all the more bitterly because, being themselves of JeWish origin, they proclaim Jesus to be the Messiah —in opposition to the other JeWs who reject Christ ").

[1] Epiphanius (*loc. cit.*) says of them : 'Ιουδαῖοι μᾶλλον καὶ οὐδὲν ἕτερον· πάνυ δὲ οὗτοι ἐχθροὶ τοῖς 'Ιουδαίοις ὑπάρχουσιν ("They are Jews more than anything else, and yet they are detested by the Jews").

[2] The Syrians are a certain exception to this rule; yet how markedly was the Syrian church Grecized, even although it retained its native language !

[3] The gospel allied itself, in a specially intimate way, to Hellenism, but not exclusively, during the period of Which we are speaking; on the contrary, the greatest stress was laid still, as by Paul of old, upon the fact that *all* peoples Were

which developed within the very earliest phases of Gentile Christianity. Though he held that the day of the Jews (πᾶσιν ἀνθρώποις ἐναντίων, 1 Thess. ii. 15) was past and gone, yet he neither could nor would believe in a final repudiation of God's people; on that point his last word is said in Rom. xi. 25, 29 :—

οὐ θέλω ὑμᾶς ἀγνοεῖν τὸ μυστήριον τοῦτο, ὅτι πώρωσις ἀπὸ μέρους τῷ Ἰσραὴλ γέγονεν ἄχρις οὗ τὸ πλήρωμα τῶν ἐθνῶν εἰσέλθῃ, καὶ οὕτως πᾶς Ἰσραὴλ σωθήσεται . . ἀμεταμέλητα γὰρ τὰ χαρίσματα καὶ ἡ κλῆσις τοῦ θεοῦ. In this sense Paul remained a Jewish Christian to the end. The duality of mankind (Jews and "nations") remained, in a way, intact, despite the *one* church of God which embraced them both. This church did not abrogate the special promises made to the Jews.

But this standpoint remained a Pauline idiosyncrasy. When people had recourse, as the large majority of Christians had, simply to the allegorical method in order to emancipate themselves from the letter, and even from the contents, of Old Testament religion, the Pauline view had no attraction for them; in fact it was quite inadmissible, since the legitimacy of the allegorical conception, and inferentially the legitimacy of the Gentile church in general, was called in question, if the Pauline view held good at any single point.[1] If the people of Israel retained a single privilege, if a single special promise still had any meaning whatsoever, if even one letter had still to remain in force—how could the whole of the Old Testament be spiritualized? How could it all be transferred to another people? The result of this mental attitude was the conviction that the Jewish

called, and the gospel accepted by members of *all* nations. Certainly the Greeks ranked as *primi inter pares*, and the esteem in which they were held was bound to increase just as tradition came to be emphasized, since it was neither possible nor permissible as yet to trace back the latter to the Jews (from the middle of the second century onwards, the appeal of tradition to the church of Jerusalem was not to a Jewish, but to a Greek church). In this sense, even the Latins felt themselves secondary as compared with the Greeks, but it was not long before the Roman church understood how to make up for this disadvantage. In the Easter controversy, about the year 190 A.D., certain rivalries between the Greeks and Latins emerged for the first time; but such differences were provincial, not national, for the Roman church at that period was still predominantly Greek.

[1] As the post-apostolic literature shows, there were wide circles in which Paul's doctrine of the law and the old covenant was never understood, and consequently was never accepted.

people was now rejected: it was Ishmael, not Isaac; Esau, not Jacob. Yet even this verdict did not go far enough. If the spiritual meaning of the Old Testament is the correct one, and the literal false, then (it was argued) *the former was correct from the very first*, since what was false yesterday cannot be true to-day. Now the Jewish people from the first persisted in adhering to the literal interpretation, practising circumcision, offering bloody sacrifices, and observing the regulations concerning food; consequently they were always in error, an error which shows that *they never were the chosen people*. The chosen people throughout was the Christian people, which always existed in a sort of latent condition (the younger brother being really the elder), though it only came to light at first with Christ. From the outset the Jewish people had lost the promise; indeed it was a question whether it had ever been meant for them at all. In any case the literal interpretation of God's revealed will proved that the people had been forsaken by God and had fallen under the sway of the devil. As this was quite clear, the final step had now to be taken, the final sentence had now to be pronounced: *the Old Testament, from cover to cover, has nothing whatever to do with the Jews*. Illegally and insolently the Jews had seized upon it; they had confiscated it, and tried to claim it as their own property. They had falsified it by their expositions and even by corrections and omissions. Every Christian must therefore deny them the possession of the Old Testament. It would be a sin for Christians to say, "This book belongs to us and to the Jews." No; *the book belonged from the outset, as it belongs now and evermore, to none but Christians*,[1] whilst Jews are the worst, the most godless and God-forsaken, of all nations upon earth,[2] the devil's own people, Satan's syna-

---

[1] It was an inconvenient fact that the book had not been taken from the Jews, who still kept and used it; but pseudo-Justin (*Cohort.* xiii.) gets over this by explaining that the Jews' retention of the Old Testament was providential. They preserved the Old Testament, so that it might afford a refutation of the pagan opponents who objected to Christianity on account of its forgeries (*i.e.*, the prophecies). In his Dialogue, Justin, however, charges the Jews with falsifying the Old Testament in an anti-Christian sense. His proofs are quite flimsy.

[2] Justin, for example, looks on the Jews not more but less favourably than on the heathen (cp. *Apol.*, I. xxxvii., xxxix., xliii.–xliv., xlvii., liii., lx.). The more friendly attitude of Aristides (*Apol.* xiv.) is exceptional.

gogue, a fellowship of hypocrites.[1] They are stamped by their crucifixion of the Lord.[2] God has now brought them to an open ruin, before the eyes of all the world; their temple is burnt, their city destroyed, their commonwealth shattered, their people scattered—never again is Jerusalem to be frequented.[3] It may be questioned, therefore, whether God still desires this people to be converted at all, and whether he who essays to win a single Jew is not thereby interfering unlawfully with his punishment. But the fact is, this people will not move; so that by their obstinacy and hostility to Christ, they relieve Christians from having to answer such a question.

This was the attitude consistently adopted by the Gentile church towards Judaism. Their instinct of self-preservation and their method of justifying their own appropriation of the Old Testament, chimed in with the ancient antipathy felt by the Greeks and Romans to the Jews. Still,[4] it was not everyone who ventured to draw the final conclusions of the epistle of Barnabas (iv. 6. f., xiv. 1 f.). Most people admitted vaguely that in earlier days a special relation existed between God and his people, though at the same time all the Old Testament promises were referred even by them to Christian people. While Barnabas held the literal observance of the law to prove a seduction of the devil to which the Jewish people had succumbed,[5]

---

[1] Cp. Rev. ii. 9, iii. 9, Did. viii., and the treatment of the Jews in the Fourth Gospel and the Gospel of Peter. Barnabas (ix. 4) declares that a wicked angel had seduced them from the very first. In 2 Clem. ii. 3, the Jews are called οἱ δοκοῦντες ἔχειν θεόν ("they that seem to have God"); similarly in the Preaching of Peter (Clem., *Strom.*, vi. 5. 41): ἐκεῖνοι μόνοι οἰόμενοι τὸν θεὸν γιγνώσκειν οὐκ ἐπίστανται ("They suppose they alone know God, but they do not understand him").

[2] Pilate was more and more exonerated.

[3] Cp. Tertull., *Apol.* xxi. : dispersi, palabundi et soli et caeli sui extorres vagantur per orbem sine homine, sine deo rege, quibus nec advenarum iure terram patriam saltim vestigio salutare conceditur ("Scattered, wanderers, exiles from their own land and clime, they roam through the world without a human or a divine king, without so much as a stranger's right to set foot even in their native land").

[4] For what follows see my *Lehrbuch der Dogmengeschichte*, I.[(3)], pp. 168 f. [Eng. trans., i. 291 f.].

[5] Cp. Barn. ix. f. The attitude of Barnabas to the Old Testament is radically misunderstood if one imagines that his expositions in vi.-x. can be passed over as the result of oddity and caprice, or set aside as destitute of any moment or

the majority regarded circumcision as a sign appointed by God;[1]
they recognized that the literal observance of the law was designed and enjoined by God for the time being, although they
held that no righteousness ever emanated from it. Still even
they held that the spiritual sense was the one true meaning,
which by a fault of their own the Jews had misunderstood; they
considered that the burden of the ceremonial law was an educational necessity, to meet the stubbornness and idolatrous tendencies of the nation (being, in fact, a safeguard of monotheism); and, finally, they interpreted the sign of circumcision
in such a way that it appeared no longer as a favour, but
rather as a mark of the judgment to be executed on Israel.[2]

Israel thus became literally a church which had been at all
times the inferior or the Satanic church. Even in point of time
the " older " people really did not precede the " younger," for
the latter was more ancient, and the " new " law was the original
law. Nor had the patriarchs, prophets, and men of God, who
had been counted worthy to receive God's word, anything in
common inwardly with the Jewish people; they were God's

method. Not a sentence in this section lacks method, and consequently there is
no caprice at all. The strictly spiritual conception of God in Barnabas, and the
conviction that all (Jewish) ceremonies are of the devil, made his expositions
of Scripture a matter of course; so far from being mere ingenious fancies to this
author's mind, they were essential to him, unless the Old Testament was to be
utterly abandoned. For example, the whole authority of the Old Testament
would have collapsed for Barnabas, unless he had succeeded in finding some fresh
interpretation of the statement that Abraham circumcised his servants. This he
manages to do by combining it with another passage from Genesis; he then discovers in the narrative, not circumcision at all, but a prophecy of the crucified
Christ (ix.).

[1] Barn. ix. 6: ἀλλ' ἐρεῖς· καὶ μὴν περιτέτμηται ὁ λαὸς εἰς σφραγῖδα ("But
thou wilt say, this people hath been certainly circumcised for a seal"). This
remark is put into the mouth of an ordinary Gentile Christian; the author himself
does not agree with it.

[2] Cp. Justin's *Dial.* xvi., xviii., xx., xxx., xl.–xlvi. He lays down these three
findings side by side: (1) that the ceremonial laws were an educational measure
on the part of God to counteract the stubbornness of the people, who were prone
to apostatize; (2) that, as in the case of circumcision, they were meant to differ-
entiate the people in view of the future judgment which was to be executed
according to divine appointment; and (3) finally, that the Jewish worship enacted
by the ceremonial law exhibited the peculiar depravity and iniquity of the people.
Justin, however, viewed the decalogue as the natural law of reason, and therefore
as definitely distinct from the ceremonial law.

elect who distinguished themselves by a holy conduct corresponding to their election, and they must be regarded as the fathers and forerunners of the latent Christian people.[1] No satisfactory answer is given by any of these early Christian writings to the question, How is it that, if these men must not on any account be regarded as Jews, they nevertheless appeared entirely or almost entirely within the Jewish nation? Possibly the idea was that God in his mercy meant to bring this wickedest of the nations to the knowledge of the truth by employing the most effective agencies at his command; but even this suggestion comes to nothing.

Such an injustice as that done by the Gentile church to Judaism is almost unprecedented in the annals of history. The Gentile church stripped it of everything; she took away its sacred book; herself but a transformation of Judaism, she cut off all connection with the parent religion. The daughter first robbed her mother, and then repudiated her! But, one may ask, is this view really correct? Undoubtedly it is, to some extent, and it is perhaps impossible to force anyone to give it up. But viewed from a higher standpoint, the facts acquire a different complexion. By their rejection of Jesus, the Jewish people disowned their calling and dealt the death-blow to their own existence; their place was taken by Christians as the new People, who appropriated the whole tradition of Judaism, giving

---

[1] This is the prevailing view of all the sub-apostolic writers. Christians are the true Israel; hence theirs are all the honourable titles of the people of Israel. They are the twelve tribes (cp. Jas. i. 1), and thus Abraham, Isaac, and Jacob are the fathers of Christians (a conception on which no doubt whatever existed in the Gentile church, and which is not to be traced back simply to Paul); the men of God in the Old Testament were Christians (cp. Ignat., *ad Magn.*, viii. 2, οἱ προφῆται κατὰ Χριστὸν Ἰησοῦν ἔζησαν, "the prophets lived according to Christ Jesus"). But it is to be noted that a considerable section of Christians, viz., the majority of the so-called gnostics and the Marcionites, repudiated the Old Testament along with Judaism (a repudiation to which the epistle of Barnabas approximates very closely, but which it avoids by means of its resolute re-interpretation of the literal sense). These people appear to be the consistent party, yet they were really nothing of the kind; to cut off the Old Testament meant that another historical basis must be sought afresh for Christianity, and such a basis could not be found except in some other religion or in another system of worship. Marcion made the significant attempt to abandon the Old Testament and work *exclusively* with the doctrine and mythology of Paulinism; but the attempt was isolated, and it proved a failure.

a fresh interpretation to any unserviceable materials in it, or else allowing them to drop. As a matter of fact, the settlement was not even sudden or unexpected; what was unexpected was simply the particular form which the settlement assumed. All that Gentile Christianity did was to complete a process which had in fact commenced long ago within Judaism itself, viz., the process by which the Jewish religion was being inwardly emancipated and transformed into a religion for the world.

About 140 A.D. the transition of Christianity to the "Gentiles," with its emancipation from Judaism, was complete.[1] It was only learned opponents among the Greeks and the Jews themselves, who still reminded Christians that, strictly speaking, they must be Jews. After the fall of Jerusalem there was no longer any Jewish counter-mission, apart from a few local efforts;[2] on the contrary, Christians established themselves in the strongholds hitherto held by Jewish propaganda and Jewish proselytes. Japhet occupied the tents of Shem,[3] and Shem had to retire.

One thing, however, remained an enigma. Why had Jesus appeared among the Jews, instead of among the "nations"?[4]

---

[1] Forty years later Irenæus was therefore in a position to treat the Old Testament and its real religion with much greater freedom, for by that time Christians had almost ceased to feel that their possession of the Old Testament was seriously disturbed by Judaism. Thus Irenæus was able even to repeat the admission that the literal observance of the Old Testament in earlier days was right and holy. The Fathers of the ancient Catholic church, who followed him, went still further: on one side they approximated again to Paulinism; but at the same time, on every possible point, they moved still further away from the apostle than the earlier generations had done, since they understood his anti-legalism even less, and had also to defend the Old Testament against the gnostics. Their candid recognition of a literal sense in the Old Testament was due to the secure consciousness of their own position over against Judaism, but it was the result even more of their growing passion for the laws and institutions of the Old Testament cultus.

[2] Attempts of the Jews to seduce Christians into apostasy are mentioned in literature, but not very often; cp. Serapion's account quoted by Eusebius (*H.E.* vi. 12), and Acta Pionii (xiii., with a Jewish criticism of Christ as a suicide and a sorcerer).

[3] The half-finished, hybrid products of Jewish propaganda throughout the empire were transmuted into independent and attractive forms of religion, far surpassing the synagogues. It was only natural that the former had at once to enter into the keenest conflict with the latter.

[4] That Jesus himself converted many people ἐν τοῦ Ἑλληνικοῦ is asserted only by a comparatively late and unauthentic remark in Josephus.

This was a vexing problem. The Fourth Gospel (see above, p. 42), it is important to observe, describes certain Greeks as longing to see Jesus (xii. 20 f.), and the words put into the mouth of Jesus on that occasion [1] are intended to explain why the Saviour did not undertake the Gentile mission. The same evangelist makes Jesus say with the utmost explicitness (x. 16), " And other sheep I have which are not of this fold ; them also I must bring, and they shall hear my voice." He himself is to bring them. The mission which his disciples carry out, is thus his mission ; it is just as if he drew them himself.[2] Indeed his own power is still to work in them, as he is to send them the Holy Spirit to lead them into all the truth, communicating to them a wisdom which had hitherto lain unrevealed.

One consequence of this attitude of mind was that the twelve were regarded as a sort of personal multiplication of Christ himself, while the Kerugma (or outline and essence of Christian preaching) came to include the despatch of the twelve into all the world—*i.e.*, to include the Gentile mission as a command of

---

[1] "The hour has come for the Son of man to be glorified. Verily, verily, I say to you, unless the grain of wheat falls into the earth and dies, it abides by itself alone ; but if it die it bears much fruit. . . . . A voice then came from heaven, ' I have glorified, and I will glorify it again.' . . . . Jesus said, ' This voice has come, not for my sake but for yours ; now is the judgment of this world, now shall the prince of this world be cast out. *Yet when I am lifted up from the earth, I will draw all men to myself.*' "

[2] Naturally, there was not entire and universal satisfaction with this explanation. Even legend did not venture in those early days to change the *locale* of Jesus to the midst of paganism, but already Magi from the East were made to come to the child Jesus and worship him, after a star had announced his birth to all the world (Matt. ii.) ; angels at the birth of Jesus announced tidings of great joy to "all peoples" (Luke ii.) ; and when that star appeared, says Ignatius (*ad Eph.*, xix.), its appearance certified that "All sorcery was dissolved and every wicked spell vanished, ignorance was overthrown and the old kingdom was destroyed, when God appeared in human guise unto newness of eternal life. Then that which had been prepared within God's counsels began to take effect. Thence were all things perturbed, because the abolition of death was being undertaken" (ἐλύετο πᾶσα μαγεία, καὶ πᾶς δεσμὸς ἠφανίζετο κακίας, ἄγνοια καθῃρεῖτο, παλαιὰ βασιλεία διεφθείρετο, θεοῦ ἀνθρωπίνως φανερουμένου εἰς καινότητα ἀιδίου ζωῆς· ἀρχὴν δὲ ἐλάμβανεν τὸ παρὰ θεῷ ἀπηρτισμένον. ἔνθεν τὰ πάντα συνεκινεῖτο διὰ τὸ μελετᾶσθαι θανάτου κατάλυσιν). The Christians of Edessa were still more venturesome. They declared in the third century that Jesus had corresponded with their king Abgar, and cured him. Eusebius (*H.E.*, i. *ad fin.*) thought this tale of great importance ; it seemed to him a sort of substitute for any direct work of Jesus among pagans.

Jesus himself. Compare the *Apology* of Aristides (ii.); Just., *Apol.*, I. xxxix.; *Ascens. Isaiae*, iii. 13 f. (where the coming of the twelve disciples belongs to the fundamental facts of the gospel); Iren., *Fragm.* 29;[1] Tertull., *Apol.* xxi., *adv. Marc.* III.| xxii. (habes et apostolorum opus praedicatum); Hippol., *de Antichr.* 61 ; Orig., *c. Cels.*, III. xxviii.; *Acta Joh.* (ed. Zahn, p. 246: "the God who chose us to be apostles of the heathen, who sent us out into the world, *who showed himself by the apostles*"); Serapion in Eus., *H.E.*, vi. 12.[2] Details on this conception of the primitive apostles will be found in Book III.

---

[1] Harvey II. p. 494: οὗτος [ὁ χριστὸς] ἐν τῇ καρδίᾳ τῆς γῆς, ἐν χώματι κρυβεὶς καὶ τριημέρῳ μέγιστον δένδρον γεννηθεὶς ἐξέτεινε τοὺς ἑαυτοῦ κλάδους εἰς τὰ πέρατα τῆς γῆς. ἐκ τούτου προκύψαντες οἱ ιβ' ἀπόστολοι, κλάδοι ὡραῖοι, καὶ εὐθαλεῖς γενηθέντες σκέπη ἐγγενήθησαν τοῖς ἔθνεσιν, ὡς πετεινοῖς οὐρανοῦ, ὑφ' ὧν κλάδων σκεπασθέντες οἱ πάντες, ὡς ὄρνεα ὑπὸ καλιὰν συνελθόντα μετέλαβον τῆς ἐξ αὐτῶν προερχομένης ἐδωδίμου καὶ ἐπουρανίου τροφῆς = "Within the heart of the earth, hidden in the tomb, he became in three days the greatest of all trees [Iren. had previously compared Christ to the seed of corn in Luke xiii. 19], and stretched out his branches to the ends of the earth. His outstretched branches, waxing ripe and fresh, even the twelve apostles, became a shelter for the birds of heaven, even for the nations. By these branches all were shadowed, like birds gathered in a nest, and partook of the food and heavenly nourishment which came forth from them."

[2] This idea suggests one of the motives which prompted people to devise tales of apostolic missions.

CHAPTER VI

1. BEFORE his last journey to Jerusalem Paul wrote from Corinth to Rome (Rom. xv. 19 f.): "From Jerusalem and round about even unto Illyricum, I have fully preached the gospel of Christ; yea, making it my aim so to preach the gospel not where Christ was already named, that I might not build upon another man's foundation. Wherefore also I was hindered these many times from coming to you; but now, having no more any place in these regions, and having these many years a longing to come unto you, I will come whenever I go to Spain. For I hope to see you on my journey and to be brought on my way thitherward by you, if first in some measure I shall have been satisfied with your company."

The preaching of the gospel within the Greek world is now complete (for this is what the words "even unto Illyria" imply); the Latin world now begins.[1] Paul thus identifies his own missionary preaching along a narrow line from Jerusalem to Illyria with the preaching of the gospel to the entire Eastern hemisphere—a conception which is only intelligible upon the supposition that the certainty of the world's near end made no other kind of mission possible than one which thus hastily covered the world's area. The fundamental idea is that the gospel has to be preached everywhere during the short remaining space of

[1] Egypt could not be passed over, for the Greek world with would have been incomplete. But Paul never alludes to Egypt ei He must have known that other missionaries were labou regard Egypt, like John (*Apoc.* xi. 8), as a land which was nothing could be hoped from it?

73

the present world-age,[1] while at the same time this is only feasible by means of mission-tours across the world. The fire it is assumed, will spread right and left spont·neously from the line of flame.[2]

This idea, that the world must be traversed, was apparently conceived by the apostle on his so-called "second" missionary tour.[3] Naturally he viewed it as a divine injunction, for it is in this sense that we must interpret the difficult passage in Acts xvi. 6–8. If Paul had undertaken this second tour with the aim of reaching the Hellenistic districts on the coast of Asia Minor, and if he had become conscious in the course of his work that he was also called to be an apostle to the Greeks, then on the western border of Phrygia this consciousness passed into the sense of a still higher duty. He is not merely the apostle of the barbarians (Syrians, Cilicians, Lycaonians), not merely the apostle even of barbarians and Greeks, but the apostle of the world. He is commissioned to bear the gospel right to the western limits of the Roman empire ; that is, he must fill up the gaps left by the missionaries in their efforts to cover the whole ground. Hence he turns aside on the frontier of Phrygia, neither westwards (to Asia) nor northward (to Bithynia), as one might expect and as he originally planned to do, but north-west. Even Mysia he only hurries through. *The decision to pass by Asia and Bithynia meant that he was undertaking a mission to Macedonia, Achaia, and beyond that to the West.*

Philippi, Thessalonica, Berœa, Athens, Corinth—or, to put it more accurately, from Paul's standpoint, Macedonia and Achaia—heard the gospel. But why did he remain for eighteen months in Corinth? Why did he not travel on at once to Rome, and thence to the far West? Why did he interpolate a fresh tour, at this point, to Asia Minor, residing no less than

---

[1] The idea recurs in the gospels (Mark xiii. 10). Was Paul the first to conceive it and to give it currency?

[2] Cp. 1 Thess. i. 8 ; Rom. i. 8 ; Col. i. 6.

[3] N   The whole of the so-called "first" mission-tour is inexplicable
· r   iis idea in his mind. Wendt is quite right in saying (on
                at this period was merely conscious of being an apostle to
                the Greeks. Otherwise, the choice of a mission-field in
                intelligible.

three years at Ephesus? The answer is obvious. While he had Rome and the West in his mind, the first time he reached Corinth (Rom. i. 13), circumstances fortunately proved too strong for any attempt to realize this ambitious scheme. If I understand the situation aright, there were three considerations which had to be borne in mind. First of all, Paul neither would nor could lose touch with the two mother-churches in Jerusalem and Antioch. This made him return upon his tracks on two occasions. In the second place, he felt irresistibly bound to build up the churches which he had founded, instead of leaving them in the lurch after a few weeks. The duty of organising and of working on a small scale prevailed over the visionary and alleged duty of hurrying over the world with the gospel; the latter duty might well have lurking in it a grain of personal ambition. Finally, it was plain that no one had raised the standard of the gospel in the great province which he had been obliged to pass by, *i.e.*, in Western Asia Minor, the kernel of the Hellenic world. Paul had certainly assumed that other agents would preach the word of God here. But his hope was disappointed. On his first return journey (from Corinth to Jerusalem) he was content to leave behind him at Ephesus the distinguished missionary Prisca with her husband Aquila; but when he came back on his so-called "third" journey, he found not only the small beginnings of a Christian community, but disciples of John, whose mission he could not afford to ignore. The local sphere proved so rich and fertile that he felt obliged to take up residence at Ephesus. Here it was that he pursued the task of that spiritual settlement between Hellenism and Christianity which he had begun at Corinth. The first epistle to the Corinthians is evidence of this relationship. At Antioch no such adjustment was possible, for Antioch was simply a large Greek colony; it was Greek only in the sense in which Calcutta is English.

Paul, however, had not abandoned his scheme for covering the world with the gospel. The realization of it was only deferred in the sense in which the return of Christ was deferred. Probably he would have remained still longer at Ephesus (in the neighbourhood of which, as well as throughout the district, new churches had sprung up) and come into closer touch with Hellenism, had he not been disturbed by news from Corinth and finally driven out of the city by a small riot.

Paul's labours made Ephesus the third capital of Christianity, / its distinctively Greek capital. For a while it looked as if Ephesus was actually destined to be the final headquarters of the faith. But already a rival was emerging in the far West, which was to eclipse the Asiatic metropolis. This was Rome, the fourth city of Christianity, destined ere long to be the first.

When he left Ephesus to journey through Macedonia and Achaia, he again became the itinerant apostle, and once more the unforgotten idea of traversing the wide world got possession of his mind. From Corinth he wrote to Rome the words with which this chapter opened — words which lose something of their hyperbolic air when we think of the extraordinary success already won by the apostle in Macedonia and Achaia, in Asia and Phrygia. He had the feeling that, despite the poor results in Athens, he had conquered the Hellenic world. Conscious of this religious and intellectual triumph, he deemed his task within that sphere already done.

Nor did God need him now in Rome or throughout Italy. There the gospel had been already preached, and a great church had been organized by unknown missionaries. The faith of this church was "heard of through the whole world." Spain alone remained, for the adjacent Gaul and Africa could be reached along this line of work. Spain is selected, instead of Gaul or Africa, because the apostle's idea was to run a transversal line right across the empire. So Clement of Rome rightly understood him (i. 5), in words which almost sound like those of the apostle himself: "Seven times imprisoned, exiled, stoned, having preached in the east and in the west, a teacher of righteousness to the whole world even to the furthest limit of the west."

Did he manage this? Not in the first instance, at any rate. He had again to return to the far East, and the gloomy forebodings with which he travelled to Jerusalem were realized. When he did reach Rome, a year or two later, it was as a prisoner. But if he could no longer work as he desired to do, his activities were undiminished, in the shape of preaching at Rome, writing letters to churches far away, and holding intercourse with friends from the East.

When he was beheaded in the summer of 64 A.D., he had fully discharged his obligations to the peoples of the world. He was the apostle κατ' ἐξοχήν. To barbarians, Greeks, and Latins he had brought the gospel. But his greatness does not lie in the mere fact that he penetrated as a missionary to Illyria, Rome, and probably Spain as well; it lies in the manner in which he trained his fellow-workers and organized, as well as created, his churches. Though all that was profoundly Hellenic remained obscure to him, yet he rooted Christianity permanently in Hellenic soil. He was not the only one to do so, but it was his ideas alone which proved a new ferment within Hellenism, as the gnostics, Irenæus, Origen, and Augustine especially show. So far as there ever was an original Christian Hellenism, it was under Pauline influences. Paul lived on in his epistles. They are not merely records of his personality and work—though even in this light few writings in the world are to be compared to them—but, as the profound outcome of a vital personal religion and an unheard-of inner conflict, they are also perennial springs of religious power. Every age has understood them in its own way. None has yet exhausted them. Even in their periods of depreciation they have been singularly influential.

Of the four centres of Christianity during the first century—Jerusalem, Antioch, Ephesus, and Rome—one alone was the work of Paul, and even Ephesus did not remain as loyal to its founder as might have been expected. As the "father" of his churches he fell into the background everywhere; in fact he was displaced, and displaced by the development of mediocrity, of that "natural" piety which gets on quite well by itself. Neither his strength nor his weakness was transmitted to his churches. In this sense Paul remained an isolated personality, but he always was the teacher of Christendom, and this he became more than ever as the years went by.

2. His legacy, apart from his epistles, was his churches. He designated them indeed as his "epistles." Neither his vocation (as a restless, pioneering missionary), nor his temperament, nor his religious genius (as an ecstatic enthusiast and a somewhat ex-

clusive theologian) seemed to fit him for the work of organization ;
nevertheless he knew better than anyone else how to found and
build up churches (cp. Weinel, *Paulus als kirchlicher Organisator*,
1899). Recognizing the supreme fruits of the Spirit in faith,
love, hope, and all the allied virtues, bringing the outbursts of
enthusiasm into the service of edification, subordinating the individual to the larger organism, claiming the natural conditions
of social life, for all their defects and worldliness, as divine
arrangements, he overcame the dangers of fanaticism and created
churches which could live in the world without being of the
world. But organization never became for Paul an end in itself
or a means to worldly aggrandizement. Such was by no means
his intention. " The aims of his ecclesiastical labours were unity
in brotherly love and the reign of God in the heart of man, not
the rule of savants or priests over the laity." In his theology
and in his controversy with the Judaists he seems often to be
like an inquisitor or a fanatical scribe, and he has been accused
of inoculating the church with the virus of theological narrowness and heresy-mongering. But in reality the only confession
he recognised, besides that of the living God, was the confession
of " Christ the Lord," and towards the close of his life he testified that he would tolerate any doctrine which occupied that
ground. The spirit of Christ, liberty, love—to these supreme
levels, in spite of his temperament and education, he won his
own way, and it was on these high levels that he sought to place
his churches.

3. There was a great disparity between him and his coadjutors.
Among the more independent, Barnabas, Silas (Silvanus), Prisca
and Aquila, and Apollos deserve mention. Of Barnabas we
have already spoken (pp. 52 f.). Silas, the prophet of the Jerusalemite church, took his place beside Paul, and held a position
during the so-called " second" missionary tour like that of
Barnabas during the " first." Perhaps the fact that Paul took
him as a companion was a fresh assurance for the church of
Jerusalem. But, so far as we can see (cp. 2 Cor. i. 19), no dis-
cord marred their intercourse. Silas shared with him the work
of founding the churches in Macedonia and Achaia. Thereafter he disappears entirely from the life of Paul and the Acts

of the Apostles, to reappear, we are surprised to find, as an author at the conclusion of the epistle to Pontus, Galatia, Cappadocia, Asia, and Bithynia, which was inspired by Peter (for such is in all probability the meaning of v. 12: διὰ Σιλουανοῦ ὑμῖν τοῦ πιστοῦ ἀδελφοῦ, ὡς λογίζομαι, δι' ὀλίγων ἔγραψα). This abrupt reference to him, which stands quite by itself, must remain an enigma. Prisca and Aquila, the wife and husband (or rather, Prisca the missionary, with her husband Aquila), who were exiled from Rome to Corinth during the reign of Claudius, had the closest relation to Paul of all the independent workers in the mission. They co-operated with him at Corinth; they prepared the way for him at Ephesus, where Prisca showed her Christian intelligence by winning over Apollos, the Alexandrian disciple of John, to Christ; they once saved the apostle's life; and, on returning to Rome, they carried on the work upon Paul's lines (cp. my study in the *Sitzungsberichte der Berliner Akademie*, Jan. 11, 1900). There is much to be said for the hypothesis that Hebrews was their composition, whether from the pen of Prisca or of Aquila (cp. my essay in the *Zeitschrift für die neutest. Wissenschaft*, vol. i. pp. 1 f., 1900). Apollos, the Alexandrian, worked independently in the field which Paul had planted at Corinth. Paul only refers to him in First Corinthians, but invariably with respect and affection; he was well aware that the Corinthians attributed a certain rivalry and coolness to himself and Apollos. At the same time it may be questioned whether the work of this able colleague, whom he had not personally chosen, was thoroughly congenial to him. The abrupt reference in Tit. iii. 13 unfortunately does not tell us anything beyond the fact that their subsequent intercourse was unimpaired.

Among the missionaries whom Paul himself secured or trained, Timothy occupies the foremost place. We learn a good deal about him, and his personality was so important even to the author of Acts that his origin and selection for this office are described (xvi. 1). Still, we cannot form any clear idea of this, the most loyal of Paul's younger coadjutors, probably because he leant so heavily on the apostle. After Paul's death at Rome he carried on his work there, having been with him in the capital, and thus came into touch with the local church. He was for a time in prison, and survived to the reign of Domitian (Heb. xiii. 23).—Mark, who belonged to the primitive church of Jerusalem, Titus, and Luke the physician, are to be singled out among the other missionaries of the second class. With regard to Mark, whom Paul did not take with him on his so-called " second " tour, but who later on is found in his company (Philemon 24, Col. iv. 10, 2 Tim. iv. 11), it is just possible (though, in my judgment, it is not likely) that tradition has made one figure out of two. He it is who, according to the presbyter John, made notes of the gospel story. Titus, of whom little is known, was a full-blooded pagan (Gal. ii. 1 f.), and laboured for some time in Crete. Luke, who came across Paul at Troas on the latter's second tour, belonged to the church of Antioch. Like Titus, he was a Gentile Christian. He furnished primitive Christianity with its most intelligent, though not its greatest, author. Paul does not appear, however, to have fully recognised the importance of this " beloved physician " (Col. iv. 15), his " fellow-worker " (Philemon 24). The last reference to his fellow-workers indeed is not enthusiastic. The epistle to the Philippians breathes an air of isolation, and in 2 Tim. iv. 9 f. we read : " Do thy diligence to come shortly unto me ; for Demas has forsaken me, having loved this present world, and is gone to Thessalonica, Crescens to Galatia, Titus to Dalmatia. Luke alone is with me [rather a mediocre consolation, it would seem !]. Take Mark and bring him with thee ; for he is useful to me for ministering. Tychicus I sent to Ephesus. Alexander the coppersmith did me much evil. At my first defence no one took my part, but all forsook me." It would be unfair, however, to judge Paul's coadjutors by these expressions of dissatisfaction. Evidently they had not done as Paul wished, but we are quite in the dark upon the reasons for their action.

4. The first epistle of Peter is a very dubious piece of evidence for the idea that Peter, either with or after Paul, took part in the mission to Asia Minor ; but there is no doubt that some prominent Palestinian Christians came to Asia and Phrygia, perhaps after the destruction of Jerusalem, and that they displayed remarkable activity in the district. At their head was a man who came to Ephesus and died there, at a ripe age, during

the first year of the reign of Trajan. This was John "the Presbyter," as he called himself, and as he was called by his own circle. He worked in the Pauline churches of Asia, both in person and by means of letters; he added to their number, organized them internally, and maintained an extraordinarily sharp opposition to heretics. He retained the oversight of the churches, and exercised it by means of itinerant emissaries. His influence was apostolic or equivalent to that of an apostolic authority, but towards the end of his life several churches, conscious of their independence, endeavoured, in conjunction with their bishops, to throw off his supervision. When he died, there was an end of the mission organisation, which had latterly survived in his own person: the independent, local authority came to the front on all hands. When Ignatius ·reached Asia, twelve or fifteen years afterwards, the former had entirely disappeared, and even the memory of this John had given place to that of Paul. The Johannine circle must therefore have been rather limited during its latter phase. Even John must have been pretty isolated.[1] The second and third epistles of John certainly belong to him, and we may therefore ascribe to him, with much probability, the Fourth gospel and the first epistle of John also—in fact, we may go a step further and claim for him the Apocalypse with its seven letters and its Christian revision of one or more Jewish apocalypses. This hypothesis is the simplest which can be framed: it meets the data of tradition better than any other, and it encounters no fatal objections. All that can be said of the personality of this John within the limits of reasonable probability, is that he was not the son of Zebedee, but a Jerusalemite of priestly origin, otherwise unknown to us, and a disciple of the Lord;[2] furthermore, as the gospel indicates,

---

[1] The same fate apparently overtook him which he had prepared for Paul. Of course we are all in a mist here, but the entire silence of the seven letters in the Apocalypse with regard to Paul is a problem which is not to be waved aside as insignificant. Even the same silence in the gospel of John, where so many other indications of recent history are to be heard, is extremely surprising. Those who wanted to refer the mission of the Paraclete to Paul (Origen mentions them; cp. addenda) were certainly wrong, but they were right in looking out for some allusion to Paul in the gospel, and they could not find any other.

[2] This title suggests, but does not prove, that he was a personal disciple of Jesus, since it occurs not in Jerusalem but in Asia.

he must at one time have been specially connected with John the son of Zebedee.[1]   If his authority collapsed towards the end of his life, or was confined to a small circle, that circle (" of presbyters ") certainly succeeded in restoring and extending his authority by editing his writings and disseminating them throughout the churches.   In all likelihood, too, they purposely identified the " apostle," presbyter, and disciple of the Lord with the son of Zebedee; or, at least, they did not oppose this erroneous tendency.

Apart from this John we can name the evangelist Philip and his four prophetic daughters, Aristion the disciple of the Lord, and probably the apostle Andrew as among those who came to Asia Minor.   As for Philip (already confused in the second century with his namesake the apostle) and his daughters, we have clear evidence for his activity in Phrygian Hierapolis.   Papias mentions Aristion together with John as primitive witnesses, and an Armenian manuscript ascribes the unauthentic ending of Mark's gospel to him—an ending which is connected with Luke and the Fourth gospel, and perhaps originated in Asia Minor. We may conjecture, from the old legends preserved in the Muratorian fragment, that Andrew came to Asia Minor, and this is confirmed by the tradition (late, but not entirely worthless) that he died in Greece.[2]

At the close of the first century Asia and Phrygia were the only two provinces in which Palestinian traditions survived in

---

[1] The most likely conjecture is that the beloved disciple was the son of Zebedee. Everything follows naturally from this view.   The Presbyter need not have gained his special relationship to John in Asia Minor : it may go back quite well to Jerusalem.   The formal difficulty of the two Johns has to be faced, but after all "John" was a common name.   If it would at all simplify the critical problem to assume that the son of Zebedee was also in Asia Minor, one might credit this tradition, which is vouched for as early as Justin Martyr.   But this would not affect the problem of the authorship of the Johannine writings, though it might explain how the author of those writings came to be identified, at a comparatively early time, with the apostle John.

[2] We may refer here to Ignat., ad Ephes., xi. : ἵνα ἐν κλήρῳ Ἐφεσίων εὑρεθῶ τῶν Χριστιανῶν, οἳ καὶ τοῖς ἀποστόλοις πάντοτε συνήνεσαν (v. I, συνῆσαν) ἐν δυνάμει Ἰησοῦ χριστοῦ ("That I may be found in the company of those Ephesian Christians who moreover were ever of one mind with the apostles in the power of Jesus Christ").   The reading συνήνεσαν does not necessarily prove the personal residence of the apostle in Ephesus, however.

the person of individual representatives. At the same time, probably, in no other part of the empire were there so many closely allied churches as here and in Pontus and Bithynia. This must have lent them, and especially the church at Ephesus, a high repute. When Clement of Alexandria was in search of early traditions, he turned to Asia; and even in Rome people were well aware of the significance with which the Asiatic churches were invested owing to their traditions, though Rome was never willing to take the second place. About 50 A.D. Christianity was an ellipse whose foci were Jerusalem and Antioch; fifty years later these foci were Ephesus and Rome. The change implied in this proves the greatness of Paul's work and of the work done by the first Christian missionaries.

BOOK II

THE MISSION-PREACHING IN
WORD AND DEED

THE unity and the variety which characterized the preaching of Christianity from the very first constituted the secret of its fascination and a vital condition of its success. On the one hand, it was so simple that it could be summed up in a few brief sentences and understood in a single crisis of the inner life; on the other hand, it was so versatile and rich, that it vivified all thought and stimulated every emotion. It was capable, almost from the outset, of vieing with every noble and worthy enterprise, with any speculation, or with any cult of the mysteries. It was both new and old; it was alike present and future. Clear and transparent, it was also profound and full of mystery. It had statutes, and yet rose superior to any law. It was a doctrine and yet no doctrine, a philosophy and yet something different from philosophy. Western Catholicism, when surveyed as a whole, has been described as a *complexio oppositorum*, but this was also true of the Christian propaganda in its earliest stages. Consequently, to exhibit the preaching and labours of the Christian mission with the object of explaining the amazing success of Christianity, we must try to get a uniform grasp of all its component factors.

We shall proceed then to describe :—

1. The religious characteristics of the mission-preaching.
2. The gospel of salvation and of the Saviour.
3. The gospel of love and charity.

4. The religion of the Spirit and power, of moral earnestness and holiness.

5. The religion of authority and of reason, of mysteries and transcendentalism.

6. The message of a new People and of a Third race (or the historical and political consciousness of Christendom).

7. The religion of a Book, and of an historical realization.

8. The conflict with polytheism and idolatry.

In the course of these chapters we hope to do justice to the wealth of the religion, without impairing or obscuring the power of its simplicity.[1] One point must be left out, of course: that is, the task of following the development of Christian doctrine into the dogmas of the church's catechism, as well as into the Christian philosophy of religion propounded by Origen and his school. Doctrine, in both of these forms, was unquestionably of great moment to the mission of Christianity, particularly after the date of its earliest definition (relatively speaking) about the middle of the third century. But such a subject would require a book to itself. I have endeavoured, in the first volume of my *History of Dogma* (third edition)[2] to deal with it, and to that work I must refer any who may desire to see how the unavoidable gaps of the present volume are to be filled up.

---

[1] At the Scilitan martyrdom the proconsul remarks : "Et nos religiosi sumus, et simplex est religio nostra" ("Our religion is simple"). To which Speratus the Christian replies: "Si tranquillas praebueris aures tuas, dico mysterium simplicitatis" ("If you give me a quiet hearing, I shall tell you the mystery of simplicity").

[2] Cp. my *Grundriss der Dogmengeschichte* (4th ed., 1905).

CHAPTER I

" MISSIONARY PREACHING " is a term which may be taken in a double sense. Its broader meaning covers all the forces of influence, attraction, and persuasion which the gospel had at its command, all the materials that it collected and endowed with life and power as it developed into a syncretistic religion during the first three centuries. The narrower sense of the term embraces simply the crucial message of faith and the ethical requirements of the gospel. Taking it in the latter sense, we shall devote the present chapter to a description of the fundamental principles of the missionary preaching. The broader conception has a wide range. The Old Testament and the new literature of Christianity, healing and redemption, gnosis and apologetic, myth and sacrament, the conquest of demons, forms of social organization and charity—all these played their part in the mission-preaching and helped to render it impressive and convincing. Even in the narrower sense of the term, our description of the mission-preaching must be kept within bounds, for the conception of the crucial message of faith and its ethical requirements is bound up naturally with the development of dogma, and the latter (as I have already remarked) cannot be exhibited without overstepping the precincts of the present volume. At the same time, these limitations are not very serious, since, to the best of our knowledge, mission-preaching (in the narrower sense of the term) was fairly extinct after the close of the second century. Its place was taken by the instruction of catechumens, by the training of the household in and for the Christian faith, and by the worship of the church. Finally, we must eschew the error of imagining that everyone who came over to Christianity was won by a missionary propaganda of dogmatic completeness. So far as our sources throw light on this point, they reveal a very different state of things, and this applies even to the entire period preceding Constantine. In countless instances, it was but one ray of light that wrought the change. One person would be brought over by means of the Old Testament, another by the exorcising of demons, a third by the purity of Christian life; others, again, by the monotheism of Christianity, above all by the prospect of complete expiation, or by the prospect which it held out of immortality, or by the profundity of its specula-tions, or by the social standing which it conferred. In the great majority of cases, so long as Christianity did not yet propagate itself naturally, one believer may well have produced another, just as one prophet anointed his successor; example (not confined to the case of the martyrs) and the *personal* manifestation of the Christian life led to imitation. A complete knowledge of Christian doctrine, which was still a plant of very tender growth in the second century, was certainly the attainment of a small minority. " Idiotae, quorum semper maior pars est," says Tertullian (" The uneducated are always in a majority with us "). Hippolytus bewails the ignorance even of a Roman bishop. Even the knowledge of the Scriptures, though they were read in private, remained of necessity the privilege of an individual here and there, owing to their extensiveness and the difficulty of understanding them.[1]

The earliest mission-preaching to Jews ran thus: "The kingdom of God is at hand; repent."[2] The Jews thought they knew what was the meaning of the kingdom of heaven and of its advent; but they had to be told the meaning of the repentance that secured the higher righteousness, so that " God's kingdom " also acquired a new meaning.

---

[1] Bishops and theologians, in the West especially, are always bewailing the defective knowledge of the Bible among the laity, and even among the clergy. Cp. also Clemens Alexandrinus.

[2] The earliest mission-preaching (Matt. x. 7 f.) with which the disciples of Jesus were charged, ran : κηρύσσετε λέγοντες ὅτι ἤγγικεν ἡ βασιλεία τῶν οὐρανῶν. Although repentance is not actually mentioned, it is to be supplied from other passages. The prospect of power to do works of healing is also held out to them (ἀσθενοῦντας θεραπεύετε, νεκροὺς ἐγείρετε, λεπροὺς καθαρίζετε, δαιμόνια ἐκβάλλετε).

The second stage in the mission-preaching to Jews was deter-mined by this tenet : " The risen [1] Jesus is the Messiah [cp. Matt. x. 32], and will return from heaven to establish his kingdom."

The third stage was marked by the interpretation of the Old Testament as a whole (*i.e.*, the law and the prophets) from the standpoint of its fulfilment in Jesus Christ, along with the accom-panying need of securing and formulating that inwardness of disposition and moral principle which members of the Messianic church, who were called and kept by the Holy Spirit, knew to be their duty.[2] This must have made them realize that the observ-ance of the law, which had hitherto prevailed, was inadequate either to cancel sin or to gain righteousness ; also that Jesus the Messiah had died that sins might be forgiven (γνωστὸν ἔστω ὑμῖν, ὅτι διὰ τούτου ὑμῖν ἄφεσις ἁμαρτιῶν καταγγέλλεται ἀπὸ πάντων ὧν οὐκ ἠδυνήθητε ἐν νόμῳ Μωϋσέως δικαιωθῆναι).[3]

---

[1] Cp. the confession of the resurrection common to primitive Christianity, in i Cor. xv. 4 f.

[2] To "imitate" or "be like" Christ did not occupy the place one would expect among the ethical counsels of the age. Jesus had spoken of imitating God and bidden men follow himself, whilst the relationship of pupil and teacher readily suggested the formula of imitation. But whenever he was recognized as Messiah, as the Son of God, as Saviour, and as Judge, the ideas of imitation and likeness had to give way, although the apostles still continued to urge both in their epistles, and to hold up the mind, the labours, and the sufferings of Jesus as an example. In the early church the imitation of Christ never became a formal principle of ethics (to use a modern phrase) except for the virtuoso in religion, the ecclesiastic, the teacher, the ascetic, or the martyr ; it played quite a subordinate rôle in the ethical teaching of the church. Even the injunction to be like Christ, in the strict sense of the term, occurs comparatively seldom. Still, it is interesting to collect and examine the passages relative to this point ; they show that whilst a parallel was fully drawn between the life of Christ and the career and conduct of distinguished Christians such as the confessors, the early church did not go the length of drawing up general injunctions with regard to the imitation of Christ. For one thing, the Christology stood in the way, involving not imitation but obedience ; for another thing, the literal details of imitation seemed too severe. Those who made the attempt were always classed as Christians of a higher order (though even at this early period they were warned against presumption), so that the Catholic theory of "evangelic counsels" has quite a primitive root.

[3] Acts xiii. 38 ; up to this point, I think, the Jewish Christian view is clearly stated in the address of Paul at Antioch, but the further development of the idea (ἐν τούτῳ πᾶς ὁ πιστεύων δικαιοῦται, "by whom everyone who believes is justified") is specifically Pauline. Taken as a whole, however, the speech affords a fine example of missionary preaching to the Jews. From i Cor. xv. 3 it follows that the tenet, "Christ died for our sins according to the scriptures," was not simply Pauline, but common to Christianity in general. Weizsäcker (*op. cit.*,

" You know that when you were pagans you were led away to dumb idols (1 Cor. xii. 2). " You turned to God from idols, to serve the living and true God, and to wait for his Son from heaven, whom he raised from the dead, even Jesus, who delivers us from the wrath to come " (1 Thess. i. 9, 10). Here we have the mission-preaching to pagans in a nutshell. The " living and true God " is the first and final thing; the second is Jesus, the Son of God, the judge, who secures us against the wrath to come, and who is therefore " Jesus the Lord." To the living God, now preached to all men, we owe faith and devoted service; to God's Son as *Lord*, our due is faith and hope.[1]

The contents of this brief message—objective and subjective, positive and negative—are inexhaustible. Yet the message itself is thoroughly compact and complete. It is objective and positive as the message which tells of the only God, who is spiritual, omnipresent, omniscient, omnipotent, the creator of heaven and earth, the Lord and Father of men, and the great disposer of human history;[2] furthermore, it is the message which tells of Jesus Christ, the Son of God, who came from heaven,

pp. 60 f. ; Eng. trans., i. 74 f.) rightly lays great stress on the fact that previous to Paul and alongside of him, even within Jewish Christian circles (as in the case of Peter), the view must have prevailed that the law and its observance were not perfectly adequate to justification before God, and that a soteriological significance attached to Jesus the Messiah or to his death.

[1] When questioned upon the "dogma" of Christians, Justin answered : ὅπερ εὐσεβοῦμεν εἰς τὸν τῶν Χριστιανῶν θεόν, ὃν ἡγούμεθα ἕνα τοῦτον ἐξ ἀρχῆς ποιητὴν καὶ δημιουργὸν τῆς πάσης κτίσεως, ὁρατῆς τε καὶ ἀοράτου, καὶ κύριον Ἰησοῦν Χριστὸν παῖδα θεοῦ, ὃς καὶ προκεκήρυκται ὑπὸ τῶν προφετῶν μέλλων παραγίνεσθαι τῷ γένει τῶν ἀνθρώπων σωτηρίας κήρυξ καὶ διδάσκαλος καλῶν μαθητῶν (*Acta Just.*, i.) ("It is that whereby we worship the God of the Christians, whom we consider to be One from the beginning, the maker and fashioner of the whole creation, visible and invisible, and also the Lord Jesus Christ the Son of God, whom the prophets foretold would come to the race of men, a herald of salvation and a teacher of good disciples ").

[2] In this respect the speech put by Luke (Acts xvii. 22–30) into the mouth of Paul at the Areopagus is typical and particularly instructive. It exhibits, at the same time, an alliance with the purest conceptions of Hellenism. We must combine this speech with First Thessalonians, in order to understand how the fundamentals of mission-preaching were laid before pagans, and also in order to get rid of the notion that Galatians and Romans are a model of Paul's preaching to pagan audiences.—The characteristic principles of the mission-preaching (both negative and positive) are also preserved, with particular lucidity, in the fragmentary *Kerugma Petri*, an early composition which, as the very title indicates, was plainly meant to be a compendium of doctrine for missionary purposes.

made known the Father, died for sins, rose, sent the Spirit hither, and from his seat at God's right hand will return *for the judgment*;[1] finally, it is the message of salvation brought by Jesus the Saviour, that is, freedom from the tyranny of demons, sin, and death, together with the gift of life eternal.

Then it is objective and negative, since it announces the vanity of all other gods, and forms a protest against idols of gold and silver and wood, as well as against blind fate and atheism.

Finally, it si subjective, as it declares the uselessness of all sacrifice, all temples, and all worship of man's devising, and opposes to these the worship of God in spirit and in truth, assurance of faith, holiness and self-control, love and brotherliness, and lastly the solid certainty of the resurrection and of life eternal, implying the futility of the present life, which lies exposed to future judgment.

This new kind of preaching excited extraordinary fears and hopes : fears of the imminent end of the world and of the great reckoning, at which even the just could hardly pass muster ; hopes of a glorious reign on earth, after the *dénouement*, and of a paradise which was to be filled with precious delights and overflowing with comfort and bliss. Probably no religion had ever proclaimed openly to men such terrors and such happiness.

To wide circles this message of the one and almighty God no

---

[1] Thaddaeus announces to Abgar a missionary address for the next day, and gives the following preliminary outline of its contents (Eus., *H.E.*, i. 13) : κηρύξω καὶ σπερῶ τὸν λόγον τῆς ζωῆς, περί τε τῆς ἐλεύσεως τοῦ Ἰησοῦ καθὼς ἐγένετο, καὶ περὶ τῆς ἀποστολῆς αὐτοῦ, καὶ ἕνεκα τίνος ἀπεστάλη ὑπὸ τοῦ πατρός, καὶ περὶ τῆς δυνάμεως καὶ τῶν ἔργων αὐτοῦ καὶ μυστηρίων ὧν ἐλάλησεν ἐν κόσμῳ, καὶ ποίᾳ δυνάμει ταῦτα ἐποίει, καὶ περὶ τῆς καινῆς αὐτοῦ κηρύξεως, καὶ περὶ τῆς μικρότητος, καὶ περὶ τῆς ταπεινώσεως, καὶ πῶς ἐταπείνωσεν ἑαυτὸν καὶ ἀπέθετο καὶ ἐσμίκρυνεν αὐτοῦ τὴν θεότητα, καὶ ἐσταυρώθη, καὶ κατέβη εἰς τὸν Ἅιδην, καὶ διέσχισε φραγμὸν τὸν ἐξ αἰῶνος μὴ σχισθέντα, καὶ ἀνήγειρεν νεκροὺς καὶ κατέβη μόνος, ἀνέβη δὲ μετὰ πολλοῦ ὄχλου πρὸς τὸν πατέρα αὐτοῦ ("I Will preach and sow the Word of God, concerning the advent of Jesus, even the manner of his birth : concerning his mission, even the purpose for which the Father sent him : concerning the power of his works and the mysteries he uttered in the world, even the nature of this power : concerning his new preaching and his abasement and humiliation, even how he humbled himself and died and debased his divinity and was crucified and Went down to Hades and burst asunder the bars Which had not been severed from all eternity, and raised the dead, descending alone but rising With many to his Father").

longer came as a surprise. It was the reverse of a surprise. What they had vaguely divined, seemed now to be firmly and gloriously realized. At the same time, as "Jesus and the Resurrection" were taken for new dæmons in Athens (according to Acts xvii. 18), and considered to be utterly strange, this doctrine must have been regarded at first as paradoxical wherever it was preached. This, however, is not a question into which we have here to enter. What is certain is, that "the *one* living God, as creator," "Jesus the Saviour,"[1] "the Resurrection" (ἡ ἀνάστασις), and ascetic "self-control" (ἡ ἐγκράτεια) formed the most conspicuous articles of the new propaganda. Along with this the story of Jesus must have been briefly communicated (in the statements of Christology), the resurrection was generally defined as the resurrection of the flesh, and self-control primarily identified with sexual purity, and then extended to include renunciation of the world and mortification of the flesh.[2]

[1] One of the distinctive ideas in Christianity was the paradox that the Saviour was also the Judge, an idea which gave it a special pre-eminence over other religions. — "Father and Son," or "Father, Son, and Holy Spirit": the dual and the triple formula interchange, but the former is rather older, though both can be traced as far back as Paul. Personally I should doubt if it was he who stamped the latter formula. Like the "Church," "the new People," "the true Israel," "apostles, prophets, and teachers," "regeneration," etc., it was probably created by the primitive circle of disciples. — The preaching of Jesus was combined with the confession of the Father, Son, and Holy Spirit, and with the church, the forgiveness of sins, and the resurrection of the body. The Roman symbol is our earliest witness to this combination, and it was probably the earliest actual witness; it hardly arose out of the work of missions, in the narrower sense of the term, but out of the earlier catechetical method.

[2] Hermas, *Mand.*, i. (πρῶτον πάντων πίστευσον, ὅτι εἷς ἐστὶν ὁ θεὸς ὁ τὰ πάντα κτίσας καὶ καταρτίσας, κ.τ.λ. : "First of all, believe that God is one, even he who created and ordered all things," etc.), is a particularly decisive passage as regards the first point (viz., the *one* living God); see *Praedic. Petri* in Clem., *Strom.*, v. 6. 48, vi. 5. 39, vi. 6. 48 (the twelve disciples despatched by Jesus with the charge to preach to all the inhabitants of the world, that they may know God is one: εὐαγγελίσασθαι τοὺς κατὰ τὴν οἰκουμένην ἀνθρώπους γινώσκειν, ὅτι εἷς θεός ἐστιν). In Chap. II. of his *Apology*, Aristides sets forth the preaching of Jesus Christ; but when he has to summarize Christianity, he is contented to say that "Christians are those who have found the *one* true God." Cp., *e.g.*, Chap. XV. : "Christians . . . . have found the truth. . . . . They know and trust in God, the creator of heaven and earth, through whom and from whom are all things, beside whom there is none other, and from whom they have received commandments which are written on their hearts and kept in the faith and expectation of the world to come." (Cp. also the *Apology* of pseudo-Melito.) The other three points are

The most overwhelming element in the new preaching was
the resurrection of the flesh, the complete "restitutio in in-
tegrum," and the kingdom of glory. Creation and resurrection
were the beginning and the end of the new doctrine. The hope
of resurrection which it aroused gave rise to a fresh estimate of
the individual's value, and at the same time to quite inferior
and sensuous desires. Faith in the resurrection of the body and
in the millennium soon appeared to pagans to be the distinguishing feature of this silly religion. And the pagans were right. It
was the distinguishing feature of Christianity at this period.
Justin explains that all orthodox Christians held this doctrine
and this hope. "Fiducia christianorum resurrectio mortuorum,
illa credentes sumus," Tertullian writes (de Resurr., i.), adding
(in ch. xxi.) that this must not be taken allegorically, as the
heretics allege, since " verisimile non est, ut ea species sacramenti,
in quam fides tota committitur, in quam disciplina tota conititur,
ambigue annuntiata et obscura proposita videatur " (the gospel
is too important to be stated ambiguously ; see further what
follows). The earliest essays of a technical character by the
teachers of the Catholic church were upon the resurrection of
the flesh. It was a hope, too, which gave vent to the ardent
desires of the oppressed, the poor, the slaves, and the disappointed
upon earth : " We want to serve no longer, our wish is to reign
soon" (Tert., de Orat., v.). "Though the times of this hope have
been determined by the sacred pen, lest it should be fixed
previous, I think, to the return of Christ, yet our prayers pant
for the close of this age, for the passing of this world to the
great day of the Lord, for the day of wrath and retribution "
(Cum et tempora totius spei fida sunt sacrosancto stilo, ne liceat
eam ante constitui quam in adventum, opinor, Christi, vota

laid down with especial clearness in the *Acta Theclae,* where Paul is said (i. 5) to
have handed down πάντα τὰ λόγια κυρίου καὶ τῆς γεννήσεως καὶ τῆς ἀναστάσεως
τοῦ ἠγαπημένου ("all the sayings of the Lord and of the birth and resurrection of
the Beloved "), and where the contents of his preaching are described as λόγος
θεοῦ περὶ ἐγκρατείας καὶ ἀναστάσεως ("the Word of God upon self-control and the
resurrection "). The last-named pair of ideas are to be taken as mutually supple-
mentary ; the resurrection or eternal life is certain, but it is conditioned by ἐγκράτεια, which is therefore put first. Cp., for example, *Vita Polycarpi,* 14 : ἔλεγεν
τὴν ἀγνείαν πρόδρομον εἶναι τῆς μελλούσης ἀφθάρτου βασιλείας ("he said that purity
was the precursor of the incorruptible kingdom to come ").

nostra suspirant in saeculi huius occasum, in transitum mundi quoque ad diem domini magnum, diem irae et retributionis.— Tert., *de Resurr.*, xxii.). " May grace come and this world pass away ! The Lord comes ! " is the prayer of Christians at the Lord's Supper (*Did.*, x.). In many circles this mood lasted even after the beginning of the third century, but it reached its height during the reign of Marcus Aurelius.[1]

From the outset " wisdom," " intelligence," " understanding," and " intellect " had a very wide scope. Indeed, there was hardly a mission propaganda of any volume which did not overflow into the " gnostic " spirit, *i.e.*, the spirit of Greek philosophy. The play of imagination was at once unfettered and urged to its highest flights by the settled conviction (for we need not notice here the circles where a different view prevailed) that Jesus, the Saviour, had come down from heaven. It was, after all, jejune to be informed, " We are the offspring of God " (Acts xvii. 28); but to be told that God became man and was incarnate in order that men might be divine—this was the apex and climax of all knowledge. It was bound up with the speculative idea (i) that, as the incarnation was a cosmic and divine event, it must therefore involve a reviving and heightened significance for the whole creation ; and (ii) that the soul of man, hitherto divided from its primal source in God by forces and barriers of various degrees, now found the way open for its return to God, while every one of those very forces which had formerly barred the path was also liberated and transformed into a step and intermediate stage on the way back. Speculations upon God, the world, and the soul were inevitable, and they extended to the nature of the church. Here, too, the earthly and historical was raised to the level of the cosmic and transcendental.

At first the contrast between a " sound " gnosis and a heretical only emerged by degrees in the propaganda, although from the very outset it was felt that certain speculations seemed to im-

---

[1] Origen (*de Princ.* II. xi. 2) has described in great detail the views of the chiliasts, whom he opposed as, even in his day, a retrograde party. His description proves that we cannot attribute too sensuous opinions to them. They actually reckoned upon "nuptiarum conventiones et filiorum procreationes." Compare the words of Irenæus in the fifth book of his large work upon the millennium, where he follows "apostolic tradition" and attaches himself to Papias.

peril the preaching of the gospel itself.[1] The extravagances of the "gnosis" which penetrated all the syncretistic religion of the age, and issued in dualism and docetism, were corrected primarily by a "sound" gnosis, then by the doctrine of Christian freedom, by a sober, rational theology and ethics, by the realism of the saving facts in the history of Jesus, by the doctrine of the resurrection of the body, but ultimately and most effectively by the church prohibiting all "innovations" and fixing her tradition. From this standpoint Origen's definition of gospel preaching (*Hom. in Joh.*, xxxii. 9) is extremely instructive. After quoting Hermas, *Mand.*, i. (the *one* God, the Creator), he adds: "It is also necessary to believe that Jesus Christ is Lord, and to believe all the truth concerning his deity and humanity, also to believe in the Holy Spirit, and that as free agents we are punished for our sins and rewarded for our good actions."

By the second century Christianity was being preached in very different ways. The evangelists of the Catholic church preached in one way throughout the East, and in another throughout the West, though their fundamental position was identical; the Gnostics and Marcionites, again, preached in yet another way. Still Tertullian was probably not altogether wrong in saying that missions to the heathen were not actively promoted by the latter; the Gnostics and the Marcionites, as a rule, confined their operations to those who were already Christians. After the gnostic controversy, the anti-gnostic rule of faith gradually became the one basis of the church's preaching. The ethical and impetuous element retreated behind

[1] One of the most remarkable and suggestive phenomena of the time is the fact that wherever a "dangerous" speculation sprang up, it was combated in such a way that part of it was taken over. For example, contrast Ephesians and Colossians with the "heresies" which had emerged in Phrygia (at Colosse); think of the "heresies" opposed by the Johannine writings, and then consider the gnostic contents of the latter; compare the theology of Ignatius with the "heresies attacked in the Ignatian epistles; think of the great gnostic systems of the second century, and then read their opponent Irenæus. "Vincendi vincentibus legem dederunt"! Such was the power of these Hellenistic, syncretistic ideas! It looks almost as if there had been a sort of disinfectant process, the "sound" doctrine being inoculated with a strong dilution of heresy, and thus made proof against virulent infection.

the dogmatic, although the emphasis upon self-control and asceticism never lost its vogue.

At the transition from the second to the third century, theology had extended widely, but the mission-preaching had then as ever to remain comparatively limited. For the "idiotæ" it was enough, and more than enough, to hold the four points which we have already mentioned. Scenes like those described in Acts (viii. 26–38) were constantly being repeated, *mutatis mutandis*, especially during the days of persecution, when individual Christians suffered martyrdom joyfully ; and this, although an orthodox doctrine of considerable range was in existence, which (in theory, at any rate) was essential. For many the sum of knowledge amounted to nothing more than the confession of the one God, who created the world, of Jesus the Lord, of the judgment, and of the resurrection ; on the other hand, some of the chief arguments in the proof from prophecy, which played so prominent a part in all preaching to Jews and pagans (see Chapter VIII.), were disseminated far and wide ; and as the apologists are always pointing in triumph to the fact that "among us," "tradesmen, slaves, and old women know how to give some account of God, and do not believe without evidence,"[1] the principles of the Christian conception

---

[1] Together with the main articles in the proof from prophecy (*i.e.*, a dozen passages or so from the Old Testament), the corresponding parts of the history of Jesus were best known and most familiar. An inevitable result of being viewed in this light and along this line was that the history of Jesus (apart from the crucifixion) represents almost entirely legendary materials (or ideal history) to a severely historical judgment. Probably no passage made so deep an impression as the birth-narratives in Matthew and especially in Luke. The fact that the story of the resurrection did not *in its details* prove a similar success, was due to a diversity of the narratives in the authoritative scriptures, which was so serious that the very exegetes of the period (and they were capable of almost anything !) failed to give any coherent or impressive account of what transpired. Hence the separate narratives in the gospels relating to the resurrection did not possess the same importance as the birth-narratives. " Raised on the third day from the dead, according to the scripture " : this brief confession was all that rivalled the popularity of Luke i.-ii. and the story of the wise men from the East.—The notion that the apostles themselves compiled a quintessence of Christian doctrine was widely current ; but the greatest difference of opinion prevailed as to what the quintessence consisted of. The Didachê marks the beginning of a series of compositions which were supposed to have been written by the apostles collectively, or to contain an authoritative summary of their regulations.

of God must have been familiar to a very large number of people.

These four points, then — the one living God, Jesus our Saviour and Judge, the resurrection of the flesh, and self-control —combined to form the new religion. It stood out in bold relief from the old religions, and above all from the Jewish ; yet in spite of its hard struggle with polytheism, it was organically related to the process of evolution which was at work throughout all religion, upon the eastern and the central coasts of the Mediterranean. The atmosphere from which those four principles drew their vitality was *the conception of recompense—* i.e., the absolute supremacy of the moral element in life on the one hand, and the redeeming cross of Christ upon the other. No account of the principles underlying the mission-preaching of Christianity is accurate, if it does not view everything from the standpoint of this conception : the sovereignty of morality, and the assurance of redemption by the forgiveness of sins, based on the cross of Christ.[1] " Grace," *i.e.*, forgiveness, did play a leading rôle, but grace never displaced recompense. From the very first, morality was inculcated within the Christian churches in two ways : by the Spirit of Christ and by the conception of judgment and of recompense. Yet both were marked by a decided bent to the future, for the Christ of both was "he who was to return." To the mind of primitive Christianity the " present " and the " future " were sharply opposed to each

---

[1] Redemption by the forgiveness of sins was, strictly speaking, considered to take place once and for all. The effects of Christ's death were conferred on the individual at baptism, and all his previous sins were blotted out. Many teachers, like Paul, presented the cross of Christ as the content of Christianity. Thus Tertullian (*de Carne*, v.), protesting against the docetism of Marcion, which impaired the death of Christ upon the cross, calls out, " O spare the one hope of the whole world" (*parce unicæ spei totius orbis*). The cross exerts a protective and defensive influence over the baptized (against demons), but it does not bestow any redeeming deliverance from sin. Speculations on the latter point do not arise till later. As a mystery, of course, it is inexhaustible, and therefore it is impossible to state its influence. Pseudo-Barnabas and Justin are already mystagogues of the cross ; cp. *Ep. Barn.*, xi.-xii., and Justin's *Apol.*, I. lv., where he triumphantly claims that " the wicked demons never imitated the crucifixion, not even in the case of any of the so-called sons of Zeus " (οὐδαμοῦ οὐδ᾽ ἐπί τινος τῶν λεγομένων υἱῶν τοῦ Διὸς τὸ σταυρωθῆναι ἐμιμήσαντο). Cp. further Minucius, *Octav.* xxix. ; Tert., *ad. Nat.* I. xii. etc.

other,[1] and it was this opposition which furnished the principle of
self-control with its most powerful motive. It became, indeed,
with many people a sort of glowing passion. The church which
prayed at every service, "May grace come and this world pass
away: maranatha," was the church which gave directions like
those which we read in the opening parable of Hermas.[2] "From

[1] Cp. 2 Clem., ad Cor. vi.: ἔστιν οὗτος ὁ αἰὼν καὶ ὁ μέλλων δύο ἐχθροί. οὗτος
λέγει μοιχείαν καὶ φθορὰν καὶ φιλαργυρίαν καὶ ἀπάτην, ἐκεῖνος δὲ τούτοις ἀποτάσ-
σεται. οὐ δυνάμεθα οὖν τῶν δύο φίλοι εἶναι. δεῖ δὲ ἡμᾶς τούτῳ ἀποταξαμένους
ἐκείνῳ χρᾶσθαι. οἰόμεθα ὅτι βέλτιόν ἐστιν τὰ ἐνθάδε μισῆσαι, ὅτι μικρὰ καὶ
ὀλιγοχρόνια καὶ φθαρτά· ἐκεῖνα δὲ ἀγαπῆσαι, τὰ ἀγαθὰ τὰ ἄφθαρτα ("This age
and the future age are two enemies. The one speaks of adultery, corruption,
avarice, and deceit; the other bids farewell to these. We cannot, therefore, be
friends of both; we must part with the one and embrace the other. We judge
it better to hate the things which are here, because they are small and transient
and corruptible, and to love the things that are yonder, for they are good and
incorruptible").

[2] Here is the passage; it will serve to represent a large class. "You know
that you servants of God dwell in a foreign land, for your city is far from this city.
If, then, you know the city where you are to dwell, why provide yourselves here
with fields and expensive luxuries and buildings and chambers to no purpose?
He who makes such provision for this city has no mind to return to his own city.
Foolish, double-minded, wretched man! seest thou not that all these things are
foreign to thee and controlled by another? For the lord of this city shall say, 'I
will not have thee in my city; leave this city, for thou keepest not my laws.'
Then, O possessor of fields and dwellings and much property besides, what wilt
thou do with field, and house, and all thine other gains, when thou art expelled
by him? For the lord of this land has a right to tell thee, 'Keep my laws, or
leave my land.' What then shalt thou do, thou who hast already a law over thee
in thine own city? For the sake of thy fields and other possessions wilt thou utterly
repudiate *thy* law and follow the law of this city? Beware! It may be unwise for
thee to repudiate thy law. For shouldst thou wish to return once more to thy city,
thou shalt not be allowed in: thou shalt be shut out, because thou didst repudiate
its law. So beware. Dwelling in a foreign land, provide thyself with nothing
more than a suitable competency; and whenever the master of this city expels
thee for opposing his law, be ready to leave his city and seek thine own, keeping
thine own law cheerfully and unmolested. So beware, you that serve God and
have him in your heart; perform his works, mindful of his commandments and of
the promises he has made, in the faith that he will perform the latter if the former
be observed. Instead of fields, then, buy souls in trouble, as each of you is able;
visit widows and orphans, and neglect them not; expend on such fields and
houses, which God has given to you [*i.e.*, on the poor], your wealth and all your
pains. The Master endowed you with riches that you might perform such
ministries for him. Far better is it to buy fields, possessions, houses of this kind;
thou wilt find them in thine own city when thou dost visit it. Such expenditure
is noble and cheerful; it brings joy, not fear and sorrow. Practise not the expenditure of pagans, then: that ill becomes you, as God's servants. Practise
your proper expenditure, in which you may rejoice. Do not stamp things falsely;

the lips of all Christians this word is to be heard: The world is crucified to me, and I to the world" (Celsus, cited by Origen, V. lxiv.).[1]

This resolute renunciation of the world was really the first thing which made the church competent and strong to tell upon the world. Then, if ever, was the saying true: "He who would do anything for the world must have nothing to do with it." Primitive Christianity has been upbraided for being too un-worldly and ascetic. But revolutions are not effected with rose-water, and it was a veritable revolution to overthrow polytheism and establish the majesty of God and goodness in the world— for those who believed in them, and also for those who did not. This could never have happened, in the first instance, had not men asserted the vanity of the present world, and practically severed themselves from it. The rigour of this attitude, however, hardly checked the mission-preaching; on the contrary, it intensified it, since instead of being isolated it was set side by side with the message of the Saviour and of salvation, of love and charity. And we must add, that for all its trenchant forms and the strong bias it imparted to the minds of men towards the future, the idea of recompense was saved from harshness and

never touch other people's property, nor lust after it, for it is evil to lust after what belongs to other people. Do thine own task and thou shalt be saved." For all the rigour of his counsel, however, it never occurs to Hermas that the distinction of rich and poor should actually cease within the church. This is plain, if further proof be needed, from the next parable. The progress of thought upon this question in the church is indicated by the tractate of Clement of Alexandria en-titled "Quis dives salvetur?" Moreover, the saying already put into the lips of Jesus in John xii. 8 ("the poor ye have always with you"), a saying which was hardly inserted without some purpose, shows that the abolition of the distinction between rich and poor was never contemplated in the church.

[1] The pessimistic attitude of the primitive Christians towards the world cannot be too strongly emphasised. (Marcion called his fellow-confessors συνταλαίπωροι καὶ συμμισούμενοι, "partners in the suffering of wretchedness and of hatred."—Tert., adv. Marc. iv. 9). This is confirmed by the evidence even of Tertullian, and of Origen himself. Let one instance suffice. In Hom. 8 ad. Levit., t. ix. pp. 316 f., Origen remarks that in the Scriptures only worldly men, like Pharaoh and Herod, celebrate their birthdays, whereas "the saints not only abstain from holding a feast on their birthdays, but, being filled with the Holy Spirit, curse that day" (Sancti non solum non agunt festivitatem in die natali suo, sed a spiritu sancto repleti exsecrantur hunc diem). The true birthday of Christians is the day of their death. Origen recalls Job, in this connection; but the form which his pessimism assumes is bound up, of course, with special speculative ideas of his own.

inertia by its juxtaposition with a feeling of perfect confidence that God was *present*, and a conviction of his *care* and of his *providence*. No mode of thought was more alien to early Christianity than what we call deism. The early Christians knew the Father in heaven; they knew that God was near them and guiding them; the more thoughtful were conscious that he reigned in their life with a might of his own. This was the God they proclaimed. And thus, in their preaching, the future became already present; hard and fast recompense seemed to disappear entirely, for what further " recompense " was needed by people who were living in God's presence, conscious in every faculty of the soul, aye, and in every sense of the wisdom, power, and goodness of their God? Moods of assured possession and of yearning, experiences of grace and phases of impassioned hope, came and went in many a man besides the apostle Paul. He yearned for the prospect of release from the body, and thus felt a touching sympathy for everything in bondage, for the whole creation in its groans. But it was no harassing or uncertain hope that engrossed all his heart and being; it was hope fixed upon a strong and secure basis in his filial relationship to God and his possession of God's Spirit.[1]

It is hardly necessary to point out that, by proclaiming repentance and strict morals on the one hand, and offering the removal of sins and redemption on the other hand, the Christian propaganda involved an inner cleavage which individual Christians must have realized in very different ways. If this removal of sins and redemption was bound up with the sacrament or specifically with the sacrament of baptism, then it came to this, that thousands were eager for this sacrament and nothing more, satisfied with belief in its immediate and magical efficacy, and devoid of any serious attention to the moral law. Upon the other hand, the moral demand could weigh so heavily on

---

[1] It was only in rare cases that the image of Christ's person as a whole produced what may be termed a " Christ-emotion," which moved people to give articulate expression to their experiences. Ignatius is really the only man we can name alongside of Paul and John. Yet in how many cases of which we know nothing, this image of Christ must have been the dominating power of human life ! In some of the dying confessions of the martyrs, and in the learned homilies of Origen, it emerges in a very affecting way.

the conscience that redemption came to be no more than the reward and prize of a holy life.   Between these two extremes a variety of standpoints was possible.   The propaganda of the church made a sincere effort to assign equal weight to both elements of its message; but sacraments are generally more welcome than moral counsels, and that age was particularly afflicted with the sacramental mania.   It added to the mysteries the requisite quality of *naïveté*, and at the same time the equally requisite note of subtlety.

CHAPTER II

THE gospel, as preached by Jesus, is a religion of redemption, but it is a religion of redemption in a secret sense. Jesus *proclaimed* a new message (the near approach of God's kingdom, God as the Father, as *his* Father), and also a new law, but he did his *work* as a Saviour or healer, and it was amid work of this kind that he was crucified. Paul, too, preached the gospel as a religion of redemption.

Jesus appeared among his people as a *physician.* "The healthy need not a physician, but the sick" (Mark ii. 17, Luke v. 31). The first three gospels depict him as the physician of soul and body, as the Saviour or healer of men. Jesus says very little about sickness; he cures it. He does not explain that sickness is health; he calls it by its proper name, and is sorry for the sick person. There is nothing sentimental or subtle about Jesus; he draws no fine distinctions, he utters no sophistries about healthy people being really sick and sick people really healthy. He sees himself surrounded by crowds of sick folk; he attracts them, and his one impulse is to help them. Jesus does not distinguish rigidly between sicknesses of the body and of the soul; he takes them both as different expressions of the *one* supreme ailment in humanity. But he knows their sources. He knows it is easier to say, "Rise up and walk," than to say, "Thy sins are forgiven thee" (Mark ii. 9).[2]

[1] This chapter is based on a fresh revision of Section VI. in my study on "Medicinisches aus der ältesten Kirchengeschichte" (*Texte und Unters.*, VIII., 1892).

[2] Or are we to interpret the passage in another way? Is it easier to say, "Thy sins are forgiven thee"? In that case, "easier" evidently must be taken in a different sense.

And he acts accordingly. No sickness of the soul repels him—he is constantly surrounded by sinful women and tax-gatherers. Nor is any bodily disease too loathsome for Jesus. In this world of wailing, misery, filth, and profligacy, which pressed upon him every day, he kept himself invariably vital, pure, and busy.

In this way he won men and women to be his disciples. The circle by which he was surrounded was a circle of people who had been healed.[1] They were healed because they had believed on him, *i.e.*, because they had gained health from his character and words. To know God meant a sound soul. This was the rock on which Jesus had rescued them from the shipwreck of their life. They knew they were healed, just because they had recognized God as the *Father* in his Son. Henceforth they drew health and real life as from a never-failing stream.

" Ye will say unto me this parable: Physician, heal thyself" (Luke iv. 23). He who helped so many people, seemed himself

---

[1] An old legend of Edessa regarding Jesus is connected with his activity as a healer of men. At the close of the third century the people of Edessa, who had become Christians during the second half of the second century, traced back their faith to the apostolic age, and treasured up an alleged correspondence between Jesus and their king Abgar. This correspondence is still extant (cp. Euseb., *H.E.*, i. 13). It is a naïve romance. The king, who is severely ill, writes thus : "Abgar, toparch of Edessa, to Jesus the excellent Saviour, who has appeared in the country of Jerusalem ; greeting. I have heard of thee and of thy cures, per- formed without medicine or herb. For, it is said, thou makest the blind to see, and the lame to walk ; thou cleansest lepers, thou expellest unclean spirits and demons, thou healest those afflicted with lingering diseases, and thou raisest the dead. Now, as I have heard all this about thee, I have concluded that one of two things must be true: either thou art God, and, having descended from heaven, doest these things, or else thou art a son of God by what thou doest. I write to thee, therefore, to ask thee to come and cure the disease from which I am suffering. For I have heard that the Jews murmur against thee, and devise evil against thee. Now, I have a very small, yet excellent city, which is large enough for both of us." To which Jesus answered : "Blessed art thou for having believed in me without seeing me. For it is written concerning me that those who have seen me will not believe in me, while they who have not seen me will believe and be saved. But as to thy request that I should come to thee, I must fulfil here all things for which I have been sent, and, after fulfilling them, be taken up again to him who sent me. Yet after I am taken up, I will send thee one of my disciples to cure thy disease and give life to thee and thine." The narrative then goes on to describe how Thaddaeus came to Edessa and cured the king by the laying on of hands, without medicine or herbs, after he had confessed his faith. "And Abdus, the son of Abdus, was also cured by him of gout."

to be always helpless. Harassed, calumniated, threatened with death by the authorities of his nation, and persecuted in the name of the very God whom he proclaimed, Jesus went to his cross. But even the cross only displayed for the first time the full depth and energy of his saving power. It put the copestone on his mission, by showing men that *the sufferings of the just are the saving force in human history.*

"Surely he hath borne our sickness and carried our sorrows; by his stripes we are healed."[1] This was the new truth that issued from the cross of Jesus. .It flowed out, like a stream of fresh water, on the arid souls of men and on their dry morality. The morality of outward acts and regulations gave way to the conception of a life which was personal, pure, and divine, which spent itself in the service of the brethren, and gave itself up ungrudgingly to death. This conception was the new principle of life. It uprooted the old life swaying to and fro between sin and virtue; it also planted a new life whose aim was nothing short of being a disciple of Christ, and whose strength was drawn from the life of Christ himself. The disciples went forth to preach the tidings of "God the Saviour,"[2] of that Saviour and physician whose person, deeds, and sufferings were man's salvation. Paul was giving vent to no sudden or extravagant emotion, but expressing with quiet confidence what he was fully conscious of at every moment, when he wrote to the Galatians (ii. 20), "I live, yet not I, but Christ liveth in me. For the life I now live in the flesh, I live by faith in the Son of God, who loved me and gave up himself for me." Conscious of this, the primitive Christian missionaries were ready to die daily. And that was just the reason why their cause did not collapse.

In the world to which the apostles preached their new

---

[1] Cp. 1 Pet. ii. 24, οὗ τῷ μώλωπι αὐτοὶ ἰάθητε.

[2] Luke ii. 11, ἐτέχθη ὑμῖν σωτήρ, ὅς ἐστιν Χριστὸς κύριος; John iv. 42, οἴδαμεν ὅτι οὗτός ἐστιν ὁ σωτὴρ τοῦ κόσμου; Tit. ii. 11, ἐπεφάνη ἡ χάρις τοῦ θεοῦ σωτήριος πᾶσιν ἀνθρώποις; Tit. iii. 4, ἡ χρηστότης καὶ ἡ φιλανθρωπία ἐπεφάνη τοῦ σωτῆρος ἡμῶν θεοῦ. By several Christian circles, indeed, the title "Saviour" was re-served for Jesus and for Jesus only. Irenæus (I. i. 3) reproaches the Valentinian Ptolemæus for never calling Jesus κύριος but only σωτήρ, and, as a matter of fact, in the epistle of Ptolemæus to Flora, Jesus is termed σωτήρ exclusively.

message, religion had not been intended originally for the sick, but for the sound. The Deity sought the pure and sound to be his worshippers. The sick and sinful, it was held, are a prey to the powers of darkness; let them see to the recovery of health by some means or another, health for soul and body—for until then they are not pleasing to the gods. It is interesting to observe how this conception is still dominant at the close of the second century, in Celsus, the enemy of Christendom (Orig., c. Cels., III. lix. f.). "Those who invite people to participate in other solemnities, make the following proclamation: 'He who hath clean hands and sensible speech (is to draw near)'; or again, 'He who is pure from all stain, conscious of no sin in his soul, and living an honourable and just life (may approach).' Such is the cry of those who promise purification from sins.[1] But let us now hear what sort of people these Christians invite. 'Anyone who is a sinner,' they say, 'or foolish, or simple-minded —in short, any unfortunate will be accepted by the kingdom of God.' By 'sinner' is meant an unjust person, a thief, a burglar, a poisoner, a sacrilegious man, or a robber of corpses. Why, if you wanted an assembly of robbers, these are just the sort of people you would summon!"[2] Here Celsus has stated, as lucidly as one could desire, the cardinal difference between Christianity and ancient religion.[3]

But, as we have already seen (Book I., Chapter III.), the

---

[1] The meaning is that even to mysteries connected with purification those only were bidden who had led upon the whole a good and a just life.

[2] Porphyry's position is rather different. He cannot flatly set aside the saying of Christ about the sick, for whose sake he came into the world. But as a Greek he is convinced that religion is meant for intelligent, just, and inquiring people. Hence his statement on the point (in Mac. Magnes, iv. 10) is rather confused.

[3] Origen makes a skilful defence of Christianity at this point. "If a Christian does extend his appeal to the same people as those addressed by a robber-chief, his aim is very different. He does so in order to bind up their wounds with his doctrine, in order to allay the festering sores of the soul with those remedies of faith which correspond to the wine and oil and other applications employed to give the body relief from pain" (III. lx.). "Celsus misrepresents facts when he declares that we hold God was sent to sinners only. It is just as if he found fault with some people for saying that some kind and gracious [φιλανθρωπότατος, an epithet of Æsculapius] monarch had sent his physician to a city for the benefit of the sick people in that city. God the Word was thus sent as a physician for sinners, but also as a teacher of divine mysteries for those who are already pure and sin no more" (III. lxi.).

religious temper which Christianity encountered, and which developed and diffused itself very rapidly in the second and third centuries, was no longer what we should term "ancient." Here again we see that the new religion made its appearance "when the time was fulfilled." The cheerful, naïve spirit of the old religion, so far as it still survived, lay a-dying, and its place was occupied by fresh religious needs. Philosophy had set the individual free, and had discovered a human being in the common citizen. By the blending of states and nations, which coalesced to form a universal empire, cosmopolitanism had now become a reality. But there was always a reverse side to cosmopolitanism, viz., individualism. The refinements of material civilization and mental culture made people more sensitive to the element of pain in life, and this increase of sensitiveness showed itself also in the sphere of morals, where more than one Oriental religion came forward to satisfy its demand. The Socratic philosophy, with its fine ethical ideas, issued from the heights of the thinker to spread across the lowlands of the common people. The Stoics, in particular, paid unwearied attention to the "health and diseases of the soul," moulding their practical philosophy upon this type of thought. There was a real demand for *purity, consolation, expiation,* and *healing,* and as these could not be found elsewhere, they began to be sought in *religion.* In order to secure them, people were on the look-out for new sacred rites. The evidence for this change which passed over the religious temper lies in the writings of Seneca, Epictetus, and many others; but a further testimony of much greater weight is afforded by the revival which attended the cult of Æsculapius during the Imperial age.[1] As far back as 290 B.C., Æsculapius of Epidaurus had been summoned to Rome on the advice of the Sibylline books. He had his sanctuary on the island in the Tiber, and close to it, just as at the numerous shrines of Asclepius in Greece, there stood a sanatorium in which sick persons waited for the injunctions

---

[1] For the cult of Æsculapius, see von Wilamowitz-Moellendorf's *Isyllos von Epidauros* (1886), pp. 36 f., 44 f., 116 f., and Usener's *Götternamen* (1896), pp. 147 f., 350, besides Ilberg's study of Æsculapius in Teubner's *Neuen Jahrbüchern*, II., 1901, and the cautious article by Thrämer in Pauly-Wissowa's *Real. Encykl.* (II. 1642 f.).

which the god imparted during sleep. Greek physicians followed the god to Rome, but it took a long time for either the god or the Greek doctors to become popular. The latter do not seem at first to have recommended themselves by their skill. "In 219 B.C. the first Greek surgeon became domiciled in Rome. He actually received the franchise, and was presented by the State with a shop 'in compito Acilio.' But this doctor made such unmerciful havoc among his patients by cutting and cauterizing, that the name of surgeon became a synonym for that of a butcher."[1] Things were different under the Cæsars. Though the Romans themselves still eschewed the art of medicine, considering it a kind of divination, skilled Greek doctors were in demand at Rome itself, and the cult of that "deus clinicus," Æsculapius, was in full vogue. From Rome his cult spread over all the West, fusing itself here and there with the cult of Serapis or some other deity, and accompanied by the subordinate cult of Hygeia and Salus, Telesphorus and Somnus. Furthermore, the sphere of influence belonging to this god of healing widened steadily; he became "saviour" pure and simple, the god who aids in all distress, the "friend of man" ($\phi\iota\lambda\alpha\nu\theta\rho\omega\pi\acute{o}\tau\alpha\tau\sigma$).[2] The more men sought deliverance and healing in religion, the greater grew this god's

---

[1] Preller-Jordan, *Röm. Mythologie,* ii. p. 243.   Pliny observes: "Mox a saevitia secandi urendique transisse nomen in carnificem et in tædium artem omnesque medicos" ("Owing to cruelty in cutting and cauterizing, the name of surgeon soon passed into that of butcher, and a disgust was felt for the profession and for all doctors").

[2] The cult was really humane, and it led the physicians also to be humane.   In a passage from the Παραγγελίαι of pseudo-Hippocrates we read: "I charge you not to show yourselves inhuman, but to take the wealth or poverty (of the patient) into account, in certain cases even to treat them gratis"—the repute of the ἰατροὶ ἀνάργυροι is well known—"and to consider future gratitude more than present fame.   If, therefore, the summons for aid happens to be the case of an unknown or impecunious man, he is most of all to be assisted; for wherever there is love to one's neighbour, it means readiness to act" (ix. 258 Littré, iii. 321 Erm.; a passage which Ilberg brought under my notice, cp. also the *Berl. Philol. Wochenschrift* for March 25, 1893).   How strongly the Christians themselves felt their affinity to humane physicians is proved by a striking instance which Ilberg quotes (*loc. cit.,* from vi. 90 Littré, ii. 123 Erm.).   Eusebius writes (*H.E.,* x. 4. 11) that Jesus, "like some excellent physician, in order to cure the sick, examines what is repulsive, handles sores, and reaps pain himself from the sufferings of others." This passage is literally taken from the treatise of pseudo-Hippocrates, περὶ φυσῶν: ὁ μὲν γὰρ ἰητρὸς ὁρεῖ τε δεινά, θιγγάνει τε ἀηδέων, ἐπ' ἀλλοτρίῃσι δὲ ξυμφορῇσιν ἰδίας καρποῦται λύπας.

repute. He belonged to the old gods who held out longest against Christianity, and therefore he is often to be met with in the course of early Christian literature. The cult of Æsculapius was one of those which were most widely diffused throughout the second half of the second century, and also during the third century. People travelled to the famous sanatoria of the god, as they travel to-day to baths. He was appealed to in diseases of the body and of the soul; people slept in his temples, to be cured; the costliest gifts were brought him as the ΘΕΟΣ ΣΩΤΗΡ ("God the Saviour"); and people consecrated their lives to him, as innumerable inscriptions and statues testify. In the case of other gods as well, healing virtue now became a central feature. Zeus himself and Apollo (cp., e.g., Tatian, Orat. viii.) appeared in a new light. They, too, became "saviours." No one could be a god any longer, unless he was also a saviour.[1] Glance over Origen's great reply to Celsus, and you soon discover that one point hotly disputed by these two remarkable men was the question whether Jesus or Æsculapius was the true Saviour. Celsus champions the one with as much energy and credulity as Origen the other. The combination of crass superstition and sensible criticism presented by both men is an enigma to us at this time of day. We moderns can hardly form any clear idea of their mental bearings. In III. iii. Origen observes: "Miracles occurred in all lands, or at least in many places. Celsus himself admits in his book that Æsculapius healed diseases and revealed the future in all cities that were devoted to him, such as Tricca, Epidaurus, Cos, and Pergamum." According to III. xxii. Celsus charged the Christians with being unable to make up their minds to call Æsculapius a god, simply because he had been first a man. Origen's retort is that the Greek tradition made Zeus slay Æsculapius with a thunderbolt. Celsus (III. xxiv.) declared it to be an authentic fact that a great number of Greeks and barbarians had seen, and still saw, no mere wraith of Æsculapius, but the god himself engaged in healing and helping man, whereas the disciples of Jesus had merely seen a phantom. Origen is very indignant at this, but his counter-assertions are

---

[1] Corresponding to this, we have Porphyry's definition of the object of philosophy as ἡ τῆς ψυχῆς σωτηρία (the salvation of the soul).

weak. Does Celsus also appeal to the great number of Greeks and barbarians who believe in Æsculapius? Origen, too, can point to the great number of Christians, to the truth of their scriptures, and to their successfnl cures in the name of Jesus. But then he suddenly alters his defence, and proceeds (III. xxv.) to make the following extremely shrewd observation: " Even were I going to admit that a demon named Æsculapius had the power of healing bodily diseases, I might still remark to those who are amazed at such cures or at the prophecies of Apollo, that such curative power is of itself neither good nor bad, but within reach of godless as well as of honest folk; while in the same way it does not follow that he who can foretell the future is on that account an honest and upright man. One is not in a position to prove the virtuous character of those who heal diseases and foretell the future. *Many instances may be adduced of people being healed who did not deserve to live, people who were so corrupt and led a life of such wickedness that no sensible physician would have troubled to cure them. . . . .* The power of healing diseases is no evidence of anything specially divine." From all these remarks of Origen, we can see how high the cult of Æsculapius was ranked, and how keenly the men of that age were on the lookout for " salvation."

Into this world of craving for salvation the preaching of Christianity made its way. Long before it had achieved its final triumph by dint of an impressive philosophy of religion, its success was already assured by the fact that it promised and offered salvation—a feature in which it surpassed all other religions and cults. It did more than set up the actual Jesus against the imaginary Æsculapius of dreamland. *Deliberately and consciously it assumed the form of " the religion of salvation or healing,"* [1] *or " the medicine of soul and body," and at the same time it recognized that one of its chief duties was to care assiduously for the sick in body.* We shall now select one or two examples out of the immense wealth of material, to throw light upon both of these points.

Take, first of all, the theory. Christianity never lost hold

---

[1] The New Testament itself is so saturated with medicinal expressions, employed metaphorically, that a collection of them would fill several pages.

of its innate principle; it was, and it remained, a religion for the sick. Accordingly it assumed that no one, or at least hardly any one, was in normal health, but that men were always in a state of disability. This reading of human nature was not confined to Paul, who looked on all men outside of Christ as dying, dying in their sins; a similar, though simpler, view was taught by the numerous unknown missionaries of primitive Christianity. The soul of man is sick, they said, a prey to death from the moment of his birth. The whole race lies a-dying. But now "the goodness and the human kindness of God the Saviour" have appeared to restore the sick soul.[1] Baptism was therefore conceived as a bath for regaining the soul's health, or for "the recovery of life";[2] the Lord's Supper was valued as "the potion of immortality,"[3] and penitence was termed "vera de satisfactione medicina" (the true medicine derived from the atonement, Cypr., *de Lapsis*, xv.). At the celebration of the sacrament, thanks were offered for the "life" therein bestowed (Did., ix.-x.). The conception of "life" acquired a new and deeper meaning. Jesus had already spoken of a "life" beyond the reach of death, to be obtained by the sacrifice of a man's earthly life. The idea and the term were taken up by Paul and by the fourth evangelist, who summed up in them the entire blessings of religion. With the tidings of immortality, the new religion confronted sorrow, misery, sin, and death. So much, at least, the world of paganism could understand. It could understand the promise of bliss and immortality resembling that of the blessed gods. And not a few pagans understood the justice of the accompanying condition, that one had to submit to the régime of the religion, that the soul had to be pure and holy before it could become immortal. Thus they grasped the message of a great Physician who preaches "abstinence" and bestows the gift of "life."[4]

---

[1] Tit. iii. 4: ἡ χρηστότης καὶ ἡ φιλανθρωπία ἐπέφανη τοῦ σωτῆρος ἡμῶν θεοῦ . . . . ἔσωσεν ἡμᾶς. See the New Testament allusions to σωτήρ.

[2] Tert., *de Baptism.*, i., etc., etc.; Clement (*Paedag.*, i. 6. 29) calls baptism παιώνιον φάρμακον. Tertullian describes it as "aqua medicinalis."

[3] Ignatius, Justin, and Irenæus.

[4] Clement of Alexandria opens his *Paedagogus* by describing his Logos as the physician who heals suffering (I. i. 1, τὰ πάθη ὁ παραμυθικὸς λόγος ἰᾶται). He

Anyone who had felt a single ray of the power and glory of the
new life reckoned his previous life to have been blindness,

distinguishes the λόγος προτρεπτικός, ὑποθετικός and παραμυθικός, to which is
added further ὁ διδακτικός.   And the Logos is Christ.   Gregory Thaumaturgus
also calls the Logos a physician, in his panegyric on Origen (xvi.).   In the pseudo-
Clementine homilies, Jesus, who is the true prophet, is always the physician ;
similarly Peter's work everywhere is that of the great physician who, by the sole
means of prayer and speech, heals troops of sick folk (see especially Bk. VII.).
Simon Magus, again, is represented as the wicked magician, who evokes disease
wherever he goes.   Origen has depicted Jesus the physician more frequently and
fully than anyone else.   One at least of his numerous passages on the subject may
be cited (from Hom. viii., *in Levit.*, ch. i. vol. ix. pp. 312 f.) : " Medicum dici in
scripturis divinis dominum nostrum Jesum Christum, etiam ipsius domini sententia
perdocemur, sicut dicit in evangeliis [here follows Matt. ix. 12 f.].   Omnis autem
medicus ex herbarum succis vel arborum vel etiam metallorum venis vel animan-
tium naturis profectura corporibus medicamenta componit.   Sed herbas istas si
quis forte, antequam pro ratione artis componantur, adspiciat, si quidem in agris
aut montibus, velut foenum vile conculcat et praeterit.   Si vero eas intra medici
scholam dispositas per ordinem viderit, licet odorem tristem, fortem et austerum
reddant, tamen suspicabitur eas curae vel remedii aliquid continere, etiamsi nondum
quae vel qualis sit sanitatis ac remedii virtus agnoverit.   Haec de communibus
medicis diximus.   Veni nunc ad Jesum coelestem medicum, intra ad hanc
stationem medicinae eius ecclesiam, vide ibi languentium iacere multitudinem.
Venit mulier, quae et partu immunda effecta est, venit leprosus, qui extra castra
separatus est pro immunditia leprae, quaerunt a medico remedium, quomodo
sanentur, quomodo mundentur, et quia Jesus hic, qui medicus est, ipse est et
verbum dei, aegris suis non herbarum succis, sed verborum sacramentis medicamenta conquirit.   Quae verborum medicamenta si quis incultius per libros tamquam
per agros videat esse dispersa, ignorans singulorum dictorum virtutem, ut vilia
haec et nullum sermonis cultum habentia praeteribit.   Qui sero ex aliqua parte
didicerit animarum apud Christum esse medicinam, intelliget profecto ex hic
libris, qui in ecclesiis recitantur, tamquam ex agris et montibus, salutares herbas
adsumere unumquemque debere, sermonum dumtaxat vim, ut si quis illi est in
anima languor, non tam exterioris frondis et corticis, quam succi interioris hausta
virtute sanetur " ("The Lord himself teaches us, in the gospels, that our Lord
Jesus Christ is called a physician in the Holy Scriptures.   Every physician com-
pounds his medicines for the good of the body from the juices of herbs or trees, or
even from the veins of metals or living creatures.   Now, supposing that anyone
sees these herbs in their natural state, ere they are prepared by skill of art, he
treads on them like common straw and passes by them, on mountain or field.
But if he chances to see them arranged in the laboratory of a herbalist or
physician, he will suspect that, for all their bitter and heavy and unpleasant
odours, they have some healing and healthful virtue, though as yet he does not
know the nature or the quality of this curative element.   So much for our
ordinary physicians.   Now look at Jesus the heavenly physician.   Come inside
his room of healing, the church.   Look at the multitude of impotent folk lying
there.   Here comes a woman unclean from childbirth, a leper expelled from the
camp owing to his unclean disease ; they ask the physician for aid, for a cure,
for cleansing ; and because this Jesus the physician is also the Word of God, he

disease, and death[1]—a view attested by both the apostolic fathers and the apologists. " He bestowed on us the light, he spoke to us as a father to his sons, he saved us in our lost estate. . . . . Blind were we in our understanding, worshipping stones and wood and gold and silver and brass, nor was our whole life aught but death."[2] The mortal will put on, nay, has already put on, immortality, the perishable will be robed in the imperishable: such was the glad cry of the early Christians, who took up arms against a sea of troubles, and turned the terror of life's last moment into a triumph. " Those miserable people," says Lucian in the *Proteus Peregrinus*, " have got it into their heads that they are perfectly immortal." He would certainly have made a jest upon it had any occurred to his mind; but whenever this nimble scoffer is depicting the faith of Christians, there is a remarkable absence of anything like jesting.

While the soul's health or the new life is a gift, however, it is a gift which must be appropriated from within. There was a great risk of this truth being overlooked by those who were accustomed to leave any one of the mysteries with the sense of

applies, not the juices of herbs, but the sacraments of the Word to their diseases. Anyone who looked at these remedies casually as they lay in books, like herbs in the field, ignorant of the power of single words, would pass them by as common things without any grace of style. But he who ultimately discovers that Christ has a medicine for souls, will find from these books which are read in the churches, as he finds from mountains and fields, that each yields healing herbs, at least strength won from words, so that any weakness of soul is healed not so much by leaf and bark as by an inward virtue and juice ").

[1] That the vices were diseases was a theme treated by Christian teachers as often as by the Stoics. Cp., *e.g.*, Origen, *in Ep. ad Rom.*, Bk. II. (Lommatzsch, vi. 91 f.) : " Languores quidem animae ab apostolo in his (Rom. ii. 8) designantur, quorum medelam nullus inveniet nisi prius morborum cognoverit causas et ideo in divinis scripturis aegritudines animae numerantur et remedia describuntur, ut hi, qui se apostolicis subdiderint disciplinis, ex his, quae scripta sunt, agnitis languoribus suis curati possint dicere : ' Lauda anima mea dominum, qui sanat omnes languores tuos ' " (" The apostle here describes the diseases of the soul ; their cure cannot be discovered till one diagnoses first of all the causes of such troubles, and consequently Holy Scripture enumerates the ailments of the soul, and describes their remedies, in order that those who submit to the apostolic discipline may be able to say, after they have been cured of diseases diagnosed by aid of what is written : ' Bless the Lord, O my soul, who healeth all thy diseases ' ").

[2] 2 Clem., *Ep. ad Cor.*, i. Similar expressions are particularly common in Tatian, but indeed no apology is wholly devoid of them.

being consecrated and of bearing with them supermundane blessings as if they were so many articles. It would be easy also to show how rapidly the sacramental system of the church lapsed into the spirit of the pagan mysteries. But once the moral demand, *i.e.*, the purity of the soul, was driven home, it proved such a powerful factor that it held its own within the Catholic church, even alongside of the inferior sacramental system. *The salvation of the soul and the lore of that salvation* never died away; in fact, the ancient church arranged all the details of her worship and her dogma with this end in view. She consistently presented herself as the great infirmary or the hospital of humanity: pagans, sinners, and heretics are her patients, ecclesiastical doctrines and observances are her medicines, while the bishops and pastors are the physicians, but only as servants of Christ, who is himself the physician of all souls.[1] Let me give one or two instances of this. "As the good of the body is health, so the good of the soul is the knowledge of God," says Justin.[2] "While we have time to be healed, let us put ourselves into the hands of God the healer, paying him a recompense. And what recompense? What but repentance from a sincere heart" (2 Clem., *ad Cor.*, ix.). "Like some excellent physician, in order to cure the sick, Jesus examines what is repulsive, handles sores, and reaps pain himself from the sufferings of others; he has himself saved us from the very jaws of death—*us* who were not merely diseased and suffering from terrible ulcers and wounds already mortified, but were also lying already among the dead . . . .; *he* who is the giver of life and of light, our great physician,[3] king and

---

[1] Celsus, who knew this kind of Christian preaching intimately, pronounced the Christians to be quacks. "The teacher of Christianity," he declares, "acts like a person who promises to restore a sick man to health and yet hinders him from consulting skilled physicians, so as to prevent his own ignorance from being exposed." To which Origen retorts, "And who are the physicians from whom we deter simple folk?" He then proceeds to show that they cannot be the philosophers, and still less those who are not yet emancipated from the coarse superstition of polytheism (III. lxxiv.).

[2] *Fragm.* ix. (Otto, *Corp. Apol.*, iii. p. 258). Cp. also the beautiful wish expressed at the beginning of 3 John : περὶ πάντων εὔχομαί σε εὐοδοῦσθαι καὶ ὑγιαίνειν, καθὼς εὐοδοῦταί σου ἡ ψυχή (ver. 2).

[3] Cp. *Ep. ad Diogn.*, ix. 6, pseudo-Justin, *de Resurr.*, x. : "Our physician, Jesus Christ"; Clem., *Paedag.*, i. 2. 6: "The Logos of the Father is the only

lord, the Christ of God."[1] "The physician cannot introduce any salutary medicines into the body that needs to be cured, without having previously eradicated the trouble seated in the body or averted the approaching trouble. Even so the teacher of the truth cannot convince anyone by an address on truth, so long as some error still lurks in the soul of the hearer, which forms an obstacle to his arguments" (Athenagoras, *de resurr.*, i.). "Were we to draw from the axiom that 'disease is diagnosed by means of medical knowledge,' the inference that medical knowledge is the cause of disease, we should be making a preposterous statement. And as it is beyond doubt that the knowledge of salvation is a good thing, because it teaches men to know their sickness, so also is the law a good thing, inasmuch as sin is discovered thereby."[2]

As early as 2 Tim. ii. 17, the word of heretics is said to eat

Paeonian physician for human infirmities, and the holy charmer (ἅγιος ἐπῳδός) for the sick soul" (whereupon he quotes Ps. lxxxii. 2-3): "The physician's art cures the diseases of the body, according to Democritus, but wisdom frees the soul from its passions. Yet the good instructor, the Wisdom, the Logos of the Father, the creator of man, cares for all our nature, healing it in body and in soul alike—he ὁ παναρκὴς τῆς ἀνθρωπότητος ἰατρὸς ὁ σωτήρ (the all-sufficient physician of humanity, the Saviour)," whereupon he quotes Mark ii. 11. See also *ibid.*, i. 6. 36, and i. 12. 100. "Hence the Logos also is called Saviour, since he has devised rational medicines for men; he preserves their health, lays bare their defects, exposes the causes of their evil affections, strikes at the root of irrational lusts, prescribes their diet, and arranges every antidote to heal the sick. For this is the greatest and most royal work of God, the saving of mankind. Patients are irritated at a physician who has no advice to give on the question of their health. But how should we not render thanks to the divine instructor," etc. (*Paedag.*, i. 8. 64-65).

[1] Eus., *H.E.*, v. 4. 11 (already referred to on p. 106). Cp. also the description of the Bible in Aphraates as "the books of the Wise Physician," and Cypr., *de Op.*, i. : "Christ was wounded to cure us of our wounds. . . . . When the Lord at his coming had healed that wound which Adam caused," etc. Metaphors from disease are on the whole very numerous in Cyprian; cp., *e.g.*, *de Habitu*, ii. ; *de Unitate*, iii. ; *de Lapsis*, xiv., xxxiv.

[2] Origen, opposing the Antinomians in *Comm. in Rom.*, iii. 6 (Lommatzsch, vi. p. 195), *Hom. in Jerem.*, xix. 3. Similarly Clem., *Paedag.*, i. 9. 88: "As the physician who tells a patient that he has fever is not an enemy to him—since the physician is not the cause of the fever but merely detects it (οὐκ αἴτιος, ἀλλ' ἔλεγχος)—neither is one who blames a diseased soul ill-disposed to that person." Cp. Methodius (Opp. I., p. 52, Bonwetsch): "As we do not blame a physician who explains how a man may become strong and well," etc. ; see also I. 65: "For even those who undergo medical treatment for their bodily pains do not at once regain health, but gladly bear pain in the hope of their coming recovery."

"like a gangrene." This expression recurs very frequently, and is elaborated in detail. "Their talk is infectious as a plague" (Cyprian, *de Lapsis*, xxxiv.). "Heretics are hard to cure," says Ignatius (*ad Ephes.*, vii., δυσθεράπευτος); . . . . there is but one physician, Jesus Christ our Lord." In the pastoral epistles the orthodox doctrine is already called "sound teaching" as opposed to the errors of the heretics.

Most frequently, however, bodily recovery is compared to penitence. It is Ignatius again who declares that "not every wound is cured by the same salve. Allay sharp pains by soothing fomentations."[1] "The cure of evil passions," says Clement at the opening of his *Paedagogus*, "is effected by the Logos through admonitions; he strengthens the soul with benign precepts like soothing medicines,[2] and directs the sick to the full knowledge of the truth." "Let us follow the practice of physicians (in the exercise of moral discipline)," says Origen,[3] "and only use the knife when all other means have failed, when application of oil and salves and soothing poultices leave the swelling still hard." An objection was raised by Christians who disliked repentance, to the effect that the public confession of sin which accompanied the penitential discipline was at once an injury to their self-respect and a misery. To which Tertullian replies (*de Poen.*, x.): "Nay, it is evil that ends in misery. Where repentance is undertaken, misery ceases, because it is turned into what is salutary. It is indeed a misery to be cut, and cauterized, and racked by some pungent powder; but the excuse for the offensiveness of means of healing that may be unpleasant, is the cure they work." This is exactly Cyprian's

---

[1] *Ad Polyc.*, ii. The passage is to be taken allegorically. It is addressed to Bishop Polycarp, who has been already (i) counselled to "bear the maladies of all"; wisely and gently is the bishop to treat the erring and the spiritually diseased. In the garb given it by Ignatius, this counsel recurs very frequently throughout the subsequent literature; see Lightfoot's learned note. Also Clem. Alex., *Fragm.* (Dindorf, iii. 499): "With *one* salve shalt thou heal thyself and thy neighbour (who slanders thee), if thou acceptest the slander with meekness"; *Clem. Hom.*, x. 18: "The salve must not be applied to the sound member of the body, but to the suffering"; and Hermes Trismeg., περὶ βοτ. χυλ., p. 331: "Do not always use this salve."

[2] i. 1. 3, ἤπια φάρμακα (see Homer).

[3] *In l. Jesu Nave*, viii. 6 (Lomm., xi. 71). Cp. *Hom. in Jerem.*, xvi. 1.

point, when he writes [1] that " the priest of the Lord must employ
salutary remedies.[2] He is an unskilled physician who handles
tenderly the swollen edges of a wound and allows the poison
lodged in the inward part to be aggraved by simply leaving it
alone. The wound must be opened and lanced ; recourse must
be had to the strong remedy of cutting out the corrupting parts.
Though the patient scream out in pain, and wail or weep,
because he cannot bear it—afterwards he will be grateful, when
he feels that he is cured." But the most elaborate comparison
of a bishop to a surgeon occurs in the *Apostolic Constitutions*
(ii. 41). " Heal thou, O bishop, like a pitiful physician, all who
have sinned, and employ methods that promote saving health.
Confine not thyself to cutting or cauterizing or the use of
corrosives, but employ bandages and lint, use mild and healing
drugs, and sprinkle words of comfort as a soothing balm. If
the wound be deep and gashed, lay a plaster on it, that it may
fill up and be once more like the rest of the sound flesh. If it
be dirty, cleanse it with corrosive powder, *i.e.*, with words of
censure. If it has proud flesh, reduce it with sharp plasters, *i.e.*,
with threats of punishment. If it spreads further, sear it, and
cut off the putrid flesh—mortify the man with fastings. And
if after all this treatment thou findest that no soothing poultice,
neither oil nor bandage, can be applied from head to foot of
the patient, but that the disease is spreading and defying all
cures, like some gangrene that corrupts the entire member ; then,
after great consideration and consultation with other skilled
physicians, cut off the putrified member, lest the whole body of
the church be corrupted. So be not hasty to cut it off, nor
rashly resort to the saw of many a tooth, but first use the lancet
to lay open the abscess, that the body may be kept free from pain
by the removal of the deep-seated cause of the disease. But if
thou seest anyone past repentance and (inwardly) past feeling,

---

[1] *De Lapsis*, xiv. Penitence and bodily cures form a regular parallel in Cyprian's
writings ; cp. *Epist.* xxxi. 6–7, lv. 16, lix. 13, and his Roman epistle xxx. 3, 5. 7.
Novatian, who is responsible for the latter, declares (in *de Trinit.*, v.) that God's
wrath acts like a medicine.

[2] Cp. pseudo-Clem., *Ep. ad Jac.*, ii. : "The president (the bishop) must hold
the place of a physician (in the church), instead of behaving with the violence of
an irrational brute."

then cut him off as an incurable with sorrow and lamentation." [1]

It must be frankly admitted that this constant preoccupation with the " diseases " of sin had results which were less favourable. The ordinary moral sense, no less than the æsthetic,[2] was deadened. If people are ever to be made better, they must be directed to that honourable activity which means moral health ; whereas endless talk about sin and forgiveness exercises, on the contrary, a narcotic influence. To say the least of it, ethical education must move to and fro between reflection on the past (with its faults and moral bondage) and the prospect of a future (with its goal of aspiration and the exertion of all one's powers). The theologians of the Alexandrian school had some sense of the latter, but in depicting the perfect Christian or true gnostic they assigned a disproportionate space to *knowledge* and correct *opinions*. They were not entirely emancipated from the Socratic fallacy that the man of *knowledge* will be invariably a *good* man. They certainly did surmount the " educated " man's intellectual pride on the field of religion and morality.[3] In Origen's treatise against Celsus, whole sections of great excellence are devoted to the duty and possibility of even the uneducated person acquir-

---

[1] Cp. Clem. Alex., *Paedag.*, i. 8. 64 f. : "Many evil passions are cured by punishment or by the inculcation of sterner commands. . . . . Censure is like a surgical operation on the passions of the soul. The latter are abscesses on the body of the truth, and they must be cut open by the lancet of censure. Censure is like the application of a medicine which breaks up the callosities of the passions, and cleanses the impurities of a lewd life, reducing the swollen flesh of pride, and restoring the man to health and truth once more." Cp. i. 9. 83 ; also Methodius, Opp. I., i. p. 115 (ed. Bonwetsch).

[2] It was at this that the Emperor Julian especially took umbrage, and not without reason. As a protest against the sensuousness of paganism, there grew up in the church an æsthetic of ugliness. Disease, death, and death's relics— bones and putrefaction—were preferred to health and beauty, whilst Christianity sought to express her immaterial spirit in terms drawn from the unsightly remnants of material decay. How remote was all this artificial subtlety of an exalted piety from the piety which had pointed men to the beauty of the lilies in the field ! The Christians of the third and fourth centuries actually begin to call sickness health, and to regard death as life.

[3] Clem. Alex., *Strom.*, vii. 7. 48 : ὡς ὁ ἰατρὸς ὑγίειαν παρέχεται τοῖς συνεργοῦσι πρὸς ὑγίειαν, οὕτως καὶ ὁ θεὸς τὴν ἀΐδιον σωτηρίαν τοῖς συνεργοῦσι πρὸς γνῶσίν τε καὶ εὐπραγίαν ("Even as the physician secures health for those who co-operate with him to that end, so does God secure eternal salvation for those who co-operate with him for knowledge *and good conduct*").

ing health of soul, and to the supreme necessity of salvation from sin and weakness.[1] Origen hits the nail upon the head when he remarks (VII. lx.) that " Plato and the other wise men of Greece, with their fine sayings, are like the physicians who confine their attention to the better classes and despise the common man, whilst the disciples of Jesus carefully study to make provision for the great mass of men." [2] Still, Origen's idea is that, as a means of salvation, religion merely forms a *stage* for those who aspire to higher levels. His conviction is that when the development of religion has reached its highest level, anything historical or positive becomes of as little value as the ideal of redemption and salvation itself. On this level the spirit, filled by God, no longer needs a Saviour or any Christ of history at all. " Happy," he exclaims (*Comm. in Joh.*, i. 22 ; Lomm., i. p. 43), " happy are they who need no longer now God's Son as the physician of the sick or as the shepherd, people who now need not any redemption, but wisdom, reason, and righteousness alone." In his treatise against Celsus (III. lxi. f.) he draws a sharp distinction between two aims and boons in the Christian

---

[1] *C. Cels.*, III. liv. : "We cure every rational being with the medicine of our doctrine."

[2] In VII. lix. there is an extremely fine statement of the true prophet's duty of speaking in such a way as to be intelligible and encouraging to the multitude, and not merely to the cultured. " Suppose that some food which is wholesome and fit for human nourishment, is prepared and seasoned so delicately as to suit the palate of the rich and luxurious alone, and not the taste of simple folk, peasants, labourers, poor people, and the like, who are not accustomed to such dainties. Suppose again that this very food is prepared, not as epicures would have it, but to suit poor folk, labourers, and the vast majority of mankind. Well, if on this supposition the food prepared in one way is palatable to none but epicures, and left untasted by the rest, while, prepared in the other way, it ministers to the health and strength of a vast number, what persons shall we believe are promoting the general welfare most successfully—those who cater simply for the better classes, or those who prepare food for the multitude ? If we assume that the food in both cases is equally wholesome and nourishing, it is surely obvious that the good of men and the public welfare are better served by the physician who attends to the health of the multitude than by him who will merely attend to a few." And Origen was far removed from anything like the narrow-mindedness of orthodoxy, as is plain from this excellent remark in III. xiii. : " As only he is qualified in medicine who has studied in various schools and attached himself to the best system after a careful examination of them all . . . . so, in my judgment, the most thorough knowledge of Christianity is his who has carefully investigated the various sects of Judaism and of Christianity."

religion, one higher and the other lower. "To no mystery, to no participation in wisdom 'hidden in a mystery,' do we call the wicked man, the thief, the burglar, etc., but to healing or salvation. For our doctrine has a twofold appeal. It provides means of healing for the sick, as is meant by the text, 'The whole need not a physician, but the sick.' But it also unveils to those who are pure in soul and body 'that mystery which was kept secret since the world began, but is now made manifest by the Scriptures of the prophets and the appearing of our Lord Jesus Christ.' . . . . God the Word was indeed sent as a physician for the sick, but also as a teacher of divine mysteries to those who are already pure and sin no more."[1]

Origen unites the early Christian and the philosophic conceptions of religion. He is thus superior to the pessimistic fancies which seriously threatened the latter view. But only among the cultured could he gain any following. The Christian people held fast to Jesus as the *Saviour*.

No one has yet been able to show that the figure of Christ which emerges in the fifth century, probably as early as the fourth, and which subsequently became the prevailing type in all pictorial representations, was modelled upon the figure of Æsculapius. The two types are certainly similar; the qualities predicated of both are identical in part; and no one has hitherto explained satisfactorily why the original image of the youthful Christ was displaced by the later. Nevertheless, we have no

---

[1] So Clem. Alex., *Paed.*, i. 1. 3 : ἴσαι οὐκ ἐστὸν ὑγίεια καὶ γνῶσις, ἀλλ' ἡ μὲν μαθήσει, ἡ δὲ ἰάσει περιγίνεται· οὐκ ἂν οὖν τις νοσῶν ἔτι πρότερόν τι τῶν διδασκαλικῶν ἐκμάθοι πρὶν ἢ τέλεον ὑγιᾶναι· οὐδὲ γὰρ ὡσαύτως πρὸς τοὺς μανθάνοντας ἢ κάμνοντας ἀεὶ τῶν παραγγελμάτων ἕκαστον λέγεται, ἀλλὰ πρὸς οὓς μὲν εἰς γνῶσιν, πρὸς οὓς δὲ εἰς ἴασιν. καθάπερ οὖν τοῖς νοσοῦσι τὸ σῶμα ἰατροῦ χρῄζει, ταύτῃ καὶ τοῖς ἀσθενοῦσι τὴν ψυχὴν παιδαγωγοῦ δεῖ, ἵν' ἡμῶν ἰάσηται τὰ πάθη, εἶτα δὲ καὶ διδασκάλου, ὃς καθηγήσεται πρὸς καθαρὰν γνώσεως ἐπιτηδειότητα εὐτρεπίζων τὴν ψυχήν, δυναμένην χωρῆσαι τὴν ἀποκάλυψιν τοῦ λόγου ("Health and knowledge are not alike ; the one is produced by learning, the other by healing. Before a sick person, then, could learn any further branch of knowledge, he must get quite well. Nor is each injunction addressed to learners and to patients alike ; the object in one case is knowledge, and in the other a cure. Thus, as patients need the physician for their body, so do those who are sick in soul need, first of all, an instructor, to heal our pains, and then a teacher who shall conduct the soul to all requisite knowledge, disposing it to admit the revelation of the Word ").

means of deriving the origin of the Callixtine Christ from
Æsculapius as a prototype, so that in the meantime we must
regard such a derivation as a hypothesis, which, however interesting, is based upon inadequate evidence.   There would be one
piece of positive evidence forthcoming, if the statue which passed
for a likeness of Jesus in the city of Paneas (Cæsarea Philippi)
during the fourth century was a statue of Æsculapius.   Eusebius
(*H.E.*, vi. 18) tells how he had seen there, in the house of the
woman whom Jesus had cured of an issue of blood, a work of
art which she had caused to be erected out of gratitude to Jesus.
" On a high pedestal beside the gates of her house there stands
the brazen image of a woman kneeling down with her hands
outstretched as if in prayer.   Opposite this stands another
brazen image of a man standing up, modestly attired in a cloak
wrapped twice round his body, and stretching out his hand to
the woman.   At his feet, upon the pedestal itself, a strange
plant is growing up as high as the hem of his brazen cloak,
which is a remedy for all sorts of disease.   This statue is said
to be an image of Jesus.   Nor is it strange that the Gentiles of
that age, who had received benefit from the Lord, should
express their gratitude in this fashion."   For various reasons it
is unlikely that this piece of art was intended to represent Jesus,
or that it was erected by the woman with an issue of blood;[1]
on the contrary, the probability is that the statuary was thus
interpreted by the Christian population of Paneas, probably at
an early period.   If the statue originally represented Æsculapius,
as the curative plant would suggest, we should have here at
least one step between " Æsculapius the Saviour" and " Christ
the Saviour."   But this interpretation of a pagan saviour or
healer is insecure; and even were it quite secure, it would not
justify any general conclusion being drawn as yet upon the
matter.   At any rate we are undervaluing the repugnance felt
even by Christians of the fourth century for the gods of paganism, if we consider ourselves entitled to think of any *conscious*
transformation of the figure of Æsculapius into that of Christ.[2]

---

[1] Cp. Hauck, *die Entstehung des Christus-typus* (1880), p. 8 f.

[2] In the eyes of Christians, Æsculapius was both a demon and an idol; no
Christian could take him as a model or have any dealings with him.   Some

Hitherto we have been considering the development of Christianity as the religion of " healing," as expressed in parables, ideas, doctrine, and penitential discipline. It now remains for us to show that this character was also stamped upon its arrangements for the care of bodily sickness.

" I was sick and ye visited me. . . . . As ye have done it unto one of the least of these my brethren, ye have done it unto me." In these words the founder of Christianity set the love that tends the sick in the centre of his religion, laying it on the hearts of all his disciples. Primitive Christianity carried it in her heart; she also carried it out in practice.[1] Even from the fragments of our extant literature, although that literature was not written with any such intention, we can still recognise the careful attention paid to works of mercy. At the outset we meet with directions everywhere to care for sick people. " Encourage the faint-hearted, support the weak," writes the apostle Paul to the church of Thessalonica (1 Thess. v. 14), which in its excitement was overlooking the duties lying close at hand. In the prayer of the church, preserved in the first epistle of Clement, supplications are expressly offered for those who are sick in soul and body.[2] " Is any man sick? let him call for the elders of

Roman Christians, who were devotees of learning, are certainly reported in one passage (written by a fanatical opponent, it is true) to have worshipped Galen (Eus., *H.E.*, v. 28); but no mention is made of them worshipping Æsculapius. In addition to the passages cited above, in which early Christian writers deal with Æsculapius (who is probably alluded to also as far back as Apoc. ii. 23), the following are to be noted : Justin, *Apol.* I., xxi., xxii., xxv., liv. (passages which are radically misunderstood when it is inferred from them that Justin is in favour of the god) ; Tatian, *Orat.* xxi. ; Theoph., *ad Autol.*, i. 9 ; Tertull., *de Anima*, i. (a passage which is specially characteristic of the aversion felt for this god) ; Cyprian's *Quod Idola*, i. ; Orig., *c. Cels.*, III. iii., xxii.–xxv., xxviii., xlii. Clement explains him in *Protr.*, ii. 26, after the manner of Euhemerus : τὸν γὰρ εὐεργετοῦντα μὴ συνιέντες θεὸν ἀνέπλασάν τινας σωτῆρας Διοσκούρους . . . . καὶ Ἀσκληπιὸν ἰατρόν ("Through not understanding the God who was their benefactor, they fashioned certain saviours, the Dioscuri and Æsculapius the physician"). A number of passages (*e.g.*, *Protr.*, ii. 20, ἰατρὸς φιλάργυρος ἦν, "he was an avaricious physician," and iv. 52) show how little Clement cared for him.

[1] Cp. the beautiful sentences of Lactantius, *Div. Inst.*, vi. 12 (especially p. 529, Brandt) : Aegros quoque quibus defuerit qui adsistat, curandos fovendosque suscipere summae humanitatis et magnae operationis est (" It is also the greatest kindness possible and a great charity to undertake the care and maintenance of the sick, who need some one to assist them ").

[2] 1 Clem. lix. : τοὺς ἀσθενεῖς (such is the most probable reading) ἴασαι . . . .

the church," says Jas. v. 14—a clear proof that all aid in cases
of sickness was looked upon as a concern of the church.[1] This
comes out very plainly also in the epistle of Polycarp (vi. 1),
where the obligations of the elders are displayed as follows:
"They must reclaim the erring, care for all the infirm, and
neglect no widow, orphan, or poor person." Particulars of this
duty are given by Justin, who, in his *Apology* (ch. lxvii.),
informs us that every Sunday the Christians brought free-will
offerings to their worship; these were deposited with the
president (or bishop), "who dispenses them to orphans and
widows, and to any who, from sickness or some other cause, are
in want." A similar account is given by Tertullian in his
Apology (ch. xxxix.), where special stress is laid on the church's
care for old people who are no longer fit for work. Justin is
also our authority for the existence of deacons whose business it
was to attend the sick.

Not later than the close of the third century, the veneration
of the saints and the rise of chapels in honour of martyrs
and saints led to a full-blown imitation of the Æsculapius-cult
within the church. Cures of sickness and infirmities were sought.
Even the practice of incubation must have begun by this time,
if not earlier; otherwise it could not not have been so widely
diffused in the fourth century. The teachers of the church had
previously repudiated it as heathenish; but, as often happens
in similar circumstances, it crept in, though with some alteration
of its ceremonies.

In its early days the church formed a permanent establishment for the relief of sickness and poverty, a function which it
continued to discharge for several generations. It was based on
the broad foundation of the Christian congregation; it acquired
a sanctity from the worship of the congregation; and its operations were strictly centralized. The bishop was the superintendent (*Apost. Constit.*, iii. 4), and in many cases, especially
in Syria and Palestine, he may have actually been a physician

ἐξανάστησον τοὺς ἀσθενοῦντας, παρακάλεσον τοὺς ὀλιγοψυχοῦντας ("Heal the
sick, ... raise up the weak, encourage the faint-hearted"). Cp. the later
formulas of prayer for the sick in *App. Constit.*, viii. 10 and onwards; cp.
Binterim, *Denkwürdigkeiten*, vi. 3, pp. 17 f.

[1] Cp. 1 Cor. xii. 26: "If one member suffer, all the members suffer with it."

himself.[1] His executive or agents were the deacons and the order of " widows." The latter were at the same time to be secured against want, by being taken into the service of the church (cp. 1 Tim. v. 16). Thus, in one instruction dating from the second century,[2] we read that, " In every congregation at least one widow is to be appointed to take care of sick women ;[3] she is to be obliging and sober, she is to report cases of need to the elders, she is not to be greedy or addicted to drink, in order that she may be able to keep sober for calls to service during the night." She is to " report cases of need to the elders," *i.e.*, she is to remain an assistant (cp. *Syr. Didasc.* xv. 79 f.). Tertullian happens to remark (*de Praescr.*, xli.) in a censure of women belonging to the heretical associations, that " they venture to teach, to debate, to exorcise, *to promise cures*, probably even to baptize." In the Eastern church the order of widows seems to have passed on into that of " deaconesses " at a pretty early date, but unfortunately we know nothing about this transition or about the origin of these " deaconesses."[4]

In the primitive church female assistants were quite thrown into the shadow by the men. The deacons were the real agents of charity. Their office was onerous ; it was exposed to grave peril, especially in a time of persecution, and deacons furnished no inconsiderable proportion of the martyrs. " Doers of good works, looking after all by day and night "—such is their description (*Texte u. Unters.*, ii. 5, p. 24), one of their

[1] Achelis (*Texte u. Unters.*, xxv. 2. 1904, p. 381) attempts to prove that the author of the *Syriac Didascalia* was at once a bishop and a physician ; he shows (p. 383) that similar combinations were not entirely unknown (cp. de Rossi's *Roma Sotter.*, tav. XXI. 9, epitaph from San Callisto, Διονυσιου ιατρου πρεσβυτερου ; Zenobius, physician and martyr in Sidon in the reign of Diocletian, Eus., *H.E.*, viii. 13 ; a physician and bishop in Tiberias, Epiph., *Hær.*, xxx. 4 ; Theodotus, physician and bishop in Laodicea Syr. ; Basilius, episcopus artis medicinae guarus, at Ancyra, Jerome, *de Vir. Ill.*, 89 ; in Can. Hipp., iii. § 18, the gift of healing is asked for the bishop and presbyter at ordination, while viii. § 53 presupposes that anyone who possessed this gift moved straightway to be enrolled among the clergy). Cp. *Texte u. Unters.*, viii. 4. pp. 1–14 (" Christian doctors ").

[2] Cp. *Texte u. Unters.*, ii. 5. p. 23.

[3] " But thou, O Widow, who art shameless, seest the widows, thy comrades, or thy brethren lying sick, yet troublest not to fast or pray for them, to lay hands on them or to visit them, as if thou wert not in health thyself or free" (*Syr. Didasc.*, xv. 80).

[4] They are first mentioned in Pliny's letter to Trajan.

main duties being to look after the poor and sick.[1]   How much
they had to do and how much they did, may be ascertained
from Cyprian's epistles[2] and the genuine Acts of the Martyrs.
Nor were the laity to be exempted from the duty of tending the
sick, merely because special officials existed for that purpose.
" The sick are not to be overlooked, nor is anyone to say that
he has not been trained to this mode of service.   No one is to
plead a comfortable life, or the unwonted character of the duty,
as a pretext for not being helpful to other people "—so runs a
letter of pseudo-Justin (c. xvii.) to Zenas and Serenus.   The
author of the pseudo-Clementine epistle " de virginitate " brings
out with special clearness the fact that to imitate Christ is to
minister to the sick, a duty frequently conjoined with that of
" visiting orphans and widows" (*visitare pupillos et viduas*).
Eusebius (*de mart. Pal.*, xi. 22) bears this testimony to the
character of Seleucus, that like a father and guardian he had
shown himself a bishop and patron of orphans and destitute
widows, of the poor and of the sick.   Many similar cases are on
record.   In a time of pestilence especially, the passion of tender
mercy was kindled in the heart of many a Christian.   Often
had Tertullian (*Apolog.* xxxix.) heard on pagan lips the remark,
corroborated by Lucian, " Look how they love one another ! "[3]

---

[1] Cp. *Ep. pseudo-Clem. ad Jacob.*, xii.   οἱ τῆς ἐκκλησίας διάκονοι τοῦ ἐπισκόπου
συνετῶς ῥεμβόμενοι ἔστωσαν ὀφθαλμοί, ἑκάστου τῆς ἐκκλησίας πολυπραγμονοῦντες
τὰς πράξεις . . . . τοὺς δὲ κατὰ σάρκα νοσοῦντας μανθανέτωσαν καὶ τῷ ἀγνοοῦντι
πλήθει προσαντιβαλλέτωσαν, ἵν᾿ ἐπιφαίνωνται, καὶ τὰ δέοντα ἐπὶ τῇ τοῦ προκα-
θεζομένου γνώμῃ παρεχέτωσαν ("Let the deacons of the church move about
intelligently and act as eyes for the bishop, carefully inquiring into the actions of
every church member . . . . let them find out those who are sick in the flesh,
and bring such to the notice of the main body who know nothing of them, that
they may visit them and supply their wants, as the president may judge fit ").

[2] In the epistles which he wrote to the church from his hiding-place, he is
always reminding them not to neglect the sick.

[3] I merely note in passing the conflict waged by the church against medical
sins like abortion (*Did.*, ii. 2 ; Barn., xix. 5 ; Tert., *Apol.* ix. ; *Minuc.
Felix.*, xxx. 2 ; Athenag., *Suppl.* xxxv. ; Clem., *Paed.*, ii. 10, 96, etc.), and the
unnatural morbid vices of paganism.   It was a conflict in which the interests of
the church were truly human ; she maintained the value and dignity of human
life, refusing to allow it to be destroyed or dishonoured at any stage of its development.   With regard to these offences, she also exerted some influence upon the
State legislation, in and after the fourth century, although even in the third
century the latter had already approximated to her teaching on such points.

As regards therapeutic methods, the case stood as it stands to-day. The more Christians renounced and hated the world, the more sceptical and severe they were against ordinary means of healing (cp., *e.g.*, Tatian's *Oratio*, xvii.–xviii.). There was a therapeutic "Christian science," compounded of old and new superstitions, and directed against more than the "dæmonic" cures (see the following section). Compare, by way of proof, Tertullian's *Scorp.*, i.: "We Christians make the sign of the cross at once over a bitten foot, say a word of exorcism, and rub it with the blood of the crushed animal." Evidently the sign of the cross and the formula of exorcism were not sufficient by themselves.

CHAPTER III

THE CONFLICT WITH DEMONS [1]

DURING the early centuries a belief in demons, and in the power they exercised throughout the world, was current far and wide. There was also a corresponding belief in demon possession, in consequence of which insanity frequently took the form of a conviction, on the part of the patients, that they were possessed by one or more evil spirits. Though this form of insanity still occurs at the present day, cases of it are rare, owing to the fact that wide circles of people have lost all belief in the existence and activity of demons. But the forms and phases in which insanity manifests itself always depend upon the general state of culture and the ideas current in the social environment, so that whenever the religious life is in a state of agitation, and a firm belief prevails in the sinister activity of evil spirits, "demon-possession" still breaks out sporadically. Recent instances have even shown that a convinced exorcist, especially if he is a religious man, is able to produce the phenomena of " possession " in a company of people against their will, in order subsequently to cure them. " Possession " is also infectious. Supposing that one case of this kind occurs in a church, and that it is connected by the sufferer himself, or even by the priest, with sin in general or with some special form of sin ; supposing that he preaches upon it, addressing the church in stirring language, and declaring that this is really devil's play, then the first case will

[1] Based on the essay from which the previous section has largely borrowed. Cp. on this point Weinel, *Die Wirkungen des Geistes und der Geister im nachapost. Zeitalter* (1899), pp. 1 f., and the article "Dämonische" in the Protest. Real-Encykl., iv.[3], by J. Weiss.

soon be followed by a second and by a third.[1] The most astounding phenomena occur, many of whose details are still inexplicable. Everything is doubled—the consciousness of the sufferer, his will, his sphere of action. With perfect sincerity on his own part (although it is always easy for frauds to creep in here), the man is at once conscious of himself and also of another being who constrains and controls him from within. He thinks and feels and acts, now as the one, now as the other ; and under the conviction that he is a double being, he confirms himself and his neighbours in this belief by means of actions which are at once the product of reflection and of an inward compulsion. Inevitable self-deception, cunning actions, and the most abject passivity form a sinister combination. But they complete our idea of a psychical disease which usually betrays extreme susceptibility to " suggestion," and, therefore, for the time being often defies any scientific analysis, leaving it open to anyone to think of special and mysterious forces in operation. In this region there are facts which we cannot deny, but which we are unable to explain.[2] Furthermore, there are " diseases " in this region which only attack superhuman individuals, who draw from this " disease " a new life hitherto undreamt of, an energy which triumphs over every obstacle, and a prophetic or apostolic zeal. We do not speak here of this kind of " possession "; it exists merely for faith — or unbelief.

In the case of ordinary people, when disease emerges in con-

---

[1] Tertullian (*de Anima*, ix.) furnishes an excellent example of the way in which morbid spiritual states (especially visions) which befel Christians in the church assemblies depended upon the preaching to which they had just listened. One sister, says Tertullian, had a vision of a soul in bodily form, just after Tertullian had preached on the soul (probably it was upon the corporeal nature of the soul). He adds quite ingenuously that the content of a vision was usually derived from the scriptures which had just been read aloud, from the psalms, or from the sermons.

[2] Cp. the biography of Blumhard by Zündel (1881) ; Ribot's *Les maladies de la personnalité* (Paris, 1885), *Les maladies de la mémoire* (Paris, 1881), and *Les maladies de la volonté* (Paris, 1883) [English translations of the second in the International Scientific Series, and of the first and third in the Religion of Science Library, Chicago]; see also Jundt's work, *Rulman Merswin : un problème de psychologie religieuse* (Paris, 1890), especially pp. 96 f. ; also the investigations of Forel and Krafft-Ebing.

nection with religion, no unfavourable issue need be anticipated. As a general rule, the religion which brings the disease to a head has also the power of curing it, and this power resides in Christianity above all other religions. Wherever an empty or a sinful life, which has almost parted with its vitality, is suddenly aroused by the preaching of the Christian religion, so that dread of evil and its bondage passes into the idea of actual " possession," the soul again is freed from the latter bondage by the message of the grace of God which has appeared in Jesus Christ. Evidence of this lies on the pages of church history, from the very beginning down to the present day. During the first three centuries the description of such cases flowed over into the margin of the page, whereas nowadays they are dismissed in a line or two. But the reason for this change is to be found in the less frequent occurrence, not of the cure, but of the disease.

The mere message or preaching of Christianity was not of course enough to cure the sick. It had to be backed by a convinced belief or by some person who was sustained by this belief. The cure was wrought by the praying man and not by prayer, by the Spirit and not by the formula, by the exorcist and not by exorcism. Conventional means were of no use except in cases where the disease became an epidemic and almost general, or in fact a conventional thing itself, as we must assume it often to have been during the second century. The exorcist then became a mesmerist, probably also a deluded impostor. But wherever a strong individuality was victimized by the demon of fear, wherever the soul was literally convulsed by the grip of that power of darkness from which it was now fain to flee, the will could only be freed from its bondage by some strong, holy, outside will. Here and there cases occur of what modern observers, in their perplexity, term " suggestion." But " suggestion " was one thing to a prophet, and another thing to a professional exorcist.

In the form in which we meet it throughout the later books of the Septuagint, or in the New Testament, or in the Jewish literature of the Imperial age, belief in the activity of demons was a comparatively late development in Judaism. But during

that period it was in full bloom.[1] And it was about this time
that it also began to spread apace among the Greeks and
Romans. How the latter came by it, is a question to which no
answer has yet been given. It is impossible to refer the form
of belief in demons which was current throughout the empire,
in and after the second century, *solely* to Jewish or even to
Christian sources. But the naturalizing of this belief, or, more
correctly, the development along quite definite lines of that
early Greek belief in spirits, which even the subsequent
philosophers (*e.g.*, Plato) had supported—all this was a process
to which Judaism and Christianity may have contributed, no less
than other Oriental religions, including especially the Egyptian,[2]
whose priests had been at all times famous for exorcism. In
the second century a regular class of exorcists existed, just as at
the present day in Germany there are " Naturärzte," or Nature-
physicians, side by side with skilled doctors. Still, sensible
people remained sceptical, while the great jurist Ulpian refused
(at a time when, as now, this was a burning question) to recognize such practitioners as members of the order of physicians.
He was even doubtful, of course, whether "specialists" were
physicians in the legal sense of the term.[3]

---

[1] Cp. the interesting passage in Joseph., *Ant.*, viii. 2. 5 : Παρέσχε Σολομῶνι
μαθεῖν ὁ θεὸς καὶ τὴν κατὰ τῶν δαιμόνων τέχνην εἰς ὠφέλειαν καὶ θεραπείαν τοῖς
ἀνθρώποις· ἐπῳδάς τε συνταξάμενος αἷς παρηγορεῖται τὰ νοσήματα καὶ τρόπους
ἐξορκώσεων κατέλιπεν, οἷς οἱ ἐνδούμενοι τὰ δαιμόνια ὡς μήκετ' ἐπανελθεῖν ἐκδιώξουσι·
καὶ αὕτη μέχρι νῦν παρ' ἡμῖν ἡ θεραπεία πλεῖστον ἰσχύει ("God enabled Solomon
to learn the arts valid against demons, in order to aid and heal mankind. He
composed incantations for the alleviation of disease, and left behind him methods
of exorcism by which demons can be finally expelled from people. A method of
healing which is extremely effective even in our own day"). Compare also the
story that follows this remark. The Jews must have been well known as exorcists
throughout the Roman empire.

[2] And also the Persian.

[3] Cp. the remarkable passage in *Dig. Leg.*, xiii. c. 1, § 3 : Medicos fortassis
quis accipiet etiam eos qui alicuius partis corporis vel certi doloris sanitatem
pollicentur : ut puta si auricularis, si fistulæ vel dentium, non tamen si incantavit,
si inprecatus est si ut vulgari verbo impostorum utar, exorcizavit : non sunt ista
medicinae genera, tametsi sint, qui hos sibi profuisse cum praedicatione adfirmant
("Perchance we should admit as physicians those also who undertake to cure
special parts of the body or particular diseases, as, for example, the ear, ulcers, or
the teeth ; yet not if they employ incantations or spells, or—to use the term
current among such impostors—if they ' exorcise.' Though there are people who
loudly maintain that they have been helped thereby.")

The characteristic features of belief in demons[1] during the second century were as follows. In the first place, the belief made its way upwards *from the obscurity of the lower classes into the upper classes of society*, and became far more important than it had hitherto been; in the second place, it was *no longer* accompanied by *a vigorous, naïve, and open religion* which kept it within bounds; furthermore, the power of the demons, which had hitherto been regarded as morally indifferent, now came to represent their *wickedness*; and finally, when the new belief was applied to the life of *individuals*, its consequences embraced psychical diseases as well as physical. In view of all these considerations, the extraordinary spread of belief in demons, and the numerous outbursts of demonic disease, are to be referred to the combined influence of such well-known factors as the dwindling of faith in the old religions, which characterized the Imperial age, together with the rise of a feeling on the part of the individual that he was free and independent, and therefore flung upon his inmost nature and his own responsibility. Free now from any control or restraint of tradition, the individual wandered here and there amid the lifeless, fragmentary, and chaotic débris of traditions belonging to a world in process of dissolution; now he would pick up this, now that, only to discover himself at last driven, often by fear and hope, to find a deceptive support or a new disease in the absurdest of them all.[2]

Such was the situation of affairs encountered by the gospel. It has been scoffingly remarked that the gospel produced the very diseases which it professed itself able to cure. The scoff is justified in certain cases, but in the main it recoils upon the scoffer. The gospel did bring to a head the diseases which it proceeded to cure. It found them already in existence, and intensified them in the course of its mission. But it also cured them, and no flight of the imagination can form any idea of what would have come over the ancient world or the Roman

---

[1] The scientific statement and establishment of this belief, in philosophy, goes back to Xenocrates; after him Posidonius deserves special mention. Cp. Apuleius, *de Deo Socratis*.

[2] Jas. iii. 15 speaks of a σοφία δαιμονιώδης.

empire during the third century, had it not been for the church. Professors like Libanius or his colleagues in the academy at Athens, are of course among the immortals; people like that could maintain themselves without any serious change from century to century. But no nation thrives upon the food of rhetoricians and philosophers. At the close of the fourth century Rome had only one Symmachus, and the East had only one Synesius. But then, Synesius was a Christian.

In what follows I propose to set down, without note or comment, one or two important notices of demon-possession and its cure from the early history of the church. In the case of one passage I shall sketch the spread and shape of belief in demons. This Tertullian has described, and it is a mistake to pass Tertullian by.—In order to estimate the significance of exorcism for primitive Christianity, one must remember that according to the belief of Christians the Son of God came into the world to combat Satan and his kingdom. The evangelists, especially Luke, have depicted the life of Jesus from the temptation onwards as an uninterrupted conflict with the devil; what he came for was to destroy the works of the devil. In Mark (i. 32) we read how many that were possessed were brought to Jesus, and healed by him, as he cast out the demons (i. 34). " He suffered not the demons to speak, for they knew him " (see also Luke iv. 34, 41). In i. 39 there is the general statement: " He preached throughout all Galilee in the synagogues and cast out the demons." When he sent forth the twelve disciples, he conferred on them the power of exorcising (iii. 15), a power which they forthwith proceeded to exercise (vi. 13 ; for the Seventy, see Luke x. 17); whilst the scribes at Jerusalem declared he had Beelzebub,[1] and that he cast out demons with the aid of their prince.[2] The tale of the " unclean spirits " who entered a herd of swine is quite familiar (v. 2), forming, as it does, one of the most curious fragments of the sacred story, which has vainly taxed the powers of believing

[1] John the Baptist was also said to have been possessed (cp. Matt. xi. 18).
[2] Jesus himself explains that he casts out demons by aid of the spirit of God (Matt. xii. 28), but he seems to have been repeatedly charged with possessing the devil and with madness (cp. John vii. 20, viii. 48 f., x. 20).

and of rationalistic criticism. Another story which more immediately concerns our present purpose is that of the Canaanite woman and her possessed daughter (vii. 25 f.). Matt. vii. 15 f. (Luke ix. 38) shows that epileptic fits, as well as other nervous disorders (*e.g.*, dumbness, Matt. xii. 22, Luke xi. 14), were also included under demon-possession. It is further remarkable that even during the lifetime of Jesus exorcists who were not authorised by him exorcised devils in his name. This gave rise to a significant conversation between Jesus and John (Mark ix. 38). John said to Jesus, " Master, we saw a man casting out demons in thy name, and we forbade him, because he did not follow us." But Jesus answered, " Forbid him not. No one shall work a deed of might in my name and then deny me presently ; for he who is not against us, is for us." On the other hand, another saying of our Lord numbers people who have never known him (Matt. vii. 22) among those who cast out devils in his name. From one woman among his followers Jesus was known afterwards to have cast out " seven demons " (Mark xvi. 9, Luke viii. 2), and among the mighty deeds of which all believers were to be made capable, the unauthentic conclusion of Mark's gospel enumerates exorcism (xvi. 17).[1]

It was as exorcisers that Christians went out into the great world, and *exorcism formed one very powerful method of their mission and propaganda. It was a question not simply of exorcising and vanquishing the demons that dwelt in individuals, but also of purifying all public life from them. For the age was ruled by the black one and his hordes (Barnabas) ; it " lieth in the evil one,"* κεῖται ἐν πονηρῷ *(John). Nor was this mere theory ; it was a most vital conception of existence.* The whole world and the circumambient atmosphere were filled with devils ; not merely idolatry, but every phase and form of life was ruled by them. They sat on thrones, they hovered around cradles. The earth was literally a hell, though it was and continued to be a creation of God. To encounter this hell and all its devils, Christians had command of weapons that were invincible. Besides the evidence drawn from the age of their holy scriptures,

_____
[1] Indeed, it is put first of all.

they pointed to the power of exorcism committed to them, which routed evil spirits, and even forced them to bear witness to the truth of Christianity. " We," says Tertullian towards the close of his *Apology* (ch. xlvi.), " we have stated our case fully, as well as the evidence for the correctness of our statement —that is, the trustworthiness and antiquity of our sacred writings, and also the testimony borne by the demonic powers themselves (in our favour)." Such was the stress laid on the activity of the exorcists.[1]

In Paul's epistles,[2] in Pliny's letter, and in the Didachê, they are never mentioned.[3] But from Justin downwards, Christian literature is crowded with allusions to exorcisms, and every large church at any rate had exorcists. Originally these men were honoured as persons endowed with special grace, but afterwards they constituted a class by themselves, in the lower hierarchy, like lectors and sub-deacons. By this change they lost their pristine standing.[4] The church sharply distinguished between exorcists who employed the name of Christ, and pagan sorcerers, magicians, etc. ;[5] but she could not protect herself adequately against mercenary impostors, and several of her exorcists were just as dubious characters as her " prophets." The hotbed of religious frauds was in Egypt, as we learn from Lucian's *Peregrinus Proteus*, from Celsus, and from Hadrian's

---

[1] In the pseudo-Clementine epistle " on Virginity " (i. 10), the reading of Scripture, exorcism, and teaching are grouped as the most important functions in religion.

[2] See, however, Eph. vi. 12 ; 2 Cor. xii. 7, etc.

[3] No explanation has yet been given of the absence of exorcism in Paul. His doctrine of sin, however, was unfavourable to such phenomena.

[4] The history of exorcism (as practised at baptism, and elsewhere on its own account) and of exorcists is far too extensive to be discussed here ; besides, in some departments it has not yet been sufficiently investigated. Much information may still be anticipated from the magical papyri, of which an ever-increasing number are coming to light. So far as exorcism and exorcists entered into the public life of the church, see Probst's *Sakramente und Sakramentalien*, pp. 39 f., and *Kirchliche Disziplin*, pp. 116 f.

[5] Cp. the apologists, Origen's reply to Celsus, and the injunction in the Canons of Hippolytus (*Texte u. Unters.*, vi. 4, pp. 83 f.): "Οἰωνιστής vel magus vel astrologus, hariolus, somniorum interpres, praestigiator . . . . vel qui phylacteria conficit . . . . hi omnes et qui sunt similes his neque instruendi neque baptizandi sunt." Observe also the polemic against the magical arts of the Gnostics.

letter to Servian.[1] At a very early period pagan exorcists appropriated the names of the patriarchs (cp. Orig., c. Cels., I. xxii.), of Solomon, and even of Jesus Christ, in their magical formulæ; even Jewish exorcists soon began to introduce the name of Jesus in their incantations.[2] The church, on the contrary, had to warn her own exorcists not to imitate the heathen. In the pseudo-Clementine de Virginitate we read (i. 12): "For those who are brethren in Christ it is fitting and right and comely to visit people who are vexed with evil spirits, and to pray and utter exorcisms over them, in the rational language of prayer acceptable to God, not with a host of fine words neatly arranged and studied in order to win the reputation among men of being eloquent and possessed of a good memory. Such folk are just like a sounding pipe, or a tinkling cymbal, of not the least use to those over whom they pronounce their exorcisms. They simply utter terrible words and scare people with them, but never act according to a true faith such as that enjoined by the Lord when he taught that 'this kind goeth not out save by fasting and prayer offered unceasingly, and by a mind earnestly bent (on God).' Let them make holy requests and entreaties to God, cheerfully, circum-spectly, and purely, without hatred or malice. For such is the manner in which we are to visit a sick (possessed) brother or a sister . . . . without guile or covetousness or noise or talkativeness or pride or any behaviour alien to piety, but with the meek and lowly spirit of Christ. Let them exorcise the sick with fasting and with prayer; instead of using elegant phrases, neatly arranged and ordered, let them act frankly like men who have received the gift of healing from God, to God's glory. By your fastings and prayers and constant watching, together with all the rest of your good works, mortify the

---

[1] Vopiscus, Saturn., 8: "Nemo illic archisynagogus Judaeorum, nemo Sama-rites, nemo Christianorum presbyter, non mathematicus, non haruspex, non aliptes."

[2] Compare the story of the Jewish exorcists in Acts xix. 13: "Now certain of the itinerant Jewish exorcists also undertook to pronounce the name of the Lord Jesus over those who were possessed by evil spirits. 'I adjure you,' they said, 'by the Jesus whom Paul preaches.'" It is admitted, in the pseudo-Cypr. de Rebapt., vii., that even non-Christians were frequently able to drive out demons by using the name of Christ.

works of the flesh by the power of the Holy Spirit. He who
acts thus is a temple of the Holy Spirit of God. Let him cast
out demons, and God will aid him therein. . . . . The Lord has
given the command to ' cast out demons' and also enjoined the
duty of healing in other ways, adding, ' Freely ye have received,
freely give.' A great reward from God awaits those who serve
their brethren with the gifts which God has bestowed upon
themselves." Justin writes (*Apol.*, II. vi.): ("The Son of God
became man in order to destroy the demons.) This you can
now learn from what transpires under your own eyes. For
many of our Christian people have healed a large number of
demoniacs throughout the whole world, and also in your own
city, exorcising them in the name of Jesus Christ, who was
crucified under Pontius Pilate; yet all other exorcists,
magicians, and dealers in drugs failed to heal such people.
Yea, and such Christians continue still to heal them, by rendering the demons impotent and expelling them from the men
whom they possessed." In his dialogue against the Jews
(lxxxv.), Justin also writes: " Every demon exorcised in the
name of the Son of God, the First-born of all creatures, who
was born of a virgin and endured human suffering, who was
crucified by your nation under Pontius Pilate, who died and
rose from the dead and ascended into heaven—every demon
exorcised in this name is mastered and subdued. Whereas if you
exorcise in the name of any king or righteous man, or prophet,
or patriarch, who has been one of yourselves, no demon will be
subject to you. . . . . Your exorcists, I have already said, are
like the Gentiles in using special arts, employing fumigation
and magic incantations." From this passage we infer that the
Christian formulæ of exorcism contained the leading facts of
the story of Christ.[1] And Origen says as much, quite unmistakably, in his reply to Celsus (I. vi.): " The power of exorcism
lies in the name of Jesus, which is uttered as the stories of his
life are being narrated." [2]

---

[1] In the formula of exorcism the most important part was the mention of the
crucifixion; cp. Justin's *Dial.* xxx., xlix., lxxvi.

[2] Ἰσχύειν δοκοῦσι . . . . τῷ ὀνόματι Ἰησοῦ μετὰ τῆς ἐπαγγελίας τῶν περὶ
αὐτὸν ἱστοριῶν.

Naturally one feels very sceptical in reading how various parties in Christianity denied each other the power of exorcism, explaining cures as due either to mistakes or to deception. So Irenæus (II. xxxi. 2): "The adherents of Simon and Carpocrates and the other so-called workers of miracles were convicted of acting as they acted, not by the power of God, nor in truth, nor for the good of men, but to destroy and deceive men by means of magical illusions and universal deceit. They do more injury than good to those who believe in them, inasmuch as they are deceivers. For neither can they give sight to the blind or hearing to the deaf, nor can they rout any demons save those sent by themselves—if they can do even that."[1] With regard to his own church, Irenæus (cp. below, ch. iv.) was convinced that the very dead were brought back to life by its members. In this, he maintains, there was neither feint, nor error, nor deception, but astounding fact, as in the case of our Lord himself. "In the name of Jesus, his true disciples, who have received grace from him, do fulfil a healing ministry in aid of other men, even as each has received the free gift of grace from him. Some surely and certainly drive out demons, so that it frequently happens that those thus purged from demons also believe and become members of the church.[2] Others, again, possess a fore-knowledge of the future, with visions and

---

[1] Cp. the sorry and unsuccessful attempts of the church in Asia to treat the Montanist prophetesses as demoniacs who required exorcism. Compare with this Firmilian's account (Cypr., *Epist.* lxxv. 10) of a Christian woman who felt herself to be a prophetess, and "deceived" many people: Subito apparuit illi unus de exorcistis, vir probatus et circa religiosam disciplinam bene semper conversatus, qui exhortatione quoque fratrum plurimorum qui et ipsi fortes ac laudabiles in fide aderant excitatus erexit se contra illum spiritum nequam revincendum . . . . ille exorcista inspiratus dei gratia fortiter restitit et esse illum nequissimum spiritum qui prius sanctus putabatur ostendit ("Suddenly there appeared before her one of the exorcists, a tried man, of irreproachable conduct in the matter of religious discipline. At the urgent appeal of many brethren present, themselves as courageous and praiseworthy in the faith, he roused himself to meet and master that wicked spirit. . . . . Inspired by the grace of God, that exorcist made a brave resistance, and showed that the spirit which had previously been deemed holy, was in reality most evil ").

[2] Still it seems to have been made a matter of reproach, in the third century, if any one had suffered from possession. Cornelius taxes Novatian (cp. Euseb., *H.E*, vi. 43) with having been possessed by a demon before his baptism, and having been healed by an exorcist.

prophetic utterances. . . . . And what shall I more say? For it is impossible to enumerate the spiritual gifts and blessings which, all over the world, the church has received from God in the name of Jesus Christ, *who was crucified under Pontius Pilate*, and which she exercises day by day for the healing of the pagan world, without deceiving or taking money from any person. For as she has freely received them from God, so also does she freely give" (ἰατροὶ ἀνάργυροι).

The popular notion prevalent among the early Christians, as among the later Jews, was that, apart from the innumerable hosts of demons who disported themselves unabashed throughout history and nature, every individual had beside him a good angel who watched over him, and an evil spirit who lay in wait for him (cp., *e.g.*, the "Shepherd" of Hermas). If he allowed himself to be controlled by the latter, he was thereby "possessed," in the strict sense of the word; *i.e.*, sin itself was possession. This brings out admirably the slavish dependence to which any man is reduced who abandons himself to his own impulses, though the explanation is naïvely simple. In the belief in demons, as that belief dominated the Christian world in the second and third centuries, it is easy to detect features which stamp it as a reactionary movement hostile to contemporary culture. Yet it must not be forgotten that the heart of it enshrined a moral and consequently a spiritual advance, viz., in a quickened sense of evil, as well as in a recognition of the power of sin and of its dominion in the world. Hence it was that a mind of such high culture as Tertullian's could abandon itself to this belief in demons. It is interesting to notice how the Greek and Roman elements are bound up with the Jewish Christian in his detailed statement of the belief (in the *Apology*), and I shall now quote this passage in full. It occurs in connection with the statement that while demons are ensconced behind the dead gods of wood and stone, they are forced by Christians to confess what they are, viz., not gods at all, but unclean spirits. At several points we catch even here the tone of irony and sarcasm over these "poor devils" which grew so loud in the Middle Ages, and yet never shook belief in them. But, on the whole, the description is extremely serious.

People who fancy at this time of day that they would possess primitive Christianity if they only enforced certain primitive rules of faith, may perhaps discover from what follows the sort of coefficients with which that Christianity was burdened.[1]

"We Christians," says Tertullian (ch. xxii. f.), "affirm the existence of certain spiritual beings. Nor is their name new. The philosophers recognize demons; Socrates himself waited on a demon's impulse, and no wonder—for a demon is said to have been his companion from childhood, detaching his mind, I have no doubt, from what was good! The poets, too, recognize demons, and even the ignorant masses use them often in their oaths. In fact, they appeal in their curses to Satan, the prince of this evil gang, with a sort of instinctive knowledge of him in their very souls. Plato himself does not deny the existence of angels, and even the magicians attest both kinds of spiritual beings. But it is our sacred scriptures which record how certain angels, who fell of their own free will, produced a still more fallen race of demons, who were condemned by God together with their progenitors and with that prince to whom we have already alluded. Here we cannot do more than merely describe their doings. The ruin of man was their sole aim. From the outset man's overthrow was essayed by these spirits in their wickedness. Accordingly they proceed to inflict diseases and evil accidents of all kinds on our bodies, while by means of violent assaults they produce sudden and extraordinary excesses of the soul. Both to soul and to body they have access by their subtle and extremely fine substance. Invisible and intangible, those spirits are not visible in the act; it is in their effects that

---

[1] Next to Tertullian, it is his predecessor Tatian who has given the most exact description of the Christian doctrine of demons (in his *Oratio ad Græcos*, vii.–xviii.). The demons introduced "Fatum" and polytheism. To believers, *i.e.*, to men of the Spirit (πνευμάτικοι), they are visible, but psychic men (ψύχικοι) are either unable to see them, or only see them at rare intervals (xv.–xvi.). Illnesses arise from the body, but demons assume the final responsibility for them. "Sometimes, indeed, they convulse our physical state with a storm of their incorrigible wickedness; but smitten by a powerful word of God they depart in terror, and the sick man is cured." Tatian does not deny, as a rule, that possessed persons are often healed, even apart from the aid of Christians. In the pseudo-Clementine Homilies (ix. 10. 16–18) there is also important information upon demons. For the Christian belief in demons, consult also Diels, *Elementum* (1899), especially pp. 50 f.

they are frequently observed, as when, for example, some mysterious poison in the breeze blights the blossom of fruit trees and
the grain, or nips them in the bud, or destroys the ripened fruit,
the poisoned atmosphere exhaling, as it were, some noxious
breath. With like obscurity, the breath of demons and of angels
stirs up many a corruption in the soul by furious passions, vile excesses, or cruel lusts accompanied by varied errors, *the worst of
which is that these deities commend themselves to the ensnared and
deluded souls of men*,[1] in order to get their favourite food of
flesh-fumes and of blood offered up to the images and statues of
the gods. And what more exquisite food could be theirs than
to divert men from the thought of the true God by means of
false illusions? How these illusions are managed, I shall now
explain. Every spirit is winged, angel and demon alike. Hence
in an instant they are everywhere. The whole world is just one
place to them. 'Tis as easy for them to know as to announce
any occurrence; and as people are ignorant of their nature, their
velocity is taken for divinity. Thus they would have themselves
sometimes thought to be the authors of the events which they
merely report—and authors, indeed, they are, not of good, but
occasionally of evil events. The purposes of Divine providence
were also caught up by them of old from the lips of the prophets,
and at present from the public reading of their works. So
picking up in this way a partial knowledge of the future, they
set up a rival divinity for themselves by purloining prophecy.
But well do your Crœsuses and Pyrrhuses know the clever
ambiguity with which these oracles were framed in view of the
future. . . . . As they dwell in the air, close to the stars, and in
touch with the clouds, they can discern the preliminary processes
in the sky, and thus are able to promise the rain whose coming
they already feel. Truly they are most kind in their concern
for health! First of all, they make you ill; then, to produce
the impression of a miracle, they enjoin the use of remedies which
are either unheard of or have quite an opposite effect; lastly, by
withdrawing their injurious influence, they get the credit of

---

[1] This ranks as the *chef-d'œuvre* of iniquity on the part of the demons; *they are
responsible for introducing polytheism, i.e.*, they get worshipped under the images
of dead gods, and profit by sacrifices, whose odour they enjoy.

having worked a cure. Why, then, should I speak further of their other tricks or even of their powers of deception as spirits —of the Castor apparitions, of water carried in a sieve, of a ship towed by a girdle, of a beard reddened at a touch—things done to get men to believe in stones as gods, instead of seeking after the true God?

"Moreover, if magicians call up ghosts and even bring forward the souls of the dead, if they strangle boys in order to make the oracle speak, if they pretend to perform many a miracle by means of their quackery and juggling, if they even send dreams by aid of those angels and demons whose power they have invoked (and, thanks to them, it has become quite a common thing for the very goats and tables to divine), how much more keen will be this evil power in employing all its energies to do, of its own accord and for its own ends, what serves another's purpose? Or, if the deeds of angels and demons are exactly the same as those of your gods, where is the pre-eminence of the latter, which must surely be reckoned superior in might to all else? Is it not a more worthy conception that the former make themselves gods by exhibiting the very credentials of the gods, than that the gods are on a level with angels and demons? Locality, I suppose you will say, locality makes a difference; in a temple you consider beings to be gods whom elsewhere you would not recognize as such! . . . .

"But hitherto it has been merely a question of words. Now for facts, now for a proof that 'gods' and 'demons' are but different names for one and the same substance. Place before your tribunals any one plainly possessed by a demon. *Bidden speak by any Christian whatsoever, that spirit will confess he is a demon, just as frankly elsewhere he will falsely pretend to be a god.*[1] Or, if you like, bring forward any one of those who are supposed to be divinely possessed, who conceive divinity from the fumes which they inhale bending over an altar, and ("ructando curantur") are delivered of it by retching, giving vent to it in gasps. Let the heavenly virgin herself, who promises rain, let that teacher of healing arts, Æsculapius, ever ready to prolong

---

[1] In this, as in some other passages of the *Apology*, Tertullian's talk is too large.

the life of those who are on the point of death, with Socordium, Tenatium (?), and Asclepiadotum—let them then and there shed the blood of that daring Christian, if—in terror of lying to a Christian—they fail to admit they are demons. Could any action be more plain? Any proof more cogent? Truth in its simplicity stands here before your eyes; its own worth supports it; suspicion there can be none. Say you, it is a piece of magic or a trick of some sort? . . . . What objection can be brought against something exhibited in its bare reality? If, on the one hand, they (the demons) are really gods, why do they pretend (at our challenge) to be demons? From fear of us? Then your so-called 'Godhead' is subordinated to us, and surely no divinity can be attributed to what lies under the control of men. . . . . So that 'Godhead' of yours proves to be no godhead at all; for if it were, demons would not pretend to it, nor would gods deny it. . . . . Acknowledge that there is but *one* species of such beings, namely, demons, and that the gods are nothing else. Look out, then, for gods! For now you find that those whom you formerly took for such, are demons."

In what follows, Tertullian declares that the demons, on being questioned by Christians, not only confess they are themselves demons, but also confess the Christian's God as the true God. "Fearing God in Christ, and Christ in God, they become subject to the servants of God and Christ. Thus at our touch and breath, overpowered by the consideration and contemplation of the (future) fire, they leave human bodies at our command, reluctantly and sadly, and—in your presence—shamefacedly. You believe their lies; then believe them when they tell the truth about themselves. When anyone lies, it is not to disgrace but to glorify himself. . . . . *Such testimonies from your so-called deities usually result in making people Christians.*"

In ch. xxvii. Tertullian meets the obvious retort that if demons were actually subject to Christians, the latter could not possibly succumb helplessly to the persecutions directed against them. Tertullian contradicts this. The demons, he declares, are certainly like slaves under the control of the Christians, but like good-for-nothing slaves they sometimes blend fear and contumacy, eager to injure those of whom they stand in awe. "At a distance they oppose us, but at close quarters they beg for mercy. Hence, like slaves that have broken loose from work-houses, or prisons, or mines, or any form of penal servitude, they break out against us, though they are in our power, well aware of their impotence, and yet rendered the more abandoned thereby. We resist this horde unwillingly, the same as if they were still unvanquished, stoutly maintaining the very position which they attack, nor is our triumph over them ever more complete than when we are condemned for our persistent faith."

In ch. xxxvii. Tertullian once more sums up the service which Christians render to pagans by means of their exorcists. "Were it not for us, who would free you from those hidden foes that are ever making havoc of your health in soul and body—from those raids of the demons, I mean, which we repel from you without reward or hire?" He says the same thing in his address to the magistrate Scapula (ii.): "We do more than repudiate the demons: we overcome them, we expose them daily to contempt, and exorcise them from their victims, *as is well known to many people*."[1] This endowment of Christians must therefore have been really acknowledged far and wide, and in a number of passages Tertullian speaks as if every Christian possessed it.[2] It would be interesting if we could only ascertain how far these cures of psychical diseases were permanent. Unfortunately, nothing is known upon the point, and yet this is a province where nothing is more common than a merely temporary success.

Like Tertullian, Minucius Felix in his "Octavius" has also treated this subject, partly in the same words as Tertullian (ch. xxvii.).[3] The apologist Theophilus (*ad Autolyc.*, ii. 8) writes:

---

[1] See also the interesting observations in *de Anima*, i.

[2] Cp., for example, *de Corona*, xi. Other Christian writers also express themselves to the same effect, *e.g.*, the speech of Peter in the pseudo-Clementine Homilies (ix. 19), which declares that Christians at baptism obtain a gift of healing other people by means of exorcisms: "Sometimes the demons will flee if you but look on them, for they know those who have surrendered themselves to God, and flee in terror because they honour such people" (ἐνίοτε δὲ οἱ δαίμονες μόνον ἐνιδόντων ὑμῶν φεύξονται· ἴσασιν γὰρ τοὺς ἀποδεδωκότας ἑαυτοὺς τῷ θεῷ, διὸ τιμῶντες αὐτοὺς πεφοβημένοι φεύγουσιν).

[3] "Adjurati (daemones) per deum verum et solum inviti miseris corporibus inhor-rescunt, et vel exiliunt statim vel evanescunt gradatim, prout fides patientis adiuvat aut gratia curantis adspirat. Sic Christianos de proximo fugitant, quos longe in coetibus per vos lacessebant," etc.

"The Greek poet spoke under the inspiration, not of a pure, but of a lying spirit, as is quite obvious from the fact that even in our own day possessed people are sometimes still exorcised in the name of the true God, whereupon their lying spirits themselves confess that they are demons, the actual demons who formerly were at work in the poets." This leads us to assume that the possessed frequently cried out the name of "Apollo" or of the Muses at the moment of exorcising. As late as the middle of the third century Cyprian also speaks, like earlier authors, of demonic cures wrought by Christians (ad Demetr., xv.): "O if thou wouldst but hear and see the demons when they are adjured by us, tormented by spiritual scourges, and driven from the possessed bodies by racking words; when howling and groaning with human voices (!), and feeling by the power of God the stripes and blows, they have to confess the judgment to come! Come and see that what we say is true. And forasmuch as thou sayest thou dost worship the gods, then believe even those whom thou dost worship. . . . . Thou wilt see how those whom thou implorest implore us; how those of whom thou art in awe stand in awe of us. Thou wilt see how they stand bound under our hands, trembling like prisoners—they to whom thou dost look up with veneration as thy lords. Verily thou wilt be made ashamed in these errors of thine, when thou seest and hearest how thy gods, when cross-questioned by us, at once yield up the secret of their being, unable, even before you, to conceal those tricks and frauds of theirs." [1] Similarly in the treatise To Donatus (ch. v.): "In Christianity there is conferred (upon pure chastity, upon a pure mind, upon pure speech) the gift of healing the sick by rendering poisonous potions harmless,

[1] See also Quod Idola Dei non sint (vii.), and Cypr., Ep. lxix. 15 : "Hodie etiam geritur, ut per exorcistas voce humana et potestate divina flagelletur et uratur et torqueatur diabolus, et cum exire se et homines dei dimittere saepe dicat, in eo tamen quod dixerit fallat . . . . cum tamen ad aquam salutarem adque ad baptismi sanctificationem venitur, scire debemus et fidere [which sounds rather hesitating], quia illic diabolus opprimitur " ("This goes on to-day as well, in the scourging and burning and torturing of the devil at the hands of exorcists, by means of the human voice and the divine power, and in his declaring that he will go out and leave the men of God alone, yet proving untrue in what he says. . . . . However, when the water of salvation and the sanctification of baptism is reached, we ought to know and trust that the devil is crushed there ").

by restoring the deranged to health, and thus purifying them from ignominious pains, by commanding peace for the hostile, rest for the violent, and gentleness for the unruly, by forcing—under stress of threats and invective—a confession from unclean and roving spirits who have come to dwell within mankind, by roughly ordering them out, and stretching them out with struggles, howls, and groans, as their sufferings on the rack increase, by lashing them with scourges, and burning them with fire. This is what goes on, though no one sees it; the punishments are hidden, but the penalty is open. Thus what we have already begun to be, that is, the Spirit we have received, comes into its kingdom." The Christian already rules with regal power over the entire host of his raging adversary.[1]

Most interesting of all are the discussions between Celsus and Origen on demons and possessed persons, since the debate here is between two men who occupied the highest level of contemporary culture.[2] Celsus declared that Christians owed the power they seemed to possess to their invocation and adjuration of certain demons.[3] Origen retorted that the power of banishing demons was actually vested in the name of Jesus and the witness of his life, and that the name of Jesus was so powerful that it operated by itself even when uttered by immoral persons (*c. Cels.*, I. vi.). Both Origen and Celsus, then, believed in demons; and elsewhere (*e.g.*, I. xxiv. f.) Origen adduces the old idea of the power exercised by the utterance of certain "names";

[1] Compare with this Lactantius, *Divin. Instit.*, ii. 15, iv. 27, who repeats in part the description of Cyprian, but lays special emphasis on the sign of the cross as a means of salvation from demons.

[2] Origen (in *Hom.* xv. 5, *in Jesu Nave*, xi. pp. 141 f.) has developed a theory of his own to explain the suppression of demons by the church, especially in the light of its bearing upon the spread of Christianity. "Anyone who vanquishes a demon in himself, *e.g.*, the demon of lewdness, puts it out of action; the demon is cast into the abyss, and cannot do any harm to anyone. Hence there are far fewer demons now than before; hence, also, a large number of demons having been overthrown, the heathen are now free to believe, as they would not be did whole legions of demons exist as formerly" ("Et inde est quod plurimo daemonum numero iam victo ad credulitatem venire gentes relaxantur, qui utique nullatenus sinerentur, si integras eorum, sicut prius fuerant, subsisterent legiones").

[3] The ethical principles of Christianity, says Celsus (I. iv. f.), are common to Christians and philosophers alike, while the apparent strength of the former lies in the names of a few demons and in incantations.

in fact, he indicates a secret " science of names "[1] which confers
power on the initiated, although of course one had to be very
careful to recite the names in the proper language. " When
recited in the Egyptian tongue, the one class is specially
efficacious in the case of certain spirits whose power does not
extend beyond such things and such a sphere, whilst the other
class is effective with some spirits if recited in Persian, and so
forth." "The name of Jesus also comes under this science of
names, as it has already expelled numerous spirits from the
souls and bodies of mankind and shown its power over those
who have thus been freed from possession."[2] Origen several
times cites the fact of successful exorcism (I. xlvi., lxvii.), and
the fact is not denied by Celsus, who admits even the " miracles "
of Jesus. Only, his explanation was very different (lxviii.).
" The magicians," he said, " undertake still greater marvels, and
men trained in the schools of Egypt profess like exploits, people
who for a few pence will sell their reverend arts in the open
market-place, expelling demons from people, blowing diseases
away with their breath, calling up the spirits of the heroes,
exhibiting expensive viands, with tables, cakes, and dainties,
which are really non-existent, and setting inanimate things in
motion as if they really possessed life, whereas they have but
the semblance of animals. If any juggler is able to perform
feats of this kind, must we on that account regard him as
' God's son ' ? Must we not rather declare that such accomplishments are merely the contrivances of knaves possessed by evil
demons ? " Christians are jugglers or sorcerers or both ; Christ
also was a master of demonic arts—such was the real opinion of
Celsus.[3] Origen was at great pains to controvert this very

---

[1] Περὶ ὀνομάτων τὰ ἐν ἀπορρήτοις φιλοσοφεῖν.

[2] See on this point the statement of Origen's pupil Dionysius, Bishop of
Alexandria (in Euseb., H.E., vii. 10. 4), for the reason why the Valerian persecution broke out. Here pagan and Christian exorcisers opposed each other.
Of the latter, Dionysius says : " There are and were among them many persons
whose very presence and look, though they merely breathed and spoke, were able
to scatter the delusive counsels of the sinful demons." Local persecution of
Christians elsewhere, and indeed the great persecution under Diocletian, arose in
this way, pagan priests affirming that the presence of Christians who attended the
sacrifices hindered their saving influence, etc.

[3] He gives his opinion of the Gnostic exorcisers in particular in VI. xxxix. f.

grievous charge (see, *e.g.*, I. lxviii.). And he succeeded. He
could appeal to the unquestionable fact that all Christ's works
were wrought with the object of benefiting men.[1] Was it so
with magicians? Still, in this reproach of Celsus there lay a
serious monition for the church and for the Christians, a monition which more than Celsus canvassed. As early as the middle
of the second century a Christian preacher had declared, "The
name of the true God is blasphemed among the heathen by
reason of us Christians; for if we fulfil not the commands of
God, but lead an unworthy life, they turn away and blaspheme,
saying that our teaching is merely a fresh myth and error."[2]
From the middle of the second century onwards the cry was often
raised against Christians, that they were jugglers and necro-
mancers, and not a few of them were certainly to blame for such
a charge.[3] Cures of demon-possession practised by unspiritual
men as a profession must have produced a repellent impression
on more serious people, despite the attractive power which they
did exercise (Tert., *Apol.*, xxiii. " Christianos facere consuerunt ").
Besides, frivolous or ignorant Christians must often have excused
themselves for their sins by pleading that a demon had seduced
them, or that it was not they who did the wrong but the
demon.[4] But there was hardly any chance of the matter being
cleared up in the third century. Christians and pagans alike
were getting more and more entangled in the belief in demons.
In their dogmas and their philosophy of religion, polytheism
certainly became more and more attenuated as a sublime mono-

---

[1] Cp., *e.g.*, III. xxviii., and I. lxviii.

[2] 2 Clem. xiii. 3, μῦθόν τινα καὶ πλάνην.

[3] Origen, who himself admits that Christian exorcists were usually uneducated
people, asserts deliberately and repeatedly that they employed neither magic nor
sorcery but prayer alone and "formulæ of exorcism which are so plain that even
the plainest man can make use of them" (*c. Cels.*, VII. iv. : σὺν οὐδενὶ περιέργῳ
καὶ μαγικῷ ἢ φαρμακευτικῷ πράγματι, ἀλλὰ μόνῃ εὐχῇ καὶ ὁρκώσεσιν ἁπλουστέραις
καὶ ὅσα ἂν δύναιτο προσάγειν ἁπλούστερος ἄνθρωπος. Cp. *Comm. in Matth.*,
xiii. 7, vol. iii. p. 224).

[4] Cp. Origen, *de Princip.* iii. 2. 1 : " Hence some of the less intelligent believers
think that all human transgressions arise from their [*i.e.*, the demons'] antagonistic
powers, which constrain the mind of the sinner" (" Unde et simpliciores quique
domino Christo credentium existimant, quod omnia peccata, quaecumque com-
miserint homines, ex istis contrariis virtutibus mentem delinquentium perurgentibus
fiant ").

theism was evolved; but in practical life they plunged more helplessly than ever into the abysses of an imaginary world of spirits. The protests made by sensible physicians [1] were all in vain.

[1] So the famous physician Posidonius at the close of the fourth century, of whom Philostorgius (*H.E.*, viii. 10) narrates: "He said, though incorrectly, that it was not by the incentive of demons that men grew frenzied, but that it was the bad juices of certain sick bodies which wrought the mischief; since the power of demons was in no whit hostile to the nature of man" (λέγειν αὐτόν, ὅμως οὐκ ὀρθῶς, οὐχὶ δαιμόνων ἐπιθέσει τοὺς ἀνθρώπους ἐκβαχεύεσθαι, ὑγρῶν δὲ τινων κακοχυμίαν τὸ πάθος ἐργάζεσθαι· μὴ γὰρ εἶναι τὸ παράπαν ἰσχὺν δαιμόνων ἀνθρώπων φύσιν ἐπηρεάζουσαν).

CHAPTER IV

THE GOSPEL OF LOVE AND CHARITY [1]

" I was hungry, and ye fed me ; I was thirsty, and ye gave me drink ; I was a stranger, and ye took me in ; naked, and ye clothed me ; I was sick, and ye visited me ; I was in prison, and ye came to me. . . . . Inasmuch as ye did it unto one of the least of these my brethren, ye did it unto me."

These words of Jesus have shone so brilliantly for many generations in his church, and exerted so powerful an influence, that one may further describe the Christian preaching as *the preaching of love and charity.* From this standpoint, in fact, the proclamation of the Saviour and of healing would seem to be merely subordinate, inasmuch as the words " I was sick, and ye visited me " form but one link in the larger chain.

Among the extant words and parables of Jesus, those which inculcate love and charity are especially numerous, and with them we must rank many a story of his life.[2] Yet, apart altogether from the number of such sayings, it is plain that whenever he had in view the relations of mankind, the gist of his

---

[1] In his work, *Die christliche Liebestätigkeit in der alten Kirche* (1st ed., 1882 ; Eng. trans., *Christian Charity in the Ancient Church*, Edinburgh), Uhlhorn presents a sketch which is thorough, but unfair to paganism. The Greeks and Romans also were acquainted with philanthropy.

[2] One recalls particularly the parable of the good Samaritan, with its new definition of " neighbour," and also the parable of the lost son ; among the stories, that of the rich young man. The gospel of the Hebrews tells the latter incident with especial impressiveness. " Then said the Lord to him, How canst thou say, ' I have kept the law and the prophets,' when it is written in the law, ' Thou shalt love thy neighbour as thyself'? And look, many of thy brethren, sons of Abraham, are lying in dirt and dying of hunger, while thy house is full of many possessions, and never a gift comes from it to them."

preaching was to enforce brotherliness and ministering love, and the surest part of the impression he left behind him was that in his own life and labours he displayed both of these very qualities. "One is your Master, and ye are all brethren"; "Whoso would be first among you shall be servant of all; for the Son of Man came not to be ministered unto, but to minister, and to give his life a ransom for many." It is in this sense that we are to understand the commandment to love one's neighbour. How unqualified it is, becomes evident from the saying, "Love your enemies, bless them that curse you, do good to them that hate you, pray for them that despitefully use you and persecute you;[1] that ye may be sons of your Father in heaven, for he maketh his sun to rise on the evil and the good, and sendeth rain on the just and the unjust." "Blessed are the merciful"—that is the keynote of all that Jesus proclaimed, and as this merciful spirit is to extend from great things to trifles, from the inward to the outward, the saying which does not pass over even a cup of cold water (Matt. x. 42) lies side by side with that other comprehensive saying, "Forgive us our debts, as we forgive our debtors." Brotherliness is love on a footing of equality; ministering love means to *give and to forgive*, and no limit is to be recognized. Besides, *ministering love is the practical expression of love to God.*

While Jesus himself was exhibiting this love, and making it a life and a power, his disciples were learning the highest and holiest thing that can be learned in all religion, namely, to believe in the love of God. To them the Being who had made heaven and earth was "the Father of mercies and the God of all comfort"—a point on which there is no longer any dubiety in the testimony of the apostolic and post-apostolic ages. Now, for the first time, that testimony rose among men, which cannot ever be surpassed, the testimony that *God is Love*. The first great statement of the new religion, into which the fourth evangelist condensed its central principle, was based entirely and exclusively on love: "We love, because He first loved us," "God so loved the world," "A new commandment give I unto you, that ye love one another." And the greatest, strongest,

[1] The saying "Fast for them that persecute you" is also traditional (Didachê, i.).

deepest thing Paul ever wrote is the hymn commencing with the words: "Though I speak with the tongues of men and angels, but have not love, I am become sounding brass or a clanging cymbal." The new language on the lips of Christians was the language of love.

But it was more than a language, it was a thing of power and action. The Christians really considered themselves brothers and sisters, and their actions corresponded to this belief. On this point we possess two unexceptionable testimonies from pagan writers. Says Lucian of the Christians: "Their original lawgiver had taught them that they were all brethren, one of another. . . . . They become incredibly alert when anything of this kind occurs, that affects their common interests. On such occasions no expense is grudged." And Tertullian (*Apolog.*, xxxix.) observes: "It is our care for the helpless, our practice of lovingkindness, that brands us in the eyes of many of our opponents. 'Only look,' they say, 'look how they love one another!' (they themselves being given to mutual hatred). 'Look how they are prepared to die for one another!' (they themselves being readier to kill each other)."[1] Thus had this saying became a fact: "Hereby shall all men know that ye are my disciples, if ye have love one to another."

The gospel thus became a social message. The preaching which laid hold of the outer man, detaching him from the world, and uniting him to his God, was also a preaching of solidarity and brotherliness. The gospel, it has been truly said, is at bottom both individualistic and socialistic. Its tendency towards mutual association, so far from being an accidental phenomenon in its history, is inherent in its character. It spiritualizes the irresistible impulse which draws one man to another, and it raises the social connection of human beings from the sphere of a convention to that of a moral obligation. In this way it serves to heighten the worth of man, and essays to recast contemporary society, to transform the socialism which involves a conflict of interests into the socialism which rests upon the consciousness of a spiritual unity and a common goal. This

[1] Also Cæcilius (in *Minuc. Felix*, ix.): "They recognise each other by means of secret marks and signs, and love one another almost before they are acquainted."

was ever present to the mind of the great apostle to the Gentiles. In his little churches, where each person bore his neighbour's burden, Paul's spirit already saw the dawning of a new humanity, and in the epistle to the Ephesians he has voiced this feeling with a thrill of exultation. Far in the background of these churches— *i.e.*, when they were what they were meant to be—like some unsubstantial semblance, lay the division between Jew and Gentile, Greek and Barbarian, great and small, rich and poor. For a new humanity had now appeared, and the apostle viewed it as Christ's body, in which every member served the rest and each was indespensable in his own place. Looking at these churches, with all their troubles and infirmities, he anticipated, in his exalted moments of enthusiasm, what was the development of many centuries.[1]

We cannot undertake to collect from the literature of the first three centuries all the passages where love and charity are enjoined. This would lead us too far afield, although we should come across much valuable material in making such a survey. We would notice the reiteration of the summons to unconditional giving, which occurs among the sayings of Jesus, whilst on the contrary we would be astonished to find that passages enforcing the law of love are not more numerous, and that they are so frequently overshadowed by ascetic counsels; we would also take umbrage at the spirit of a number of passages in which the undisguised desire of being rewarded for benevolence stands out in bold relief.[2] Still, this craving for reward is not in every

---

[1] Warnings against unmercifulness, and censures of this temper, must have begun, of course, at quite an early period; see the epistle of James (iv.-v.) and several sections in the "Shepherd" of Hermas.

[2] All these points are illustrated throughout the literature, from the Didachê and Hermas doWnwards. For unconditional giving, see Did. I. 5 f.: παντὶ τῷ αἰτοῦντί σε δίδου καὶ μὴ ἀπαίτει · πᾶσι γὰρ θέλει δίδοσθαι ὁ πατὴρ ἐκ τῶν ἰδίων χαρισμάτων. μακάριος ὁ διδοὺς κατὰ τὴν ἐντολήν · ἀθῷος γάρ ἐστιν · οὐαὶ τῷ λαμβάνοντι · εἰ μὲν γὰρ χρείαν ἔχων λαμβάνει τις, ἀθῷος ἔσται · ὁ δὲ μὴ χρείαν ἔχων δώσει δίκην, ἵνα τί ἔλαβε καὶ εἰς τί · ἐν συνοχῇ δὲ γενόμενος ἐξετασθήσεται περὶ ὧν ἔπραξε, καὶ οὐκ ἐξελεύσεται ἐκεῖθεν μέχρις οὗ ἀποδῷ τὸν ἔσχατον κοδράντην ("Give to everyone who asks of thee, and ask not back again; for the Father desireth gifts to be given to all men from his own bounties. Blessed is he who gives according to the commandment, for he is guiltless. But woe to him who receives; for if a man receives who is in need, he is guiltless, but if he is not in need he shall give satisfaction as to Why and Wherefore he received, and

case immoral, and no conclusion can be drawn from the number of times when it occurs. The important thing is to determine what actually took place within the sphere of Christian

being confined he shall be examined upon his deeds, and shall not come out till he has paid the uttermost farthing "). The counsel of unconditional giving, which is frequently repeated, is closely bound up with the question of earthly possessions in the early church, and consequently with the question of asceticism. Theoretically, from the very outset, there was to be neither property nor wealth at all ; such things belong to the world which Christians were to renounce. Consequently, to devote one's means to other people was a proceeding which demanded a fresh point of view ; to part with one's property was the authorised and most meritorious course of action, nor did it matter, in the first instance, who was the recipient. In practical life, however, things were very different, and this was constantly the result of the very theory just mentioned, since it never gave up the voluntary principle (even the attempt at communism in Jerusalem, if there even was such an attempt, did not exclude the voluntary principle). It was by means of this principle that Christian love maintained its power. In practical life, complete renunciation of the world was achieved only by a few ; these were the saints and heroes. Other people were in precisely the same position, with the same feelings and concern, as serious, devoted Catholics at the present day ; they were actuated by motives of asceticism and of love alike. It is needless, therefore, to depict this state of matters in closer detail. The extreme standpoint is represented by Hermas, *Sim.*, I. (see above, pp. 97 f.).

A great deal has been written upon early Christian "communism," but nothing of the kind ever existed in the great Gentile church—for we need not take any account of an isolated phenomenon like the semi-pagan sect of the Carpocratians and their communism. Monastic "communism" is only called such by a misuse of the term, and, besides, it is irrelevant to our present subject. Even on the soil of Jewish Christianity, no communism flourished, for the example of the Essenes was never followed. Uhlhorn remarks truly (*op. cit.*, p. 68 ; Eng. trans., 74) that "we cannot more radically misconceive the so-called 'communism' of early Christianity than by conceiving it as an institution similar to those which existed among the Essenes and the Therapeutæ. It is far more correct to represent the state of things as an absence of all institutions whatsoever." Directions not infrequently occur (*e.g.*, *Barn.*, xix. 8 ; Tert., *Apol.*, xxxix.) which have a communistic ring, but they are not to be taken in a communistic sense. The common formula οὐκ ἐρεῖς ἴδια εἶναι ("thou shalt not say these things are thine own ") simply enjoins liberality, forbidding a man to use his means merely for his own advantage.

I have already remarked that, upon the whole, the voluntary principle was never abandoned in the matter of Christian giving and the scale of gifts. This statement, however, admits of one qualification. While the West, so far as I can judge, knew nothing as yet of the law of first-fruits and tithes throughout our epoch (for Cyprian, *de Unit.*, xxvi., is not to be understood as implying the law of tithes), in some quarters of the East the law of first-fruits was taken over at a very early period (see *Didachê*, xiii.). From the Didachê it passed, as an apostolic regulation, into all the Oriental apostolic constitutions. Origen, however, does not appear to regard it yet as a law of the church, though even he admits the legitimacy of it (*in Num. Hom.*, xi. 1 ; *in Jos. Nav. Hom.*, xvii.).

charity and active love, and this we shall endeavour to ascertain.

Three passages may be brought forward to show the general activities which were afoot.

In the official writing sent by the Roman to the Corinthian church *c.* 96 A.D., there is a description of the first-rate condition of the latter up till a short time previously (1 Clem., i., ii.), a description which furnishes the pattern of what a Christian church should be, and the approximate realization of this ideal at Corinth. "Who that had stayed with you did not approve your most virtuous and stedfast faith? Who did not admire your sober and forbearing Christian piety? Who did not proclaim the splendid style of your *hospitality*? Who did not congratulate you on your perfect and assured knowledge? For you did everything *without respect of persons*; you walked by the ordinances of God, submitting to your rulers and rendering due honour to your senior men. Young persons also you charged to have a modest and grave mind; women you instructed to discharge all their tasks with a blameless, grave, and pure conscience, and to cherish a proper affection for their husbands, teaching them further to look after their households decorously, with perfect discretion. You were all lowly in mind, free from vainglory, yielding rather than claiming submission, *more ready to give than to take*; content with the supplies provided by God and holding by them, you carefully laid up His words in your hearts, and His sufferings were ever present to your minds. Thus a profound and unsullied peace was bestowed on all, with *an insatiable craving for beneficence.* . . . . Day and night you agonized for all the brotherhood, that *by means of compassion and care* the number of God's elect might be saved. You were sincere, guileless, and void of malice among yourselves. Every sedition and every schism was an abomination to you. *You lamented the transgressions of your neighbours and judged their shortcomings to be your own. You never rued an act of kindness, but were ready for every good work.*"

Then Justin concludes the description of Christian worship in his *Apology* (c. lxvii.) thus: "Those who are well-to-do and willing, give as they choose, each as he himself purposes; the collection is then deposited with the president, who succours orphans, widows, those who are in want owing to sickness or any other cause, those who are in prison, and strangers who are on a journey."

Finally, Tertullian (*Apolog.*, xxxix.) observes : " Even if there does exist a sort of common fund, it is not made up of fees, as though we contracted for our worship.   Each of us puts in a small amount one day a month, or whenever he pleases ; but only if he pleases and if he is able, for there is no compulsion in the matter, everyone contributing of his own free will.   These monies are, as it were, the deposits of piety.   They are expended upon no banquets or drinking-bouts or thankless eating-houses, but on feeding and burying poor people, on behalf of boys and girls who have neither parents nor money, in support of old folk unable now to go about, as well as for people who are shipwrecked, or who may be in the mines or exiled in islands or in prison—so long as their distress is for the sake of God's fellowship—themselves the nurslings of their confession."

In what follows we shall discuss, so far as may be relevant to our immediate purpose—

1. Alms in general, and their connection with the cultus and officials of the church.

2. The support of teachers and officials.

3. The support of widows and orphans.

4. The support of the sick, the infirm, and the disabled.

5. The care of prisoners and people languishing in the mines.

6. The care of poor people needing burial, and of the dead in general.

7. The care of slaves.

8. The care of those visited by great calamities.

9. The churches furnishing work, and insisting upon work.

10. The care of brethren on a journey (hospitality), and of churches in poverty or any peril.

1. *Alms in general and in connection with the cultus.*—Liberality was steadily enjoined upon Christians ; indeed, the headquarters of this virtue were to lie within the household, and its proof was to be shown in daily life.   From the apostolic counsels

down to Cyprian's great work *de Opere et Eleemosynis*, there stretches one long line of injunctions, in the course of which ever-increasing stress is laid upon the importance of alms to the religious position of the donor, and upon the prospect of a future recompense. These points are already prominent in Hermas, and in 2 Clem. we are told that "almsgiving is good as a repentance from sin; fasting is better than prayer, but almsgiving is better than either" (καλὸν ἐλεεμοσύνη ὡς μετάνοια ἁμαρτίας, κρείσσων νηστεία προσευχῆς, ἐλεεμοσύνη δὲ ἀμφοτέρων). Cyprian develops alms[1] into a formal means of grace, the only one indeed which remains to a Christian after baptism; in fact he goes still further, representing alms as a spectacle which the Christian offers to God.[2]

[1] *De Op. et Eleem.*, i. : "Nam cum dominus adveniens sanasset illa quae Adam portaverat vulnera et venena serpentis antiqui curasset, legem dedit sano et pracepit ne ultra jam peccaret, ne quid peccanti gravius eveniret. Coartati eramus et in angustum innocentiae praescriptione conclusi, nec haberet quid fragilitatis humanae infirmitas atque imbecillitas faceret ; nisi *iterum* pietas divina subveniens justitiae et misericordiae operibus ostensis viam quandam tuendae salutis aperiret ut sordes postmodum, quascumque contrahimus, *eleemosynis* abluamus ("For when the Lord had at his advent cured the wounds which Adam brought, and healed the poison of the old serpent, he gave a law to the sound man and bade him sin no more, lest a worse thing should befall the sinner. We were restrained and bound by the commandment of innocence. Nor would human weakness and impotence have any resource left to it, unless the divine mercy should *once more* come to our aid, by pointing out works of righteousness and mercy, and thus opening a way to obtain salvation, so that by means of *alms* we may wash off any stains subsequently contracted ").

[2] *Op. cit.*, xxi. : "Quale munus cuius editio deo spectante celebratur ! Si in gentilium munere grande et gloriosum videtur proconsules vel imperatores habere presentes, et apparatus ac sumptus apud munerarios maior est ut possint placere maioribus—quanto inlustrior muneris et maior est gloria deum et Christum spectatores habere, quanto istic et apparatus uberior et sumptus largior exhibendus est, ubi ad spectaculum conveniunt caelorum virtutes, conveniunt angeli omnes, ubi munerario non quadriga vel consulatus petitur sed vita aeterna praestatur, nec captatur inanis et temporarius favor vulgi sed perpetuum praemium regni caelestis accipitur " ("What a gift is it which is set forth for praise in the sight of God ! If, when the Gentiles offer gifts, it seems a great and glorious thing to have proconsuls or emperors present, and if their better classes make greater preparations and display in order to please the authorities—how much more illustrious and splendid is the glory of having God and Christ as the spectators of a gift ! How much more lavish should be 'the preparation, how much more liberal the outlay, in such a case, when the powers of heaven muster to the spectacle, when all the angels gather, when the donor seeks no chariot or consulship, but life eternal is the boon ; when no fleeting and fickle popularity is craved for, but the lasting reward of the kingdom of heaven is received ! ").

It is not our business to follow up this aspect of almsgiving, or to discuss the amount of injury thus inflicted on a practice which was meant to flow from a pure love to men. The point is that a great deal, a very great deal, of alms was given away privately throughout the Christian churches.[1] As we have already seen, this was well known to the heathen world.[2]

But so far from being satisfied with private almsgiving,[3] early Christianity instituted, apparently from the first, a church fund (Tertullian's *arca*), and associated charity very closely with the cultus and officials of the church. From the ample materials at our disposal, the following outline may be sketched :—Every Sunday (cp. already I Cor. xvi. 2), or once a month (Tertullian),

[1] The pagan in Macarius Magnes (iii. 5) declares that several Christian women had become beggars by their lavish donations. "Not in the far past, but only yesterday, Christians read Matt. xix. 21 to prominent women and persuaded them to share all their possessions and goods among the poor, to reduce themselves to beggary, to ask charity, and then to sink from independence into unseemly pauperism, reducing themselves from their former good position to a woebegone condition, and being finally obliged to knock at the doors of those who were better off."

[2] With Clement of Alexandria, the motive of love to men is steadily kept in the front rank ; cp. *Paed.*, iii., and in particular the fine saying in iii. 7. 39 : καθάπερ τῶν φρεάτων ὅσα πέφυκεν βρύειν ἀπαντλούμενα εἰς τὸ ἀρχαῖον ἀναπιδύει μέτρον, οὕτως ἡ μετάδοσις, ἀγαθὴ φιλανθρωπίας ὑπάρχουσα πηγή, κοινωνοῦσα τοῖς διψῶσι ποτοῦ αὔξεται πάλιν καὶ πίμπλαται ("Even as such wells as spring up rise to their former level even after they have been drained, so that kindly spring of love to men, the bestowal of gifts, imparts its drink to the thirsty, and is again increased and replenished"). Cyprian (in *de Unit.*, xxvi.) complains of a lack of benevolence : "Largitas operationis infracta est . . . . nunc de patrimonio nec decimas damus et cum vendere jubeat dominus, emimus potius et augemus" ("Liberality in benevolence is impaired . . . . we do not now give even the tithe of our patrimony away. The Lord bids us sell, but we prefer to buy and lay up ").

[3] One recommendation very frequently made, was to stint oneself by means of fasting in order to give alms. In this way, even the poor could afford something. See Hermas, *Sim.*, v. ; Aristides, *Apol.*, xv. ("And if anyone among them is poor or needy, and they have no food to spare, they fast for two or three days, that they may meet the poor man's need of sustenance") ; *Apost. Constit.*, v. 1, etc. The habit also prevailed in pre-Christian ages. Otherwise, whenever the question is raised, how alms are to be provided, one is pointed to work ; in fact, this is almost the only point at which work is taken into consideration at all within the sphere of the religious estimate. See Eph. iv. 28 ("Let him that stole, steal no more, but rather work with his hands at honest work, *so that he may have something to give the needy*") ; and Barn. xix. 10 : διὰ χειρῶν σου ἐργάσῃ εἰς λύτρον ἁμαρτιῶν σου [the reference being to alms]. Cp. my short study (in the "Evangelisch-Sozial" Magazine, 1905, pp. 48 f.) on "The Primitive Christian Conception of the Worth of Labour."

or whenever one chose, gifts in money or kind (*stips*) were brought to the service and entrusted to the president, by whom they were laid on the Lord's table and so consecrated to God.[1] Hence the recipient obtained them from the hand of God. " 'Tis God's grace and philanthropy that support you," wrote bishop Cornelius (Eus., *H.E.*, vi. 43). The president decided who were to be the recipients, and how much was to be allocated to each, a business in which he had the advice of the deacons, who were expected to be as familiar as possible with the circumstances of each member, and who had the further task of distributing the various donations, partly at the close of worship, partly in the homes of the indigent. In addition to the regular voluntary assessments—for, as the principle of liberty of choice was strictly maintained, we cannot otherwise describe these offerings—there were also extraordinary gifts, such as the present of 200,000 sesterces brought by Marcion when, as a Christian from Asia, he entered the Roman church about the year 139.[2]

Among these methods of maintenance we must also include the love-feasts, or *agapæ*, with which the Lord's Supper was originally associated, but which persisted into a later age. The idea of the love-feast was that the poor got food and drink, since a common meal, to which each contributed as he was able, would unite rich and poor alike. Abuses naturally had to be corrected at an early stage (cp. 1 Cor. xi. 18 f.), and the whole affair (which was hardly a copy of the pagan feasts at the Thiasoi) never seems to have acquired any particular importance upon the whole.[3]

---

[1] The relation of *stips* and *oblationes* is a question which has not been cleared up yet, and need not be raised here.

[2] See on this point Book IV. Chap. I. (1). The money was returned.

[3] Cp. also Jude ver. 12 ; Tert., *Apol.*, xxxix. ; *de Ieiun.*, xvii. ; Clem., *Paed.*, ii. 1. We need not enter into the controversies over the *agapæ* ; cp. Keating's *The Agape and the Eucharist* (1901), Batiffol's *Études d'hist. et de théol. positive* (1902), pp. 279 f., and Funk on " L'Agape " (*Rev. d'hist. ecclésiastique*, t. iv. 1, 1903). In later days the feasts served to satisfy the poor at the graves of the martyrs. Constantine justified this·practice of feasts in honour of the dead against objections which were apparently current ; cp. his address to the council (xii.), where he dwells expressly on their charitable uses : τὰ συμπόσια (for the martyrs, at their graves) πρὸς ἔλεον καὶ ἀνάκτησιν τῶν δεομένων ποιούμενα καὶ πρὸς βοήθειαν τῶν ἐκπεσόντων. ἅπερ ἄν τις φορτικὰ εἶναι νομίζῃ, οὐ κατὰ τὴν θείαν καὶ

From the very first, the president appears to have had practically an absolute control over the donations;[1] but the deacons had also to handle them as executive agents. The responsibility was heavy, as was the temptation to avarice and dishonesty; hence the repeated counsel, that bishops (and deacons) were to be ἀφιλάργυροι, "no lovers of money." It was not until a later age that certain principles came to be laid down with regard to the distribution of donations as a whole, from which no divergence was permissible.

This system of organized charity in the churches worked side by side with private benevolence—as is quite evident from the letters and writings of Cyprian. But it was inevitable that the former should gradually handicap the latter, since it wore a superior lustre of religious sacredness, and therefore, people were convinced, was more acceptable to God. Yet, in special cases, private liberality was still appealed to. One splendid instance is cited by Cyprian (*Epist.* lxii.), who describes how the Carthaginian churches speedily raised 100,000 sesterces (between £850 and £1000).[2]

In 250 A.D. the Roman church had to support about 100 clergy and 1500 poor persons. Taking the yearly cost of supporting one man at £7, 10s. (which was approximately the upkeep of one slave), we get an annual sum of £12,000. If, however (like Uhlhorn, *op. cit.*, p. 153; Eng. trans., p. 159), we allow sixty Roman bushels of wheat per head a year at 7s. 6d., we get a total of about £4300. It is safe to say, then, that about 250 A.D. the Roman church had to expend from half a million to a million sesterces (*i.e.*, from £5000 to £10,000) by way of relief.

The demands made upon the church funds were heavy, as will appear in the course of the following classification and discussion.

μακαρίαν διδασκαλίαν φρονεῖ ("These feasts are held for the purpose of helping and restoring the needy, and in aid of the outcast. Anyone who thinks them burdensome, does not judge them by the divine and blessed rule of life").

[1] On the traces of an exception to this rule in the *Apostolic Constitutions*, see *Texte u. Untersuch.*, ii. 5, pp. 12 f., 58.

[2] For special collections ordered by the bishop, see Tertull., *de Jejun.* xiii., and Clem., *Hom.*, iii. 71: ὁπότε χρεία τινὸς πόρου πρὸς τὸ ἀναγκαῖον γένοιτο, ἅμα οἱ πάντες συμβάλλεσθε ("Whenever any funds are needed, club together, all of you").

2. *The support of teachers and officials.* — The Pauline principle[1] that the rule about a "labourer being worthy of his hire" applied also to missionaries and teachers, was observed without break or hesitation throughout the Christian churches. The conclusion drawn was that teachers could lay claim to a plain livelihood, and that this claim must always have precedence of any other demand upon the funds. When a church had chosen permanent officials for itself, these also assumed the right of being allowed to claim a livelihood, but only so far as their official duties made inroads upon their civil occupations. Here, too, the bishop had discretionary power; he could

---

[1] Paul even describes the principle as a direction of Jesus himself; see I Cor. ix. 14: ὁ κύριος διέταξεν τοῖς τὸ εὐαγγέλιον καταγγέλλουσιν ἐκ τοῦ εὐαγγελίου ζῆν.

[2] The circumstances are not quite clear; still, enough is visible to corroborate what has been said above. Church officials were not, in the first instance, obliged to abandon their civil calling, and so far as that provided them with a livelihood they had no claim upon the church's funds. But in the course of time it became more and more difficult, in the larger churches, to combine civil employment with ecclesiastical office. There is one very instructive account in the Clementine Homilies (iii. 71) which indicates that some people were sceptical upon the duty of supporting the bishop and clergy. The author writes: Ζακχαῖος [the bishop] μόνος ὑμῖν ὅλος ἑαυτὸν ἀσχολεῖν ἀποδεδωκώς, κοιλίαν ἔχων καὶ ἑαυτῷ μὴ εὐσχολῶν, πῶς δύναται τὴν ἀναγκαίαν πορίζειν τροφήν; οὐχὶ δὲ εὔλογόν ἐστιν πάντας ὑμᾶς τοῦ ζῆν αὐτοῦ πρόνοιαν ποιεῖν, οὐκ ἀναμένοντας αὐτὸν ὑμᾶς αἰτεῖν, τοῦτο γὰρ προσαιτοῦντός ἐστιν· μᾶλλον δὲ τεθνήξεται λιμῷ ἢ τοῦτο ποιεῖν ὑποσταίη· πῶς δὴ καὶ ὑμεῖς οὐ δίκην ὑφέξετε, μὴ λογισάμενοι ὅτι "ἄξιός ἐστιν ὁ ἐργάτης τοῦ μισθοῦ αὐτοῦ"; καί μὴ λεγέτω τις· Οὐκοῦν ὁ δωρεὰν παρασχεθεὶς λόγος πωλεῖται; μὴ γένοιτο· εἰ τις γὰρ ἔχων πόθεν ζῆν λάβοι, οὗτος πωλεῖ τὸν λόγον—εἰ δὲ μὴ ἔχων τοῦ ζῆν χάριν λαμβάνει τροφήν, ὡς καὶ ὁ κύριος ἔλαβεν ἔν τε δείπνοις καὶ φίλοις, οὐδὲν ἔχων ὁ εἰς αὖθις πάντα ἔχων, οὐχ ἁμαρτάνει. ἀκολούθως οὖν τιμᾶτε [by an honorarium] πρεσβυτέρους κατηχητάς, διακόνους χρησίμους, χήρας εὖ βεβιω-κυίας, ὀρφανοὺς ὡς ἐκκλησίας τέκνα ("Zacchæus alone has devoted himself wholly to your interests; he needs food, and yet has no time to provide for himself; how then is he to get the requisitive provisions for a livelihood? Is it not reasonable that you should all provide for his support? Do not wait for him to ask you— asking is a beggar's rôle, and he would rather die than stoop to that. Shall not you also incur punishment for failing to consider that 'the labourer is worthy of his hire'? Let no one say, 'Then is the word which was given freely, to be sold?' God forbid. If any man has means and yet accepts any help, *he* sells the Word. But there is no sin in a man without means accepting support in order to live—as the Lord also accepted gifts at supper and among his friends, he who had nothing though he was the Lord of all things. Honour, then, in appropriate fashion the elder catechists, useful deacons, respectable widows, and orphans as children of the church"). A fixed monthly salary, such as that assigned by the church of Theodotus to her bishop Natalis, was felt to be obnoxious. (Cp. the primitive story in Eus., *H.E.*, v. 28).

appropriate and hand over to the presbyters and deacons whatever he thought suitable and fair, but he was bound to provide
the teachers (*i.e.*, missionaries and prophets) with enough to live
on day by day.   Obviously, this could not fail to give rise to
abuses.   From the Didachê and Lucian we learn that such
abuses did arise, and that privileges were misemployed.[1]

3. *The support of widows and orphans.*[2]—Wherever the early
Christian records mention poor persons who require support,
widows and orphans are invariably in the foreground.   This
corresponds, on the one hand, with the special distress of their
position in the ancient world, and on the other hand with the
ethical injunctions which had passed over into Christianity from
Judaism.   As it was, widows and orphans formed the poor κατ'
ἐξοχήν.   The church had them always with her.   "The Roman
church," wrote bishop Cornelius, "supports 1500 widows and
poor persons" (Eus., *H.E.*, vi. 43).   Only widows, we note, are
mentioned side by side with the general category of recipients
of relief.   Inside the churches, widows had a special title of
honour, viz., "God's altar,"[3] and even Lucian the pagan was
aware that Christians attended first and foremost to orphans
and to widows (*Peregrin.*, xii.).   The true worship, James had
already urged (i. 27), is to visit widows and orphans in their
distress, and Hermas (*Mand.*, viii. 10) opens his catalogue of
virtues with the words: χήραις ὑπηρετεῖν, ὀρφανοὺς καὶ
ὑστερημένους ἐπισκέπτεσθαι ("to serve widows and visit the
forlorn and orphans").[4]   It is beyond question that the early

---

[1] Details will be found below, in the chapter [Book III. Chap. I.] on the
mission-agents.

[2] In the liturgy, widows and orphans are also placed immediately after the
servants of the church.

[3] See Polycarp, *ad Phil.*, iv. ; Tert., *ad Uxor.*, i. 7 ; pseudo-Ignat., *Tars.*, 9 ;
and *Apos. Constit.*, ii. 26 (where the term is applied also to orphans ; cp. iv. 3).
I shall not discuss the institution of Widows, already visible in the first epistle to
Timothy, which also tended to promote their interests.   The special attention
devoted to Widows was also meant to check the undesirable step of re-marriage.

[4] In *Vis.*, II. 4. 3, it is remarkable also how prominent are widows and orphans.
See Aristides, *Apol.*, xv. : "They do not avert their attention from widows, and
they deliver orphans from anyone who oppresses them."   Instances of orphans
being adopted into private families are not wanting.   Origen, for example, was
adopted by a Christian woman (Eus., *H.E.*, vi. 2) ; cp. *Acta Perpet. et Felic.*,
xv. ; *Apost. Const.*, iv. 1.   Lactantius (*Instit.*, vi. 12) adduces yet another

church made an important contribution to the amelioration of social conditions among the lower classes, by her support of widows.[1] We need not dwell on the fact, illustrated as early as the epistles to Timothy, that abuses crept into this department. Such abuses are constantly liable to occur wherever human beings are relieved, in whole or in part, of the duty of caring for themselves.[2]

4. *The support of the sick, the infirm, the poor, and the disabled.*—Mention has already been made of the cure of sick people; but where a cure was impossible the church was bound to support the patient by consolation (for they were remembered in the prayers of the church from the very first; cp. 1 Clem. lix. 4), visitation,[3] and charitable gifts (usually in kind). Next to the sick came those in trouble (ἐν θλίψει) and people sick in soul (κάμνοντες τῇ ψυχῇ, Herm., *Mand.*, viii. 10) as a rule,

special argument for the duty of supporting widows and orphans : "God commands them to be cared for, in order that no one may be hindered from going to his death for righteousness' sake on the plea of regard for his dear children, but that he may promptly and boldly encounter death, knowing that his beloved ones are left in God's care and will never lack protection."

[1] See, further, Herm., *Simil.* i., v. 3, ix. 26-27, x. 4 ; Polyc., *Epist.* vi. 1 ; Barn., xx. 2 ; Ignat., *Smyrn.*, vi. (*a propos* of heretics : "They care not for love, or for the Widow, or for the orphan, or for the afflicted, or for the prisoner or ransomed, or for the hungry or thirsty"—περὶ ἀγάπης οὐ μέλει αὐτοῖς, οὐ περὶ χήρας, οὐ περὶ ὀρφανοῦ, οὐ περὶ θλιβομένου, οὐ περὶ δεδεμένου ἢ λελυμένου, ἢ περὶ πεινῶντος ἢ διψῶντος), *ad Polyc.*, iv. ; Justin's *Apol.*, I. lxvii. ; Clem., *Ep. ad Jacob.* 8 (τοῖς μὲν ὀρφανοῖς ποιοῦντες τὰ γονέων, ταῖς δὲ χήραις τὰ ἀνδρῶν, "acting the part of parents to orphans and of husbands to widows") ; Tert., *ad Uxor.*, i. 7-8 ; *Apost. Constit.* (Bks. III., IV.) ; and pseudo-Clem., *de Virgin.*, i. 12 ("pulchrum et utile est visitare pupillos et viduas, imprimis pauperes qui multos habent liberos"). For the indignation roused by the heartlessness of many pagan ladies, who were abandoned to luxury, read the caustic remark of Clement (*Paedag.*, iii. 4. 30) : παιδίον δὲ οὐδὲ προσίενται ὀρφανὸν αἱ τοὺς ψιττακοὺς καὶ τοὺς χαραδριοὺς ἐκτρέφουσαι ("They bring up parrots and curlews, but will not take in the orphan child").

[2] Scandalmongering, avarice, drunkenness, and arrogance had all to be dealt with in the case of widows who were being maintained by the church. It even happened that some widows put out to usury the funds they had thus received (cp. *Didasc. Apost.*, xv. ; *Texte u. Unters.*, xxv. 2. pp. 78, 274 f.) But there were also highly gifted widows. In fact (cp. *Apost. Constit.*), it was considered that true widows who persevered in prayer received revelations.

[3] See Tert., *ad Uxor.*, ii. 4, on the difficult position of a Christian woman whose husband was a pagan : "Who would be willing to let his wife go through street after street to other men's houses, and indeed to the poorest cottages, in order to visit the brethren ?"

then the helpless and disabled (Tertullian singles out expressly *senes domestici*), finally the poor in general. To quote passages would be superfluous, for the duty is repeatedly inculcated; besides, concrete examples are fairly plentiful, although our records only mention such cases incidentally and quite accidentally.[1] Deacons, "widows," and deaconesses (though the last-named were apparently confined to the East) were set apart for this work. It is said of deacons in the *Apostolic Constitutions* (see *Texte u. Unters.*, ii. 5. 8 f.): "They are to be doers of good works, exercising a general supervision day and night, neither scorning the poor nor respecting the person of the rich; they must ascertain who are in distress and not exclude them from a share in the church funds, compelling also the well-to-do to put money aside for good works." Of "widows" it is remarked, in the same passage, that they should render aid to women afflicted by disease, and the trait of φιλόπτωχος (a lover of the poor) is expected among the other qualities of a bishop.[2] In an old legend dating from the Decian persecution, there is a story of the deacon Laurentius in Rome, who, when desired to hand over the treasures of the church, indicated the poor as its only treasures. This was audacious, but it was not incorrect; from the very first, any possessions of the church were steadily characterized as poor-funds, and this remained true during the early centuries.[3] The excellence of the church's charitable system, the deep impression made by it, and the numbers that it won over to the faith, find their best voucher in the action of Julian the Apostate, who attempted an exact reproduction of it in that artificial creation

---

[1] Naturally, neither private nor, for the matter of that, church charity was to step in where a family was able to support some helpless member; but it is evident, from the sharp remonstrance in 1 Tim. v. 8, that there were attempts made to evade this duty ("If anyone does not provide for his own people, and especially for his own household, he has renounced the faith and is worse than an infidel").

[2] *Apost. Constit.*, in *Texte u. Unters.*, ii. 5. 8 f. In the *Vita Polycarpi* (Pionius) traits of this bishop are described which remind us of St Francis. On the female diaconate, see Uhlhorn (*op. cit.*, 159-171 ; Eng. trans., 165 f.).

[3] It was not possible, of course, to relieve all distress, and Tertullian (*de Idolat.*, xxiii.) mentions Christians who had to borrow money from pagans. This does not seem to have been quite a rare occurrence.

of his, the pagan State-church, in order to deprive the Christians of this very weapon. The imitation, of course, had no success.[1]

Julian attests not only the excellence of the church's system of relief, but its extension to non-Christians. He wrote to Arsacius (Sozom. v. 16): " These godless Galileans feed not only their own poor but ours; our poor lack our care." This testimony is all the more weighty inasmuch as our Christian sources yield no satisfactory data on this point. Cp., however, under (8), and Paul's injunction in Gal. vi. 10: "Let us do good *to all*, especially to those who belong to the household of the faith." "True charity," says Tertullian (*Apol.*, xlii.), " disburses more money in the streets than your religion in the temples." The church-funds were indeed for the use of the brethren alone, but private beneficence did not restrict itself to the household of faith. In a great calamity, as we learn from reliable evidence (see below), Christians did extend their aid to non-Christians, even exciting the admiration of the latter.

5. *Care for prisoners and for people languishing in the mines.*— The third point in the catalogue of virtues given by Hermas is: ἐξ ἀναγκῶν λυτροῦσθαι τοὺς δούλους τοῦ θεοῦ (" Redeem the servants of God from their bonds "). Prisoners might be innocent for various reasons, but above all there were people incarcerated for their faith or imprisoned for debt, and both classes had to be reached by charity. In the first instance, they had to be visited and consoled, and their plight alleviated by gifts of food.[2] Visiting prisoners was the regular work of

---

[1] We may certainly conclude that a register was kept of those who had to be maintained. This very fact, however, was a moral support to poor people, for it made them sure that they were not being neglected.

[2] Heb. x. 34, τοῖς δεσμίοις συνεπαθήσατε; Clem. Rom., lix. 4 (in the church's prayer), λύτρωσαι τοὺς δεσμίους ἡμῶν ; Ignat., *Smyrn.*, vi. (the duty of caring περὶ δεδεμένου ἢ λελυμένου) ; Clem., *Ep. ad Jacob.*, 9 (τοῖς ἐν φυλακαῖς ἐπιφαινόμενοι ὡς δύνασθε βοηθεῖτε) ; Arist., *Apol.*, xv. ("And if they hear that anyone of their number is imprisoned or in distress for the sake of their Christ's name, they all render aid in his necessity, and if he can be redeemed, they set him free"). Of the young Origen we are told (Eus., *H.E.*, vi. 3) that "not only was he at the side of the holy martyrs in their imprisonment, and until their final condemnation, but when they were led to death he boldly accompanied them into danger." Cp. Tert., *ad Mart.*, i. f. (both the church and charitable individuals supplied prisoners with food), *Acta Pass. Perpet.*, iii. ; Petri Alex., *Ep.* c. 2 (Lagarde's *Reliq. jur. eccles.*, p. 64, 14 f.), c. 11 (*ibid.*, p. 70, 1 f.), c. 12 (*ibid.*, p. 70, 20 f.).

the deacons, who had thus to run frequent risks; but ordinary Christians were also expected to discharge this duty. If the prisoners had been arrested for their faith, and if they were rather distinguished teachers, there was no hardship in obeying the command; in fact, many moved heaven and earth to get access to prisoners,[1] since it was considered that there was something sanctifying about intercourse with a confessor. In order to gain admission they would even go the length of bribing the gaolers,[2] and thus manage to smuggle in decent meals and crave a blessing from the saints. The records of the martyrs are full of such tales. Even Lucian knew of the practice, and pointed out the improprieties to which it gave rise. Christian records, particularly those of a later date,[3] corroborate this, and as early as the Montanist controversy it was a burning question whether or no any prominent confessor was really an impostor, if, after being imprisoned for misdemeanours, he made out as if he had been imprisoned on account of the Christian faith. Such abuses, however, were inevitable, and upon the whole their number was not large. The keepers, secretly impressed by the behaviour of the Christians, often consented of their own accord to let them communicate with their friends (*Acta Perpet.*, ix.: " Pudens miles optio, praepositus carceris, nos magnificare coepit, intelligens magnam virtutem esse in nobis; qui multos ad nos admittebat,

---

[1] Thekla, in the *Acta Theclæ*, is one instance, and there are many others; *e.g.*, in Tertull., *ad Uxor.*, ii. 4.

[2] As in Thekla's case; see also Lucian's *Peregr.*, xii., and the *Epist. Lugd.*, in Euseb., *H.E.*, v. 1. 61.

[3] Cp. Lucian, *Peregr.*, xii., xiii., xvi. ("costly meals"). Tertullian, at the close of his life, when he was filled with bitter hatred towards the Catholic church, wrote thus in *de Jejun.*, xii.: "Plainly it is your way to furnish restaurants for dubious martyrs in the gaols, lest they miss their wonted fare and so grow weary of their life, taking umbrage at the novel discipline of abstinence! One of your recent martyrs (no Christian he!) was by no means reduced to this hard régime. For after you had stuffed him during a considerable period, availing yourselves of the facilities of free custody, and after he had disported himself in all sorts of baths (as if these were better than the bath of baptism), and in all resorts of pleasure in high life (as if these were the secret retreats of the church), and with all the seductive pursuits of such a life (preferable, forsooth, to life eternal)—and all this, I believe, just in order to prevent any craving for death—then on the last day, the day of his trial, you gave him in broad daylight some medicated wine (in order to stupefy him against the torture)!"

ut et nos et illi invicem refrigeraremus " (" Pudens, a military
subordinate in charge of the prison, began to have a high
opinion of us, since he recognized there was some great power
of God in us. He let many people in to see us, that we and
they might refresh one another ").

If any Christian brethren were sentenced to the mines, they
were still looked after, even there.[1] Their names were carefully
noted; attempts were made to keep in touch with them ; efforts
were concocted to procure their release,[2] and brethren were sent
to ease their lot, to edify and to encourage them.[3] The care
shown by Christians for prisoners was so notorious that (according to Eusebius, *H.E.*, v. 8) Licinius, the last emperor
before Constantine who persecuted the Christians, passed a law
to the effect that " no one was to show kindness to sufferers in
prison by supplying them with food, and that no one was to
show mercy to those who were starving in prison." " In addition to this," Eusebius proceeds to relate, " a penalty was
attached, to the effect that those who showed compassion were
to share the fate of the objects of their charity, and that those
who were humane to the unfortunate were to be flung into
bonds and imprisonment and endure the same suffering as the
others." This law, which was directly aimed at Christians, shows,
more clearly than anything else could do, the care lavished by
Christians upon their captive brethren, although much may have
crept in in connection with this which the State could not tolerate.

---

[1] Cp. Dionysius of Corinth (in Eus., *H.E.*, iv. 23), who pays a brilliant testimony to the Roman church in this connection.

[2] Cp. the story told by Hippolytus (*Philos.*, ix. 12) of the Roman bishop Victor,
who kept a list of all Christians sentenced to the mines in Sardinia, and actually
procured their liberty through the intercession of Marcia to the Emperor Commodus.

[3] Some extremely beautiful examples of this occur in the treatise of Eusebius
upon the Palestinian martyrs during the Diocletian persecution. The Christians
of Egypt went to the most remote mines, even to Cilicia, to encourage and edify
their brethren who were condemned to hard labour in these places. In the mines
at Phæno a regular church was organized. Cp. also *Apost. Constit.*, v. I: εἴ τις
Χριστιανὸς διὰ τὸ ὄνομα τοῦ χριστοῦ . . . . κατακριθῇ ὑπὸ ἀσεβῶν εἰς . . . .
μέταλλον, μὴ παρίδητε αὐτόν, ἀλλ᾽ ἐκ τοῦ κόπου καὶ τοῦ ἱδρῶτος ὑμῶν πέμψατε
αὐτῷ εἰς διατροφὴν αὐτοῦ καὶ εἰς μισθοδοσίαν τῶν στρατιωτῶν ("If any Christian
is condemned for Christ's sake . . . . to the mines by the ungodly, do not overlook him, but from the proceeds of your toil and sweat send him something to
support himself and to reward the soldiers ").

But they did more than try to merely alleviate the lot of prisoners. Their aim was to get them ransomed. Instances of this cannot have been altogether rare, but unfortunately it is difficult for us to form any judgment on this matter, since in a number of instancces, when a ransom is spoken of, we cannot be sure whether prisoners or slaves are meant. Ransoming captives, at any rate, was regarded as a work which was specially noble and well-pleasing to God, but it never appears to have been undertaken by any church. To the last it remained a monopoly of private generosity, and along this line individuals displayed a spirit of real heroism.[1]

6. *Care of poor people requiring burial, and of the dead in general.*—We may begin here with the words of Julian, in his letter to Arsacius (*Soz.*, v. 15): "This godlessness (*i.e.*, Christianity) is mainly furthered by its philanthropy towards strangers and its careful attention to the bestowal of the dead." Tertullian declares (see p. 153) that the burial of poor brethren was performed at the expense of the common fund, and Aristides (*Apol.*, xv.) corroborates this, although with him it takes the form of private charity. "Whenever," says Aristides,

---

[1] Herm., *Sim.*, I. : ἀντὶ ἀγρῶν ἀγοράζετε ψυχὰς θλιβομένας, καθά τις δυνατός ἐστιν ("Instead of fields buy souls in trouble, as each of you is able"); *Sim.*, X. v. 2 f. ; *Clem. Rom.*, lv. 2: ἐπιστάμεθα πολλοὺς ἐν ἡμῖν παραδεδωκότας ἑαυτοὺς εἰς δεσμά, ὅπως ἑτέρους λυτρώσονται · πολλοὶ ἑαυτοὺς ἐξέδωκαν εἰς δουλείαν, καὶ λαβόντες τὰς τιμὰς αὐτῶν ἑτέρους ἐψώμισαν ("We know that many of our own number have given themselves up to be captives, in order to ransom others ; many have sold themselves to slavery, and with the price of their own bodies they have fed others"); *Apost. Constit.*, iv. 9: τὰ ἐκ τοῦ δικαίου κόπου ἀθροιζόμενα χρήματα διατάσσετε διακονοῦντες εἰς ἀγορασμοὺς τῶν ἁγίων ῥυόμενοι δούλους καὶ αἰχμαλώ-τους, δεσμίους, ἐπηρεαζομένους, ἥκοντας ἐκ καταδίκης, κ.τ.λ. ("All monies accruing from honest labour do ye appoint and apportion to the redeeming of the saints, ransoming thereby slaves and captives, prisoners, people who are sore abused or condemned by tyrants," etc.), cp. v. 1-2. In *Idolol.*, xxiii., Tertullian refers to release from imprisonment for debt, or to the efforts made by charitable brethren to prevent such imprisonment. When the Numidian robbers carried off the local Christians, the Carthaginian church soon gathered the sum of 100,000 sesterces as ransom-money, and declared it was ready to give still ampler aid (Cypr., *Ep.* lxii.). When the Goths captured the Christians in Cappadocia about the year 255, the Roman church sent contributions in aid of their ransom (Basil., *Ep. ad Dam.* lxx.). See below (10) for both of these cases. The ransoming of captives continued even in later days to be reckoned a work of special merit. Le Blant has published a number of Gallic inscriptions dating from the fourth and fifth centuries, in which the dead person is commended because "he ransomed prisoners."

"one of their poor passes from the world, one of them looks after him and sees to his burial, according to his means." We know the great importance attached to an honourable burial in those days, and the pain felt at the prospect of having to forego this privilege. In this respect the Christian church was meeting a sentiment which even its opponents felt to be a human duty. Christians, no doubt, were expected to feel themselves superior to any earthly ignominy, but even they felt it was a ghastly thing not to be buried decently. The deacons were specially charged with the task of seeing that everyone was properly interred (*Const. Ap.*, iii. 7),[1] and in certain cases they did not restrict themselves to the limits of the brotherhood. "We cannot bear," says Lactantius (*Instit.*, vi. 12), "that the image and workmanship of God should be exposed as a prey to wild beasts and birds, but we restore it to the earth from which it was taken,[2] and do this office of relatives even to the body of a

---

[1] A certain degree of luxury was even allowed to Christians ; cp. Tertull., *Apol.*, xlii. : "If the Arabians complain of us [for giving them no custom], let the Sabeans be sure that the richer and more expensive of their wares are used as largely in burying Christians as in fumigating the gods." Another element in a proper burial was that a person should lie among his companions in the faith. Anyone who buried his people beside non-Christians needlessly, incurred severe blame. Yet about the middle of the third century we find a Spanish bishop burying his children among the heathen ; cp. Cyprian, *Ep.* lxvii. 6 : "Martialis [episcopus] praeter gentiliam turpia et lutulenta conviva in collegio diu frequentata filios in eodem collegio exterarum gentium more apud profana sepulcra deposuit et alieni-genis consepelivit" ("Martialis himself frequented for long the shameful and filthy banquets of the heathen in their college, and placed his sons in the same college, after the custom of foreign nations, amid profane sepulchres, burying them along with strangers"). Christian graves have been found now and then in Jewish cemeteries.

[2] Christians were therefore opposed to cremation, and tried to gather even the fragments of their brethren who had been martyred in the flames. The belief of the "simplices" about the resurrection of the body wavered a little in view of the burning of the body, but the theologians always silenced any doubts, though even they held that burning was a piece of wickedness. Cp. *Epist. Lugd.* (Eus., *H.E.*, v. 1, towards the close ; Tert., *de Anima*, li. : "Nec ignibus funerandum aiunt (*i.e.*, some pagans), parcentes superfluo animae (*i.e.*, because particles of the soul still clung to the body). Alia est autem ratio pietatis istius (*i.e.*, of Christianity), non reliquiis animae adulatrix, sed crudelitatis etiam corporis nomine aversatrix, quod et ipsum homo non mereatur poenali exitu impendi" ; Tert., *de Resurr.*, i : "Ego magis ridebo vulgus, tum quoque, cum ipsos defunctos atrocissime exurit, quos postmodum gulisossime nutrit. . . . . O pietatem de crudelitate ludentem !" ("I have greater derision for the crowd, particularly when it inhumanely burns its

person whom we do not know, since in their room humanity must step in."[1] At this point also we must include the care of the dead after burial. These were still regarded in part as destitute and fit to be supported. Oblations were presented in their name and for the welfare of their souls, which served as actual intercessions on their behalf. This primitive custom was undoubtedly of immense significance to the living; it comforted many an anxious relative, and added greatly to the attractive power of Christianity.[2]

7. *Care for slaves.*—It is a mistake to suppose that any " slave question" occupied the early church. The primitive Christians looked on slavery with neither a more friendly nor a more hostile eye than they did upon the State and legal ties.[3] They never dreamt of working for the abolition of the State, nor did it ever occur to them to abolish slavery for humane or other reasons— not even amongst themselves. The New Testament epistles already assume that Christian masters have slaves (not merely that pagan masters have Christian slaves), and they give no directions for any change in this relationship. On the contrary, slaves are earnestly admonished to be faithful and obedient.[4]

dead, only to pamper them afterwards with luxurious indulgence. . . . . Out upon the piety which mocks its victims with cruelty !"). The reasons which seem to have led Christians from the first to repudiate cremation have not been preserved. We can only surmise what they were.

[1] The question of the relation between the churches and the collegia tenuiorum (collegia funeraticia) may be left aside. Besides, during the past decade it has passed more and more out of notice. No real light has been thrown by such guilds upon the position of the churches, however convincing may be the inference that the rights obtained by these collegia may have been for a time available to Christians as well. Cp. Neumann, *Röm. Staat und Kirche*, i. 102 f.

[2] Tertullian is our first witness for this custom. It did not spring up independently of pagan influence, though it may have at least *one* root within the Christian cultus itself. Tertullian attacked the common pagan feasts of the dead and the custom of bringing food to the graves ; but this rooted itself as early as the third century, and was never dislodged.

[3] The Didachê (iv. 11) even bids slaves obey their (Christian) masters ὡς τύπῳ θεοῦ (" as a type of God ").

[4] The passages in Paul's epistles are well known ; see also 1 Peter. In his letter to Philemon, Paul neither expects nor asks the release of the slave Onesimus. The only possible sense of 1 Cor. vii. 20 f. (ἕκαστος ἐν τῇ κλήσει ᾗ ἐκλήθη, ἐν ταύτῃ μενέτω· δοῦλος ἐκλήθης; μή σοι μελέτω· ἀλλ᾽ εἰ καὶ δύνασαι ἐλεύθερος γενέσθαι, μᾶλλον χρῆσαι) is that the apostle counsels slaves not even to avail themselves of the chance of freedom. Any alteration of their position would

Still, it would not be true to assert that primitive Christianity was indifferent to slaves and their condition. On the contrary, the church did turn her attention to them, and effected some change in their condition. This follows from such considerations as these :—

(*a*) Converted slaves, male or female, were regarded in the full sense of the term as brothers and sisters from the standpoint of religion. Compared to this, their position in the world was reckoned a matter of indifference.[1]

(*b*) They shared the rights of church members to the fullest extent. Slaves could even become clergymen, and in fact bishops.[2]

(*c*) As personalities (in the moral sense) they were to be just as highly esteemed as freemen. The sex of female slaves had to be respected, nor was their modesty to be outraged.

divert their minds to the things of earth—such seems to be the writer's meaning. It is far from certain whether we may infer from this passage that Christian slaves begged from Christian masters the chance of freedom more often than their pagan fellows. Christian slave-owners often appear in the literature of the second and third centuries. Cp. Athenag., *Suppl.*, xxxv. ; *Acta Perpetuæ* ; etc.

[1] Paul is followed on this point by others ; *e.g.*, Tatian, *Orat.*, xi. ; Tertull., *de Corona*, xiii. ; and Lactantius, *Instit.*, v. 16, where, in reply to the opponents who cry out, "You too have masters and slaves ! Where then is your so-called equality ?" the answer is given, "Alia causa nulla est cur nobis invicem fratrum nomen impertiamus nisi quia pares esse nos credimus. Nam cum omnia humana non corpore sed spiritu metiamur, tametsi corporum sit diversa condicio, nobis tamen servi non sunt, sed eos et habemus et dicimus spiritu fratres, religione con-servos" ("Our sole reason for giving one another the name of brother is because we believe we are equals. For since all human objects are measured by us after the spirit and not after the body, although there is a diversity of condition among human bodies, yet slaves are not slaves to us; we deem and term them brothers after the spirit, and fellow-servants in religion"). De Rossi (*Boll. di Arch. Christ.*, 1866, p. 24) remarks on the fact that the title "slave" never occurs in the sepulchral inscriptions of Christianity. Whether this is accidental or intentional, is a question which I must leave undecided. On the duty of Christian masters to instruct their slaves in Christianity, cp. Arist., *Apol.*, xv. : "Slaves, male and female, are instructed so that they become Christians, on account of the love felt for them by their masters; and when this takes place, they call them brethren without any distinction whatsoever."

[2] The Roman presbyter or bishop, Pius, the brother of Hermas, must have belonged to the class of slaves. Callistus, the Roman bishop, was originally a slave. Cp. the eightieth canon of Elvira : "Prohibendum ut liberti, quorum patroni in saeculo fuerint, ad clerum non promoveantur" ("It is forbidden to hinder freemen from being advanced to the rank of clergy, whose owners may be still alive").

The same virtues were expected from slaves as from freemen, and consequently their virtues earned the same honour.[1]

(d) Masters and mistresses were strictly charged to treat all their slaves humanely,[2] but, on the other hand, to remember that

[1] Ample material on this point is to be found in the Acts of the Martyrs. Reference may be made in especial to Blandina, the Lyons martyr, and to Felicitas in the Acts of Perpetua. Not a few slaves rank among "the holy martyrs" of the church. Unless it had been set down, who would imagine that Blandina was a slave—Blandina, who is held in high honour by the church, and whose character has such noble traits? In Euseb., *Mart. Pal.* (*Texte u. Unters.*, xxiv. 2. p. 78), we read : " Porphyry passed for a slave of Pamphilus, but in love to God and in amazing confession of his faith he was a brother, nay more, a beloved son, to Pamphilus, and was like his teacher in all things."—Cp., however, the penitential ordinance appointed for those astute Christian masters who had forced their Christian slaves to offer sacrifice during the Diocletian persecution (canons 6 and 7 of Peter Alex., in Routh's *Reliq. Sacr.*, iv. 29 f.). The masters are to do penance for three years καὶ ὡς ὑποκρινάμενοι καὶ ὡς καταναγκάσαντες τοὺς ὁμοδούλους θῦσαι, ἅτε δὴ παρακούσαντες τοῦ ἀποστόλου τὰ αὐτὰ θέλοντος ποιεῖν τοὺς δεσπότας τοῖς δούλοις, ἀνιέντας τὴν ἀπειλήν, εἰδότας, φησίν, ὅτι καὶ ὑμῶν καὶ αὐτῶν ὁ κύριός ἐστιν ἐν οὐρανοῖς, καὶ προσωπολήψια παρ᾽ αὐτῷ οὐκ ἔστιν (Eph. vi. 9 ; then follows Col. iii. 11) . . . . σκοπεῖν ὀφείλουσιν ὃ κατειργάσαντο θελήσαντες τὴν ψυχὴν ἑαυτῶν σῶσαι, οἱ τοὺς συνδούλους ἡμῶν ἑλκύσαντες ἐπὶ εἰδωλολατρείαν δυναμένους καὶ αὐτοὺς ἐκφυγεῖν, εἰ τὸ δίκαιον καὶ τὴν ἰσότητα ἦσαν αὐτοῖς παρασχόντες, ὡς πάλιν ὁ ἀπόστολος λέγει (Col. iv. 1) ("for having played the hypocrite and for having compelled their fellow-servants to sacrifice—in disobedience to the apostle, who enjoins masters and servants to do the same things, and to forbear threatening, knowing, saith he, that you and they have a Lord in heaven, with whom there is no respect of persons. . . . . They ought to consider this compulsion of theirs, due to their desire to save their own lives, by which they drag our fellow-servants into idolatry, when they could themselves avoid it— that is, if masters treated them justly and equitably, as the apostle once more observes "). Only a single year's penance was imposed on slaves thus seduced. Tertullian, on the contrary (*de Idol.*, xvii.), shows that the same courage and loyalty was expected from Christian slaves and freedmen as from the highly born. The former were not to hand the wine or join in any formula when they attended their pagan lords at sacrifice. Otherwise they were guilty of idolatry. For attempts on the part of pagan masters to seduce their slaves from the faith, cp. *Acta Pionii*, ix., etc.

[2] A beautiful instance of the esteem and position enjoyed by a Christian female slave in a Christian home, is afforded by Augustine in his description of the old domestic ("famula decrepita") belonging to his maternal grandfather's house, who had nursed his grandfather as a child ("sicut dorso grandiuscularum puellarum parvuli portari solent"=as little children are often carried on the backs of older girls) ; *i.e.*, she was active as early as the year 300 A.D. "On account of her age and her excellent character, she was highly respected by the heads of that Christian home. Hence the charge of her master's daughters [*i.e.*, including Monica] was given her, and she fulfilled her duty thoroughly [better than the mother did]. When necessary, she was strict in restraining the girls with a holy firmness, and in teaching them with a sober judgment " ("Propter senectam ac

Christian slaves were their own brethren.[1] Christian slaves, for their part, were told not to disdain their Christian masters, *i.e.*, they were not to regard themselves as their equals.[2]

(*e*) To set a slave free was looked upon, probably from the very beginning, as a praiseworthy action;[3] otherwise, no Christian slave could have had any claim to be emancipated. Although the primitive church did not admit any such claim on their part, least of all any claim of this kind on the funds of the church, there were cases in which slaves had their ransom paid for out of such funds.[4] The church never condemned the rights of masters over slaves as sinful; it simply saw in them a natural relationship. In this sphere the source of reform lay, not in Christianity, but in general considerations derived from moral philosophy and in economic necessities.

From one of the canons of the Council of Elvira (*c.* 300 A.D.), as well as from other minor sources, we learn that even in the Christian church, during the third century in particular, cases unfortunately did occur in which slaves were treated with revolting harshness and barbarity.[5] In general, one has to

---

mores optimas in domo christiana satis a dominis honorabatur ; unde etiam curam filiarum dominicarum commissam diligenter gerebat, et erat in eis coercendis, cum opus esset, sancta severitate vehemens atque in docendis sobria prudentia," *Confess.*, ix. 8. 17). The basis of Augustine's own piety rested on this slave !

[1] A long series of testimonies, from the Lyons epistle onwards, witnesses to the fact that Christian masters had heathen slaves. Denunciations of their Christian masters by such slaves, and calumnies against Christian worship, cannot have been altogether uncommon.

[2] As early as 1 Tim. vi. 1 f. It proves that Christianity must have been in many cases "misunderstood" by Christian slaves.

[3] Authentic illustrations of this are not available, of course.

[4] From the epistle of Ignatius to Polycarp (iv.) two inferences may be drawn : (1) that slaves were ransomed with money taken from the church collections, and (2) that no *claim* to this favour was admitted. Δούλους καὶ δούλας μὴ ὑπερηφάνει · ἀλλὰ μηδὲ αὐτοὶ φυσιούσθωσαν [Christian slaves could easily lose their feelings of deference towards Christian owners], ἀλλ' εἰς δόξαν θεοῦ πλέον δουλευέτωσαν, ἵνα κρείττονος ἐλευθερίας ἀπὸ θεοῦ τύχωσιν · μὴ ἐράτωσαν ἀπὸ τοῦ κοινοῦ ἐλευθεροῦσθαι, ἵνα μὴ δοῦλοι εὑρεθῶσιν ἐπιθυμίας ("Despise not male or female slaves. Yet let not these again be puffed up, but let them be all the better servants to the glory of God, that they may obtain a better freedom from God. Let them not crave to be freed at the public cost, lest they be found to be slaves of lust ").

[5] Canon v. : "Si qua femina furore zeli accensa flagris verberaverit ancillam suam, ita ut intra tertium diem animam cum cruciatu effundat," etc. (" If any

recollect that even as early as the second century a diminution
of the great slave-establishment can be detected—a diminution
which, on economic grounds, continued during the third century.
The liberation of slaves was frequently a necessity; it must not
be regarded, as a rule, in the light of an act prompted by compassion or brotherly feeling.

8. *Care for people visited by great calamities.*—As early as
Hebrews x. 32 f. a church is commended for having nobly stood
the test of a great persecution and calamity, thanks to sympathy
and solicitous care. From that time onward, we frequently
come across counsels to Christian brethren to show themselves
specially active and devoted in any emergencies of distress; not
counsels merely, but also actual proofs that they bore fruit. We
shall not, at present, go into cases in which churches lent aid to
sister churches, even at a considerable distance; these fall to be
noticed under section 10. But some examples referring to
calamities within a church itself may be set down at this stage
of our discussion.

When the plague raged in Alexandria (about 259 A.D.),
bishop Dionysius wrote (Euseb., *H.E.*, vii. 22): "The most of
our brethren did not spare themselves, so great was their
brotherly affection. They held fast to each other, visited the
sick without fear, ministered to them assiduously, and served
them for the sake of Christ. Right gladly did they perish with
them. . . . Indeed many did die, after caring for the sick and
giving health to others, transplanting the death of others, as it
were, into themselves. In this way the noblest of our brethren

mistress, in a fit of passion, scourges her handmaid, so that the latter expires
within three days," etc.). Canon xli. also treats of masters and slaves. We do
not require to discuss the dispensation given by Callistus, bishop of Rome, to
matrons for entering into sexual relations with slaves, as the object of this
dispensation was to meet the case of high-born ladies who were bent on marriage,
and not to admit that slaves had equal rights. Hippol. *Philos.*, ix. 12 : καὶ
γυναιξὶν ἐπέτρεψεν, εἰ ἄνανδροι εἶεν καὶ ἡλικίᾳ γε ἐκκαίοιντο ἀναξίᾳ ἢ ἑαυτῶν ἀξίαν
μὴ βούλοιντο καθαιρεῖν διὰ τὸ νομίμως γαμηθῆναι, ἔχειν ἕνα ὃν ἂν αἱρήσωνται,
σύγκοιτον, εἴτε οἰκέτην, εἴτε ἐλεύθερον, καὶ τοῦτον κρίνειν ἀντὶ ἀνδρὸς μὴ νόμῳ
γεγαμημένην ("He even permitted women, if unmarried and inflamed with a
passion unworthy of their age, or unwilling to forfeit their position for the sake
of a legal marriage, to have any one they liked as a bedfellow, either slave or
free, and to reckon him their husband although he was not legally married to
them").

died, including some presbyters and deacons and people of the highest reputation. . . . . Quite the reverse was it with the heathen. They abandoned those who began to sicken, fled from their dearest friends, threw out the sick when half dead into the streets, and let the dead lie unburied."

A similar tale is related by Cyprian of the plague at Carthage. He exclaims to the pagan Demetrianus (x.) : " Pestem et luem criminaris, cum peste ipsa et lue vel detecta sint vel aucta crimina singulorum, dum nec infirmis exhibetur misericordia et defunctis avaritia inhiat ac rapina. Idem ad pietatis obsequium timidi,[1] ad impia lucra temerarii, fugientes morientium funera et adpetentes spolia mortuorum (" You blame plague and disease, when plague and disease either swell or disclose the crimes of individuals, no mercy being shown to the weak, and avarice and rapine gaping greedily for the dead. The same people are sluggish in the discharge of the duties of affection, who rashly seek impious gains ; they shun the deathbeds of the dying, but make for the spoils of the dead "). Cyprian's advice is seen in his treatise *de Mortalitate*. His conduct, and the way he inspired other Christians by his example, are narrated by his biographer Pontianus (*Vita*, ix. f.) : " Aggregatam primo in loco plebem de misericordiae bonis instruit. Docet divinae lectionis exemplis . . . . tunc deinde subiungit non esse mirabile, si nostros tantum debito caritatis obsequio foveremus ; cum enim perfectum posse fieri, qui plus aliquid publicano vel ethnico fecerit, qui malum bono vincens et divinae clementiae instar exercens inimicos quoque dilexerit. . . . . Quid Christiana plebs faceret, cui de fide nomen est ? distributa sunt ergo continuo pro qualitate hominum atque ordinum ministeria [organized charity, then]. Multi qui paupertatis beneficio sumptus exbibere non poterant, plus sumptibus exhibebant, compensantes proprio labore mercedem divitiis omnibus cariorem . . . . fiebat itaque exuberantium operum largitate, quod bonum est ad omnes, non ad solos domesticos fidei (" The people being assembled together, he first of all urges on them the benefits of

---

[1] Cp. Cyprian, *per Pont.*, ix. : "Jacebant interim tota civitate vicatim non jam corpora, sed cadavera plurimorum" ("Meanwhile all over the city lay, not bodies now, but the carcases of many ").

mercy. By means of examples drawn from the sacred lessons, he teaches them. . . . . Then he proceeds to add that there is nothing remarkable in cherishing merely our own people with the due attentions of love, but that one might become perfect who should do something more than heathen men or publicans, one who, overcoming evil with good, and practising a merciful kindness like to that of God, should love his enemies as well. . . . . What should a Christian people do, a people whose very name was derived from faith ? The contributions are always distributed then according to the degree of the men and of their respective ranks. Many who, on the score of poverty, could not make any show of wealth, showed far more than wealth, as they made up by personal labour an offering dearer than all the riches in the world. Thus the good done was done to all men, and not merely to the household of faith, so richly did the good works overflow ").

We hear exactly the same story of practical sympathy and self-denying love displayed by Christians even to outsiders, in the great plague which occurred during the reign of Maximinus Daza (Eus., *H.E.*, ix. 8) : " Then did they show themselves to the heathen in the clearest light. For the Christians were the only people who amid such terrible ills showed their fellow-feeling and humanity by their actions. Day by day some would busy themselves with attending to the dead and burying them (for there were numbers to whom no one else paid any heed); *others gathered in one spot all who were afflicted by hunger throughout the whole city, and gave bread to them all.* When this became known, people glorified the Christians' God, and, convinced by the very facts, confessed the Christians alone were truly pious and religious."

It may be inferred with certainty, as Eusebius himself avows, that cases of this kind made a deep impression upon those who were not Christians, and that they gave a powerful impetus to the propaganda.

9. *The churches furnishing work and insisting upon work.*— Christianity at the outset spread chiefly among people who had to work hard. The new religion did not teach its votaries " the dignity of labour," or " the noble pleasure invariably afforded

by work." What it inculcated was just the *duty* of work.[1] "If any will not work, neither let him eat" (2 Thess. iii. 10). Over and again it was enunciated that the duty of providing for others was conditioned by their incapacity for work. The brethren had soon to face the fact that some of their number were falling into restless and lazy habits, as well as the sadder fact that these very people were selfishly trying to trade upon the charity of their neighbours. This was so notorious that even in the brief compass of the Didachê there is a note of precautions which are to be taken to checkmate such attempts, while in Lucian's description of the Christians he singles out, as one of their characteristic traits, a readiness to let cunning impostors take advantage of their brotherly love.[2]

Christianity cannot be charged at any rate with the desire of promoting mendicancy or with underestimating the duty of work.[3] Even the charge of being "infructuosi in negotiis" (of no use in practical affairs) was repudiated by Tertullian. "How so?" he asks. "How can that be when such people dwell beside you, sharing your way of life, your dress, your habits, and the same needs of life? We are no Brahmins or Indian gymnosophists, dwelling in woods and exiled from life. . . . . We stay beside you in this world, making use of the forum, the provision-market, the bath, the booth, the workshop, the inn, the weekly market, and all other places of commerce. We sail with you, fight at your side, till the soil with you, and traffic with you; we likewise join our technical skill to that of others, and make our works public property for your use" (*Apol.* xlii.).[4] Even clerics were not exempted from making a

---

[1] At the same time there was a quiet undercurrent of feeling expressed by the maxim that absolute devotion to religion was a higher plane of life—"The heavenly Father who feeds the ravens and clothes the lilies will provide for us." Apostles and prophets (with the heroes of asceticism, of course, from the very outset) did not require to work. The idea was that their activity in preaching demanded their entire life and occupied all their time.

[2] The pseudo-Clementine *de Virgin.*, i. 11, contains a sharp warning against the "otiosi," or lazy folk, who chatter about religion instead of attending to their business.

[3] Cp. 2 Thess. iii. 6: παραγγέλλομεν ὑμῖν ἐν ὀνόματι τοῦ κυρίου I. X. στέλλεσθαι ὑμᾶς ἀπὸ παντὸς ἀδελφοῦ ἀτάκτως περιπατοῦντος, cp. ver. 12.

[4] Tertullian at this point is suppressing his personal views; he speaks from the standpoint of the majority of Christians. In reality, as we see from the treatise

livelihood,[1] and admirable sayings on the need of labour occur
in Clement of Alexandria as well as in other writers.   We have
already observed (pp. 155 f.) that one incentive to work was
found in the consideration that money could thus be gained for
the purpose of supporting other people, and this idea was by no
means thrown out at random.   Its frequent repetition, from the
epistle to the Ephesians onwards, shows that people recognized
in it a powerful motive for the industrious life.   It was also
declared in simple and stirring language that the labourer was
worthy of his hire, and a fearful judgment was prophesied for
those who defrauded workmen of their wages (see especially Jas.
v. 4 f.).   It is indeed surprising that work was spoken of in such
a sensible way, and that the duty of work was inculcated so
earnestly, in a society which was so liable to fanaticism and
indolence.

But we have not yet alluded to what was the really noticeable
feature in this connection.   We have already come across several
passages which would lead us to infer that, together with the
recognition that every Christian brother had the right to a bare
provision for livelihood, the early Christian church also admitted
its obligation to secure this minimum either by furnishing him
with work or else by maintaining him.   Thus we read in the
pseudo-Clementine homilies (cp. *Clem.*, viii.): "For those able
to work, provide work; and to those incapable of work, be
charitable."[2]   Cyprian also (*Ep.* ii.) assumes that if the church

de Idololatria, he was convinced that there was hardly a single occupation or
business in which any Christian could engage without soiling his conscience with
idolatry.

[1] The earliest restrictions on this point occur in the canons of the Synod of
Elvira (canon xix.).   They are very guarded.   " Episcopi, presbyteres et diacones
de locis suis [this is the one point of the prohibition] negotiandi causa non
discedant . . . . sane ad victum sibi conquirendum aut filium, aut libertum, aut
mercenarium, aut amicum, aut quemlibet mittant ; et si voluerint negotiari, intra
provinciam negotientur " ("Let no bishop or presbyter or deacon leave his place
for the purpose of trading . . . . he can, of course, send his son, or his freedman,
or his hired servant, or a friend, or anyone else, to procure provisions ; but if he
wishes to transact business, he must confine himself to his own sphere ").

[2] Παρέχοντες μετὰ πάσης εὐφροσύνης τὰς τροφάς . . . . τοῖς ἀτέχνοις διὰ τῶν
ἐπιτηδευμάτων ἐννούμενοι τὰς προφάσεις τῆς ἀναγκαίας τροφῆς· τεχνίτῃ ἔργον,
ἀδρανεῖ ἔλεος ("Providing supplies with all kindliness . . . . furnishing those
who have no occupation with employment, and thus with the necessary means of
livelihood.   To the artificer, work ; to the incapable, alms ").

forbids some teacher of dramatic art to practise his profession, it must look after him, or, in the event of his being unable to do anything else, provide him with the necessaries of life.[1] We were not aware, however, if this was really felt to be a duty by the church at large, till the discovery of the Didachê. This threw quite a fresh light on the situation. In the Didaché (xii.) it is ordained that no brother who is able to work is to be maintained by any church for more than two or three days. The church accordingly had the right of getting rid of such brethren. But the reverse side of this right was a duty. " If any brother has a trade, let him follow that trade and earn the bread he eats. If he has no trade, exercise your discretion in *arranging for him to live among you as a Christian, but not in idleness*. If he will not do this (*i.e.*, engage in the work with which you furnish him), he is trafficking with Christ ($\chi\rho\iota\sigma\tau\acute{\epsilon}\mu\pi\rho\rho\sigma$). Beware of men like that." It is beyond question, therefore, that a Christian brother could demand work from the church, and that the church had to furnish him with work. What bound the members together, then, was not merely the duty of supporting one another—that was simply the *ultima ratio*; it was the fact that they formed a guild of workers, in the sense that the churches had to provide work for a brother whenever he required it. This fact seems to me of great importance, from the social standpoint. The churches were also labour unions. The case attested by Cyprian proves that there is far more here than a merely rhetorical maxim. The Church did prove in this way a refuge for people in distress who were prepared to work. Its attractive power was consequently intensified, and from the economic standpoint we must attach very high value to a union which provided work for those who were able to work, and at the same time kept hunger from those who were unfit for any labour.

---

[1] " Si paenurian talis et necessitatem paupertatis obtendit, potest inter ceteros qui ecclesiae alimentis sustinentur huius quoque necessitatis adiuvari, si tamen contentus sit frugalioribus et innocentibus cibis nec putet salario se esse redimendum, ut a peccatis cesset " (" Should such a person allege penury and the necessities of poverty, his wants may also be met among those of the other people who are maintained by the church's aliment—provided always that he is satisfied with plain and frugal fare. Nor is he to imagine he must be redeemed by means of an allowance of money, in order to cease from sins ").

10. *Care for brethren on a journey (hospitality) and for churches in poverty or peril.*[1]—The diaconate went outside the circle of the individual church when it deliberately extended its labours to include the relief of *strangers, i.e.,* in the first instance of Christian brethren on their travels. In our oldest account of Christian worship on Sunday (Justin, *Apol.,* I. lxvii.; see above, p. 153), strangers on their travels are included in the list of those who receive support from the church-collections. This form of charity was thus considered part of the church's business, instead of merely being left to the goodwill of individuals; though people had recourse in many ways to the private method, while the virtue of hospitality was repeatedly inculcated on the faithful.[2] In the first epistle of Clement to the Corinthian

[1] I have based this section on a study of my own which appeared in the *Monatsschrift f. Diakonie und innere Mission* (Dec. 1879, Jan. 1880); but, as the relations of the individual church with Christendom in general fall to be noticed in this section, I have thought it appropriate to treat the subject in greater detail. The ideal background of all this enterprise and activity may be seen in Tertullian's remark (*de Præscr.,* xx.) : " Omnes ecclesiae una ; probant unitatem ecclesiarum communicatio pacis et appellatio fraternitatis et contesseratio hospitalitatis " (" All churches are one, and the unity of the churches is shown by their peaceful intercommunion, the title of brethren, and the bond of hospitality ").

[2] Rom. xii. 13, "Communicating to the necessities of the saints, given to hospitality"; 1 Pet. iv. 9, "Using hospitality one towards another without murmuring"; Heb. vi. 10, xiii. 2, "Forget not to show love to strangers, for thereby some have entertained angels unawares." Individuals are frequently commended by Paul to the hospitality of the church; *e.g.,* Rom. xvi. 1 f., " Receive her in the Lord, *as becometh the saints.*" See also 3 John 5–8. In the "Shepherd" of Hermas (*Mand.,* viii. 10) hospitality is distinctly mentioned in the catalogue of virtues, with this remarkable comment : ἐν γὰρ τῇ φιλοξενίᾳ εὑρίσκεται ἀγαθοποίησίς ποτε ("for benevolence from time to time is found in hospitality"), while in *Sim.,* viii. 10. 3, praise is assigned to those Christians who εἰς τοὺς οἴκους αὐτῶν ἡδέως ὑπεδέξαντο τοὺς δούλους τοῦ θεοῦ (" gladly welcomed God's servants into their houses"). Aristides, in his *Apology* (xv.), says that if Christians " see any stranger, they take him under their roof and rejoice over him as over a very brother " (ξένον ἐὰν ἴδωσιν, ὑπὸ στέγην εἰσάγουσι καὶ χαίρουσιν ἐπ' αὐτῷ ὡς ἐπὶ ἀδελφῷ ἀληθινῷ). The exercise of hospitality by private individuals towards Christian brethren is assumed by Tertullian to be a duty which no one dare evade; for, in writing to his wife (*ad Uxor.,* ii. 4), he warns her against marrying a heathen, should he (Tertullian) predecease her, on the ground that no Christian brother would get a spiritual reception in an alien household. But hospitality was inculcated especially upon officials of the church, such as elders (bishops) and deacons, who practised this virtue in the name of the church at large; cp 1 Tim. iii. 2, Tit. i. 8 (1 Tim. v. 10). In Hermas (*Sim.,* ix. 27. 2) hospitable bishops form a special class among the saints, since " they gladly received God's servants into their houses at all times, and without hypocrisy." In

church, it is particularly noted, among the distinguishing virtues of the church, that anyone who had stayed there praised their splendid sense of hospitality.[1] But during the early centuries of Christianity it was the Roman church more than any other which was distinguished by the generosity with which it practised this virtue. In one document from the reign of Marcus Aurelius, a letter of Dionysius the bishop of Corinth to the Roman church, it is acknowledged that the latter has maintained its *primitive* custom of showing kindness to *foreign* brethren. " Your worthy bishop Soter has not merely kept up this practice, but even extended it, by aiding the saints with rich supplies, which he sends from time to time, and also by addressing blessed words of comfort to brethren coming up to Rome, like a loving father to his children " (Eus., *H.E.*, iv. 23. 10). We shall return to this later on ; meanwhile it may be

the Didachê a comparatively large amount of space is taken up with directions regarding the care of travellers, and Cyprian's interest in strangers is attested by his seventh letter, written to his clergy at Carthage from his place of retreat during the Decian persecution. He. writes : " I beg you will attend carefully to the widows, and sick people, and all the poor. You may also pay the expenses of any strangers who may be in need, out of my own portion which I left with my fellow-presbyter Rogatianus. In case it should be all used, I hereby forward by the hands of Naricus the acolyte another sum of money, so that the sufferers may be dealt with more promptly and liberally" ("Viduarum et infirmorum et omnium pauperum curam peto diligenter habeatis, sed et peregrinis si qui indigentes fuerint sumptus suggeratis de quantitate mea propria quam apud Rogatianum compresbyterum nostrum dimisi. Quae quantitas ne forte iam erogata sit, misi eidem per Naricum acoluthum aliam portionem, ut largius et promptius circa laborantes fiat operatio "). Cp. also *Apost. Const.*, iii. 3 (P. 98, 9 f., ed. Lagarde), and *Ep. Clem. ad Jacob.* (P. 9, 10 f., ed. Lagarde): τοὺς ξένους μετὰ πάσης προθυμίας εἰς τοὺς ἑαυτῶν οἴκους λαμβάνετε ("Receive strangers into your homes with all readiness"). In his satire on the death of Peregrinus (xvi.), Lucian describes how his hero, on becoming a Christian, was amply provided for on his travels : " Peregrinus thus started out for the second time, and betook himself to travelling ; he had an ample allowance from the Christians, who constituted themselves his bodyguard, so that he lived in clover. Thus for some time he provided for himself in this fashion." From the pseudo-Clementine epistle *de Virginitate* one also learns to appreciate the appeal and exercise of hospitality. Finally, Julian (*Ep. ad Arsac.*) emphasises ἡ περὶ τοὺς ξένους φιλανθρωπία among Christians, and wishes that his own party would imitate it (see above, p. 162).

[1] 1 Clem. i. 2: τίς γὰρ παρεπιδημήσας πρὸς ὑμᾶς . . . . τὸ μεγαλοπρεπὲς τῆς φιλοξενίας ὑμῶν ἦθος οὐκ ἐκήρυξεν ("What person who has sojourned among you . . . . has not proclaimed your splendid, hospitable disposition?") ; cp. above, p. 152.

pointed out, in this connection, that the Roman church owed
its rapid rise to supremacy in Western Christendom, not simply
to its geographical position within the capital of the empire, or
to the fact of its having been the seat of apostolic activity
throughout the West, but also to the fact that it recognized
the special obligation of caring for Christians in general, which
fell to it as the church of the imperial capital. A living interest
in the collective church of Christ throbbed with peculiar intensity
throughout the Roman church, as we shall see, from the very
outset, and the practice of hospitality was one of its manifestations. At a time when Christianity was still a homeless religion, the occasional travels of the brethren were frequently the
means of bringing churches together which otherwise would
have had no common tie; while in an age when Christian
captives were being dragged off, and banished to distant spots
throughout the empire, and when brethren in distress sought
shelter and solace, the practical proof of hospitality must have
been specially telling. As early as the second century one
bishop of Asia Minor even wrote a book upon this virtue.[1]
So highly was it prized within the churches that it was put next
to faith as the genuine proof of faith. "For the sake of his
faith and hospitality, Abraham had a son given him in his old
age." "For his hospitality and piety was Lot saved from
Sodom." "For the sake of her faith and hospitality was Rahab
saved." Such are the examples of which, in these very words,
the Roman church reminds her sister at Corinth.[2] Nor was this
exercise of hospitality merely an aid in passing. The obligation
of work imposed by the Christian church has been already
mentioned (cp. pp. 173 f.); if any visitors wished to settle down,
they had to take up some work, as is plain from the very provision made for such cases. Along roads running through
waste country hospices were erected. The earliest case of this
occurs in the *Acta Archelai*[3] (fourth century).

It was easy to take advantage of a spirit so obliging and

---

[1] Melito of Sardes, according to Eusebius (*H.E.*, iv. 26. 2).

[2] I Clem. x. 7, xi. I, xii. I.

[3] Ch. iv. : " Si quando veluti peregrinans ad hospitium pervenisset, quae quidem
diversoria hospitalissimus Marcellus instruxerat."

unsparing (*e.g.*, the case of Proteus Peregrinus, and especially the churches' sad experience of so-called prophets and teachers). Heretics could creep in, and so could loafers or impostors. We note, accordingly, that definite precautions were taken against these at quite an early period. The new arrival is to be tested to see whether or not he is a Christian (cp. 2 and 3 John; Did., xii.). In the case of an itinerant prophet, his words are to be compared with his actions. No brother is to remain idle in any place for more than two days, or three at the very most; after that, he must either leave or labour (Did., xii.). Later on, any brother on a journey was required to bring with him a passport from his church at home. Things must have come to a sad pass when (as the Didachê informs us) it was decreed that any visitor must be adjudged a false prophet without further ado, if during an ecstasy he ordered a meal and then partook of it, or if in an ecstasy he asked for money. Many a traveller, however, who desired to settle down, did not come with empty hands; such persons did not ask, they gave. Thus we know (see above) that when Marcion came from Pontus and joined the Roman church, he contributed 200,000 sesterces to its funds (Tert., *de Præscr.*, xxx.). Still, such cases were the exception; as a rule, visitors were in need of assistance.

Care lavished on brethren on a journey blossomed naturally into a sympathy and care for any distant churches in poverty or peril. The keen interest shown in a guest could not cease when he left the threshold of one's house or passed beyond the city gates. And more than this, the guest occupied the position of a representative to any church at which he arrived; he was a messenger to them from some distant circle of brethren who were probably entire strangers and were yet related to them. His account of the distress and suffering of his own church, or of its growth and spiritual gifts, was no foreign news. The primitive churches were sensible that their faith and calling bound them closely together in this world; they felt, as the apostle enjoined, that "if one member suffer, all the members suffer with it, while if one member is honoured, all the members rejoice with it" (1 Cor. xii. 26). And there is no doubt whatever that the consciousness of this was most vigorous and vital in the very ages during which no external bond as yet united the various churches, the latter standing side by side in almost entire independence of each other. These were the ages when the primitive article of the common symbol, " I believe in one holy church," was really nothing more than an *article of faith.* And of course the effect of the inward ties was all the stronger when people were participating in a common faith which found expression ere long in a brief and vigorous confession, or practising the same love and patience and Christian discipline, or turning their hopes in common to that glorious consummation of Christ's kingdom of which they had each received the earnest and the pledge. These common possessions stimulated brotherly love; they made strangers friends, and brought the distant near. " By secret signs and marks they manage to recognize one another, loving each other almost before they are acquainted"; such is the description of Christians given by the pagan Cæcilius (*Min. Felix,* ix. 3). Changes afterwards took place; but this vital sense of belonging to *one brotherhood* never wholly disappeared.

In the great prayers of thanksgiving and supplication offered every Sabbath by the churches, there was a fixed place assigned to intercession for the whole of Christendom throughout the earth. Before very long this kindled the consciousness that every individual member belonged to the holy unity of Christendom, just as it also kept them mindful of the services which they owed to the general body. In the epistles and documents of primitive Christianity, wherever the church-prayers emerge their œcumenical character becomes clear and conspicuous.[1] Special means of intercourse were provided by epistles, circular letters, collections of epistles, the transmission of acts or of official records, or by travellers and special messengers. When matters of importance were at stake, the bishops themselves went forth to settle controversial questions or to arrange a common basis of agreement. It is not our business in these pages to describe all this varied intercourse. We shall confine ourselves to the task of gathering and explaining those passages in which one church comes to the aid of another in any case of need.

[1] Cp. 1 Clem. lix. 2 f. with my notes *ad loc.* Polyc., *Phil.*, xii. 2 f.

Poverty, sickness, persecution, and suffering of all kinds formed one class of troubles which demanded constant help on the part of churches that were better off; while, in a different direction, assistance was required in those internal crises of doctrine and of conduct which might threaten a church and in fact endanger its very existence. Along both of these lines the brotherly love of the churches had to prove its reality.

The first case of one church supporting another occurs at the very beginning of the apostolic age. In Acts xi. 27 f. we read that Agabus in Antioch foretold a famine. On the news of this, the young church at Antioch made a collection on behalf of the poor brethren in Judæa, and despatched the proceeds to them by the hands of Barnabas and Paul.[1] It was a Gentile Christian church which was the first, so far as we are aware, to help a sister church in her distress. Shortly after this, the brotherly love felt by young Christian communities drawn from pagans in Asia and Europe is reported to have approved itself on a still wider scale. Even after the famine had passed, the mother church at Jerusalem continued poor. Why, we do not know. An explanation has been sought in the early attempt by which that church is said to have introduced a voluntary community of goods; it was the failure of this attempt, we are to believe, that left the local church impoverished. This is merely a vague conjecture. Nevertheless, the poverty at Jerusalem remains a fact. At the critical conference in Jerusalem, when the three pillar-apostles definitely recognized Paul's mission to the Gentiles, the latter pledged himself to remember the poor saints at Jerusalem in distant lands; and the epistles to the Galatians, the Corinthians, and the Romans, show how widely and faithfully the apostle discharged this obligation. His position in this matter was by no means easy. He had made himself responsible for a collection whose value depended entirely on the *voluntary* devotion of the churches which he founded. But he was sure he could rely on them, and in this he did not deceive himself. Paul's churches made his concerns

---

[1] No doubt, the account (in Acts) of the Antiochene donation and of the journey of Barnabas and Paul to Jerusalem does lie open to critical suspicion (see Overbeck, *ad loc.*).

their own, and money for the brethren far away at Jerusalem was collected in Galatia, Macedonia, and Achaia.   Even when the apostle had to endure the prospect of all his work in Corinth being endangered by a severe local crisis, he did not fail to remember the business of the collection along with more important matters.   The local arrangements for it had almost come to a standstill by the time he wrote, and the aim of his vigorous, affectionate, and graceful words of counsel to the church is to revive the zeal which had been allowed to cool amid their party quarrels (2 Cor. viii. 9).   Not long afterwards he is able to tell the Romans that " those of Macedonia and Achaia *freely chose* to make a certain contribution for the poor saints at Jerusalem.   They have done it willingly, and indeed it was a debt.   For if the Gentiles have been made partakers of their spiritual things, they owe it to them also to minister to them in secular things" (Rom. xv. 26 f.).   In this collection Paul saw a real duty of charity which rested on the Gentile churches, and one has only to realize the circumstances under which the money was gathered in order to understand the meaning it possessed for the donors themselves.   As yet, there was no coming or going between the Gentile and the Judean Christians, though the former had to admit that the latter were one with themselves as brethren and as members of a single church.   The churches in Asia and Europe were imitators of the churches of God in Judæa (1 Thess. ii. 14), yet they had no fellowship in worship, life, or customs.   This collection formed, therefore, the one visible expression of that brotherly unity which otherwise was rooted merely in their common faith.   This was what lent it a significance of its own.   For a considerable period this devotion of the Gentile Christians to their distressed brethren in Jerusalem was the sole manifestation, even in visible shape, of the consciousness that all Christians shared an inner fellowship.   We do not know how long the contributions were kept up.   The great catastrophes which occurred in Palestine after 65 A.D. had a disastrous effect at any rate upon the relations between Gentile Christians and their brethren in Jerusalem and Palestine.[1]—Forty years later the age of perse-

---

[1] The meaning of Heb. vi. 10 is uncertain. I may observe at this point that

cutions burst upon the churches, though no general persecution occurred until the middle of the third century. When some churches were in distress, their possessions seized[1] and their existence imperilled, the others could not feel happy in their own undisturbed position. Succour of their persecuted brethren seemed to them a duty, and it was a duty from which they did not shrink. Justin (*loc. cit.*) tells us that the maintenance of imprisoned Christians was one of the regular objects to which the church collections were devoted, a piece of information which is corroborated and enlarged by the statement of Tertullian, that those who languished in the mines or were exiled to desert islands or lay in prison all received monies from the church.[2] Neither statement explains if it was only members of the particular church in question who were thus supported. This, however, is inherently improbable, and there are express statements to the contrary, including one from a pagan source. Dionysius of Corinth (Eus., *H.E.*, iv. 23. 10) writes thus to the Roman Christians about the year 170 : "From the very first you have had this practice of aiding *all* the brethren in various ways and of sending contributions to *many* churches in *every* city, thus in one case relieving the poverty of the needy, or in another providing for brethren in the mines. By these gifts, which you have sent from the very first, you Romans keep up the hereditary customs of the Romans, a practice your bishop Soter has not merely maintained but even extended." A hundred years later Dionysius, the bishop of Alexandria, in writing to Stephen the bishop of Rome, has occasion to mention the churches in Syria and Arabia. Whereupon he remarks in passing, "To them you send help regularly, and you have just

more than three centuries later Jerome employed this Pauline collection as an argument to enforce the duty of all Christians throughout the Roman empire to support the monastic settlements at the sacred sites of Jerusalem and Bethlehem. In his treatise against Vigilantius (xiii.), who had opposed the squandering of money to maintain monks in Judæa, Jerome argues from 2 Cor. viii., etc., without more ado, as a scriptural warrant for such collections.

[1] Even by the time of Domitian, Christian churches were liable to poverty, owing to the authorities seizing their goods ; cp. Heb. x. 34 (if the epistle belongs to this period), and Eus., *H.E.*, iii. 17.

[2] Tert., *Apol.*, xxxix. : "Si qui in metallis et si qui in insulis, vel in custodiis, dumtaxat ex causa dei sectae, alumni suae confessionis fiunt" (cp. p. 153).

written them another letter " (Eus., *H.E.*, vii. 5. 2).   Basil the
Great informs us that under bishop Dionysius (259-269 A.D.)
the Roman church sent money to Cappadocia to purchase the
freedom of some Christian captives from the barbarians, an act
of kindness which was still remembered with gratitude in
Cappadocia at the close of the fourth century.[1]   Thus Corinth,
Syria, Arabia, and Cappadocia, all of them churches in the
East, unite in testifying to the praise of the church at Rome;
and we can understand, from the language of Dionysius of
Corinth, how Ignatius could describe that church as the
προκαθημένη τῆς ἀγάπης, "the leader of love."[2]   Nor were
other churches and their bishops behindhand in the matter.
Similar stories are told of the church at Carthage and its
bishop Cyprian.   From a number of letters written shortly
before his execution, it is quite clear that Cyprian sent money
to provide for the Christians who then lay captive in Numidia
(*Ep.* lxxvi.–lxxix.), and elsewhere in his correspondence there is
similar evidence of his care for stranger Christians and foreign
churches.   The most memorable of his letters, in this respect,
is that addressed to the bishops of Numidia in 253 A.D.   The
latter had informed him that wild hordes of robbers had invaded
the country and carried off many Christians of both sexes into
captivity.   Whereupon Cyprian instituted a collection on their
behalf and forwarded the proceeds to the bishops along with
the following letter (*Ep.* lxii.).   It is the most elaborate and
important document from the first three centuries bearing upon
the support extended to one church by another, and for that
reason we may find space for it at this point.

"Cyprian to Januarius, Maximus, Proculus, Victor, Modianus,
Nemesianus, Nampulus, and Honoratus, the brethren: greeting.

"With sore anguish of soul and many a tear have I read the
letter which in your loving solicitude you addressed to me, dear
brethren, with regard to the imprisonment of our brothers and
sisters.   Who would not feel anguish over such misfortunes?

---

[1] Basil, *Ep. ad Damasum Papam* (lxx).

[2] Ign., *ad Rom.*, procemium.   Cp. Zahn, *ad loc.* : "In caritatis operibus semper
primum locum sibi. vindicavit ecclesia Romana" ("The Roman church always
justified her primacy in works of charity ").

Who would not make his brother's grief his own? For, says the apostle Paul: Should one member suffer, all the others suffer along with it; and should one member rejoice, the others rejoice with it also. And in another place he says: Who is weak, and I am not weak? We must therefore consider the present imprisonment of our brethren as our imprisonment, reckoning the grief of those in peril as our grief. We form a single body in our union, and we ought to be stirred and strengthened by religious duty as well as by love to redeem our members the brethren.

" For as the apostle Paul once more declares: Know ye not that ye are God's temple and that the Holy Spirit dwelleth in you? Though love failed to stir us to succour the brethren, we must in this case consider that it is temples of God who are imprisoned, nor dare we by our procrastination and neglect of fellow-feeling allow temples of God to remain imprisoned for any length of time, but must put forth all our energies, and with all speed manage by mutual service to deserve the grace of Christ our Lord, our Judge, our God. For since the apostle Paul says: So many of you as are baptized into Christ have put on Christ, we must see Christ in our imprisoned brethren, redeeming from the peril of imprisonment him who redeemed us from the peril of death. He who took us from the jaws of the devil, who bought us with his blood upon the cross, who now abides and dwells in us, he is now to be redeemed by us for a sum of money from the hands of the barbarians. . . . . Will not the feeling of humanity and the sense of united love incline each father among you to look upon those prisoners as his sons, every husband to feel, with anguish for the marital tie, that his wife languishes in that imprisonment?" Then, after an account of the special dangers incurred by the consecrated " virgins "—" our church, having weighed and sorrowfully examined all those matters in accordance with your letter, has gathered donations for the brethren speedily, freely, and liberally; for while, according to its powers of faith, it is ever ready for any work of God, it has been raised to a special pitch of charity on this occasion by the thought of all this suffering. For since the Lord says in his gospel: I was sick and ye visited

me, with what ampler reward for our alms will he now say:
I was in prison and ye redeemed me? And since again he says:
I was in prison and ye visited me, how much better will it be
for us on the day of judgment, when we are to receive the
Lord's reward, to hear him say: I was in the dungeon of
imprisonment, in bonds and fetters among the barbarians, and
ye rescued me from that prison of slavery! Finally, we thank
you heartily for summoning us to share your trouble and your
noble and necessary act of love, and for offering us a rich
harvest-field wherein to scatter the seeds of our hope, in the
expectation of reaping a very plentiful harvest from this
heavenly and helpful action. We transmit to you a sum of a
hundred thousand sesterces [close upon £1000] collected and
contributed by our clergy and people here in the church over
which by God's mercy we preside; this you will dispense in the
proper quarter at your own discretion.

" In conclusion, we trust that nothing like this will occur in
future, but that, guarded by the power of God, our brethren
may henceforth be quit of all such perils. Still, should the
like occur again, for a test of love and faith, do not hesitate to
write of it to us; be sure and certain that while our own church
and the whole of the church pray fervently that this may not
recur, they will gladly and generously contribute even if it does
take place once more. In order that you may remember in
prayer our brethren and sisters who have taken so prompt and
liberal a share in this needful act of love, praying that they may
be ever quick to aid, and in order also that by way of return
you may present them in your prayers and sacrifices, I add
herewith the names of all. Further, I have subjoined the
names of my colleagues (the bishops) and fellow-priests, who
like myself were present and made such contributions as they
could afford in their own name and in the name of their people;
I have also noted and forwarded their small sums along with
our own total. It is your duty—faith and love alike require it
—to remember all these in your prayers and supplications.

" Dearest brethren, we wish you unbroken prosperity in the
Lord. Remember us."

Plainly the Carthaginian church is conscious here of having

done something out of the common. But it is intensely conscious also of having thus discharged a *duty* of Christian love, and the religious basis of the duty is laid down in exemplary fashion.   It is also obvious that so liberal a grant could not be taken from the proceeds of the ordinary church-collections.

Yet another example of Cyprian's care for a foreign church is extant. In the case (cp. above, p. 175) already mentioned of the teacher of the histrionic art who is to give up his profession and be supported by the church, if he has no other means of livelihood, Cyprian (*Ep.* ii.) writes that the man may come to Carthage and find maintenance in the local church if his own church is too poor to feed him.[1]

Lucian's satire on the death of Peregrinus, in the days of Marcus Aurelius, is a further witness to the alert and energetic temper of the interest taken in churches at the outbreak of persecution or during a period of persecution. The governor of Syria had ordered the arrest of this character, who is discribed by Lucian as a nefarious impostor. Lucian then describes the honour paid him, during his imprisonment, by Christians, and proceeds as follows : " In fact, people actually came from several Asiatic townships, sent by Christians, in the name of their churches, to render aid, to conduct the defence, and to encourage the man. They become incredibly alert when anything of this kind occurs that affects their common interests. On such occasions no expense is grudged. Thus they pour out on Peregrinus, at this time, sums of money which were by no means trifling, and he drew from this source a considerable income."[2] What Lucian relates in this passage cannot, therefore, have been an infrequent occurrence. Brethren arrived from afar in the name of their churches, not merely to bring donations for the support of prisoners, but also to visit them in

---

[1] " Si illic ecclesia non sufficit ut laborantibus praestat alimenta, poterit se ad nos transferre (*i.e.*, to Carthage), et hic quod sibi ad victum atque ad vestitum necessarium fuerit accipere " (" If the local church is not able to support those who labour, let it send them on to us to get the needful food and clothing ").

[2] It may be observed at this point that there were no *general collections* in the early church, like those maintained by the Jews in the Imperial age. The organization of the churches would not tend greatly to promote any such undertakings, since Christians had no headquarters such as the Jews possessed in Palestine.

prison, and to encourage them by evidences of love; they actually endeavoured to stand beside them in the hour of trial. The seven epistles of Ignatius form, as it were, a commentary upon these observations of the pagan writer. In them we find the keen sympathy shown by the churches of Asia Minor as well as by the Roman church in the fortunes of a bishop upon whom they had never set eyes before: we also get a vivid sense of their care for the church at Antioch, which was now orphaned. Ignatius is being taken from Antioch to Rome in order to fight with beasts at the capital, and meanwhile the persecution of Christians at Antioch proceeds apace. On reaching Smyrna, he is greeted by deputies from the churches of Ephesus, Magnesia, and Tralles. After several days' intercourse, he entrusts them with letters to their respective churches, in which, among other things, he warmly commends to the brethren of Asia Minor his own forlorn church. "Pray for the church in Syria," he writes to the Ephesians. "Remember the church in Syria when you pray," he writes to the Trallians; "I am not worthy to belong to it, since I am the least of its members." And in the letter to the Magnesians he repeats this request, comparing the church at Antioch to a field scorched by the fiery heat of persecution, which needs some refreshing dew: the love of the brethren is to revive it.[1] At the same time we find him turning to the Romans also. There appears to have been some brother from Ephesus who was ready to convey a letter to the Roman church, but Ignatius assumes they will learn of his fortunes before the letter reaches them. What he fears is, lest they should exert their influence at court on his behalf, or rob him of his coveted martyrdom by appealing to the Emperor. The whole of the letter is written with the object of blocking the Roman church upon this line of action.[2] But all that concerns us here is the fact that a stranger bishop from abroad could assume that the Roman church would interest itself in him, whether he was thinking of a legal appeal or of the Roman Christians moving

[1] *Eph.*, xxi. 2 ; *Trall.*, xiii. 1 ; *Magn.*, xiv.

[2] Even here Ignatius remembers to commend the church at Antioch to the church of Rome (ix.): "Remember in your prayers the Syrian church, which has God for its shepherd now instead of me. Jesus Christ alone shall be its over-seer (bishop)—he and your love together."

in his favour along some special channels open to themselves.
A few days afterwards Ignatius found himself at Troas, accompanied by the Ephesian deacon Burrhus, and provided with contributions from the church of Smyrna.[1] Thence he writes to
the churches of Philadelphia and Smyrna, with both of which he
had become acquainted during the course of his journey, as well
as to Polycarp, the bishop of Smyrna. Messengers from Antioch
reached him at Troas with news of the cessation of the
persecution at the former city, and with the information that
some churches in the vicinity of Antioch had already despatched
bishops or presbyters and deacons to congratulate the local church
(*Philad.*, x. 2). Whereupon, persuaded that the church of
Antioch had been delivered from its persecution through the
prayers of the churches in Asia Minor, Ignatius urges the latter
also to send envoys to Antioch in order to unite with that church
in thanking God for the deliverance. "Since I am informed,"
he writes to the Philadelphians (x. 1 f.), "that, in answer to
your prayers and love in Jesus Christ, the church of Antioch is
now at peace, it befits you, as a church of God, to send a deacon
as your delegate with a message of God for that church, so that
he may congratulate the assembled church and glorify the Name.
Blessed in Jesus Christ is he who shall be counted worthy of
such a mission ; and ye shall yourselves be glorified. Now it is
not impossible for you to do this for the name of God, if only
you have the desire." The same counsel is given to Smyrna.
The church there is also to send a messenger with a pastoral letter
to the church of Antioch (*Smyrn.*, xi.). The unexpected sudden-
ness of his departure from Troas prevented Ignatius from
addressing the same request to the other churches of Asia Minor.
He therefore begs Polycarp not only himself to despatch a
messenger with all speed (*Polyc.*, vii. 2), but to write in his
name to the other churches and ask them to share the general
joy of the Antiochene Christians either by messenger or by letter
(*Polyc.*, viii. 1). A few weeks later the church at Philippi wrote
to Polycarp that it also had made the acquaintance of Ignatius
during that interval ; it requested the bishop of Smyrna, therefore, to forward its letter to the church of Antioch whenever

---

[1] *Philad.*, xi. 2 ; *Smyrn.*, xii. 1.

he sent his own messenger. Polycarp undertakes to do so. In fact, he even holds out the prospect of conveying the letter himself. As desired by them, he also transmits to them such letters of Ignatius as had come to hand, and asks for reliable information upon the fate of Ignatius and his companions.[1]

Such, in outline, is the situation as we find it in the seven letters of Ignatius and in Polycarp's epistle to the Philippians. What a wealth of intercourse there is between the churches! What public spirit! What brotherly care for one another! Financial support retires into the background here. The foreground of the picture is filled by proofs of that personal co-operation by means of which whole churches, or again churches and their bishops, could lend mutual aid to one another, consoling and strengthening each other, and sharing their sorrows and their joys. Here we step into a whole world of sympathy and love.

From other sources we also learn that after weathering a persecution the churches would send a detailed report of it to other churches. Two considerable documents of this kind are still extant. One is the letter addressed by the church of Smyrna to the church of Philomelium and to all Christian churches, after the persecution which took place under Antonius Pius. The other is the letter of the churches in Gaul to those in Asia Minor and Phrygia, after the close of the bloody persecution under Marcus Aurelius.[2] In both letters the persecution is described in great detail, while in the former the death of bishop Polycarp is specially dwelt on, since the glorious end of a bishop who was well known in the East and West alike had to be announced to all Christendom. The events which transpired in Gaul had a special claim upon the sympathy of the Asiatic brethren, for at least a couple of the latter, Attalus of Pergamum and Alexander, a Phrygian, had suffered a glorious martyrdom in the Gallic persecution. The churches also took advantage of the opportunity to communicate to the brethren

---

[1] Polyc., *ad Phil.*, xiii.

[2] It is preserved, though not in an entirely complete form, by Eusebius (*H.E.*, v. 1 f.). The Smyrniote letter also occurs in an abbreviated form in Eusebius (iv. 15); the complete form, however, is also extant in a special type of text, both in Greek and Latin.

certain notable experiences of their own during the period of
persecution, as well as any truths which they had verified.
Thus the Smyrniote church speaks very decidedly against the
practice of people delivering themselves up and craving for
martyrdom.   It gives one melancholy instance of this error
(*Mart. Polyc.*, iv.).   The churches of Gaul, for their part
(in Eus., *H.E.*, v. 2), put in a warning against excessive
harshness in the treatment of penitent apostates.   They are
able also to describe the tender compassion shown by their
own confessors.   It was otherwise with the church of Rome.
She exhorted the church of Carthage to stand fast and firm
during the Decian persecution,[1] and at a subsequent period
conferred with it upon its mode of dealing with apostates.[2]
Here a special case was under discussion.   Cyprian, the bishop
of Carthage, had fled during the persecution ; nevertheless, he
had continued to superintend his church from his retreat, since
he could say with quite a good conscience that he was bound
to look after his own people.   The Romans, who had not been
at first informed of the special circumstances of the case,
evidently viewed the bishop's flight with serious misgiving ;
they thought themselves obliged to write and encourage the
local church.   The fact was, no greater disaster could befall
a church in a period of distress than the loss of its clergy or
bishop by death or dereliction of duty.   In his treatise on
"Flight during a Persecution," Tertullian relates how deacons,
presbyters, and bishops frequently ran away at the outbreak of
a persecution, on the plea of Matt. x. 23 : "If they persecute
you in one city, flee unto another."   The result was that the
church either collapsed or fell a prey to heretics.[3]   The more

---

[1] Ep. viii. in Cyprian's correspondence (ed. Hartel).

[2] Cp. my study (in the volume dedicated to Weizsäcker, 1892) on "The letters
of the Roman clergy from the age of the papal vacancy in 250 A.D."   There is
also an interesting remark of Dionysius of Alexandria in a letter addressed to
Germanus which Eusebius has preserved (*H.E.*, VII. xi. 3).   Dionysius tells
how "one of the brethren who were present from Rome accompanied" him to
his examination before Æmilianus the governor (during the Valerian persecution).

[3] "Sed cum ipsi auctores, id est ipsi diaconi et presbyteri et episcopi fugiunt,
quomodo laicus intellegere potuerit, qua ratione dictum : Fugite de civitate in
civitatem ?   (Tales) dispersum gregem faciunt et in praedam esse omnibus bestiis
agri, dum non est pastor illis.   Quod nunquam magis fit, quam cum in persecutione

dependent the church became upon its clergy, the more serious were the consequences to the church of any failure or even of any change in the ranks of the latter.   This was well understood by the ardent persecutors of the church in the third century, by Maximin I., by Decius, by Valerian, and by Diocletian.   Even a Cyprian could not retain control of his church from a place of retreat!   He had to witness it undergoing shocks of disastrous force.   It was for this very reason that the sister churches gave practical proof of their sympathy in such crises, partly by sending letters of comfort during the trial, as the Romans did, partly by addressing congratulations to the church when the trial had been passed.   In his church history Eusebius furnishes us with selections from the ample correspondence of Dionysius, bishop of Corinth, and one of these letters, addressed to the church of Athens, is relevant to our present purpose.   Eusebius writes as follows (*H.E.*, IV. xxiii. 2 f.): "The epistle exhorts them to the faith and life of the gospel, which Dionysius accuses them of undervaluing.   Indeed, he almost says they have fallen away from the faith since the martyrdom of Publius, their bishop, which had occurred during the persecution in those days.   He also mentions Quadratus, who was appointed bishop after the martyrdom of Publius, and testifies that by the zeal of Quadratus they were gathered together again and had new zeal imparted to their faith."   The persecution which raged in Antioch during the reign of Septimius Severus claimed as its victim the local bishop of that day, one Serapion.   His death must have exposed the church to great peril, for when the episcopate was happily filled up again, the bishop of Cappadocia wrote a letter of his own from prison to congratulate the church of Antioch, in the following terms: "The Lord has lightened and smoothed my bonds in this time of captivity, by letting me hear that, through the providence of God, the bishopric of your holy church has been undertaken by Asclepiades, whose services

---

destituitur ecclesia a clero " (" But when the very authorities themselves—deacons, I mean, and presbyters and bishops—take to flight, how can a layman see the real meaning of the saying, ' Flee from city to city'?   Such shepherds scatter the flock and leave it a prey to every wild beast of the field, by depriving it of a shepherd.   And this is specially the case when a church is forsaken by the clergy during persecution ").—*De Fuga*, xi.

to the faith qualify him thoroughly for such a position " (Eus., *H.E.*, VI. xi. 5).

Hitherto we have been gleaning from the scanty remains of the primitive Christian literature whatever bore upon the material support extended by one church to another, or upon the mutual assistance forthcoming in a time of persecution. But whenever persecutions brought about internal crisis and perils in a church, as was not infrequently the case, the sympathetic interest of the church extended to this sphere of need as well, and attempts were made to meet the situation. Such cases now fall to be considered—cases in which it was not poverty or persecution, but internal abuses and internal dangers, pure and simple, which drew a word of comfort or of counsel from a sister church or from its bishop.

In this connection we possess one document dating from the very earliest period, viz., the close of the first century, which deserves especial notice. It is the so-called first epistle of Clement, really an official letter sent by the Roman church to the Corinthian.[1] Within the pale of the latter church a crisis had arisen, whose consequences were extremely serious. All we know, of course, is what the majority of the church thought of the crisis, but according to their account certain newcomers, of an ambitious and conceited temper, had repudiated the existing authorities and led a number of the younger members of the church astray.[2] Their intention was to displace the presbyters and deacons, and in general to abolish the growing authority of the officials (xl.–xlviii.). A sharp struggle ensued, in which even the women took some part.[3] Faith, love, and brotherly feeling were already threatened with extinction (i.–iii.). The scandal became notorious throughout Christendom, and indeed there was a danger of the heathen becoming acquainted with the quarrel, of the name of Christ being blasphemed, and of the church's security being imperilled.[4] The Roman Church stepped in. It had not been asked by the Corinthian church to interfere in the matter ; on the contrary, it spoke out of its own accord.[5] And it did so with an affection and solicitude equal

---

[1] Cp. the inscription.　　[2] Cp. i. 1, iii. 3, xxxix. 1, xlvii. 6, etc.

[3] This is probable, from i. 3, xxi. 6.　　[4] Cp. xlvii. 7, i. 1.　　[5] i. 1, xlvii 6-7.

to its candour and dignity.   It felt bound, for conscience' sake, to give a serious and brotherly admonition, conscious that God's voice spoke through its words for peace,[1] and at the same time for the strict maintenance of respect towards the authority of the officials (cp. xl. f.).   Withal it never forgets that its place is merely to point out the right road to the Corinthians, not to lay commands upon them;[2] over and again it expresses most admirably its firm confidence that the church knows the will of God and will bethink itself once more of the right course.[3]   It even clings to the hope that the very agitators will mend their ways (cp. liv.).   But in the name of God it asks that a speedy end be put to the scandal.   The transmission of the epistle is entrusted to the most honoured men within its membership. "They shall be witnesses between us and you.   And we have done this that you may know we have had and still have every concern for your speedy restoration to peace" (lxiii. 3).   The epistle concludes by saying that the Corinthians are to send back the envoys to Rome as soon as possible in joy and peace, so that the Romans may be able to hear of concord regained with as little delay as possible and to rejoice speedily on that account (lxv. 1).   There is nothing in early Christian literature to compare with this elaborate and effective piece of writing, lit up with all the brotherly affection and the public spirit of the church.   But similar cases are not infrequent.   The church at Philippi, for example, sent a letter across the sea to the aged Polycarp at Smyrna, informing him of a sad affair which had occurred in their own midst.   One of their presbyters, named Valens, had been convicted of embezzling the funds of the church.   In his reply, which is still extant, Polycarp treats this melancholy piece of news (Polyc., *ad Phil.*, xi.).   He does not interfere with the jurisdiction of the church, but he exhorts and counsels the Philippians.   They are to take warning from this case and avoid avarice themselves.   Should the presbyter and his wife repent, the church is not to treat them as enemies, but as ailing and erring members, so that the whole body may be

---

[1] Cp. lix. 1, lvi. 1, lxiii. 2.

[2] Cp. especially lviii. 2 : δέξασθε τὴν συμβουλὴν ἡμῶν ("accept our counsel").

[3] Cp. xl. 1, xlv. 2 f., liii. 1, lxii. 3.

saved. The bishop lets it be seen that the church's treatment
of the case does not appear to him to have been entirely correct.
He exhorts them to moderate their passion and to be gentle.
But, at the same time, in so doing he is perfectly conscious of
the length to which he may venture to go in opposing an outside church. When Ignatius, bishop of Antioch, is being
conveyed across Asia Minor, he takes the opportunity of writing
brief letters to encourage the local churches in any perils to
which they may be exposed. He warns them against the
machinations of heretics, exhorts them to obey the clergy, urges
a prudent concord and firm unity, and in quite a thorough
fashion gives special counsels for any emergency. At the
opening of the second century a Roman Christian, the brother
of the bishop, desires to lay down the *via media* of proper order
and discipline at any crisis in the church, as he himself had
found that *via*, between the extremes of laxity and rigour. His
aim is directed not merely to the Roman church but to
Christendom in general (to the " foreign cities "); he wishes all
to learn the counsels which he claims to have personally received
from the Holy Spirit through the church (Herm., *Vis.*, ii. 4).
In the days of Marcus Aurelius it was bishop Dionysius of
Corinth in particular who sought (no doubt in his church's
name as well as in his own) by means of an extensive correspondence to confirm the faith of such churches, even at a great
distance, as were in any peril. Two of his letters, those to the
Athenians and the Romans, we have already noticed, but
Eusebius gives us the contents of several similar writings, which
he calls "catholic" epistles. Probably these were meant to be
circulated throughout the churches, though they were collected
at an early date and also (as the bishop himself is forced
indignantly to relate) were interpolated. One letter to the
church at Sparta contains an exposition of orthodox doctrine
with an admonition to peace and unity. In the epistle to the
church of Nicomedia in Bithynia he combats the heresy of
Marcion. " He also wrote a letter to the church in Gortyna,
together with the other churches in Crete, praising their bishop
Philip for the testimony borne to the great piety and steadfastness of his church, and warning them to guard against the

aberrations of heretics. He also wrote to the church of Amastris, together with the other churches in Pontus. . . . . Here he adds explanations of some passages from Holy Scripture, and mentions Palmas, their bishop, by name. He gives them long advice, too, upon marriage and chastity, enjoining them also to welcome again into their number all who come back after any lapse whatsoever, be it vice or heresy. There is also in his collection of letters another addressed to the Cnosians (in Crete), in which he exhorts Pinytus, the bishop of the local church, not to lay too heavy and sore a burden on the brethren in the matter of continence, but to consider the weakness of the majority" (Eus., *H.E.*, iv. 23). Such is the variety of contents in these letters. Dionysius seems to have spoken his mind on every question which agitated the churches of his day, nor was any church too remote for him to evince his interest in its inner fortunes.

After the close of the second century a significant change came over these relationships, as the institution of synods began to be adopted. The free and unconventional communications which passed between the churches (or their bishops) yielded to an intercourse conducted upon fixed and regular lines. A new procedure had already come into vogue with the Montanist and Quartodeciman controversies, and this was afterwards developed more highly still in the great Christological controversies and in the dispute with Novatian. Doubtless we still continue to hear of cases in which individual churches or their bishops displayed special interest in other churches at a distance, nor was there any cessation of *voluntary* sympathy with the weal and woe of any sister church. But this gave place more than ever both to an interest in the position taken up by the church at large in view of individual and particular movements, and also to the support of the provincial churches.[1] Keen interest was shown in the attitude taken up by the churches throughout the empire (or their bishops) upon any critical question. On such matters harmony could be arranged, but otherwise the provincial churches began to form groups of their

---

[1] Instances of this occur, *e.g.*, in the correspondence of Cyprian and of Dionysius of Alexandria.

own. Still, for all this, fresh methods emerged in the course of the third century by which one church supported or rallied another, and these included the custom of inviting the honoured teachers of one church to deliver addresses in another, or of securing them, when controversies had arisen, to pronounce an opinion, to instruct the parties, and to give a judgment in the matter. Instances of this are to be found, for example, in the career of the great theologian Origen.[1] Even in the fourth and fifth centuries, the material support of poor churches from foreign sources had not ceased; Socrates, in his church history (vii. 25), notes one very brilliant example of the practice.

[1] Cp. Eus., *H.E.*, vi. 19. 15 ; 33. 2 ; 37 ; 32. 2.

CHAPTER V

In its missionary activities the Christian religion presented
itself as something more than the gospel of redemption and of
ministering love; it was also the religion of the Spirit and of
power. No doubt, it verified its character as Spirit and power
by the very fact that it brought redemption and succour to
mankind, freeing them from demons (see above, pp. 125 f.) and
from the misery of life. But the witness of the Spirit had a
wider reach than even this. " I came to you in weakness and
fear and with great trembling; nor were my speech and preaching in persuasive words of wisdom but in demonstration of the
Spirit and of power" (1 Cor. ii. 3, 4). Though Paul in these
words is certainly thinking of his conflict with demons and of
their palpable defeat, he is by no means thinking of that alone,
but also of all the wonderful deeds that accompanied the labours
of the apostles and the founding of the church. These were
not confined to his own person. From all directions they were
reported in connection with other missionaries as well. Towards
the close of the first century, when people came to look back
upon the age in which the church had been established, the
course of events was summed up in these words (Heb. ii. 3):
" Salvation began by being spoken through the Lord, and was
confirmed for us by those who heard it, while God accompanied

---

[1] In presenting this aspect of the Christian religion, one has either to be extremely
brief or very copious. In the volume which has been already mentioned (on
p. 125), Weinel has treated it with great thoroughness. Here I shall do no more
than adduce the salient points.

their witness by signs and wonders and manifold miracles and distributions of the holy Spirit."

The variety of expressions [1] here is in itself a proof of the number of phenomena which emerge in this connection. Let us try to single out the most important of them.

(1) God speaks to the missionaries in visions, dreams, and ecstasy, revealing to them affairs of moment and also trifles, controlling their plans, pointing out the roads on which they are to travel, the cities where they are to stay, and the persons whom they are to visit. Visions occur especially after a martyrdom, the dead martyr appearing to his friends during the weeks that immediately follow his death, as in the case of Potamiæna (Eus., *H.E.*, vi. 5), or of Cyprian, or of many others.

It was by means of dreams that Arnobius (Jerome, *Chron.*, p. 326) and others were converted. Even in the middle of the third century, the two great bishops Dionysius and Cyprian [2] were both visionaries. Monica, Augustine's mother, like many a Christian widow, saw visions frequently ; she could even detect, from a certain taste in her mouth, whether it was a real revelation or a dream-image that she saw (Aug., *Conf.*, vi. 13. 23 : " Dicebat discernere se nescio quo sapore, quem verbis explicare non poterat, quid interesset inter revelantem te et animam suam somniantem "). She was not the first who used this criterion.

(2) At the missionary addresses of the apostles or evangelists, or at the services of the churches which they founded, sudden movements of rapture are experienced, many of them being simultaneous seizures ; these are either full of terror and dismay, convulsing the whole spiritual life, or exultant outbursts of a joy that sees heaven opened to its eyes. The simple question, " What must I do to be saved ? " also bursts upon the mind with an elemental force.

---

[1] Cp. Justin's *Dial.* xxxix. : φωτιζόμενοι διὰ τοῦ ὀνόματος τοῦ χριστοῦ τούτου · ὁ μὲν γὰρ λαμβάνει συνέσεως πνεῦμα, ὁ δὲ βουλῆς, ὁ δὲ ἰσχύος, ὁ δὲ ἰάσεως, ὁ δὲ προγνώσεως, ὁ δὲ διδασκαλίας, ὁ δὲ φόβου θεοῦ (" Illuminated by the name of Christ. For one receives the spirit of understanding, another the spirit of counsel, another the spirit of might, another the spirit of healing, another the spirit of foreknowledge, another the spirit of teaching, another the spirit of the fear of God ").

[2] Cp. my essay on " Cyprian als Enthusiast " in the *Zeitschrift fur die neutest. Wissenschaft*, iii. (1902), pp. 177 f.

(3) Some are inspired who have power to clothe their experience in words—prophets to explain the past, to interpret and to fathom the present, and to fortell the future.[1] Their prophecies relate to the general course of history, but also to the fortunes of individuals, to what individuals are to do or leave undone.

(4) Brethren are inspired with the impulse to improvise prayers and hymns and psalms.

(5) Others are so filled with the Spirit that they lose consciousness and break out in stammering speech and cries, or in unintelligible utterances—which can be interpreted, however, by those who have the gift.

(6) Into the hands of others, again, the Spirit slips a pen, either in an ecstasy or in exalted moments of spiritual tension; they not merely speak but write as they are bidden.

(7) Sick persons are brought and healed by the missionaries, or by brethren who have been but recently awakened; wild paroxysms of terror before God's presence are also soothed, and in the name of Jesus demons are cast out.

(8) The Spirit impels men to an immense variety of extraordinary actions—to symbolic actions which are meant to reveal some mystery or to give some directions for life, as well as to deeds of heroism.

(9) Some perceive the presence of the Spirit with every sense; they see its brilliant light, they hear its voice, they smell the fragrance of immortality and taste its sweetness. Nay more; they see celestial persons with their own eyes, see them and also hear them; they peer into what is hidden or distant or to come; they are even rapt into the world to come, into heaven itself, where they listen to " words that cannot be uttered."[2]

---

[1] These prophecies do *not* include, however, the Christian Sibylline oracles. The Jewish oracles were accepted in good faith by Christians, and quoted by them (ever since Hermas) as prophetic; but the production of Christian Sibyllines did not begin, in all likelihood, till after the middle of the third century. These oracles are an artificial and belated outcome of the primitive Christian enthusiasm, and are simply a series of forgeries. Cp. my *Chronologie*, i. pp. 581 f., ii. pp. 184 f.

[2] Cp., however, Orig., Hom. xxvii. 11, *in Num.* (vol. 10, p. 353): " In visions there is wont to be temptation, for the angel of evil sometimes transforms himself into an angel of light. Hence you must take great care to discriminate the kind of vision, just as Joshua the son of Nun on seeing a vision knew there was

(10) But although the Spirit manifests itself through marvels like these, it is no less effective in heightening the religious and the moral powers, which operate with such purity and power in certain individuals that they bear palpably the stamp of their divine origin. A heroic faith or confidence in God is visible, able to overthrow mountains, and towering far above the faith that lies in the heart of every Christian; charitable services are rendered which are far more moving and stirring than any miracle; a foresight and a solicitude are astir in the management of life, that operate as surely as the very providence of God. When these spiritual gifts, together with those of the apostles, prophets, and teachers, are excited, they are the fundamental means of edifying the churches, proving them thereby to be " churches of God."

The amplest evidence for all these traits is to be found in the pages of early Christian literature from its earliest record down to Irenæus, and even further. The apologists allude to them as a familiar and admitted fact, and it is quite obvious that they were of primary importance for the mission and propaganda of the Christian religion. Other religions and cults could doubtless point to some of these actions of the Spirit, such as ecstasy, vision, demonic and anti-demonic manifestations, but nowhere do we find such a wealth of these phenomena presented to us as in Christianity; moreover, and this is of supreme importance, the fact that their Christian range included the exploits of moral heroism, stamped them in this field with a character which was all their own and lent them a very telling power. What existed elsewhere merely in certain stereotyped and fragmentary forms, appeared within Christianity in a wealth of expression where every function of the spiritual, the mental, and the moral life seemed actually to be raised above itself.[1]

a temptation in it, and at once asked the figure, Art thou on our side, or on our foes'?" ("Solet in visionibus esse tentatio; nam nonnunquam angelus iniquitatis transfigurat se in angelum lucis, et ideo cavendum est et sollicite agendum, ut scienter discernas visionum genus, sicut et Iesus Nave, cum visionem viderit, sciens in hoc esse tentationem, statim requisit ab eo qui apparuit et dicit : Noster es an adversariorum?"). See also what follows.

[1] We must not ignore the fact that these proofs of "the Spirit and power" were not favourable to the propaganda in all quarters. Celsus held that they were trickery, magic, and a gross scandal, and his opinion was shared by other sensible

In all these phenomena there was an implicit danger, due to the great temptation which people felt either to heighten them artificially, or credulously to exaggerate them,[1] or to imitate them fradulently, or selfishly to turn them to their own account.[2]

pagans, although the latter were no surer of their facts than Celsus himself. Paul had observed long ago that, instead of recommending Christianity, speaking with tongues might on the contrary discredit it among pagans (see 1 Cor. xiv. 23 : "If the whole congregation assemble and all speak with tongues, then will not uneducated or unbelieving men, who may chance to enter, say that you are mad?").

[1] At that period, as all our sources show, belief in miracles was strong upon the whole; but in Christian circles it seems to have been particularly robust and unlimited, tending more and more to deprive men of any vision of reality. Compare, for example, the apocryphal Acts, a genre of literature whose roots lie in the second century. We must also note how primitive popular legends which were current acquired a Christian cast and got attached to this or that Christian hero or apostle or saint. One instance of this may be seen in the well-known stories of corpses which moved as if they could still feel and think. Tertullian (de Anima, li.) writes thus : " I know of one woman, even within the church itself, who fell peacefully asleep, after a singularly happy though short married life, in the bloom of her age and beauty. Before her burial was completed, when the priest had begun the appointed office, she raised her hands from her side at the first breath of his prayer, put them in the posture of devotion, and, when the holy service was concluded, laid them back in their place. Then there is the other story current among our people, that in a certain cemetery one corpse made way of its own accord for another to be laid alongside of it " (this is also told of the corpse of bishop Reticius of Autun at the beginning of the fourth century).

[2] Cp. what has been already said (p. 132) on exorcists being blamed, and also the description of the impostor Marcus given by Irenæus in the first book of his great work. When the impostor Peregrinus joined the Christians, he became (says Lucian) a " prophet," and as such secured for himself both glory and gain. The Didachê had already endeavoured to guard the churches against men of this kind, who used their spiritual gifts for fraudulent ends. There were even Christian minstrels; cp. the pseudo-Clementine epistle de Virginitate, ii. 6 : " Nec proicimus sanctum canibus nec margaritas ante porcos ; sed dei laudes celebramus cum omnimoda disciplina et cum omni prudentia et cum omni timore dei atque animi intentione. Cultum sacrum non exercemus ibi, ubi inebriantur gentiles et verbis impuris in conviviis suis blasphemant in impietate sua. Propterea non psallimus gentilibus neque scripturas illis praelegimus, ut ne tibicinibus aut cantoribus aut hariolis similes simus, sicut multi, qui ita agunt et haec faciunt, ut buccella panis saturent sese et propter modicum vini cunt et cantant cantica domini in terra aliena gentilium ac faciant quod non licet " (" We do not cast what is holy to the dogs nor throw pearls before swine, but celebrate the praises of God with perfect self-restraint and discretion, in all fear of God and with deliberate mind. We do not practise our sacred worship where the heathen get drunk and impiously blaspheme with impure speech at their banquets. Hence we do not sing to the heathen, nor do we read aloud our scriptures to them, that we may not be like flute-players, or singers, or soothsayers, as many are who live and act thus in order to get a mouthful of bread, going for a sorry cup of wine to sing the songs of the

It was in the primitive days of Christianity, during the first sixty years of its course, that their effects were most conspicuous, but they continued to exist all through the second century, although in diminished volume.[1] Irenæus confirms this view.[2] The Montanist movement certainly gave new life to the " Spirit," which had begun to wane; but after the opening of the third century the phenomena dwindle rapidly, and instead of being the hall-mark of the church at large, or of every individual community, they become no more than the endowment of a few favoured individuals. The common life of the church has now its priests, its altar, its sacraments, its holy book and rule of faith. But it no longer possesses " the Spirit and power."[3]

Lord in the strange land of the heathen and doing what is unlawful "). See also the earlier passage in i. 13 : May God send workmen who are not " operarii mercenarii, qui religionem et pietatem pro mercibus habeant, qui simulent lucis filios, cum non sint lux sed tenebrae, qui operantur fraudem, qui Christum in negotio et quaestu habeant " (" mere hirelings, trading on their religion and piety, imitating the children of light although they themselves are not light but darkness, acting fraudulently, and making Christ a matter of profit and gain ").

[1] They must have been generally and inevitably discredited by the fact that the various parties in Christianity during the second century each denied that the other possessed the Spirit and power, explaining that when such phenomena occurred among its opponents they were the work of the devil, and unauthentic.

[2] He actually declares (see above, p. 135) that people are still raised from the dead within the Christian church (ii. 31. 2). On the spiritual gifts still operative in his day, cp. ii. 32. 4 : Διὸ καὶ ἐν τῷ ἐκείνου ὀνόματι (that of Jesus) οἱ ἀληθῶς αὐτοῦ μαθηταὶ παρ' αὐτοῦ λαβόντες τὴν χάριν ἐπιτελοῦσιν ἐπ' ἐνεργεσίᾳ τῇ τῶν λοιπῶν ἀνθρώπων, καθὼς εἷς ἕκαστος αὐτῶν δωρεὰν εἴληφε παρ' αὐτοῦ · οἱ μὲν γὰρ δαίμονας ἐλαύνουσι βεβαίως καὶ ἀληθῶς, ὥστε πολλάκισ καὶ πιστεύειν αὐτοὺς ἐκείνους τοὺς καθαρισθάντας ἀπὸ τῶν πονηρῶν πνευμάτων καὶ εἶναι ἐν τῇ ἐκκλησίᾳ · οἱ δὲ καὶ πρόγνωσιν ἔχουσι τῶν μελλόντων καὶ ὀπτασίας καὶ ῥήσεις προφητικάς · ἄλλοι δὲ τοὺς κάμνοντας διὰ τῆς τῶν χειρῶν ἐπιθέσεως ἰῶνται καὶ ὑγιεῖς ἀποκαθιστᾶσιν · ἤδη δὲ καὶ νεκροὶ ἠγέρθησαν καὶ παρέμειναν σὺν ἡμῖν ἱκανοῖς ἔτεσι · καὶ τί γάρ; οὐκ ἔστιν ἀριθμὸν εἰπεῖν τῶν χαρισμάτων ὧν κατὰ παντὸς τοῦ κόσμου ἡ ἐκκλησία παρὰ θεοῦ λαβοῦσα ἐν τῷ ὀνόματι Ἰησοῦ Χριστοῦ τοῦ σταυρωθέντος ἐπὶ Ποντίου Πιλάτου ἑκάστης ἡμέρας ἐπ' ἐνεργεσίᾳ τῇ τῶν ἐθνῶν ἐπιτελεῖ (cp. above, p. 135). Irenæus distinctly adds that these gifts were gratuitous. Along with other opponents of heresy, he blames the Gnostics for taking money and thus trading upon Christ. A prototype of this occurs as early as Acts viii. 15 f. (the case of Simon Magus), where it is strongly reprimanded (τὸ ἀργύριόν σου σὺν σοὶ εἴη εἰς ἀπώλειαν, "Thy money perish with thee !").

[3] All the higher value was attached to such people as appeared to possess the Spirit. The more the phenomena of Spirit and power waned in and for the general mass of Christians, the higher rose that cultus of heroes in the faith (i.e., ascetics, confessors, and workers of miracles) which had existed from the very first. These all bear unmistakable signs of the Christ within them, in consequence

Eusebius is not the first (in the third book of his history) to look back upon the age of the Spirit and of power as the bygone heroic age of the church,[1] for Origen had already pronounced this verdict on the past out of an impoverished present.[2] Yet this impoverishment and disenchantment hardly inflicted any injury now upon the mission of Christianity. During the third century that mission was being prosecuted in a different way from that followed in the first and second centuries. There were no longer any regular missionaries—at least we never hear of any such. And the propaganda was no longer an explosive force, but a sort of steady fermenting process. Quietly but surely Christianity was expanding from the centres it had already occupied, diffusing itself with no violent shocks or concussions in its spread.

If the early Christians always looked out for the proofs of the Spirit and of power, they did so from the standpoint of their *moral* and *religious* energy, since it was for the sake of the latter object that these gifts had been bestowed upon the church.

of which they enjoy veneration and authority. Gradually, during the second half of the third century in particular, they took the place of the dethroned deities of paganism, though as a rule this position was not gained till after death.—Though Cyprian still made great use of visions and dreams, he merely sought by their means to enhance his episcopal authority. In several cases, however, they excited doubts and incredulity among people ; cp. *Ep.* lxvi. 10 : " Scio somnia ridicula et visiones ineptas quibusdam videri " ("I know that to some people dreams seem absurd and visions senseless "). This is significant.

[1] *H.E.*, iii. 37 : "A great many wonderful works of the Holy Spirit were wrought in the primitive age through the pupils of the apostles, so that whole multitudes of people, on first hearing the word, suddenly accepted with the utmost readiness faith in the Creator of the universe."

[3] In *c. Cels.*, II. viii., he only declares that he himself has seen still more miracles. The age of miracles therefore lay for Origen in earlier days. In II. xlviii. he puts a new face on the miracles of Jesus and his apostles by interpreting them not only as symbolic of certain truths, but also as intended to win over many hearts to the wonderful doctrine of the gospel. Exorcisms and cures are represented by him as still continuing to occur (frequently ; cp. I. vi.). From I. ii. we see how he estimated the present and the past of Christianity : "For our faith there is one especial proof, unique and superior to any advanced by aid of Grecian dialectic. This diviner proof is characterised by the apostle as 'the demonstration of the Spirit and of power'—'the demonstration of the Spirit' on account of the prophecies which are capable of producing faith in hearer and reader, 'the demonstration of power' on account of the extraordinary wonders, whose reality can be proved by this circumstance, among many other things, that *traces of them still exist among those who live according to the will of the Logos.*"

Paul describes this object as the edification of the entire church,[1] while, as regards the individual, it is the new creation of man from death to life, from a worthless thing into a thing of value. This edification means a growth in all that is good (cp. Gal. v. 22 : " *The fruit of the Spirit* is love, joy, peace, long-suffering, gentleness, goodness, faith, meekness, self-control "), and the evidence of *power* is that God has not called many wise after the flesh, nor many noble, but poor and weak men, whom he has transformed into morally robust and intelligent natures. Moral regeneration and the moral life were not merely *one* side of Christianity to Paul, but its very *fruit* and goal on earth. The entire labour of the Christian mission might be described as a *moral* enterprise, as the awakening and strengthening of the moral sense. Such a description would not be inadequate to its full contents.

Paul's opinion was shared by Christians of the sub-apostolic age, by the apologists and great Christian fathers like Tertullian [2]

---

[1] Cp. pseudo-Clem., *de Virgin.*, I. xi. : "Illo igitur charismate, quod a domino accepisti, illo inservi fratribus pneumaticis, prophetis, qui dignoscant dei esse verba ea, quae loqueris, et enarra quod accepisti charisma in ecclesiastico conventu ad aedificationem fratrum tuorum in Christo" ("Therefore with that spiritual gift which thou hast received from the Lord, serve the spiritual brethren, even the prophets, who know that the words thou speakest are of God, and declare the gift thou hast received in the church-assembly to the edification of thy brethren in Christ").

[2] The highly characteristic passage in *Apol.*, xlv., may be quoted in this connection : " Nos soli innocentes, quid mirum, si necesse est ? enim vero necesse est. Innocentiam a deo edocti et perfecte eam novimus, ut a perfecto magistro revelatam, et fideliter custodiamus, ut ab incontemptibili dispectore mandatam. Vobis autem humana aestimatio innocentiam tradidit, humana item dominatio imperavit, inde nec plenae nec adeo timendae estis disciplinae ad innocentiae veritatem. Tanta est prudentia hominis ad demonstrandum bonum quanta auctoritas ad exigendum ; tam illa falli facilis quam ista contemni. Atque adeo quid plenius, dicere : Non occides, an docere : ne irascaris quidem ? " etc. ("We, then, are the only innocent people. Is that at all surprising, if it is inevitable? And inevitable it is. Taught of God what innocence is, we have a perfect knowledge of it as revealed by a perfect teacher, and we also guard it faithfully as commanded by a judge who is not to be despised. But as for you, innocence has merely been introduced among you by human opinions, and it is enjoined by nothing better than human rules ; hence your moral discipline lacks the fulness and authority requisite for the production of true innocence. Human skill in pointing out what is good is no greater than human authority in enforcing obedience to what is good ; the one is as easily deceived as the other is disobeyed. And so, which is the ampler rule—to say, ' Thou shalt not kill,' or ' Thou shalt not so much as be angry ' ?").

and Origen. Read the Didachê and the first chapter of *Clemens Romanus*, the conclusion of Barnabas, the homily entitled "Second Clement," the "Shepherd" of Hermas, or the last chapter of the *Apology* of Aristides, and everywhere you find the ethical demands occupying the front rank. They are thrust forward almost with weariesome diffuseness and with a rigorous severity. Beyond all question, these Christian communities seek to regulate their common life by principles of the strictest morality, tolerating no unholy members in their midst,[1] and well aware that with the admission of immorality their very existence at once ceases. The fearful punishment to which Paul sentences the incestuous person (1 Cor. v.) is not exceptional. Gross sinners were always ejected from the church. Even those who consider all religions, including Christianity, to be merely idiosyncrasies, and view progress as entirely identical with the moral progress of mankind—even such observers must admit that in these days progress did depend upon the Christian churches, and that history then had recourse to a prodigious and paradoxical system of levers in order to gain a higher level of human evolution. Amid all the convulsions of the soul and body produced by the preaching of a judgment which was imminent, and amid the raptures excited by the Spirit of Christ, morality advanced to a position of greater purity and security. Above all, the conflict undertaken by Christianity was one against sins of the flesh, such as fornication, adultery, and unnatural vices. In the Christian communities monogamy was held to be the sole permissible union of the sexes.[2] The indissoluble character of marriage

---

[1] *Martyr. Apoll.*, xxvi. : "There is a distinction between death and death. For this reason the disciples of Christ die daily, torturing their desires and mortifying them according to the divine scriptures ; for we have no part at all in shameless desires, or scenes impure, or glances lewd, or ears attentive to evil, lest our souls thereby be wounded."

[2] It formed part of the preparation for Christianity that monogamy had almost established itself by this time among the Jews and throughout the Empire as the one legal form of union between the sexes. Christianity simply proclaimed as an ordinance of God what had already been carried out. Contrary practices, such as concubinage, were still tolerated, but they counted for little in the social organism. Of course the verdict on "fornicatio" throughout the Empire generally was just as lax as it had always been, and even adultery on the man's side was hardly condemned. The church had to join issue on these points.

was inculcated (apart from the case of adultery),[1] and marriage was also secured by the very difficulties which second marriages encountered.[2] Closely bound up with the struggle against carnal sins was the strict prohibition of abortion and the exposure of infants.[3] Christians further opposed covetousness, greed, and dishonesty in business life; they attacked mammon-worship in every shape and form, and the pitiless temper which is its result. Thirdly, they combated double-dealing and falsehood. It was along these three lines, in the main, that Christian preaching asserted itself in the sphere of morals. Christians were to be pure men, who do not cling to their possessions and are not self-seeking; moreover, they were to be truthful and brave.

The apologists shared the views of the sub-apostolic fathers. At the close of his *Apology*, addressed to the public of paganism, Aristides exhibits the Christian life in its purity, earnestness, and love, and is convinced that in so doing he is expressing all that is most weighty and impressive in it. Justin follows suit. Lengthy sections of his great *Apology* are devoted to a statement of the moral principles in Christianity, and to a proof that these are observed by Christians. Besides, all the apologists rely on the fact that even their opponents hold goodness to be good and wickedness to be evil. They consider it superfluous to waste their time in proving that goodness is really goodness; they can be sure of assent to this proposition. What they seek to prove is that goodness among Christians is not an impotent claim or a pale ideal, but a power which is developed on all sides and actually exercised in life.[4] It was of special import-

---

[1] We may ignore casuistry in this connection.

[2] The second century was filled with discussions and opinions about the permissibility of second marriages.

[3] Cp. the Didachê; Athenag., *Suppl.*, xxxv., etc. (above, p. 123).

[4] Celsus distinctly admits that the ethical ideas of Christianity agree with those of the philosophers (I. iv.); cp. Tert., *Apol.*, xlvi. : "Eadem, inquit, et philosophi monent atque profitentur" ("These very things, we are told, the philosophers also counsel and profess"). Here too we must, however, recognize a *complexio oppositorum*, and that in a twofold sense. On the one hand, morality, viewed in its essence, is taken as self-evident; a general agreement prevails on this (purity in all the relationships of life, perfect love to one's neighbours, etc.). On the other hand, under certain circumstances it is still maintained that Christian ethics are qualitatively distinct from all other ethics, and that they cannot be understood

ance to them to be able to show (cp. the argument of the apostle Paul) that what was weak and poor and ignoble rose thereby to strength and worth. "They say of us, that we gabble nonsense among females, half-grown people, girls, and old women.[1] Not so. Our maidens ' philosophize,' and at their distaffs speak of things divine" (Tatian, *Orat.*, xxxiii.). "The poor, no less than the well-to-do, philosophize with us" (*ibid.*, xxxii.). "Christ has not, as Socrates had, merely philosophers and scholars as his disciples, but also artizans and people of no education, who despise glory, fear, and death."[2] "Among us are uneducated folk, artizans, and old women who are utterly unable to describe the value of our doctrines in words, but who attest them by their deeds."[3] Similar retorts are addressed by

---

or practised apart from the Spirit of God. This estimate answers to the double description given of Christian morality, which on one side is correct behaviour in every relationship on earth, while on the other side it is a divine life and conduct, which is supernatural and based on complete asceticism and mortification. This extension of the definition of morality, which is most conspicuous in Tatian, was not, however, the original creation of Christianity ; it was derived from the ethics of the philosophers. Christianity merely took it over and modified it. This is easily understood, if we read Philo, Clement, and Origen.

[1] Celsus, III. xliv. : "Christians must admit that they can only persuade people destitute of sense, position, or intelligence, only slaves, women, and children, to to accept their faith."

[2] Justin, *Apol.*, II. x. He adds: δύναμίς ἐστιν τοῦ ἀρρήτου πατρὸς καὶ οὐχὶ ἀνθρωπείου λόγου κατασκευή (" He is a power of the ineffable Father, and no mere instrument of human reason "). So Diognet., vii. : ταῦτα ἀνθρώπου οὐ δοκεῖ τὰ ἔργα, ταῦτα δύναμίς ἐστι θεοῦ (" These do not look like human works ; they are the power of God ").

[3] Athenag., *Suppl.*, xi. ; cp. also Justin, *Apol.*, I. lx. : παρ' ἡμῖν οὖν ἐστι ταῦτα ἀκοῦσαι καὶ μαθεῖν παρὰ τῶν οὐδὲ τοὺς χαρακτῆρας τῶν στοιχείων ἐπισταμένων, ἰδιωτῶν μὲν καὶ βαρβάρων τὸ φθέγμα, σοφῶν δὲ καὶ πιστῶν τὸν νοῦν ὄντων, καὶ πηρῶν καὶ χήρων τινῶν τὰς ὄψεις · ὡς συνεῖναι οὐ σοφίᾳ ἀνθρωπείᾳ ταῦτα γεγονέναι, ἀλλὰ δυνάμει θεοῦ λεγέσθαι (" Among us you can hear and learn these things from people who do not even know the forms of letters, who are uneducated and barbarous in speech, but wise and believing in mind, though some of them are even maimed and blind. From this you may understand these things are due to no human wisdom, but are uttered by the power of God "). Tertull., *Apo..*, xlvi. : " Deum quilibet opifex Christianus et invenit, et ostendit, et exinde totum quod in deum quaeritur re quoque adsignat, licet Plato adfirmet factitatorem universitatis neque inveniri facilem et inventum enarrari in omnes difficilem " (" There is not a Christian workman who does not find God, and manifest him, and proceed to ascribe to him all the attributes of deity, although Plato declares the maker of the universe is hard to find, and hard, when found, to be expounded to all and sundry ").

Origen to Celsus (in his second book), and by Lactantius (*Instit.*, VI. iv.) to his opponents.

A whole series of proofs is extant, indicating that the high level of morality enjoined by Christianity and the moral conduct of the Christian societies were intended to promote, and and actually did promote, the direct interests of the Christian mission.[1] The apologists not infrequently lay great stress on this.[2] Tatian mentions "the excellence of its moral doctrines" as one of the reasons for his conversion (*Orat.*, xxix.), while Justin declares that the steadfastness of Christians convinced him of their purity, and that these impressions proved decisive in bringing him over to the faith (*Apol.*, II. xii.). We frequently read in the Acts of the Martyrs (and, what is more, in the genuine sections) that the steadfastness and loyalty of Christians made an overwhelming impression on those who witnessed their trial or execution ; so much so, that some of these spectators suddenly decided to become Christians themselves.[3]

---

[1] Ignat., *ad Ephes.*, x. : ἐπιτρέψατε αὐτοῖς (*i.e.*, the heathen) κἂν ἐκ τῶν ἔργων ὑμῖν μαθητευθῆναι · πρὸς τὰς ὀργὰς αὐτῶν ὑμεῖς πραεῖς, πρὸς τὰς μεγαλορρημοσύνας αὐτῶν ὑμεῖς ταπεινόφρονες, πρὸς τὰς βλασφημίας αὐτῶν ὑμεῖς τὰς προσευχάς.. . . . μὴ σπουδάζοντες ἀντιμιμήσασθαι αὐτούς · ἀδελφοὶ αὐτῶν εὑρεθῶμεν τῇ ἐπιεικείᾳ · μιμηταὶ τοῦ κυρίου σπουδάζωμεν εἶναι ("Allow them to learn a lesson at least from your works. Be meek when they break out in anger, be humble against their vaunting words, set your prayers against their blasphemies . . . . ; be not zealous to imitate them in requital. Let us show ourselves their brethren by our forbearance, and let us be zealous to be imitators of the Lord ").

[2] Cp. also 2 Clem., lxiii. : τὰ ἔθνη ἀκούοντα ἐκ τοῦ στόματος ἡμῶν τὰ λόγια τοῦ θεοῦ ὡς καλὰ καὶ μεγάλα θαυμάζει · ἔπειτα καταμαθόντα τὰ ἔργα ἡμῶν ὅτι οὐκ ἔστιν ἄξια τῶν ῥημάτων ὧν λέγομεν, ἔνθεν εἰς βλασφημίαν τρέπονται, λέγοντες εἶναι μῦθόν τινα καὶ πλάνην ("When the Gentiles hear from our mouth the words of God, they wonder at their beauty and greatness ; then, discovering our deeds are not worthy of the words we utter, they betake themselves to blasphemy, declaring it is all a myth and error "). Such instances therefore did occur. Indirectly, they are a proof of what is argued above.

[3] Even the second oldest martyrdom of which we know, that of James, the son of Zebedee, as related by Clement of Alexandria in his Hypotyposes (cp. Eus., *H.E.*, ii. 9), tells how the accuser himself was converted and beheaded along with the apostle.—All Christians recognised that the zenith of Christian morality was reached when the faith was openly confessed before the authorities, but the sectarian Heracleon brought forward another view, which of course they took seriously amiss. His contention was that such confession in words might be hypocritical as well as genuine, and that the only conclusive evidence was that afforded by the steady profession which consists in words and actions answering to the faith itself (Clem. Alex., *Strom.*, IV. ix. 71 f.).

But it is in Cyprian's treatise "to Donatus" that we get the most vivid account of how a man was convinced and won over to Christianity, not so much by its moral principles, as by the moral energy which it exhibited. Formerly he considered it impossible to put off the old man and put on the new. But "after I had breathed the heavenly spirit in myself, and the second birth had restored me to a new manhood, then doubtful things suddenly and strangely acquired certainty for me. What was hidden disclosed itself; darkness became enlightened; what was formerly hard seemed feasible, and what had appeared impossible seemed capable of being done."

Tertullian and Origen speak in similar terms.

But it is not merely Christians themselves who bear witness that they have been lifted into a new world of moral power, of earnestness, and of holiness; even their opponents bear testimony to their purity of life. The abominable charges circulated by the Jews against the moral life of Christians did hold their own for a long while, and were credited by the common people as well as by many of the educated classes.[1] But anyone who examined the facts found something very different. Pliny told Trajan that he had been unable to prove anything criminal or vicious on the part of Christians during all his examination of them, and that, on the contrary, the purpose of their gatherings was to make themselves more conscientious and virtuous.[2]

[1] Probably, *e.g.*, by Fronto, the teacher of M. Aurelius (cp. the *Octavius* of Minutius Felix), and also by Apuleius, if the woman described in *Metam.*, ix. 14 (omnia prorsus ut in quandam caenosam latrinam in eius animam flagitia confluxerant—"every vice had poured into her soul, as into some foul cesspool") was a Christian (spretis atque calcatis divinis numinibus invicem certae religionis mentita sacrilega presumptione dei, quem praedicaret unicum—"scorning and spurning the holy deities in place of the true religion, she affected to entertain a sacrilegious conception of God—the only God, as she proclaimed"). The orator Aristides observed in the conduct of Christians a mixture of humility and arrogance, in which he finds a resemblance between them and the Jews (*Orat.*, xlvi.). This is his most serious charge, and Celsus raises a similar objection (see Book III., Chapter V.).

[2] "Adfirmabant autem [*i.e.*, the Christians under examination] hanc fuisse summam vel culpae suae vel erroris, quod essent soliti stato die ante lucem convenire carmenque Christo quasi deo dicere secum invicem, seque sacramento non in scelus aliquod obstringere, sed ne furta, ne latrocinia, ne adulteria committerent, ne fidem fallerent, ne depositum appellati abnegarent" ("They maintained that the head and front of their offending or error had been this, that they were accustomed on

Lucian represents the Christians as credulous fanatics, but also as people of a pure life, of devoted love, and of a courage equal to death itself. The last-named feature is also admitted by Epictetus and Aurelius.[1] Most important of all, however, is the testimony of the shrewd physician Galen. He writes (in his treatise[2] "de Sententiis Politiæ Platonicæ") as follows :— "Hominum plerique orationem demonstrativam continuam morte assequi nequeunt, quare indigent, ut instituantur parabolis. veluti nostro tempore videmus homines illos, qui Christiani vocantur, fidem suam e parabolis petiisse. Hi tamen interdum talia faciunt, qualia qui vere philosophantur. Nam quod mortem contemnunt, id quidem omnes ante oculos habemus ; item quod verecundia quadam ducti ab usu rerum venerearum abhorrent. sunt enim inter eos et feminae et viri, qui per totam vitam a concubitu abstinuerint ;[3] sunt etiam qui in

a stated day to assemble ere daylight and sing in turn a hymn to Christ as a god, and also that they bound themselves by an oath, not for any criminal end, but to avoid theft or robbery or adultery, never to break their word, or to repudiate a deposit when called upon to refund it ").

[1] Both of course qualify their admission. Epictetus (Arrian, *Epict. Diss.*, iv. 7. 6) declares that the Galileans' ἀφοβία before tyrants was due to habit, while Aurelius attributes the readiness of Christians to die, to ostentation (*Med.*, xi. 3).

[2] Extant in Arabic in the *Hist. anteislam. Abulfedae* (ed. Fleischer, p. 109). Cp. Kalbfleisch in the *Festschrift für Gomperz* (1902), pp. 96 f., and Norden's *Kunstprosa*, pp. 518 f.

[3] From the time of Justin (and probably even earlier) Christians were always pointing, by way of contrast to the heathen, to the group of their brethren and sisters who totally abjured marriage. Obviously they counted on the fact that such conduct would evoke applause and astonishment even among their opponents (even castration was known, as in the case of Origen and of another person mentioned by Justin). Nor was this calculation quite mistaken, for the religious philosophy of the age was ascetic. Still, the applause was not unanimous, even among strict moralists. The pagan in Macarius Magnes, III. xxxvi. (*i.e.*, Porphyry) urged strongly against Paul that in 1 Tim. iv. 1 he censures those who forbid marriage, while in 1 Cor. vii. he recommends celibacy, even although he has to admit he has no word of the Lord upon virgins. " Then is it not wrong to live as a celibate, and also to refrain from marriage at the order of a mere man, seeing that there is no command of Jesus extant upon celibacy ? And how can some women who live as virgins boast so loudly of the fact, *declaring they are filled with the Holy Ghost* like her who bore Jesus?" The suspicious attitude of the early Christians towards sexual intercourse (even in marriage) comes out in Paul unmistakably. On this point the apocryphal Acts of the Apostles (beginning with the Acts of Paul) are specially significant, as they mirror the popular ideas on the subject. The following facts may be set down in this connection. (1) Marriage was still tolerated as a concession to human weakness. (2) The

animis regendis coercendisque et in acerrimo honestatis studio eo progressi sint, ut nihil cedant vere philosophantibus."[1] One can hardly imagine a more impartial and brilliant testimony to the morality of Christians.   Celsus, too, a very prejudiced critic of Christians, finds no fault with their moral conduct.   Everything about them, according to him, is dull, mean, and deplorable; but he never denies them such morality as is possible under the circumstances.

As the proof of " the Spirit and of power" subsided after the beginning of the third century, the extraordinary moral tension also became relaxed, paving the way gradually for a morality which was adapted to a worldly life, and which was no longer equal to the strain of persecution.[2] This began as far back as the second century, in connection with the question, whether any, and if so what, post-baptismal sins could be forgiven.

restriction of sexual intercourse, or even entire abstinence from it, was advocated and urgently commended.   (3) Second marriage was designated "a specious adultery" (εὐπρεπὴς μοιχεία).   (4) Virgins were persuaded to remain as they were.   (5) Instead of marriage, platonic ties (" virgines subintroductæ") were formed, audaciously and riskily.   Cp. Tertull., de Resurr., viii. : " Virginitas et viduitas et modesta in occulto matrimonii dissimulatio et una notitia eius (" Virginity and widowhood and secret self-restraint upon the marriage-bed and the sole practical recognition of that restraint [i.e., monogamy]").   Such, in the order of diminuendo, were the four forms assumed by sexual asceticism.

[1] " As a rule, men are unable to follow consecutively any argumentative speech, so that they need to be educated by means of parables. Just as in our own day we see the people who are called Christians seeking their faith from parables. Still, they occasionally act just as true philosophers do. For their contempt of death is patent to us all, as is their abstinence from the use of sexual organs, by a certain impulse of modesty. For they include women and men who refrain from cohabiting all through their lives, and they also number individuals who in ruling and controlling themselves, and in their keen pursuit of virtue, have attained a pitch not inferior to that of real philosophers."   Galen, of course, condemns the faith of Christians as a mere obstinate adherence to what is quite unproven : περὶ διαφορᾶς σφυγμῶν, II. iv. (ἵνα μή τις εὐθὺς κατ' ἀρχάς, ὡς εἰς Μωυσοῦ καὶ Χριστοῦ διατριβὴν ἀφιγμένος, νόμων ἀναποδείκτων ἀκούῃ—" That no one may hastily give credence to unproven laws, as if he had reached the way of life enjoined by Moses and Christ "), and III. iii. (θᾶττον ἄν τις τοὺς ἀπὸ Μωυσοῦ καὶ Χριστοῦ μεταδιδάξειεν ἢ τοὺς ταῖς αἵρεσι προστετηκότας ἰατρούς τε καὶ φιλοσόφους —" One could more easily teach novelties to the adherents of Moses and Christ than to doctors and philosophers who are stuck fast in the schools ").

[2] The number of those who lapsed during the persecutions of Decius and Diocletian was extraordinarily large; but Tertullian had already spoken of "people who are only Christians if the wind happens to be favourable " (Scorp., i.).

But the various stages of the process cannot be exhibited in these pages. It must suffice to remark that from about 230 A.D. onwards, many churches followed the lead of the Roman church in forgiving gross bodily sins, whilst after 251 A.D. most churches also forgave sins of idolatry. Thus the circle was complete; only in one or two cases were crimes of exceptional atrocity denied forgiveness, implying that the offender was not re-admitted to the church. It is quite obvious from the later writings of Tertullian ("nostrorum bonorum status iam mergitur," *de Pudic.*, i.), and from many a stinging remark in Origen's commentaries, that even by 220 A.D. the Christian churches, together with their bishops and clergy, were no longer what they had previously been, from a moral point of view;[1] nevertheless (as Origen expressly emphasizes against Celsus; cp. III. xxix.–xxx.) their morals still continued to excel the morals of other guilds within the empire and of the population in the cities, whilst the penitential ordinances between 251 and 325, of which we possess no small number, point to a very earnest endeavour being made to keep up morality and holiness of life. Despite their moral deterioration, the Christian churches must have still continued to wield a powerful influence and fascination for people of a moral disposition.

But here again we are confronted with the *complexio oppositorum*. For the churches must have also produced a powerful effect upon people in every degree of moral weakness, just on account of that new internal development which had culminated about the middle of the third century. If the churches hitherto had been societies which admitted people under the burden of sin, not denying entrance even to the worst offender, but securing him forgiveness with God *and thereafter requiring him to continue pure and holy, now they had established themselves voluntarily or involuntarily as societies based upon unlimited forgiveness.* Along with baptism, and subsequent to it, they had now developed a second sacrament; it was still without form, but they relied upon it as a thing which had form, and considered themselves justified in applying it in almost every

---

[1] The "Shepherd" of Hermas shows, however, the amount of trouble which even at an earlier period had to be encountered.

case—it was *the sacrament of penitence.* Whether this development enabled them to meet the aims of their Founder better than their more rigorous predecessors, or whether it removed them further from these aims, is not a question upon which we need to enter. The point is, that now for the first time the attractive power of Christianity as a religion of pardon came fully into play. No doubt, everything depended on the way in which pardon was applied, but it was not merely a frivolous scoff on the part of Julian the apostate when he pointed out that the way in which the Christian churches preached and administered forgiveness was injurious to the best interests of morality, and that there were members in the Christian churches whom no other religious societies would tolerate within their bounds. The feature which Julian censured had arisen upon a wide scale as far back as the second half of the third century. When clerics of the same church started to quarrel with each other, as in the days of Cyprian at Carthage, they instantly flung at each other the most heinous charges of fraud, of adultery, and even of murder. One asks, in amazement and indignation, why the offending presbyter or deacon had not been long ago expelled from the church, if such accusations were correct? To this question no answer can be given. Besides, even if these repeated and almost stereotyped charges were not in every case well founded, the not less serious fact remains that one brother wantonly taxed another with the most heinous crimes. It reveals a laxity that would not have been possible, had not a fatal influence been already felt from the reverse side of the religion of the merciful heart and of forgiveness.

Still, this forgiveness is not to be condemned by the mere fact that it was extended to worthless characters. We are not called upon to be its judges. We must be content to ascertain, as we have now ascertained, that while the character of the Christian religion, as a religion of morality, suffered some injury in the course of the third century, this certainly did not impair its powers of attraction. It was now sought after as the religion which formed a permanent channel of forgiveness to mankind. Which was partly due, no doubt, to the fact that different groups of people were now appealing to it.

Yet, if this sketch of the characteristics of Christianity is not to be left unfinished two things must still be noted. One is this: the church never sanctioned the thesis adopted by most of the gnostics,[1] that there was a qualitative distinction of human beings according to their moral capacities, and that in consequence of this there must also be different grades in their ethical conduct and in the morality which might be expected from them. But there was a primitive distinction between a morality for the perfect and a morality which was none the less adequate, and this distinction was steadily maintained. Even in Paul there are evident traces of this view alongside of a strictly uniform conception. The Catholic doctrine of "præcepta" and "consilia" prevailed almost from the first within the Gentile church, and the words of the Didachê which follow the description of "the two ways" (c. vi: "If thou canst bear the whole yoke of the Lord, thou shalt be perfect: but if thou canst not, do what thou canst") only express a conviction which was very widely felt. The distinction between the "children" and the "mature" (or perfect), which originally obtained within the sphere of Christian knowledge, overflowed into the sphere of conduct, since both spheres were closely allied.[2] Christianity had always her heroic souls in asceticism and poverty and so forth. They were held in exceptional esteem (see above), and they had actually to be warned, even

---

[1] It is surprising that the attractiveness of these (gnostic) ideas was not greater than it seems to have been. But by the time that they sought to establish their position on Christian soil or to force their way in, the church's organisation was well knit together, so that gnosticism could do no more in the way of breaking it up or creating a rival institution.

[2] The ascetics are not only the "perfect" but also the "religious," strictly speaking. Cp. Origen (Hom. ii. *in Num.*, vol. x. p. 20), who describes virgins, ascetics, and so forth, as those "qui in professione religionis videntur"; also Hom. xvii. *in Luc.* (vol. v. p. 151), where, on 1 Cor. i. 2, he observes: "Memini cum interpretarer 1 Cor. i. 2 dixisse me diversitatem ecclesiae et eorum qui invocant nomen domini. Puto enim monogamum et virginem et eum, qui in castimonia perseverat, esse de ecclesia dei, eum vero, qui sit digamus, licet bonam habeat conversationem et ceteris virtutibus polleat, tamen non esse de ecclesia et de numero, qui non habent rugam aut maculam aut aliquid istius modi, sed esse de secundo gradu et de his qui invocant nomen domini, et qui salvantur quidem in nomine Jesu Christi, nequaquam tamen coronantur ab eo" (church=virgins, ascetics, and the once married: those who call on the name of the Lord=the second rank, *i.e.*, the twice married, even though their lives are pure otherwise).

in the sub-apostolic age, against pride and boasting (cp. Ignat.,
ad Polyc. v. : εἴ τις δύναται ἐν ἁγνείᾳ μένειν εἰς τιμὴν τῆς σαρκὸς
τοῦ κυρίου, ἐν ἀκαυχησίᾳ μενέτω· ἐάν καυχήσηται, ἀπώλετο—" If
anyone is able to remain in purity to the honour of the flesh of
the Lord, let him remain as he is without boasting of it. If he
boast, he is a lost man ; " also Clem. Rom., xxxviii. : ὁ ἁγνὸς ἐν
τῇ σαρκὶ ἤτω καὶ μὴ ἀλαζονευέσθω—" Let him that is pure in
the flesh remain so and not boast about it "). It was in these
ascetics of early Christianity that the first step was taken towards
monasticism.

Secondly, veracity in matters of fact is as liable to suffer as
righteousness in every religion : every religion gets encumbered
with fanaticism, the indiscriminate temper, and fraud. This is
writ clear upon the pages of church history from the very first.
In the majority of cases, in the case of miracles that have never
happened, of visions that were never seen, of voices that were
never heard, and of books that were never written by their
alleged authors, we are not in a position at this time of day to
decide where self-deception ended and where fraud began, where
enthusiasm became deliberate and then passed into conventional
deception, any more than we are capable of determining, as a rule,
where a harsh exclusiveness passes into injustice and fanaticism.
We must content ourselves with determining that cases of this
kind were unfortunately not infrequent, and that their number
increased. What we call priestcraft and miracle-fraud were not
absent from the third or even from the second century. They
are to be found in the Catholic church as well as in several of
the gnostic conventicles, where water was changed into wine (as
by the Marcosians) or wine into water (cp. the books of Jeû).

Christianity, as the religion of the Spirit and of power, contained another element which proved of vital importance, and
which exhibited pre-eminently the originality of the new faith.
This was its reverence for the lowly, for sorrow, suffering, and
death, together with its triumphant victory over these contradictions of human life. The great incentive and example alike
for the eliciting and the exercise of this virtue lay in the
Redeemer's life and cross. Blent with patience and hope, this
reverence overcame any external hindrance ; it recognised in

suffering the path to deity, and thus triumphed in the midst of all its foes. "Reverence for what is beneath us—this is the last step to which mankind were fitted and destined to attain. But what a task it was, not only to let the earth lie beneath us, we appealing to a higher birthplace, but also to recognize humility and poverty, mockery and despite, disgrace and wretchedness, suffering and death—to recognize these things as divine."[1] Here lies the root of the most profound factor contributed by Christianity to the development of the moral sense, and contributed with perfect strength and delicacy. It differentiates itself, as an entirely original element, from the similar phenomena which recur in several of the philosophical schools (*e.g.*, the Cynic). Not until a much later period, however,—from Augustine onwards,—did this phase of feeling find expression in literature.

Even what is most divine on earth has its shadow nevertheless, and so it was with this reverence. It was inevitable that the new æsthetic which it involved should become an æsthetic of lower things, of death and its grim relics ; in this way it ceased to be æsthetic by its very effort to attain the impossible, until finally a much later period devised an æsthetic of spiritual agony and raptures over suffering. But there was worse behind. Routine and convention found their way even into this phase of feeling. What was most profound and admirable was gradually stripped of its inner spirit and rendered positively repulsive[2] by custom, common talk, mechanical tradition, and ritual practices. Yet, however strongly we feel about the unsightly phlegm of this corruption, and however indignantly we condemn it, we should never forget that it represented the shadow thrown by the most profound and at the same time the most heroic mood of the human soul in its spiritual exaltation ; it is, in fact, religion itself, fully ripe.

[1] Goethe, *Wanderjahre*, xxiv. p. 243.

[2] Goethe (*ibid.*, p. 255) has said the right word on this as well : "We draw a veil over those sufferings (the sufferings of Christ in particular), just because we reverence them so highly. We hold it is a damnable audacity to take these mysterious secrets, in which the depth of the divine sorrow lies hid, and play with them, fondle them, trick them out, and never rest until the supreme object of reverence appears vulgar and paltry."

CHAPTER VI

THE RELIGION OF AUTHORITY AND OF REASON, OF THE MYSTERIES AND OF TRANSCENDENTALISM

I

" Some Christians [evidently not all] will not so much as give or accept any account of what they believe. They adhere to the watchwords ' Prove not, only believe,' and ' Thy faith shall save thee.' Wisdom is an evil thing in the world, folly a good thing." So Celsus wrote about the Christians (I. ix.). In the course of his polemical treatise he brings forward this charge repeatedly in various forms; as in I. xii., "They say, in their usual fashion, ' Enquire not'"; I. xxvi. f., "That ruinous saying of Jesus has deceived men. With his illiterate character and lack of eloquence he has gained of course almost no one but illiterate people";[1] III. xliv., "The following rules are laid down by Christians, even by the more intelligent among them. ' Let none draw near to us who is educated, or shrewd, or wise. Such qualifications are in our eyes an evil. But let the ignorant, the idiots, and the fools come to us with confidence'"; vi. x. f., "Christians say, ' Believe first of all that he whom I announce to thee is the Son of God.'" " All are ready to cry out, ' Believe if thou wilt be saved, or else begone.' What, is wisdom among men they describe as foolishness with God, and their reason for this is their desire to win over none but the uneducated and simple by means of this saying." Justin also represents Christians being charged by their opponents with

---

[1] Still Celsus adds that there are also one or two discreet, pious, reasonable people among the Christians, and some who are experts in intelligent argument.

making blind assertions and giving no proof (*Apol.*, I. lii.),
while Lucian declares (*Peregr.*, xiii.) that they "received such
matters on faith without the slightest enquiry" (ἄνευ τινὸς
ἀκριβοῦς πίστεως τὰ τοιαῦτα παρεδέξαντο).

A description and a charge of this kind were not entirely
unjustified. Within certain limits Christians have maintained,
from the very first, that the human understanding has to be
captured and humbled in order to obey the message of the
gospel. Some Christians even go a step further. Bluntly,
they require a blind faith for the word of God. When the
apostle Paul views his preaching, not so much in its content as
in its origin, as *the word of God*, and even when he notes the
contrast between it and the wisdom of this world, his demand
is for a firm, resolute faith, and for nothing else. "We bring
every thought into captivity to the obedience of Christ" (2 Cor.
x. 5), and—the word of the cross tolerates no σοφία λόγου
(no wisdom of speech), it is to be preached as foolishness and
apprehended by faith (1 Cor. i. 17 f.). Hence he also issues
a warning against the seductions of philosophy (Col. ii. 8).
Tertullian advanced beyond this position much more boldly.
He prohibited Christians (*de Præscr.*, viii. f.) from ever applying
to doctrine the saying, "Seek, and ye shall find." "What,"
he exclaims (*op. cit.*, vii.), "what has Athens to do with
Jerusalem, or the Academy with the church? What have
heretics to do with Christians? Our doctrine originates with
the porch of Solomon, who had himself taught that men must
seek the Lord in simplicity of heart. Away with all who
attempt to introduce a mottled Christianity of Stoicism and
Platonism and dialectic! Now that Jesus Christ has come, no
longer need we curiously inquire, or even investigate, since the
gospel is preached. When we believe, we have no desire to
sally beyond our faith. For our belief is the primary and
palmary fact. There is nothing further that we have still to
believe beyond our own belief. . . . . To be ignorant of everything outside the rule of faith, is to possess all knowledge."[1]

---

[1] Cp. *de Carne Christi*, ii. : "Si propheta es, praenuntia aliquid ; si apostolus,
praedica publice ; si apostolicus, cum apostolis senti ; si tantum Christianus es,
crede quod traditum est " ("If you are a prophet, predict something ; if an apostle,

Many missionaries may have preached in this way, not merely after but even previous to the stern conflict with gnosticism. Faith is a matter of resolve, a resolve of the will and a resolve to obey. Trouble it not by any considerations of human reason!

Preaching of this kind is only possible if at the same time some powerful authority is set up. And such an authority was set up. First and foremost (cp. Paul), it was the authority of the revealed will of God as disclosed in the mission of the Son to earth. Here external and internal authority blended and coincided, for while the divine will is certainly an authority in itself (according to Paul's view), and is also capable of making itself felt as such, without men understanding its purpose and right (Rom. ix. f.), the apostle is equally convinced that God's gracious will makes itself intelligible *to the inner man.*

Still, even in Paul, the external and internal authority vested in the cross of Christ is accompanied by other authorities which claim the obedience of faith. These are the written word of the sacred documents and the sayings of Jesus. In their case also neither doubt nor contradiction is permissible.

For all that, the great apostle endeavoured to reason out everything, and in the last resort it is never a question with him of any "sacrifice of the intellect" (see below). Some passages may seem to contradict this statement, but they only seem to do so. When Paul demands the obedience of faith and sets up the authority of "the word" or of "the cross," he simply means that obedience of faith which is inseparable from any religion whatsoever, no matter how freely and spiritually it may be set forth. But, as Celsus and Tertullian serve to remind us (if any reminder at all is necessary on this point), many missionaries and teachers went about their work in a very different manner. They simply erected their authority wherever they went; it was the letter of Scripture more and more,[1]

preach openly; if a follower of the apostles, think as they thought; if you are merely a Christian individual, believe tradition"). But faith was many a time more rigorous among the masses (the "simpliciores" or "simplices et idiotae") than theologians—even than Tertullian himself—cared. Origen's laments over this are numerous (cp., *e.g.*, *de Princip.*, iv. 8).

[1] For details on the significance of the Bible in the mission, see Chapter VIII.

but ere long it became the rule of faith, together with the church (the church as "the pillar and ground of the truth," στῦλος καὶ ἑδραίωμα τῆς ἀληθείας, as early as 1 Tim. iii. 15). True, they endeavoured to buttress the authority of these two magnitudes, the Bible and the church, by means of rational arguments (the authority of the Bible being supported by the proof from the fulfilment of prophecy, and that of the church by the proof from the unbroken tradition which reached back to Christ himself and invested the doctrine of the church with the value of Christ's own words). In so doing they certainly did not demand an absolutely blind belief. But, first of all, it was assuredly not every missionary or teacher who was competent to lead such proofs. They were adduced only by the educated apologists and controversialists. And in the second place, no *inner* authority can ever be secured for the Bible and the church by means of external proofs. The latter really remained a sort of alien element. At bottom, the faith required was blind faith.

Still, it would be a grave error to suppose that for the majority of people the curt demand that authorities must be simply believed and reason repudiated, acted as a serious obstacle to their acceptance of the Christian religion.[1] In reality, it was the very opposite. The more peremptory and exclusive is the claim of faith which any religion makes, the more trustworthy and secure does that religion seem to the majority; the more it relieves them of the duty and responsibility of reflecting upon its truth, the more welcome it is. Any firmly established authority thus acts as a sedative. Nay more. The most welcome articles of faith are just the most paradoxical, which are a mockery of all experience and rational reflection; the reason for this being that they appear to guarantee the

---

[1] Naturally it did repel highly cultured men like Celsus and Porphyry. For Celsus, see above, p. 219. Porphyry, the pagan in Macarius Magnes (IV. ix.), writes thus on Matt. xi. 25: "As the mysteries are hidden from the wise and thrown down before minors and senseless sucklings (in which case, of course, even what is written for minors and senseless people should have been clear and free from obscurity), it is better to aim at a lack of reason and of education! And this is the very acme of Christ's sojourn upon earth, to conceal the ray of knowledge from the wise and to unveil it to the senseless and to small children!"

disclosure of divine wisdom and not of something which is merely human and therefore unreliable. "Miracle is the favourite child of faith." That is true of more than miracles; it applies also to the miraculous doctrines which cannot be appropriated by a man unless he is prepared to believe and obey them blindly.

But so long as the authorities consisted of books and doctrines, the coveted haven of rest was still unreached. The meaning of these doctrines always lies open to some doubt. Their scope, too, is never quite fixed. And, above all, their application to present-day questions is often a serious difficulty, which leads to painful and disturbing controversies. "Blind faith" never gains its final haven until its authority is *living*, until questions can be put to it, and answers promptly received from it. During the first generations of Christendom no such authority existed; but in the course of the second century and down to the middle of the third, it was gradually taking shape —I mean, *the authority of the church as represented in the episcopate*. It did not dislodge the other authorities of God's saving purpose and the holy Scripture, but by stepping to their side it pushed them into the background. *The auctoritas interpretiva is invariably the supreme and real authority.* After the middle of the third century, the church and the episcopate developed so far that they exercised the functions of a sacred authority. And it was after that period that the church first advanced by leaps and bounds, till it became a church of the masses. For while the system of a living authority in the church had still defects and gaps of its own—since in certain circumstances it either exercised its functions very gradually or could not enforce its claims at all—these defects did not exist for the masses. In the bishop or priest, or even in the ecclesiastical fabric and the cultus, the masses were directly conscious of something holy and authoritative to which they yielded submission, and this state of matters had prevailed for a couple of generations by the time that Constantine granted recognition and privileges to Christianity. *This* was the church on which he conferred privileges, this church with its enormous authority over the masses! *These* were the Christians whom he declared

to be the support of the throne, people who clung to the
bishops with submissive faith and who would not resist their
divinely appointed authority! The Christianity that triumphed
was the Christianity of blind faith, which Celsus has depicted.
When would a State ever have shown any practical interest in
any other kind of religion?

II

Christianity is a *complexio oppositorum*. The very Paul who
would have reason brought into captivity, proclaimed that
Christianity, in opposition to polytheism, was a "reasonable
service of God" (Rom. xii. 1, λογικὴ λατρεία), and declared
that what pagans thought folly in the cross of Christ seemed
so to those alone who were blinded, whereas what Christians
preached was in reality the profoundest wisdom. He went on
to declare that this was not merely reserved for us as a wisdom
to be attained in the far future, but capable of being understood
even at present by believers as such. He promised that he
would introduce the "perfect" among them to its mysteries.[1]
This promise (cp., *e.g.*, 1 Cor. ii. 6 f., σοφίαν ἐν τοῖς τελείοις) he
made good; yet he never withheld this wisdom from those who
were children or weak in spiritual things. He could not, indeed
he dared not, utter all he understood of God's word and the
cross of Christ—λαλοῦμεν θεοῦ σοφίαν ἐν μυστηρίῳ τὴν ἀποκεκ-
ρυμμένην ("We speak the wisdom of God in a mystery, even the
hidden wisdom")—but he moved freely in the realm of history
and speculation, drawing abundantly from "the depths of the
riches and wisdom and knowledge of God." In Paul one feels
the joy of the thinker who enters into the thoughts of God, and
who is convinced that in and with and through his faith he has

---

[1] For the "perfect," see p. 216. They constitute a special class for Paul. The
distinction came to be sharply drawn at a later period, especially in the Alexandrian
school, where one set of Christian precepts was formed for the "perfect" ("those
who know"), another for believers. Christ himself was said by the Alexandrians
(not merely by the gnostics) to have committed an esoteric doctrine to his intimate
disciples, and to have provided for its transmission. Cp. Clement of Alexandria,
as quoted in Eus., *H.E.*, ii. 1: Ἰακώβῳ τῷ δικαίῳ καὶ Ἰωάννῃ καὶ Πέτρῳ μετὰ τὴν
ἀνάστασιν παρέδωκεν τὴν γνῶσιν ὁ κύριος, οὗτοι τοῖς λοιποῖς ἀποστόλοις παρέδωκαν,
κ.τ.λ. ("The Lord delivered all knowledge after the resurrection to James the
Just, and John, and Peter; they delivered it to the rest of the apostles," etc.).

passed from darkness into light, from confusion, cloudiness, and oppression into the lucid air that frees the soul.

" We have been rescued from darkness and lifted into the light "—such was the chant which rose from a chorus of Christians during those early centuries. It was *intellectual truth and lucidity* in which they revelled and gloried. Polytheism seemed to them an oppressive night ; now that it was lifted off them, the sun shone clearly in the sky! Wherever they looked, everything became clear and sure in the light of spiritual mono-theism, owing to the living God. Read, for example, the epistle of Clemens Romanus,[1] the opening of the Clementine Homily,[2] or the epistle of Barnabas ;[3] listen to the apologists, or study Clement of Alexandria and Origen. They gaze at Nature, only to rejoice in the order and unity of its movement ; heaven and earth are a witness to them of God's omnipotence and unity. They ponder the capacities and endowments of human nature, and trace in them the Creator. In human reason and liberty they extol his boundless goodness ; they com-pare the revelations and the will of God with this reason and freedom, and lo, there is entire harmony between them ! Noth-ing is laid on man which does not already lie within him, nothing is revealed which is not already presupposed in his inward being. The long-buried religion of nature, religion μετὰ λόγου, has been rediscovered.[4] They look at Christ, and scales fall, as it were, from their eyes ! What wrought in him was the Logos, the very Logos by which the world had been created and with which the spiritual essence of man was bound up inextric-ably, the Logos which had wrought throughout human history in all that was noble and good, and which was finally obliged to reveal its power completely in order to dissipate the obstacles

---

[1] Especially chap. xix. f.

[2] 2 Clem. i. 4 f. : τὸ φῶς ἡμῶν ἐχαρίσατο . . . . πηροὶ ὄντες τῇ διανοίᾳ προσ-κυνοῦντες λίθους καὶ ξύλα καὶ χρυσὸν καὶ ἄργυρον καὶ χαλκὸν, ἔργα ἀνθρώπων . . . . ἀμαύρωσιν οὖν περικείμενοι καὶ τοιαύτης ἀχλύος γέμοντες ἐν τῇ ὁράσει ἀνεβλέψαμεν (" He bestowed on us the light . . . . we were blind in understanding, worship-ping stones and stocks and gold and silver and brass, the works of men. . . . . Thus, girt with darkness and oppressed by so thick a mist in our vision, we regained our sight "). There are numerous passages of a similar nature.

[3] Cp. chap. i., chap. ii. 2 f.

[4] Cp. Justin's *Apology*, Tertullian's tract *de Testimonio Animæ*, etc.

and disorders by which man was beset—so weak was he, for all the glory of his creation. Lastly, they contemplate the course of history, its beginning, middle, and end, only to find a common purpose everywhere, which is in harmony with a glorious origin and with a still·more glorious conclusion. The freedom of the creature, overcome by the allurements of demons, has occasioned disorders, but the disorders are to be gradually removed by the power of the Christ-Logos. At the commencement of history humanity was like a child, full of good and divine instincts, but as yet untried and liable to temptation; at the close, a perfected humanity will stand forth, fitted to enter immortality. Reason, freedom, immortality—these are to carry the day against error, failure, and decay.

Such was the Christianity of many people, a bright and glad affair, the doctrine of pure reason. The new doctrine proved a deliverance, not an encumbrance, to the understanding. Instead of imposing foreign matter on the understanding, it threw light upon its own darkened contents. *Christianity is a divine revelation, but it is at the same time pure reason; it is the true philosophy.*

Such was the conception entertained by most of the apologists, and they tried to show how the entire content of Christianity was embraced by this idea. Anything that did not fit in, they left out. It was not that they rejected it. They simply explained it afresh by means of their "scientific" method, *i.e.*, the method of allegorical spiritualizing, or else they relegated it to that great collection of evidence, the proof from prophecy. In this way, anything that seemed obnoxious or of no material value was either removed or else enabled to retain a formal value as part of the striking proof which confirmed the divine character of Christianity. It is impossible in these pages to exhibit in detail the rational philosophy which thus emerged;[1] for our immediate purpose it is enough to state that a prominent group of Christian teachers existed as late as the opening of the fourth century (for Lactantius was among their number) who held this conception of Christianity. As apologists and as

---

[1] I have endeavoured to expound it in my *Dogmengeschichte*, I.(3) pp. 462-507 [Eng. trans., iii. 267 f.].

teachers *ex cathedra* they took an active part in the Christian mission. Justin,[1] for example, had his " school," no less than Tatian. The theologians in the royal retinue of Constantine also pursued this way of thinking, and it permeated any decree of Constantine that touched on Christianity, and especially his address to the holy council.[2] When Eusebius wishes to make the new religion intelligible to the public at large, he describes it as the religion of reason and lucidity; see, for example, the first book of his church history and the life of Constantine with its appendices. We might define all these influential teachers as "rationalists of the supernatural," to employ a technical term of modern church history; but as the revelation was continuous, commencing with creation, never ceasing, and ever in close harmony with the capacities of men, the term "supernatural" is really almost out of place in this connection. The outcome of it all was a pure religious rationalism, with a view of history all its own, in which, as was but natural, the final phenomena of the future tallied poorly with the course traversed in the earlier stages. From Justin, Commodian, and Lactantius, we learn how the older apocalyptic and the rationalistic moralism were welded together, without any umbrage being taken at the strange blend which this produced.

III

But authority and reason, blind faith and clear insight, do not sum up all the forms in which Christianity was brought

---

[1] See the *Acta Justini*, and his *Apology*. We know that Tatian had Rhodon as one of his pupils (Eus., *H.E.*, v. 13).

[2] This address, even apart from its author, is perhaps the most impressive apology ever written (for its genuineness, see my *Chronologie*, ii. pp. 116 f., and Wendland in *Philolog. Wochenschr.*, 1902, No. 8). It was impressive for half-educated readers, *i.e.*, for the educated public of those days. Very effectively, it concludes by weaving together the (fabricated) prophecies of the Sibylline oracles and the (interpolated) Eclogue of Virgil, and by contrasting the reign of Constantine with those of his predecessors. The Christianity it presents is exclusive; even Socrates finds no favour, and Plato is sharply censured (ch. ix.) as well as praised. Still, it is tinged with Neoplatonism. The Son of God as such and as the Christ is put strongly in the foreground; he is God, at once God's Son and the hero of a real myth. But everything shimmers in a sort of speculative haze which corresponds to the style, the latter being poetic, flowery, and indefinite.

before the world. The mental standpoint of the age and its religious needs were so manifold that it was unwilling to forgo any form, even in Christianity, which was capable of transmitting anything of religious value. It was a complex age, and its needs made even the individual man complex. The very man who longed for an authority to which he might submit blindfold, often longed at the same moment for a reasonable religion; nor was he satisfied even when he had secured them both, but craved for something more, for sensuous pledges which gave him a material representation of holy things, and for symbols of mysterious power. Yet, after all, was this peculiar to that age? Was it only in these days that men have cherished such desires?

From the very outset of the Christian religion, its preaching was accompanied by two outward rites, neither less nor more than two, viz., baptism and the Lord's supper. We need not discuss either what was, or what was meant to be, their original significance. The point is, that whenever we enter the field of Gentile Christianity, their meaning is essentially fixed; although Christian worship is to be a worship in spirit and in truth, these sacraments are sacred actions *which operate on life*, containing the forgiveness of sins, knowledge, and eternal life.[1] No doubt, the elements of water, bread, and wine are symbols, and the scene of operation is not external; still, the symbols do actually convey to the soul all that they signify. Each symbol has a mysterious but real connection with the fact which it signifies.

To speak of water, bread, and wine as holy elements, or of being immersed in water that the soul might be washed and purified: to talk of bread and wine as body and blood, or as the body and the blood of Christ, or as the soul's food for immortality: to correlate water and blood—all this kind of language was quite intelligible to that age. It was intelligible to the blunt realist, as well as to the most sublime among what may be called "the spiritualists." *The two most sublime spiritualists of the church, namely, John and Origen, were the most profound exponents of the mysteries,* while the great gnostic

---

[1] See the gospel of John, the epistle of John, and the Didachê with its sacramental prayer.

theologians linked on their most abstract theosophies to realistic mysteries. *They were all sacramental theologians.* Christ, they held, had connected, and in fact identified, the benefits he brought to men with symbols; the latter were the channel and vehicle of the former; the man who participates in the unction of the holy symbol gets grace thereby. This was a fact with which people were familiar from innumerable mysteries; in and with the corporeal application of the symbol, unction or grace was poured into the soul. The connection seemed like a predestined harmony, and in fact the union was still more inward. The sentence of the later schoolmen, "Sacramenta continent gratiam," is as old as the Gentile church, and even older, for it was in existence long before the latter sprang into being.

The Christian religion was intelligible and impressive, owing to the fact that it offered men sacraments.[1] Without its

---

[1] Many, of course, took umbrage at the Lord's supper as the eating and drinking of flesh and blood. The criticism of the pagan (Porphyry) in Mac. Magnes, III. xv., is remarkable. He does not attack the mystery of the supper in the Synoptic tradition, but on John vi. 53 ("Except ye eat my flesh and drink my blood, ye have no life in yourselves") he observes: "Is it not, then, bestial and absurd, surpassing all absurdity and bestial coarseness, for a man to eat human flesh and drink the blood of his fellow tribesman or relative, and thereby win life eternal? [Porphyry, remember, was opposed to the eating of flesh and the tasting of blood in general.] Why, tell me what greater coarseness could you introduce into life, if you practise that habit? What further crime will you start, more accursed than this loathsome profligacy? The ear cannot bear to hear it mentioned—and by 'it,' I am far from meaning the action itself, I mean the very name of this strange, utterly unheard of offence. Never, even in extraordinary emergencies, was any-thing like this offence enacted before mankind in the most fantastic presentations of the Erinyes. Not even would the Potidæans have admitted anything like this, although they had been debilitated by inhuman hunger. Of course we know about Thyestes and his meals, etc. [then follow similar cases from antiquity]. All these persons unintentionally committed this offence. But no civilized person ever served up such food, none ever got such gruesome instructions from any teacher. And if thou wert to pursue thine inquiries as far as Scythia or the Macrobii of Ethiopia, or to travel right round the margin of the sea itself, thou wouldst find people who eat lice and roots, or live on serpents, and make mice their food, but all refrain from human flesh. What, then, does this saying mean? *For even although it was meant to be taken in a more mystical or allegorical (and therefore profitable) sense,* still the mere sound of the words upon the ear grates inevitably on the soul, and makes it rebel against the loathsomeness of the saying. . . . . Many teachers, no doubt, attempt to introduce new and strange ideas. But none has ever devised a precept so strange and horrible as this, neither

mysteries, people would have found it hard to appreciate the new religion. But who can tell how these mysteries arose? No one was to blame, no one was responsible. Had not baptism chanced to have been instituted, had not the observance of the holy supper been enjoined (and can any one maintain that these flowed inevitably from the essence of the gospel?), then some sacrament would have been created out of a parable of Jesus, out of a word or act of some kind or another. The age for material and certainly for bloody sacrifices was now past and gone; these were no longer the alloy of any religion. But the age of sacraments was very far from being over; it was in full vigour and prime. Every hand that was stretched out for religion, tried to grasp it in sacramental form; the eye saw sacraments where sacraments there were none, and the senses gave them body.[1]

Water and blood, bread and wine—though the apostle Paul was far from being a sacramental theologian, yet even he could not wholly avoid these mysteries, as is plain if one will but read the tenth chapter of First Corinthians, and note his speculations upon baptismal immersion. But Paul was the first and almost[2] the last theologian of the early church with whom sacramental theology was really held in check by clear ideas and strictly spiritual considerations. After him all the flood-gates were opened, and in poured the mysteries with their lore. In Ignatius, who is only sixty years later than Paul, they had already dragged down and engulfed the whole of intelligent theology. A man like the author of Barnabas believes he has fathomed the depths of truth when he connects his ideas with the water, the blood, and the cross. And the man who wrote

historian nor philosopher, neither barbarian nor primitive Greek. See here, what has come over you that you foolishly exhort credulous people to follow such a faith? Look at all the mischief that is set thus afoot to storm the cities as well as the villages! Hence it was, I do believe, that neither Mark nor Luke nor Matthew mentioned this saying, just because they were of opinion that it was unworthy of civilized people, utterly strange and unsuitable and quite alien to the habits of honourable life."

[1] By the end of the second century, at the very latest, the *disciplina arcani* embraced the sacraments, partly owing to educational reasons, partly to the example of pagan models. It rendered them still more weighty and impressive.

[2] Not quite the last, for Marcion and his disciples do not seem to have been sacramental theologians at all.

these words—"There are three that bear witness, the Spirit and the water and the blood, and these three agree in one" (1 John v. 8)—had a mind which lived in symbols and in mysteries. In the book of Revelation the symbols generally are not what we call "symbols" but semi-real things—*e.g.*, the Lamb, the blood, the washing and the sprinkling, the seal and the sealing. Much of this still remains obscure to us. What is the meaning, for example, of the words (1 John ii. 27) about the "unction," an unction conveying knowledge which is so complete that it renders any further teaching quite unnecessary?

But how is this, it may be asked? Is not John a thorough "spiritualist"? And are not Origen, Valentinus, and Basilides also "spiritualists"? How, then, can we assert that their realistic expressions meant something else to them than mere symbols? In the case of John this argument can be defended with a certain amount of plausibility, since we do not know his entire personality. All we know is John the author. And even as an author he is known to us merely on one side of his nature, for he cannot have always spoken and written as he does in his extant writings. But in regard to the rest, so far as they are known to us on several sides of their characters, the plea is untenable. This is plain from a study of Clement and Origen, both of whom are amply accessible to us. In their case the combination of the mysterious realistic element with the spiritual is rendered feasible by the fact that they have simply no philosophy of religion at all which is capable of being erected upon one level, but *merely one which consists of different stories built one upon the other.*[1] In the highest of these stories, realism of every kind certainly vanishes; in fact, even the very system of intermediate agencies and forces, including the Logos itself, vanishes entirely, leaving nothing but God and the souls that are akin to him. These have a reciprocal knowledge of each other's essence, they love each other, and thus are absorbed in one another. But ere this consummation is reached, a ladder must be climbed. And every stage or rung has special forces which correspond to it, implying a theology, a metaphysic, and

[1] This construction is common to them and to the idealist philosophers of their age.

an ethic of its own.   On the lowest rung of the ascent, religion stands in mythological guise accompanied by sacraments whose inward value is as yet entirely unknown.   Even so, this is not falsehood but truth.   It answers to a definite state of the soul, and it satisfies this by filling it with bliss.   Even on this level the Christian religion is therefore true.   Later on, this entirely ceases, and yet it does not cease.   It ceases, because it is transcended; it does not cease, because the brethren still require this sort of thing, and because the foot of the ladder simply cannot be pulled away without endangering its upper structure.

After this brief sketch we must now try to see the significance of the realistic sacramental theology for these spiritualists. Men like Origen are indeed from our standpoint the most obnoxious of the theologians who occupied themselves with the sacraments, the blood, and the atonement.   In and with these theories they brought back a large amount of polytheism into Christianity by means of a back-door, since the lower and middle stories of their theological edifice required[1] to be furnished with angels and archangels, æons, semi-gods, and deliverers of every sort.   This was due both to cosmological and to soteriological reasons, for the two correspond like the lines AB and BA.[2]   But, above all, theology was enabled by this means to respond to the very slightest pressure of popular religion, and it is here, of course, that we discover the final clue to the singular enigma now before us.   This theology of the mysteries and of these varied layers and stages afforded the best means of conserving the spiritual character of the Christian

---

[1] For a considerable length of time one of the charges brought by Christians against the Jews was that of *angel-worship* (Preaching of Peter, in Clem. Alex., *Strom.*, vi. 5; Arist., *Apol.*, xiv. Celsus also is acquainted with this charge, and angel-worship is, of course, a note of the errorists combated in Colossians).   Subsequently the charge came to be levelled against the Christians themselves, and Justin had already written rather incautiously (*Apol.*, I. vi.): [τὸν θεὸν] καὶ τὸν παρ' αὐτοῦ υἱὸν ἐλθόντα καὶ διδάξαντα ἡμᾶς ταῦτα καὶ τὸν τῶν ἄλλων ἑπομένων καὶ ἐξομοιουμένων ἀγαθῶν ἀγγέλων στρατόν, πνεῦμά τε τὸ προφητικὸν σεβόμεθα καὶ προσκυνοῦμεν ("Both God and the Son who came from him and taught us these things, also the host of the other good angels who follow and are made like to him, and also the prophetic Spirit—these we worship and adore ").   The four words πνεῦμα τε τὸ προφητικὸν are supposed by some to be an interpolation.

[2] As to the "descent" and "ascent" of the soul, cp. Anz., "Zur Frage nach dem Ursprung des Gnosticismus" (*Texte u. Unters.*, xv. 4, 1897).

religion upon the upper level, and at the same time of arranging any compromise that might be desirable upon the lower. This was hardly the result of any conscious process. It came about quite naturally, for everything was already present in germ at the very first when sacraments were admitted into the religion.[1]

So much for the lofty theologians. With the inferior men the various stages dropped away and the sacramental factors were simply inserted in the religion in an awkward and unwieldy fashion. Read over the remarks made even in that age by Justin the rationalist upon the "cross," in the fifty-fifth chapter of his *Apology*. A more sturdy superstition can hardly be imagined. Notice how Tertullian (*de Bapt.*, i.) speaks of "water" and its affinity with the holy Spirit! One is persuaded, too, that all Christians with one consent attributed a magical force, exercised especially over demons, to the mere utterance of the name of Jesus and to the sign of the cross. One can also read the stories of the Lord's supper told by Dionysius of Alexandria, a pupil of Origen, and all that Cyprian is able to narrate as to the miracle of the host. Putting these and many similar traits together, one feels driven to conclude that Christianity has become a religion of magic, with its centre of gravity in the sacramental mysteries. "Ab initio sic non erat" is the protest that will be entered. "From the beginning it was not so." Perhaps. But one must go far back to find that initial stage—so far back that its very brief duration now eludes our search.

Originally the water, the bread and wine (the body and the blood), the name of Jesus, and the cross were the sole sacraments of the church, whilst baptism and the Lord's supper were the sole mysteries. But this state of matters could not continue. For different reasons, including reasons of philosophy, the scope of all sacraments tended to be enlarged, and so our period witnesses the further rise of sacramental details—anointing, the laying on of hands, sacred oil and salt, etc. But the most

---

[1] The necessity of priests and sacrifices was an idea present from the first in Gentile Christianity—even at the time when Christians sought with Paul to know of spiritual sacrifices alone and of the general priesthood of believers. Cp. Justin's *Dial.* cxvi : οὐ δέχεται παρ' οὐδενὸς θυσίας ὁ θεός, εἰ μὴ διὰ τῶν ἱερέων αὐτοῦ ("God receives sacrifices from no one, save through his priests").

momentous result was the gradual assimilation of the entire Christian worship to the ancient mysteries. By the third century it could already rival the most imposing cultus in all paganism, with its solemn and precise ritual, its priests, its sacrifices, and its holy ceremonies.

These developments, however, are by no means to be judged from the standpoint of Puritanism. Every age has to conceive and assimilate religion as it alone can; it must understand religion for itself, and make it a living thing for its own purposes. If the traits of Christianity which have been described in the preceding chapters have been correctly stated, if Christianity remained the religion of God the Father, of the Saviour and of salvation, of love and charitable enterprise, then it was perhaps a misfortune that the forms of contemporary religion were assumed. But the misfortune was by no means irreparable. Like every living plant, religion only grows inside a bark. Distilled religion is not religion at all.

Something further, however, still remains to be considered.

We have already seen how certain influential teachers— teachers, in fact, who founded the whole theology of the Christian Church—felt a strong impulse, and made it their definite aim, to get some *rational* conception of the Christian religion and to present it as the reasonable religion of mankind. This feature proved of great importance to the mission and extension of Christianity. Such teachers at once joined issue with contemporary philosophers, and, as the example of Justin proves, they did not eschew even controversy with these opponents. They retained all that they had in common with Socrates, Plato, and the Stoics; they showed how far people could go with them on the road; they attempted to give an historical explanation[1] of the points in common between themselves and pagan-

---

[1] The Jewish Alexandrian philosophers had been the pioneers in this direction, and all that was really needed was to copy them. But they had employed a variety of methods in their attempt, amongst which a choice had to be made. All these attempts *save one* were childish. One was quite appropriate, viz., that which explained the points of agreement by the sway of the same Logos which worked in the Jewish prophets and in the pagan philosophers and poets. One attempt, again, was naïve, viz., that which sought to expose the Greek philosophers and poets as plagiarists—though Celsus tried to do the same thing with

ism; and in this way they inaugurated the great adjustment of terms which was inevitable, unless Christians chose to remain a tiny sect of people who refused to concern themselves with culture and scientific learning. Still, as these discussions were carried on in a purely rational spirit, and as there was a frankly avowed partiality for the idea that Christianity was a transparently rational system, vital Christian truths were either abandoned or at any rate neglected. This meant a certain impoverishment, and a serious dilution, of the Christian faith.

Such a type of knowledge was certainly different from Paul's idea of knowledge, nor did it answer to the depths of the Christian religion. In one passage, perhaps, the apostle himself employs rational considerations of a Stoic character, when those were available for the purposes of his apologetic (cp. the opening sections of Romans), but he was hardly thinking about such ideas when he dwelt upon the Christian σοφία, σύνεσις, ἐπιστήμη, and γνῶσις ("wisdom," "intelligence," "understanding," and "knowledge"). Something very different was present to his mind at such moments. He was thinking of absorption in the being of God as revealed in Christ, of progress in the knowledge of his saving purpose, manifested in revelation and in history, of insight into the nature of sin or the power of demons (those "spirits of the air") or the dominion of death, of the boundless knowledge of God's grace, and of the clear anticipation of life eternal. In a word, he had in view a knowledge that soared up to God himself above all thrones, dominions, and principalities, and that also penetrated the depths from which we are delivered—a knowledge that traced human history from Adam to Christ, and that could, at the same time, define both faith and love, both sin and grace.

Paradoxical as it may appear, these phases of knowledge were actually fertilized and fed by the mysteries. From an early period they attached themselves to the mysteries. It was in the train of the mysteries that they crossed from the soil of heathenism, and it was by dint of the mysteries that they grew and developed

reference to Christ. Finally, it was both naïve and fanatical to undertake to prove that all agreements of the philosophers with Christian doctrine were but a delusion and the work of the devil.

upon the soil of Christianity. The case of the mysteries was at that time exactly what it was afterwards in the sixteenth and the seventeenth centuries. Despite all their acuteness, it was not the rationalists among the schoolmen who furthered learning and promoted its revival—it was the cabbalists, the natural philosophers, the alchemists, and the astrologers. What was the reason of this, it may be asked? How can learning develop itself by aid of the mysteries? The reply is very simple. Such development is possible, because learning or knowledge is attained by aid of the emotions and the imagination. Both are therefore able to arouse and to revive it. The great speculative efforts of the syncretistic philosophy of religion, whose principles have been already outlined (cp. pp. 30 f.), were based upon the mysteries (*i.e.*, upon the feelings and fancies, whose products were thrown into shape by the aid of speculation). The gnostics, who to a man were in no sense rationalists, attempted to transplant these living and glowing speculations to the soil of Christianity, and withal to preserve intact the supremacy of the gospel. The attempt was doomed to fail. Speculations of this kind contained too many elements alien to the spirit of Christianity which could not be relinquished.[1] But as separate fragments, broken up as it were into their constituent elements, they were able to render, and they did render, very signal services to a fruitful Christian philosophy of religion—these separate elements being originally prior perhaps to the combinations of later ages. All the more profound conceptions generated within Christianity subsequently to the close of the first century, all the transcendental knowledge, all those tentative ideas, which nevertheless were of more value than mere logical deductions—all this sprang in large measure from the contact of Christianity with the ancient lore

---

[1] These included the distinction between the god of creation (the demiurgus) and the god of redemption (redemption corresponding to emanation, not to creation), the abandonment of the Old Testament god, the dualistic opposition of soul and body, the disintegration of the redemptive personality, etc. Above all, redemption to the syncretist and the gnostic meant the separation of what had been unnaturally conjoined, while to the Christian it meant the union of what had been unnaturally divided. Christianity could not give up the latter conception of redemption, unless she was willing to overturn everything. Besides, this conception alone was adequate to the monarchical position of God.

of the mysteries. It disengaged profound conceptions and rendered them articulate. This is unmistakable in the case of John or of Ignatius or of Irenæus, but the clearest case is that of the great Alexandrian school. Materials valuable and useless alike, sheer fantasy and permanent truth which could no longer be neglected, all were mixed up in a promiscuous confusion—although this applies least of all to John, who, more than anyone, managed to impress a lofty unity even upon the form and expression of his thoughts. Such ideas will, of course, be little to the taste of anyone who holds that empiricism or rationalism confines knowledge within limits which one must not so much as try to overleap; but anyone who assigns greater value to tentative ideas than to a deliberate absence of all ideas whatsoever, will not be disposed to underestimate the labour expended by the thinkers of antiquity in connection with the mysteries. At any rate, it is beyond question that this phase of Christianity, which went on developing almost from the very hour of its birth, proved of supreme importance to the propaganda of the religion. Christianity gained special weight from the fact that in the first place it had mysterious secrets of its own, which it sought to fathom only to adore them once again in silence, and secondly, that it preached to the perfect in another and a deeper sense than it did to simple folk. These mysterious secrets may have had, as it is plain that they did have, a deadening effect on thousands of people by throwing obstacles in the way of their access to a rational religion; but on other people they had a stimulating effect, lending them wings to soar up into a supra-sensible world.[1]

[1] With this comparative appreciation of speculation in early Christianity, we concede the utmost that can be conceded in this connection. It is a time-honoured view that the richest fruit of Christianity, and in fact its very essence, lies in that " Christian" metaphysic which was the gradual product of innumerable alien ideas dragged into contact with the gospel. But this assertion deserves respect simply on the score of its venerable age. If it were true, then Jesus Christ would not be the founder of his religion, and indeed he would not even be its forerunner, since he neither revealed any philosophy of religion nor did he lay stress on anything which from such a standpoint is counted as cardinal. The Greeks certainly forgot before very long the Pauline saying ἐκ μέρους γινώσκομεν . . . . βλέπομεν γὰρ ἄρτι δι' ἐσόπτρου ἐν αἰνίγματι ("We know in part . . . . for now we see in a mirror, darkly"), and they also forgot that as knowledge (γνῶσις) and wisdom (σοφία) are charismatic gifts, the product of these gifts affords no definition of what

This ascent into the supra-sensible world ($\theta\epsilon o\pi o i\eta\sigma\iota\varsigma$, apotheosis) was the last and the highest word of all. The supreme message of Christianity was its promise of this divine state to every believer. We know how, in that age of the twilight of the gods, all human hopes concentrated upon this aim, and consequently a religion which not only taught but realized this apotheosis of human nature (especially in a form so complete that it did not exclude even the flesh) was bound to have an enormous success. Recent investigations into the history of dogma have shown that the development of Christian doctrine down to Irenæus must be treated in this light, viz., with the aim of proving how the idea of apotheosis—that supreme desire and dream of the ancient world, whose inability to realize it cast a deep shadow over its inner life—passed into Christianity, altered the original lines of that religion, and eventually dominated its entire contents.[1] The presupposition for it in primitive Christianity was the promise of a share in the future kingdom of God. As yet no one could foresee what was to fuse itself with this promise and transform it. But Paul co-ordinated with it the promise of life eternal in a twofold way : as given to man in justification (*i.e.*, in the Spirit, as an indissoluble inner union with the love of God), and as infused into man through holy media in the shape of a new nature. The fourth evangelist has grasped this double idea still more vividly, and given it sharper outline. His message is the spiritual and physical immanence of life eternal for believers. Still, the idea of love outweighs that of a natural transformation in his conception of the unity of believers with the Father and the Son, so that he only approaches the verge of the conception, " We have become gods." He still seems to prefer the expression " children of God." The apologists also keep the idea of apotheosis secondary to that of a full knowledge of God,[2] but even after the great epoch when " gnosticism " was opposed and assimilated, the church went

Christianity really is. Of the prominent teachers, Marcion, Apelles, and to some extent Irenæus, were the only ones who remained conscious of the limitations of knowledge.

[1] Cp. my *Dogmengeschichte* (third ed.), i., especially pp. 516 f. [Eng. trans., iii. 275 f.].

[2] Yet cp. Justin., *Dial.* cxxiv., a parallel to the great section in John. x. 33 f.

forward in the full assurance that she understood and preached apotheosis as the distinctive product of the Christian religion. When she spoke of "adoptio" by God, or of "participatio dei," for example, although a spiritual relationship continued to be understood, yet its basis and reality lay in a sacramental renewal of the physical nature : " Non ab initio dii facti sumus ; sed primo quidem homines, tunc demum dii " (We were not made gods at first ; at first we were men, thereafter we became gods at length). These are the words of Irenæus (cp. IV. xxxviii. 4, and often elsewhere), and this was the doctrine of Christian teachers after him. " Thou shalt avoid hell when thou hast gained the knowledge of the true God. Thou shalt have an immortal and incorruptible body as well as a soul, and shalt obtain the kingdom of heaven. Thou who hast lived on earth and known the heavenly King, shalt be a friend of God and a joint-heir with Christ, no longer held by lusts, or sufferings, or sicknesses. *For thou hast become divine*, and all that pertains to the God-life hath God promised to bestow on thee, seeing that thou, now become immortal, art deified."[1] This was the sort of preaching which anyone could understand, and which could not be surpassed.

Christianity, then, is a revelation which has to be believed, an authority which has to be obeyed, the rational religion which may be understood and proved, the religion of the mysteries or the sacraments, the religion of transcendental knowledge. So it was preached. It was not that every missionary expressed but one aspect of the religion. The various presentations of it were all mixed up together, although every now and then one of them would acquire special prominence. It is with amazement that we fathom the depths of this missionary preaching ; yet those who engaged in it were prepared at any moment to put everything else aside and rest their whole faith on the confession that " There is *one* God of heaven and earth, and Jesus is the Lord."

---

[1] Hippol., *Philos.*, x. 34. Cp. pseudo-Hippolytus, *Theoph.*, viii : εἰ ἀθάνατος γέγονεν ὁ ἄνθρωπος, ἔσται καὶ θεός (" If man become immortal, he shall also be divine ").

CHAPTER VII

THE TIDINGS OF THE NEW PEOPLE AND OF THE THIRD RACE:
THE HISTORICAL AND POLITICAL CONSCIOUSNESS OF CHRISTENDOM

I

THE gospel was preached simultaneously as the consummation of Judaism, as a new religion, and as the re-statement and final expression of man's original religion. Nor was this triple aspect preached merely by some individual missionary of dialectic gifts; it was a conception which emerged more or less distinctly in all missionary preaching of any scope. Convinced that Jesus, the teacher and the prophet, was also the Messiah who was to return ere long to finish off his work, people passed from the consciousness of being his *disciples* into that of being his *people*, the people of God: ὑμεῖς γένος ἐκλεκτόν, βασίλειον ἱεράτευμα, ἔθνος ἅγιον, λαὸς εἰς περιποίησιν (1 Pet. ii. 9: "Ye are a chosen *race*, a *royal* priesthood, a holy *nation*, a *people* for possession"); and in so far as they felt themselves to be a *people*, Christians knew they were the *true Israel*, at once the *new* people and the *old*.

This conviction that they were a *people*—*i.e.*, the transference of all the prerogatives and claims of the Jewish people to the new community as a new creation which exhibited and realized whatever was old and original in religion—this at once furnished adherents of the new faith with a *political and historical* self-consciousness. Nothing more comprehensive or complete or impressive than this consciousness can be conceived. Could there be any higher or more comprehensive conception than that of the complex of momenta afforded by the Christians'

estimate of themselves as " the true Israel," " the new people,"
" the original people," and " the people of the future," *i.e.*, of
eternity? This estimate of themselves rendered Christians
impregnable against all attacks and movements of polemical
criticism, while it further enabled them to advance in every
direction for a war of conquest. Was the cry raised, " You are
renegade Jews "—the answer came, " We are the community of
the Messiah, and therefore the true Israelites." If people said,
" You are simply Jews," the reply was, " We are a new creation
and a new people." If, again, they were taxed with their
recent origin and told that they were but of yesterday, they
retorted, " We only seem to be the younger People; from the
beginning we have been latent; we have always existed, previous
to any other people; we are the original people of God." If
they were told, " You do not deserve to live," the answer ran,
" We would die to live, for we are citizens of the world to come,
and sure that we shall rise again."

There were one or two other quite definite convictions of a
general nature specially taken over by the early Christians at
the very outset from the stores accumulated by a survey of
history made from the Jewish standpoint. Applied to their
own purposes, these were as follows:—(1) Our people is older
than the world; (2) the world was created for our sakes;[1] (3)
the world is carried on for our sakes; we retard the judgment
of the world; (4) everything in the world is subject to us and
must serve us; (5) everything in the world, the beginning and
course and end of all history, is revealed to us and lies transparent to our eyes; (6) we shall take part in the judgment of
the world and ourselves enjoy eternal bliss. In various early
Christian documents, dating from before the middle of the
second century, these convictions find expression, in homilies,
apocalypses, epistles, and apologies,[2] and nowhere else did

---

[1] By means of these two convictions, Christians made out their case for a
position superior to the world, and established a connection between creation and
history.

[2] Cp. the epistles of Paul, the apocalypse of John, the " Shepherd " of Hermas,
(*Vis.*, ii. 4. 1), the second epistle of Clement (xiv.), and the *Apologies* of
Aristides and Justin (II. vii.). Similar statements occur earlier in the Jewish
apocalypses.

Celsus vent his fierce disdain of Christians and their shameless, absurd pretensions with such keenness as at this point.[1]

But for Christians who knew they were the old and the new People, it was not enough to set this self-consciousness over against the Jews alone, or to contend with them for the possession of the promises and of the sacred book ;[2] settled on the soil of the Greek and Roman empires, they had to define

---

[1] He is quite aware that these pretensions are common to Jews and Christians, that the latter took them over from the former, and that both parties contended for the right to their possession. Μετὰ ταῦτα, observes Origen (c. Cels., IV. xxiii.), συνήθως ἑαυτῷ γελῶν τὸ Ἰουδαίων καὶ Χριστιανῶν γένος πάντας παραβέβληκε νυκτερίδων ὁρμαδῷ ἢ μύρμηξιν ἐκ καλιᾶς προελθοῦσιν ἢ βατράχοις περὶ τέλμα συνεδρεύουσιν ἢ σκώληξιν ἐν βορβόρου γωνίᾳ ἐκκλησιάζουσι καὶ πρὸς ἀλλήλους διαφερομένοις, τίνες αὐτῶν εἶεν ἁμαρτωλότεροι, καὶ φάσκουσιν ὅτι πάντα ἡμῖν ὁ θεὸς προδηλοῖ καὶ προκαταγγέλλει, καὶ τὸν πάντα κόσμον καὶ τὴν οὐράνιον φορὰν ἀπολιπὼν καὶ τὴν τοσαύτην γῆν παριδὼν ἡμῖν μόνοις πολιτεύεται καὶ πρὸς ἡμᾶς μόνους ἐπικηρυκεύεται καὶ πέμπων οὐ διαλείπει καὶ ζητῶν, ὅπως ἀεὶ συνῶμεν αὐτῷ. καὶ ἐν τῷ ἀναπλάσματί γε ἑαυτοῦ παραπλησίους ἡμᾶς ποιεῖ σκώληξι, φάσκουσιν ὅτι ὁ θεός ἐστιν, εἶτα μετ' ἐκεῖνον ἡμεῖς ὑπ' αὐτοῦ γεγονότες πάντῃ ὅμοιοι τῷ θεῷ, καὶ ἡμῖν πάντα ὑποβέβληται, γῆ καὶ ὕδωρ καὶ ἀὴρ καὶ ἄστρα, καὶ ἡμῶν ἕνεκα πάντα, καὶ ἡμῖν δουλεύειν τέτακται. λέγουσι δέ τι παρ' αὐτῷ οἱ σκώληκες, ἡμεῖς δηλαδή, ὅτι νῦν, ἐπειδή τινες [ἐν] ἡμῖν πλημμελοῦσιν, ἀφίξεται θεὸς ἢ πέμψει τὸν υἱόν, ἵνα καταφλέξῃ τοὺς ἀδίκους καὶ οἱ λοιποὶ σὺν αὐτῷ ζωὴν αἰώνιον ἔχωμεν. καὶ ἐπιφέρει γε πᾶσιν ὅτι ταῦτα [μᾶλλον] ἀνεκτὰ σκωλήκων καὶ βατράχων ἢ Ἰουδαίων καὶ Χριστιανῶν πρὸς ἀλλήλους διαφερομένων (" In the next place, laughing as usual at the race of Jews and Christians, he likens them all to a flight of bats, or a swarm of ants crawling out of their nest, or frogs in council on a marsh, or worms in synod on the corner of a dunghill, quarrelling as to which of them is the greater sinner, and declaring that 'God discloses and announces all things to us beforehand ; God deserts the whole world and the heavenly region and disregards this great earth in order to domicile himself among us alone ; to us alone he makes his proclamations, ceasing not to send and seek that we may company with him for ever.' And in his representation of us, he likens us to worms that declare 'there is a God, and next to him are we whom he has made in all points like unto himself, and to whom all things are subject—land and water, air and stars ; all things are for our sakes, and are appointed to serve us.' As he puts it, the worms, i.e., we Christians, declare also that 'since certain of our number commit sin, God will come or send his son to burn up the wicked and to let the rest of us have life eternal with himself.' To all of which he subjoins the remark that such discussions would be more tolerable among worms and frogs than among Jews and Christians ").

[2] This controversy occupies the history of the first generation, and stretches even further down. Although the broad lines of the position taken up by Christians on this field were clearly marked out, this did not exclude the possibility of various attitudes being assumed, as may be seen from my study in the third section of the first volume of the *Texte u. Untersuchungen* (1883), upon "the anti-Jewish polemic of the early church."

their position with regard to this realm and its "people." The apostle Paul had already done so, and in this he was followed by others.

In classifying mankind Paul does speak in one passage of "Greeks and barbarians" alongside of Jews (Rom. i. 14), and in another of "barbarians and Scythians" alongside of Greeks (Col. iii. 11); but, like a born Jew and a Pharisee, he usually bisects humanity into circumcised and uncircumcised—the latter being described, for the sake of brevity, as "Greeks."[1] Beside or over against these two "peoples" he places the church of God as a new creation (cp., *e.g.*, 1 Cor. x. 32, "Give no occasion of stumbling to Jews or Greeks or to the church of God"). Nor does this mere juxtaposition satisfy him. He goes on to the conception of this new creation as that which is to embrace both Jews and Greeks, rising above the differences of both peoples into a higher unity. The people of Christ are not a third people to him beside their neighbours. They represent the new grade on which human history reaches its consummation, a grade which is to supersede the previous grade of bisection, cancelling or annulling not only national but also social and even sexual distinctions.[2] Compare, *e.g.*, Gal. iii. 28: οὐκ ἔνι Ἰουδαῖος οὐδὲ Ἕλλην, οὐκ ἔνι ἄρσεν καὶ θῆλυ· πάντες γὰρ ὑμεῖς εἷς ἐστε ἐν Χριστῷ Ἰησοῦ, or Gal. v. 6: ἐν Χριστῷ Ἰησοῦ οὔτε περιτομή τι ἰσχύει οὔτε ἀκροβυστία, ἀλλὰ πίστις δι' ἀγάπης ἐνεργουμένη (cp. vi. 15, οὔτε γὰρ περιτομή τι ἐστιν οὔτε ἀκροβυστία, ἀλλὰ καινὴ κτίσις, and 2 Cor. v. 17). 1 Cor. xii. 13: ἐν ἑνὶ πνεύματι ἡμεῖς πάντες εἰς ἓν σῶμα ἐβαπτίσθημεν, εἴτε Ἰουδαῖοι εἴτε Ἕλληνες, εἴτε δοῦλοι εἴτε ἐλεύθεροι.

---

[1] Even in the passage from Colossians the common expression "Greek and Jew, circumcision and uncircumcision" (Ἕλλην καὶ Ἰουδαῖος, περιτομὴ καὶ ἀκροβυστία) is put first; "barbarian, Scythian, bond and free" (βάρβαρος, Σκύθης, δοῦλος, ἐλεύθερος) follows as a rhetorical amplification.

[2] It was in the conception of Christ as the second Adam that the conception of the new humanity as opposed to the old, a conception which implies a dual division, was most deeply rooted. The former idea obviously played a leading part in the world of Pauline thought, but it was not introduced for the first time by him; in the Messianic system of the Jews this idea already held a place of its own. In Paul and in other Christian thinkers the idea of a dual classification of mankind intersects that of a triple classification, but both ideas are at one in this, that the new humanity cancels the old.

Coloss. iii. 11 : ὅπου οὐκ ἔνι Ἕλλην καὶ Ἰουδαῖος, περιτομὴ καὶ ἀκροβυστία, βάρβαρος, Σκύθης, δοῦλος, ἐλεύθερος. Most impressive of all is Ephes. ii. 11 f. : μνημονεύετε ὅτι ποτὲ ὑμεῖς τὰ ἔθνη . . . . ἦτε ἀπηλλοτριωμένοι τῆς πολιτείας τοῦ Ἰσραήλ . . . . (ὁ Χριστός) ἐστιν ἡ εἰρήνη ἡμῶν, ὁ ποιήσας τὰ ἀμφότερα ἐν καὶ τὸ μεσότοιχον τοῦ φραγμοῦ λύσας . . . . ἵνα τοὺς δύο κτίσῃ ἐν αὐτῷ εἰς ἕνα καινὸν ἄνθρωπον ποιῶν εἰρήνην, καὶ ἀποκαταλλάξῃτοὺς ἀμφοτέρους ἐν ἑνὶ σώματι· Finally, in Rom. ix.–xi. Paul promulgates a philosophy of history, according to which the new People, whose previous history fell within the limits of Israel, includes the Gentile world, now that Israel has been rejected, but will embrace in the end not merely " the fulness of the Gentiles " (πλήρωμα τῶν ἐθνῶν) but also " all Israel " (πᾶς Ἰσραήλ).

Greeks (Gentiles), Jews, and the Christians as the new People (destined to embrace the two first)—this triple division now becomes frequent in early Christian literature, as one or two examples will show.[1]

---

[1] For Christians as the new People, see the " Shepherd " of Hermas, and *Barn.* v. 7 (Χριστὸς ἑαυτῷ τὸν λαὸν τὸν καινὸν ἑτοιμάζων (Christ preparing himself the new people) ; vii. 5, ὑπὲρ ἁμαρτιῶν μέλλων τοῦ λαοῦ τοῦ καινοῦ προσφέρειν τὴν σάρκα (Christ about to offer his flesh for the sins of the new people) ; xiii. 6, βλέπετε . . " . τὸν λαὸν τοῦτον [new and evidently young] εἶναι πρῶτον (ye see that this people is the first) ; 2 Clem. ad Cor. ii. 3, ἔρημος ἐδόκει εἶναι ἀπὸ τοῦ θεοῦ ὁ λαὸς ἡμῶν, νυνὶ δὲ πιστεύσαντες πλείονες ἐγενόμεθα τῶν δοκούντων ἔχειν θεόν (" Our people seemed to be forsaken of God, but now we have become more numerous by our faith than those who seemed to possess God ") ; Ignat., *ad Ephes.*, xix.–xx. ; Aristides, *Apol.*, xvi. (" truly this people is new, and a divine admixture is in them ") ; *Orac. Sibyll.*, i. 383 f., βλαστὸς νέος ἀνθήσειεν ἐξ ἐθνῶν (" a fresh growth shall blossom out of the Gentiles "). Bardesanes also calls the Christians a new race. Clement (*Paed.*, I. v. 15, on Zech. ix. 9) remarks : οὐκ ἤρκει τὸ πῶλον εἰρηκέναι μόνον, ἀλλὰ καὶ τὸ νέον προσέθηκεν αὐτῷ, τὴν ἐν Χριστῷ νεολαίαν τῆς ἀνθρωπότητος . . . . ἐμφαίνων (" To say ' colt ' was not enough ; ' young ' had to be added, in order to bring out the youth of humanity ") ; and in I. v. 20 he observes, νέοι ὁ λαὸς ὁ καινὸς πρὸς ἀντιδιαστολὴν τοῦ πρεσβυτέρου λαοῦ τὰ νέα μαθόντες ἀγαθά (" In contradistinction to the older people, the new people are young because they have learned the new blessings "). See also I. vii. 58, καὶ γὰρ ἦν ὡς ἀληθῶς διὰ μὲν Μωυσέως παιδαγωγὸς ὁ κύριος τοῦ λαοῦ τοῦ παλαιοῦ, δι' αὐτοῦ δὲ τοῦ νέου καθηγεμὼν λαοῦ, πρόσωπον πρὸς πρόσωπον (" For it was really the Lord who instructed the ancient people by Moses ; but the new people he directs himself, face to face "). The expression " new people " was retained for a long while in those early days ; cp., *e.g.*, Constant., *ad s. Coet.* xix., κατὰ χρόνον τοῦ Τιβερίου ἡ τοῦ σωτῆρος ἐξέλαμψε παρουσία . . . . ἥ τε νέα τοῦ δήμου διαδοχὴ συνέστη, κ.τ.λ. (" About the time of Tiberius the advent of the

The fourth evangelist makes Christ say (x. 16): "And other sheep have I which are not of this fold; them also I must bring, and they shall hear my voice, and there shall be one flock, one shepherd." And again, in a profound prophetic utterance (iv. 21 f.): "The hour cometh when neither in this mountain [that of the Samaritans, who stand here as representatives of the Gentiles] nor in Jerusalem shall ye worship the Father; ye worship what ye know not; we worship what we know, for salvation is of the Jews. But the hour cometh and now is, when the true worshippers shall worship the Father in spirit and truth." This passage is of importance, because it is something more than a merely formal classification: it defines, in a positive manner, the three possible religious standpoints and apportions them among the different peoples. First of all, there is ignorance of God, together with an external and therefore an erroneous worship (= the Gentiles, or Samaritans); secondly, there is a true knowledge of God together with a wrong, external worship (= the Jews); and thirdly, there is true knowledge of God together with worship that is inward and

Saviour flashed on the World . . . . and the new succession of the people arose," etc.). On the other hand, Christians are also the "non-gens," since they are not a nation; cp. Orig., Hom. I. in Ps. xxxvi. (vol. xii. p. 155): "Nos sumus ' non gens' [Deut. xxxii. 21], qui pauci ex ista civitate credimus, et alii ex alia, et nusquam gens integra ab initio credulitatis videtur assumpta. Non enim sicut Iudaeorum gens erat vel Aegyptiorum gens ita etiam Christianorum genus gens est una vel integra, sed sparsim ex singulis gentibus congregantur."—For Christians as a distinctive genus, or as the genus of the truly pious, see *Mart. Polyc.*, iii., ἡ γενναιότης τοῦ θεοφιλοῦς καὶ θεοσεβοῦς γένους τῶν Χριστιανῶν ("the brave spirit of the God-beloved and God-fearing race of Christians"); xiv., πᾶν τὸ γένος τῶν δικαίων ("the whole race of the righteous"); *Martyr. Ignat. Antioch.*, ii., τὸ τῶν Χριστιανῶν θεοσεβὲς γένος (the pious race of Christians). Also Melito, in Eus., *H.E.*, iv. 26. 5, τὸ τῶν θεοσεβῶν γένος ("the race of the pious"), Arnobius, i. 1 ("Christiana gens"), pseudo-Josephus, *Testim. de Christo* (τὸ φῦλον τῶν Χριστιανῶν—the tribe of the Christians); *Orac. Sibyll.*, iv. 136, εὐσεβέων φῦλον, etc. Several educated Christians correlated the idea of a new and at the same time a universal people with the Stoic cosmopolitan idea, as, for example, Tertullian, who points out more than once that Christians only recognise *one* state, *i.e.*, the World. Similarly, Tatian writes (*Orat.* xxviii.): "I repudiate your legislation; there ought to be only one common polity for all men" (τῆς παρ' ὑμῖν κατέγνων νομοθεσίας · μίαν μὲν γὰρ ἐχρῆν εἶναι καὶ κοινὴν ἀπάντων τὴν πολιτείαν). This democratic and cosmopolitan feature of Christianity was undoubtedly of great use to the propaganda among the lower and middle classes, particularly throughout the provinces. Religious equality was felt, up to a certain degree, to mean political and social equality as well.

therefore true (=the Christians). This view gave rise to many similar conceptions in early Christianity; it was the precursor of a series of cognate ideas which formed the basis of early Christian speculations upon the history of religion. It was the so-called "gnostics" in particular who frankly built their systems upon ideas of this kind. In these systems, Greeks (or pagans), Jews, and Christians sometimes appear as different grades; sometimes the two first are combined, with Christians subdivided into "psychic" (ψύχικοι) and "pneumatic" (πνευμάτικοι) members; and finally a fourfold division is also visible, viz., Greeks (or pagans), Jews, churchfolk, and "pneumatic" persons.[1] During that period, when religions were undergoing transformation, speculations on the history of religion were in the air; they are to be met with even in inferior and extravagant systems of religion.[2] But from all this we must turn back to writers of the Catholic church with their triple classification.

In one early Christian document from the opening of the second century, of which unfortunately we possess only a few fragments (i.e., the Preaching of Peter, in Clem., *Strom.*, vi. 5. 41), Christians are warned not to fashion their worship on the model of the Greeks or of the Jews (μὴ κατὰ τοὺς Ἕλληνας σέβεσθε τὸν θεόν . . . . μηδὲ κατὰ Ἰουδαίους σέβεσθε). Then we read: ὥστε καὶ ὑμεῖς ὁσίως καὶ δικαίως μανθάνοντες ἃ παραδίδομεν ὑμῖν, φυλάσσεσθε καινῶς τὸν θεὸν διὰ τοῦ Χριστοῦ σεβόμενοι· εὕρομεν γὰρ ἐν ταῖς γραφαῖς καθὼς ὁ κύριος λέγει· ἰδοὺ διατίθεμαι ὑμῖν καινὴν διαθήκην οὐχ ὡς διεθέμην τοῖς πατράσιν ὑμῶν ἐν ὄρει Χωρήβ· νέαν ὑμῖν διέθετο, τὰ γὰρ Ἑλλήνων καὶ Ἰουδαίων παλαιά, ὑμεῖς δὲ οἱ καινῶς αὐτὸν τρίτῳ γένει σεβόμενοι Χριστιανοί ("So

---

[1] It is impossible here to go into the question of how this ethnological division of humanity intersected and squared with the other religious division made by the gnostics, viz., the psychological (into "hylic," "psychic," and "pneumatic" persons).

[2] With regard to the religious system of the adherents of Simon Magus, we have this fragmentary and obscure piece of information in Irenæus (I. xxiii.): Simon taught that "he himself was he who had appeared among the Jews as the Son, who had descended in Samaria as the Father, and made his advent among other nations as the holy Spirit" ("Semetipsum esse qui inter Judaeos quidem quasi filius apparuerit, in Samaria autem quasi pater descenderit, in reliquis vero gentibus quasi spiritus sanctus adventaverit").

do you keep what you have learnt from us holily and justly, worshipping God *anew* through Christ. For we find in the scriptures, as the Lord saith, Behold I make a new covenant with you, not as I made it with your fathers in Mount Horeb. A *new* covenant he has made with us, for that of the Greeks and Jews is old, but *ye who worship him anew in the third manner* are Christians ").[1]

This writer also distinguishes Greeks, Jews, and Christians, and distinguishes them, like the fourth evangelist, by the degree of their knowledge and worship of God. But the remarkable thing is his explicit assumption that there are *three* classes, neither more nor less, and his deliberate description of Christianity as the new or *third* genus of worship. There are several similar passages which remain to be noticed, but this is the earliest of them all. Only, it is to be remarked that Christians do not yet call themselves " the third race "; it is their worship which is put third in the scale. The writer classifies humanity, not into three peoples, but into three groups of worshippers.

Similarly the unknown author of the epistle to Diognetus. Only, with him the conception of three classes of worshippers is definitely carried over into that of three peoples (" Christians esteem not those whom the Greeks regard as gods, nor do they observe the superstition of the Jews . . . . [thou enquirest] about the nature of this fresh development or interest which has entered life now and not previously," ch. i. ; cp. also ch. v. : " They are attacked as aliens by the Jews, and persecuted by the Greeks "). This is brought out particularly in his endeavour to prove that as Christians have a special manner of life, existing socially and politically by themselves, they have a legitimate claim to be ranked as a special " nation."

In his Apology to the Emperor Pius, Aristides distinctly arranges human beings in three " orders," which are equivalent to nations, as Aristides assigns to each its genealogy—*i.e.*, its historical origin. He writes (ch. ii.): φανερὸν γάρ ἐστιν ἡμῖν, ὦ βασιλεῦ, ὅτι τρία γένη εἰσὶν ἀνθρώπων ἐν τῷδε τῷ κόσμῳ· ὧν

---

[1] The term " religio Christiana " does not occur till Tertullian, who uses it quite frequently. The apologists speak of the distinctive θεοσέβεια of Christians.

εἰσιν οἱ παρ' ὑμῖν λεγομένων θεῶν προσκυνηταὶ καὶ Ἰουδαῖοι καὶ Χριστιανοί· αὐτοὶ δὲ πάλιν οἱ τοὺς πολλοὺς σεβόμενοι θεοὺς εἰς τρία διαρροῦνται γένη, Χαλδαίους τε καὶ ῞Ελληνας καὶ Αἰγυπτίους (then follows the evidence for the origin of these nations, whilst the Christians are said to "derive their genealogy from Jesus Christ").[1]

How seriously Irenæus took this idea of the Christians as a special people, is evident from his remarks in iv. 30. The gnostics had attacked the Jews and their God for having appropriated the gold and silver vessels of the Egyptians. To which Irenæus retorts that it would be much more true to accuse Christians of robbery, inasmuch as all their possessions originated with the Romans. "Who has the better right to gold and silver? The Jews, who took it as a reward for their labour in Egypt? or we, who have taken gold from the Romans and the rest of the nations, though they were not our debtors?" This argument would be meaningless unless Irenæus regarded Christians as a nation which was sharply differentiated from the rest of the peoples and had no longer anything to do with them. As a matter of fact, he regarded the exodus of Israel from Egypt as a type of the "profectio ecclesiae e gentibus" (iv. 30. 4).

The religious philosophy of history set forth by Clement of Alexandria rests entirely upon the view that these two nations,

---

[1] "It is clear to us, O king, that there are three orders of mankind in this world; these are, the worshippers of your acknowledged gods, the Jews, and the Christians. Furthermore, those who worship a plurality of gods are again divided into three orders, viz., Chaldeans, Greeks, and Egyptians." In the Syrian and Armenian versions the passage runs somewhat otherwise. "This is clear, O king, that there are four races of men in the world, barbarians and Greeks, Jews and Christians" (omitting altogether the further subdivision of the Greeks into three classes). Several scholars prefer this rendering, though it should be noted that Hippolytus also, in *Philos.*, x. 30 (twice) and 31 (twice), contrasts the Egyptians, Chaldeans, and Greeks with the Jews and Christians. Still, the question is one of minor importance for our present purpose.—Justin (*Dial.* cxxiii.) also derives Christians from Christ, not as their teacher but as their progenitor: ὡς ἀπὸ τοῦ ἑνὸς Ἰακὼβ ἐκείνου, τοῦ καὶ Ἰσραὴλ ἐπικληθέντος, τὸ πᾶν γένος ὑμῶν προσηγόρευτο Ἰακὼβ καὶ Ἰσραήλ, οὕτω καὶ ἡμεῖς ἀπὸ τοῦ γεννήσαντος ἡμᾶς εἰς θεὸν Χριστοῦ . . . . καὶ θεοῦ τέκνα ἀληθινὰ καλούμεθα καὶ ἐσμέν . . . . ("As all your nation has been called Jacob and Israel from the one man Jacob, who was surnamed Israel, so *from Christ who begat us unto God* . . . . we are called, and we are, God's true children").

Greeks and Jews, were alike trained by God, but that they are
now (see Paul's epistle to the Ephesians) to be raised into the
higher unity of a third nation. It may suffice to bring forward
three passages bearing on this point. In *Strom.*, iii. 10. 70, he
writes (on the saying " where two or three are gathered together,"
etc.) : εἴη δ' ἂν καὶ ἡ ὁμόνοια τῶν πολλῶν ἀπὸ τῶν τριῶν ἀριθ-
μουμένη μεθ' ὧν ὁ κύριος, ἡ μία ἐκκλησία, ὁ εἷς ἄνθρωπος, τὸ γένος
τὸ ἕν. ἢ μή τι μετὰ μὲν τοῦ ἑνὸς τοῦ Ἰουδαίου ὁ κύριος νομοθετῶν
ἦν, προφητεύων δὲ ἤδη καὶ τὸν Ἰερεμίαν ἀποστέλλων εἰς Βαβυ-
λῶνα, ἀλλὰ καὶ τοὺς ἐξ ἐθνῶν διὰ τῆς προφητείας καλῶν, συνῆγε
λαοὺς τοὺς δύο, τρίτος δὲ ἦν ἐκ τῶν δυεῖν κτιζόμενος εἰς καινὸν
ἄνθρωπον, ᾧ δὴ ἐμπεριπατεῖ τε καὶ κατοικεῖ ἐν αὐτῇ τῇ ἐκκλησίᾳ
(" Now the harmony of the many, calculated from the three
with whom the Lord is present, might signify the one church,
the one man, the one race. Or was the Lord legislating with
the one Jew [at Sinai], and then, when he prophesied and sent
Jeremiah to Babylon, calling some also from the heathen, did
he collect the two peoples together, while the third was created
out of the twain into a new man, wherein he is now resident,
dwelling within the church "). Again, in *Strom.*, v. 14. 98, on
Plato's *Republic*, iii. p. 415 : εἰ μή τι τρεῖς τινας ὑποτιθέμενος
φύσεις, τρεῖς πολιτείας, ὡς ὑπέλαβόν τινες, διαγράφει, καὶ Ἰουδαίων
μὲν ἀργυρᾶν, Ἑλλήνων δὲ τρίτην [a corrupt passage, incorrectly
read as early as Eus., *Prepar.*, xiii. 13 ; on the margin of L there
is the lemma, Ἑλλήνων σιδηρὰν ἢ χαλκήν, Χριστιανῶν χρυσῆν],
Χριστιανῶν δέ, οἷς ὁ χρυσὸς ὁ βασιλικὸς ἐγκαταμέμικται, τὸ ἅγιον
πνεῦμα (" Unless he means by his hypothesis of three natures to
describe, as some conjecture, three polities, the Jews being the
silver one, and the Greeks the third [the lemma running thus :—
" The Greeks being the iron or brass one, and the Christians
the gold one "], along with the Christians, with whom the regal
gold is mixed, even the holy Spirit "). Finally, in *Strom.*, vi.
5. 42 : ἐκ γοῦν τῆς Ἑλληνικῆς παιδείας, ἀλλὰ καὶ ἐκ τῆς νομικῆς
εἰς τὸ ἓν γένος τοῦ σωζομένου συνάγονται λαοῦ οἱ τὴν πίστιν
προσιέμενοι, οὐ χρόνῳ διαιρουμένων τῶν τριῶν λαῶν, ἵνα τις
φύσεις ὑπολάβοι τριττάς, κ.τ.λ. (" From the Hellenic discipline,
as also from that of the law, those who accept the faith are
gathered into the one race of the people who are saved—not

that the peoples are separated by time, as though one were to suggest three different natures," etc.).[1]

Evidence may be led also from other early Christian writers to show that the triad of "Greeks (Gentiles), Jews, and Christians" was the church's basal conception of history.[2] It was employed with especial frequency in the interpretation of biblical stories. Thus Tertullian enlists it in his exposition of the prodigal son (de Pudic., viii. f.); Hippolytus (Comm. in Daniel, ed. Bonwetsch, p. 32) finds the Christians in Susanna, and the Greeks and Jews in the two elders who lay snares for her; while pseudo-Cyprian (de Mont. Sina et Sion, vii.) explains that the two thieves represent the Greeks and Jews. But, so far as I am aware, the blunt expression "We Christians are the third race" only occurs once in early Christian literature subsequent to the Preaching of Peter (where, moreover, it is simply Christian worship which is described as the third class), and that is in the pseudo-Cyprianic tract de Pascha Computus (c. 17), written in 242–243 A.D. Unfortunately, the context of the expression is not quite clear. Speaking of hell-fire, the author declares it has consumed the opponents of Ananias, Azarias, and Misael, "et ipsos tres pueros a dei filio protectos—in mysterio nostro qui sumus tertium genus hominum — non vexavit" ("Without hurting, however, those three lads, protected by the Son of God—in the mystery which pertains to us who are the third race of mankind"). It is hard to see how the writer could feel he was reminded of Christians as the third race of men by the three children who were all-pleasing in God's sight, although they were cast into the fiery furnace; still, reminded he was, and at any rate the inference to be drawn from the passage is that he must have been familiar with the description of Christians as a "third race." What sense he attached to it, we

---

[1] Clement (Strom., ii. 15. 67) once heard a "wise man" explain that Gentiles ("seat of the ungodly"), Jews ("way of sinners"), and heretics ("seat of the scornful") Were meant in Ps. i. 1. This addition of "heretics" is simply due to the passage under discussion.

[2] The letter of Hadrian to Servianus (Vopisc., Saturnin., viii.) is to be included among these Witnesses, if it is a Christian fabrication: "Hunc (nummum) Christiani, hunc Judaei, hunc omnes venerantur et gentes" ("Christians, Jews, and all nations Worship this one thing, money").

are not yet in a position to determine with any certainty ; but
we are bound to assume, in the first instance, from our previous
investigations, that Christians were to him a third race alongside
of the Greeks (Gentiles) and Jews.   Whether this assumption is
correct·or false, is a question to be decided in the second section
of our inquiry.

II

The consciousness of being a *people*,[1] and of being indeed
the primitive and the new people, did not remain abstract or
unfruitful in the church ; it was developed in a great variety
of directions.   In this respect also the synagogue had led
the way at every point, but Christianity met its claim by
making that claim her own and extending it, wherever this
was possible, beyond the limits within which Judaism had confined it.

There were three cardinal directions in which the church
voiced her peculiar consciousness of being the primitive people.
(1) She demonstrated that, like any other people, she had a
characteristic life.   (2) She tried to show that so far as the
philosophical learning, the worship, and the polity of other
peoples were praiseworthy, they were plagiarized from the
Christian religion.   (3) She began to set on foot, though merely
in the shape of tentative ideas, some political reflections upon
her own actual importance within the world-empire of Rome,
and also upon the positive relation between the latter and herself
as the new religion for the world.

1. The proofs advanced by early Christianity with regard to
its πολιτεία were twofold.   The theme of one set was stated by
Paul in Philippians iii. 20: " Our citizenship (πολιτεία) is in

---

[1] Cp. the first book of the Church History of Eusebius, especially ch. iv. : τῆς
μὲν γὰρ τοῦ σωτῆρος ἡμῶν Ἰησοῦ Χριστοῦ παρουσίας νεωστὶ πᾶσιν ἀνθρώποις ἐπι-
λαμψάσης, νέον ὁμολογουμένως ἔθνος, οὐ μικρὸν οὐδ᾽ ἀσθενὲς οὐδ᾽ ἐπὶ γωνίας που
γῆς ἰδρυμένον, ἀλλὰ καὶ πάντων τῶν ἐθνῶν πολυανθρωπότατόν τε καὶ θεοσεβέστατον
. . . τὸ παρὰ τοῖς πᾶσι τῇ τοῦ Χριστοῦ προσηγορίᾳ τετιμημένον ("*It is agreed*
that when the appearance of our Saviour Jesus Christ recently broke upon all men,
there appeared *a new nation*, admittedly neither small nor weak nor dwelling in
any corner of the earth, but the most numerous and pious of all nations . . . .
honoured by all men with the title of Christ ").

heaven" (cp. Heb. xiii. 13 f. : "Let us go outside the camp
. . . . for here we have no permanent city, but we seek one
which is to come "). On this view Christians feel themselves
pilgrims and sojourners on earth, walking by faith and not by
sight ; their whole course of life is a renunciation of the world,
and is determined solely by the future kingdom towards which
they hasten. This mode of life is voiced most loudly in the
first similitude of Hermas, where two cities with their two lords
are set in opposition—one belonging to the present, the other
to the future. The Christian must have nothing whatever to
do with the former city and its lord the devil ; his whole course
of life must be opposed to that of the present city, with its
arrangements and laws. In this way Christians were able
emphatically to represent themselves as really a special people,
with a distinctive course of life ; but they need not have felt
surprised when people took them at their word, and dismissed
them with the remark : πάντες ἑαυτοὺς φονεύσαντες πορεύεσθε
ἤδη παρὰ τὸν θεὸν καὶ ἡμῖν πράγματα μὴ παρέχετε (" Go and
kill yourselves, every one of you ; begone to God at once, and
leave us in peace "), quoted by Justin, *Apol.*, II. iv.

This, however, represented but one side of the proof that
Christianity had a characteristic life and order of its own.
With equal energy an attempt was made to show that there was
a polity realized in Christianity which was differentiated from
that of other nations by its absolute morality (see above, pp.
205 f.). As early as the apostolic epistles, no point of dogma
is more emphatically brought forward than the duty of a holy
life, by means of which Christians are to shine as lights amid a
corrupt and crooked generation. "Not like the Gentiles," nor
like the Jews, but as the people of God—that is the watchword.
Every sphere of life, down to the most intimate and trivial, was
put under the control of the Spirit and re-arranged ; we have
only to read the Didachê in order to find out the earnestness
with which Christians took "the way of life." In line with
this, a leading section in all the Christian apologies was occupied
by the exposition of the Christian polity as a polity which was
purely ethical, the object being in every case to show that this
Christian polity was in accordance with the highest moral

standards, standards which even its opponents had to recognize, and that for this very reason it was opposed to the polity of the other nations. The *Apologies* of Justin (especially I. xiv. f.), Aristides (xv.), Tatian and Tertullian especially, fall to be considered in this light.[1] The conviction that they are in possession of a distinctive polity is also voiced in the notion of Christians as the army of the true God and of Christ.[2]

2. The strict morality, the monotheistic view of the world, and the subordination of the entire life of man, private and social, to the regulations of a supreme ethical code—all this is "what has been from the very first" ("quod ab initio fuit"). Now as the church finds this once more repeated in her own life, she recognizes in this phenomenon the guarantee that she herself, though apparently the youngest of the nations, is in reality the oldest. Furthermore, as she undertakes to bring forward proof for this conviction by drawing upon the books of Moses, which she appropriated for her own use (cp. Tatian, Theophilus,

---

[1] The belauded description in the epistle to Diognetus (v. 6) is a fine piece of rhetoric, but not much more than that. The author manages to express three aspects, as it were, in a single breath : the Christian polity as the climax of morals, the Christian aloofness from the world, and the inwardness by which this religion was enabled to live in the midst of the world and adapt itself to all outward conditions without any loss of purity. A man who is able to weave these ideas into one perfect woof, either stands on the high level of the fourth evangelist—a position to which the author can hardly be promoted—or else incurs the suspicion of paying no serious attention to any one of the three ideas in question.

[2] Hermas (*Sim.*, ix. 17) brings forward one most important aspect of the Christian polity, viz., its power of combining in a mental and moral *unity* peoples of the most varied capacities and customs. The stones built into the tower (*i.e.*, the church) from the various mountains (the nations) are at first many-coloured, but upon being built in, they all acquire the same white colour : λαβόντες τὴν σφραγῖδα μίαν φρόνησιν ἔσχον καὶ ἕνα νοῦν, καὶ μία πίστις αὐτῶν ἐγένετο καὶ μία ἀγάπη . . . . διὰ τοῦτο ἡ οἰκοδομὴ τοῦ πύργου μιᾷ χρόᾳ ἐγένετο λαμπρὰ ὡς ὁ ἥλιος ("On receiving the seal they had one understanding and one mind, one faith and one love became theirs . . . . wherefore the fabric of the tower became of one colour, bright as the sun ") ; cp. also Iren., I. 10. 2. Celsus (*c. Cels.*, VIII. lxxii.) longed ardently for such a unity of mankind, instead of humanity being split up into nationalities. But he regarded it as a mere Utopia. Εἰ γὰρ δὴ οἷόν τε εἰς ἕνα συμφρονῆσαι νόμον τοὺς τὴν 'Ασίαν καὶ Εὐρώπην καὶ Λιβύην ῞Ελληνάς τε καὶ βαρβάρους ἄχρι περάτων νενεμημένους ("Were it at all possible that the inhabitants of Asia, Europe, and Libya, Greeks and barbarians alike, should unite to obey one law"). On which Origen remarks : ἀδύνατον τοῦτο νομίσας εἶναι ἐπιφέρει [sc. Celsus] ὅτι ὁ τοῦτο οἰόμενος οἶδεν οὐδέν (" Judging this an impossibility, he adds that anyone who thinks it possible knows nothing at all").

Clement, Tertullian, and Julius Africanus),[1] she is thereby dethroning the Jewish people and claiming for herself the primitive revelation, the primitive wisdom, and the genuine worship. Hence she acquires the requisite insight and courage, not merely to survey and appropriate for herself the content of all connected with revelation, wisdom, and worship that had appeared on the horizon of other nations, but to survey and estimate these materials as if they were merely copies made from an original in her own possession. We all know the space devoted by the early Christian apologies to the proof that Greek philosophy, so far as it merited praise and was itself correct, had been plagiarized from the primitive literature which belonged to Christians. The efforts made in this direction culminate in the statement that " Whatever truth is uttered anywhere has come from us." The audacity of this assertion is apt to hide from us at this time of day the grandeur and vigour of the self-consciousness to which it gives expression. Justin had already claimed any true piece of knowledge as " Christian," whether it occurred in Homer, the tragedians, the comic poets, or the philosophers. Did it never dawn on him, or did he really suspect, that his entire standpoint was upset by such an extension of its range, and that what was specifically " Christian " was transformed into what was common to all men? Clement of Alexandria, at any rate, who followed him in this line of thought, not merely foresaw this inference, but deliberately followed it up.

By comparing itself with philosophy, early Christianity gave itself out as a " philosophy," while those who professed it were " philosophers." This, however, is one form of its self-consciousness which must not be overrated, for it is almost exclusively confined to the Christian apologetic and polemic. Christians never doubted, indeed, that their doctrine was really the truth, and therefore the true philosophy. But then it was infinitely more than a philosophy. It was the wisdom of God. They too were different from mere philosophers; they were God's

---

[1] Note in passing that this marks the beginning in general of the universal chronography of history, and consequently of the general Christian outlook upon the entire course of human history.

people, God's friends.   It suited their polemic, however, to designate Christianity as philosophy, or "barbarian" philosophy, and adherents of Christianity as "philosophers."   And that for two reasons.   In the first place, it was the only way of explaining to outsiders the nature of Christian doctrine—for to institute a positive comparison between it and pagan *religions* was a risky procedure.   And in the second place, this presupposition made it possible for Christians to demand from the State as liberal treatment for themselves as that accorded to philosophy and to philosophic schools.   It is in this light, pre-eminently; that we must understand the favourite parallel drawn by the apologists between Christianity and philosophy. Individual teachers who were at the head either of a school (διδασκαλεῖον) within the church or of an independent school, did take the parallel more seriously ;[1] but such persons were in a certain sense merely adjuncts of catholic Christendom.[2]

The charge of plagiarism was not merely levelled against philosophy, so far as philosophy was genuine, but also against any rites and methods of worship which furnished actual or alleged parallels to those of Christianity.   Little material of this kind was to be found in the official cults of the Greeks and Romans, but this deficiency was more than made up for by the rich spoil which lay in the mysteries and the exotic cults, the cult of Mithra, in particular, attracting the attention of Christian apologists in this connection at a very early period. The verdict on all such features was quite simple : the demons, it was argued, had imitated Christian rites in the cults of paganism.   If it could not be denied that those pagan rites and sacraments were older than their Christian parallels, the plea readily suggested itself that the demons had given a

---

[1] Such teachers, with their small groups, hardly felt themselves to be the "primitive people."   Their consciousness of entire independence was expressed in the titles of "gifted" and "learned."   We shall have to discuss the Christian διδασκαλεῖα and its significance for the Christian propaganda in another connection ; but we can well understand how pagans found the Christians' claim to be "learned" and "philosophers" a peculiarly ridiculous and presumptuous pretension.   On their part, they dubbed Christians as credulous, and scoffed at them as πιστοί ("believers"), who put faith in foreign fables and old wives' gossip.

[2] They have nothing to do with the primitive shape assumed by Christianity, that of Jesus as the teacher and the disciples as his pupils.

distorted copy of Christianity previous to its real appearance, with the object of discrediting it beforehand. Baptism, the Lord's supper, the rites of expiation, the cross, etc., are instances in point. The interests of dogma are always able to impinge on history, and they do so constantly. But here we have to consider some cases which are specially instructive, since the Christian rites and sacraments attained their final shape under the influence of the mysteries and their rites (not, of course, the rites of any special cultus, but those belonging to the general type of the mysteries), so that dogma made the final issue of the process its first cause. Yet even in this field the *quid pro quo* appears in a more favourable light when we notice that Christendom posits itself as the original People at the dawn of human history, and that this consciousness determines their entire outlook upon that history. For, in the light of this presupposition, the Christians' confiscation of those pagan rites and ceremonies simply denotes the assertion of their character as ideally human and therefore divine. Christians embody the fundamental principles of that divine revelation and worship which are the source of human history, and which constitute the primitive possession of Christianity, although that possession has of course lain undiscovered till the present moment.

3. The most interesting side of the Christian consciousness of being a people, is what may be termed, in the narrower sense of the word, the political. Hitherto, however, it has been studied less than the others. The materials are copious, but up till now little attention has been paid to them. I shall content myself here with laying bare the points of most importance.[1]

The political consciousness of the primitive church was based on three presuppositions. There was first of all the political element in the Jewish apocalyptic, which was called forth by the demand of the imperial cultus and the terror of the persecution. Then there was the rapid transference of the gospel from

[1] Tertullian's sentence (*Apol.*, xxxviii.): "Nulla magis res nobis aliena quam publica ; unam omnium rempublicam agnoscimus, mundum " ("Nothing is more alien to us than politics ; we acknowledge but one universal state, the world ") has a Stoic tinge ; at best, it may be taken with a grain of salt. Besides, people who despise the state always pursue a very active policy of their own.

the Jews to the Greeks, and the unmistakable affinity between Christianity and Hellenism, as well as between the church and the world-wide power of Rome.   Thirdly, there was the fall and ruin of Jerusalem and the Jewish state.   The first of these elements stood in antithesis to the two others, so that in this way the political consciousness of the church came to be defined in opposite directions and had to work itself out of initial contradictions.

The politics of Jewish apocalyptic viewed the world-state as a diabolic state, and consequently took up a purely negative attitude towards it.   This political view is put uncompromisingly in the apocalypse of John, where it was justified by the Neronic persecution, the imperial claim for worship, and the Domitianic reign of terror.   The largest share of attention, comparatively speaking, has been devoted by scholars to this political standpoint, in so far as it lasted throughout the second and the third centuries, and quite recently (1901) Neumann has discussed it thoroughly in his study of Hippolytus.   The remarkable thing is that although Christians were by no means numerous till after the middle of the second century, they recognized that Christianity formed the central point of humanity as the field of political history as well as its determining factor.   Such a self-consciousness is perfectly intelligible in the case of Judaism, for the Jews were really a large nation and had a great history behind them.   But it is truly amazing that a tiny set of people should confront the entire strength of the Roman empire,[1] that it should see in the persecution of the Christians the chief rôle of that empire, and that it should make

---

[1] Tertullian was the first who was able to threaten the state with the great number of Christians (*Apol.*, xxxvii., written shortly before 200 A.D.), for up till then people had merely endeavoured to hold out the terrors of the calamities at the close of the world and the return of Christ.   Although Christians still lacked a majority in the empire, still (from the outset) a substitute for this, so to speak, was found in the telling fact of the broad diffusion of Christianity throughout the whole empire and beyond its bounds.   Even as early as the first generations, the fact that Christians were to be found everywhere strengthened and moulded their self-consciousness.   In contrast to nations shut up within definite boundaries, even though these were as large as those of the Parthians, Tertullian calls Christians (*Apol.*, xxxvii.) the "gens totius orbis," *i.e.*, the people of the whole world.   And this had been felt long before even Tertullian wrote.

the world's history culminate in such a conflict. The only explanation of this lies in the fact that the church simply took the place of Israel, and consequently felt herself to be a *people*; this implied that she was also a political factor, and indeed the factor which ranked as decisive alongside of the state and by which in the end the state was to be overcome. Here we have already the great problem of " church and state " making its appearance, and the uncompromising form given to it at this period became normal for succeeding ages. The relationship between these two powers assumed other forms, but this form continued to lie concealed beneath them all.

This, however, is only one side of the question. The transition of the gospel from the Jews to the Greeks, the unmistakable affinity between Christianity and Hellenism, as well as between the church and the Roman world-power, and finally the downfall of the Jewish state at the hands of Rome—these factors occasioned ideas upon the relation of the empire to the church which were very different from the aims of the accepted apocalyptic. Any systematic treatment of this view would be out of place, however; it would give a wrong impression of the situation. The better way will be, as we are dealing merely with tentative ideas, to get acquainted with the most important features and look at them one after another.

2 Thess. ii. 5–7 is the oldest passage in Christian literature in which a positive meaning is attached to the Roman empire. It is represented there, not as the realm of antichrist, but, on the contrary, as the restraining power by means of which the final terrors and the advent of antichrist are held in check. For by τὸ κατέχον (ὁ κατέχων), " that which (or he who) restrains," we must understand the Roman empire. If this be so, it follows that the church and the empire could not be considered merely as diametrically opposed to each other.

Rom. xiii. 1 f. makes this quite plain, and proceeds to draw the inference that civil authority is θεοῦ διάκονος (" a minister of God "), appointed by God for the suppression of wickedness; resistance to it means resistance to a divine ordinance. Consequently one must not merely yield to its force, but obey it for conscience' sake. The very payment of taxes is a moral duty. The author of 1 Pet. ii. 13 f.[1] expresses himself in similar terms. But he goes a step further, following up the fear of God directly with honour due to the emperor (πάντας τιμήσατε, τὴν ἀδελφότητα ἀγαπᾶτε, τὸν θεὸν φοβεῖσθε, τὸν βασιλέα τιμᾶτε).[2] Nothing could be more loyal than this conception, and it is noticeable that the author was writing in Asia Minor, among the provinces where the imperial cultus flourished.

Luke begins his account of Christ with the words (iii. 1): ἐγένετο ἐν ταῖς ἡμέραις ἐκείναις ἐξῆλθεν δόγμα παρὰ Καίσαρος Αὐγούστου ἀπογράφεσθαι πᾶσαν τὴν οἰκουμένην. As has been correctly surmised, the allusion to the emperor Augustus is meant to be significant. It was the official and popular idea that with Augustus a new era dawned for the empire; the imperial throne was its " peace," the emperor its saviour (σωτήρ). Behind the earthly saviour, Luke makes the heavenly appear— he, too, is bestowed upon the whole world, and what he brings is peace (ver. 14, ἐπὶ γῆς εἰρήνη).[3] Luke hardly intended to set Augustus and Christ in hostile opposition; even Augustus and his kingdom are a sign of the new era. This may also be

---

[1] Cp. Tit. iii. 1. With regard to Paul's language in Romans, one may recollect what a quiet and happy time the early years of Nero were.

[2] Greek Christians usually called the emperor βασιλεύς (" king "), a common title in the East, where it had not the same servile associations as " rex " had on the lips of people in the West. But βασιλεύς was also a title of the Lord Christ (κύριος Χριστός) which Christians dared not avoid uttering (not merely on account of " the kingdom of God," βασιλεία τοῦ θεοῦ, but also because Jesus had called himself by this name: John xviii. 33 f.). This occasioned a painful dilemma, though prudent Christians made strenuous efforts to repudiate the apparent treason which their religious usage of this title inevitably suggested, and to make it clear that by " kingdom " and " king" they understood nothing earthly or human, but something divine (so already Justin's *Apol.*, I. vi.). Some hotspurs, no doubt, declared to their judges that they recognised only *one* king or emperor (God or Christ), and so drew upon themselves just punishment. But these cases were very rare. Christ was also called " imperator" in the West, but not in writings intended for publicity.

[3] Even the expression used in Eph. ii. 14, αὐτός ἐστιν ἡ εἰρήνη ἡμῶν (" he is our peace "), is modelled on the language applied to the emperor in Asia Minor. I have shown elsewhere how strongly this language has influenced the terminology of Luke in the above-mentioned passage of his gospel. No doubt we have to think of Micah v. 4, in connection with Eph. ii. 14 and Luke ii. 14. But this converging of different lines was quite characteristic of the age and the idea in question.

gathered from the book of Acts, which in my opinion has not
any consciously political aim ; it sees in the Roman empire, as
opposed to Judaism, the sphere marked out for the new religion,
it stands entirely aloof from any hostility to the emperor, and
it gladly lays stress upon such facts as prove a tolerant mood
on the part of the authorities towards Christians in the past.

Justin (*Apol.*, I. xii.) writes to the emperor : ἀρωγοὶ ὑμῖν καὶ
σύμμαχοι πρὸς εἰρήνην ἐσμὲν πάντων μᾶλλον ἀνθρώπων ("We,
more than any others, are your helpers and allies in promoting
peace"), admitting thereby that the purpose of the empire was
beneficial (*pax terrena*), and that the emperors sought to effect
this purpose. Also, in describing Christians as the power [1] best
adapted to secure this end—inasmuch as they shun all crime,
live a strictly moral life, and teach a strict morality, besides
scaring and exorcising those supreme enemies of mankind, the
demons—he too, in a certain sense, affirms a positive relationship between the church and the state.

When the author of the epistle to Diognetus differentiates
Christians from the world (the state) as the soul from the body
(vi.) and elaborates his account of their relationship in a series
of antitheses, he is laying down at the same time a positive
relation between the two magnitudes in question : ἐγκέκλεισται
μὲν ἡ ψυχὴ τῷ σώματι, συνέχει δὲ αὐτὴ τὸ σῶμα · καὶ Χριστιανοὶ
κατέχονται μὲν ὡς ἐν φρουρᾷ τῷ κόσμῳ, αὐτοὶ δὲ συνέχουσι
τὸν κόσμον ("The soul is shut up in the body, and yet holds
the body together ; so Christians are kept within the world as
in a prison, yet they hold the world together"). Similarly
Justin (*Apol.*, II. vii.).

All this implies already a positive political standpoint,[2] but

---

[1] Wherever mention is made of the power of the Christian people which
upholds the state and frees humanity, it is always these two factors which are in
view—their strict morality and their power over demons. Others also wield the
former weapon, though not so well. But the second, the power over demons,
pertains to Christians alone, and therefore they render an incomparable service to
the state and to the human race, small though their numbers may be. From this
conviction there grew up in Christianity the consciousness of being the power
which conserves and emancipates mankind in this world.

[2] I might also include here the remark of Athenagoras in his "Supplicatio" to
the emperors (xviii.) :· ἔχοιτε ἀφ᾽ ἑαυτῶν καὶ τὴν ἐπουράνιον βασιλείαν ἐξετάζειν·
ὡς γὰρ ὑμῖν πατρὶ καὶ υἱῷ πάντα κεχείρωται, ἄνωθεν τὴν βασιλείαν εἰληφόσι—

the furthest step in this direction was taken subsequently by
Melito (in Eus., *H.E.*, iv. 26). It is no mere accident that he
writes in loyal Asia Minor. By noting Luke's suggestion with
regard to Augustus, as well as all that had been already said elsewhere upon the positive relations subsisting between the church
and the world-empire, Melito could advance to the following
statement of the situation in his *Apology* to Marcus Aurelius:—

"This philosophy of ours certainly did flourish at first among
a barbarian people. But springing up in the provinces under
thy rule during the great reign of thy predecessor Augustus,
it brought rich blessings to thine empire in particular. For
ever since then the power of Rome has increased in size and
splendour; to this hast thou succeeded as its desired possessor,
and as such shalt thou continue with thy son if thou wilt
protect the philosophy which rose under Augustus and has risen
with the empire, a philosophy which thine ancestors also held
in honour along with other religions. The most convincing
proof that the flourishing of our religion has been a boon to
the empire thus happily inaugurated, is this—that the empire
has suffered no mishap since the reign of Augustus, but, on the
contrary, everything has increased its splendour and fame, in
accordance with the general prayer."

Melito's ideas [1] need no analysis; they are plainly and clearly
stated. The world-empire and the Christian religion are foster-
sisters; they form a pair; they constitute a new stage of human
history; the Christian religion means blessing and welfare to the
empire, towards which it stands as the inward to the outward.
Only when Christianity is protected and permitted to develop

βασιλέως γὰρ ψυχὴ ἐν χειρὶ θεοῦ, φησὶ τὸ προφητικὸν πνεῦμα—οὕτως ἐνὶ τῷ θεῷ καὶ
τῷ παρ' αὐτοῦ λόγῳ υἱῷ νοουμένῳ ἀμερίστῳ πάντα ὑποτέτακται ("May you be able to
discover the heavenly kingdom by considering yourselves! For as all things are
subject to you, father and son, who have received the kingdom from above—since
the king's soul is in the hand of God, saith the spirit of prophecy,—so are all
things subordinate to the one God and to the Logos proceeding from him, even
the Son, who is not apprehended apart from him").

[1] Tertullian's opinion was different. He knew of no solidarity of Christianity
and the empire : "Sed et Caesares credidissent super Christo, si aut Caesares non
essent necessarii saeculo, aut si et Christiani potuissent esse Caesares" (*Apol.* xxi. :
"Yes, the very Cæsars would have believed on Christ, if Cæsars had not been
necessary to the world, or if they could have been Cæsars and Christians as well").

itself freely, does the empire continue to preserve its size and splendour. Unless one is to suppose that Melito simply wanted to flatter—a supposition for which there is no ground, although there was flattery in what he said—the inference is that in the Christianity which formed part of the world-empire he really recognized a co-ordinate and sustaining inward force. Subsequent developments justified this view of Melito, and in this light his political insight is marvellous. But still more marvellous is the fact that at a time like this, when Christians were still a feeble folk, he actually recognized in Christianity the one magnitude parallel to the state, and that simply on the ground of religion—*i.e.*, as being a spiritual force which was entrusted with the function of supporting the state.[1]

There is yet another early Christian writer on whom the analogy of Christendom and the world-empire dawned (*a propos* of its œcumenical range); only, he attempted to explain it in a very surprising fashion, which betrayed a deep hostility towards the empire. Hippolytus writes (*in Dan.*, iv. 9): " For as our Lord was born in the forty-second year of the emperor Augustus, whence the Roman empire developed, and as the Lord also called all nations and tongues by means of the apostles and fashioned believing Christians into a *people*, the people of the Lord, and the people which consists of those who bear a new name—so was all this imitated to the letter by the empire of that day, ruling ' according to the working of Satan ': for it also collected to itself the noblest of every nation, and, dubbing them Romans, got ready for the fray. And that is the reason why the first census took place under Augustus, when our Lord was born at Bethlehem; it was to get the men of this world, who enrolled for our earthly king, called Romans, while those who believed in a heavenly king were termed Christians, bearing on their foreheads the sign of victory over death."

---

[1] Cp. also Orig., *c. Cels.*, VIII. lxx. : ἀλλ' οἱ καθ' ὑπόθεσιν Κέλσου πάντες ἂν πεισθέντες Ῥωμαῖοι εὐχόμενοι περιέσονται τῶν πολεμίων ἢ οὐδὲ τὴν ἀρχὴν πολεμήσουνται, φρουρούμενοι ὑπὸ θείας δυνάμεως, τῆς διὰ πεντήκοντα δικαίους πέντε πόλεις ὅλας ἐπαγγειλαμένης διασῶσαι ("According to the notion of *C*elsus, if all the Romans are brought to believe, they will either overcome their foes by praying, or refrain from fighting altogether, being guarded by that power divine which promised to save five entire cities for the sake of fifty just persons ").

The œcumenical range of the Roman empire is, therefore, a Statanic aping of Christianity.   As the demons purloined Christian philosophy and aped the Christian cultus and sacraments, so also did they perpetrate a plagiarism against the church by founding the great imperial state of Rome!   This is the self-consciousness of Christendom expressed in perhaps the most robust, but also in the most audacious form imaginable!   The real cosmopolitan character of Christianity is stated by Octavius (*Min. Felix*, xxxiii.) thus: "Nos gentes nationesque distinguimus: deo una domus est mundus hic totus" ("We draw distinctions between nations and races, but to God the whole of this world is one household").

Origen's political views are more accurate, but how extravagant are his ideas!   In chapters lxvii.–lxxv. of his eighth book against Celsus, by dint of a fresh interpretation given to a primitive Christian conception, and a recourse to a Platonic idea, he propounds the idea that the church, this κόσμος τοῦ κόσμου (*in Joh.*, vi. 38), or universe of the universe, is the future kingdom of the whole world, destined to embrace the Roman empire and humanity itself, to amalgamate and to replace the various realms of this world.   Cp. ch. lxviii.: "For if, in the words of Celsus, all were to do as we do, then there is no doubt whatever that even the barbarians would become law-abiding and humane, so soon as they obeyed the Word of God; then would all religions vanish, leaving that of Christ alone to reign.   And reign it will one day, as the Word never ceases to gain soul after soul."   This means the reversal of the primitive Christian hope.   The church now presents itself as the civilizing and cohesive power which is to create, even in the present age, a state that shall embrace an undivided humanity.   Origen, of course, is not quite sure whether this is feasible in the present age.   No further away than ch. lxxii., *a propos* of the question (to which Celsus gave a negative answer) whether Asia, Europe, and Libya, Greeks and barbarians alike, could agree to recognize one system of laws, we find him writing as follows: "Perhaps," he says, "such a result would not indeed be possible to those who are still in the body; but it would not be impossible to those who are released from the body" (καὶ τάχα ἀληθῶς ἀδύνατον μὲν τὸ τοιοῦτο τοῖς ἔτι ἐν

σώμασι, οὐ μὲν ἀδύνατον καὶ ἀπολυθεῖσιν αὐτῶν).[1] In II. xxx.
he writes: "In the days of Jesus, righteousness arose and fulness of peace, beginning with his birth. God prepared the
nations for his teaching, by causing the Roman emperor to rule
over all the world; there was no longer to be a plurality of
kingdoms, else would the nations have been strangers to one
another, and so the apostles would have found it harder to
carry out the task laid on them by Jesus, when he said, 'Go and
teach all nations.'"

In his reply to Celsus (III. xxix.–xxx.), this great father of the
church, who was at the same time a great and sensible statesman,
submits a further political consideration, which is not high-flown
this time, but sober. It has also the advantage of being impressive and to the point. Although the passage is somewhat
lengthy. I quote it here, as there is nothing like it in the
literature of early Christianity [Greek text in *Hist. Dogma*,
ii. 126]:—

"Apollo, according to Celsus, required the Metapontines to
consider Aristeas as a god. But the Metapontines considered
Aristeas was a man, and perhaps not even a respectable man,
and this conviction of theirs seemed to them more valid than the
declaration of the oracle that Aristeas was a god and deserving
of divine honour. Consequently they would not obey Apollo,
and no one regarded Aristeas as a god. But with regard to
Jesus, we may say that it proved a blessing to the human race
to acknowledge him as God's son, as God appearing in a human
soul and body. . . . . God, who sent Jesus, brought to nought all
the conspiracies of the demons and gave success to the gospel
of Jesus over the whole earth for the conversion and amelioration of mankind, causing churches everywhere to be established,
which should be ruled by other laws than those of superstitious,
licentious, and evil men. For such is the character of the
masses who constitute the assemblies throughout the various
towns. Whereas, the churches or assemblies of God, whom
Christ instructs, are 'lights in the world,' compared to the

---

[1] I do not understand, any more than Origen did, the political twaddle which
Celsus (lxxi.) professes to have heard from a Christian. It can hardly have come
from a Christian, and it is impossible nowadays to ascertain what underlay it. I
therefore pass it by.

assemblies of the districts among which they live as strangers. For who would not allow that even the inferior members of the church, and such as take a lower place when judged by the standard of more eminent Christians—even these are far better people than the members of profane assemblies?

"Take the church of God at Athens; it is a peaceable and orderly body, as it desires to please God, who is over all. Whereas the assembly of the Athenians is refractory, nor can it be compared in any respect to the local church or assembly of God. The same may be said of the church of God at Corinth and the local assembly of the people, as also of the church of God at Alexandria and the local assembly in that city. And if any candid person hears this and examines the facts of the case with a sincere love for the truth, he will admire him who conceived the design and was able to realize it, establishing churches of God to exist as strangers amid the popular assemblies of the various cities. Furthermore, if one compares the council of the Church of God with that of the cities, one by one, it would be found that many a councillor of the church is worthy to be a leader in God's city, if such a city exists in the world; whereas other councillors in all parts of the world show not a trait of conduct to justify the superiority born of their position, which seems to give them precedence over their fellow-citizens. Such also is the result of any comparison between the president of the church in any city and the civic magistrates. It will be found that, in the matter of conduct, even such councillors and presidents of the church as are extremely defective and indolent compared to their more energetic colleagues, are possessed of virtues which are in general superior to those of civic councillors and rulers."

At this point I shall break off the present part of our investigation. The evidence already brought forward will suffice to give some idea of how Christians held themselves to be the new People and the third race of mankind, and also of the inferences which they drew from these conceptions. But how did the Greeks and Romans regard this phenomenon of Christianity with its enormous claims? This is a question to which justice must be done in an excursus.

EXCURSUS

CHRISTIANS AS A THIRD RACE, IN THE JUDGMENT OF THEIR OPPONENTS

For a proper appreciation of the Greek and Roman estimate of Christianity, it is essential, in the first instance, to recollect how the Jews were regarded and estimated throughout the empire, since it was generally known that the Christians had emanated from the Jews.

Nothing is more certain than that the Jews were distinguished throughout the Roman empire as a special people in contrast to all others. Their imageless worship (ἀθεότης), their stubborn refusal to participate in other cults, together with their exclusiveness (ἀμιξία), marked them off from all nations as a unique people.[1] This uniqueness was openly acknowledged by the

---

[1] There were also their special customs (circumcision, prohibition of swine's flesh, the sabbath, etc.), but these did not contribute so seriously as ἀθεότης and ἀμιξία to establish the character of the Jews for uniqueness ; for customs either identical or somewhat similar were found among other Oriental peoples as well. For ἀθεότης (cp. my essay on "The Charge of Atheism in the First Three Centuries," *Texte u. Unters.*, xxviii. 4), see Pliny, *Hist. Nat.*, xiii. 4. 46 : "gens contumelia numinum insignis" ("a race distinguished by its contempt for deities") ; Tacit., *Hist.*, v. 5 : "Judaei mente sola unumque numen intellegunt . . . . igitur nulla simulacra urbibus suis, nedum templis sistunt ; non regibus haec adulatio non Caesaribus honor" ("the Jews conceive of their deity as one, by the mind alone . . . . hence there are no images erected in their cities or even in their temples. This reverence is not paid to kings, nor this honour to the Cæsars") ; Juv., *Satir.*, xiv. 97 : "nil praeter nubes et caeli numen adorant" ("they venerate simply the clouds and the deity of the sky"), etc. For μισανθρωπία and ἀμιξία, see Tacit. (*loc. cit.*) : "Apud ipsos fides obstinata, misericordia in promptu, sed adversus omnes alios hostile odium" ("Among themselves their honesty is inflexible, their compassion quick to move, but to all other persons they show the hatred of antagonism ") ; and earlier still, Apollonius Molon (in Joseph., *Apion.*, ii. 14). Cp. Schürer's *Gesch. des jüd. Volk.*, III.[3], p. 418 [Eng. trans., II. ii. 295].

legislation of Cæsar. Except for a brief period, the Jews were certainly never expected to worship the emperor. Thus they stood alone by themselves amid all the other races who were included in, or allied to, the Roman empire. The blunt formula "We are Jews" never occurs in the Greek and Roman literature, so far as I know;[1] but the fact was there, i.e., the view was widely current that the Jews were a national phenomenon by themselves, deficient in those traits which were common to the other nations.[2] Furthermore, in every province and town the Jews, and the Jews alone, kept themselves aloof from the neighbouring population by means of their constitutional position and civic demeanour. Only, this very uniqueness of character was taken to be a defect in public spirit and patriotism, as well as an insult and a disgrace, from Apollonius Molon and Posidonius down to Pliny, Tacitus, and later authors,[3] although one or two of the more intelligent writers did not miss the "philosophic" character of the Jews.[4]

Disengaging itself from this Jewish people, Christianity now encountered the Greeks and Romans. In the case of Christians, some of the sources of offence peculiar to the Jews were absent; but the greatest offence of all appeared only in heightened colours, viz., the ἀθεότης and the ἀμιξία (μισανθρωπία). Consequently the Christian religion was described as a "superstitio nova et malefica" (Suet., Nero, 16), as a "superstitio prava, immodica" (Plin., Ep. x. 96, 97), as an "exitiabilis superstitio" (Tacit., Annal., xv. 44), and as a "vana et demens superstitio" (Min. Felix, 9), while the Christians themselves were characterized

---

[1] Yet, cp. Epist. Aristeas, § 16 (ed. Wendland, 1900, p. 6): τὸν πάντων ἐπόπτην καὶ κτίστην θεὸν οὗτοι σέβονται, ὃν καὶ πάντες, ἡμεῖς δὲ προσονομάζοντες ἑτέρως Ζῆνα καὶ Δία.

[2] In Egypt a clear-cut triple division obtained—Egyptians, Greeks, and Jews. Cp. Schürer, III.(3), p. 23 [Eng. trans., II. ii. 231].

[3] Apollonius Molon in Joseph., Apion., II. 15, "The most stupid of the barbarians, ἄθεοι, μισάνθρωποι"; Seneca (in August., de Civit., vi. 11), "sceleratissima gens"; Tacitus (Hist., v. 8), "despectissima pars servientium—taeterrima gens"; Pliny (loc. cit.), Marcus Aurelius (in Ammian, xxii. 5), and Cæcilius (in Min. Felix, x.), "Judaeorum misera gentilitas."

[4] Aristotle (according to Clearchus), φιλόσοφοι παρὰ Σύροις; Theophrastus (according to Porphyry), ἅτε φιλόσοφοι τὸ γένος ὄντες; Strabo (xvi. 2. 35, pp. 760 f.); and Varro (in August., de Civit., iv. 31).

as "per flagitia invisi," and blamed for their "odium generis humani." [1]

Several sensible people during the course of the second century certainly took a different view. Lucian saw in Christians half crazy, credulous fanatics, yet he could not altogether refuse them his respect. Galen explained their course of life as philosophic, and spoke of them in terms of high esteem.[2] Porphyry also treated them, and especially their theologians, the gnostics and Origen, as respectable opponents.[3] But the vast majority of authors persisted in regarding them as an utter abomination. "Latebrosa et lucifuga natio," cries the pagan Cæcilius (in *Minut. Felix*, viii. f.), "in publicum muta, in angulis garrula ; templa ut busta despiciunt, deos despuunt, rident sacra . . . . occultis se notis et insignibus noscunt et amant mutuo paene antequam noverint . . . . cur nullas aras habent, templa nulla, nulla nota simulacra . . . . nisi illud quod colunt et interprimunt, aut puniendum est aut pudendum ? unde autem vel quis ille aut ubi deus unicus, solitarius, destitutus, quem non

---

[1] Tacitus (*loc. cit.*); cp. Tertull., *Apol.*, xxxv., "publici hostes"; xxxvii., "hostes maluistis vocare generis humani Christianos" (you prefer to call Christians the enemies of the human race); *Minuc.*, x., "pravae religionis obscuritas" ; viii., "homines deploratae, inlicitae ac desperatae factionis" (reprobate characters, belonging to an unlawful and desperate faction); " plebs profanae coniurationis " ; ix., "sacraria taeterrima impiae citionis" (abominable shrines of an impious assembly); "eruenda et execranda consensio " (a confederacy to be rooted out and detested).

[2] The passage is extant only in the Arabic (see above, p. 212).

[3] Of the historical basis of the Christian religion and its sacred books in the New Testament, Porphyry and the Neoplatonists in general formed no more favourable opinion than did Celsus, while even in the Old Testament they found (agreeing thus far with the Christian gnostics) a great deal of folly and falsehood. The fact is, no one, not even Celsus, criticised the gospel history so keenly and disparagingly as Porphyry. Still, much that was to be found in the books of Moses and in John appeared to them of value. Further, they had a great respect for the Christian philosophy of religion, and endeavoured in all seriousness to come to terms with it, recognizing that it approximated more nearly than that of the gnostics to their own position. The depreciatory estimate of the world and the dualism which they found in gnosticism seemed to them a frivolous attack upon the Godhead. *Per contra* Porphyry says of Origen: "His outward conduct was that of a Christian and unlawful. *But he thought like a Greek in his views of matter and of God*, and mingled the ideas of the Greeks with foreign fables" (in Eus., *H.E.*, vi. 19). On the attitude of Plotinus towards the gnosis of the church and gnosticism, cp. Karl Schmidt in *Texte u. Unters.*, N.F. v., part 4.

gens libera, non regna, non saltem Romana superstitio noverunt ?
Judaeorum sola et misera gentilitas unum et ipsi deum, sed
palam, sed templis, aris, victimis caeremoniisque coluerunt, cuius
adeo nulla vis ac potestas est, ut sit Romanis numinibus cum
sua sibi natione captivus. At iam Christiani quanta monstra,
quae portenta confingunt."[1] What people saw—what Cæcilius
saw before him—was a descending series, with regard to the
numina and cultus : first Romans, then Jews, then Christians.

So monstrous, so repugnant are those Christians (of whose
faith and life Cæcilius proceeds to tell the most evil tales), that
they drop out of ordinary humanity, as it were. Thus Cæcilius
indeed calls them a "natio," but he knows that they are re-
cruited from the very dregs of the nations, and consequently
are no "people" in the sense of a "nation." The Christian
Octavius has to defend them against this charge of being a
non-human phenomenon, and Tertullian goes into still further
details in his *Apology* and in his address *ad Nationes*. In both
of these writings the leading idea is the refutation of the charge
brought against Christianity, of being something exceptional
and utterly inhuman. "Alia nos opinor, natura, Cyropennæ
[Cynopae ?] aut Sciapodes," we read in *Apol.*, viii., "alii ordines
dentium, alii ad incestam libidinem nervi ? . . . . homo est
enim et Christianus et quod et tu" ("We are of a different
nature, I suppose! Are we Cyropennæ or Sciapodes? Have
we different teeth, different organs for incestuous lust? . . . .
Nay, a Christian too is a man, he is whatever you are." In
Apol., xvi., Tertullian is obliged to refute wicked lies told about
Christians which, if true, would make Christians out to be quite

---

[1] " A *people* who skulk and shun the light of day, silent in public but talkative in
holes and corners.   They despise the temples as dead-houses, they scorn the
gods, they mock sacred things . . . . they recognize each other by means of
secret tokens and marks, and love each other almost before they are acquainted.
Why have they no altars, no temples, no recognized images . . . . unless what
they worship and conceal deserves punishment or is something to be ashamed of?
Moreover, whence is he, who is he, where is he, that one God, solitary and forsaken, whom no free people, no realm, not even a Roman superstition, has ever
known?   The lonely and wretched race of the Jews worshipped one God by
themselves, but they did it openly, with temples, altars, victims, and ceremonies,
and he has so little strength and power that he and all his nation are in bondage
to the deities of Rome ! But the Christians ! What marvels, what monsters, do
they feign ! "

an exceptional class of human beings. Whereas, in reality, "Christiani homines sunt vobiscum degentes, eiusdem victus, habitus, instructus, eiusdem ad vitam necessitatis. neque enim Brachmanae aut Indorum gymnosophistae sumus, silvicolae et exules vitae . . . . si caeremonias tuas non frequento, attamen et illa die *homo* sum" (*Apol.* xlii. : "Christian men live beside you, share your food, your dress, your customs, the same necessities of life as you do. For we are neither Brahmins nor Indian gymnosophists, inhabiting the woods, and exiles from existence. If I do not attend your religious ceremonies, none the less am I a human being on the sacred day"). "Cum concutitur imperium, concussis etiam ceteris membris eius utique et nos, *licet extranei a turbis aestimemur*,[1] in aliquo loco casus invenimur" (*Apol.*, xxxi. : "When the state is disturbed and all its other members affected by the disturbance, surely we also are to be found in some spot or another, *although we are supposed to live aloof from crowds.*" It is evident also from the nicknames and abusive epithets hurled at them, that Christians attracted people's attention as something entirely strange (cp., e.g., *Apol.* l.).

In his two books *ad Nationes*, no less than in the *Apology*, all these arguments also find contemporary expression. Only in the former *one* further consideration supervenes, which deserves

---

[1] Hence the request made to Christians is quite intelligible : "Begone from a world to which you do not belong, and trouble us not." Cp. the passage already cited from Justin's *Apol.*, II. iv., where Christians are told by their opponents, πάντες ἑαυτοὺς φονεύσαντες πορεύεσθαι ἤδη παρὰ τὸν θεὸν καὶ ἡμῖν πράγματα μὴ παρέχετε. Tertullian relates (*ad Scap.* v.) how Arrius Antoninus, the proconsul of Asia, called out to the Christians who crowded voluntarily to his tribunal in a time of persecution, "You miserable wretches; if you want to die, you have precipices and ropes." Celsus (in Orig., *c. Cels.*, VIII. lv.) writes : "If Christians decline to render due honour to the gods or to respect those appointed to take charge of the religious services, let them not grow up to manhood or marry wives or have children or take any part in the affairs of this life, but rather be off with all speed, leaving no posterity behind them, that such a race may become utterly extinct on earth." Hatred of the empire and emperor, and uselessness from the economic standpoint—these were standing charges against Christians, charges which the apologists (especially Tertullian) were at great pains to controvert. Celsus tries to show Christians that they were really trying to cut off the branch on which they sat (VIII. lxviii.): "Were all to act as you do, the emperor would soon be left solitary and forlorn, and affairs would presently fall into the hands of the wildest and most lawless barbarians. Then it would be all over with the glory of

special attention, namely, the assertion of Tertullian that Christians were called "genus tertium" (the Third race) by their opponents. The relevant passages are as follows :—

Ad Nat., I. viii. : "Plane, *tertium genus* dicimur. An Cyropennae aliqui vel Sciapodes vel aliqui de subterraneo Antipodes ? Si qua istic apud vos saltem ratio est, edatis velim primum et secundum genus, ut ita de tertio constet. Psammetichus quidem putavit sibi se de ingenio exploravisse prima generis. dicitur enim infantes recenti e partu seorsum a commercio hominum alendos tradidisse nutrici, quam et ipsam propterea elinguaverat, ut in totum exules vocis humanae non auditu formarent loquellam, sed de suo promentes eam primam nationem designarent cuius sonum natura dictasset. Prima vox ' beccos ' renuntiata est ; interpretatio eius ' panis ' apud Phrygas nomen est ; Phryges primum genus exinde habentur . . . . sint nunc primi Phryges, non tamen tertii Christiani. Quantae enim aliae gentium series post Phrygas ? verum recogitate, ne quos *tertium genus* dicitis principem locum obtineant, siquidem non ulla gens non Christiana. itaque quaecunque gens prima, nihilominus Christiana. ridicula dementia novissimos diciti et *tertios* nominatis. *sed de superstitione tertium genus deputamur, non de natione, ut sint Romani, Judaei, dehinc Christiani.* ubi autem Graeci ? vel si in Romanorum suberstitionibus censentur, quoniam quidem etiam deos Graeciae Roma sollicitavit, ubi

your Worship and the true Wisdom among men." As the Christians Were almost alone among religionists in being liable to this charge of enmity to the empire, they Were held responsible by the populace, as everybody knoWs, for any great calamities that occurred. The passages in Tertullian bearing on this point are quite familiar ; but one should also compare the parallel statements in Origen (*in Matt. Comment Ser.*, xxxix.). Henceforth Christians appear a special group by themselves. Maximinus Daza, in his rescript to Sabinus (Eus., *H.E.*, ix. 9), speaks of the ἔθνος τῶν Χριστιανῶν (the nation of the Christians), and the edict of Galerius reluctantly admits that Christians succeeded in combining the various nations into a relative unity by means of their commandments (Eus., *H.E.*, viii. 17. 7) : τοσαύτη αὐτοὺς πλεονεξία παρεσχήκει καὶ ἄνοια κατειλήφει, ὡς μὴ ἕπεσθαι τοῖς ὑπὸ τῶν πάλαι καταδειχθεῖσιν . . . . ἀλλὰ κατὰ τὴν αὐτῶν πρόθεσιν καὶ ὡς ἕκαστος ἐβούλετο, οὕτως ἑαυτοῖς καὶ νόμους ποιῆσαι καὶ τούτους παραφυλάττειν καὶ ἐν διαφόροις διάφορα πλήθη συνάγειν ("Such arrogance had seized them and such senselessness had mastered them, that instead of folloWing the institutions of their ancestors . . . . they framed laWs for themselves according to their own purpose, as each desired, and observed these laWs, and thus held various gatherings in various places ").

saltem Ægyptii, et ipsi, quod sciam, privatae curiosaeque religionis? *porro si tam monstruosi, qui tertii loci, quales habendi,
qui primo et secundo antecedunt?*" (" We are indeed called the
third race of men! Are we monsters, Cyropennæ, or Sciopades,
or some Antipodeans from the underworld? If these have any
meaning for you, pray explain the first and second of the races,
that we may thus learn the ' third.' Psammetichus thought he
had ingeniously hit upon primeval man. He removed, it is
said, some newly born infants from all human intercourse and
entrusted their upbringing to a nurse whom he had deprived of
her tongue, in order that being exiled entirely from the sound
of the human voice, they might form their words without
hearing it, and derive them from their own nature, thus indicating what was the first nation whose language was originally
dictated by nature. The first word they uttered was ' beccos,'
the Phrygian word for bread. The Phrygians, then, are held
to be the first race. . . . . If, then, the Phrygians are the first
race, still it does not follow that the Christians are the third.
For how many other races successively came after the Phrygians ?
But take heed lest those whom you call *the third race* take first
place, since there is no nation which is not Christian. Whatever nation, therefore, is the first, is nevertheless Christian now.
It is senseless absurdity for you to call us the latest of nations
and then to dub us the *Third*. *But*, you say, *it is on the score
of religion and not of nationality that we are considered to be
third; it is the Romans first, then the Jews, and after that the
Christians.* What about the Greeks then? Or supposing that
they are reckoned among the various Roman religions (since it
was from Greece that Rome borrowed even her deities), where do
the Egyptians at any rate come in, since they possess a religion
which, so far as I know, is all their own, and full of secrecy?
*Besides, if those who occupy the third rank are such monsters,
what must we think of those who precede them in the first and
second?* ").

Further, in *ad Nat.*, I. xx. (after showing that the charges
brought against Christians recoil upon their adversaries the
heathen), Tertullian proceeds: " *Habetis et vos tertium genus
etsi non de tertio ritu*, attamen de tertio sexu. Illud aptius de

viro et femina viris et feminis iunctum" (" You too have your 'third race' [i.e., of eunuchs], though it is not in the way of a third religion, but of a third sex.   Made up of male and female in conjunction, it is better suited to pander to men and women ! ")

Add also a passage from the treatise *Scorpiace* (x. : a word to heretics who shunned martyrdom) : " Illic constitues et syna-gogas Judaeorum fontes persecutionum, apud quas apostoli flagella perpessi sunt, et populos nationum cum suo quidem circo, *ubi facile conclamant*: ' *Usque quo genus tertium ?* ' " (" Will you set up there [i.e., in heaven] also synagogues of the Jews— which are fountains of persecution—before which the apostles suffered scourging, and heathen crowds with their circus, for-sooth, where all are ready to shout, ' How long are we to endure this third race ? ' ").

From these passages we infer :—

i. That " the third race" (*genus tertium*) as a designation of Christians on the lips of the heathen was perfectly common in Carthage about the year 200.   Even in the circus people cried, " Usque quo genus tertium ? "

ii. That this designation referred exclusively to the Christian method of conceiving and worshipping God.   The Greeks, Romans, and all other nations passed for the first race (*genus primum*), in so far as they mutually recognized each other's gods or honoured foreign gods as well as their own, and had sacrifices and images.   The Jews (with their national God, their ex-clusiveness, and a worship which lacked images but included sacrifice)[1] constituted the second race (*genus alterum*).   The Christians, again (with their spiritual God, their lack of images and sacrifices, and the contempt for the gods—*contemnere deos*— which they shared with the Jews[2]), formed the Third race (*genus tertium*).

iii. When Tertullian talks as if the whole system of classifica-

[1] Cp. *ad Nat.*, I. viii.

[2] Cp. what is roundly asserted in *ad Nat.*, I. viii. : "It is on the score of *religion* and not of nationality that we are considered to be third ; it is the Romans first, then the Jews, and after that the Christians." Also, I. xx. : "Tertium genus [dicimur] de ritu " (" We are called a third race on the ground of religion "). It seems to me utterly impossible to suppose that Tertullian might have been mistaken in this interpretation of the title in question.

tion could denote the chronological series of the nations, it is merely a bit of controversial dialectic. Nor has the designation of "the Third race" (*genus tertium*) anything whatever to do either with the virginity of Christians, or, on the other hand, with the sexual debaucheries set down to their credit.[1]

All these results[2] were of vital importance to the impression made by Christianity (and Judaism[3]) upon the pagan world. As early as the opening of the second century Christians designate their religion as "the third method" of religion (cp. the

---

[1] Passages may indeed be pointed out in which either virginity (or unsexual character) or unnatural lust is conceived as "genus tertium" (a third race), or as a race (*genus*) in general (Tertull., *de Virg. Vel.*, vii. : "Si caput mulieris vir est, ubique et virginis, de qua fit mulier illa quae nupsit, nisi si virgo *tertium genus* est monstrosum aliquod sui capitis." "If the man is the head of the woman, he is also the head of the virgin, for out of a virgin comes the woman who marries ; unless she is some monstrosity with a head of its own, *a third race*"). Cp. *op cit.*, v., where the female sex is "genus secundi hominis" ; pseudo-Cypr., *de Pudic.*, vii., "Virginitas neutrius est sexus"; and Clem. Alex., *Paedag.*, II. x. 85, οὐδὲ γὰρ αἰδοῖα ἔχει ἡ ὕαινα ἅμα ἄμφω, ἄρρενος καὶ θήλεος, καθὼς ὑπειλήφασί τινες, ἑρμαφροδίτους τερατολοῦντες καὶ τρίτην ταύτην μεταξὺ θηλείας καὶ ἄρρενος ἀνδρόγυνον καινοτομοῦντες φύσιν [a similar sexual analogy]. Cp., on the other hand, *op. cit.*, I. iv. 11, where there is a third condition common to both sexes, viz., that of being human beings and also children ; also Lampridius, *Alex. Sever.*, xxiii. : "Idem tertium genus hominum eunuchos dicebat" ("He said eunuchs were a third race of mankind"). Obviously, however, such passages are irrelevant to the point now under discussion.

[2] It is remarkable that Tertullian is only aware of the title "tertium genus" as a pagan description of Christians, and not as one also applied by Christians to themselves. But despite his silence on the fact that Christians also designated their religion as "the third kind" of religion, we must nevertheless assume that the term rose as spontaneously to the lips of Christians as of their opponents, since it is unlikely, though not impossible, that the latter borrowed it from Christian literature. (Consequently Fronto, in his lost treatise against the Christians, must have made polemical use of the title "genus tertium" which he found in Christian writings, and by this means the term passed out into wider currency among the heathen. Yet in Minucius Felix it does not occur.) To recall the chronological succession of its occurrences once again : at the opening of the second century one Christian writer (the author of the Preaching of Peter) calls the Christian religion "the third kind" of religion ; in the year 197, Tertullian declares, "Tertium genus *dicimur*" ("*We are called* the third race") ; while in 242-243 A.D. a Roman or African Christian (pseudo-Cyprian) writes, "Tertium genus *sumus*" ("*We are* the third race ").

[3] I add, Judaism—for hitherto in our discussion we could not determine with absolute certainty whether any *formula* was current which distinguished the Jews from all other peoples with regard to their conception and worship of God. Now it is perfectly plain. The Jews ranked in this connection as an independent magnitude, a "genus alterum."

evidence above furnished by the Preaching of Peter), and frankly declare, about the year 240 A.D., "We are the third race of mankind" (cp. the evidence of the treatise *de Pascha Computus*).[1] Which proves that the pagans did borrow this conception, and that (even previously to 200 A.D.)[2] they described the Jews as the second and the Christians as the third race of men. This they did for the same reason as the Christians, on account of the nature of the religion in question.

It is indeed amazing! One had certainly no idea that in the consciousness of the Greeks and Romans the Jews stood out in such bold relief from the other nations, and the Christians from both, or that they represented themselves as independent "genera," and were so described in an explicit formula. Neither Jews nor Christians could look for any ample recognition,[3] little as the demarcation was intended as a recognition at all.

The polemical treatises against Christians prove that the triple formula "Romans, etc., Jews, and Christians" was really never absent from the minds of their opponents. So far as we are

---

[1] It is now clear that we were right in conjecturing above that the Romans were to pseudo-Cyprian the first race, and the Jews the second, as opposed to the Third race.

[2] How long before we do not know. By the end of the second century, at any rate, the title was quite common. It is therefore hardly possible to argue against the authenticity of Hadrian's epistle to Servianus (see above) on the ground that it contains this triple division : " Hunc [nummum] *Christiani*, hunc Judaei, hunc omnes venerantur *et gentes* " ("This pelf is revered by the Christians, the Jews, and the nations "). But the description of Romans, Greeks, etc., as " gentes " is certainly very suspicious ; it betrays, unless I am mistaken, the pen of a Christian writer.

[3] Thanks to Varro, who had a genius for classification, people had been accustomed among literary circles, in the first instance, to grade the gods and religions as well. Perhaps it was under the influence of his writings (and even Tertullian makes great play with them in his treatise *ad Nationes*) that the distinction of Jews and Christians as "the second and third ways" obtained primarily among the learned, and thence made its way gradually into the minds of the common people. It is utterly improbable that this new classification was influenced by the entirely different distinction current among the Egyptians (see above), of the three γένη (Egyptians, Greeks, and Jews). Once it was devised, the former conception must have gone on working with a logic of its own, setting Judaism and Christianity in a light which was certainly not intended at the outset. It developed the conception of three circles, of three possible religions ! Strangely enough, Tertullian never mentions the "genus tertium" in his *Apology*, though it was contemporaneous with the *ad Nationes*. Was the fact not of sufficient importance to him in encountering a Roman governor?

acquainted with these treatises, they one and all adopt this scheme of thought: the Jews originally parted company with all other nations, and after leaving the Egyptians, they formed an ill-favoured species by themselves, whilst it is from these very Jews that the Christians have now broken off, retaining all the worst features of Judaism and adding loathsome and repulsive elements of their own. Such was the line taken by Celsus, Porphyry, and Julian in their anti-Christian writings. Celsus speaks of the γένος of the Jews, and opposes both γένη in the sharpest manner to all other nations, in order to show that when Christians, as renegade Jews, distinguish themselves from this γένος—a γένος which is, at least, a people—they do so to their own loss. He characterizes Christians (VIII. ii.) as ἀποτειχίζοντες ἑαυτοὺς καὶ ἀπορρηγνύντες ἀπὸ τῶν λοιπῶν ἀνθρώπων ("people who separate themselves and break away from the rest of mankind"). For all that, everything in Christianity is simply plagiarized from a plagiarism, or copied from a copy. Christians *per se* have no new teaching (μάθημα, I. iv.; cp. II. v. and IV. xiv.). That they have any teaching at all to present, is simply due to the fact that they have kept back the worst thing of all, viz., their στασιάζειν πρὸς τὸ κοινόν ("their revolt against the common weal").[1] Porphyry — who, I imagine, is the anti-Christian controversialist before the mind of Eusebius [2]—in his *Preparatio*, i. 2, begins by treating Christians as a sheer impossibility, inasmuch as they will not and do not belong to the Greeks or to the barbarians. Then he goes on to say: καὶ μηδ' αὐτῷ τῷ παρὰ Ἰουδαίοις τιμουμένῳ θεῷ κατὰ τὰ παρ' αὐτοῖς προσανέχειν νόμιμα, καινὴν δέ τινα καὶ ἐρήμην ἀνοδίαν ἑαυτοῖς συντεμενεῖ μήτε τὰ Ἑλλήνων μήτε τὰ Ἰουδαίων φυλάττουσαν ("Nor do they adhere to the rites of the God worshipped by the Jews according to their customs, but fashion some new and solitary vagary for themselves of which there is no trace in Hellenism or Judaism"). So that he also gives the triple classification. Finally, Julian (Neumann, p. 164) likewise

---

[1] The τρίτον γένος which Celsus mentions rather obscurely in V. lxi. has nothing to do with the third race which is our present topic. It refers to distinctions within Christianity itself.

[2] Cp. von Wilamowitz-Moellendorf in the *Zeitschrift für neutestamentliche Wissenschaft*, i. 2, pp. 101 f.

follows the division of Ἕλληνες, Ἰουδαῖοι, and Γαλιλαῖοι. The Galileans are neither Greeks nor Jews ; they have come from the Jews, but have separated from them and struck out a path of their own.   " They have repudiated every noble and significant idea current among us Greeks, and among the Hebrews who are descended from Moses ; yet they have lifted from both sources everything that adhered to these nations like an ill-omened demon, taking their godlessness from the levity of the Jews, and their careless and lax way of living from our own thoughtlessness and vulgarity."

Plainly, then, Greek and Jews and Christians were distinguished throughout upon the ground of religion, although the explicit formula of " the third race " occurs only in the West.   After the middle of the third century, both empire and emperor learnt to recognize and dread the third race of worshippers as a " nation," as well as a race.   They were a state within the state.   The most instructive piece of evidence in this connection is the account of Decius given by Cyprian (*Ep.* lv. 9): " Multo patientius et tolerabilius audivit levari adversus se aemulum principem quam constitui Romae dei sacerdotem " (" He would hear of a rival prince being set up against himself with far more patience and equanimity than of a priest of God being appointed at Rome "). The terrible edict issued by this emperor for the persecution of Christians is in the first instance the practical answer given by the state to the claims of the " New People " and to the political view advocated by Melito and Origen.   The inner energy of the new religion comes out in its self-chosen title of " the New People " or " the Third race " just as plainly as in the testimony extorted from its opponents, that in Christianity a new *genus* of religion had actually emerged side by side with the religions of the nations and of Judaism.   It does not afford much direct evidence upon the outward spread and strength of Christianity, for the former estimate emerged, asserted itself, and was recognized at an early period, when Christians were still, in point of numbers, a comparatively small society.[1]   But it must have been

---

[1] They could not have been utterly insignificant, however ; otherwise this estimate would be incredible. In point of numbers they must have already rivalled the Jews at any rate.

of the highest importance for the propaganda of the Christian religion, to be so distinctly differentiated from all other religions and to have so lofty a consciousness of its own position put before the world.[1] Naturally this had a repelling influence as well on certain circles. Still it was a token of power, and power never fails to succeed.

[1] Judaism already owed no small amount of her propaganda to her apologetic and, within her apologetic, to the valuation of herself which it developed. Cp. Schürer, *Gesch. des Volkes Israel*, III.[3], pp. 107 f. [Eng. trans., II. iii. 249 f.].

CHAPTER VIII

THE RELIGION OF A BOOK AND A HISTORICAL REALIZATION

CHRISTIANITY, unlike Islam, never was and never became the religion of a book in the strict sense of the term (not until a much later period, that of rigid Calvinism, did the consequences of its presentation as the religion of a book become really dangerous, and even then the rule of faith remained at the helm). Still, the book of Christianity—*i.e.*, in the first instance, the Old Testament—did exert an influence which brought it to the verge of becoming the religion of a book. Paul, of course, when we read him aright, was opposed to this development, and wide circles throughout Christendom—both the gnostics and the Marcionites—even went the length of entirely repudiating the Old Testament or of ascribing it to another god altogether, though he too was righteous and dependent on the most high God.[1] But in the catholic church this gnostic criticism was indignantly rejected, whilst the complicated position adopted by the apostle Paul towards the book was not understood at all. The Old Testament, interpreted allegorically, continued to be *the sacred* book for these Christians, as it was for the Jews, from whom they aimed to wrest it.

This attitude to the Old Testament is quite intelligible. What other religious society could produce a book like it?[2] How overpowering and lasting must have been the impression made by it on Greeks, educated and uneducated alike, once they

[1] Cp., for example, the letter of Ptolemæus to Flora, with my study of it in the *Sitzungsberichte d. K. Pr. Akad. d. Wiss.*, May 15, 1902.

[2] It had this double advantage, that it was accessible in Greek, and also that the Hebrew original was familiar. On the Septuagint, see the studies by Nestle and Deissmann, besides the epistle of Aristeas (ed. Wendland, 1900).

learnt to understand it! Many details might be strange or obnoxious, but the instruction and inspiration of its pages amply made up for that. Its great antiquity—stretching in some parts, as men held, to thousands of years[1]—was already proof positive of its imperishable value; its contents seemed in part a world of mysteries and in part a compendium of the profoundest wisdom. By its inexhaustible wealth, by its variety, comprehensiveness, and extensive character, it seemed like a literary cosmos, a second creation which was the twin of the first.[2] This indeed was the deepest impression which it made. The opinion most widely held by Greeks who came in contact with the Old Testament was that this was a book which was to be coupled with the universe, and that a similar verdict could be passed upon both of them. Variously as they might still interpret it, the fact of its being a parallel creation to the world, equally great and equally comprehensive, and of both issuing from a single author, appeared indubitable even to the gnostics and the Marcionites, whilst the members of the catholic church recognized in this divine author the most high God himself![3] In the entire history of human thought, when did any other book earn such an opinion?[4]

The Old Testament certainly was an enormous help to the Christian propaganda, and it was in vain that the Jews protested.[5]

---

[1] In his treatise *de Pallio* Tertullian exclaims triumphantly, " Your history only reaches back to the Assyrians ; we are in possession of the history of the whole world " (" Ferme apud vos ultra stilus non solet. ab Assyriis, si forte, aevi historiae patescunt. qui vero divinas lectitamus, ab ipsius mundi natalibus compotes sumus ").

[2] Hence the numerous names for the book, partly due to its origin, partly to its contents (σωτήρια γράμματα).

[3] Certain gnostics distinguished the god of creation and the god of the Old Testament. This distinction prevailed wherever nature was depreciated in comparison with the religious attainments of the pre-Christian era. Nature is fierce and fatal ; the law is, relatively speaking, moral.

[4] Attacks by gnostics and pagans were not awanting, but the latter must have seldom assailed it on the whole. When they busied themselves seriously with the book, they almost invariably respected it. " Unde scis illos libros (veteri Testamenti) unius veri et veracissimi dei spiritu esse humano generi ministratos ? " (Aug., *Confess.*, vi. 5, 7. : " Whence knowest thou that these books have been imparted to mankind by the spirit of the one true and most truthful God ? ")—this is a Manichæan or gnostic objection.

[5] Their right to the book was simply denied ; their misinterpretation of it proved that it was no longer theirs ; the opinion was even current (cp. Barnabas

We have one positive testimony, in the following passage from Tatian (*Orat.* xxix.), that for many people the Old Testament formed the real bridge by which they crossed to Christianity. " When I was paying earnest heed to what was profitable," he writes, " some barbarian writings came into my hands which were too old for Greek ideas and too divine for Greek errors. *These I was led to trust,* owing to their very simplicity of expression and the unstudied character of their authors, owing to their intelligible description of creation, their foreknowledge of the future, the excellence of their precepts, and the fact of their embracing the universe under the sole rule of God. Thus was my soul instructed by God, and I understood how other teachings lead to condemnation, whilst these writings abolish the bondage that prevails throughout the world and free us from a plurality of rulers and tyrants innumerable. They furnish us, not with something which we had not already received, but with something which had been received but which, thanks to error, had been lost." [1]

This confession is particularly noticeable, not merely on account of the explicit manner in which it brings out the significance of the Old Testament for the transition to Christianity, but also for its complete and clear statement of the

epist.) that it never had been theirs, and that they had appropriated it unfairly. " In Judaeorum oleastro insiti sumus," says Tertullian (*de Testim.*, v., after Rom. xi.); but the oleaster had thereby lost its very right to exist.

[1] Cp. also Justin, *Dial. c. Tryph.*, vii. f. : Ἐγένοντό τινες πρὸ πολλοῦ χρόνου πάντων τούτων τῶν νομιζομένων φιλοσόφων παλαιότεροι, μακάριοι καὶ δίκαιοι καὶ θεοφιλεῖς, θείῳ πνεύματι λαλήσαντες καὶ τὰ μέλλοντα θεσπίσαντες, ἃ δὴ νῦν γίνεται· προφήτας δὲ αὐτοὺς καλοῦσιν· οὗτοι μόνοι τὸ ἀληθὲς καὶ εἶδον καὶ ἐξεῖπον ἀνθρώποις, μήτ’ εὐλαβηθέντες μήτε δυσωπηθέντες τινά .... ἀλλὰ μόνα ταῦτα εἰπόντες ἃ ἤκουσαν καὶ ἃ εἶδον ἁγίῳ πληρωθέντες πνεύματι· συγγράμματα δὲ αὐτῶν ἔτι καὶ νῦν διαμένει, κ.τ.λ. .... Ἐμοῦ δὲ παραχρῆμα πῦρ ἐν τῇ ψυχῇ ἀνήφθη καὶ ἔρως εἶχε με τῶν προφητῶν καὶ τῶν ἀνδρῶν ἐκείνων, οἵ εἰσι Χριστοῦ φίλοι (" Long ago there were certain men, more ancient than all those who are esteemed philosophers, men blessed and righteous and beloved of God, who spoke by the spirit of God, and foretold what would come to pass, even what is now coming to pass. Their name is that of prophets. They alone saw the truth and proclaimed it to men, neither reverencing nor dreading any man .... but only saying what they saw and heard, being filled with the holy spirit. Writings of theirs are still extant. .... A fire was at once kindled in my soul, and I was seized with a passion for the prophets and for those who are the friends of Christ ").

reasons for this influence. In the first place, the _form_ of this
book made a deep impression, and it is characteristic of Tatian
the Greek, though he would remain a Greek no longer, that its
form is the first point which he singles out. The vigorous style
of the prophets and psalmists captivated the man who had
passed through the schools of rhetoric and philosophy. Vigour
coupled with simplicity—this was what made the book seem to
him so utterly different from those treatises and unwieldy tomes
in which their authors made desperate efforts to attain clearness
of thought upon questions of supreme moment. The second
item mentioned by the apologist is the narrative of creation in
Genesis. This also is significant and quite intelligible. Every
Greek philosopher had his cosmology, and here was a narrative
of creation that was both lucid and comprehensible. It did not
look like a philosophy, nor did it look like an ordinary myth;
it was an entirely new _genre_, something between and above them
both. It can only have been inspired by God himself! The
third feature which struck Tatian was the prophecies of the
book. A glance at the early Christian writers, and especially
at the apologists, reveals the prominent and indeed the commanding rôle played by the argument from prophecy, and this
argument could only be led by means of the Old Testament.
The fourth item was the moral code. Here Tatian was certainly thinking in the first instance of the decalogue, which even
the gnostics, for all their critical attitude towards the book as a
whole, considered only to require completion, and which was
therefore distinguished by them from the rest of the Old Testament.[1] To Gentile Christians the decalogue invariably meant
the sum of morals, which only the sayings of the Sermon on the
Mount could render more profound.[2] Finally, the fifth item
mentioned by the apologist is the rigid monotheism which
stamps the whole volume.

This list really includes all the elements in the Old Testament which seemed of special weight and marked its origin as
divine. But in a survey of the services rendered by it to the
Christian church throughout the first two centuries, the following points stand out clearly.

[1] Cp. the epistle of Ptolemæus to Flora.   [2] Cp. the Didachê.

1. Christians borrowed from the Old Testament its mono-theistic cosmology and view of nature. Though the gospels and epistles presuppose this, they do not expressly state it, and in the Old Testament books people found exactly what they required, viz., in the first place, innumerable passages proclaiming and inculcating monotheism, and also challenging polytheism, and in the second place many passages which extolled God as the creator of heaven and earth and depicted his creation.

2. From the Old Testament it could be proved that the appearance and the entire history of Jesus had been predicted hundreds and even thousands of years ago; and further, that the founding of the New People which was to be fashioned out of all nations upon earth,[1] had from the very beginning been prophesied and prepared for (cp. pp. 240 f.).[2]

Their own religion appeared, on the basis of this book, to be the religion of a history which was the fulfilment of prophecy; what remained still in the future could only be a brief space of time, and even in its course everything would be fulfilled in accordance with what had been prophesied. The certain

---

[1] The apologists refute the idea that the Jewish proselytes were this new people. It was an obvious objection. But Christians alone have adherents ἐκ παντὸς γένους ἀνθρώπων.

[2] To cite but a single passage, compare the Preaching of Peter (Clem. Alex., Strom., VI. xv.): Ἡμεῖς ἀναπτύξαντες τὰς βίβλους ἃς εἴχομεν τῶν προφητῶν, ἃ μὲν διὰ παραβολῶν, ἃ δὲ δι' αἰνιγμάτων, ἃ δὲ αὐθεντικῶς καὶ αὐτολεξεὶ τὸν Χριστὸν Ἰησοῦν ὀνομαζόντων, εὔρομεν καὶ τὴν παρουσίαν αὐτοῦ καὶ τὸν θάνατον καὶ τὸν σταυρὸν καὶ τὰς λοιπὰς κολάσεις πάσας, ὅσας ἐποίησαν αὐτῷ οἱ Ἰουδαῖοι, καὶ τὴν ἔγερσιν καὶ τὴν εἰς οὐρανοὺς ἀνάληψιν πρὸ τοῦ Ἱεροσόλυμα κριθῆναι, καθὼς ἐγέγραπτο ταῦτα πάντα ἃ ἔδει αὐτὸν παθεῖν καὶ γεγραμμένων εἰς αὐτόν (" Unrolling the books of the prophets in our possession, which name Christ Jesus partly in parables, partly in enigmas, and partly in plain expressions and in so many words, we find his advent, death, cross, and the other punishments inflicted on him by the Jews, his resurrection and his ascension into heaven, previous to the fall of Jerusalem, even as it is written, 'All these things which he had to suffer, and which shall be after him.' Learning all this, we believed in God by means of what had been written about him "). This writer explains, then, that on the ground of the Old Testament he came to believe in God the Father of Jesus Christ. Tertull., Apol., xlvi.: " Ostendimus totum statum nostrum, et quibus modis probare possimus ita esse sicut ostendimus, ex fide scilicet et antiquitate divinarum litterarum, item ex confessione spiritualium potestatum " [i.e., the testimony which the demons exorcised by us are forced to bear] (" We have stated all our case, and also shown you how we are able to prove it, viz., from the trustworthy character and great age of our sacred writings, and likewise from the confession of the powers of spiritual evil "). These, then, were the two decisive proofs.

guarantee for this was afforded by what had already been fulfilled. By aid of the Old Testament, Christian teachers dated back their religion to the very beginning of things, and connected it with the creation. This formed one of the most impressive articles of the mission-preaching among educated people, and thereby Christianity got a hold which was possessed by no religion except Judaism. But one must take good care not to imagine that to the minds of these Christians the Old Testament was pure prophecy which still lacked its fulfilment. The Old Testament was indeed a book of prophecies, but for that very reason it had didactic significance as the *complete* revelation of God, which needed no manner of addition whatsoever, and excluded any subsequent modification. The historical fulfilment—"lex radix evangeliorum" (Tert., *Scorp.*, ii.)—of these revelations merely attested their truth in the eyes of all the world. Indeed, the whole gospel was thus put together from the Old Testament. Handbooks of this kind must have been widely circulated in different though similar editions.

3. Proofs from the Old Testament were increasingly employed to justify principles and institutions adopted by the Christian church (not merely imageless, spiritual worship, the abolition of the ceremonial law and its precepts, with baptism and the Lord's supper, but also—though hesitatingly—the Christian priesthood, the episcopate, and the new organizations within the cultus).

4. The book was used for the purpose of exhortation, following the formula of "a minori ad maius." If God had praised or punished this or that in the past, how much more, it was argued, are we to look for similar treatment from him, we who are now living in the last days and who have received "the calling of promise."

5. From the Old Testament (*i.e.*, from its prophetic denunciations) Christians proved [1] that the Jewish people had no covenant with God (cp. pp. 66 f.).

---

[1] How impressive was the argument—you see, the Jewish nation is dispersed, the temple is destroyed, the sacrifices have ceased, the princes of the house of Juda have disappeared! Compare the extensive use of these facts by Eusebius in his Church History.

6. Christians edified themselves by means of the Old Testament and its sayings about trust in God, about God's aid, about humility, and about holy courage, as well as by means of its heroic spirits and its prophets, above all, by the psalms.

What has been summarized in these paragraphs is enough to indicate the importance of the Old Testament for primitive Christianity and its mission.[1]   Be it remembered, however, that

---

[1] No thorough statement of the significance and employment of the Old Testament in the early church is available even at this time of day.   In his *Untersuchungen zum ersten Clemensbrief* (1891), Wrede, however, has shown how such an essay should be planned and executed.   His summary there (p. 75) agrees with what I have stated above.   "Clement's use of Scripture," he writes, "depends wholly on the presupposition common to all Christians, that the Old Testament is the *one* holy book given by God to Christians, and to Christians directly and expressly ; its words can lay claim to absolute authority, and they furnish the primary and most important basis of all Christian παράδοσις (tradition). Historically, it would be a totally inadequate account of the real facts of the case to declare that the Old Testament in whole or part *still* retained its value for Christians, as though the recognition of this was the result of some kind of reflection.   The possession of this wonderful infallible volume was really, in the eyes of Christians, one of the most convincing and attractive features of the new religion.   We simply cannot possess our minds too fully of the view that in those days there was not the slightest idea of a second sacred scripture ever rising one day to rank with the Old Testament, much less to round off the earlier book." In worship, readings were regularly given from the Old Testament, and further acquaintance with it was certainly promoted by means of brief selections and writings like the *Testimonia* of Cyprian.   Private reading of the Bible was also practised, as is plain from the Acts of the Scillitan Martyrs, several passages in Tertullian and Origen, and other sources.   Origen (Hom. II. *in Num.*, vol. x. p. 19) thinks that from one to two hours of prayer and Bible-reading is barely an adequate minimum for the individual Christian ; in Hom. *in Levit.*, ix. 7, he describes "divina lectio, orationes assiduae, et sermo doctrinae" as "nutrimenta spiritus."   In pseudo-Clem., *de Virginit.*, I. x., the reading of the Bible at small devotional gatherings held in private houses is mentioned.   Justin assumes, in his Apology, that the Old Testament is easily accessible, and that the emperor could readily procure a copy.   But the description of Pamphilus at Cæsarea (Jerome, *adv. Rufin.*, I. ix.) is particularly illuminating : "Scripturas sanctas non ad legendum tantum, sed et ad habendum tribuebat promptissime, nec solum viris sed et feminis quas vidisset lectioni deditas, unde et multos codices praeparabat, ut cum necessitas poposcisset, volentibus largiretur" ("He readily provided Bibles not only to read but to keep, not only for men but for any women whom he saw addicted to reading.   Hence he would prepare a large number of volumes, so that, when any demand was made upon him, he might be in a position to gratify those who applied to him)."   For the diffusion of Scripture knowledge by means of reading (in small circles or publicly), cp. pseudo-Clem., *de Virg.*, II. vi.   Yet Augustine was not alone in his complaint (*Conf.*, vi. 11. 18): "Ubi ipsos codices quaerimus? Unde aut quomodo comparamus? A quibus sumimus? ("Where are we to find

a large portion of its contents was allegorized, *i.e.*, criticised and re-interpreted. Without this, a great deal of the Old Testament would have been unacceptable to Christians. Anyone who refused such re-reading of its contents had to reject the book in whole or part.[1]

After the rise of the New Testament, which was the most important and independent product of the primitive church, and which legitimized its faith as a new religion, certain aspects of

even the books [*i.e.*, of Scripture]? Where and how can we procure them? From whom can we get them?").

[1] Like Barnabas before him, Origen has shown with perfect clearness that the literal sense is in many cases inadmissible. Compare, for example, Hom. VII. 5 *in Levit.* (vol. ix. pp. 306 f.): "Si adsideamus literae, et secundum hoc vel quod Judaeis vel id quod vulgo videtur accipiamus, quae in lege scripta sunt, erubesco dicere et confiteri, quia tales leges dederit deus. videbuntur enim magis elegantes et rationabiles hominum leges, verbi gratia vel Romanorum vel Atheniensium vel Lacedaemoniorum. si vero secundum hanc intelligentiam, quam docet ecclesia, accipiatur dei lex, tunc plane omnes humanas supereminet leges et veri dei lex esse creditur." It may not be superfluous to recall that any authoritative text, especially one which was explained as of divine authority, *demanded* the allegorical interpretation, since those who recognized or maintained its authority usually connected the text with ideas which were quite different from the interpretation sanctioned by the historical interpretation. Nay more. Authority was desired and devised for such ideas themselves. For example, to treat the Song of Solomon as a love-song and then to vindicate the authority of its sacred text, is the acme of absurdity; it became an intolerable burden for the church to do so. But the same difficulty arose in connection with a book like Genesis. Those who admitted the book to the canon had no desire to canonize a wretched Jacob, etc.; but they were prepared for all such contingencies, and employed the allegorical method to remove any stumbling-blocks. Here, indeed, one may even ask whether the final redactor did not smooth over his work with allegorical expositions; in that event, only the sources of the book would need to be explained historically, whereas the book itself (apart from its canonization) would invite the allegorical method—the latter going back to the age of the book's final redaction. Once a Bible text is explained as possessing divine authority, no one needs to trouble any longer about the allegorical interpretation of those who had canonized it; the acceptance of it as a divine authority tacitly enjoined the faithful to read it in such a way as to draw the maximum of edifying matter from it. This was the true method of interpretation! A few connecting links, be they ever so slender and arbitrary, had to be made between certain parts of the literal text and the fine ideas which were attached to the letter. But, once this was done, everything was in order, and those ideas now ranked as the ideas of the text itself. So it is at bottom with all books of human law, *mutatis mutandis*. They all invite an "allegorical" interpretation alongside of the historical (*i.e.*, the sense of the original lawgiver). They not only permit but involve the acceptance of any explanation as legitimate which can at all be reconciled with the letter of their writing, even though the reconciliation be rather forced.

the Old Testament fell into the background. Still, these were
not numerous. Plainly, there were vital points at which the
former could not undertake to render the service done by the
latter. No doubt any statement of Christian morality always
went back to the words of Jesus as its primary source. Here
the Old Testament had to retire. But elsewhere the latter held
its own. It was only in theory, not in practice, that an imper-
ceptible revolution occurred. The conflict with gnosticism, and
the formation of the New Testament which took place in and
with that conflict, made it plain to the theologians of the
catholic church that the simple identification of the Old Testament and the gospel was by no means a matter of course. The
first theologians of the ancient catholic church, Irenæus and
Tertullian, already relax this absolute identification; they
rather approximate to the conception of the apostle Paul, viz.,
that the Old Testament and the old covenant mark quite a
different level from that of the New. The higher level of the
new covenant is recognized, and therewith the higher level of
the New Testament as well. Now in theory this led to many
consequences of no small moment, for people learned to assign
higher value to the specific significance of the Christian religion
when it was set in contrast to the Old Testament—a point on
which the gnostics had insisted with great energy. But in
practice this change of estimate did not seriously affect the use
of the Old Testament. If one could now hold theoretically
that much of the Old Testament was "demutatum, suppletum,
impletum, perfectum," and even "expunctum" by the New
Testament (Tert., *de Orat.*, i.), the third century saw the Old
Testament allegorized and allegorically employed as direct
evidence for the truths of Christianity. Indeed, people really
ceased to allegorize it. As the churches became stocked with
every kind of sacred ceremony, and as they carefully developed
priestly, sacrificial, and sacramental ideas, people now began to
grow careless and reckless in applying the *letter* of Old Testament ceremonial laws to the arrangements of the Christian
organization and worship. In setting itself up as a legislative
body, the church had recourse to the Old Testament in a way
that Paul had severely censured; it fell back on the law,

though all the while it blamed the Jews and declared that their observance of the law was quite illicit. In dogma there was now greater freedom from the Old Testament than had been the case during the second century ; Christological problems occupied the foreground, and theological interests shifted from problems of θεός and λόγος to those of the Trinity and of Christology, as well as to Christocentric mysteries. In the practice of the church, however, people employed the Old Testament more lavishly than their predecessors, in order to get a basis for usages which they considered indispensable. For a purpose of this kind the New Testament was of little use.

The New Testament as a whole did not generally play the same rôle as the Old Testament in the mission and practice of the church. The gospels certainly ranked on a level with the Old Testament, and actually eclipsed it ; through them the words of Jesus gleamed and sparkled, and in them his death and resurrection were depicted. But the epistles never enjoyed the same importance—particularly as many passages in them, in Paul especially, landed the fathers of the church in sore difficulties,[1] above all during the conflict with gnosticism. Augustine was the first to bring the Pauline gospel into prominence throughout the West ; in the East, it never emerged at all from the shadow. As for the Johannine theology, it left hardly any traces upon the early church. Only one or two sections of it proved effective. As a whole, it remained a sealed book, though the same may be said of the Pauline theology.[2]

---

[1] The second epistle of Peter already bewails this, and one can see from the great work of Irenæus what difficulties were raised by the Pauline doctrines of predestination, sin, freedom, and grace. Tertullian felt these difficulties still more keenly than Irenæus, but as a Montanist he could solve them by means of the Paraclete ; cp., e.g., *de Resurr.*, lxiii. : "Deus pristina instrumenta manifestis verborum et sensuum luminibus ab omni ambiguitatis obscuritate purgavit" ("God has now purged from all the darkness of ambiguity those ancient scriptures, by the plain light of their language and their meanings, *i.e.*, by the new prophecy).

[2] Along with the Bible, *i.e.*, primarily with the Old Testament, a considerable literature of apocalypses and allied writings entered the Christian churches. These also contained cosmological and philosophical materials. Tertullian conjectures that pagan philosophers may have been acquainted with them, but he speaks very slightingly of them (*de Anima*, ii.): " Quid autem, si philosophi etiam illa incursaverunt quae penes nos apocryphorum confessione damnantur, certos nihil recipiendum quod non conspiret germanae, et ipso iam aevo pronatae propheticae paraturae,

quando et pseudoprophetarum meminerimus et multo prius apostatarum spirituum," etc. ("What if the philosophers have also attacked those Writings Which we condemn under the title of 'apocryphal,' convinced as we are that nothing should be received unless it tallies With the true prophetic system Which has also arisen in the present age, since we do not forget the existence of false prophets and apostate spirits long before them," etc.); cp. *de Resurr.*, lxiii., Where he says that the gnostics "arcana apocryphorum superducunt, blasphemiae fabulas" ("introduce apocryphal mysteries and blasphemous fables ").

CHAPTER IX

1. In combating "demons" (pp. 125 f.) and in taking the field against the open immorality which was part and parcel of polytheism (pp. 205 f.), the early church was waging war against polytheism. But it did not rest content with this onset. Directly, no doubt, the "dumb idols" were weakened by this attack; still, they continued to be a real power, particularly in the circles from which the majority of Christians were drawn. Nowadays, the polemic against the gods of Olympus, against Egyptian cats and crocodiles, or against carved and cast and chiselled idols, seems to our eyes to have been cheap and superfluous. It was not a difficult task, we may fairly add; philosophers like the Cynics and satirists like Lucian supplied a wealth of material, and the intellect and moral sense alike had long ago outgrown that sort of deity. But it was by no means superfluous. Had it been unnecessary, the apologists from Aristides to Arnobius would never have pursued this line of controversy with such zest, the martyr Apollonius would never have troubled to deliver his long polemic before the senate, and Tertullian, an expert in heathen laws and customs, would never have deemed it necessary to refute polytheism so elaborately in his defence before the presiding magistrate. Yet even from this last-named refutation we see how disreputable (we might almost say, how shabby) the public system of gods and sacrifices had already become. It was scoffed at on the stage; half-dead animals of no value were offered in sacrifice;[1] the idols were

---

[1] Tert., *Apol.*, xiv. : "I wish now to review your sacred rites. I do not censure your methods of sacrifice, offering what is worn-out, scabbed, and corrupting,

dishonoured, the temples were profaned.[1] The whole business lay under a mass of disgust, disdain, derision, and nausea. But it would be a serious mistake to suppose that this feeling was universal. Not merely was everything kept going officially, but many minds still clung to such arrangements and ceremonies. The old cults were freshened by the influx of the new religions, and a new significance was often lent even to their most retrograde elements. Besides, whether the public system of religion was flourishing or entirely withered, it by no means represented the sole existing authority. In every town and province, at Rome as well as at Alexandria, in Spain, in Asia, in Egypt, there were household gods and family gods, with household customs of religion, and all manner of superstitions and ceremonies. These rarely rise above the surface of literature, but inscriptions, tombs, and magical papyri have brought them nearer us. Here every household function has its guardian spirit; every event is under one controlling god. And this religious world, this second-class religion, it must be remembered, was living and active everywhere.

As a rule, the apologists contented themselves with assailing the official world of gods.[2] Their method aimed, in the first place, at rousing the moral sense against these so-called "gods" by branding their abominable vices; in the second place, it sought to exhibit the folly and absurdity of what was taught or told about the gods; and, thirdly, it aimed at exposing the origin of the latter. The apologists showed that the gods were an empty nothing, illusions created by the demons who lay in wait behind their dead puppets and introduced them in order

cutting off for the altar the useless parts from the fat and sound—*e.g.*, head and hoofs, which you would hand at home to your dogs and children —not giving a third part of the tithe of Hercules," etc.

[1] Tert., *Apol.*, xlii. : " Every day, you complain, the temple-receipts are dwindling away. How few people nowadays put in their contributions !" Cp. Arnobius, I. xxiv.

[2] Household superstitions perhaps seemed to them too unimportant, or else they counted upon these being dragged down of their own accord in the collapse of the public superstitions. On this point they certainly made a miscalculation.—A scene at Ephesus is related in Acts, which may be adduced at this point. Thanks to Paul's preaching, the converts were roused to bring out the books of magic which they had at home and to burn them (Acts xix. 19). But there are few parallels to this scene in the literature of early Christianity.

to control men by this means. Or, following the track of Euhemerus, they showed that the so-called gods were nothing but dead men.[1] Or, again, they pointed out that the whole thing was a compound of vain fables and deceit, and very often the product of covetous priestcraft. In so doing they displayed both wit and irony, as well as a very strong feeling of aversion. We do not know, of course, how much of all this argument and feeling was original. As has been already remarked, the Stoic, Sceptic, and Cynic philosophers (in part, the Epicureans also) had preceded Christianity along this line, and satires upon the gods were as cheap as blackberries in that age. Consequently, it is needless to illustrate this point by the citation of individual passages. A perusal of the *Apology* of Aristides, which is of no great size, is quite sufficient to give one an idea of this kind of polemic; the *Oratio ad Graecos* of pseudo-Justin may also be consulted, and especially the relevant sections in the *Apology* of Tertullian.

The duty of keeping oneself free from all contamination with polytheism ranked as the *supreme* duty of the Christian. It took precedence of all others. It was regarded as the negative side of *the duty of confessing one's faith*, and the "sin of idolatry" was more strictly dealt with in the Christian church than any sin whatsoever.[2] Not for long, and not without great difficulty, did the church make up her mind to admit that forgiveness could be extended to this offence, and what forced her first to this conclusion was the stress of the terrible consequences of the Decian outburst (*i.e.*, after 250 A.D.).[3] This we can well understand, for exclusiveness was the condition of her existence as a church. If she made terms with polytheism at a single point,

---

[1] The Euhemeristic vein was neither the oldest nor the most popular, however, among Christian writers.

[2] Cp. Tertull., *de Idol.*, i. : "Principale crimen generis humani, summus sacculi reatus, tota causa iudicii, idolatria" ("Idolatry is the principal crime of mankind, the supreme guilt of the world, the entire reason of judgment"). In the opening chapter of this treatise Tertullian endeavours to prove that all the cardinal vices (*e.g.*, adultery, murder, etc.) are included in idolatry.

[3] Hitherto it had only dawned on Tertullian, during his conflict with the laxity displayed by the church in her treatment of fleshly sins, that under certain circumstances a denial of the faith extorted by means of torture was a lesser sin than adultery and fornication. A similar position was afterwards adopted by Cyprian.

it was all over with her distinctive character. Such was the position of affairs, at any rate until about the middle of the third century. After that she could afford to be less anxious, since the church as an institution had grown so powerful, and her doctrine, cultus, and organization had developed in so characteristic a fashion by that time, that she stood out as a sharply defined magnitude *sui generis*, even when, consciously or unconsciously, she went half-way to meet polytheism in disguise, or showed herself rather lenient towards it.

But as the duty of confession did not involve the duty of pushing forward to confess, or indeed of denouncing oneself[1] (in the epistle of the church of Smyrna to the church of Philomelium an explicit protest is even entered against this practice, while elsewhere[2] the Montanist craving for martyrdom is also censured),[3] so to protest against polytheism did not involve the obligation of publicly protesting against it of one's own accord. There were indeed cases in which a Christian who was standing as a spectator in court audibly applauded a confessor, and in cousequence of this was himself arrested. Such cases were mentioned with approval, for it was held that the Spirit had impelled the spectator. But open abuse of the emperor or of the gods was not sanctioned any more than rebellion; in fact, all unprovoked insults and all upsetting of images were rebuked.[4] Here and there, however, such incidents must have occurred, for in the

---

[1] Even to escape in time was permissible, according to Matt. x. 23, but the Montanists and Tertullian would not allow this; cp. the latter's treatise "de Fuga in Persecutione." Clement speaks very thoughtfully on the point; cp. *Strom.*, IV. x., lxxvi.–lxxvii., and VII. xi.–xii.

[2] The Acts of Perpetua relate, without any censure, how Saturus voluntarily announced that he was a Christian. But then these Acts are Montanist.

[3] It was not quite the same thing when Christians trooped into court, in order to force the magistrate either to have them all killed or to spare them all; cp. Tertull., *ad Scap.* v. : Arrius Antoninus in Asia cum persequeretur instanter, omnes illius civitatis Christiani ante tribunalia eius se manu facta obtulerunt. tum ille paucis duci jussis reliquis ait : ὦ δειλοί, εἰ θέλετε ἀποθνήσκειν, κρημνοὺς ἢ βρόχους ἔχετε (cp. above, p. 270).

[4] Still, there were some Christians who exulted in this kind of thing, as is plain from several records (from a late period, of course) of the martyrs. Eusebius narrates approvingly (*de Mart. Pal.*, ii.) the action of the martyr Romanus, who, just after the Diocletian persecution had broken out, saw in Antioch a procession of men, women, and children on their way to the temples, and tried to stop them by means of loud warnings.

sixtieth canon of Elvira we read: " Si quis idola fregerit et
ibidem fuerit occisus, quatenus in evangelio scriptum non est
neque invenietur sub apostolis unquam factum, placuit in
numerum eum non recipi martyrum " (" If anyone shall have
broken an idol and been slain in the act, he shall not be reckoned
among the martyrs, seeing that no such command is to be found
in scripture, nor will any such deed be found to be apostolic ").

2. In order to combat polytheism effectively, one could not
stop short of the philosophers, not even of the most distinguished
of their number, for they had all some sort of connection with
idol-worship.   But at this stage of their polemic the apologists
diverged in different directions.   All were agreed that no philosopher had discovered the truth in its purity and perfection ;
and further, that no philosopher was in a position to demonstrate
with certainty the truth which he had discovered, to spread it
far and wide, or to make men so convinced of it as to die for
it.   But one set of apologists were quite content with making
this strict proviso ; moreover, they delighted in the harmony of
Christianity and philosophy ; indeed, like Justin, they would
praise philosophers for their moral aims and profound ideas.
The Christian teachers in Alexandria even went the length of
finding a parallel to the Jewish law in Greek philosophy.[1]   They
found affinities with Plato's doctrine of God and metaphysics,
and with the Stoic ethic.   They recognized philosophers like
Seneca[2] as their fellows to some extent.   They saw in Socrates a
hero and forerunner of the truth.   Others, again, would not
hear of philosophy or philosophers ; the best service they could
render the gospel-mission was, in their opinion, to heap coarse
abuse on both.   Tatian went to incredible lengths in this line, and
was guilty of shocking injustice.   Theophilus fell little short of
him, while even Tertullian, for all his debt to the Stoics, came
dangerously near to Tatian.   But these apologists were under
an entire delusion if they imagined they were accomplishing
very much by dint of all their calumnies.   So far as we are in a
position to judge, it was the methods, not of these extremists,
but of Justin, Clement, and Origen, that impressed the Greek

[1] Cp. my lecture on "Socrates and the Early Church" (1900).
[2] Cp. Tert., de Anima, xx. : "Seneca saepe noster."

world of culture.   Yet even the former had probably a public of their own.   Most people either do not think at all, or else think in the crudest antitheses, and such natures would likely be impressed by Tatian's invectives.   Besides, it is impossible to ignore the fact that neither he nor Tertullian were mere calumniators.   They were honest men.   Wherever they came upon the slightest trace of polytheism, all their moral sense rose in revolt ; in polytheism, they were convinced, no good was to be found, and hence they gave credit to any calumnies which a profligate literature put at their disposal.   Now traces of polytheism were thickly sown throughout all the philosophers, including even the most sublime of their number.   Why, Socrates himself had ordered a cock to be slain, after he was dead, in honour of Æsculapius !   The irony of the injunction was not understood. It was simply viewed as a recognition of idolatry.   So even Socrates the hero had to be censured.   Yet, whether half-admirers or keen opponents of philosophy, the apologists to a man occupied philosophic ground, and indeed Platonic ground.   They attacked philosophy, but they brought it inside the church and built up the doctrinal system of the church on the outlines of Platonism and with the aid of Platonic material (see below, the epilogue of this book).

3. From the practical point of view, what was of still greater moment than the campaign against the world and worship of the gods, was the campaign against *the apotheosis of men*.   This struggle, which reached its height in the uncompromising rejection of the imperial cultus, marked at the same time the resolute protest of Christianity against *the blending of religion and patriotism*, and consequently against that cultus of the state in which the state (personified in the emperor) formed itself the object of the cultus.   One of the cardinal aims and issues of the Christian religion was to draw a sharp line between the worship of God and the honour due to the state and to its leaders. *Christianity tore up political religion by the roots.*

The imperial cultus[1] was of a twofold nature.   In both aspects it was an Oriental, not a Greek or a Roman phenomenon ;

[1] In addition to the well-known German literature on the subject, see Beurlier's *Essai sur le culte rendu aux empereurs romain* (1890).

yet this worship of the dead Cæsars and of the living Cæsar, with its adoration of the imperial images, was dovetailed, not only without any difficulty, but inevitably, into the " caeremoniae Romanae," once the empire had become imperial. From the first the headquarters of the former (*i.e.*, the worship of the dead Cæsars) were in Rome, whence it passed into the provinces as the most vital element of the state religion. The latter (*i.e.*, the worship of the living Cæsar) originated in the East, but as early as the first century it was adopted by Caligula and Domitian, and during the second century it became quite common (in the shape of adoration paid to the imperial images). The rejection of either cult was a crime which came under the head of sacrilege as well as of high treason, and *it was here that the repressive measures taken by the state against Christianity almost invariably started*, inasmuch as the state did not concede Christianity the same liberty on this point as she granted to Judaism. Had the Christians merely turned round against Olympus and hit upon some compromise with the imperial cultus, they would in all probability have been left entirely unmolested—such is Tertullian's blunt assertion in his *Apology* (xxviii. f.). Nearly all the encounters between individual Christians and the regulations of the empire resolved themselves into a trial for treason. The positive value of the imperial cultus for the empire has been stated recently and impressively by von Wilamowitz-Moellendorf.[1]

[1] In *Geschichte des gerich. Religion* ("Jahrbuch des Freien deutschen Hochstifts," 1904 ; reprint, pp. 23 f.): "The idea by which Augustus brought renewal to the world was the religion of Poseidonius : faith in a universal reason and the unity of all life, in the Stoic universal deity, providence and necessity. He could regard himself as the organ or representative of this cosmic law ; he could expect the personal survival of his soul as a reward for his clemency, since this corresponded exactly to the doctrine of Poseidonius. Hence the cult of the "divus" was its justification. No one can understand the age or the man if he regards the "divi filius" claim as merely ornamental or an imposture. Naturally enough, it ran counter to the taste and reason of Tiberius, who was averse to anything mystical, though he was addicted to a superstitious faith in astrology. Caligula's belief in his divine nature made him a fool, and sensible people only saw a farce in Claudius being consecrated to divine honours by his murderers. Yet even they took it very seriously. The cultus of the person inevitably passed once more, as it had done after Alexander the Great, into the cultus of the office. The emperor was god, because he was emperor ; he was not the viceroy of the universe because the god in him possessed the strength and the authority of lord-

The Christians repudiated the imperial cultus in every shape and form, even when they met it in daily life, in the very oaths and turns of expression which made the emperor appear a super-human being. Unhesitatingly they reckoned it a phase of idolatry. Withal, they guarded themselves against the charge of being disrespectful and disloyal, by pointing to their prayers for the emperor and for the state.[1] These prayers, in fact, constituted a fixed part of Christian worship from the very

ship. His person embodied the supreme power of the empire, and this made itself felt by the smallest and most remote of his subjects. This personal embodiment was as unapproachable to the million as a universal god in heaven, further removed from each individual than the gods of his village or his district. And if one could not manage to understand the unity of all life in heaven and on earth, still on earth this unity of the state, the church, the law, and morals was a fact ; it might deserve the predicate of "divine," and, if so, then the worship of its personal exponents was an irresistible religious obligation. Thus the imperial cultus, or the cultus of the empire, was the cardinal article of religion. To deny it was tantamount to the ancient crime of denying the πάτριοι θεοί of the city-republics. All other deities who shared the worship of civil or municipal bodies fell into their place within and below this religion ; henceforth their cultus had no meaning save as part of the larger cultus which the state enjoined. Even in the West the imperial cultus absorbed within itself the older deities, whether Fortuna, Silvanus, the Mater Augusti or Augustæ. The content of this faith was great indeed, for all the benefits of civilisation, from the security of physical life up to the highest pleasures of the human spirit, were viewed as gifts of the deity, who was at once immanent in the empire and also for the time being in the emperor or in his genius or fortune as the personal embodiment of the divine. . . . . It followed quite logically that the refusal to sacrifice to the emperor was high treason. The Christians refused this from the firm and clear sense that they were resisting the πολιτεία τοῦ κόσμου in so doing. They felt that they were citizens of another empire. It was equally logical to regard them as ἄθεοι, since their denial of the state-religion meant a denial of all the gods whose existence was due to the favour of the state."

[1] Cp. the familiar passages from the New Testament, the apostolic fathers, and the apologists. The content of these intercessions, which was current in Carthage, is given by Tertullian in *Apol.*, xxxix. ("Oramus etiam pro imperatoribus, pro ministris eorum et potestatibus, pro statu sacculi, pro rerum quiete, pro mora finis"—"We pray too for the emperors, for their subordinates, and for all authorities, for the welfare of the world, for peace, for the delay of the end"); and xxx. ("Precantes sumus semper pro omnibus imperatoribus : vitam illis prolixam, imperium securum, domum tutam, exercitus fortes, senatum fidelem, populum probum, orbem quietum, quaecumque hominis et Caesaris vota sunt [a deo oramus]"—"We ever pray to God for all the emperors, for length of life to them, for the safety of the empire, for the protection of the royal household, for bravery in the army, loyalty in the senate and virtue among the people, for peace throughout the world ; in short, for whatever, as man or emperor, the Cæsars would desire").

first,[1] while the saying of Christ, " Render unto Cæsar the things
that are Cæsar's," was generally referred, not merely to obedience and the punctual payment of taxes, but also to intercession.
The sharpest strictures passed by individual Christian teachers
upon the character of the Roman state and the imperial office
never involved the neglect of intercession or dissuaded Christians
from this duty.   Numerous passages, in which the emperor is
mentioned immediately after God, attest the fact that he was
held by Christians to be " a deo secundus ante omnes et super
omnes deos " (Tertull., *Apol.*, xxx. : " second only to God, before
and above all the gods ").[2]   Christians, in fact, could declare
that they tolerated no defect, either in the theory or in the
practice of their loyalty.   They taught—and they made their
teaching an inherent element of history—that worship paid to
God was one thing, and honour paid to a ruler quite another ;
also, that to worship a monarch was a detestable and humiliating
offence.   Nevertheless, they strictly inculcated obedience to all
authority, and respect for the emperor.

The general position of the church did not alter upon this
point during the third century ;[3] it adhered to its sharp denial
of apotheosis in the shape of the imperial cultus.   But at
another point apotheosis gradually filtered into the church with
elemental force, namely, through the worship of the apostles
and the martyrs.   As early as the apocryphal Acts, written
towards the close of the second and the opening of the third
century, we find the apostles appearing as semi-divine ; in fact,

---

[1] Their origin dates from the very earliest times, but we do not know what
considerations led to their institution.

[2] This high estimate of the emperors as "second to God alone " does not, however, affect the conviction that they could never be Christians.   At least it does
not in the case of Tertullian (cp. *Apol.*, xxi. : " Et Caesares credidissent super
Christo, si aut Caesares non essent necessarii sacculo, aut si et Christiani potuissent
esse Caesares ".—" The Cæsars, too, would have believed in Christ, if they had not
been necessary to the world as Cæsars, or if they could have been Cæsars and
Christians as well ").   Sixty years later a different view prevailed throughout the
East.   Not only was it reported widely that Alexander Severus and Philip had
become secretly Christians, but even so prominent a teacher as Dionysius of
Alexandria believed this legend and did not take umbrage at it.

[3] Dionysius of Alexandria (Eus., *H.E.*, vii. 23) no doubt applied Isa. xliii. 19
to Gallienus, who was friendly disposed towards the Christians.   But this was
mere rhetoric.

even by the year 160 A.D., the pagans in Smyrna were afraid
that the Christians would pay divine honours to the martyred
Polycarp, while Lucian scoffs at the impostor Peregrinus, with
his cheap martyrdom, passing for a god amongst the Christians.
Both fear and scoff were certainly baseless as yet. But they
were not baseless three generations afterwards. Towards the
close of the third century there were already a number of chapels
in existence, consecrated[1] to the apostles, patriarchs, martyrs,
and even the archangels; people had a predilection for passing
the night at the graves of the saints, and a cultus of the saints
had been worked out in a wide variety of local forms, which
afforded an indispensable means of conserving those ancient
cults to which the common people still clung. Theoretically,
the line between the worship of God and this cultus of deliverers
and intercessors was sharply drawn throughout the third century,
although one Christian root for the latter cultus is evident in
the communion of the saints. As things stood, however, the
distinction between the two was constantly blurred in the course
of practical experience.[2] For all its monotheism, the Christian
religion at the close of the third century represented a religion
which was exceptionally strong in saints and angels and deliverers, in miraculous relics, and so forth; on this score it was
able to challenge any cult whatsoever. Porphyry (the pagan
quoted in Macar. Magnes, IV. xxi.) was quite alive to this. He
wrote as follows: "If, therefore, you declare that beside God
there are angels who are not subject to suffering and death, and
are incorruptible in nature—*just the beings we call gods*, inas-

---

[1] Cp. Eus., *Mart. Pal.*, p. 102 (*Texte u. Unters.*, xv. 4).

[2] Origen attacks only a moiety of polytheistic superstition and its expressions;
cp. Hom. viii. 4 *in Jesum Nave* (vol. xi. p. 67): "Illi qui, cum Christiani sint,
solemnitates gentium celebrant, anathema in ecclesias introducunt. Qui de
astrorum cursibus vitam hominum et gesta perquirunt, qui volatus avium et cetera
huiusmodi, quae in sacculo prius observabantur, inquirunt, de Jericho anathema
inferunt in ecclesiam, et polluunt castra domini et vinci faciunt populum dei"
("Those who, even though they are Christians, celebrate the festivals of pagans,
bring anathema into the churches. Those who make out the life and deeds of
men from the courses of the stars, who study the flight of birds, and engage in similar
practices, which they formerly observed in the world, bring the anathema of
Jericho on the church; they pollute the camp of the Lord, and cause God's people
to be overcome"). He could and should have mentioned a great deal more;
only in such directions he was no longer sensitive to polytheism.

múch as they stand near the godhead—then what is all the dispute about, with regard to names? Or are we to consider it merely a difference of terminology? . . . . So, if anyone likes to call them either gods or angels—for names are, on the whole, of no great moment, one and the same goddess, for example, being called Athenê and Minerva, and by still other names among the Egyptians and the Syrians—then it makes no great difference, as their divine nature is actually attested even by yourselves in Matt. xxii. 29–31." [1]

4. The warfare against polytheism was also waged by means of a thoroughgoing opposition to the theatre and to all the games. Anyone who considers the significance [2] of these features in ancient life and their close connection with idolatry,[3] knows

[1] Porphyry then proceeds, in his attack upon the cheap criticism levelled by Christians (see above) at idolatry : " When, therefore, it is admitted that the angels share in the divine nature, it is not, on the other hand, the belief of those who pay seemly honour to the gods, that God is composed of the wood or stone or brass from which the image is manufactured, nor is it their opinion that, whenever a bit of the image is broken off, some injury is thereby inflicted on the power of the god in question. Images and temples of the gods have been created from all antiquity for the sake of forming reminders to men. Their object is to make those who draw near them think of God thereby, or to enable them, after ceasing from work, and abstaining from anything else, to address their vows and prayers to him, that each may obtain from him whatever he is in need of. For when any person gets an image or picture of some friend prepared for himself, he certainly does not believe that his friend is to be found in the image, or that his members exist actually inside the different portions of the representation. His idea rather is that the honour which he pays to his friend finds expression in the image. And while the sacrifices offered to the gods do not bring them any honour, they are meant as a testimony to the goodwill of their worshippers, implying that the latter are not ungrateful to the gods." The majority of Christians by this time scarcely held so pure and spiritual a view of the matter as this " worshipper of idols."

[2] For what follows, see Bigelmair's *Die Beteiligung der Christen am öffentlichen Leben in vorconstantinischer Zeit* (1902).

[3] Tert., *de Spect.*, iv. : " Quid erit summum ac praecipuum, in quo diabolus et pompae et angeli eius censeantur, quam idololatria ? . . . . Igitur si ex idololatria universam spectaculorum paraturam constare constiterit, indubitate praeiudicatum erit etiam ad spectacula pertinere renuntiationis nostrae testimonium in lavacro, quae diabolo et pompae et angelis eius sint mancipata, scil. per idololatriam. Commemorabimus origines singulorum, quibus incunabilis in sacculo adoleverint, exinde titulos quorundam, quibus nominibus nuncupentur, exinde apparatus, quibus superstitionibus instruantur, tum loca, quibus praesidibus dicantur, tum artes, quibus auctoribus deputentur. Si quid ex his non ad idolum pertinuerit, id neque ad idololatriam neque ad nostram eiurationem pertinebit " (" Where, more than in idolatry, will you find the devil with his pomp and

what a polemic against them implied. But we may point out that existence, in case of vast numbers of people, was divided into daily drudgery and—"panis et circenses" (free food and the theatre). No member of the Christian church was allowed to be an actor or gladiator, to teach acting (see Cypr., *Epist.* ii.), or to attend the theatre.[1] The earliest flash of polemic occurs in the *Oratio* of Tatian (xxii.-xxiii.), and it was followed by others, including the treatises of Tertullian and pseudo - Cyprian (Novatian) *de Spectaculis*, and the discussions of Lactantius.[2]

angels? . . . . Therefore, if it can be proven that the whole business of the shows depends upon idolatry, unquestionably we shall have anticipated the conclusion that the confession of renouncing the world which we make in baptism, refers to these shows which have been handed over to the devil and his pomp and angels, *i.e.*, on account of their idolatry. We shall now exhibit their separate sources, the nurseries in which they have grown to maturity in the world; next the titles of some of them, the names by which they are called; after that, their contents, the superstitions by which they are supported; then their seats, the patrons to which they are dedicated; and finally their arts, the authors to whom they are to be referred. If any of these is found to have no connection with an idol, then it is irrelevant to idolatry and irrelevant also to our oath of abjuration"). Novatian, *de Spect.*, ii. : " Quando id quod in honore alicuius idoli ab ethnicis agitur [sc. the theatrical spectacles] a fidelibus christianis spectaculo frequentatur, et idololatria gentilis asseritur et in contumeliam dei religio vera et divina calcatur" ("Since whatever is performed by pagans in honour of any idol is attended by faithful Christians in the public spectacles, and thus pagan idolatry is maintained, whilst the true and divine religion is trodden under foot in contempt of God").

[1] *Minuc. Felix*, xii. : " Vos vero suspensi interim atque solliciti honestis volup-tatibus abstinetis, non spectacula visitis, non pompis interestis, convivia publica absque vobis, sacra certamina " ("But meantime, anxious and unsettled, you are abstaining from respectable enjoyments ; you attend no spectacles, you take no part in public displays, public banquets and the sacred contest you decline ").

[2] *Instit.*, vi. 20-21 ; see also Arnob., iv. 35 f.—Along with the games, partici-pation in public festivals was also forbidden, as these were always bound up with polytheism. Cp. the seventh canon of Ancyra : περὶ τῶν συνεστιαθέντων ἐν ἑορτῇ ἐθνικῇ, ἐν τόπῳ ἀφωρισμένῳ τοῖς ἐθνικοῖς, ἴδια βρώματα ἐπικομισαμένων καὶ φαγόντων, ἔδοξε διετίαν ὑποπεσόντας δεχθῆναι ("With regard to those who have sat down at a pagan banquet, in a place set apart for pagans, even though they brought and ate their own food, it seems good to us that they be received after they have done penance for two years"). In this connection, Tertullian, *de Idol.*, xiii.-xvi., is particularly important. All public festivals, he declares, are to be avoided, since they are held either owing to wantonness or to timidity. " If we rejoice with the world, it is to be feared that we shall also mourn with the world." Here, of course, it is plain that Tertullian is in a minority. The majority of Christians at Carthage saw nothing wrong in attending public or private feasts ; in fact, it was considered rather a dangerous mark of the factious spirit to abstain from them. " ' Let your works shine,' is Christ's rule," says Tertullian in his cry of complaint.

These writings by themselves are enough to show that the above prohibitions were not universally obeyed.[1] The passion for public games was almost irresistible, and Tertullian has actually to hold out hopes of the spectacle afforded by the future world as a compensation to Christians who were robbed of their shows in the present.[2] Still, the conflict with these shows was by no means in vain. On the contrary, its effects along this line were greater than along other lines. By the time that Constantine granted privileges to the church, public opinion had developed

"But here are all our shops and doors shining! Nowadays you will find more doors unilluminated and unwreathed among the pagans than among the Christians! What do you think about the custom? If it is meant as honour to an idol, then certainly it is idolatry to honour an idol. If, again, it is done for the sake of some man, then let us remember that all idolatry is worship paid to men (the gods of the pagans having been formerly men themselves)." "I know how one Christian brother was severely punished in a vision on that very night, because his slaves had decorated his gateway with wreaths on the sudden proclamation of some public thanksgiving." Tertullian only draws the line at well-established family feasts such as those at the assumption of the toga virilis, betrothals, marriages, and name-givings, since these are not necessarily contaminated with idolatry, and since the command to observe no particular days does not apply in these instances. "One may accept an invitation to such functions, provided that the title of the invitation does not run 'to assist at a sacrifice.' Except in the latter event, I can please myself as much as I like. Since Satan has so thoroughly entangled the world in idolatry, it must be allowable for us to attend certain ceremonies, if thereby we stipulate that we are under obligations to a man and not to an idol."

[1] Novatian, *de Spect.*, i. : "Quoniam non desunt vitiorum assertores blandi et indulgentes patroni qui praestant vitiis auctoritatem *et quod est deterius censuram scripturarum caelestium in advocationem criminum convertunt*, quasi sine culpa innocens spectaculorum ad remissionem animi appetatur voluptas—nam et eo usque enervatus est ecclesiasticae disciplinae vigor et ita omni languore vitiorum praecipitatur in peius ut non iam vitiis excusatio sed auctoritas detur—placuit paucis vos non nunc instruere [*i.e.*, de spectaculis], sed instructos admonere" ("Plausible advocates of vice are not awanting, nor are complaisant patrons who lend their authority to vice and—*what is worse*—*twist the rebuke of scripture into a defence of crimes*; as if any innocent pleasure could be sought from public shows by way of relaxation for the mind. The vigour of ecclesiastical discipline has become so weakened and so deteriorated by all the languor produced by vices, that wickedness wins no longer an apology but actual authority for itself. Consequently I have determined not now to instruct you [on public shows], but in a few words to admonish those who have been instructed").

[2] *De Spect.*, xxx., with its closing sentence, "Ceterum qualia illa sunt, quae nec oculus vidit nec auris audivit nec in cor hominis ascenderunt? Credo, circa et utraque cavea et omni stadio gratiora" ("But what are the things that eye hath not seen, nor ear heard, nor have entered into the heart of man? Superior, I imagine, to the circus, the theatre, the amphitheatre, and any racecourse!").

to such a pitch that the state immediately adopted measures for curtailing and restricting the public spectacles.[1]

5. A sharp attack was also made upon luxury, in so far as it was bound up in part with polytheism and certainly betrayed a senseless and pagan spirit. Cp. the *Paedagogus* of Clement, and Tertullian's writings "de cultu feminarum." It was steadily maintained that the money laid out upon luxuries would be better spent in charity. But no special regulations for the external life of Christians were as yet drawn up.

6. With regard to the question of how far a Christian could take part in the manners and customs and occupations of daily life without denying Christ and incurring the stain of idolatry, there was a strict attitude as well as a lenient, freedom as well as narrowness, even within the apostolic age. Then the one burning question, however, seems to have been that of food offered to idols, or whether one could partake of meals provided by unbelievers. In those days, as the large majority of Christians belonged to the lower classes, they had no representative duties, but were drawn from working people of the lower orders, from day-labourers, in fact, whose simple occupation hardly brought them into any kind of relation to public life, and consequently exempted them from any conflict in this sphere. Presently, however, a change came over the situation. A host of difficult and vexatious problems poured upon the churches. Even the laxer party would do nothing that ran counter to the will of God. They, too, had scriptural proofs ready to support their position, and corollaries from scriptural principles. "Flee from one city to another" was the command they pled when they prudently avoided persecution. "I have power over all things," "We must be all things to all men"— so they followed the apostle in declaring. They knew how to defend even attendance at public spectacles from scripture. Novatian (*de Spect.*, ii.) sorrowfully quotes their arguments as follows: "Where, they ask, are such scriptures? Where are such things prohibited? Nay, was not Elijah the charioteer of Israel? Did not David himself dance before the ark? We read

---

[1] Against games of chance, cp. the treatise of pseudo-Cyprian (Victor) *adversus Aleatores*, and a number of cognate passages in other writings.

of horns, psalteries, trumpets, drums, pipes, harps, and choral dances. The apostle, too, in his conflict with evil sets before us the struggle of the cæstus and our wrestling with the spiritual powers of wickedness. Again, he takes illustrations from the racecourse, and holds out to us the prize of the crown. Why, then, may not a faithful Christian look at things of which the sacred books could write?"

This defence of attendance at the games sounds almost frivolous. But there were many graver conflicts on this subject, which one can follow with serious interest.

Participation in feasts and in convivial gatherings already occasioned such conflicts to a large extent, but it was the question of one's occupation that was really crucial. Can a Christian engage in business generally in the outside world without incurring the stain of idolatry? Though the strict party hardly tabooed a single occupation on the score of principle, yet they imposed such restrictions as amounted almost to a prohibition. In his treatise *de Idololatria*, Tertullian goes over a series of occupations, and his conclusion is the same in almost every case: better leave it alone, or be prepared to abandon it at any moment. To the objection, "But I have no means of livelihood," the reply follows, "A Christian need never be afraid of starving."[1]

Tertullian especially prohibits the manufacture of idols (iv. f.), as was only natural. Yet there were Christian workmen who knew no other trade, and who tried to shelter themselves behind the text, "Let every man abide in the calling wherein he was called" (1 Cor. vii. 20). They also pointed out that Moses had a serpent manufactured in the wilderness. From

---

[1] Cp. especially the sharp remarks in ch. xii f. *a propos* of the passages from the gospels, which conclude: "Nemo corum, quos dominus allegit, non habeo, dixit, quo vivam. Fides famem non timet. Scit etiam famem non minus sibi contemnendam propter deum quam omne mortis genus; didicit non respicere vitam, quanto magis victum? Quotusquisque haec adimplevit? sed quae penes homines difficilia, penes deum facilia?" ("None of those whom the Lord chose for himself ever said, I have no means of livelihood. Faith has no fear of starvation. Faith knows it must despise starvation as much as any kind of death, for the sake of God. Life it has learnt not to respect; how much more, food? How many, you ask, have answered to these conditions? Ah well, what is hard with men is easy with God").

Tertullian's charges it is quite evident that the majority in the church connived at such people and their practices. "From idols they pass into the church; from the workshop of the adversary they come to the house of God; to God the Father they raise hands that fashion idols; to the Lord's body they apply hands that have conferred bodies upon idols. Nor is this all. They are not content to contaminate what they receive from other hands, but even hand on to others what they have themselves contaminated. Manufacturers of idols are actually elected to ecclesiastical office!" (vii.).

As against these lax members of the church, Tertullian prohibits the manufacture, not only of images and statues, but also of anything which was even indirectly employed in idol-worship. Carpenters, workers in stucco, joiners, slaters, workers in gold-leaf, painters, brass-workers, and engravers—all must refrain from manufacturing the slightest article required for idol-worship; all must refuse to participate in any work (e.g., in repairs) connected therewith (ch. viii.).

Similarly, no one is allowed to practise as an astrologer or a magician. Had not the magi to depart home "by another way"?[1] Nor can any Christian be a schoolmaster or a professor of learning, since such professions frequently bring people into contact with idolatry.[2] Knowledge of the pagan gods has to be diffused; their names, genealogy and myths have to be

---

[1] Tertullian, de Anima, lvii.: "Quid ergo dicemus magiam? Quod omnes paene—fallaciam! Sed ratio fallaciae solos non fugit Christianos, qui spiritualia nequitiae, non quidem socia conscientia, sed inimica scientia novimus, nec invitatoria operatione, sed expugnatoria dominatione tractamus multiformem luem mentis humanae, totius erroris artificem, salutis pariter animaeque vastatorem. Sic etiam magiae, secundae scilicet idololatriae," etc. ("What then shall we say about magic? Just what almost everybody says—that it is sheer imposture! The nature of the imposture has been detected by more than Christians, though we have discovered these spirits of iniquity, not because we are in league with them, but by a hostile instinct, not because our methods of work attract them, but on the contrary because we handle them by means of a power which vanquishes them. This protean pest of the human mind! This deviser of all error! This destroyer alike of our salvation and of our soul! For thus it is, by magic, which is simply a second idolatry," etc.).

[2] Mathematics was also suspect. Even in the beginning of the fourth century there was opposition offered in Emesa to Eusebius being promoted to the episcopate, on the ground that he practised mathematical studies (Socrates, H.E., ii. 9).

imparted; their festivals and holy days have to be observed, "since it is by means of them that the teacher's fees are reckoned." The first payment of any new scholar is devoted by the teacher to Minerva. Is the contamination of idolatry any the less because in this case it leads to something else? It may be asked, if one is not to be a teacher of pagan learning, ought one then to be a pupil? But Tertullian is quite ready to be indulgent on this point, for—"how can we repudiate secular studies which are essential to the pursuit of religious studies?" A remarkable passage (x.).[1]

Then comes trade. Tertullian is strongly inclined to pro-

---

[1] The perusal of bad and seductive literature was, of course, always prohibited, so soon as this danger became felt. If one must not listen to blasphemous or heretical speeches, far less must one handle books of this character. What Dionysius of Alexandria relates about his own practice, only proves the rule (Eus., *H.E.*, vii. 7): "I have busied myself," he writes to Philemon, the Roman presbyter, "with the writings and also the traditions of the heretics, staining my soul for a little with their utterly abominable ideas, yet deriving this benefit from them, that I refute them for myself and loathe them all the more. One of the presbyters sought to dissuade me, fearing lest I might become mixed up with the mire of their iniquity and so injure my own soul. I felt he was quite right, but a divine vision came to confirm me, and a voice reached me with the clear command : 'Read all that you come across, for you can estimate and prove every-thing ; and this capacity has been from the first the explanation of your faith.' I accepted the vision, as it tallied with the apostolic word spoken to the stronger Christians, 'Be skilled moneychangers.'" Cp. *Didasc. Apost.*, ii. (ed. Achelis, p. 5): "Keep away from all heathen writings, for what hast thou to do with strange words or laws and false prophecies, which indeed seduce young people from the faith? What dost thou miss in God's Word, that thou dost plunge into these pagan histories? If thou wilt read histories, there are the books of Kings ; if wise men and philosophers, there are the prophets, with whom thou shalt find more wisdom and understanding than in all the wise men and philosophers ; for these are the words of the one and the only wise God. If thou cravest hymns, there are the psalms of David; and if thou wantest information about the begin-ning of all things, there is the book of Genesis by the great Moses ; if thou wilt have laws and decrees, there are his laws. . . . . Keep thyself therefore from all those strange things, which are contrary." General prohibitions of definite books under pain of punishment begin with Constantine's order regarding the writings of Arius and other heretics (Eus., *Vita Const.*, iii. 66 ; for the prohibition of the writings of Eunomius, cp. Philostorgius, *H.E.*, xi. 5).—Whether one should quote pagan philosophers and poets, and, if so, how, remained a problem. The apologists made ample use of them, as we know. Paul's citations from profane literature are striking (Tit. i. 12, 1 Cor. xv. 33, Acts xvii. 28); since Origen's treatment of them, they have often been discussed and appealed to by the more liberal. Origen (Hom. xxxi., *in Luc.*, vol. v. p. 202) thought: "Ideo assumit Paulus verba etiam de his qui foris sunt, ut sanctificet eos."

hibit trade altogether,[1] owing to its origin in covetousness and its connection, however indirectly, with idolatry. It provides material for the temple services. What more need be said? "Even supposing that these very wares—frankincense, I mean, and other foreign wares—used in sacrificing to idols, are also of use to people as medicinal salves, and particularly to us Christians in our preparations for a burial, still you are plainly promoting idolatry, so long as processions, ceremonies, and sacrifices to idols are furnished at the cost of danger, loss, inconvenience, schemes, discussion, and commercial ventures." "With what face can a Christian dealer in incense, who happens to pass by a temple, spit on the smoking altars, and puff aside their fumes, when he himself has provided material for those very altars?" (xi.).[2] The taking of interest on money was not differentiated from usury, and was strictly prohibited. But the prohibition was not adhered to. Repeatedly, steps had to be taken against even the clergy, the episcopate, and the church-widows for taking interest or following occupations tinged with usury.[3]

Can a Christian hold a civil appointment? Joseph and Daniel did; they kept themselves free from idolatry, said the liberal party in the church. But Tertullian is unconvinced. "Supposing," he says, "that any one holder of an office were to succeed in coming forward with the mere title of the office, without either sacrificing or lending the sanction of his presence to a sacrifice, without farming out the supply of sacrificial victims, without handing over to other people the care of the temples or superintending their revenues, without holding spectacles either at his own or at the state's expense, without presiding at such spectacles, without proclaiming or announcing any ceremony, without even taking an oath, and moreover—in

---

[1] Tertullian stands here pretty much by himself. We find even a man like Irenæus (cp. iv. 30. 1) had no objections to a Christian engaging in trade.

[2] The clergy themselves were not absolutely forbidden to trade; only restrictions were laid on them (cp. the nineteenth canon of Elvira).

[3] Cp. Funk, "Interest and Usury in Christian Antiquity" (*Tübingen Theol. Quartalschrift*, vol. lvii., 1875, pp. 214 f.). See Eus., *H.E.*, v. 21; Cyprian, *de Lapsis*, vi., and *Testim.*, iii. 48; Commod., *Instruct.*, ii. 24; and the twentieth canon of the Council of Elvira.

regard to other official business—without passing judgment of
life or death on anyone or on his civil standing . . . . without
either condemning or laying down ordinances of punishment,
without chaining or imprisoning, or torturing a single person—
well, supposing all that to be possible, then there is nothing to
be said against a Christian being an official!" Furthermore,
the badges of officials are all mixed up with idolatry. "If you
have abjured the pomp of the devil, know that whatever part
of it you touch is idolatry to you" (xvii.–xviii.).

This involves the impossibility of any Christian being a
military officer. But may he not be a private and fill subordinate positions in the army? "'The inferior ranks do not need
to sacrifice, and have nothing to do with capital punishments.'
True, but it is unbecoming for anyone to accept the military
oath of God and also that of man, or to range himself under the
standard of Christ and also under that of the devil, or to bivouac
in the camp of light and also in the camp of darkness; no soul
can be indebted to both, to Christ and to the devil." You point
to the warriors of Israel, to Moses and Joshua, to the soldiers
who came to John the Baptist, to the centurion who believed.
But "subsequently the Lord disarmed Peter, and in so doing
unbuckled the sword of every soldier. Even in peace it is not
to be worn" (xix.).

Furthermore, in ordinary life a good deal must be entirely
proscribed. One must abjure any phrase in which the gods are
named. Thus one dare not say "by Hercules," or "as true as
heaven" (*medius fidius*), or use any similar expletive (xx.). And
no one is tacitly to accept an adjuration addressed to himself,
from fear of being recognised as a Christian if he demurs to it.[1]
Every pagan blessing must be rejected; accept it, and you are
accursed of God. "It is a denial of God for anyone to
dissemble on any occasion whatsoever and let himself pass for a
pagan. All denial of God is idolatry, just as all idolatry is denial
of God, be it in word or in deed" (xxi.–xxii.). Even the pledge

---

[1] "I know one Christian who, on being publicly addressed during a law-suit
with the words 'Jove's wrath be on you,' answered, 'Nay, on *you.*'" The
unlawfulness of this answer, according to Tertullian, consisted, not simply in the
malediction, but in the recognition of Jupiter which it implied.

exacted from Christians as a guarantee when money is borrowed, is a denial of God, though the oath is not sworn in words (xxiii.).

"Such are the reefs and shoals and straits of idolatry, amid which faith has to steer her course, her sails filled by the Spirit of God." Yet after the close of the second century the large majority of Christians took quite another view of the situation, and sailed their ship with no such anxieties about her track.[1] Coarse forms of idolatry were loathed and severely punished, but during the age of Tertullian, at least, little attention was paid any longer to such subtle forms as were actually current. Moreover, when it suits his point to do so, Tertullian himself in the *Apology* meets the charge of criminal isolation brought against Christians, by boasting that "we share your voyages and battles, your agriculture and your trading" (xlii.), remarking in a tone of triumph that Christians are to be met with everywhere, in all positions of state, in the army, and even in the senate. "We have left you nothing but the temples." Such was indeed the truth. The facts of the case show that Christians were to be found in every line of life,[2] and that troubles occasioned by one's occupation must have been on the whole very rare (except in the case of soldiers; see below, Bk. IV. Ch. IL). Nor was the sharp criticism passed by Tatian, Tertullian, Hippolytus, and even (though for different reasons, of course) by Origen, upon the state as such, and upon civil relations, translated very often into practice.[3] The kingdom of

[1] Read the second and third books of Clement's *Paedagogus*. The author certainly does not belong to the lax party, but he does not go nearly the length of Tertullian. On the other hand, he lashes (*Paed.*, III. xi. 80) mere "Sunday Christianity": "They drop the heavenly inspiration of the congregation when they leave the meeting-place, and become like the great majority with whom they associate. Or rather, in laying aside the affected and specious mask of solemnity, they show their real nature, undisguised. After listening reverently to the Word of God, they leave what they have heard within the church itself, and go outside to amuse themselves in godless society with music," etc.

[2] Of course, as Tertullian sarcastically observes (*Apol.*, xliii.), "pimps, panders, assassins, poisoners and sorcerers, with sacrificial augurs, diviners, and astrologers, very reasonably complain of Christians being a profitless race!" As early as Acts xix. we read of tradesmen in Ephesus who lived by the cult of Diana feeling injured by Christians.

[3] Still, Cæcilius (in *Min. Felix*, viii.) describes Christians as a "natio in publico muta, in angulis garrula (a people tongue-tied in public, but talkative in corners), honores et purpuras despiciunt (despising honours and purple robes)."

Christ, or the world-empire of the Stoics, or some platonic republic of Christian philosophy, might be played off against the existing state, as the highest form of social union intended by God, but all this speculation left life untouched, at least from the close of the second century onwards. The *Paedagogus* of Clement already furnishes directions for managing to live a

Cp. Tatian, *Orat.*, xi. : βασιλεύειν οὐ θέλω, πλουτεῖν οὐ βούλομαι, τὴν στρατηγίαν παρῄτημαι . . . . δοξομανίας ἀπήλλαγμαι ("I have no desire to reign—no wish to be rich. I decline all leadership. . . . . I am void of any frenzy for fame"); Speratus (in *Martyr. Scil.*): "Ego imperium huius sacculi non cognosco" ("of the kingdom of this world I know nothing"); Tertull., *Apol.*, xlii. : "Christianus nec aedilitatem affectat ("the Christian has no ambition to be aedile"), and his critique of Roman laws in chaps. iv.–vi. of the *Apology*. On the charge of "infructuositas in negotio" (barrenness in affairs), see Tert., *de Pallio*, v., where all that is said of the pallium applies to Christians: "Ego, inquit, nihil foro, nihil campo, nihil curiae debeo, nihil officio advigilo, nulla rostra praeoccupo, nulla praetoria observo, canales non odoro, cancellos non adoro, subsellia non contundo, iura non conturbo, causas non elatro, non iudico, non milito, non regno, secessi de populo. in me unicum negotium mihi est ; nisi aliud non curo quam ne curem. vita meliore magis in secessu fruare quam in promptu. sed ignavam infamabis. scilicet patriae et imperio reique vivendum est. erat olim ista sententia. nemo alii nascitur moriturus sibi. certe cum ad Epicuros et Zenones ventum est, sapientes vocas totum quietis magisterium, qui eam summae atque unicae voluptatis nomine consecravere," etc. ("I," quoth the cloak, "I owe no duty to the forum, the hustings, or the senate-house. I keep no obsequious vigils, I haunt no platforms, I boast no great houses, I scent no cross-roads, I worship no lattices, I do not wear out the judicial bench, I upset no laws, I bark in no pleadings at the bar ; no judge am I, no soldier, and no king. I have withdrawn from the people. My peculiar business is with myself. No care have I save to shun care. You, too, would enjoy a better life in retreat than in publicity. But you will decry me as indolent. 'We must live,' forsooth, 'for country, empire, and estate.' Well, our view prevailed in days gone by. None, it was said, is born for another's ends, since to himself he is to die. At all events, when you come to the Epicureans and Zenos, you dub all the teachers of quietism 'sages'; and they have hallowed quietism with the name of the 'unique' and 'supreme' pleasure"). *Apolog.*, xxxviii. f. : "Nec ulla magis res aliena quam publica . . . . unam omnium rempublicam agnoscimus, mundum ("Nothing is so alien to us as political affairs. . . . . We recognize but one universal commonwealth, viz., the universe"). On the absence of any home-feeling among Christians, see Diognet., v. 5: πατρίδας οἰκοῦσιν ἰδίας, ἀλλ' ὡς πάροικοι. μετέχουσι πάντων ὡς πολῖται, καὶ πάνθ' ὑπομένουσιν ὡς ξένοι · πᾶσα ξένη πατρίς ἐστιν αὐτῶν, καὶ πᾶσα πατρὶς ξένη ("They inhabit their own countries, but merely as sojourners; they share in everything as citizens and endure everything as strangers. Every foreign country is a fatherland to them, and every fatherland is foreign"); also Clem., *Paed.*, iii. 8. 41: πατρίδα ἐπὶ γῆν οὐκ ἔχομεν ("On earth we have no fatherland"); *Vita Polycarpi*, vi.: παντὶ δούλῳ θεοῦ πᾶς ὁ κόσμος πόλις, πατρὶς δὲ ἡ ἐπουράνιος Ἱερουσαλήμ· ἐνταῦθα δὲ παροικεῖν, ἀλλ' οὐ κατοικεῖν, ὡς ξένοι καὶ παρεπίδημοι τετάγμεθα (cp. also xxx.). Not without reason does Celsus (*Orig.*, VIII. lxviii.)

Christian life in the world. By the close of our period, the court, the civil service, and the army were full of Christians.[1]

Still, it was significant, highly significant indeed, that gross and actual idolatry was combated to the bitter end. With it Christianity never came to terms.[2]

remark to his Christian opponent : "Were all to behave as you do, the emperor would ere long be left solitary and deserted, and the affairs of this world would presently fall into the hands of the most wild and lawless barbarians." He proceeds to point out that, in the event of this, Christianity would cease to exist, and that the Roman empire consequently was the support of Christianity. To which Christians replied that, on the contrary, it was they alone who upheld the empire.

Between the second century and the third (the line may be drawn about 180 A.D.) a vital change took place. In the former, Christians for the most part had the appearance of a company of people who shunned the light and withdrew from public life, an immoral, nefarious set who held aloof from actual life; in the third century, paganism, to its alarm, discovered in Christianity a foe which openly and energetically challenged it in every sphere, political, social, and religious. By this time the doctrine of Christianity was as familiar as its cultus, discipline, and organization ; and just as Christian basilicas rose everywhere after the reign of Gallienus beside the older temples, so Christians rose to every office in the state. So far as regards the civil and social status of Christianity, the period dating from 250 A.D. belongs on the whole to the fourth century rather than to the preceding age.

[1] It is not surprising that Origen proves the existence of a numerous class of Christians who believed everything, were devoted to the priests, and yet were destitute of any moral principle. What does surprise us is that he assigns heaven to them, simply because they were believers ! (Hom. x. 1, *in Jesum Nave*, vol. xi. p. 102, Hom. xx. 1, pp. 182 f.). It is also significant, in this connection, that Augustine's mother, Monica, was concerned about the adultery of her young son, but that she did not warn him about banquets till he became a Manichean (cp. *Confess.*, iii.).

[2] Nor did the sects of Christianity, with rare exceptions. In one or two cases the rarefied intellectualism and spiritual self-confidence of the gnostics made all external conduct, including any contact with idols, a matter of entire indifference, while open confession of one's faith was held to be useless and, in fact, suicidal (cp. the polemic against this in Iren., iv. 33. 9 ; Clem., *Strom.*, iv. 4. 16; and Tertull., *Scorpiace adv. Gnost.*). But the opponents of heresy taxed the gnostics in such cases also with a denial of their Christian position on principle, where no such denial existed whatsoever (cp. what has been said on Heracleon, p. 210), while at the same time they described the freer attitude of the gnostics towards the eating of sacrificial meat as an apostasy.

EPILOGUE

CHRISTIANITY IN ITS COMPLETED FORM AS SYNCRETISTIC RELIGION

How rich, then, and how manifold, are the ramifications of the Christian religion as it steps at the very outset on to pagan soil! And every separate point appears to be the main point; every single aspect seems to be the whole! It is the preaching of God the Father Almighty ($\theta\epsilon\grave{o}\varsigma$ $\pi\alpha\tau\grave{\eta}\rho$ $\pi\alpha\nu\tau\sigma\kappa\rho\acute{\alpha}\tau\omega\rho$), of his Son the Lord Jesus Christ, and of the resurrection. It is the gospel of the Saviour and of salvation, of redemption and the new creation. It is the message of man becoming God. It is the gospel of love and charity. It is the religion of the Spirit and power, of moral earnestness and holiness. It is the religion of authority and of an unlimited faith; and again, the religion of reason and of enlightened understanding. Besides that it is a religion of " mysteries." It proclaims the origin of a new people, of a people which had existed in secret from the very beginning. It is the religion of a sacred book. It possessed, nay, it was, everything that can possibly be considered as religion.

Christianity thus showed itself to be syncretistic. But it revealed to the world a special kind of syncretism, namely, the syncretism of a universal religion. Every force, every relationship in its environment, was mastered by it and made to serve its own ends—a feature in which the other religions of the Roman empire make but a poor, a meagre, and a narrow show. Yet, unconsciously, it learned and borrowed from many quarters; indeed, it would be impossible to imagine it existing amid all the wealth and vigour of these religions, had it not drawn pith and flavour even from them. These religions fertilized the ground for it, and the new grain and seed which fell upon that soil sent down its roots and grew to be a mighty tree. Here is a religion which embraces everything. And yet it can always be expressed with absolute simplicity: one name, the name of Jesus Christ, still sums up everything.

The syncretism of this religion is further shown by its faculty for incorporating the most diverse nationalities — Parthians, Medes and Elamites, Greeks and barbarians. It mocked at the barriers of nationality. While attracting to itself all popular elements, it repudiated only *one*, viz., that of *Jewish nationalism*. But this very repudiation was a note of universalism, for, although Judaism had been divested of its nationalism and already turned into a universal religion, its universalism had remained for two centuries confined to narrow limits. And how universal did Christianity show itself, in relation to the capacities and culture of mankind! Valentinus is a contemporary of Hermas, and both are Christians; Tertullian and Clement of Alexandria are contemporaries, and both are teachers in the church; Eusebius is a contemporary of St Antony, and both are in the service of the same communion.

Even this fails to cover what may be termed "syncretism," in the proper sense of the word. After the middle of the third century A.D., Christianity falls to be considered as syncretistic religion [1] in the fullest sense; as such it faced the two other syncretistic products of the age, Manicheanism and the Neoplatonic religion which was bound up with the sun-cult.[2] Henceforward,

---

[1] One of my reviewers, de Grandmaison (in *Études, Rev. par les pères de la comp. de Jésus*, vol. xcvi., 5th Aug. 1903, p. 317) asks, "How can a syncretistic religion continue to be exclusive? That is what one fails to see." But if it gives out as its own inherent possession whatever it has taken over and assimilated ; nay more, if it makes this part of its very being—why should it not be able to remain exclusive?

[2] See my *Lehrbuch der Dogmengeschichte*, Bd. I.[3], pp. 766 f., 785 f. (Eng. trans., iii. 316 f.) : "Three great religious systems confronted each other in Western Asia and Southern Europe from the close of the third century : *Neoplatonism, Catholicism*, and *Manicheanism*. All three may be characterized as the final products of a history which had lasted for over a thousand years, the history of the religious development of the civilized nations from Persia to Italy. In all three the old national and particular character of religion was laid aside ; they were *world-religions* of the most universal tendency, with demands whose consequences transformed the whole life of man, both public and private. For the national

Christianity may be just as truly called a Hellenic religion as an Oriental, a native religion as a foreign. From the very outset it had been syncretistic upon pagan soil; it made its appearance, not as gospel pure and simple, but equipped with all that Judaism had already acquired during the course of its long history, and entering forthwith upon nearly every task in which Judaism was defective. Still, it was the middle of the third century that first saw the new religion in full bloom as the syncretistic religion *par excellence*, and yet, for all that, as an exclusive religion. As a church, it contained everything the age could proffer, a powerful priesthood, with a high priest and subordinate clergy, a priesthood which went back to Christ and the apostles, and led bishops to glory in their succession and apostolic ordination. Christianity possessed every element included in the conception of "priesthood." Its worship and its sacraments together represented a real energy of the divine nature. The world to come and the powers of an endless life

cultus they substituted a system which aspired to be at once a theology, a theory of the universe, and a science of history, while at the same time it embraced a definite ethic and a ritual of worship. Formally, therefore, all these religions were alike; they were also alike in this, that each had appropriated the elements of different older religions. Further, they showed their similarity in bringing to the front the ideas of *revelation, redemption, ascetic virtue,* and *immortality*. But Neoplatonism was natural religion spiritualized, the polytheism of Greece transfigured by Oriental influences and developed into pantheism. Catholicism was the monotheistic world-religion based on the Old Testament and the gospel, but built up with the aid of Hellenic speculation and ethics. Manicheanism was the dualistic world-religion, resting on Chaldæism, but interspersed with Christian, Parsi, and perhaps Buddhist ideas. Manicheanism lacked the Hellenic element, while Catholicism almost entirely lacked the Chaldee and Persian. Here are three world-religions developing in the course of two centuries (*c.* A.D. 50-250), Catholicism coming first and Manicheanism last. Both of these were superior to Neoplatonism, for the very reason that the latter had no *founder*; it therefore developed no elemental force, and never lost the character of being an artificial creation. Attempts were made to *invent* a founder for it, but naturally they came to nothing. Yet, even apart from its contents as a religion, Catholicism was superior to Manicheanism, because its founder was venerated, not merely as the bearer of revelation, but as the redeemer in person and the Son of God." These three syncretistic religions all opposed the imperial cultus. Christianity was its only open foe, for the Neoplatonic religion of the sun was indeed designed to confirm it. Yet Neoplatonism also proved a foe to it, by transferring religion to the inward life. This cut at the roots of the imperial cultus. It was a supreme delusion on the part of Julian to imagine that he could link political religion with the Neoplatonic religion of the sun.

were in operation in the cultus, and through it upon the world; they could be laid hold of and appropriated in a way that was at once spiritual and corporeal. To believers, Christianity disclosed all that was ever embraced under the terms "revealed knowledge," "mysteries," and "cultus." In its doctrine it had incorporated everything offered by that contemporary syncretism which we have briefly described (pp. 30 f.). And while it certainly was obliged to re-arrange this syncretism and correct it in some essential points, upon the whole it did appropriate the system. In the doctrinal system of Origen which dominated thoughtful Christians in the East during the second half of the third century, the combination of the gospel and of syncretism is, a *fait accompli*. Christianity possessed in a more unsullied form the contents of what is meant by "the Greek philosophy of religion."[1] Powerful and vigorous, assured of her own distinctive character, and secure from any risk of being dissolved into contemporary religions, she believed herself able now to deal more generously and complaisantly with men, provided only that they would submit to her authority. Her missionary methods altered slowly but significantly in the course of the third century. Gregory Thaumaturgus, who shows himself a pupil of Origen in his religious philosophy with its comprehensive statement of Christianity, but who, as a Hellenist, excels his master, accommodated himself as a bishop in a truly surprising way to the pagan tendencies of those whom he converted. We shall hear of him later on. Saints and intercessors, who were thus semi-gods, poured into the church.[2] Local cults and

[1] The philosophy of religion which men like Posidonius and Philo founded, and which culminated in Neoplatonism, was rounded off by the Christian philosophy of religion which developed until the beginning of the third century. Its final statement was given by Origen. It led to an alarming increase of dulness towards the reality of the senses and fostered an indiscriminate attitude towards life, but it deepened the inner life and modified the philosophical conception of God by introducing the doctrine of creation. The idea of the Incarnation was also brought within the range of speculation, and even at the present day there are many distinguished thinkers who venture to see in that idea the distinctive worth of the Christian religion as well as its main significance for the history of the human spirit. The contest with the materialists, the sceptics, and the Epicureans was waged by the apologists, especially by Origen and Dionysius of Alexandria.

[2] The habit of seeking oracular hints from the Scriptures is part and parcel of this movement. So far as I know, the earliest evidence for it comes from the

holy places were instituted. The different provinces of life were distributed afresh among guardian spirits. The old gods returned; only, their masks were new. Annual festivals were noisily celebrated. Amulets and charms, relics and bones of the saints, were cherished eagerly.[1] And the very religion which erstwhile in its strictly spiritual temper had prohibited and resisted any tendency towards materialism, now took material shape in every one of its relationships. It had mortified the world and nature. But now it proceeded to revive them, not of course in their entirety, but still in certain sections and details, and—what is more—in phases that were dead and repulsive. Miracles

fourth century, but it is certainly later than that period. Cp Aug., *Epist.* lv. 37 : " Hi qui de paginis evangelicis sortes legunt, etsi optandum est, ut hoc potius faciant quam ad daemonia concurrant, tamen etiam ista mihi displicet *consuetudo*, ad negotia saecularia et ad vitae huius vanitatem propter aliam vitam loquentia oracula divina velle convertere " (" As for those who read fortunes out of the pages of the gospel, though it were better they should do this than betake themselves to the demons, still, I dislike the custom of trying to turn divine oracles which speak of another life into counsels upon secular affairs and the vanity of this life "). This, however, is more lax than the attitude of Hermas (*Mand.*, xi.) towards the false prophets. Cp., too, the famous " tolle, lege " of Augustine's own history.

[1] The question is not what amount of mythology, superstition, and sacramentalism the church took over, but rather what was the result of its borrowings, and what it did not borrow. In regard to the first point, we have to reckon not only with the amount of analogous ideas and practices current here and there from the very first within the churches (for, of course, the fact that here or there a few Syrians were converted, does not mean that the entire cast of things was Syrian, any more than the incorporation of Greek converts means a peculiarly Hellenic tinge), but with the problem, When were such ideas and practices consecrated by the church and admitted to public use, or to public expression in prayer and doctrine (in a city, in a province, or throughout the entire church)? The story of this process remains to be written, and it can only be written in part. Besides, many elements came in side by side from the very first. Yet we can explain in certain cases, perhaps, when definite pieces of pagan mythology and ritual were taken over into the public representation of the church's religion, with the requisite alterations of their garb. The answer to such problems, however, needs to be sought with much more caution and care than is usual at present. Attempts to refer the primitive Christian Sabbath and Lord's supper, and the doctrines of the virgin birth, the resurrection on the third day, the ascension, etc., to the influence of a definite pagan origin (whether obscure or open), seem to me radically unsound and as yet entirely unsuccessful. (How these institutions and ideas came into existence at so early a period is another question.) Generally, we may say that if the catholic churches and not individual gnostic circles are kept in view (though even this distinction may be disputed), the fundamental principles of the idealistic philosophy were received, only to be followed by mythology and ritual. As for the second point, the most important thing is to determine for how long and with what

in the churches became more numerous, more external, and more coarse. Whatever fables the apocryphal Acts of the Apostles had narrated, were dragged into contemporary life and predicated of the living present.

This church, whose religion Porphyry blamed for its audacious critique of the universe, its doctrine of the incarnation,[1] and its assertion of the resurrection of the flesh [2]—this church laboured at her mission in the second half of the third century, and she won the day. But had she been summoned to the bar and asked what right she had to admit these novelties, she could have

strenuousness the church resisted astrology, the deadly foe of morals and religion. Anyone who will consider the influence of astrology during the imperial period, when the natural sciences had in general decayed, its knack of assuming the garb of science, its widespread diffusion, and its adaptation to the active and passive moods of the age, will be able to appreciate aright the resistance offered by the church (for gnosticism in this department too was pretty defenceless). Here we recognise a great achievement of the church. Schürer, in his recent essay on the seven-day week of the church during the first centuries (*Zeits. f. die neutest. Wiss.*, vi., 1905, pp. 1 f., 43 f.), has thoroughly investigated the position of the church towards astrology. In the second century, practically nothing was heard of it ; *i.e.*, it was attacked as pagan pseudo-science, as bad as polytheism, or worse. In the third century it raised its head within the church. In the fourth, it had to be sharply refuted. The theologians of the church always condemned it with indignation, but after the third century they no longer controlled the Christian communities, and they could not prevent it filtering in, and permeating alike the ideas and the speech of the people.

[1] Cp. the pagan in *Macarius Magnes*, IV. xxii. : εἰ δὲ καὶ τις τῶν Ἑλλήνων οὕτω κοῦφος τὴν γνώμην, ὡς ἐν τοῖς ἀγάλμασιν ἔνδον οἰκεῖν νομίζειν τοὺς θεούς, πολλῷ καθαρώτερον εἶχεν τὴν ἔννοιαν τοῦ πιστεύοντος ὅτι εἰς τὴν γαστέρα Μαρίας τῆς παρθένου εἰσέδυ τὸ θεῖον, ἔμβρυόν τε ἐγένετο καὶ τεχθὲν ἐσπαργανώθη, μεστὸν αἵματος χόριον καὶ χολῆς καὶ τῶν ἔτι πολλῷ τούτων ἀτοπώτερον ("A Greek might be silly enough to believe that the gods dwelt in their shrines, but he would at least be more reverent than the man who believes that the deity entered the womb of the Virgin Mary, became an embryo, was born and swaddled as from the fœtus full of blood and bile and all the rest of it ").

[2] The points of agreement between Celsus and Origen are already striking and instructive, although Celsus's was not a religious nature; still more striking are the points of agreement between Porphyry and the Oriental church teachers of his age. Porphyry's acute criticism of the gospels (especially the Fourth gospel), which is at many points quite justified, as well as of the apostle Paul, with whom he had little sympathy, cannot blind us to the fact that, apart from these three points, he was substantially of *one* mind with the Christians, and that he and they breathed the same religious atmosphere. The main point of difference lay in the fact that he reverently combined the entire universe with the Godhead, refusing to separate the Godhead from it, although he hated "the garment spotted by the flesh " as thoroughly as did the Christian teachers.

replied, " I am not to blame. I have only developed the germ which was planted in my being from the very first!" *This* religion was the first to cut the ground from under the feet of all other religions, and by means of her religious philosophy, as a civilizing power, to displace ancient philosophy.[1] But the reasons for the triumph of Christianity in that age are no guarantee for the permanence of that triumph throughout the history of mankind. Such a triumph rather depends upon the simple elements of the religion, on the preaching of the living God as the Father of men, and on the representation of Jesus Christ. For that very reason it depends also on the capacity of Christianity to strip off repeatedly such a collective syncretism and unite itself to fresh coefficients. The Reformation made a beginning in this direction.

[1] Cp. the question started by Henrici in his *Das Urchristenthum* (1902), p. 3.

BOOK III

THE MISSIONARIES: THE METHODS
OF THE MISSION AND THE
COUNTER-MOVEMENTS

CHAPTER I

THE CHRISTIAN MISSIONARIES (APOSTLES, EVANGELISTS, AND PROPHETS OR TEACHERS: THE INFORMAL MISSIONARIES)

I

BEFORE entering upon the subject proper, let us briefly survey the usage of the term "apostle," in its wider and narrower senses, throughout the primitive Christian writings.[1]

1. In Matthew, Mark, and John, "apostle" is not a special and distinctive name for the inner circle of the disciples of Jesus. These are almost invariably described as "the twelve,"[2] or the

---

[1] Though it is only apostles of Christ who are to be considered, it may be observed that Paul spoke (2 Cor. viii. 23) of ἀπόστολοι ἐκκλησιῶν, and applied the title "apostle of the Philippians" to Epaphroditus, who had conveyed to him a donation from that church (Philip. ii. 25). In Heb. iii. 1 Jesus is called "the apostle and high-priest of our confession." But in John xiii. 16 "apostle" is merely used as an illustration: οὐκ ἔστι δοῦλος μείζων τοῦ κυρίου αὐτοῦ, οὐδὲ ἀπόστολος μείζων τοῦ πέμψαντος αὐτόν. For the literature on this subject, see my edition of the Didachê (*Texte u. Untersuchungen*, vol. ii., 1884) and my *Dogmengeschichte* I.[3] (1894), pp. 153 f. [Eng. trans., vol. i. pp. 212 f.], Seufert on *Der Ursprung und die Bedeutung des Apostolats in d. Christliche Kirche* (1887), Weizsäcker's *Der Apost. Zeitalter*[2] (1892, s.v.), Zahn's *Skizzen aus dem Leben der alten Kirche*[2] (1898), p. 338, Haupt on *Zum Verständnisse des Apostolats im N.T.* (1896), Wernle's *Anfänge unserer Religion*[2] (1904), and Monnier's *La notion de l'Apostolat des origines à Irénée* (1903).

[2] Matt. x. 5, xx. 17, xxvi. 14, 47 ; Mark (iii. 14), iv. 10, vi. 7, ix. 35, x. 32, xi 11, xiv. 10, 17, 20, 43 ; John vi. 67, 70, 71, xx. 24.

twelve disciples.[1] As may be inferred from Matt. xix. 28, the
choice of this number probably referred to the twelve tribes of
Israel.[2] In my opinion the fact of their selection is historical, as
is also the tradition that even during his lifetime Jesus once
despatched them to preach the gospel, and selected them with
that end in view. At the same time, the primitive church
honoured them pre-eminently not as apostles but as the twelve
disciples (chosen by Jesus). In John they are never called the
apostles;[3] in Matthew they are apparently called "the twelve
apostles" (x. 2) once,[4] but this reading is a. correction, Syr. Sin.
giving "disciples." At one place Mark writes "the apostles"
(vi. 30), but this refers to their temporary missionary labours
during the life of Jesus. All three evangelists are thus ignorant
of "apostle" as a designation of the twelve: there is but *one*
instance where the term is applied to them *ad hoc*.[5]

2. With Paul it is quite otherwise. He never employs the
term "the twelve" (for in 1 Cor. xv. 5 he is repeating a formula
of the primitive church),[6] but confines himself to the idea of
"apostles." His terminology, however, is not unambiguous on
this point.

---

[1] Matt. x. i, xi. 1, xxvi. 20.—Add further the instances in which they are called
"the eleven" (Mark xvi. 14) or "the eleven disciples" (Matt. xxviii. 16).

[2] This is explicitly stated in Barn. 8: οὖσιν δεκαδύο εἰς μαρτύριον τῶν φυλῶν
ὅτι ιβ′ αἱ φυλαὶ τοῦ Ἰσραήλ ("They are twelve for a testimony to the tribes, for
there are twelve tribes in Israel").

[3] This is a remarkable fact. In the Johannine epistles "apostle" never occurs
at all. Yet these letters were composed by a man who, whatever he may have
been, claimed and exercised apostolic authority over a large number of the
churches, as is plain from the third epistle (see my study of it in the fifteenth
volume of the *Texte und Untersuchungen*, part 3). More on this point afterwards.

[4] Not "the twelve" pure and simple. Elsewhere the term, "the twelve
apostles," occurs only in Apoc. xxi. 14, and there the "twelve" is not superfluous,
as the Apocalypse uses "apostle" in a more general sense (see below).

[5] The phrasing of Mark iii. 14 (ἐποίησεν δώδεκα ἵνα ὦσιν μετ᾽ αὐτοῦ καὶ ἵνα
ἀποστέλλῃ αὐτοὺς κηρύσσειν καὶ ἔχειν ἐξουσίαν ἐκβάλλειν τὰ δαιμόνια) corresponds
to the original facts of the case. The mission (within Israel) was one object of
their election from the very first; see, further, the saying upon "fishers of men"
(Mark i. 17).—In this connection we must also note those passages in the gospel
where ἀποστέλλειν is used, *i.e.*, where it is applied by Jesus to his own commissions
and to the disciples whom he commissions (particularly John xx. 21, καθὼς
ἀπέσταλκέν με ὁ πατήρ, κἀγὼ πέμπω ὑμᾶς).

[6] From the absence of the term "twelve" in Paul, one might infer (despite the
gospels) that it did not arise till later; 1 Cor. xv. 5, however, proves the reverse.

(a) He calls himself an apostle of Jesus Christ, and lays the greatest stress upon this fact.[1] He became an apostle, as alone one could, through God (or Christ); God called him and gave him his apostleship,[2] and his apostleship was proved by the work he did and by the way in which he did it.[3]

(b) His fellow-missionaries—e.g., Barnabas and Silvanus—are also apostles; not so, however, his assistants and pupils, such as Timothy and Sosthenes.[4]

(c) Others also—probably, e.g., Andronicus and Junias [5]—are apostles. In fact, the term cannot be sharply restricted at all; for as God appoints prophets and teachers "in the church," so also does he appoint apostles to be the front rank

---

[1] See the opening of all the Pauline epistles, except 1 and 2 Thess., Philippians and Philemon; also Rom. i. 5, xi. 13, 1 Cor. iv. 9, ix. 1 f., xv. 9 f., 2 Cor. xii. 12, Gal. i. 17 (ii. 8). It may be doubted whether, in 1 Cor. iv. 9 (δοκῶ, ὁ θεὸς ἡμᾶς τοὺς ἀποστόλους ἐσχάτους ἀπέδειξεν ὡς ἐπιθανατίους), ἐσχάτους is to be taken as an attribute of ἀποστόλους or as a predicative. I prefer the former construction (see 1 Cor. xv. 8 f.), and it seems to me therefore probable that the first person plural here is an epistolary plural.

[2] Gal. i. 1 f., Rom. i. 5 (ἐλάβομεν χάριν καὶ ἀποστολήν). It is hard to say whether ἐλάβομεν is a real plural, and, if so, what apostles are here associated with Paul.

[3] 1 Cor. ix. 1, 2, xv. 9 f., 2 Cor. xii. 12, Gal. 1. 2.

[4] 1 Cor. ix. 4 f. and Gal. ii. 9 prove that Barnabas was an apostle, whilst 1 Thess. ii. 7 makes it very probable that Silvanus was one also. In the greetings of the Thessalonian and Philippian epistles Paul does not call himself an apostle, since he is associating himself with Timothy, who is never given this title (1 Thess. ii. 7 need not be taken as referring to him). It is therefore quite correct to ascribe to him (as in 2 Tim. iv. 5) the work of an evangelist. Apollos, too [see p. 79], is never called an apostle. As for εὐαγγελιστής, it is to be noted that, apart from 2 Timothy, it occurs twice in the New Testament; namely, in the We-journal in Acts (xxi. 8, as a title of Philip, one of the seven), and in Ephes. iv. 11, where the reason for evangelists being mentioned side by side with apostles is that the epistle is addressed to churches which had been founded by non-apostolic missionaries, and not by Paul himself—just as the term οἱ ἀκούσαντες (sc. τὸν κύριον) is substituted for "apostles" in Heb. ii. 3, because the readers for whom the epistle was originally designed had not received their Christianity from apostles.

[5] Rom. xvi. 7 (ἐπίσημοι ἐν τοῖς ἀποστόλοις, οἳ καὶ πρὸ ἐμοῦ γέγοναν ἐν Χριστῷ); ἐν is probably (with Lightfoot, as against Zahn) to be translated "among" rather than "by," since the latter would render the additional phrase rather superfluous and leave the precise scope of ἀπόστολοι unintelligible. If ἐν means "by," this passage is to be correlated with those which use οἱ ἀπόστολοι for the original apostles, since in the present case this gives the simplest meaning to the words. At any rate, the οἳ refers to Andronicus and Junias, not to ἀποστόλοις.

therein,[1] and since such charismatic callings depend upon the church's needs, which are known to God alone, their numbers are not fixed. To the apostleship belong (in addition to the above-mentioned call of God or Christ) the wonderful deeds which accredit it (2 Cor. xii. 12) and a work of its own (1 Cor. ix. 1-2), in addition to special rights.[2] He who can point to such is an apostle. The very polemic against false apostles (2 Cor. xi. 13) and "super-apostles" (2 Cor. xi. 5, xii. 11) proves that Paul did not regard the conception of "apostle" as implying any fixed number of persons, otherwise the polemic would have been differently put. Finally, a comparison of 1 Cor. xv. 7 with verse 5 of the same chapter shows, with the utmost clearness, that Paul distinguished a circle of apostles which was wider than the twelve—a distinction, moreover, which prevailed during the earliest period of the church and within Palestine.[3]

(d) But in a further, strict, sense of the term, "apostle" is reserved for those with whom he himself works,[4] and here some significance attaches to the very chronological succession of those who were called to the apostleship (Rom. xvi. 7). The twelve who were called during the lifetime of Jesus fall to be considered as the oldest *apostles*;[5] with their qualities and functions they

---

[1] 1 Cor. xii. 28 f. ; Eph. iv. 11. Even Eph. ii. 20 and iii. 5 could not be understood to refer exclusively to the so-called "original apostles," otherwise Paul would simply be disavowing his own position.

[2] It cannot be proved—at least not with any great degree of probability—from 1 Cor. ix. 1 that one *must* have seen the Lord in order to be able to come forward as an apostle. The four statements are an ascending series (οὐκ εἰμὶ ἐλεύθερος ; οὐκ εἰμὶ ἀπόστολος; οὐχὶ Ἰησοῦν τὸν κύριον ἡμῶν ἑόρακα ; οὐ τὸ ἔργον μου ὑμεῖς ἐστε ἐν κυρίῳ), as is proved by the relation of the second to the first. It is clear that the third and fourth statements are meant to attest the second, but it is doubtful if they contain an attestation which is absolutely necessary.

[3] Cp. Origen, Hom. *in Num.*, xxvii. 11 (vol. x. p. 353, ed. Lommatzsch) : "In quo apostolus ostendit [sc. 1 Cor. xv. 7] esse et alios apostolos exceptis illis duodecim."

[4] 1 Cor. ix. 2 and Gal. ii. (a Jewish and a Gentile apostolate); cp. also Rom. xi. 13, ἐθνῶν ἀπόστολος. Peter (Gal. ii. 8) has the ἀποστολὴ τ. περιτομῆς. Viewed ideally, there is only *one* apostolate, since there is only *one* church ; but the concrete duties of the apostles vary.

[5] The apostolate is the highest rank (1 Cor. xii. 28); it follows that the main thing even about the twelve is the fact of their being apostles.

form the pattern and standard for all subsequent apostles. *Thus the twelve, and (what is more) the twelve as apostles, come to the front.* As *apostles* Paul put them in front; in order to set the dignity of his own office in its true light, he embraced the twelve under the category of the *original apostolate* (thereby allowing their personal discipleship to fall into the background, in his terminology), and thus raised them above all other apostles, although not higher than the level which he claimed to occupy himself. That the twelve henceforth rank in history as the twelve apostles, and in fact as *the* apostles, was a result brought about by Paul; and, paradoxically enough, this was brought about by him in his very effort to fix the value of his own apostleship. He certainly did not work out this conception, for he neither could nor would give up the more general conception of the apostleship. Thus the term "apostle" is confined to the twelve only twice in Paul,[1] and even in these passages the reference is not absolutely certain. They occur in the first chapter of Galatians and in 1 Cor. ix. 5. Gal. i. 17 speaks of οἱ πρὸ ἐμοῦ ἀπόστολοι ("those who were apostles before me"), where in all likeliehood the twelve are alone to be understood. Yet the subsequent remark in verse 19 (ἕτερον τῶν ἀποστόλων οὐκ εἶδον εἰ μὴ Ἰάκωβον τὸν ἀδελφὸν τοῦ κυρίου) shows that it was of no moment to Paul to restrict the conception rigidly. In I Cor. ix. 5 we read, μὴ οὐκ ἔχομεν ἐξουσίαν ἀδελφὴν γυναῖκα περιάγειν, ὡς καὶ οἱ λοιποὶ ἀπόστολοι καὶ οἱ ἀδελφοὶ τοῦ κυρίου καὶ Κηφᾶς; the collocation of λοιπῶν ἀποστολῶν with the Lord's brothers renders it very probable that Paul here is thinking of the twelve exclusively, and not of all the existing apostles, when he mentions "the apostles." To sum up our results: Paul holds fast to the wider conception of the apostolate, but the twelve disciples form in his view its original nucleus.

3. The terminology of Luke is determined as much by that of the primitive age (the Synoptic tradition) as by the post-Pauline Following the former, he calls the chosen disciples of

---

[1] Apart from I Cor. xv. 7 (cp. verse 5), where the twelve appear as the original nucleus of the apostles; probably also apart from Rom. xvi. 7 (cp. p. 321, note) and i. 5.

Jesus "the twelve,"[1] or "the eleven;"[2] but he reproduces the latter in describing these disciples almost invariably throughout Acts as simply "the apostles"—just as though there were no other[3] apostles at all—and in relating, in his gospel, how Jesus himself called them apostles (vi. 13). Accordingly, even in the gospel he occasionally calls them "the apostles."[4] This would incline one to assert that Luke either knew, or wished to know, of no apostles save the twelve; but the verdict would be precipitate, for in Acts xiv. 4, 14, he describes not merely Paul but also Barnabas as an apostle.[5] Obviously, the terminology was not yet fixed by any means. Nevertheless it is surprising that Paul is only described as an "apostle" upon *one* occasion in the whole course of the book. He does not come[6] under the description of the qualities requisite for the apostleship which Luke has in view in Acts i. 21 f., a description which became more and more normative for the next age. Consequently he cannot have been an apostle for Luke, except in the wider sense of the term.

4. The apocalypse of John mentions those who call themselves

---

[1] Luke viii. 1, ix. 1, 12, xviii. 31, xxii. 3, 47 ; Acts vi. 2. Only once, then, are they called by this title in Acts, and that in a place where Luke seems to me to be following a special source.

[2] Luke xxiv. 9, 33 (cp. Acts ii. 14, Πέτρος σὺν τοῖς ἔνδεκα).

[3] Acts i. 2, ii. 37, 42-43, iv. 33, 35, 36, 37, v. 2, 12, 18, 29, 40, vi. 6, viii. 1, xiv. 18, ix. 27, xi. 1, xv. 2, 4, 6, 22, 23, xvi. 4. In the later chapters "apostle" no longer occurs at all. Once we find the expression οἱ ἔνδεκα ἀπόστολοι (Acts i. 26).

[4] Luke ix. 10, xvii. 5, xxii. 14, xxiv. 10. The gospel of Peter is more cautious ; it speaks of μαθηταί (30), or of οἱ δώδεκα μαθηταί (59), but never of ἀπόστολοι. Similarly, the apocalypse of Peter (5) writes, ἡμεῖς οἱ δώδεκα μαθηταί.

[5] With both Paul (see above) and Luke, then, the apostolic dignity of Barnabas is well established.—In regard to the Seventy disciples Luke does speak of an ἀποστέλλειν and calls them "seventy other" apostles, in allusion to the twelve. Yet he does not call them explicitly apostles. Irenæus (II. xxi. 1), Tertullian (*adv. Marc.*, iv. 24), Origen (on Rom. xvi. 7), and other writers, however, describe them as apostles, and people who were conjectured to have belonged to the Seventy were also named apostles by a later age.

[6] The apostle to be elected must have companied with Jesus from the date of John's baptism until the ascension ; he must also have been a witness of the resurrection (cp. also Luke xxiv. 48, Acts i. 8). (Paul simply requires an apostle to have "seen" the Lord.) This conception of the apostolate gradually displaced the original conception entirely, although Paul still retained his apostolic dignity as an exception to the rule.

apostles and are not (ii. 2),[1] which implies that they *might* be apostles. Obviously the writer is following the wider and original conception of the apostolate. The reference in xviii. 20 does not at least contradict this,[2] any more than xxi. 14 (see above), although only the twelve are named here "apostles," while the statement with its symbolic character has certainly contributed largely to win the victory for the narrower sense of the term.

5. In First Peter and Second Peter (i. 1), Peter is called an apostle of Jesus Christ. As for Jud. 17 and 2 Peter iii. 2 (τὰ ῥήματα τὰ προειρημένα ὑπὸ τῶν ἀποστόλων τοῦ κυρίου ἡμῶν Ἰησοῦ Χριστοῦ, τὰ προειρημένα ῥήματα ὑπὸ τῶν ἁγίων προφητῶν καὶ ἡ τῶν ἀποστόλων ὑμῶν ἐντολὴ τοῦ κυρίου καὶ σωτῆρος), in the first passage it is certain, and in the second very likely, that only the twelve disciples are to be understood.

6. That the epistle of Clement uses "apostles" merely to denote the original apostles and Paul, is perfectly clear from xlii. 1 f. (the apostles chosen previous to the resurrection) and xlvii. 4 (where Apollos, as ἀνὴρ δεδοκιμάσμενος παρ' ἀποστόλοις, a man approved by the apostles, is definitely distinguished from the apostles); cp. also v. 3 and xliv. 1. For Clement's conception of the apostolate, see below. The epistle of Barnabas (v. 9) speaks of the Lord's choice of his own apostles (ἴδιοι ἀπόστολοι), and therefore seems to know of some other apostles; in viii. 3 the author only mentions the twelve " who preached to us the gospel of the forgiveness of sins [3] and were empowered to preach the gospel," without calling them expressly " apostles."[4]   As the Preaching of Peter professes to be an actual composition of

---

[1] Cp. (above) Paul's judgment on the false apostles.

[2] Εὐφραίνου οὐρανὲ καὶ οἱ ἅγιοι καὶ οἱ ἀπόστολοι καὶ οἱ προφῆται. For the collocation of the Old Testament prophets, cp. also Luke xi. 49, 2 Pet. iii. 2. But in our passage, as in Eph. iii. 20, iii. 5, iv. 11, the Writer very possibly means Christian prophets.

[3] οἱ ῥαντίζοντες παῖδες οἱ εὐαγγελισάμενοι ἡμῖν τὴν ἄφεσιν ἁμαρτιῶν καὶ τὸν ἁγνισμὸν τῆς καρδίας, οἷς ἔδωκεν τοῦ εὐαγγελίου τὴν ἐξουσίαν—οὖσιν δεκαδύο εἰς μαρτύριον τῶν φυλῶν, ὅτι δεκαδύο φυλαὶ τοῦ Ἰσραήλ—εἰς τὸ κηρύσσειν ("The children who sprinkle are those who preached to us the gospel of the forgiveness of sins and purification of heart ; those whom he empowered to preach the gospel, being twelve in number for a testimony to the tribes—since there are twelve tribes in Israel").

[4] As v. 9 shows, this is merely accidental.

Peter, it is self-evident that whenever it speaks of apostles, the twelve are alone in view.[1]

7. The passage in *Sim.* IX. xvii. 1 leaves it ambiguous whether Hermas meant by "apostles" the twelve or some wider circle. But the other four passages in which the apostles emerge (*Vis.*, III. v. 1; *Sim.*, IX. xv. 4, xvi. 5, xxv. 2) make it perfectly clear that the author had in view a wider, although apparently a definite, circle of persons, and that he consequently paid no special attention to the twelve (see below, Sect. III., for a discussion upon this point and upon the collocation of apostles, bishops, and teachers, or of apostles and teachers). Similarly, the Didachê contemplates nothing but a wider circle of apostles. It certainly avows itself to be, as the title suggests, a διδαχὴ κυρίου διὰ τῶν ιβ′ ἀποστόλων (an instruction of the Lord given through the twelve apostles), but the very addition of the number in this title is enough to show that the book knew of other apostles as well, and xi. 3–6 takes apostles exclusively in the wider sense of the term (details of this in a later section).

8. In the dozen or so passages where the word "apostle" occurs in Ignatius, there is not a single one which renders it probable that the word is used in its wider sense. On the contrary, there are several in which the only possible allusion is to the primitive apostles. We must therefore conclude that by "apostle" Ignatius simply and solely understood[2] the twelve and Paul (*Rom.* iv. 3). Any decision in the case of Polycarp (*Ep.*, vi. 3, viii. 1) is uncertain, but he would hardly have occupied a different position from that of Ignatius. His church added to his name the title of an "*apostolic* and prophetic teacher" (*Ep. Smyrn.*, xvi. 2).

This survey of the primitive usage of the word "apostle"

---

[1] See von Dobschütz in *Texte u. Unters.*, xi. I. Jesus says in this Preaching : Ἐξελεξάμην ὑμᾶς δώδεκα μαθητὰς κρίνας ἀξίους ἐμοῦ καὶ ἀποστόλους πιστοὺς ἡγησάμενος εἶναι, πέμπων ἐπὶ τὸν κόσμον εὐαγγελίσασθαι τοὺς κατὰ τὴν οἰκουμένην ἀνθρώπους, κ.τ.λ. ("I have chosen you *twelve disciples*, judging you to be worthy of me and esteeming you to be faithful *apostles*, sending you out into the world to preach the gospel to all its inhabitants," etc.).

[2] Ignatius disclaims apostolic dignity for himself, in several passages of his epistles ; which nevertheless is a proof that there was a possibility of one who had not been an original apostle being none the less an apostle.

shows that while two conceptions existed side by side, the narrower was successful in making headway against its rival.[1]

II

One other preliminary inquiry is necessary before we can proceed to the subject of this chapter. We are to discuss apostles, prophets, and teachers as the missionaries or preachers of Christianity ; the question is, whether this threefold group can be explained from Judaism.

Such a derivation is in any case limited by the fact that these classes did not form any triple group in Judaism, their close association being a characteristic of primitive Christianity. With regard to each group, the following details are to be noted :—

1. *Apostles*.[2]—Jewish officials bearing this title are unknown to us until the destruction of the temple and the organization of the Palestinian patriarchate ; but it is extremely unlikely that no " apostles " previously existed, since the Jews would hardly have created an official class of " apostles " after the appearance of the Christian apostles. At any rate, the fact was there, as also, beyond question, was the name[3]—*i.e.*, of authoritative officials who collected contributions from the Diaspora for the temple and kept the churches in touch with Jerusalem and with each other. According to Justin (*Dial.* xvii., cviii., cxvii.), the thoroughly systematic measures which were initiated from

---

[1] During the course of the second century it became more rare than ever to confer the title of "apostles" on any except the biblical apostles or persons mentioned as apostles in the Bible. But Clement of Rome is called an apostle by Clement of Alexandria (*Strom.*, IV. xvii. 105), and Quadratus is once called by this name.

[2] The very restricted use of the word in classical (Attic) Greek is well known (Herod., I. 21. v. 38 ; Hesychius : ἀπόστολος· στρατηγὸς κατὰ πλοῦν πεμπόμενος). In the LXX. the word occurs only in 1 Kings xiv. 6 (describing the prophet Abijah : Hebrew שלוח). Justin has to fall back on ἀποστέλλειν in order to prove (*Dial.* lxxv.) that the prophets in the Old Testament were called ἀπόστολοι. Josephus calls Varus, the head of a Jewish deputation to Rome, ἀπόστολος αὐτῶν (*Antiq.*, xvii. 11. 1). The classical usage does not explain the Jewish-Christian. Hence it is probable that ἀπόστολος on Jewish soil retained the technical sense of " messenger."

[3] If Judaism had never known apostles, would Paul have spoken of "apostles" in 2 Cor. viii. 23 and Phil. ii. 25?

Jerusalem in order to counteract the Christian mission even in
Paul's day were the work of the high priests and teachers, who
despatched men (ἄνδρας χειροτονήσαντες ἐκλεκτούς) all over the
world to give correct information about Jesus and his disciples.
These were "apostles" [1]; that is, this task was entrusted to the
"apostles" who kept Jerusalem in touch with the Diaspora.[2]

Eusebius (*in Isa.* xviii. 1 f.) proves that the chosen persons
whom Justin thus characterizes are to be identified with the
"apostles" of Judaism. The passage has been already printed
(cp. p. 59), but in view of its importance it may once moré
be quoted: εὕρομεν ἐν τοῖς τῶν παλαιῶν συγγράμμασιν, ὡς οἱ
τὴν Ἰερουσαλὴμ οἰκοῦντες τοῦ τῶν Ἰουδαίων ἔθνους ἱερεῖς καὶ
πρεσβύτεροι γράμματα διαχαράξαντες εἰς πάντα διεπέμψαντο
τὰ ἔθνη τοῖς ἀπανταχοῦ Ἰουδαίοις διαβάλλοντες τὴν Χριστοῦ
διδασκαλίαν ὡς αἵρεσιν καινὴν καὶ ἀλλοτρίαν τοῦ θεοῦ, παρήγγελλόν τε δι᾽ ἐπιστολῶν μὴ παραδέξασθαι αὐτήν . . . . οἵ τε
ἀπόστολοι αὐτῶν ἐπιστολὰς βιβλίνας κομιζόμενοι[3] ἀπανταχοῦ
γῆς διέτρεχον, τὸν περὶ τοῦ σωτῆρος ἡμῶν ἐνδιαβάλλοντες λόγον.
ἀποστόλους δὲ εἰσέτι καὶ νῦν (so that the institution was no
novelty) ἔθος ἐστὶν Ἰουδαίοις ὀνομάζειν τοὺς ἐγκύκλια γράμματα
παρὰ τῶν ἀρχόντων αὐτῶν ἐπικομιζομένους. The primary
function, therefore, which Eusebius emphasized in the Jewish
"apostles" of his own day, was their duty of conveying encyclical epistles issued by the central authority for the instruction
and direction of the Diaspora. In the law-book (*Theodosianus
Codex*, xvi. 8. 14), as is only natural, another side is presenteḋ:
"Superstitionis indignae est, ut archisynagogi sive presbyteri
Judaeorum vel quos ipsi *apostolos* vocant, qui ad exigendum
aurum atque argentum a patriarcha certo tempore. diriguntur,"

---

[1] The passages have been printed above, on pp. 57 f. ; χειροτονήσαντες denotes
the apostolate (cp. Acts xiii. 3).

[2] For this intercommunication see, *e.g.*, Acts, xxviii. 21 : οὔτε γράμματα περὶ
σοῦ ἐδέξαμεθα ἀπὸ τῆς Ἰουδαίας (say the Roman Jews, with regard to Paul) οὔτε
παραγενόμενος τις τῶν ἀδελφῶν ἀπήγγειλεν. A cognate reference is that of 2 Cor.
iii. 1, to ἐπιστολαὶ συστατικαί.

[3] The allusion is to Isa. xviii. 1–2, where the LXX. reads : οὐαὶ . . . . ὁ
ἀποστέλλων ἐν θαλάσσῃ ὅμηρα καὶ ἐπιστολὰς βιβλίνας ἐπάνω τοῦ ὕδατος, while
Symmachus has not ὅμηρα but ἀποστόλους. Eusebius therefore refers this passage
to the false "apostles" of Judaism, and the words πορεύσονται γὰρ ἄγγελοι κοῦφοι,
κ.τ.λ., to the true apostles.

etc. ("It is part of this worthless superstition that the Jews have chiefs of their synagogues, or elders, or persons whom they call *apostles*, who are appointed by the patriarch at a certain season to collect gold and silver "). The same aspect is adduced, as the context indicates, by Julian (*Epist.* xxv.; Hertlein, p. 513), when he speaks of "the apostleship you talk about" (λεγομένη παρ' ὑμῖν ἀποστολή). Jerome (*ad Gal.*, i. 1) merely remarks: "Usque hodie a patriarchis Judaeorum apostolos mitti" ("To this day apostles are despatched by the Jewish patriarchs "). But we gain much more information from Epiphanius, who, in speaking of a certain Joseph (*adv. Hær.*, xxx. 4), writes: οὗτος τῶν παρ' αὐτοῖς ἀξιωματικῶν ἀνδρῶν ἐναρίθμιος ἦν· εἰσὶ δὲ οὗτοι μετὰ τὸν πατριάρχην ἀπόστολοι καλούμενοι, προσεδρεύουσι δὲ τῷ πατριάρχῃ καὶ σὺν αὐτῷ πολλάκις καὶ ἐν νυκτὶ καὶ ἐν ἡμέρα συνεχῶς διάγουσι, διὰ τὸ συμβουλεύειν καὶ ἀναφέρειν αὐτῷ τὰ κατὰ τὸν νόμον.[1] He tells (chap. xi.) when this Joseph became an apostle (or, got the εὐκαρπία τῆς ἀποστολῆς), and then proceeds: καὶ μετ' ἐπιστολῶν οὗτος ἀποστέλλεται εἰς τὴν Κιλίκων γῆν· ὃς ἀνελθὼν ἐκεῖσε ἀπὸ ἑκάστης πόλεως τῆς Κιλικίας τὰ ἐπιδέκατα καὶ τὰς ἀπαρχὰς παρὰ τῶν ἐν τῇ ἐπαρχίᾳ Ἰουδαίων εἰσέπραττεν . . . . ἐπεὶ οὖν, οἷα ἀπόστολος (οὕτως γὰρ παρ' αὐτοῖς, ὡς ἔφην, τὸ ἀξίωμα καλεῖται), ἐμβριθέστατος καὶ καθαρεύων δῆθεν τὰ εἰς κατάστασιν εὐνομίας, οὕτως ἐπιτελεῖν προβαλλόμενος, πολλοὺς τῶν κακῶν κατασταθέντων ἀρχισυναγώγων καὶ ἱερέων καὶ πρεσβυτέρων καὶ ἀξανιτῶν . . . . καθαιρῶν τε καὶ μετακινῶν τοῦ ἀξιώματος ὑπὸ πολλῶν ἐνεκοτεῖτο, κ.τ.λ. ("He was despatched with epistles to Cilicia, and on arriving there proceeded to levy from every city of Cilicia the titles and first-fruits paid by the Jews throughout the province. When, therefore, in virtue of his apostleship (for so is this order of men entitled by the Jews, as I have said), he acted with great rigour, forsooth, in his reforms and restoration of good order—*which was the very business before him*—deposing and removing from office many wicked chiefs of the synagogue and priests and

---

[1] " He belonged to the order of their distinguished men. These consist of men called 'apostles'; they rank next to the patriarch, with whom they are associated and with whom they often spend whole nights and days taking counsel together and consulting him on matters concerning the law."

presbyters and ministers . . . . he became hated by many people ").

Putting together these functions of the "apostles,"[1] we get the following result. (1) They were consecrated persons of a very high rank; (2) they were sent out into the Diaspora to collect tribute for headquarters; (3) they brought encyclical letters with them, kept the Diaspora in touch with the centre and informed of the intentions of the latter (or of the patriarch), received orders about any dangerous movement, and had to organize resistance to it; (4) they exercised certain powers of surveillance and discipline in the Diaspora; and (5) on returning to their own country they formed a sort of council which aided the patriarch in supervising the interests of the law.

In view of all this one can hardly deny a certain connection between these Jewish apostles and the Christian. It was not simply that Paul[2] and others had hostile relations with them: their very organization afforded a sort of type for the Christian apostleship, great as were the differences between the two. But, one may ask, were not these differences too great? Were not the Jewish apostles just financial officials? Well, at the very moment when the primitive apostles recognized Paul as an apostle, they set him also a financial task (Gal. ii. 10); he was to collect money throughout the Diaspora for the church at Jerusalem. The importance henceforth attached by Paul to this side of his work is well known; on it he spent unceasing care, although it involved him in the sorest vexations and led finally to his death. Taken by itself, it is not easy to understand exactly how the primitive apostles could impose this task on Paul, and how he could quietly accept it. But the thing becomes intelligible whenever we assume that the church at Jerusalem, together with the primitive apostles, considered

---

[1] Up till now only one inscription has been discovered which mentions these apostles, viz., the epitaph of a girl of fourteen at Venosa: "Quei dixerunt trenus duo apostuli et duo rebbites" (Hirschfeld, *Bullett. dell Instit. di corrisp. archæol.*, 1867, p. 152).

[2] Was not Paul himself, in his pre-Christian days [cp. p. 59], a Jewish "apostle"? He bore *letters* which were directed against Christians in the Diaspora, and had assigned to him by the highpriests and Sanhedrin certain disciplinary powers (see Acts viii. 2, xxii. 4 f., xxvi. 10 f., statements which deserve careful attention).

themselves the central body of Christendom, and also the representatives of the true Israel. That was the reason why the apostles whom they recognized were entrusted with a duty similar to that imposed on Jewish "apostles," viz., the task of collecting the tribute of the Diaspora. Paul himself would view it, one imagines, in a somewhat different light, but it is quite probable that this was how the matter was viewed by the primitive apostles. In this way the connection between the Jewish and the Christian apostles, which on other grounds is hardly to be denied in spite of all their differences, becomes quite evident.[1]

These statements about the Jewish apostles have been contested by Monnier (*op. cit.*, pp. 16 f.): "To prop up his theory, Harnack takes a text of Justin and fortifies it with another from Eusebius. That is, he proves the existence of an institution in the first century by means of a second-century text, and interprets the latter by means of a fourth-century writer. This is too easy." But it is still more easy to let such confusing abstractions blind us to the reasons which in the present instance not only allow us but even make it obvious to explain the testimony of Justin by that of Eusebius, and again to connect it with what we know of the antichristian mission set on foot by the Jerusalemites, and of the false apostles in the time of Paul. I have not ignored the fact that we possess no direct evidence for the assertion that Jewish emissaries like Saul in the first century bore the name of "apostles."

(2) *Prophets.*—The common idea is that prophets had died out in Judaism long before the age of Jesus and the apostles, but the New Testament itself protests against this erroneous idea. Reference may be made especially to John the Baptist, who certainly was a prophet and was called a prophet; also to the prophetess Hanna (Luke ii. 36), to Barjesus the Jewish prophet

---

[1] We do not know whether there were also "apostles" among the disciples of John—that narrow circle of the Baptist which, as the gospels narrate, was held together by means of fasting and special prayers; we merely know that adherents of this circle existed in the Diaspora (at Alexandria: Acts xviii. 24 f., and Ephesus: Acts xix. 1 f.). Apollos (see above, p. 79) would appear to have been originally a regular missionary of John the Baptist's movement; but the whole narrative of Acts at this point is singularly coloured and obscure.

in the retinue of the pro-consul at Cyprus (Acts xiii. 7), and to the warnings against false prophets (Matt. vii. 15, xxiv. 11, 25 = Mark xiii. 22, 1 John iv. 1, 2 Pet. ii. 1). Besides, we are told that the Essenes possessed the gift of prophecy;[1] of Theudas, as of the Egyptian,[2] it is said, προφήτης ἔλεγεν εἶναι ("he alleged himself to be a prophet," Joseph., *Antiq.*, xx. 5. 1); Josephus the historian played the prophet openly and successfully before Vespasian;[3] Philo called himself a prophet, and in the Diaspora we hear of Jewish interpreters of dreams, and of prophetic magicians.[4] What is still more significant, the wealth of contemporary Jewish apocalypses, oracular utterances, and so forth shows that, so far from being extinct, prophecy was in luxuriant bloom, and also that prophets were numerous, and secured both adherents and readers. There were very wide circles of Judaism who cannot have felt any surprise when a prophet appeared: John the Baptist and Jesus were hailed without further ado as prophets, and the imminent return of ancient prophets was an article of faith.[5] From its earliest awakening, then, Christian prophecy was no novelty, when formally considered, but a phenomenon which readily co-ordinated itself with similar contemporary phenomena in Judaism. In both cases, too, the high value attached to the prophets follows as a matter of course, since they are the voice of God; recognized as genuine prophets, they possess an absolute authority in their preaching and counsels. They were not

---

[1] Cp. Josephus' *Wars*, i. 3. 5, ii. 7. 3, 8. 12; *Antiq.*, xiii. 11. 2, xv. 10. 5, xvii. 3. 3.

[2] Acts xxi. 38; Joseph., *Antiq.*, xx. 8. 6; *Wars*, ii. 13. 5.

[3] *Wars*, iii. 8. 9; cp. Suet., *Vespas.*, v., and *Dio Cass.*, lxvi. 1.

[4] Cp. Hadrian, *Ep. ad Servian.* (Vopisc., *Saturn.*, viii.).—One cannot, of course, cite the gospel of pseudo-Matthew, ch. xiii. (" et prophetae qui fuerant in Jerusalem dicebant hanc stellam indicare nativitatem Christi "), since the passage is merely a late paraphrase of the genuine Matthew.

[5] Only it is quite true that the Sadducees would have nothing to do with prophets, and that a section of the strict upholders of the law would no longer hear of anything ranking beside the law. It stands to reason also that the priests and their party did not approve of prophets. After the completion of the canon there must have been a semi-official doctrine to the effect that the prophets were complete (cp. Ps. lxxiv. 9 : τὰ σημεῖα ἡμῶν οὐκ εἴδομεν, οὐκ ἔστιν ἔτι προφήτης, καὶ ἡμᾶς οὐ γνώσεται ἔτι, also 1 Macc. iv. 46, ix. 27, xiv. 41), and this conviction passed over into the church (cp. Murator. Fragm., "completo numero"); the

merely deemed capable of miracles, but even expected to perform them. It even seemed credible that a prophet could rise from the dead by the power of God; Herod and a section of the people were quite of opinion that Jesus was John the Baptist *redivivus* (see also Rev. xi. 11).[1]

(3) *Teachers.*—No words need be wasted on the importance of the scribes and teachers in Judaism, particularly in Palestine; but in order to explain historically the prestige claimed and enjoyed by the Christian διδάσκαλοι it is necessary to allude to the prestige of the Jewish teachers. " The rabbis claimed from their pupils the most unqualified reverence, a reverence which was to exceed even that paid to father and mother." " Let esteem for thy friend border on respect for thy teacher, and respect for thy teacher on reverence for God." " Respect for a teacher surpasses respect for a father; for son and father alike owe respect to a teacher." " If a man's father and teacher have lost anything, the teacher's loss has the prior claim; for while his father has only brought the man into the world, his teacher has taught him wisdom and brought him to life in the world to come. If a man's father and teacher are bearing burdens, he must help the teacher first, and then his father. If father and teacher are both in captivity, he must ransom the teacher first." As a rule, the rabbis claimed everywhere the highest rank. " They love the uppermost places at feasts and the front seats

---

book of Daniel was no longer placed among the prophets, and the later apocalypses were no longer admitted at all into the canon. Josephus is undoubtedly echoing a widely spread opinion when he maintains that the "succession of the prophets" is at an end (*Apion.*, i. 8 ; cp. also Euseb., *H.E.*, iii. 10. 4 : " From the time of Artaxerxes to our own day all the events have been recorded, but they do not merit the same confidence as we repose in the events that preceded them, since there has not been during this time an exact succession of prophets "—ἀπὸ δὲ 'Αρταξέρξου μέχρι τοῦ καθ' ἡμᾶς χρόνου γέγραπται μὲν ἕκαστα, πίστεως δ' οὐχ ὁμοίας ἠξίωται τοῖς πρὸ αὐτῶν, διὰ τὸ μὴ γενέσθαι τὴν τῶν προφητῶν ἀκριβῆ διαδοχήν). Julian, *c. Christ.*, 198 C: τὸ παρ' Ἑβραίοις [προφητικὸν πνεῦμα] ἐπέλιπεν ("the prophetic spirit failed among the Hebrews "). But although the line of the "canonical" prophets had been broken off before the appearance of Jesus, prophecy need not therefore have been extinguished.

[1] The saying of Jesus, that all the prophets and the law prophesied until John (Matt. xi. 13), is very remarkable (see below) ; he appears to have been thinking of the cessation of prophecy, probably owing to the nearness of the end. But the word also admits of an interpretation which does not contemplate the cessation of prophecy.

in the synagogues, and greetings in the market-place, and to be called by men 'rabbi'" (Matt. xxiii. 6 f. and parallel passages). "Their very dress was that of people of quality."[1]

Thus the three members of the Christian group—apostles, prophets, teachers—were already to be met with in contemporary Judaism, where they were individually held in very high esteem. Still, they were not grouped together, otherwise the prophets would have been placed in a more prominent position. The grouping of these three classes, and the special development of the apostleship, were the special work of the Christian church. It was a work which had most vital consequences.

III

As we are essaying a study of the missionaries and teachers, let us take the Didachê into consideration.[2]

In the fourth chapter, where the author gathers up the special duties of Christians as members of the church, this counsel is put forward as the first commandment: τέκνον μου, τοῦ λαλοῦντός σοι τὸν λόγον τοῦ θεοῦ μνησθήσῃ νυκτὸς καὶ ἡμέρας, τιμήσεις δὲ αὐτὸν ὡς κύριον· ὅθεν γὰρ ἡ κυριότης λαλεῖται, ἐκεῖ κύριός ἐστιν ("My son, thou shalt remember him that speaketh to thee the word of God by night and day; thou shalt honour him as the Lord. For whencesoever the lordship is lauded, there is the Lord present").[3] As is plain from the whole book (particularly from what is said in chap. xv. on the bishops and deacons), the writer knew only *one* class of people who were to be honoured in the church, viz., those alone who preached the word of God in their capacity of *ministri evangelii*.[4]

---

[1] Schürer, *Gesch. d. jüd. Volkes*, II.[3] pp. 317 f. (Eng. trans., II. i. 317).

[2] In what follows I have drawn upon the section in my larger edition of the Didachê (1884), which occupies pp. 93 f.

[3] Compare the esteem above mentioned in which the Jews held their teachers. Barnabas (xix. 9-10), in a passage parallel to that of the Didachê, writes: ἀγαπήσεις ὡς κόρην τοῦ ὀφθαλμοῦ σου πάντα τὸν λαλοῦντά σοι τὸν λόγον κυρίου, μνησθήσῃ ἡμέραν κρίσεως νυκτὸς καὶ ἡμέρας: ("Thou shalt love as the apple of thine eye everyone who speaks to thee the Word of the Lord; night and day shalt thou remember the day of judgment").

[4] The author of Hebrews also depicts the ἡγούμενοι more closely, thus: οἵτινες ἐλάλησαν ὑμῖν τὸν λόγον τοῦ θεοῦ (xiii. 7). The expression ἡγούμενοι or προηγούμενοι (see also Heb. xiii. 17), which had a special vogue in the Roman church,

But who are these λαλοῦντες τὸν λόγον τοῦ θεοῦ in the Didachê? Not permanent, elected officials of an individual church, but primarily independent teachers who ascribed their calling to a divine command or charism. Among them we distinguish (I) apostles, (2) prophets, and (3) teachers. These preachers, at the time when the author wrote, and for the circle of churches with which he was familiar, were in the first place the regular missionaries of the gospel (apostles), in the second place the men who ministered to edification, and consequently sustained the spiritual life of the churches (prophets and teachers).[1]

(1) *They were not elected by the churches,* as were bishops and deacons alone (xv. 1, χειροτονήσατε ἑαυτοῖς ἐπισκόπους καὶ διακόνους). In 1 Cor. xii. 28 we read: καὶ οὓς μὲν ἔθετο ὁ θεὸς ἐν τῇ ἐκκλησίᾳ πρῶτον ἀποστόλους, δεύτερον προφήτας, τρίτον διδασκάλους (cp. Ephes. iv. 11: καὶ αὐτὸς ἔδωκεν τοὺς μὲν ἀποστόλους, τοὺς δὲ προφήτας, τοὺς δὲ εὐαγγελιστάς, τοὺς δὲ ποιμένας καὶ διδασκάλους). The early source incorporated in Acts xiii. gives a capital idea of the way in which this divine appointment is to be understood in the case of the apostles. In that passage we are told how after prayer and fasting five prophets and teachers resident in the church at Antioch (Barnabas, Simeon, Lucius, Manäen, and Saul) received instructions from the holy Spirit to despatch Barnabas and Saul as missionaries or apostles.[2] We may assume that in other cases also the apostles could fall back on such an exceptional commission.[3]

---

although it is not unexampled elsewhere, did not become a technical expression in the primitive age; consequently it is often impossible to ascertain in any given case who are meant by it, whether bishops or teachers.

[1] According to chap. xv., bishops and deacons belong to the second class, in so far as they take the place of prophets and teachers in the work of edifying the church by means of oral instruction.

[2] The despatch of these two men appears to be entirely the work of the holy Spirit. Ἀφορίσατε δή μοι τὸν Βαρνάβαν καὶ Σαῦλον εἰς τὸ ἔργον ὃ προσκέκλημαι αὐτούς, says the Spirit. The envoys thus act simply as executive organs of the Spirit.

[3] In the epistles to Timothy, Timothy is represented as an "evangelist," *i.e.*, as an apostle of the second class, but he is also the holder of a charismatic office. Consequently, just as in Acts xiii., we find in I. i. 18 these words: ταύτην τὴν παραγγελίαν παρατίθεμαί σοι, τέκνον Τιμόθεε, κατὰ τὰς προαγούσας ἐπὶ σὲ προφητείας; and in iv. 14, the following: μὴ ἀμέλει τοῦ ἐν σοὶ χαρίσματος, ὃ ἐδόθη σοι διὰ προφητείας [μετὰ ἐπιθέσεως τῶν χειρῶν τοῦ πρεσβυτερίου].

The prophets were authenticated by what they delivered in the form of messages from the holy Spirit, in so far as these addresses proved spiritually effective. But it is impossible to determine exactly how people were recognized as teachers. One clue seems visible, however, in Jas. iii. 1, where we read: μὴ πολλοὶ διδάσκαλοι γίνεσθε, εἰδότες ὅτι μεῖζον κρίμα λημψόμεθα. From this it follows that to become a teacher was a matter of personal choice—based, of course, upon the individual's consciousness of possessing a charisma. The teacher also ranked as one who had received the holy Spirit[1] for his calling; whether he was a genuine teacher (Did., xiii. 2) or not, was a matter which, like the genuineness of the prophets (Did., xi. 11, xiii. 1), had to be decided by the churches. Yet they merely verified the existence of a divine commission; they did not in the slightest degree confer any office by their action. As a rule, the special and onerous duties which apostles and prophets had to discharge (see below) formed a natural barrier against the intrusion of a crowd of interlopers into the office of the preacher or the missionary.

(2) *The distinction of "apostles, prophets, and teachers" is very old, and was common in the earliest period of the church.* The author of the Didachê presupposes that apostles, prophets, and teachers were known to all the churches. In xi. 7 he specially mentions prophets; in xii. 3 f. he names apostles and prophets, conjoining in xiii. 1-2 and xvi. 1-2 prophets and teachers (never apostles and teachers: unlike Hermas). The inference is that although this order—" apostles, prophets, and teachers "—was before his mind, the prophets and apostles formed in certain aspects a category by themselves, while in other aspects the prophets had to be ranked with the teachers (see below). This order is identical with that of Paul (1 Cor. xii. 28), so that its origin is to be pushed back to the sixth decade of the first century; in fact, it goes back to a still earlier

---

[1] This may probably be inferred even from 1 Cor. xiv. 26, where διδαχή follows ἀποκάλυψις, and it is made perfectly clear by Hermas. who not only is in the habit of grouping ἀπόστολοι and διδάσκαλοι, but also (*Sim.*, ix. 25. 2) writes thus of the apostles and teachers : " They taught the Word of God soberly and purely . . . . even as also they had received the holy Spirit " (διδάξαντες σεμνῶς καὶ ἁγνῶς τὸν λόγον τοῦ θεοῦ . . . . καθὼς καὶ παρέλαβον τὸ πνεῦμα τὸ ἅγιον).

period, for in saying οὓς μὲν ἔθετο ὁ θεὸς ἐν τῇ ἐκκλησίᾳ πρῶτον ἀποστόλους, κ.τ.λ., Paul is thinking without doubt of some arrangement in the church which held good among Jewish Christian communities founded apart from his co-operation, no less than among the communities of Greece and Asia Minor. This assumption is confirmed by Acts xi. 27, xv. 22, 32, and xiii. 1. f. In the first of these passages we hear of *prophets* who had migrated from the Jerusalem-church to the Antiochene;[1] the third passage implies that five men, who are deseribed as *prophets* and *teachers*, occupied a special position in the church at Antioch, and that two of their number were elected by them as apostles at the injunction of the Spirit (see above).[2] Thus the apostolic vocation was not necessarily involved in the calling to be a prophet or teacher; it required for itself a further special injunction of the Spirit. From Acts xiii. 1 f. the order—"apostles, prophets, teachers"—follows indirectly but quite obviously; we have therefore evidence for it (as the notice may be considered historically reliable) in the earliest Gentile church and at a time which was probably not even one decade distant from the year of Paul's conversion.

A century may have elapsed between the event recorded in Acts xiii. 1 f. and the final editing of the Didachê. But intermediate stages are not lacking. First, we have the evidence of 1 Cor. (xii. 28),[3] with two witnesseses besides in Ephesians (whose

[1] On a temporary visit. One of them, Agabus, was permanently resident in Judæa about fifteen years later, but journeyed to meet Paul at Cæsarea in order to bring him a piece of prophetic information (Acts xxi. 10 f.).

[2] From the particles employed in the passage, it is probable that Barnabas, Simeon, and Lucius were the prophets, while Manäen and Saul were the teachers. One prophet and one teacher were thus despatched as apostles. As the older man, Barnabas at first took the lead (his prophetic gift may be gathered from the name assigned to him, " Barnabas "=υἱὸς παρακλήσεως [Acts iv. 36]; for in 1 Cor. xiv. 3 we read, ὁ προφητεύων ἀνθρώποις λαλεῖ παράκλησιν).

[3] Observe that after enumerating apostles, prophets, and teachers, Paul does not proceed to give any further category of persons with charismatic gifts, but merely adds charismatic gifts themselves; note further that he gives no classification of these gifts, but simply arranges them in one series with a double ἔπειτα, whereas the apostles, prophets, and teachers are enumerated in order with πρῶτον, δεύτερον, and τρίτον. The conclusion is that the apostolate, the prophetic office (not, speaking with tongues), and teaching were the only offices which made their occupants persons of rank in the church, whilst the δυνάμεις, ἰάματα, ἀντιλήμψεις, κ.τ.λ., conferred no special standing on those who were gifted with such charis-

evidence is all the more weighty if the epistle is not genuine) and Hermas. Yet neither of these witnesses is of supreme importance, inasmuch as both fail to present in its pristine purity the old class of the regular λαλοῦντες τὸν λόγον τοῦ θεοῦ as apostles, prophets, and teachers ; both point to a slight modification of this class, owing to the organization of individual churches, complete within themselves, which had grown up on other bases.

Like Did. xi. 3, Eph. ii. 20 and iii. 5 associate apostles and prophets, and assign them an extremely high position. All believers, we are told, are built up on the foundation of the apostles and prophets, to whom, in the first instance, is revealed the secret that the Gentiles are fellow-heirs of the promise of Christ. That prophets of the gospel, and not of the Old Testament, are intended here is shown both by the context and by the previous mention of apostles. Now in the list at iv. 11 the order " apostles, prophets, and teachers " is indeed preserved, but in such a way that " evangelists " are inserted after " prophets," and " pastors " added to " teachers " (preceding them, in fact, but constituting with them a single group or class).[1] From these intercalated words it follows (1) that the author (or Paul) knew missionaries who did not possess the dignity of apostles,[2] but that he did not place them immediately after the apostles, inasmuch as the collocation of " apostles and prophets " was a sort of noli me tangere (not so the collocation of " prophets and teachers "); (2) that he reckoned the leaders of an individual church (ποιμένες) among the preachers bestowed upon the church as a whole (the individual church in this way made its influence felt); (3) that he looks upon the teachers as persons belonging to a definite church, as is evident from the close connection of teachers with ποιμένες and the subsequent mention (though in

mata. Hence with Paul, too, it is the preaching of God's Word which constitutes a position in the ἐκκλησία of God. This agrees exactly with the view of the author of the Didachê.

[1] It does not follow that the " teachers " are to be considered identical with the " pastors," because τοὺς δὲ does not immediately precede διδάσκαλους. The inference is merely that Paul or the author took both as comprising a single group.

[2] I have already tried (p. 321) to explain exactly why evangelists are mentioned in Ephesians.

collocation) of the former. The difference between the author of Ephesians and the author of the Didachê on these points, however, ceases to have any significance when one observes two things: (a) first, that even the latter places the ποιμένες (ἐπίσκοποι) of the individual church side by side with the teachers, and seeks to have like honour paid to them (xv. 1-2); and secondly (b), that he makes the permanent domicile of teachers in an individual church (xiii. 2) the rule, as opposed to any special appointment (whereas, with regard to prophets, domicile would appear, from xiii. 1, to have been the exception). It is certainly obvious that the Didachê's arrangement approaches more nearly than that of Ephesians to the arrangement given by Paul in Corinthians, but it would be more than hasty to conclude that the Didachê must therefore be older than the former epistle. We have already seen that the juxtaposition of the narrower conception of the apostolate with the broader is very early, and that the latter, instead of being simply dropped, kept pace for a time with the former. Furthermore, it must be borne in mind that passages like Acts xiii. 1, xi. 27, xxi. 10, etc., prove that although the prophets, and especially the teachers, had to serve the whole church with their gifts, they could possess, even in the earliest age, a permanent residence and also membership of a definite community, either permanently or for a considerable length of time. Hence at an early period they could be viewed in this particular light, without prejudice to their function as teachers who were assigned to the church in general.

As for Hermas, the most surprising observation suggested by the book is that the prophets are never mentioned, for all its enumeration of classes of preachers and superintendents in Christendom.[1] In consequence of this, apostles and teachers (ἀπόστολοι and διδάσκαλοι) are usually conjoined.[2] Now as

---

[1] In Sim. ix. 15. 4a Old Testament prophets are meant.

[2] Cp. Sim., ix. 15, 4b: οἱ δὲ μ' ἀπόστολοι καὶ διδάσκαλοι τοῦ κηρύγματος τοῦ υἱοῦ τοῦ θεοῦ ("the forty are apostles and teachers of the preaching of the Son of God"); 16. 5: οἱ ἀπόστολοι καὶ οἱ διδάσκαλοι οἱ κηρύξαντες τὸ ὄνομα τοῦ υἱοῦ τοῦ θεοῦ ("the apostles and teachers who preached the name of the Son of God"); 25. 2: ἀπόστολοι καὶ διδάσκαλοι οἱ κηρύξαντες εἰς ὅλον τὸν κόσμον καὶ οἱ διδάξαντες σεμνῶς καὶ ἁγνῶς τὸν λόγον τοῦ κυρίου ("apostles and teachers who preached to

Hermas comes forward in the rôle of prophet, as his book contains one large section (*Mand.* xi.) dealing expressly with false and genuine prophets, and finally as the vocation of the genuine prophet is more forcibly emphasized in Hermas than in any other early Christian writing and presupposed to be universal, the absence of any mention of the prophet in the " hierarchy " of Hermas must be held to have been deliberate. In short, *Hermas passed over the prophets because he reckoned himself one of them.* If this inference be true [1] we are justified in supplying "prophets" wherever Hermas names "apostles and teachers," so that he too becomes an indirect witness to the threefold group of "apostles, prophets, teachers." [2] In that case the conception expounded in the ninth similitude of the " Shepherd " is exactly parallel to that of the man who wrote the Didachê. Apostles (prophets) and teachers are the preachers appointed by God to establish the spiritual life of the churches ; next to them come (chapters xxv.–xxvii.) the bishops and deacons.[3] On the other hand, the author alters this order in *Vis.*, III. v. 1, where he writes:[4] οἱ μὲν οὖν λίθοι οἱ τετράγωνοι καὶ λευκοὶ καὶ συμφωνοῦντες ταῖς ἁρμογαῖς αὐτῶν, οὗτοι εἰσιν οἱ ἀπόστολοι

---

all the world, and taught soberly and purely the Word of the Lord "). *Vis.*, III. v. 1. (see below) is also relevant in this connection. Elsewhere the collocation of " ἀπόστολος, διδάσκαλος " occurs only in the Pastoral epistles (1 Tim. ii. 7, 2 Tim. i. 11); but these passages prove nothing, as Paul either is or is meant to be the speaker.

[1] Lietzmann (*Götting. Gelehrte Anz.*, 1905, vi. p. 486) proposes another explanation: "Apostles and teachers belong to the past generation for Hermas ; he recognises a prophetic office also, but only in the Old Testament (*Sim.*, ix. 15. 4). He does occupy himself largely with the activities of the true prophet, and feels he is one himself ; but he conceives this προφητεύειν as a private activity which God's equipment renders possible, but which lacks any official character. So with his censor in the Muratorian Fragment." Perhaps this is the right explanation of the difficulty. But can Hermas have really estimated the prophets like the Muratorian Fragmentist?

[2] Hermas, like the author of the Didachê, knows nothing about "evangelists" as distinguished from "apostles" ; he, too, uses the term "apostle" in its wider sense (see above, p. 326).

[3] In conformity with the standpoint implied in the parable, the order is reversed in chapters xxvi.–xxvii. ; for the proper order, see *Vis.*, III. v. 1.

[4] "The squared white stones that fit together in their joints, are the apostles and bishops and teachers and deacons who walked after the holiness of God and acted as bishops, teachers, and deacons, purely and soberly for the elect of God. Some have already fallen asleep, and others are still living."

(add καὶ προφῆται) καὶ ἐπίσκοποι καὶ διδάσκαλοι καὶ διάκονοι
οἱ πορευθέντες κατὰ τὴν σεμνότητα τοῦ θεοῦ καὶ ἐπισκοπήσαντες
καὶ διδάξαντες καὶ διακονήσαντες ἁγνῶς καὶ σεμνῶς τοῖς ἐκλεκτοῖς
τοῦ θεοῦ, οἱ μὲν κεκοιμημένοι, οἱ δὲ ἔτι ὄντες. According to the
author of the Didachê also, the ἐπίσκοποι and διάκονοι are to
be added to the ἀπόστολοι., προφῆται, and διδάσκαλοι, but the
difference between the two writers is that Hermas has put the
bishops, just as the author of Ephesians has put the ποιμένες,
before the teachers. The reasons for this are unknown to us;
all we can make out is that at this point also the actual organization of the individual communities had already modified the
conception of the organization of the collective church which
Hermas shared with the author of the Didachê.[1]

Well then ; one early source of Acts, Paul, Hermas, and the
author of the Didachê all attest the fact that in the earliest
Christian churches " those who spoke the word of God " (the
λαλοῦντες τὸν λόγον τοῦ θεοῦ) occupied the highest position,[2]
and that they were subdivided into apostles, prophets, and
teachers. They also bear evidence to the fact that these apostles
prophets, and teachers were not esteemed as officials of an individual community, but were honoured as preachers who had been
appointed by God and assigned to the church *as a whole*. The
notion that the regular preachers in the church were *elected* by
the different churches is as erroneous as the other idea that they
had their " office " transmitted to them through a human channel
of some kind or other. So far as men worked together here, it
was in the discharge of a direct command from the Spirit.

Finally, we have to consider more precisely the bearings of
this conclusion, viz., that, to judge from the consistent testimony
of the earliest records, the apostles, prophets, and teachers were
allotted and belonged, not to any individual community, but to
the church as a whole. By means of this feature Christendom

---

[1] It is to be observed, moreover, that *Sim.* ix. speaks of apostles and teachers
as of a bygone generation, whilst *Vis.* iii. declares that one section of the whole
group have already fallen asleep, while the rest are still alive. We cannot, however, go into any further detail upon the important conceptions of Hermas.

[2] So, too, the author of Hebrews. Compare also I Pet. iv. 11 : εἴ τις λαλεῖ,
ὡς λόγια θεοῦ · εἴ τις διακονεῖ, ὡς ἐξ ἰσχύος ἧς χορηγεῖ ὁ θεός [a passage which
illustrates the narrative in Acts vi.].

possessed, amid all its scattered fragments, a certain cohesion and a bond of unity which has often been underestimated. These apostles and prophets, wandering from place to place, and received by every community with the utmost respect, serve to explain how the development of the church in different provinces and under very different conditions could preserve, as it did, such a degree of homogeneity. Nor have they left their traces merely in the scanty records, where little but their names are mentioned, and where witness is borne to the respect in which they were held. In a far higher degree their self-expression appears throughout a whole *genre* of early Christian literature, namely, *the so-called catholic epistles and writings*. It is impossible to understand the origin, spread, and vogue of a literary *genre* so peculiar and in many respects so enigmatic, unless one correlates it with what is known of the early Christian " apostles, prophets, and teachers." When one considers that these men were set by God within the *church*—*i.e.*, in Christendom as a whole, and not in any individual community, their calling being meant for *the church collective*—it becomes obvious that the so-called catholic epistles and writings, addressed to the whole of Christendom, form a *genre* in literature which corresponds to these officials, and which must have arisen at a comparatively early period. An epistle like that of James, addressed " to the twelve tribes of the dispersion," with its prophetic passages (iv.–v.), its injunctions uttered even to presbyters (v. 14), and its emphatic assertions (v. 15 f.), this epistle, which cannot have come from the apostle James himself, becomes intelligible so soon as we think of the wandering prophets who, conscious of a divine calling which led them to all Christendom, felt themselves bound to serve the church as a whole. We can well understand how catholic epistles must have won great prestige, even although they were not originally distinguished by the name of any of the twelve apostles.[1]

---

[1] This period, of course, was past and gone, when one of the charges levelled at the Montanist Themison was that he had written a catholic epistle and thus invaded the prerogative of the original apostles : see Apollonius (in Euseb., *H.E.*, v. 18. 5)—Θεμίσων ἐτόλμησε, μιμούμενος τὸν ἀπόστολον, καθολικήν τινα συνταξάμενος ἐπιστολὴν κατηχεῖν τοὺς ἄμεινον αὐτοῦ πεπιστευκότας (" Themison ventured, in imitation of the apostles, to compose a catholic epistle for the instruction of people whose faith was better than his own ").

Behind these epistles stood the teachers called by God, who were to be reverenced like the Lord himself. It would lead us too afar afield to follow up this view, but one may refer to the circulation and importance of certain "catholic" epistles throughout the churches, and to the fact that they determined the development of Christianity in the primitive period hardly less than the Pauline epistles. During the closing decades of the first century, and at the opening of the second, the extraordinary activity of these apostles, prophets, or teachers left a lasting memorial of itself in the "catholic" writings; to which we must add other productions like the "Shepherd" of Hermas, composed by an author of whom we know nothing except the fact that his revelations were to be communicated to *all* the churches. He is really not a *Roman* prophet; being a prophet, he is a teacher for Christendom as a *whole*.

It has been remarked, not untruly, that Christendom came to have *church officials*—as distinct from local officials of the communities—only after the episcopate had been explained as an organization intended to perpetuate the apostolate in such a way that every bishop was held, not simply to occupy an office in the particular community, but to rank as a bishop of the catholic church (and, in this sense, to be a follower of the apostles). This observation is correct. But it has to be supplemented by the following consideration, that in the earliest age special forms of organization did arise which in *one* aspect afford an analogy to ecclesiastical office in later catholicism. For "those who spake the word of God" (the λαλοῦντες τὸν λόγον τοῦ θεοῦ) were catholic teachers (διδάσκαλοι καθολικοί).[1] Yet

---

[1] I shall at this point put together the sources which prove the threefold group.

(1) The λαλοῦντες τὸν λόγον τοῦ θεοῦ (and they alone at first, it would appear; *i.e.*, apostles, prophets, and teachers) are the ἡγούμενοι or τετιμήμενοι in the churches; this follows from (*a*) Did., iv. 1, xi. 3 f., xiii., xv. 1-2, when taken together; also (*b*) from Heb. xiii. 7, 17, 24, where the ἡγούμενοι are expressly described as λαλοῦντες τὸν λόγον τοῦ θεοῦ; probably (*c*) from *Clem. Rom.*, i. 3, xxi. 6; (*d*) from Acts xv. 22, 32, where the same persons are called ἡγούμενοι and then προφῆται; and (*e*) from the "Shepherd" of Hermas.

(2) Apostles, prophets, and teachers: cp. Paul (1 Cor. xii. 28 f., where he tacks on δυνάμεις, χαρίσματα ἰαμάτων, ἀντιλήψεις, κυβερνήσεις, γένη γλωσσῶν). When the fathers allude to this passage during later centuries, they do so as if the threefold group still held its own, oblivious often of the presence of the hierarchy. Novatian, after speaking of the apostles who had been comforted by the Paraclete,

even when these primitive teachers were slowly disappearing, a development commenced which ended in the triumph of the monarchical episcopate, *i.e.*, in the recognition of the apostolic and catholic significance attaching to the episcopate. The preliminary stages in this development may be distinguished wherever in Ephesians, Hermas, and the Didachê the permanent

proceeds (*de Trinit.*, xxix.): "Hic est qui prophetas in ecclesia constituit, magistro. erudit" ("This is he who places prophets in the church and instructs teachers"). Cyril of Jerusalem (*Catech.*, xviii. 27) will recognize no officials as essential to the church, not even bishops, except the persons mentioned in the above passage. Ambrose (*Hexaëm*, iii. 12, 50) writes: "God has girt the vine as it were with a trench of heavenly precepts and the custody of angels ; . . . . he has set in the church as it were a tower of apostles, prophets, and teachers, who are wont to safeguard the peace of the church" ("Circumdedit enim vincam velut vallo quodam caelestium praeceptorum et angelorum custodia . . . . posuit in ecclesia velut turrim apostolorum et prophetarum atque doctorum, qui solent pro ecclesiae pace praetendere"; see *in Ps.* cxviii., *Sermo* xxii., ch. 15). Vincent of Lerin (*Commonit.* 37, 38) speaks of false apostles, false prophets, false teachers ; in ch. 40, where one expects to hear of bishops, only apostles and prophets and teachers are mentioned. Paulinus of Nola (*Opera*, ed. Hartel, i. p. 411 f.) addressed an inquiry to Augustine upon apostles, prophets and teachers, evangelists and pastors. He remarks very significantly : "In omnibus his diversis nominibus simile et prope unum doctrinae officium video fruisse tractatum" ("Under all these different names I see that a like and almost identical order of doctrine has been preserved"), and rightly assumes that the prophets cannot be those of the Old Testament, but must be Christian prophets.

(3) Prophets and teachers, who select apostles from their number (Acts xiii. 1).

(4) Apostles, prophets, and teachers: the Didachê (adding bishops and deacons).

(5) Apostles, prophets, evangelists, pastors, and teachers: Ephes. iv. 11.

(6) Apostles and teachers (prophets being purposely omitted), with bishops and deacons in addition : Hermas, *Sim.*, ix.

(7) Apostles (prophets), bishops, teachers, deacons: Hermas, *Vis.*, iii.

(8) Apostles, teachers, prophets : *Clem. Hom.*, xi. 35, μέμνησθε ἀπόστολον ἢ διδάσκαλον ἢ προφήτην.

(9) Apostles and prophets (the close connection of the two follows at an early period from Matt. x. 41): Rev. xviii. 20 (ii. 2, 20), Ephes. ii. 20, iii. 5, Did., xi. 3. (According to Irenæus, III. ii. 4, John the Baptist was at once a prophet and an apostle : "et prophetae et apostoli locum habuit " ; according to Hippolytus, *de Antichr.*, 50, John the disciple was at once an apostle and prophet.) So the opponent of the Alogi, in Epiph., *Hær.*, 51. 35, etc. ; cp. Didasc., *de Charism.* [Lagarde, *Reliq.*, pp. 4, 19 f.]: οἱ προφῆται ἐφ' ἡμῶν προφητεύσαντες οὐ παρεξέτειναν ἑαυτοὺς τοῖς ἀποστόλοις ("our prophets did not measure themselves with the apostles ").

(10) Prophets and teachers: Acts xiii. 1 (2 Pet. ii. 1), Did., xiii. 1–2, xiv. 1–2, Pseudo-Clem., *de Virg.*, I. 11 : "Ne multi inter vos sint doctores neque omnes sitis prophetae" (*loc. cit.*, λόγος διδαχῆς ἢ προφητείας ἢ διακονίας). In the later literature, the combination (false prophets and false teachers) still occurs fre-

officials of the individual community are promoted to the class
of apostles, prophets, and teachers," or already inserted among
them. When this happened, the fundamental condition was
provided which enabled the bishops at last to secure the prestige
of "apostles, prophets, and teachers." If one looks at 1 Cor.

quently; see, *e.g.*, Orig., Hom. ii. *in Ezek.* (Lommatzsch, xiv. pp. 33, 37),
and Vincent of Lerin., *loc. cit.*, 15. 23. In the pseudo-Clementine Homilies
Jesus himself is called "our teacher and prophet."

(11) Apostles and teachers (Hermas): 1 Tim. ii. 7, 2 Tim. i. 11, Clem., *Strom.*,
vii. 16. 103 : οἱ μακάριοι ἀπόστολοί τε καὶ διδάσκαλοι, *Eclog.* 23.

(12) Polycarp is described in the epistle of his church (xvi. 2) as ἐν τοῖς καθ'
ἡμᾶς χρόνοις διδάσκαλος ἀποστολικὸς καὶ προφητικός, γενόμενος ἐπίσκοπος τῆς ἐν
Σμύρνῃ καθολικῆς ἐκκλησίας (cp. *Acta Pion.* 1 : ἀποστολικὸς ἀνὴρ τῶν καθ' ἡμᾶς
γενόμενος). Here the ancient and honourable predicates are conjoined and
applied to a "bishop." But it is plain that there was something wholly exceptional in an apostolic and prophetic teacher surviving "in our time." The
way in which Eusebius speaks is very noticeable (*Mart. Pal.*, yi. 1) : of one
group of twelve martyrs he says, they partook of προφητικοῦ τινος ἢ καὶ ἀποστολικοῦ χαρίσματος καὶ ἀριθμοῦ (a prophetic or apostolic grace and number).

(13) Alexander the Phrygian is thus described in the epistle from Lyons
(Eus., *H.E.*, v. 1. 49): γνωστὸς σχεδὸν πᾶσι διὰ τὴν πρὸς θεὸν ἀγάπην καὶ
παρρησίαν τοῦ λόγου · ἦν γὰρ καὶ οὐκ ἄμοιρος ἀποστολικοῦ χαρίσματος ("Well
known to all on account of his love to God and boldness of speech—for he was
not without a share of apostolic grace ").

An admirable proof that the prophets were bestowed on the church as a whole,
instead of on any individual congregation (that it was so with the apostles, goes
without saying), is furnished by Valentinian circles (*Excerpta ex Theodot.*, 24):
"The Valentinians declare that the Spirit possessed by each individual of the
prophets for service is poured out on all members of the church; wherefore the
tokens of the Spirit, *i.e.*, healing and prophecy, are performed by the church"
(λέγουσιν οἱ Οὐαλεντινιανοὶ ὅτι ὁ κατὰ εἷς τῶν προφητῶν ἔσχεν πνεῦμα ἐξαίρετον
εἰς διακονίαν, τοῦτο ἐπὶ πάντας τοὺς τῆς ἐκκλησίας ἐξεχύθη · διὸ καὶ τὰ σημεῖα τοῦ
πνεύματος ἰάσεις καὶ προφητεῖαι διὰ τῆς ἐκκλησίας ἐπιτελοῦνται). Compare the
claims of the Montanist prophets and the history of the "Shepherd" of Hermas
in the church.

The passage from the *Eclogues* of Clement, referred to under (11), reads as
follows : ὥσπερ διὰ τοῦ σώματος ὁ σωτὴρ ἐλάλει καὶ ἰατο, οὕτως καὶ πρότερον "διὰ
τῶν προφητῶν," νῦν δὲ "διὰ τῶν ἀποστόλων καὶ διδασκάλων" . . . . καὶ πάντοτε
ἄνθρωπον ὁ φιλάνθρωπος ἐνδύεται θεὸς εἰς τὴν ἀνθρώπων σωτηρίαν, πρότερον μὲν τοὺς
προφήτας, νῦν δὲ τὴν ἐκκλησίαν ("Even as the Saviour spake and healed through
his body, so did he formerly by the prophets and so does he now by the apostles
and teachers. . . . . Everywhere the God who loves men equips man to save men,
formerly the prophets and now the church"). This passage is very instructive ;
but, as is evident, the old threefold group is already broken up, the prophets
being merely admitted and recognized as Old Testament prophets. I leave it an
open question whether the πνευματικοί of Origen (*de Orat.*, xxviii.) are connected
with our group of teachers. The τάξις προφητῶν μαρτύρων τε καὶ ἀποστόλων
(Hipp., *de Antichr.*, 59) is irrelevant in this connection.

xii. 28 or Did. xiii. (" the prophets are your high-priests "), and then at the passages in Cyprian and the literature of the following period, where the bishops are extolled as the apostles, prophets, teachers, and high-priests of the *church*, one has before one's eyes the start and the goal of one of the most important developments in early Christianity. In the case of prominent bishops like Polycarp of Smyrna, the end had long ago been anticipated ; for Polycarp was honoured by his church and throughout Asia as an " apostolic and prophetic teacher."

As for the origin of the threefold group, we have shown that while its component parts existed in Judaism, their combination cannot be explained from such a quarter. One might be inclined to trace it back to Jesus Christ himself, for he once sent out his disciples as missionaries (apostles), and he seems (according to Matt. x. 41) to have spoken of itinerant preaching prophets whom he set on foot. But the historicity of the latter passage is disputed ; [1] Jesus expressely denied the title " teacher " to his disciples (Matt. xxiii. 8) ; and an injunction such as that implied in the creation of this threefold group does not at all tally with the general preaching of Jesus or with the tenor of his instructions. We must therefore assume that the rise of the threefold group and the esteem in which it was held by the community at Jerusalem (and that from a very early period) were connected with the " Spirit " which possessed the community. Christian prophets are referred to in the context of Acts ii. (cp. verse 18) ; they made their appearance very soon (Acts iv. 36). Unfortunately, we do not know any further details, and the real origin of the enthusiastic group of " apostles, prophets, and teachers " is as obscure as that of the ecclesiastical group of " bishops, deacons, and presbyters," or of the much later complex of the so-called inferior orders of the clergy. In each case it is a question of something *consciously* created, which starts from a definite point, although it may have sprung up under pressure exerted by the actual circumstances of the situation.

---

[1] I would point, not to the words of Matt. xi. 13 ($\pi\acute{a}\nu\tau\epsilon\varsigma$ oἱ $\pi\rho o\phi\hat{\eta}\tau a\iota$ καὶ ὁ νόμος ἕως 'Ιωάννου ἐπροφήτευσαν), since that saying perhaps (see p. 333) covers a new type of prophets, but certainly to the situation in which Matt. x. 40 f. is uttered ; the latter seems to presuppose the commencement and prosecution of missionary labours.

IV

The Didachê begins by grouping together apostles and prophets (xi. 3), and directing that *the ordinance of the gospel* is to hold good as regards both of them ; but in its later chapters it groups prophets and teachers together and is silent on the apostles. From this it follows, as has been already pointed out, that the prophets had something in common with apostles on the one hand and with teachers on the other. The former characteristic may be inferred from the expression κατὰ τὸ δόγμα τοῦ εὐαγγελίου, as well as from the detailed injunctions that follow.[1] The " ordinance of the gospel " can mean only the rules which we read in Mark vi. (and parallels),[2] and this assumption is corroborated by the fact that in Matt. x., which puts together the instructions for apostles, itinerant prophets also are mentioned, who are supposed to be penniless. *To be penniless, therefore, was considered absolutely essential for apostles and prophets*; this is the view shared by 3 John, Origen, and Eusebius. John remarks that the missionaries wandered about and preached, without accepting anything from pagans. They must therefore have been instructed to " accept " from Christians. Origen (*contra Cels.*, III. ix.) writes : " Christians do all in their power to spread the faith all over the world. Some of them accordingly make it the business of their life to wander not only from city to city but from township to township and village to village, in order to gain fresh converts for the Lord. Nor could

---

[1] "Let every apostle who comes to you be received as the Lord. But he shall not remain more than one day, or, if need be, two ; if he remains for three days, he is a false prophet. And on his departure let the apostle receive nothing but bread, till he finds shelter ; if he asks for money, he is a false prophet" (Πᾶς ὁ ἀπόστολος ἐρχόμενος πρὸς ὑμᾶς δεχθήτω ὡς κύριος· οὐ μενεῖ δὲ εἰ μὴ ἡμέραν μίαν· ἐὰν δὲ ᾖ χρεία, καὶ τὴν ἄλλην· τρεῖς δὲ ἐὰν μείνῃ, ψευδοπροφήτης ἐστίν· ἐξερχόμενος δὲ ὁ ἀπόστολος μηδὲν λαμβανέτω εἰ μὴ ἄρτον ἕως οὗ αὐλισθῇ· ἐὰν δὲ ἀργύριον αἰτῇ, ψευδοπροφήτης ἐστίν, xi. 4–6).

[2] Lietzmann (*loc. cit.*, p. 486) objects that the words could not mean what apostles and prophets had to do, but simply how the community was to treat them. We are to think of passages like Matt. x. 40 f. But this view seems to me excluded by what follows (4 f.) in Did. xi. Here there is certainly an injunction to the community, but the latter is to make the δόγμα the norm for its treatment of these officials, the δόγμα laid down in the gospel ; and this is to be found in Mark vi. (and parallels).

one say they do this for the sake of gain, since they often refuse
to accept so much as the bare necessities of life ; even if necessity drives them sometimes to accept a gift, they are content
with getting their most pressing needs satisfied, although many
people are ready to give them much more than that. And if
at the present day, owing to the large number of people who
are converted, some rich men of good position and delicate
high-born women give hospitality to the messengers of the
faith, will any one venture to assert that some of the latter
preach the Christian faith merely for the sake of being honoured ?
In the early days, when great peril threatened the preachers of
the faith especially, such a suspicion could not easily have been
entertained ; and even at the present day the discredit with
which Christians are assailed by unbelievers outweighs any
honour that some of their fellow-believers show to them."
Eusebius (H.E., iii. 37) writes : " Very many of the disciples of
that age (pupils of the apostles), whose heart had been ravished
by the divine Word with a burning love for philosophy [i.e.,
asceticism], had first fulfilled the command of the Saviour and
divided their goods among the needy. Then they set out on
long journeys, performing the office of evangelists, eagerly
striving to preach Christ to those who as yet had never heard
the word of faith, and to deliver to them the holy gospels. In
foreign lands they simply laid the foundations of the faith.
That done, they appointed others as shepherds, entrusting them
with the care of the new growth, while they themselves proceeded with the grace and co-operation of God to other countries
and to other peoples." See, too, H.E., v. 10. 2, where, in connection with the end of the second century, we read : " There
were even yet many evangelists of the word eager to use their
divinely inspired zeal, after the example of the apostles, to
increase and build up the divine Word. One of these was
Pantænus " (ἔνθεον ζῆλον ἀποστολικοῦ μιμήματος συνεισφέρειν
ἐπ᾽ αὐξήσει καὶ οἰκοδομῇ τοῦ θείου λόγου προμηθούμενοι, ὧν εἷς
γενόμενος καὶ Πανταῖνος).[1] The second essential for apostles,

---

[1] The Word "evangelist" occurs in Ephes. iv. 11, Acts xxi. 8, 2 Tim. iv. 5, and
then in the Apost. Canons (ch. 19). Then it recurs in Tertull., de Præscr., iv.,
and de Corona, ix. (Hippol., de Antichr., 56, calls Luke apostle and evangelist).

laid down by the Didachê side by side with poverty, namely, *indefatigable missionary activity* (no settling down), is endorsed by Origen and Eusebius also.[1]

The Didachê informs us that these itinerant missionaries were still called apostles at the opening of the second century. Origen and Eusebius assure us that they existed during the second century, and Origen indeed knows of such even in his own day ; but the name of "apostle" was no longer borne,[2] owing to the heightened reverence felt for the original apostles, and also owing to the idea which gained currency even in the course of the second century, that the original apostles had already preached the gospel to the whole world. This idea prevented any subsequent missionaries from being apostles, since they were no longer the first to preach the gospel to the nations.[3]

We have already indicated how the extravagant estimate of the primitive apostles arose.[4] Their labours were to be looked upon as making amends for the fact that Jesus Christ did not himself labour as a missionary in every land. Furthermore, the belief that the world was near its end produced, by a sort of inevitable process, the idea that the gospel had by this time been preached everywhere; for the end could not come until

This proves that any distinction between apostles and evangelists was rarely drawn in the early ages of the church ; on the contrary, the apostles themselves were frequently described as οἱ εὐαγγελισάμενοι (cp. Gal. i. 8, *Clem. Rom.*, xliii. 1, and Polyc., *Epist.* vi. 3 ; in Barn. viii. 3 the twelve indeed, without the designation of "apostles," are thus described). Eusebius calls the evangelists the imitators of the apostles, but in the earliest period they were held by most people simply to be apostles.

[1] Apostles have merely to preach the word ; that is literally their one occupation. This conception, which Acts vi. 6 already illustrates, lasted as long as the era of the actual apostles was remembered. The Abgar-source, transcribed by Eusebius (*H.E.*, i. 13), also confirms the idea that no apostle was to receive any money, and makes one notable addition to the duties of the apostolate. When Thaddæus was summoned to preach God's word to a small group, he remarked : " I shall say nothing in the meantime, for I am sent to preach the word of God (κηρῦξαι) publicly. But assemble all thy citizens in the morning, and I will preach to them."

[2] It is, of course, merely by way of sarcasm that Cyprian speaks of Novatian's apostles (*Ep.* lv. 24).

[3] Naturally, Eusebius thus comes into conflict with his own conception of the situation ; compare ii. 3, iii. 1-4, and iii. 37.

[4] The idea of collective statements made by the apostles occurs as early as the Didachê (cp. its title), Jude and 2 Peter, and Justin (*Apol.*, i. 62).

this universal proclamation had been accomplished, and the credit of this wonderful extension was assigned to the apostles.[1] On these grounds the prestige of the primitive apostles shot up to so prodigious a height, that their commission to the whole world was put right into the creed.[2] We are no longer in a position nowadays to determine the degree of truth underlying the belief in the apostles' world-wide mission. In any case it must have been extremely slight, and any representation of the twelve apostles as a unity organized for the purpose of world-wide labours among the Gentile churches is to be relegated without hesitation to the province of legend.[3]

Unfortunately, we know next to nothing of any details con-

---

[1] Cp. Tert., *de Carne*, ii. : "Apostolorum erat tradere." The idea of the apostolic tradition is primitive and not destitute of an historical germ ; it was first of all in Rome, and certainly under the influence of the genius of the city and the empire, that this idea was condensed and applied to the conception and theory of a tradition which transmitted itself through an apostolic succession. Afterwards this theory became the common possession of Christianity and constituted the idea of "catholicity." Origen (cp. *de Princ.*, iv. 9) defends it as confidently as Tertullian ("Regula et disciplina quam ab Jesu Christo traditam sibi apostoli per successionem posteris quoque suis sanctam ecclesiam docentibus tradidcrunt ").

[2] Details in my *Lehrbuch der Dogmengeschichte*, I.[(3)] pp. 153-156 [Eng. trans,. i. pp. 160 f.] ; I shall return to the legends of the mission in Book IV. Chap. I., but without attempting to exhaust the endless materials ; all I shall do is to touch upon them. The most extreme and eccentric allusion to the importance of the twelve apostles occurs in the *Pistis Sophia*, ch. 7 (Schmidt, p. 7), where Jesus says to the twelve : "Be glad and rejoice, for when I set about making the world, I was in command of twelve powers from the very first (as I have told you from the beginning), which I had taken from the twelve saviours (σωτῆρες) of the treasure of light according to the commandment of the first mystery. These, then, I deposited in the womb of your mother, while I entered the world—these that live now in your bodies. For these powers were given to you in the sight of all the world, since ye are to be the deliverers of the world, that ye may be able to endure . . . . the threats of the archons of the world, and the sufferings of the world, your perils and all your persecutions." Compare ch. 8 (p. 9) : "Be glad then and rejoice, for ye are blessed above all men on earth, since it is ye who are to be the deliverers of the world." In Clement's *Eclogues* (c. 16) also the apostles are usually called σωτῆρες τῶν ἀνθρώπων ("saviours of men"). Origen calls them "kings" (Hom. xii. 2, *in Num.*, vol. x. pp. 132 f.), and he does not reject the interpretation (*de Princ.*, ii. 8. 5) of the saying "My soul is sorrowful even unto death" which made Jesus think of the apostles as his soul. The "multitudo credentium" are the body of Christ, the apostles are his soul !

[3] It is worth noting that, according to the early Christian idea, the Mosaic law also had spread over the whole world. In their world-wide preaching, the apostles therefore came upon the results produced by that law (see, for example, the statements of Eusebius in the first book of his church-history).

cerning the missionaries (apostles) and their labours during the second century; their very names are lost, with the exception of Pantænus, the Alexandrian teacher, and his mission to "India" (Eus., *H.E.*, v. 10). Perhaps we should look upon Papylus in the Acts of Carpus and Papylus as a missionary; for in his cross-examination he remarks: ἐν πάσῃ ἐπαρχίᾳ καὶ πόλει εἰσίν μου τέκνα κατὰ θεόν (ch. 32, " in every province and city I have children according to God "). Attalus in Lyons was probably a missionary also (Eus., *H.E.*, v. i.). Neither of these cases is, however, beyond doubt. If we could attach any value to the romance of Paul and Thecla (in the *Acta Pauli*), *one* name would come up in this connection, viz., that of Thecla, the only woman who was honoured with the title of ἡ ἀπόστολος. But it is extremely doubtful if any basis of fact, apart from the legend itself, underlies the veneration felt for her, although the legend itself *may* contain some nucleus of historic truth. Origen knows of cases within his own experience in which a missionary or teacher was subsequently chosen to be bishop by his converts,[1] but the distinction between missionary and teacher had been blurred by this time, and the old triad no longer existed.

Yet even though we cannot describe the labours of the apostles during the second century—and by the opening of the third century only stragglers from this class were still to be met with—the creation and the career of this heroic order form of themselves a topic of supreme interest. Their influence need not, of course, be overestimated. For, in the first place, we find the Didachè primarily concerned with laying down rules to prevent abuses in the apostolic office; so that by the beginning of the second century, as we are not surprised to learn, it must have been already found necessary to guard against irregularity. In the second place, had apostles continued to play an important part in the second century, the stereotyped conception of the primitive apostles, with their fundamental and really exhaustive labours in the mission-field, could never have arisen at all or become so widely current. Probably, then, it is

---

[1] Cp. Hom. xi. 4, *in Num.*, vol. x. p. 113: "Sicut in aliqua, verbi gratia, civitate, ubi nondum Christiani nati sunt, si accedat aliquis et docere incipiat, laboret, instruat, adducat ad fidem, et ipse postmodum iis quos docuit princeps et episcopus fiat."

not too hazardous to affirm that the church really had never more than two apostles in the true sense of the term, one great and the other small, viz., Paul and Peter—unless perhaps we add John of Ephesus. The chief credit for the spread of Christianity scarcely belongs to the other regular apostles, penniless and itinerant, otherwise we should have heard of them, or at least have learnt their names; whereas even Eusebius was as ignorant about them as we are to-day. The chief credit for the spread of Christianity is due to those who were *not* regular apostles, and also to the "teachers."

<h2 style="text-align:center">V</h2>

Though the prophets,[1] according to the Didachê and other witnesses, had also to be penniless like the apostles, they are not to be reckoned among the regular missionaries. Still, like the teachers, they were indirectly of importance to the mission, as their charismatic office qualified them for preaching the word of God, and, indeed, put them in the way of such a task. Their inspired addresses were listened to by pagans as well as by Christians, and Paul assumes (1 Cor. xiv. 24), not without reason, that the former were specially impressed by the prophet's harangue and by his power of searching the hearer's heart. Down to the close of the second century the prophets retained their position in the church;[2] but the Montanist movement brought

---

[1] In the Gentile church they were steadily differentiated from the seers or μάντεις (cp. Hermas, *Mand.*, xi.; Iren. Fragm., 23 [cd. Harvey]: οὗτος οὐκέτι ὡς προφήτης ἀλλ᾽ ὡς μάντις λογισθήσεται). Still, the characteristics are not always distinctive or distinct. The faculty of prediction ("aliquid praenuntiare"), *e.g.*, belongs to the prophet as well as to the seer, according to Tertullian (*de Carne*, ii.).

[2] Tertullian (*de Præscr.*, iii.) no longer reckons them as a special class: "Quid ergo, si episcopus, si diaconus, si vidua, si virgo, si doctor, si etiam martyr lapsus a regula fuerit?" ("What if a bishop, a deacon, a widow, a virgin, a teacher, or even a martyr, have fallen away from the rule of faith?"). In a very ancient Christian fragment discovered by Grenfell and Hunt (*The Oxyrhynchus Papyri*, I., 1898, No. 5, pp. 8 f.; cp. *Sitzungsber. der Preuss. Akad.*, 1898, pp. 516 f.) these words occur: τὸ προφητικὸν πνεῦμα τὸ σωματεῖόν ἐστιν τῆς προφητικῆς τάξεως, ὃ ἐστιν τὸ σῶμα τῆς σαρκὸς Ἰησοῦ Χριστοῦ τὸ μιγὲν τῇ ἀνθρωπότητι διὰ Μαρίας. The fragment perhaps belongs to Melito's last treatise περὶ προφητείας, but unfortunately it is so short and abrupt that no certain opinion is possible. For the expression ἡ προφητικὴ τάξις, cp. Serapion of Antioch's *Ep. ad Caricum et Pontium* (Eus., *H.E.*, v. 19. 2): ἡ ἐνέργεια τῆς ψευδοῦς ταύτης τάξεως τῆς ἐπιλεγομένης νέας προφητείας. The expression must have been common about 200 A.D.

early Christian prophecy at once to a head and to an end. Sporadic traces of it are still to be found in later years,[1] but such prophets no longer possessed any significance for the church; in fact, they were quite summarily condemned by the clergy as false prophets. Like the apostles, the prophets occupied a delicate and risky position. It was easy for them to degenerate. The injunctions of the Didachê (ch. xi.) indicate the sort of precautions which were considered necessary, even in the opening of the second century, to protect the churches against fraudulent prophets of the type sketched by Lucian in *Proteus Peregrinus*; and the latter volume agrees with the Didachê, inasmuch as it describes Peregrinus in his prophetic capacity as now settled in a church, now itinerating in company with Christians who paid him special honour—for prophets were not confined to any single church. Nor were even prophetesses awanting; they were to be met with inside the catholic church as well as among the gnostics in particular.[2]

The materials and sources available for a study of the early Christian prophets are extremely voluminous, and the whole subject is bound up with a number of questions which are still unsettled; for example, the relation of the Christian prophets to the numerous categories of the pagan prophets (Egyptian, Syrian, and Greek) who are known to us from the literature and inscriptions of the period, is a subject which has never yet been investigated.[3] However, these materials are of no use for

---

[1] Cp. Firmilian in Cyprian's *Epist.* lxxv. 10.

[2] From the Coptic version of the *Acta Pauli* (Paul's correspondence with the Corinthian church) we find that the prophet of the Corinthian church who is mentioned there was not a man but a woman (named Theonœ, not Theonas). Another prophetess, called Myrte, occurs in these Acts. Origen writes (Hom. v. 2, *in Judic.*, vol. xi. p. 250): "Though many judges in Israel are said to have been men, none is mentioned as a prophet save Deborah. This very fact affords great comfort to the female sex, and incites them not to despair by any means of being capable of prophetic grace, despite the weakness of their sex; they are to understand and believe that purity of mind, not difference of sex, wins this grace" (Cum plurimi iudices viri in Israel fuisse referuntur, de nullo eorum dicitur quia propheta fuerit, nisi de Debbora muliere. praestat et in hoc non minimam consolationem mulierum sexui etiam prima ipsius literae facies, et provocat eas, ut nequaquam pro infirmitate sexus desperent, etiam prophetiae gratiae capaces se fieri posse, sed intelligant et credant quod meretur hanc gratiam puritas mentis non diversitas sexus).

[3] As impostors mingled here and there with the prophets, no sharp distinction can have existed. Celsus (Orig., *c. Cels.* VII., ix., xi.) gives an extremely

our immediate purpose, as no record of the missionary labours of the prophets is extant.

VI.

The Didachê mentions teachers twice (xiii. 2, xv. 1-2), and, what is more, as a special class within the churches. Their ministry was the same as that of the prophets, a ministry of the word ; consequently they belonged to the "honoured" class, and, like the prophets, could claim to be supported. On the other hand, they were evidently not obliged to be penniless ;[1] nor did they wander about, but resided in a particular community.

These statements are corroborated by such passages in our sources (see above, pp. 336 f.) as group apostles, prophets, and teachers together, and further, by a series of separate testimonies which show that to be a teacher was a vocation in Christianity, and that the teacher enjoyed great repute not only in the second century, but partly also, as we shall see, in later years. First of all, the frequency with which we find authors protesting that they are not writing in the capacity of teachers (or issuing instructions) proves how serious was the veneration paid to a

interesting description of the prophets, as follows : "There are *many* who, though they are people of no vocation, with the utmost readiness, and on the slightest occasion, both within and without the sacred shrines, behave as if they were seized by the prophetic ecstasy. Others, roaming like tramps throughout cities and camps, perform in the same fashion in order to excite notice. Each is wont to cry, each is glib at proclaiming, 'I am God,' 'I am the Son of God' (παῖς θεοῦ), or 'I am the Spirit of God,' 'I have come because the world is on the verge of ruin, and because you, O men, are perishing in your iniquities. But I would save you, and ye shall see me soon return with heavenly power ! Blessed is he who now honours me ! All others I will commit to everlasting fire, cities and lands and their inhabitants. Those who will not now awake to the punishments awaiting them, shall repent and groan in vain one day. But those who believe in me, I will preserve eternally. . . . .' These mighty threats are further mixed up with weird, half-crazy, and perfectly senseless words, in which no rational soul can discover any meaning, so obscure and unintelligible they are. Yet the first comer who is an idiot or an impostor can interpret them to suit his own fancy ! . . . . These so-called prophets, whom more than once I have heard with my own ears, confessed their foibles to me, after I had exposed them, and acknowledged that they had themselves invented their incomprehensible jargon."

[1] When Origen, in the story told by Eusebius (*H.E.*, vi. 3), carried out the gospel saying, not to have two staves, etc., it was a voluntary resolve upon his part. Shortly before that, we are told how he purchased an annuity by selling his books, in order to free himself from all care about a livelihood.

true teacher, and how he was accorded the right of issuing injunctions that were universally valid and authoritative. Thus Barnabas asserts: ἐγὼ δὲ οὐχ ὡς διδάσκαλος ἀλλ' ὡς εἷς ὑμῶν ὑποδείξω (i. 8, " I am no teacher, but as one of yourselves I will demonstrate "); and again, " Fain would I write many things, but not as a teacher" (πολλὰ δὲ θέλων γράφειν οὐχ ὡς διδάσκαλος, iv. 9).[1] Ignatius explains, οὐ διατάσσομαι ὑμῖν ὡς ὤν τις . . . . προσλαλῶ ὑμῖν ὡς συνδιδασκαλίταις μου (" I do not command you as if I were somebody . . . . I address you as my school-fellows," ad Eph., iii. 1);[2] and Dionysius of Alexandria in the third century still writes (Ep. ad Basil.): ἐγὼ δὲ οὐχ ὡς διδάσκαλος, ἀλλ' ὡς μετὰ πάσης ἁπλότητος προσῆκον ἡμᾶς ἀλλήλοις διαλέγεσθαι (" I speak not as a teacher, but with all the simplicity with which it befits us to address each other ").[3] The warning of the epistle of James (iii. 1): μὴ πολλοὶ διδάσκαλοι γίνεσθε, proves how this vocation was coveted in the church, a vocation of which Hermas pointedly remarks (Sim., IX. xxv. 2) that its members had received the holy Spirit.[4] Hermas also refers (Mand., IV. iii. I) to a saying which he had heard from certain teachers with regard to baptism, and which the angel proceeds deliberately to endorse; this proves that there were teachers of high repute at Rome in the days of Hermas. An elaborate charge to teachers is given in the pseudo-Clementine Epist. de Virginitate (I. 11): " Doctores esse volunt et disertos sese ostendere . . . . neque adtendunt ad id quod dicit [Scriptura]: 'Ne multi inter vos sint doctores, fratres, neque omnes sitis prophetæ.' . . . . Timeamus ergo iudicium quod imminet doctoribus; grave enim vero iudicium subituri sunt doctores illi, qui docent[5] et non faciunt, et illi

---

[1] On the other hand, in ix. 9 he Writes: οἶδεν ὁ τὴν ἔμφυτον δωρεὰν τῆς διδαχῆς αὐτοῦ θέμενος ἐν ὑμῖν (" He knoweth, who hath placed in you the innate gift of his teaching ").

[2] Note διατάσσομαι in this passage, the term used by Ignatius of the apostles (Trall, iii. 3, Rom., iv. 3; cp. Trall., vii. 1, τὰ διατάγματα τῶν ἀποστόλων).

[3] See further, Commodian, Instruct., ii. 22. 15 : " Non sum ego doctor, sed lex docet "; ii. 16. 1 : " Si quidem doctores, dum exspectant munera vestra aut timent personas, laxant singula vobis ; et ego non doceo."

[4] Διδάσκαλοι οἱ διδάξαντες σεμνῶς καὶ ἁγνῶς τὸν λόγον τοῦ κυρίου. . . . . καθὼς καὶ παρέλαβον τὸ πνεῦμα τὸ ἅγιον.

[5] Cp. Did., xi. 10: προφήτης, εἰ ἃ διδάσκει οὐ ποιεῖ, ψευδοπροφήτης ἐστί (" If a prophet does not practise what he teaches, he is a false prophet ").

qui Christi nomen mendaciter assumunt dicuntque se docere veritatem, at circumcursant et temere vagantur seque exaltant atque gloriantur in sententia carnis suae. . . . . Verumtamen si accepisti sermonem scientiae aut sermonem doctrinae aut prophetias aut ministerii, laudetur deus . . . . illo igitur charismate, quod a deo accepisti (sc. χαρίσματι διδαχῆς), illo inservi fratribus pneumaticis, prophetis, qui dignoscant dei esse verba ea, quae loqueris, et enarra quod accepisti charisma in ecclesiastico conventu ad aedificationem fratrum tuorum in Christo" ("They would be teachers and show off their learning . . . . and they heed not what the Scripture saith : ' Be not many teachers, my brethren, and be not all prophets.' . . . . Let us therefore dread that judgment which hangs over teachers. For indeed a severe judgment shall those teachers undergo who teach but do not practise, as also those who falsely take on themselves the name of Christ, and say they are speaking the truth, whereas they gad round and wander rashly about and exalt themselves and glory in the mind of their flesh. . . . . But if thou hast received the word of knowledge, or of teaching, or of prophecy, or of ministry, let God be praised. . . . . Therefore with that spiritual gift received from God, do thou serve thy brethren the spiritual ones, even the prophets who detect that thy words are the words of God ; and publish the gift thou hast received in the assembly of the church to edify thy brethren in Christ"). From this passage it is plain that there were still teachers (and prophets) in the churches, that the former ranked below the latter (or had to submit to a certain supervision), and that, as we see from the whole chapter, gross abuses had to be dealt with in this order of the ministry. As was natural, this order of independent teachers who were in the service of the entire church produced at an early period prominent individuals who credited themselves with an exceptionally profound knowledge of the δικαιώματα τοῦ θεοῦ (ordinances of God), and consequently addressed themselves, not to all and sundry, but to the advanced or educated, i.e., to any select body within Christendom. *Insensibly, the charismatic teaching also passed over into the profane,* and this marked the point at which Christian teachers as an institution had to undergo, and did undergo, a change. It was inevitable that within Christianity schools should be founded similar to the numerous contemporary schools which had been established by Greek and Roman philosophers. They might remain embedded, as it were, in Christianity; but they might also develop very readily in a sectarian direction, since this divisive tendency beset any school whatsoever. Hence the efforts of itinerant Christian apologists who, like Justin [1] and Tatian,[2] set up schools in the larger towns; hence scholastic establishments such as those of Rhodon and the two Theodoti at Rome;[3] hence the enterprise of many so-called "gnostics"; hence, above all, the Alexandrian catechetical school (with its offshoots in Cæsarea Palest.), whose origin, of course, lies buried in obscurity,[4] and the school of Lucian at Antioch (where we hear of Συλλουκιανισταί, i.e., a union similar to those of the philosophic schools). But as a direct counterpoise to the danger of having the church split up into schools, and the gospel handed over to the secular culture, the acumen, and the

---

[1] Justin's are best known from the *Acta Justini*. He stands with his scholars before the judge Rusticus, who inquires, "Where do you meet?" Justin at first gives an evasive answer; his aim is to avoid any suggestion of the misleading idea that the Christians had a sacred spot for worship. Then, in reply to the urgent demand, "Where dost thou assemble thy scholars?" he declares: ἐγὼ ἐπάνω μένω τινὸς Μαρτίνου τοῦ Τιμωτίνου βαλανείου, καὶ παρὰ πάντα τὸν χρόνον τοῦτον—ἐπεδήμησα δὲ τῇ Ῥωμαίων πόλει τοῦτο δεύτερον—οὐ γινώσκω ἄλλην τινὰ συνέλευσιν εἰ μὴ τὴν ἐκείνου ("I stay above a certain Martinus at the Timotinian bath, and during all the time—for this is my second visit to Rome—I know of no other meeting-place but this"). Justin had also a school at Ephesus.

[2] On Tatian's school, which became sectarian, see Iren., i. 28: οἰήματι διδασ- κάλου ἐπαρθεὶς . . . . ἴδιον χαρακτῆρα διδασκαλείου συνεστήσατο. Tatian came from Justin's school.

[3] For Rhodon, see Eus., *H.E.*, v. 13 (he came from Tatian's school); for the Theodoti, whose school became sectarian and then attempted to transform itself into a church, see Eus., *H.E.*, v. 28. Praxeas, who propagated his doctrine in Asia, Rome, and Carthage, is called a "doctor" by Tertullian; cp. also the schools of Epigonus, Cleomenes, and Sabellius, in Rome.

[4] Cp. Eus., *H.E.*, v. 10: ἡγεῖτο ἐν Ἀλεξανδρείᾳ τῆς τῶν πιστῶν αὐτόθι διατριβῆς τῶν ἀπὸ παιδείας ἀνὴρ ἐπιδοξότατος, ὄνομα αὐτῷ Πανταῖνος, ἐξ ἀρχαίου ἔθους διδασκαλείου τῶν ἱερῶν λόγων παρ' αὐτοῖς συνεστῶτος ("The school of the faithful in Alexandria was under the charge of a man greatly distinguished for his learning; his name was Pantænus. A school of sacred letters has been in existence there from early days, and still survives"). Jerome (*Vir. Illust.*, 36) remarks: "Alexandriae Marco evangelista instituente semper ecclesiastici fuere doctores" ("There have always been ecclesiastical teachers instituted by Mark the evangelist at Alexandria"); Clem., *Strom.*, I. i. 11.

ambition of individual teachers,[1] the consciousness of the church finally asserted its powers, and the word "school" became almost a term of reproach for a separatist ecclesiastical community.[2] Yet the "doctors" (διδάσκαλοι)—I mean the charismatic teachers who were privileged to speak during the service, although they did not belong to the clergy—did not become extinct all at once in the communities; indeed, they maintained their position longer than the apostles or the prophets. From the outset they had been free from the "enthusiastic" element which characterized the latter and paved the way for their suppression. Besides, the distinction of "milk" and "strong meat," of different degrees of Christian σοφία, σύνεσις, ἐπιστήμη, and γνῶσις, was always indispensable.[3] In consequence of this, the διδάσκαλοι had naturally to continue in the churches till the bulk of the administrative officials or priests came to possess the qualification of teachers, and until the bishop (together with the presbyters) assumed the task of educating and instructing the church. In several even of the large churches this did not take place till pretty late, i.e., till the second half of the third

---

[1] Hermas boasts that the good teachers (Sim., ix. 25. 2) "kept nothing at all back for evil intent—μηδὲν ὅλως ἐνοσφίσαντο εἰς ἐπιθυμίαν πονηράν : on such teachers as introduced διδαχαὶ ξέναι (strange doctrines), however, see Sim., ix. 19. 2-3, viii. 6. 5 ; Vis., iii. 7. 1. It is noticeable that in the famous despatch of Constantine to Alexandria, which was intended to quiet the Arian controversy, the emperor holds up the practice of the philosophic schools as an example to the disputants (Eus., Vita Const., ii. 71) ; still, he does so in a way that shows plainly that nothing lay farther from him than any idea of the church as a philosophic school : ἵνα μικρῷ παραδείγματι τὴν ὑμετέραν σύνεσιν ὑπομνήσαιμι, ἴστε δήπου καὶ τοὺς φιλοσόφους αὐτοὺς ὡς ἑνὶ μὲν ἅπαντες δόγματι συντίθενται, πολλάκις δὲ ἐπειδὰν εἴ τινι τῶν ἀποφάσεων μέρει διαφωνῶσιν, εἰ καὶ τῇ τῆς ἐπιστήμης ἀρετῇ χωρίζονται, τῇ μέντοι τοῦ δόγματος ἑνώσει πάλιν εἰς ἀλλήλους συμπνέουσιν ("Let me recall to your minds a slight example of what I mean. You know, of course, that while the philosophers all agree in one principle, they often differ in details of their argument. Yet, for all their disagreement upon the virtue of knowledge, the unity of their principles seems to reconcile them once more"). The distinction drawn between ἡ χωρίζουσα τῆς ἐπιστήμης ἀρετή and ἡ τοῦ δόγματος ἕνωσις is interesting.

[2] The Theodotian church at Rome was dubbed a school by its opponents (cp. Euseb., H.E., v. 28) ; Hippolytus inveighs against the church of Callistus, his opponent, as a διδασκαλεῖον (Philos., ix. 12, p. 458. 9 ; p. 462. 42) ; and Rhodon similarly mentions a Marcionite διδασκαλεῖον (Eus., H.E., v. 13. 4).

[3] Cp. the Pauline epistles, Hebrews, Barnabas, etc., also Did. xi. 2. : διδάσκειν εἰς τὸ προσθεῖναι δικαιοσύνην καὶ γνῶσιν κυρίου ("Teach to the increase of righteousness and the knowledge of the Lord").

century, or the beginning of the fourth. Up to that period
" teachers " can still be traced here and there.[1] Beside the new
and compact organization of the churches (with the bishops, the
college of presbyters, and the deacons) these teachers rose like
pillars of some ruined edifice which the storm had spared. They
did not fit into the new order of things, and it is interesting to
notice how they are shifted from one place to another. Tertullian's order [2] (de Præscr., iii.) is : " bishop, deacon, widow,
virgin, teacher, martyr " ! Instead of putting the teacher among
the clergy, he thus ranks him among the spiritual heroes, and,
what is more, assigns him the second place amongst them, next
to the martyrs—for the order of the list runs up to a climax.
In the Acta Perpetuæ et Felic., as well as in the Acta Saturnini
et Dativi (under Diocletian ; cp. Ruinart's Acta Martyr.,
Ratisbon, 1859, p. 418), both of African origin, we come across
the title " presbyter doctor," and from Cyprian (Ep. xxix.) we
must also infer that in some churches the teachers were ranked
in the college of presbyters, and entrusted in this capacity with
the duty of examining the readers.[3] On the other hand, in the
account given by Hippolytus in Epiph., Hær., xlii. 2 (an account
which refers to Rome in the days of Marcion), the teachers stand
beside the presbyters (not inside the college of presbyters): οἱ
ἐπιεικεῖς πρεσβύτεροι καὶ διδάσκαλοι, a position which is still
theirs in Egyptian villages after the middle of the third century.
Dionysius of Alexandria (Eus., H.E., vii. 24. 6), speaking of

---

[1] Cp. Bonwetsch's remarks on Melito (Festschrift f. Oettingen, 1898, p. 51):
"The teachers still occupy a prominent position in the church, alongside of
the bishop. Together with him, they constitute the fixed order of the church.
The same monition applies to both, that they nourish themselves on sacred knowledge and be heavenly minded. Teachers are also described as experts in Scripture,
and tenants of the teacher's chair, who are exposed by their position to the danger
of self-assumption. The bishops also occupy the teacher's chair, as the same
passages show ; but the teachers were able to retain their special position alongside
of them, perhaps because not all bishops as yet possessed the teaching gift."

[2] In de Præscr., xiv., the " doctor " is also mentioned.

[3] Cyprian (loc. cit.) also speaks of " doctores audientium," but it is impossible
to determine the relationship which he implies between these and the readers. As
catechists, the doctors were now and then ranked among the clergy, and, in fact,
in the college of presbyters. As against Lagarde, no comma is to be placed in
Clem. Homil. III. 71 after πρεσβυτέρους : τιμᾶτε πρεσβυτέρους κατηχητάς,
διακόνους χρησίμους, χήρας εὖ βεβιωκυίας (cp. above, p. 158).

his sojourn in such villages, observes, " I called together the presbyters and teachers of the brethren in the villages " (συνεκάλεσα τοὺς πρεσβυτέρους καὶ διδασκάλους τῶν ἐν ταῖς κώμαις ἀδελφῶν). As there were no bishops in these localities at that period, it follows that the teachers still shared with the presbyters the chief position in these village churches.

This item of information reaches us from Egypt; and, unless all signs deceive us, we find that in Egypt generally, and especially at Alexandria, the institution of teachers survived longest in juxtaposition with the episcopal organization of the churches (though their right to speak at services of worship had expired; see below). Teachers still are mentioned frequently in the writings of Origen,[1] and what is more, the " doctores " constitute for him, along with the " sacerdotes," quite a special order, parallel to that of priests within the church. He speaks of those " who discharge the office of teachers wisely in our midst" c. Cels., IV. lxxii.), and of "doctores ecclesiae" (Hom. XIV. in Gen., vol. ii. p. 97). In Hom. II. in Num. (vol. ii. p. 278) he remarks : " It often happens that a man of low mind, who is base and of an earthly spirit, creeps up into the high rank of the priesthood or into the chair of the doctorate, while he who is spiritual and so free from earthly ties that he can prove all things and yet himself be judged by no man—he occupies the rank of an inferior minister, or is even left among the common throng" (" Nam saepe accidit, ut is qui humilem sensum gerit et abiectum et qui terrena sapit, excelsum sacerdotii gradum vel cathedram doctoris insideat, et ille qui spiritualis est et a terrena conversatione tam liber ut possit examinare omnia et ipse a nemine iudicari, vel inferioris ministerii ordinem teneat vel etiam in plebeia multitudine relinquatur ").[2] In Hom. VI. in Levit (vol. ix. p. 219) we read : " Possunt enim et in ecclesia sacerdotes et

---

[1] And in those of Clement. According to Quis Div. Salv. xli., the Christian is to choose for himself a teacher who shall watch over him as a confessor. In Paed. III. 12. 97 Clement discusses the difference between a pedagogue and a teacher, placing the latter above the former.

[2] Here " spiritalis " (γνωστικός, πνευματικός) is in contrast to the teachers as well as to the priests. According to Clement of Alexandria, the " spiritual" person is apostle, prophet, and teacher, superior to all earthly dignitaries—a view which Origen also favours.

doctores filios generare sicut et ille qui dicebat (Gal. iv. 19), et iterum alibi dicit (1 Cor. iv. 15). Isti ergo doctores ecclesiae in huiusmodi generationibus procreandis aliquando constrictis femoralibus utuntur et abstinent a generando, cum tales invenerint auditores, in quibus sciant se fructum habere non posse!"[1] These passages from Origen, which might be multiplied (see, *e.g.*, *Hom. II. in Ezek.* and *Hom. III.* for the difference between magistri and presbyteri), show that during the first thirty years of the third century there still existed at Alexandria an order of teachers side by side with the bishop, the presbyters, and the deacons. But indeed we scarcely need the writings of Origen at all. There is Origen himself, his life, his lot—and that is the plainest evidence of all. For what was the man himself but a διδάσκαλος τῆς ἐκκλησίας, busily travelling as a teacher upon endless missions, in order to impress true doctrine on the mind, or to safeguard it? What was the battle of his life against that "ambitious" and utterly uneducated bishop Demetrius, but the conflict of an independent teacher of *the church* with the bishop of an *individual community*? And when, in the course of this conflict, which ended in a signal triumph for the hierarchy, a negative answer was given to this question among other things, viz., whether the "laity" could give addresses in the church, in presence of the bishops—was not the affirmative answer, which was still given by bishops like Alexander and Theoktistus, who pointed to the primitive usage,[2] simply the final echo of an organization of the Christian churches older

---

[1] " For even in the church, priests and doctors can beget children, even as he who wrote Gal. iv. 19, and again in another place 1 Cor. iv. 15. Therefore such doctors of the church refrain from begetting offspring, when they find an irresponsive audience!"

[2] Eus., *H.E.*, vi. 19. Their arguments prove that the right of "laymen" (for the teachers were laymen) to speak at services of worship had become extinct throughout Egypt, Palestine, and most of the provinces, for the two bishops friendly to this proposal had to bring evidence for the practice from a distance, and from comparatively remote churches. They write thus : "Wherever people are to be found who are able to profit the brethren, they are exhorted by the holy bishops to give addresses to the congregation ; as, for example, Euelpis has been invited by Neon in Laranda, Paulinus by Celsus in Iconium, and Theodorus by Atticus in Synnada, all of whom are our blessed brethren. Probably this has also been done in other places unknown to us." The three persons mentioned in this passage are the last of the "ancient" teachers who are known to us.

and more venerable than the clerical organization which was already covering all the field? During the course of the third century, the "teachers" were thrust out of the church, *i.e.*, out of the service;[1] some of them may have even been fused with the readers.[2] No doubt, the order of teachers had developed in such a way as to incur at a very early stage the exceptionally grave risk of sharply Hellenizing and thus secularizing Christianity. The διδάσκαλοι of the third century may have been very unlike the διδάσκαλοι who had ranked as associates of the prophets. But Hellenizing was hardly the decisive reason for abolishing the order of teachers in the churches; here, as elsewhere, the change was due to the episcopate with its intolerance of any office that would not submit to its strict control and allow itself to be incorporated in the simple and compact organization of the hierarchy headed by the bishop. After the middle of the third century, not all, but nearly all, the teachers of the church were clerics, while the instruction of the catechumens was undertaken either by the bishop himself or by a presbyter. The organizing of the catechetical system gradually put an end to the office of independent teachers.

The early teachers of the church were missionaries as well;[3] pagans as well as catechumens entered their schools and listened to their teaching. We have definite information upon this point in the case of Justin (see above), but Tatian also delivered

---

[1] In this connection reference may perhaps be made to the important statement of Alexander, bishop of Alexandria (in Theodoret's *H.E.*, i. 3), that Lucian remained outside the church at Antioch (ἀποσυνάγωγος) during the régime of three bishops. Lucian was the head of a school.

[2] On this order and office, originally a charismatic one, which under certain circumstances embraced the further duty of explaining the Scriptures, cp. the evidence I have stated in *Texte u. Untersuch.*, ii. 5, pp. 57 f., "On the Origin of the Readership and the other Lower Orders" [Eng. trans. in *Sources of the Apostolic Canons*, by Wheatley and Owen (Messrs A. & C. Black)].

[3] Tertullian complains that the heretical teachers, instead of engaging in mission work, merely tried to win over catholic Christians; cp. *de Præscr.*, xlii. : "De verbi autem administratione quid dicam, cum hoc sit negotium haereticis, non ethnicos convertendi, sed nostros evertendi. Ita fit, ut ruinas facilius operentur stantium aedificiorum quam exstructionem iacentium ruinarum " ("But concerning the ministry of the Word, What shall I say? for heretics make it their business not to convert pagans but to subvert our people. . . . . Thus they can effect the ruin of buildings which are standing more easily than the erection of ruins that lie low "). See also *adv. Marc.*, ii. 1. I shall return to this complaint later on.

his "Address" in order to inform the pagan public that he had
become a Christian teacher, and we have a similar tradition of
the missionary work done by the heads of the Alexandrian
catechetical school in the way of teaching. Origen, too, had
pagan hearers whom he instructed in the elements of Christian
doctrine (cp. Eus., *H.E.*, vi. 3); indeed, it is well known that
even Julia Mamæa, the queen-mother, had him brought to
Antioch that she might listen to his lectures (Eus., *H.E.*, vi. 21).
Hippolytus also wrote her a treatise, of which fragments have
been preserved in a Syriac version. When one lady of quality
in Rome was arraigned on a charge of Christianity, her teacher
Ptolemæus (διδάσκαλος ἐκείνης τῶν Χριστιανῶν μαθημάτων
γενόμενος) was immediately arrested also (Justin, *Apol.*, II. ii.).
In the African *Acta Saturnini et Dativi*, dating from Diocletian's
reign, we read (Ruinart's *Acta Mart.*, Ratisbon, 1859, p. 417)
the following indictment of the Christian Dativus, laid by
Fortunatianus (" vir togatus ") with regard to his sister who had
been converted to Christianity : " This is the fellow who during
our father's absence, while we were studying here, perverted our
sister Victoria, and took her away from the glorious state of
Carthage with Secunda and Restituta as far as the colony of
Abitini ; he never entered our house without beguiling the girls'
minds with some wheedling arguments" (" Hic est qui per
absentiam patris noster, nobis hic studentibus, sororem nostram
Victoriam seducens, hinc de splendidissima Carthaginis civitate
una cum Secunda et Restituta ad Abitinensem coloniam secum
usque perduxit, quique nunquam domum nostram ingressus est,
nisi tunc quando quibusdam persuasionibus puellares animos
illiciebat ").   This task also engaged the whole activity of
the Christian apologists. The effects upon the inner growth
of Christianity we may estimate very highly.[1] But we know

---

[1] It was the task of apologists and teachers to exhibit the Christian faith in its
various stages, and to prove it.   Rhodon (Eus., *H.E.*, v. 13) says of the gnostic
Apelles : διδάσκαλος εἶναι λέγων οὐκ ᾔδει τὸ διδασκόμενον ὑπ' αὐτοῦ κρατύνειν
(" Though calling himself a teacher, he knew not how to confirm what he
taught ").   "Non difficile est doctori," says Cyprian (*Ep.* lxxiii. 3), "vera et
legitima insinuare ci qui haeretica pravitate damnata et ecclesiastica veritate
comperta ad hoc venit ut discat, ad hoc discit ut vivat" (" It is not hard for a
teacher to instil what is true and genuine into the mind of a man who, having
condemned heretical evil and learnt the church's truth, comes to learn, and learns

nothing of the scale on which they worked among pagans. We have no information as to whether the apologies really reached those to whom they were addressed, notably the emperors ; or, whether the educated public took any notice of them. Tertullian bewails the fact that only Christians read Christian literature ("ad nostras litteras nemo venit nisi iam Christianus," *de Testim.*, i.), and this would be true of the apologies as well. Celsus, so far as I know, never takes them into account, though there were a number of them extant in his day. He only mentions the dialogue of Aristo of Pella ; but that cannot have been typical, otherwise it would have been preserved.

The apologists set themselves a number of tasks, emphasizing and elucidating now one, now another aspect of the truth. They criticized the legal procedure of the state against Christians ; they contradicted the revolting charges, moral and political, with which they were assailed ; they criticized the pagan mythology and the state-religion ; they defined, in very different ways, their attitude to Greek philosophy, and tried

in order that he may live "). Everyone knows the importance of apologetic to the propaganda of Judaism, and Christians entered on a rich inheritance at this and at other points, since their teachers were able to take over the principles and material of Jewish apologetic. Directly or indirectly, most of the Christian apologists probably depended on Philo and the apologetic volumes of selections made by Alexandrian Judaism as well as philosophical compendia of criticisms upon ancient mythology. As for the dissemination of apologies throughout the church, Justin's at least was read very soon in very different sections of the church ; Irenæus knew it in Gaul, Tertullian in Carthage, probably Athenagoras in Athens and Theophilus in Antioch. By the end of the second century Tertullian had a whole corpus of apologetic writings at his command ; cp. *de Testim.*, i. : "Nonnulli quidem, quibus de pristina litteratura et curiositatis labor et memoriae tenor perseveravit, ad eum modum opuscula penes nos condiderunt, commemorantes et contestificantes in singula rationem et originem et traditionem et argumenta sententiarum, per quae recognosci possit nihil nos aut novum aut portentosum suscepisse, de quo non etiam communes et publicae litterae ad suffragium nobis patrocinentur, si quid aut erroris eiecimus aut aequitatis admisimus" ("Some, indeed, who have busied themselves inquisitively with ancient literature, and kept it in their memories, have published works of this very kind which we possess. In these they record and attest the exact nature, origin, tradition, and reasons of their opinions, from which it is plain that we have not admitted any novelty or extravagance, for which we cannot claim the support of ordinary and familiar writings ; this applies alike to our exclusion of error and to our admission of truth ").

partly to side with it, partly to oppose it ;[1] they undertook an analysis of ordinary life, public and private ; they criticized the achievements of culture and the sources as well as the consequences of conventional education. Still further, they stated the essence of Christianity, its doctrines of God, providence, virtue, sin, and retribution, as well as the right of their religion to lay claim to revelation and to uniqueness. They developed the Logos-idea in connection with Jesus Christ, whose ethics, preaching, and victory over demons they depicted. Finally, they tried to furnish proofs for the metaphysical and ethical content of Christianity, to rise from a mere opinion to a reasoned conviction, and at the same time—by means of the Old Testament—to prove that their religion was not a mere novelty but the primitive religion of mankind.[2] The most important of these proofs included those drawn from the fulfilment of prophecy, from the moral energy of the faith, from its enlightenment of the reason, and from the fact of the victory over demons.

The apologists also engaged in public discussions with pagans (Justin, *Apol.* II., and the Cynic philosopher Crescens; Minucius Felix and Octavius) and Jews (Justin, *Dial. with Trypho*; Tertull., *adv. Jud.*, i.). In their writings some claimed the right of speaking in the name of God and truth; and although (strictly speaking) they do not belong to the charismatic teachers, they describe themselves as " taught of God."[3]

The schools established by these teachers could only be regarded by the public and the authorities as philosophic schools;

---

[1] Three different attitudes to Greek philosophy were adopted : it contained real elements of truth, due to the working of the Logos ; or these were plagiarized from the Old Testament ; or they were simply demonic replicas of the truth, as in the case of pagan mythology.

[2] Literary fabrications, which were not uncommon in other departments (cp. the interpolation in Josephus, etc.), played a rôle of their own here. But the forgeries which appeared in the second century seem to me to be for the most part of Jewish origin. In the third century things were different.

[3] Compare, *e.g.*, Aristides, *Apol.* ii. : " God himself granted me power to speak about him wisely." Diogn., *Ep.* I : τοῦ θεοῦ τοῦ καὶ τὸ λέγειν καὶ τὸ ἀκούειν ἡμῖν χορηγοῦντος αἰτοῦμαι δοθῆναι ἐμοὶ μὲν εἰπεῖν οὕτως, κ.τ.λ. ("God, who supplies us both with speech and hearing, I pray to grant me utterance so as," etc.).

indeed, the apologists avowed themselves to be philosophers [1] and their doctrine a philosophy,[2] so that they participated here and there in the advantages enjoyed by philosophic schools, particularly in the freedom of action they possessed. This never can have lasted any time, however. Ere long the Government was compelled to note that the preponderating element in these schools was not scientific but practical, and that they were the outcome of the illegal " religio Christiana."[3]

VII

"Plures efficimur quotiens metimur a vobis; semen est sanguis Christianorum . . . . illa ipsa obstinatio, quam exprobratis magistra est"—so Tertullian cries to the authorities (*Apol.*, l. : "The oftener we are mown down by you, the larger grow our numbers. The blood of Christians is a seed. . . . . That very obstinacy which you reprobate is our instructress "). The most numerous and successful missionaries of the Christian religion were not the regular teachers but Christians themselves, in virtue of their loyalty and courage. How little we hear of the former and their results! How much we hear of the effects

---

[1] Some of them even retained the mantle of the philosopher ; at an early period in the church Justin was described as "philosopher and martyr."

[2] Τὶ γάρ, says Justin's (*Dial. c. Tryph.*, i.) Trypho, *a propos* of contemporary philosophy, οὐχ οἱ φιλόσοφοι περὶ θεοῦ τὸν ἅπαντα ποιοῦνται λόγον, καὶ περὶ μοναρχίας αὐτοῖς καὶ προνοίας αἱ ζητήσεις γίγνονται ἑκάστοτε; ἢ οὐ τοῦτο ἔργον ἐστὶ φιλοσοφίας, ἐξετάζειν περὶ τοῦ θείου; ("Why not? do not the philosophers make all their discourses turn upon the subject of God, and are they not always engaged in questions about his sole rule and providence? Is not this the very business of philosophy, to inquire concerning the Godhead?"). Cp. Melito's phrase, ἡ καθ' ἡμᾶς φιλοσοφία. Similarly others.

[3] The apologists, on the one hand, complain that pagans treat Christianity *at best* as a human philosophy, and on the other hand claim that, as such, Christianity should be conceded the liberty enjoyed by a philosophy. Tertullian (*Apol.*, xlvi. f.) expatiates on this point at great length. Plainly, the question was one of practical moment, the aim of Christians being to retain, as philosophic schools and as philosophers, at least some measure of freedom, when a thoroughgoing recognition of their claims could not be insisted upon. "Who forces a philosopher to sacrifice or take an oath or exhibit useless lamps at noon? No one. On the contrary, they pull down your gods openly, and in their writings arraign your religious customs, and you applaud them for it ! Most of them even snarl at the Cæsars." The number of sects in Christianity also confirmed well-disposed opponents in the belief that they had to deal with philosophic schools (c. xlvii.)

produced by the latter ! Above all, every confessor and martyr was a missionary; he not merely confirmed the faith of those who were already won, but also enlisted new members by his testimony and his death. Over and again this result is noted in the Acts of the martyrs, though it would lead us too far afield to recapitulate such tales. While they lay in prison, while they stood before the judge, on the road to execution, and by means of the execution itself, they won people for the faith. Ay, and even after death. One contemporary document (cp. Euseb. vi. 5) describes how Potamiæna, an Alexandrian martyr during the reign of Septimius Severus, appeared immediately after death even to non-Christians in the city, and how they were converted by this vision. This is by no means incredible. The executions of the martyrs (legally carried out, of course) must have made an impression which startled and stirred wide circles of people, suggesting to their minds the question: Who is to blame, the condemned person or the judge?[1] Looking at the earnestness, the readiness for sacrifice, and the steadfastness of these Christians, people found it difficult to think that *they* were to blame. Thus it was by no means an empty phrase, when Tertullian and others like him asserted that the blood of Christians was a seed.

Nevertheless, it was not merely the confessors and martyrs who were missionaries. It was characteristic of this religion that everyone who seriously confessed the faith proved of service to its propaganda.[2] Christians are to "let their light shine, that pagans may see their good works and glorify the Father in heaven." If this dominated all their life, and if they lived

---

[1] In the ancient epistle of the Smyrniote church on the death of Polycarp, we already find Polycarp a subject of general talk among the pagans. In the *Vita Cypriani* (ch. i.), also, there is the following allusion: "Non quo aliquem gentilium lateat tanti viri vita" ("Not that the life of so great a man can be unknown to any of the heathen").

[2] "Bonum huius sectae usu iam et de commercio innotuit," says Tertullian (*Apol.* xlvi.) very distinctly ("The worth of this sect is now well known for its benefits as well as from the intercourse of life"); *de Pallio*, vi. : "Elinguis philosophia vita contenta est" ("Life is content with even a tongueless philosophy"). What Tertullian makes the *pallium* say (ch. v.) is true of Christians (cp. above, p. 310). Compare also what has been already specified in Book II. Chap. IV., and what is stated afterwards in Chap. IV. of this Book.

according to the precepts of their religion, they could not be hidden at all; by their very mode of living they could not fail to preach their faith plainly and audibly.[1] Then there was the conviction that the day of judgment was at hand, and that they were debtors to the heathen. Furthermore, so far from narrowing Christianity, the exclusiveness of the gospel was a powerful aid in promoting its mission, owing to the sharp dilemma which it involved.

We cannot hesitate to believe that the great mission of Christianity was in reality accomplished by means of informal missionaries. Justin says so quite explicitly. What won him over was the impression made by the moral life which he found among Christians in general. How this life stood apart from that of pagans even in the ordinary round of the day, how it had to be or ought to be a constant declaration of the gospel— all this is vividly portrayed by Tertullian in the passage where he adjures his wife not to marry a pagan husband after he is dead (ad Uxor., II. iv.–vi.). We may safely assume, too, that women did play a leading rôle in the spread of this religion (see below, Book IV. Chap. II.). But it is impossible to see in any one class of people inside the church the chief agents of the Christian propaganda. In particular, we cannot think of the army in this connection. Even in the army there were Christians, no doubt, but it was not easy to combine Christianity and military service. Previous to the reign of Constantine, Christianity cannot possibly have been a military religion, like Mithraism and some other cults.[2]

---

[1] In the Didasc. Apost. (cp. Achelis in *Texte u. Untersuchungen*, xxv. 2. pp. 276, 80, 76 f.) we find that the church-widows made proselytes.

[2] Africa is the only country where we may feel inclined to conjecture that the relations between Christianity and the army were at all intimate.

EXCURSUS

THE apostles, as well as many of the prophets, travelled unceasingly in the interests of their mission. The journeys of
Paul from Antioch to Rome, and probably to Spain, lie in the
clear light of history, but—to judge from his letters—his
fellow-workers and companions were also continually on the

[1] Cp. Zahn's *Weltkehr und Kirche während der drei ersten Jahrhunderte* (1877);
Ramsay in *Expositor*, vol. viii., Dec. 1903, pp. 401 f. ("Travel and Correspondence
among the Early Christians") [also reproduced in his *Letters to the Seven Churches*,
1904, ch. i.], his *Church in the Roman Empire*, pp. 364 f., and his article on
"Travel" in Hastings' *Dictionary of the Bible*. "It is the simple truth that
travelling, whether for business or for pleasure, was contemplated and performed
under the empire with an indifference, confidence, and, above all, certainty which
were unknown in after centuries until the introduction of steamers and the consequent increase in ease and sureness of communication." Compare the direct and
indirect evidence of Philo, Acts, Pliny, Appian, Plutarch, Epictetus, Aristides, etc.
Iren., iv. 30. 3 : "Mundus pacem habet per Romanos, et nos sine timore in viis
ambulamus et navigamus quocumque voluerimus" ("The world enjoys peace, thanks
to the Romans, and we can travel by road and sea wherever we wish, unafraid").
One merchant boasts, in an inscription on a tomb at Hierapolis in Phrygia, that
he voyaged from Asia to Rome seventy-two times (*C.I.G.*, 3920). The author of
Acts treats Paul's journey from Ephesus to Jerusalem and his return by land as a
simple excursion (xviii. 21-32). No excessive length of time was needed to cover
the distances. In twelve days one could reach Alexandria from Neapolis, in seven
from Corinth. With a favourable wind, the voyage from Narbo in Southern
France to Africa occupied only five days (Sulpic. Sever., *Dial.*, i. 3) ; from the
Syrtes to Alexandria took six days (*ibid.*, i. 6). The journey by land from Ephesus
to Antioch in Syria certainly took a month (cp. Evagrius, *Hist. Eccles.*, i. 3) ; but
there were rapid messengers who traversed the empire with incredible speed. Of
one it is said (Socrates, *H.E.*, vii. 19), οὗτος ὁ Παλλάδιος μεγίστην οὖσαν τῶν
Ῥωμαίων ἀρχὴν μικρὰν ἔδειξε τῇ ταχύτητι ("This Palledius made the huge empire
of Rome seem small by his speed"). Cp. Friedländer's *Sittengeschichte* (vol. ii.,
at the beginning). For the letters, cp. Deissmann's *Bible Studies* (Eng. trans.,
1901) and Wehofer's *Untersuch. zur altchristl. Epistolographie* (in "Wiener akad.
Sitzungsber., Philos.-Hist. Klasse, cxliii., 1901," pp. 102 f). Norden (*Antike*

move, partly along with him, and partly on their own account.[1]
One thinks especially of that missionary couple, Aquila and
Priscilla. To study and state in detail the journeys of Paul
and the rest of these missionaries would lead us too far afield,
nor would it be relevant to our immediate purpose. Paul felt
that the Spirit of God drove him on, revealing his route and
destination; but this did not supersede the exercise of delibera-
tion and reflection in his own mind, and evidences of the latter
may be found repeatedly throughout his travels. Peter also
journeyed as a missionary; he too reached Rome.

However, what interests us at present is not so much the
travels of the regular missionaries as the journeys undertaken
by other prominent Christians, from which we may learn the
vitality of personal communication and intercourse throughout
the early centuries. In this connection the Roman church
became surprisingly prominent. The majority of the Christians
with whose travels we are acquainted made it their goal.[2]

Justin, Hegesippus, Julius Africanus, and Origen were
Christian teachers who were specially travelled men, i.e., men
who had gone over a large number of the churches. Justin,
who came from Samaria, stayed in Ephesus and Rome. Hegesippus reached Rome via Corinth after starting, about the
middle of the second century, on an Eastern tour occupying
several years, during which he visited many of the churches.
Julius Africanus from Emmaus in Palestine also appeared in
Edessa, Rome, and Alexandria. But the most extensive travels
were those of Origen, who, from Alexandria and Cæsarea (in
Palestine) respectively, made his appearance in Sidon, Tyre,
Bostra, Antioch, Cæsarea (in Cappadocia), Nikomedia, Athens,
Nicopolis, Rome, and other cities[3] (sometimes more than once).

Kunstprosa, p. 492) observes : " The epistolary literature, even in its artless
forms, had a far greater right to exist, according to the ideas of the age, than we
can understand at the present day. The epistle gradually became a literary
form into which any material, even of a scientific nature, could be thrown loosely
and freely."

[1] Read the sixteenth chapter of Romans in particular, and see what a number
of Paul's acquaintances were in Rome.

[2] See Caspari, Quellen z. Taufsymbol, vol. iii. (1875).

[3] Abercius turned up at Rome and on the Euphrates from Hieropolis in
Phrygia.

The following notable Christians[1] journeyed from abroad to . Rome :—

Polycarp, bishop of Smyrna (Eus., *H.E.*, iv. 14, v. 24).

Valentinus the gnostic, from Egypt (Iren., iii. 4. 3).

Cerdo the gnostic, from Syria (Iren., i. 27. 1, iii. 4. 3).

Marcion the heretic, from Sinope (Hippolytus, cited in Epiph., *Hær.*; xlii. 1 f.).

Marcellina the heretic (Iren., i. 25. 6).

Justin the apologist, from Samaria (see his *Apology*; also Euseb., *H.E.*, iv. 11).

Tatian the Assyrian (*Orat.* xxxv.).

Hegesippus, from the East (Eus., *H.E.*, iv. 22, according to the ὑπομνήματα of Hegesippus).

Euelpistus, Justin's pupil, from Cappadocia (*Acta Justini*).

Hierax, Justin's pupil, from Cappadocia (*Acta Justini*).[2]

Rhodon, from Asia (Eus., *H.E.*, v. 13).

Irenæus, from Asia (Eus., *H.E.*, v. 1–4; [*Martyr. Polyc.*, append.]).

Apelles, Marcion's pupil (Tertull., de *Præscr.*, xxx. ; though Apelles may have been born at Rome), from —— ?

Florinus, from Asia (Eus., *H.E.*, v. 15. 20).

Proclus and other Montanists from Phrygia or Asia (Eus., *H.E.*, ii. 25, iii. 31, vi. 20; Tertull., *adv. Prax.*, 1).

[Tertullian, from Carthage (de *Cultu Fem.*, i. 7; Eus., *H.E.*, ii. 2).]

Theodotus, from Byzantium (Epiph., *Hær.*, liv. 1).

Praxeas, from Asia (Tert., *adv. Prax.*, 1).

Abercius, from Hieropolis (see his inscription).

Julius Africanus, from Emmaus (Κεστοί).

Alcibiades, from Apamea in Syria (Hippol., *Philos.*, ix. 13).

[Prepon the Marcionite, an Assyrian (Hippol., *Philos.*, vii. 31).]

Epigonus, from Asia (Hipp., *Philos.*, ix. 7).

---

[1] The apostolic age is left out of account. It is very probable, I think, that Simon Magus also really came to Rome. Ignatius was taken thither from Antioch against his will, but several Christians accompanied him of their own accord. John, too, is said to have come to Rome, according to an early but poorly authenticated legend.

[2] Euelpistus and Hierax, however, were probably involuntary travellers ; they seem to have come to Rome as slaves.

Sabellius, from Pentapolis (Theodoret, *Hær. Fab.*, ii. 9).

Origen, from Alexandria (Eus., *H.E.*, vi. 14).

Many Africans, about the year 250 (Cyprian's epistles).[1]

Shortly after the middle of the second century, Melito of Sardes journeyed to Palestine (Eus., *H.E.*, iv. 26), as did Alexander from Cappadocia (Eus., *H.E.*, vi. 11) and Pionius from Smyrna (about the middle of the third century: see the *Acta Pionii*); Julius Africanus travelled to Alexandria (Eus., *H.E.*, vi. 31); Hermogenes, a heretic, emigrated from the East to Carthage (Theophilus of Antioch opposed him, as did Tertullian); Apelles went from Rome to Alexandria (Tert., *de Præscr.*, xxx.); during the Decian persecution and afterwards, Roman Christians were despatched to Carthage (see Cyprian's epistles); at the time of Valerian's persecution, several Roman brethren were in ˉAlexandria ˙(Dionys. Alex., cited by Euseb., *H.E.*, vii. 11); while Clement of Alexandria got the length of Cappadocia (Eus., *H.E.*, vi. 11). This list is incomplete, but it will give some idea of the extent to which the travels of prominent teachers promoted intercommunication.

As for the exchange of letters,[2] I must content myself with noting the salient points. Here, too, the Roman church occupies the foreground. We know of the following letters and despatches issued from it :—

The pastoral letter to Corinth (*i.e.*, the first epistle of Clement), *c.* 96 A.D.

The " Shepherd " of Hermas, which (according to *Vis.*, ii. 4) was sent to the churches abroad.

The pastoral letter of bishop Soter to Corinth (*i.e.*, the homily he sent thither, or 2 Clem.). The letter in reply, from Dionysius of Corinth, shows that Rome had for decades been in the habit of sending letters and despatches to a number of churches.

---

[1] Different motives prompted a journey to Rome. Teachers came to prosecute their vocation, others to gain influence in the local church, or to see this famous church, and so forth. Everyone was attracted to the capital by that tendency to make for the large towns which characterizes each new religious enterprise. How eagerly Paul strove to get to Rome !

[2] The churches also communicated to each other the eucharist. The earliest evidence is that of Irenæus in the letter to Victor of Rome (Eus., *H.E.*, v. 24. 15).

During the Montanist controversy, under (Soter) Eleutherus and Victor, letters passed to Asia, Phrygia, and Gaul.

During the Easter controversy, Victor issued letters to all the churches abroad.

Pontian wrote to Alexandria, assenting to the condemnation of Origen.

During the vacancy in the Papacy after bishop Fabian's death, letters passed to Carthage, to the other African churches, and to Sicily ; the Roman martyrs also wrote to the Carthaginian.

Bishop Cornelius wrote numerous letters to Africa, as well as to Antioch and Alexandria.

Bishop Stephanus wrote to Africa, Alexandria, Spain, and Gaul, as well as to all the churches abroad during the controversy over the baptism of heretics.   He also sent letters and despatches to Syria and Arabia, following the custom of his predecessors.

Letters of bishop Xystus II. to Alexandria.

Letters of bishop Dionysius to Alexandria.

A letter and despatches of bishop Dionysius to Cappadocia.

A letter of bishop Felix to Alexandria.

Letters to Antioch during the trouble caused by Paul of Samosata.

Among the non-Roman letters are to be noted : those of Ignatius to the Asiatic churches and to Rome, that written by Polycarp of Smyrna to Philippi and other churches in the neighbourhood, the large collection of those written by Dionysius of Corinth (to Athens, Lacedæmon, Nicomedia, Crete, Pontus, Rome), the large collections of Origen's letters (no longer extant), of Cyprian's (to the African churches, to Rome, Spain, Gaul, Cappadocia), and of Novatian's (to a very large number of churches throughout all Christendom : no longer extant), and of those written by Dionysius of Alexandria (preserved in fragments).[1]   Letters were sent from Cappadocia, Spain, and Gaul to Cyprian (Rome) ; the synod which gathered in Antioch to deal with Paul of Samosata, wrote to all the churches of Christendom ; and Alexander of Alexandria, as well

[1] He even wrote to the brethren in Armenia.

as Arius, wrote letters to a large number of churches in the Eastern empire.[1]

The more important Christian writings also circulated with astonishing rapidity.[2] Out of the wealth of material at our disposal, the following instances may be adduced :—

Ere the first half of the second century expired, the four gospels appear to have reached the majority, or at any rate a very large number, of churches throughout the empire.

A collection of Paul's letters was already known to Clement of Rome, Ignatius, Polycarp, and all the leading gnostics.

The first epistle of Clement (addressed to Corinth) was in the hands of Polycarp (at Smyrna), and was known to Irenæus at Lyons, as well as to Clement of Alexandria.

A few weeks or months after the epistles of Ignatius were composed, they were collected and despatched to Philippi; Irenæus in Lyons and Origen in Alexandria were acquainted with them.

The Didachê was circulated in the second century through East and West alike.

The "Shepherd" of Hermas, in its complete form, was well known in Lyons, Alexandria, and Carthage, even in the second century

The *Apology* and other works of Justin were known to Irenæus at Lyons, and to Tertullian at Carthage, etc. Tatian was read in Alexandria.

By the close of the second century, writings of Melito, bishop of Sardes (during the reign of Marcus Aurelius) were read in Ephesus, Alexandria, Rome, and Carthage.

As early as about the year 200 A.D., writings of Irenæus (who wrote *c.* 190) were read in Rome and Alexandria, whilst, like Justin, he was known at a later period to Methodius in Lycia.

The writings of several authors in Asia Minor during the

---

[1] Evidence for all these letters will be found in my *Geschichte der altchristlichen Litteratur*, vol. i.

[2] On this point also I may refer to my History of the literature, where the ancient testimony for each writing is carefully catalogued. Down to about the reign of Commodus the number of Christian writings is not very striking, if one leaves out the heretical productions ; but when the latter are included, as they must be, it is very large.

reign of Marcus Aurelius were read in Alexandria, Carthage, and Rome.

The "Antitheses" of the heretic Marcion were known to all the larger churches in the East and West by the end of the second century.

The apocryphal *Acta Pauli*, originating in Asia, was probably read in all the leading churches, and certainly in Rome, Carthage, and Alexandria, by the end of the second century.

Numerous writings of the Roman Hippolytus were circulated throughout the East. What a large number of Christian writings were gathered from all parts of the world in the library at Cæsarea (in Palestine) is known to us from the Church History of Eusebius, which was written from the material in this collection. It is owing primarily to this library, which in its way formed a counterpart of the Alexandrian, that we possess to-day a coherent, though very limited, knowledge of Christian antiquity.[1] And even previous to that, if one takes the trouble (and it is no trouble) to put together, from the writings of Celsus, Tertullian, Hippolytus, Clement of Alexandria, and Origen, their library of *Christian* works, it becomes evident that they had access to an extensive range of Christian books from all parts of the church.

These data are merely intended to give an approximate idea of how vital was the intercourse, personal and epistolary and literary, between the various churches, and also between prominent teachers of the day. It is not easy to exaggerate the significance of this fact for the mission and propaganda of Christianity. The co-operation, the brotherliness, and more-

---

[1] Compare on this point the two tables, given in my *Litteratur-Geschichte*, vol. i. pp. 883–886, of "Early Christian Greek Writings in old Latin Versions," and "Early Christian Greek Writings in old Syriac Versions." No writing is translated into a foreign language until it appears to be indispensable for the purposes of edification or of information. Compare, in the light of this, the extraordinary amount of early Christian literature which was translated at an early period into Latin or Syriac. It is particularly interesting to ascertain what writings were rendered into Latin as well as into Syriac. Their number was considerable, and this forms an unerring aid in answering the question, which of the early Christian writings were most widely circulated and most influential. Very little was translated into Greek from Latin (Tertullian's *Apology*, Cyprian's epistles) in the pre-Constantine period.

over the mental activity of Christians, are patent in this connection, and they were powerful levers in the extension of the
cause. Furthermore, they must have made a powerful impression
on the outside spectator, besides guaranteeing a certain unity
in the development of the religion and ensuring the fact that
when a Christian passed from the East to the West, or from
one distant church to another, he never felt himself a stranger.
Down to the age of Constantine, or at any rate until the middle
of the third century, the centripetal forces in early Christianity
were, as a matter of fact, more powerful than the centrifugal.
And Rome was the centre of the former tendencies. The
Roman Church was *the* catholic church. It was more than the
mere symbol and representative of Christian unity; to it more
than to any other Christians owed unity itself.

So far as I know, the technical side of the spread of early
Christian literature has not yet been investigated, and any results
that can be reached are far from numerous.[1] We must realize,
however, that a large number of these writings, not excluding
the oldest and most important of them, together with almost
all the epistolary literature, was never " edited " in the technical
sense of the term—never, at any rate, until after some generations

---

[1] Cp. however, what Sulpicius Severus (*Dial.*, i. 23, in the light of iii. 17)
says of his little volume on "The Life of S. Martin." Postumianus, the inter-
rogator, says: "Nunquam a dextera mea liber iste discedit. nam si agnoscis, ecce
—et aperit librum qui veste latebat—en ipsum ! hic mihi, inquit, terra ac mari
comes, hic in peregrinatione tota socius et consolator fuit. sed referam tibi sane,
quo liber iste penetrarit, et quam nullus fere in orbe terrarum locus sit, ubi non
materia tam felicis historiae pervulgata teneatur. primus eum Romanae urbi vir
studiossimus tui Paulinus invexit; deinde cum tota certatim urbe raperetur,
exultantes librarios vidi, quod nihil ab his quaestiosius haberetur, siquidem nihil
illo promptius, nihil carius venderetur. hic navigationis meae cursum longe ante
praegressus, cum ad Africam veni, iam per totam Carthaginem legebatur. solus
eum Cyrenensis ille presbyter non habebat, sed me largiente descripsit. nam quid
ego de Alexandria loquar ? ubi paene omnibus magis quam tibi notus est. hic
Aegyptum, Nitriam, Thebaidam ac tota Memphitica regna transivit. hunc ego in
eremo a quodam sene legi vidi," etc. ("That book never leaves my right hand.
Look, said he—and he showed the book under his cloak—here it is, my companion by land and sea, my ally and comforter in all my wanderings. I'll tell you
where it has penetrated ; let me tell you, pray, how there is no single spot where
this blessed story is not known. Paulinus, your great admirer, brought it first to
Rome. The whole city seized on it, and I found the booksellers in delight,
because no demand was more profitable, no book sold so keenly and quickly as

had passed. There were no editions of the New Testament (or of the Old?) until Origen (*i.e.*, the Theodotian), although Marcion's New Testament deserves to be called a critical revision and edition, while revised editions were meant by those early fathers who bewailed the falsification of the Bible texts by the gnostics. For the large majority of early Christian writings the exemplars in the library at Cæsarea served as the basis for editions (*i.e.*, transcripts) from the fourth and fifth centuries onwards. Yet even after editions of the Scriptures were published they were frequently transcribed at will from some rough copy. From the outset the apologies, the works of the gnostics (which were meant for the learned), and any ecclesiastical writings designed, from Irenæus downwards, for the educated Christian public, were published and circulated. The first instance of a bishop collecting and editing his own letters is that of Dionysius of Corinth, during the reign of Marcus Aurelius (Eus., *H.E.*, iv. 23).

Unedited or unpublished writings were naturally exposed in a special degree to the risk of falsification. The church-fathers are full of complaints on this score. Yet even those which were edited were not preserved with due care.[1]

yours. I found it before me wherever I sailed. When I reached Africa, it was being read in Carthage. That presbyter of Cyrene did not only possess it; at my expense, he wrote it out. And what shall I say of Alexandria, where nearly everyone knows it better than you do yourself. Through Nitria, the Thebais, and all the Memphis district it has circulated. I saw it also being read in the desert by an old anchorite," etc.). This refers, of course, to a book which appeared about 400 A.D., but the description, even when modified, is significant for an earlier period.

[1] To give one or two instances. Dionysius of Corinth found that his letters were circulating in falsified shape even during his own lifetime; he comforts himself naïvely with the thought that even the Scriptures shared the same fate (so, apropos of Origen's writings, Sulpic. Sever., *Dial.*, i. 7). Irenæus adjures all future copyists of his works not to corrupt them, and to copy out his adjuration (Eus., *H.E.*, v. 20). But the most striking proof of the prevailing uncertainty in texts is afforded by the fact that only a century and a half after Cyprian an attempt was actually made to set aside all his letters on the baptism of heretics as forgeries. Augustine's remarks on the matter are quite as remarkable (*Ep.* xciii. 38). He regards the hypothesis as possible, though he does not agree with it: "Non desunt, qui hoc Cyprianum prorsus non sensisse contendant, sed sub eius nomine a praesumptoribus atque mendacibus fuisse confictum. neque enim sic potuit integritas atque notitia litterarum unius quamlibet inlustris episcopi custodivi quemadmodum scriptura canonica tot linguarum litteris et ordine ac successione celebrationis

To what extent the literature of Christianity fell into the hands of its opponents, is a matter about which we know next to nothing. Tertullian speaks quite pessimistically on the point (*de Testim.*, i.), and Norden's verdict is certainly true (*Kunstprosa*, pp. 517 f.): " We cannot form too low an estimate of the number of pagans who read the New Testament. . . . . I believe I am correct in saying that pagans only read the New Testament when they wanted to refute it." Celsus furnished himself with quite a considerable Christian library, in which he studied deeply before he wrote against the Christians; but it is merely a rhetorical phrase, when Athenagoras assumes (*Suppl.*, ix.) that the emperors knew the · Old Testament. The attitude of the apologists to the Scriptures, whether they are quoting them or not, shows that they do not pre-suppose any knowledge of their contents (Norden, *loc. cit.*). Writings of Origen were read by the Neoplatonist philosophers, who had also in their hands the Old Testament, the gospels, and the Pauline epistles. We may say the same of Porphyry and Amelius. One great obstacle to the diffusion of the Scriptures lay in the Greek version, which was inartistic and offensive (from the point of view of style),[1] but still more in

---

ecclesiasticae custoditur, contra quam tamen non defuerat qui sub nominibus apostolorum multa confingerent frustra quidem, quia illa sic commendata, sic celebrata, sic nota est " (" There are, indeed, some people who assert that Cyprian did not hold such opinions at all, but that the correspondence has been composed in his name by daring forgers. For the writings of a bishop, however distinguished, could not indeed be preserved in their integrity, like the holy canonical Scriptures, by ecclesiastical order and use and regular succession—though even here there have actually been people who issued many fabrications under the names of apostles. It was useless, however, for Scripture was too well attested, too well known, too familiar, to permit of them succeeding in their designs ").—How Tertullian fared with the second edition of his anti-Marcion, he tells us himself : " Hanc composi-tionem *nondum exemplariis suffectam* fraude tunc fratris, dehinc apostatae, amisi, qui forte descripserat quaedam mendosissime et exhibuit frequentiae " (" I lost it, before it was finally published, by the fraud of one who was then a Christian brother but afterwards apostatized. He happened to have transcribed part of it very inaccurately, and then he published it ").—The author of the *Life of Polycarp* observes that the works, sermons, and letters of that writer were pilfered during the persecution by the knavery of unbelievers.

[1] Nearly all the apologists (cp. even Clem. Alex., *Protrept.*, viii. 77) tried to justify the "unadorned" style of the prophets, and thus to champion the defect. Origen (Hom. viii. 1, *in Jesum Nave*, vol. xi. p. 74) observes : " We appeal to you, O readers of the sacred books, not to hearken to their contents with weariness

the old Latin version of the Bible, which in many parts was simply intolerable. How repellent must have been the effect produced, for example, by reading (Baruch ii. 29) "Dicens: si non audieritis vocis meae, si sonos magnos hagminis iste avertatur in minima in gentibus, hubi dispergam ibi."[1] Nor could Christianity in the West boast of writers whose work penetrated far into the general literature of the age, at a time when Origen and his pupils were forcing an entrance for themselves. Lactantius, whose evidence is above suspicion,[2] observes that in Latin society Christians were still considered "stulti" (*Instit.*, v. 1 f.),[3] and personally vouches for the lack of suitable and skilled teachers and authors ; Minucius Felix and Tertullian could not secure "satis celebritatis," whilst, for all his admirable qualities as a speaker and writer, Cyprian "is unable to satisfy those who are ignorant of all but the words of our religion, since his language is mystical and designed only for the ears of the faithful. In short, the learned of this world who chance to

and disdain for what seems to be their unpleasing method of narration" ("Deprecamur vos, O auditores sacrorum voluminum, non cum taedio vel fastidio ea quae leguntur, audire pro eo quod minus delectabilis corum videtur esse narratio"); cp. Hom. viii. 1, *in Levit.*, vol. ix. p. 313, *de Princip.*, iv. 1. 7, iv. 26 [the divine nature of the Bible all the more plain from its defective literary style], *Cohort. ad Græc.*, xxxv.–xxxvi., xxxviii.

[1] Even the Greek text, of course, is unpleasing : λέγων· ἐὰν μὴ ἀκούσητε τῆς φωνῆς μου, εἰ μὴν ἡ βόμβησις ἡ μεγάλη ἡ πολλὴ αὕτη ἀποστρέψει εἰς μικρὰν ἐν τοῖς ἔθνεσιν οὗ διασπερῶ αὐτοὺς ἐκεῖ. On the style of the New Testament, cp. Norden, *Die antike Kunstprosa* (1898), pp. 516 f. ("Educated people could not but view the literary records of the Christians as stylistic monstrosities").—Arnobius (i. 58) writes of the Scriptures : "They were written by illiterate and uneducated men, and therefore are not readily to be credited" ("Ab indoctis hominibus et rudibus scripta sunt et idcirco non sunt facili auditione credenda"). When he writes (i. 59) : "Barbarismis, soloecismis obsitae sunt res vestrae et vitiorum deformitate pollutae" ("Your narratives are overrun by barbarisms and solecisms, and disfigured by monstrous blunders"), he is reproducing pagan opinions upon the Bible. Compare the remarks of Sulpicius Severus, and the reasons which led him to compose his Chronicle of the World ; also Augustine's *Confess.*, iii. 5 (9). The correspondence between Paul and Seneca was fabricated in order to remove the obstacles occasioned by the poor style of Paul's letters in the Latin version (cp. my *Litt. Geschichte*, i. p. 765).

[2] No doubt he is anxious to bring out his own accomplishments.

[3] Cp. on this the extremely instructive treatise "ad Paganos" in the pseudo-August. *Quæst. in Vet. et Nov. Test.*, No. 114. Underlying it is the charge of stupidity levelled at Christians, who are about thirty times called "stulti." The author naturally tries to prove that it is the pagans who are the stupid folk.

become acquainted with his writings are in the habit of deriding him. I myself once heard a really cultured person call him 'Coprianus' [dung-man] by the change of a single letter in his name, as if he had bestowed on old wives' fables a polished intellect which was capable of better things" ("placere ultra verba sacramentum ignorantibus non potest, quoniam mystica sunt quae locutus est et ad id praeparata, ut a solis fidelibus audiantur: denique a doctis huius sacculi, quibus forte scripta eius innotuerant, derideri solet. audivi ego quendam hominem sane disertum, qui eum immutata una litera 'Coprianum' vocaret, quasi quod elegans ingenium et melioribus rebus aptum ad aniles fabulas contulisset").

In the Latin West, although Minucius Felix and Cyprian (*ad Donatum*) wrote in a well-bred style, Christian literature had but little to do with the spread of the Christian religion; in the East, upon the contrary, it became a factor of great importance from the third century onwards.

CHAPTER II

ANYONE who inquires about the missionary methods in general, must be referred to what has been said in our Second Book (pp. 86 f.). For the missionary *preaching* includes the missionary *methods*. The *one* God, Jesus Christ as Son and Lord according to apostolic tradition, future judgment and the resurrection—these truths were preached. So was the gospel of the Saviour and of salvation, of love and charity. The new religion was stated and verified as Spirit and power, and also as the power to lead a new moral life, and to practise self-control. News was brought to men of a divine revelation to which humanity must yield itself by faith. A new people, it was announced, had now appeared, which was destined to embrace all nations; withal a primitive, sacred book was handed over, in which the world's history was depicted from the first day to the last.

In 1 Cor. i.–ii. Paul expressly states that he gave a central place to the proclamation of the crucified Christ. He summed up everything in this preaching; that is, he proclaimed Christ as *the Saviour* who wiped sins away. But preaching of this kind implies that he began by revealing and bringing home to his hearers their own impiety and unrighteousness (ἀσέβεια καὶ ἀδικέια), otherwise the preaching of redemption could never have secured a footing or done its work at all. Moreover, as the decisive proof of men's impiety and unrighteousness, Paul adduced their ignorance regarding God and also regarding idolatry, an ignorance for which they themselves were to blame. To prove that this was their own fault, he appealed to the conscience of his hearers, and to the remnant of divine knowledge which they still possessed. The opening of the epistle to the Romans (chaps. i.–iii.) may therefore be considered to represent the way in which Paul began his missionary preaching. First of all, he brought his hearers to admit " we are sinners, one and all." Then he led them to the cross of Christ, where he developed the conception of the cross as the power and the wisdom of God. And interwoven with all this, in characteristic fashion, lay expositions of the flesh and the Spirit, with allusions to the approaching judgment.

So far as we can judge, it was Paul who first threw into such sharp relief the significance of Jesus Christ as a Redeemer, and made this the central point of Christian preaching. No doubt, the older missionaries had also taught and preached that Christ died for sins (1 Cor. xv. 3); but in so far as they addressed Jews, or people who had for some time been in contact with Judaism, it was natural that they should confine themselves to preaching the imminence of judgment, and also to proving from the Old Testament that the crucified Jesus was to return as judge and as the Lord of the messianic kingdom. Hence quite naturally they could summon men to acknowledge him, to join his church, and to keep his commandments.

We need not doubt that this was the line taken at the outset, even for many people of pagan birth who had already become familiar with some of the contents and characteristics of the Old Testament. The Petrine speeches in Acts are a proof of this. As for the missionary address ascribed to Paul in ch. xiii., it is plainly a blend of this popular missionary preaching with the Pauline manner; but in that model of a mission address to educated people which is preserved in ch. xvii.,[1] the Pauline manner of missionary preaching is perfectly distinct, in spite of what seems to be one vital difference. First we have an exposition of the true doctrine of God, whose main aspects are successively presented (monotheism, spirituality, omnipresence and omnipotence, creation and providence, the unity of the human race and their religious capacities, spiritual worship). The state of mankind hitherto is described as " ignorance," and therefore

---

[1] The address in xiv. 15 f. is akin to this.

to be repented of; God will overlook it. But the new era has dawned: an era of repentance and judgment, involving faith in Jesus Christ, who has been sent and raised by God and who is at once redeemer and judge.[1] Many of the more educated missionaries, and particularly Luke himself, certainly preached in this fashion, as is proved by the Christian apologies and by writings like the " Preaching of Peter." Christian preaching was bent on arousing a feeling of godlessness and unrighteousness; it also worked upon the natural consciousness of God; but it was never unaccompanied by references to the coming judgment.

The address put into the mouth of Paul by the " Acta Pauli "

---

[1] Whatever be the origin of the address in Acts xvii. 22–31 and the whole narrative of Paul's preaching at Athens, it remains the most wonderful passage in the book of Acts; in a higher sense (and probably in a strictly historical sense, at some vital points) it is full of truth. No one should have failed especially to recognize how closely the passage fits into the data which can be gathered from 1 Cor. i. f. and Rom. i. f., with regard to the missionary preaching of Paul. The following points may be singled out :—

(a) According to Acts xvii. 18, "Jesus and the Resurrection" were decidedly put in the front rank of Paul's preaching. This agrees with what may be inferred from 1 Cor. i. f.

(b) As Rom. i. 19 f. and ii. 14 f. prove, the exposition of man's natural knowledge of God formed a cardinal feature in the missionary preaching of Paul. It occupies most of the space in the address at Athens.

(c) In this address the Judgeship of Jesus is linked on directly to the "ignorance" which has replaced the primitive knowledge of God (καθότι ἔστησεν ἡμέραν ἐν ᾗ μέλλει κρίνειν τὴν οἰκουμένην ἐν δικαιοσύνῃ ἐν ἀνδρὶ ᾧ ὥρισεν), precisely as Rom. ii. 14 f. is followed by ver. 16 (ἐν ἡμέρᾳ ὅτε κρίνει ὁ θεὸς τὰ κρυπτὰ τῶν ἀνθρώπων διὰ Χριστοῦ Ἰησοῦ).

(d) According to the Athenian address, between the time of "ignorance" and the future judgment there is a present interval which is characterized by the offer of saving faith (ver. 31). The genuinely Pauline character of this idea only needs to be pointed out.

(e) The object of this saving faith is the risen Jesus (ver. 31)—a Pauline idea of which again no proof is necessary.

The one point at which the Athenian address diverges from the missionary preaching which we gather from the Pauline letters, is the lack of prominence assigned by the former to the *guilt* of mankind. Still, it is clear enough that their "ignorance" is implicitly condemned, and the starting-point of the address (ὃ ἀγνοοῦντες εὐσεβεῖτε, τοῦτο ἐγὼ καταγγέλλω ὑμῖν) made it almost impossible to lay any greater emphasis upon the negative aspect of the matter.

Several important features of Paul's work as a pioneer missionary may be also recognised in 1 Thessalonians (cp. Acts xx. 18 f.). But it does not come within the scope of the present volume to enter more fully into such details.

(*Acta Theclæ*, v.-vi.) is peculiar and quite un-Pauline (compare, however, the preaching of Paul before Nero). Strictly speaking, it cannot even be described as a missionary address at all. The apostle speaks in beatitudes, which are framed upon those of Jesus but developed ascetically. A more important point is that the content of Christian preaching is described as "the doctrine of the generation and resurrection of the Beloved" (διδασκαλία τῆς τε γεννήσεως καὶ τῆς ἀναστάσεως τοῦ ἠγαπημένου), and as "the message of self-control and of resurrection" (λόγος τῆς ἐγκρατείας καὶ ἀναστάσεως).[1]

The effect of connected discourses, so far as regards the Christian mission, need not be overestimated; in every age a single stirring detail that moves the heart is of greater weight than a long sermon. The book of Acts describes many a person being converted all at once, by a sort of rush. And the description is not unhistorical. Paul was converted, not by a missionary, but by means of a vision. The Ethiopian treasurer was led to believe in Jesus by means of Isaiah liii., and how many persons

---

[1] A brief and pregnant missionary address, delivered by an educated Christian, is to be found in the *Acta Apollonii* (xxxvi. f.). The magistrate's demand for a brief statement of Christianity is met thus : οὗτος ὁ σωτὴρ ἡμῶν Ἰησοῦς Χριστὸς ὡς ἄνθρωπος γενόμενος ἐν τῇ Ἰουδαίᾳ κατὰ πάντα δίκαιος καὶ πεπληρωμένος θείᾳ σοφίᾳ, φιλανθρώπως ἐδίδαξεν ἡμᾶς τίς ὁ τῶν ὅλων θεὸς καὶ τί τέλος ἀρετῆς ἐπὶ σεμνὴν πολιτείαν ἁρμόζον πρὸς τὰς τῶν ἀνθρώπων ψυχάς · ὃς διὰ τοῦ παθεῖν ἔπαυσεν τὰς ἀρχὰς τῶν ἁμαρτιῶν ("This Jesus Christ our Saviour, on becoming man in Judæa, being just in all respects and filled with divine wisdom, taught us—in his love for men—who was the God of all, and what was that end of virtue which promoted a holy life and was adapted to the souls of men ; by his sufferings he stopped the springs of sin "). Then follows a list of all the virtues, including the duty of honouring the emperor, with faith in the immortality of the soul and in retribution ; all of these were taught by Jesus μετὰ πολλῆς ἀποδείξεως. Like the philosophers and just men before him, however, Jesus was persecuted and slain by "the lawless," even as one of the Greeks had also said that the just man would be tortured, spat upon, bound, and finally crucified. As Socrates was unjustly condemned by the Athenian sycophants, so did certain wicked persons vilify and condemn our Teacher and Saviour, just as already they had done to the prophets who foretold his coming, his work, and his teaching (προεῖπον ὅτι τοιοῦτός τις ἀφίξεται πάντα δίκαιος καὶ ἐνάρετος, ὃς εἰς πάντας εὖ ποιήσας ἀνθρώπους ἐπ᾿ ἀρετῇ πείσει σέβειν τὸν πάντων θεόν, ὃν ἡμεῖς φθάσαντες τιμῶμεν, ὅτι ἐμάθομεν σεμνὰς ἐντολὰς ἃς οὐκ ᾔδειμεν, καὶ οὐ πεπλανήμεθα : they predicted that "such an one will come, absolutely righteous and virtuous, who in beneficence to all men shall persuade them to reverence that God of all men whom we now by anticipation honour, because we have learnt holy commands which we knew not, and have not been deceived ").

may have found this chapter a bridge to faith! Thecla was won over from paganism by means of the "word of virginity and prayer" (λόγος τῆς παρθενίας καὶ τῆς προσευχῆς, *Acta Theclæ*, ch. vii.), a motive which is so repeatedly mentioned in the apocryphal Acts that its reality and significance cannot be called in question. Asceticism, especially in the sexual relationship, did prevail in wide circles at that period, as an outcome of the religious syncretism. The apologists had good grounds also for declaring that many were deeply impressed and eventually convinced by the exorcisms which the Christians performed, while we may take it for granted that thousands were led to Christianity by the stirring proclamation of judgment, and of judgment close at hand. Besides, how many simply succumbed to the authority of the Old Testament, with the light thrown on it by Christianity! Whenever a proof was required, here was this book all ready.[1]

The mission was reinforced and actively advanced by the behaviour of Christian men and women. Paul often mentions this, and in 1 Pet. iii. 1 we read that men who do not believe the Word are to be won over without a word by means of the conduct of their wives.[2] The moral life of Christians appealed

---

[1] Strictly speaking, we have no mission-literature, apart from the fragments of the " Preaching of Peter " or the Apologies, and the range of the latter includes those who are already convinced of Christianity. The New Testament, in particular, does not contain a single missionary work. The Synoptic gospels must not be embraced under this category, for they are catechetical works, intended for the instruction of people who are already acquainted with the principles of doctrine, and who require to have their faith enriched and confirmed (cp. Luke i. 4). One might with greater reason describe the Fourth gospel as a missionary work ; the prologue especially suggests this view. But even here the description would be inapplicable. Primarily, at any rate, even the Fourth gospel has Christian readers in view, for it is certainly Christians and not pagans who are addressed in xx. 31. Acts presents us with a history of missions ; such was the deliberate intention of the author. But ch. i. 8 states what is merely the cardinal, and by no means the sole, theme of the book.

[2] Details upon Christian women follow in Book IV. Chap. II. But here we may set down the instructive description of a Christian woman's daily life, from the pen of Tertullian (*ad Uxor.*, II. iv. f.). Its value is increased by the fact that the woman described is married to a pagan.

"If a vigil has to be attended, the husband, the first thing in the morning, makes her an appointment for the baths ; if it is a fast-day, he holds a banquet on that very day. If she has to go out, household affairs of urgency at once come in the way. For who would be willing to let his wife go through one street after another to other men's houses, and indeed to the poorer cottages, in order to visit

to a man like Justin with peculiar force, and the martyrdoms made a wide impression. It was no rare occurrence for outsiders to be struck in such a way that on the spur of the moment they suddenly turned to Christianity. But we know of no cases in which Christians desired to win, or actually did win, adherents by means of the charities which they dispensed. We are quite aware that impostors joined the church in order to profit by the brotherly kindness of its members; but even pagans never charged Christianity with using money as a missionary bribe. What they did allege was that Christians won credulous people to their religion with their words of doom, and that they promised the heavy-laden a vain support, and the guilty an unlawful pardon. In the third century the channels of the mission among the masses were multiplied. At one moment in the crisis of the struggle against gnosticism it looked as if the church could only continue to exist by prohibiting any intercourse with that devil's courtezan, philosophy; the "simplices et idiotae," indeed, shut their ears firmly against all learning.[1] But even a Tertullian found himself compelled to oppose this standpoint, while the pseudo-Clementine Homilies made a vigorous attack upon the methods of those who would

---

the brethren? Who would like to see her being taken from his side by some duty of attending a nocturnal gathering? At Easter time who will quietly tolerate her absence all the night? Who will unsuspiciously let her go to the Lord's supper, that feast which they heap such calumnies upon? Who will let her creep into gaol to kiss the martyrs' chains? or even to meet any one of the brethren for the holy kiss? or to bring water for the saints' feet? If a brother arrives from abroad, what hospitality is there for him in such an alien house, if the very larder is closed to one for whom the whole storeroom ought to be thrown open! . . . . Will it pass unnoticed, if you make the sign of the cross on your bed or on your person? or when you blow away with a breath some impurity? or even when you rise by night to pray? Will it not look as if you were trying to engage in some work of magic? Your husband will not know what it is that you eat in secret before you taste any food." The description shows us how the whole daily life of a Christian was to be a confession of Christianity, and in this sense a propaganda of the mission as well.

[1] Tert., *adv. Prax.* iii.: "Simplices quique, ne dixerim imprudentes et idiotae, quae maior semper credentium pars est" ("The simple—I do not call them senseless or unlearned—who are always the majority"); cp. *de Resurr.*, ii. Hippolytus, at the beginning of the third century, calls Zephyrinus, the bishop of Rome, an ἰδιώτης and ἀγράμματος (*Philos.*, ix. 11), and Origen often bewails the large number of ignorant Christians.

substitute dreams and visions for instruction and doctrine. That, they urge, is the method [1] of Simon Magus! Above all, it was the catechetical school of Alexandria, it was men like Clement and Origen, who by their patient and unwearied efforts won the battle for learning, and vindicated the rights of learning in the Christian church. Henceforward, Christianity used her learning also, in the shape of word and book, for the purpose of her mission (*i.e.*, in the East, for in the West there is little trace of this). But the most powerful agency of the mission during the third century was the church herself in her entirety. As she assumed the form of a great syncretistic religion and managed cautiously to bring about a transformation which gnosticism would have thrust upon her violently, the mere fact of her existence and the influence exerted by her very appearance in history wielded a power that attracted and captivated men.

When a newcomer was admitted into the Christian church he was baptized. This rite ("purifici roris perfusio," Lactant., iv. 15), whose beginnings lie wrapt in obscurity, certainly was not *introduced* in order to meet the pagan craving for the mysteries, but as a matter of fact it is impossible to think of any symbolic action which would prove more welcome to that craving than baptism with all its touching simplicity. The mere fact of

---

[1] See *Homil.* xvii. 14-19, where censure is passed on the view that it is safer "to learn by means of an apparition than from the clearness of truth itself" (ὑπὸ ὀπτασίας ἀκούειν ἢ παρ' αὐτῆς ἐναργείας, 14); ὁ ὀπτασίᾳ πιστεύων, we read, ἢ ὁράματι καὶ ἐνυπνίῳ ἀγνοεῖ τίνι πιστεύει ("He who believes in an apparition or vision and dreams, does not know in whom he is believing"). Cp. 17: καὶ ἀσεβεῖς ὁράματα καὶ ἐνύπνια ἀληθῆ βλέπουσιν . . . . τῷ εὐσεβεῖ ἐμφύτῳ καὶ καθαρῷ ἀναβλύζει τῷ νῷ τὸ ἀληθές, οὐκ ὀνείρῳ σπουδαζόμενον, ἀλλὰ συνέσει ἀγαθοῖς διδόμενον ("Even impious men have true visions and dreams . . . . but truth bubbles up to the natural and pure mind of the pious; it is not worked up through dreams, but vouchsafed to the good through their understanding"). In § 18 Peter explains that his own confession (Matt. xvi.) first became precious to himself when Jesus told him it was the Father who had allowed him to participate in this revelation. Τὸ ἔξωθεν δι' ὀπτασιῶν καὶ ἐνυπνίων δηλωθῆναί τι οὐκ ἔστιν ἀποκαλύψεως ἀλλὰ ὀργῆς ("The declaration of anything external by means of apparitions and dreams is the mark, not of revelation, but of wrath divine"). In § 19 a negative answer is given to the question "whether anyone can be rendered fit for instruction by means of an apparition" (εἴ τις δι' ὀπτασίαν πρὸς διδασκαλίαν σοφισθῆναι δύναται).

such a rite was a great comfort in itself, for few indeed could be satisfied with a purely spiritual religion. The ceremony of the individual's immersion and emergence from the water served as a guarantee that old things were now washed away and gone, leaving him a new man. The utterance of the name of Jesus or of the three names of the Trinity during the baptismal act brought the candidate into the closest union with them; it raised him to God himself. Speculations on the mystery at once commenced.[1] Immersion was held to be a death; immersion in relation to Christ was a dying with him, or an absorption into his death; the water was the symbol of his blood. Paul himself taught this doctrine, but he rejected the speculative notions of the Corinthians (1 Cor. i. 13 f.) by which they further sought to bring the person baptized into a mysterious connection with the person who baptizes. It is remarkakle how he thanks God that personally he had only baptized a very few people in Corinth. This is not, of course, to be taken as a depreciation of baptism. Like his fellows, Paul recognized it to be simply indispensable. The apostle is merely recollecting, and recollecting in this instance with satisfaction, the limitation of his apostolic calling, in which no duty was imposed on him beyond the preaching of the word of God. Strictly speaking, baptism does not fall within his jurisdiction. He may perform the rite, but commonly it is the business of other people. In the majority of cases it implies a lengthy period of instruction and examination, and the apostle has no time for that: his task is merely to lay the foundation. Baptism marks therefore not the act of initiation but the final stage of the initiation.

"Fiunt, non nascuntur Christiani"; men are not born Christians, but made Christians. This remark of Tertullian (*Apol.*, xviii.)[2] may have applied to the large majority even after the middle of the second century, but thereafter a companion feature arose in the shape of the natural extension of Christianity through parents to their children. Subsequently to that period the practice

---

[1] Magical ideas were bound up from the very first with baptism; cp. the baptism ὑπὲρ τῶν νεκρῶν at Corinth and Paul's attitude towards it (1 Cor. xv. 29).

[2] Cp. *de Testim.*, i. : "Fieri non nasci solet christiana anima." Those born in Christian homes are called "vernaculi ecclesiae" (cp. *de Anima*, li.).

of infant baptism was also inaugurated; at least we are unable
to get certain evidence for it at an earlier date.[1]   But whether
infants or adults were baptized, baptism in either case was held
to be a mystery which involved decisive consequences of a
natural and supernatural kind.   The general conviction was
that baptism effectually cancelled all past sins of the baptized
person, apart altogether from the degree of moral sensitiveness
on his own part ; he rose from his immersion a perfectly pure
and perfectly holy man.   Now this sacrament played an extremely important rôle in the mission of this church.   It was
an act as intelligible as it was consoling ; the ceremony itself
was not so unusual as to surprise or scandalize people like
circumcision or the taurobolium, and yet it was something
tangible, something to which they could attach themselves.[2]

[1] Here, too, I am convinced that the saying holds true, " Ab initio sic non erat."
[2] At the same time, of course, people of refined feeling were shocked by the
rite of baptism and the declaration involved in it, that all sins were now wiped
out.   Porphyry, whose opinion in this matter is followed by Julian, writes thus
in Macarius Magnes (iv. 19) : " We must feel amazed and truly concerned about
our souls, if a man thus shamed and polluted is to stand out clean after a single
immersion, if a man whose life is stained by so much debauchery, by adultery,
fornication, drunkenness, theft, sodomy, murder by poisoning, and many another
shameful and detestable vice—if such a creature, I say, is lightly set free from it
all, throwing off the whole guilt as a snake sheds its old scales, merely because he
has been baptized and has invoked the name of Christ.   Who will not commit
misdeeds, mentionable and unmentionable, who will not do things which can
neither be described nor tolerated, if he learns that he can get quit of all these
shameful offences merely by believing and getting baptized, and cherishing the
hope that he will hereafter find forgiveness with him who is to judge the living and
the dead ?   Assertions of this kind cannot but lead to sin on the part of anyone
who understands them.   They teach men constantly to be unrighteous.   They
lead one to understand that they proscribe even the discipline of the law and
righteousness itself, so that these have no longer any power at all against unrighteousness.   They introduce a lawless life into an ordered world.   They raise
it to the rank of a first principle, that a man has no longer to shun godlessness at
all—if by the simple act of baptism he gets rid of a mass of innumerable sins.
Such, then, is the position of matters with regard to this boastful fable."   But is
Porphyry quite candid in this detestation of sacraments and their saving efficiency
in general, as well as in his description of the havoc wrought upon morals by
baptism ?   As to the latter point, it is of course true that the practice of postponing
baptism became more and more common, even as early as the second century, in
order to evade a thorough-going acceptance of the Christian life, and yet to have
the power of sinning with impunity (cp., e.g., Tert., de Pœnit., vi.).   Even strict
teachers advised it, or at least did not dissuade people from it, so awful seemed
the responsibility of baptism.   No safe means could be found for wiping off post-

Furthermore, if one added the story of Jesus being baptized by John—a story which was familiar to everyone, since the gospel opened with it—not merely was a fresh field thrown open for profound schemes and speculations, but, thanks to the precedent of this baptism of Jesus, the baptism to which every Christian submitted acquired new unction and a deeper content. As the Spirit had descended upon Jesus at his own baptism, so God's Spirit hovered now upon the water at every Christian's baptism, converting it into a bath of regeneration and renewal. How much Tertullian has already said about baptism in his treatise *de Baptismo*! Even that simple Christian, Hermas, sixty years previous to Tertullian, cannot say enough on the topic of baptism; the apostles, he exclaims, went down into the underworld and there baptized those who had fallen asleep long ago.

It was as a mystery that the Gentile church took baptism from the very first,[1] as is plain even from the history of the way in which the sacrament took shape. People were no longer satisfied with the simple bath of baptism. The rite was amplified; new ceremonies were added to it; and, like all the mysteries, the holy transaction underwent a development. Gradually the new ceremonies asserted their own independence, by a process which also is familiar. In the treatise I have just mentioned, Tertullian exhibits this development at an advanced stage,[2] but

baptismal sins. Yet this landed them in a sore dilemma, of which they were themselves quite conscious. They had to fall in with the light-minded! Cp. Tertullian, *loc. cit.* and *de Baptismo*; at a later date, the second book of Augustine's *Confessions*. Justin, however, declares that baptism is only for those who have actually ceased to sin (*Apol.*, i. 61 f.).

[1] This sacrament was not, of course, performed in secret at the outset, nor indeed for some time to come. It is not until the close of the second century that the secrecy of the rite commences, partly for educative reasons, partly because more and more stress came to be laid on the nature of baptism as a mystery. The significance attaching to the correct ritual as such is evident as early as the Didachê (vii.), where we read that in the first instance running water is to be used in baptism; failing that, cold standing water; failing that, warm water; failing a sufficient quantity even of that, mere sprinkling is permissible. The comparative freedom of such regulations was not entirely abolished in later ages, but it was scrupulously restricted. Many must have doubted the entire efficacy of baptism by sprinkling, or at least held that it required to be supplemented.

[2] On the conception and shaping of baptism as a mystery, see Anrich's *Das antike Mysterienwesen in seinem Einfluss auf das Christentum* (1894), pp. 84 f., 168 f., 179 f., and Wobbermin's *Religionsgeschich. Studien z. Frage d. Beein-*

on the main issue there was little or no alteration ; baptism was essentially the act by which past sins were entirely cancelled.

It was a *mysterium salutare*, a saving mystery ; but it was also a *mysterium tremendum*, an awful mystery, for the church had no second means of grace like baptism. The baptized person must remain pure, or (as 2 Clem., *e.g.*, puts it) "keep the seal pure and intact." Certain sects attempted to introduce repeated baptism, but they never carried their point ; baptism, it was steadily maintained, could never be repeated. True, the sacrament of penance gradually arose, by means of which the grace lost after baptism could be restored. Despite this, however, there was a growing tendency in the third century to adopt the custom of postponing baptism until immediately before death, in order to make the most of this comprehensive means of grace.

No less important than baptism itself was the preparation for it. Here the spiritual aspect of the Christian religion reached its highest expression ; here its moral and social force was plainly shown. The Didachê at once corroborates and elucidates the uncertain information which we possess with regard to this point in the previous period. The pagan who desired to become a Christian was not baptized there and then. When his heart had been stirred by the broad outlines of the preaching of the *one* God and the Lord Jesus Christ as saviour and redeemer, he was then shown the will and law of God, and what was meant by renouncing idolatry. No summary doctrines were laid down, but the "two ways" were put before him in a most comprehensive and thoroughgoing fashion ; every sin was tracked to its lurking-place within. He had to renounce all sins and assent to the law of God, nor was he baptized until the church was convinced that he knew the moral code and desired to follow it (Justin, *Apol.*, I. lxvii. : λοῦσαι τὸν πεπεισμένον καὶ συγκατατε- θειμένον, " to wash him who is convinced and who has assented to our teaching ").[1] The Jewish synagogue had already drawn

flussung des Urchristentums durch das antike Mysterienwesen (1896), pp. 143 f. The latter discusses σφραγίς, σφραγίζειν, φωτισμός, φωτίζειν, and σύμβολον, the technical baptismal terms. The mysteries are exhibited in greatest detail by the *Pistis Sophia*.

[1] Cp. Orig., *c. Cels.*, III. li. : " Having previously tested, as far as possible, the hearts of those who desire to become their hearers, and having given them

up a catechism for proselytes and made morality the condition of religion; it had already *instituted a training* for religion. Christianity took this up and deepened it. In so doing it was actuated by the very strongest motives, for otherwise it could not protect itself against the varied forms of "idolatry" or realize its cherished ideal of being the *holy* church of God. For over a century and a half it ranked everything almost secondary to the supreme task of maintaining its morality. It recognized no faith and no forgiveness that might serve as a pillow for the conscience, and one reason why the church did not triumph over gnosticism at an earlier period was simply because she did not like to shut out people who owned Christ as their Lord and led a strictly moral life. Her power lay in the splendid and stringent moral code of her baptismal training, which at once served as an introduction to the Scriptures;[1] moreover, every brother was backed up and assisted in order that he might continue to be fit for the duties he had undertaken to fulfil.[2] Ever since the great conflict with gnosticism and Marcionitism, some instruction in the rule of faith was added. People were no longer satisfied with a few fundamental truths about God and Christ;

preliminary instruction by themselves, Christians admit them into the community whenever they evince adequate evidence of their desire to lead a virtuous life. Certain persons are entrusted by Christians with the duty of investigating and testing the life and conduct of those who come forward, in order to prevent people of evil behaviour from entering the community, and at the same time to extend a hearty welcome to people of a different stamp, and to improve them day by day."

[1] Cp. the *Testimonia* of Cyprian.

[2] Origen distinctly remarks (III. liii.) that the moral and mental training of catechumens and of young adherents of the faith varied according to the require-ments of their position and the amount of their knowledge. After Zezschwitz, Holtzmann, in his essay on "The Catechising of the Early Church" (*Abhandl. f. Weizsäcker*, 1892, pp. 53 f.), has given the most thorough account of the pedagogy of the church. But we must refrain from imagining that catechetical instruction was uniformly as thoroughgoing and comprehensive during the third century as it was, say, in Jerusalem under Cyril in the fourth. In the majority of churches there were no clergy capable of taking part in this work. Still, the demand was there, and this demand for initiation into religion by means of regular, public, and individual instruction in morals and religion raised Christianity far above all pagan religions and mysteries, while at the same time it allied Christianity to knowledge and education. Even when it clothed part of its doctrine in mysteries (as in the third century), the message still remained open and accessible to all. The letter of Ptolemæus to Flora shows the graded instruction in Christianity given by the Valentinians.

a detailed exposition of the dogmatic creed, based on the baptismal formula, and presented in apologetic and controversial shape, was also laid before the catechumen. At the same time, prior to Constantine, while we have requirements exacted from the catechumens (or those recently baptized), we possess no catechisms of a dogmatic character.

It is deeply to be deplored that the first three centuries yield no biographies depicting the conversion or the inner rise and growth of any Christian personality. It is not as if such documents had perished: they were never written. We do not even know the inner history of Paul up to the day on which he reached Damascus; all we know is the rupture which Paul himself felt to be a sudden occurrence. Justin indeed describes (in his *Dialogue with Trypho*, i. f.) the steps leading up to his secession to Christianity, his passage through the philosophic schools, and finally his apprehension of the truth which rested on revelation; but the narrative is evidently touched up and it is not particularly instructive. Thanks to Tatian's *Oratio*, we get a somewhat deeper insight into that writer's inner growth, but here, too, we are unable to form any real idea of the change. Otherwise, Cyprian's little treatise *ad Donatum* is of the greatest service. What he sought for was a power to free him from an unworthy life, and in the Christian faith he found this power.

How deeply must conversion have driven its wedge into marriage and domestic life! What an amount of strain, dispeace, and estrangement conversion must have produced, if one member was a Christian while another clung to the old religion! "Brother shall deliver up brother to death, and the father his child: children shall rise up against their parents and have them put to death." "I came not to bring peace on earth, but a sword. For I came to set a man at variance with his father, and the daughter against her mother, and the daughter-in-law against her mother-in-law; and a man's foes shall be they of his own household. He who loveth father and mother more than me is not worthy of me; and he who loves son or daughter more than me is not worthy of me" (Matt. x. 21, 34–37). These prophecies, says Tertullian (*Scorp.*, ix.), were fulfilled in none of the apostles; therefore they apply to us. "Nemo enim apostolorum aut fratrem aut patrem passus est traditorem, quod plerique iam nostri" ("None of the apostles was betrayed by father or brother, *as most of us to-day are*"). Cp. ch. xi.: "We are betrayed by our next of kin." Justin (*Dial.* xxxv.) says the same: "We are put to death by our kindred." "The father, the neighbour, the son, the friend, the brother, the husband, the wife, are imperilled; if they seek to maintain discipline, they are in danger of being denounced" (*Apol.*, II. i.). "If anyone," says Clement (*Quis Dives*, xxii.), "has a godless father or brother or son, who would be a hindrance to faith and an obstacle to the higher life, he must not associate with him or share his position; he must abjure the fleshly tie on account of the spiritual hostility."[1] In the *Recognitions* of Clement (ii. 29) we read: "In unaquaque domo, cum inter credentem et non credentem coeperit esse diversitas, necessario pugna fit, incredulis quidem contra fidem dimicantibus, fidelibus vero in illis errorem veterem et peccatorum vitia confutantibus" ("When differences arise in any household between a believer and an unbeliever, an inevitable conflict arises, the unbelievers fighting against the faith, and the faithful refuting their old error and sinful vices"). Eusebius (*Theophan.*, iv. 12) writes, on Luke xii. 51 f.: "Further, we see that no word of man, whether philosopher or poet, Greek or barbarian, has ever had the force of these words, whereby Christ rules the entire world, breaking up every household, parting and separating all generations, so that some think as he thinks whilst others find themselves opposed to him." A very meagre record of these tragedies has come down to us. The orator Aristides (*Orat.*, xlvi.) alludes to them in a passage which will come up before us later on. Justin (*Apol.*, II.) tells us of an aristocratic couple in Rome who were leading a profligate life. The woman became a Christian, and, unable ultimately to put up with her profligate husband any

---

[1] He continues (ch. xxiii.): "Suppose it is a lawsuit. Suppose your father were to appear to you and say, 'I begot you, I reared you. Follow me, join me in wickedness, and obey not the law of Christ,' and so on, as any blasphemer, dead by nature, would say."

longer, proposed a divorce; whereupon he denounced her and her teacher to the city prefect as Christians.[1] When Thecla became a Christian, she would have nothing to do with her bridegroom—a state of matters which must have been fairly common, like the refusal of converted wives to admit a husband's marital rights. Thecla's bridegroom denounced her teacher to the magistrates, and she herself left her parents' house. Celsus (Orig., *adv. Cels.*, III. lv.) gives a drastic account of how Christian fanatics of the baser classes sowed dispeace in families of their own standing. The picture is at least drawn from personal observation, and on that account it must not be left out here. " As we see, workers in wool and leather, fullers and cobblers, people entirely uneducated and unpolished, do not venture in private houses to say a word in presence of their employers, who are older and wiser than themselves. But as soon as they get hold of young people and such women as are as ignorant as themselves, in private, they become wonderfully eloquent. ' You must follow us,' they say, ' and not your own father or teachers; the latter are deranged and stupid ; in the grip of silly prejudices, how can they conceive or carry out anything truly noble or good ? Let the young people follow us, for so they will be happy and make the household happy also!' If they see, as they talk so, a teacher or intelligent person or the father himself coming, the timorous among them are sore afraid, while the more forward incite the young folks to fling off the yoke. ' So long as you are with *them*,' they whisper, ' we cannot and will not impart any good to you ; we have no wish to expose ourselves to their corrupt folly and cruelty, to their abandoned sinfulness and vindictive tempers ! If you want to pick up any good, leave your fathers and teachers. Come with your playmates and the women to the women's apartments, or to the cobbler's stall, or to the fuller's shop ! There you will attain the perfect life !' Such are their wheedling words." A sketch like this, apart from its malice, was certainly applicable to the time of the Antonines ; hardly so, when Origen wrote. Origen is quite indignant that Christian teachers should be

---

[1] Tertullian distinctly says (*ad Uxor.*, II. v.) that heathen husbands held their wives in check by the fact that they could denounce them at any moment.

mixed up with wool-dressers, cobblers, and fullers, but he cannot deny that young people and women were withdrawn from their teachers and parents. He simply declares that they were all the better for it (III. lvi.).

The scenes between Perpetua[1] and her father are most affecting. He tried at first to bring her back by force,[2] and then besought her with tears and entreaties (ch. v.).[3] The crowd called out to the martyr Agathonikê, " Have pity on thy son!" But she replied, " He has God, and God is able to have pity on his own." Pagan spectators of the execution of

---

[1] " Honeste nata, liberaliter instituta, matronaliter nupta, habens patrem et matrem et fratres duos, alterum aeque catechuminum, et filium infantem ad ubera" (" A woman of respectable birth, well educated, a married matron, with a father, mother, and two brothers alive, one of the latter being, like herself, a catechumen, and with an infant son at the breast").

[2] " Tunc pater mittit se in me, ut oculos mihi erueret, sed vexavit tantum . . . . tunc paucis diebus quod caruissem patrem, domino gratias egi et refrigeravi absentia illius" (" Then my father flung himself upon me as if he would tear out my eyes. But he only distressed me . . . . then a few days after my father had left me, I thanked the Lord, and his absence was a consolation to me "), ch. iii.

[3] " Supervenit de civitate pater meus, consumptus taedio et adscendit ad me, ut me deiiceret dicens: Filia, miserere canis meis, miserere patri, si dignus sum a te pater vocari ; si his te manibus ad hunc florem aetatis provexi, si te praeposui omnibus fratribus tuis ; ne me dederis in dedecus hominum. aspice fratres tuos, aspice matrem tuam et materteram, aspice filium tuum, qui post te vivere non poterit . . . . haec dicebat quasi pater pro sua pietate, basians mihi manus, et se ad pedes meos jactans et lacrimans me iam non filiam nominabat, sed dominam" (" Then my father arrived from the city, worn out with anxiety. He came up to me in order to overthrow my resolve, saying, 'Daughter, have pity on my grey hairs ; have pity on your father, if I am worthy to be called your father ; if with these hands I have brought you up to this bloom of life, if I have preferred you to all your brothers, hand me not over to the scorn of men. Consider your brothers, your mother, your aunt, your son who will not be able to survive you.' . . . . So spake my father in his affection, kissing my hands and throwing himself at my feet, and calling me with tears not daughter, but lady"). Cp. vi. : " Cum staret pater ad me deiciendam jussus est ab Hilariano (the judge) proici, et virga percussus est. et doluit mihi casus patri mei, quasi ego fuissem percussa : sic dolui pro senecta eius misera" (" As my father stood there to cast me down from my faith, Hilarianus ordered him to be thrown on his face and beaten with rods ; and my father's ill case grieved me as if it had been my own, such was my grief for his pitiful old age "); also ix. : " Intrat ad me pater consumptus taedio et coepit parbam suam evellere et in terram mittere et prosternere se in faciem et inproperare armis suis et dicere tanta verba quae moverent universam creaturam" (" My father came in to me, worn out with anxiety, and began to tear his beard and to fling himself on the earth, and to throw himself on his face and to reproach his years, and utter such words as might move all creation ").

Christians would cry out pitifully: "Et puto liberos habet. nam est illi societas in penatibus coniunx, et tamen nec vinculo pignerum cedit nec obsequio pietatis abductus a proposito suo deficit" (Novat., *de Laude Mart.*, xv.: "Yet I believe the man he has a wife at home. In spite of this, however, he does not yield to the bond of his offspring, nor withdraw from his purpose under the constraint of family affection"). "Uxorem iam pudicam maritus iam non zelotypus, filium iam subiectum pater retro patiens abdicavit, servum iam fidelem dominus olim mitis ab oculis relegavit" (Tert., *Apol.*, iii.: "Though jealous no longer, the husband expels his wife who is now chaste; the son, now obedient, is disowned by his father who was formerly lenient; the master, once so mild, cannot bear the sight of the slave who is now faithful"). Similar instances occur in many of the Acts of the Martyrs.[1] Genesius (Ruinart, p. 312), for example, says that he cursed his Christian parents and relatives. But the reverse also happened. When Origen was young, and in fact little more than a lad, he wrote thus to his father, who had been thrown into prison for his faith: "See that you do not change your mind on our account" (Eus., *H.E.*, vi. 2).[2]

---

[1] During the persecution of Diocletian, Christian girls of good family (from Thessalonica) ran off and wandered about, without their fathers' knowledge, for weeks together in the mountains ("Acta Agapes, Chioniæ, Irenes," in Ruinart's *Acta Mart.*, Ratisbon, 1859, p. 426). How bitterly does the aristocratic Fortunatianus complain before the judge, in the African *Acts of Saturninus and Dativus* (dating from Diocletian's reign; cp. above, p. 363), that Dativus crept into the house and converted his (the speaker's) sister to Christianity during the absence of her father, and then actually took her with him to Abitini (Ruinart, p. 417). Compare the scene between the Christian soldier Marcianus and his wife, a woman of pagan opinions, in the *Acts of Marcianus and Nicander* (Ruinart, p. 572). When her husband goes off to be executed, the woman cries: "Vae miserae mihi! non mihi respondes? miserator esto mei, domine; aspice filium tuum dulcissimum, convertere ad nos, noli nos spernere. Quid festinas? quo tendis? cur nos odisti?" ("Ah, woe is me! will you not answer me? pity me, sir. Look at your darling son. Turn round to us; ah, scorn us not. Why hasten off? Whither do you go? Why hate us?") See also the *Acta Irenæi*, ch. iii. (*op. cit.*, p. 433), where parents and wife alike adjure the young bishop of Sirmium not to sacrifice his life.—Of the martyr Dionysia we read (in Eus., *H.E.*, vi. 41. 18): ἡ πολύπαις μέν, οὐχ ὑπὲρ τὸν κύριον δὲ ἀγαπήσασα ἑαυτῆς τὰ τέκνα ("She had a large family, but she loved not her own children above the Lord").

[2] Cp. Daria, the wife of Nicander, in the *Acts of Marcianus and Nicander*, who exhorted her husband to stand firm. Also the *Acts of Maximilianus*, where the martyr is encouraged by his father, who rejoices in the death of his son; and

In how many cases the husband was a pagan and the wife a Christian (see below, Book IV. Chap. II.). Such a relationship may have frequently[1] been tolerable, but think of all the distress and anguish involved by these marriages in the majority of cases. Look at what Arnobius says (ii. 5): " Malunt solvi conjuges matrimoniis, exheredari a parentibus liberi quam fidem rumpere Christianam et salutaris militiae sacramenta deponere " (" Rather than break their Christian troth or throw aside the oaths of the Christian warfare, wives prefer to be divorced, children to be disinherited ").

A living faith requires no special " methods " for its propagation ; on it sweeps over every obstacle ; even the strongest natural affections cannot overpower it. But it is only to a very limited extent that the third century can be regarded in this ideal aspect. From that date Christianity was chiefly influential as the monotheistic religion of mysteries and as a powerful church which embraced holy persons, holy books, a holy doctrine, and a sanctifying cultus. She even stooped to meet the needs of the masses in a way very different from what had hitherto been followed ; she studied their traditional habits of worship and their polytheistic tendencies by instituting and organizing festivals, deliverers, saints, and local sacred sites, after the popular fashion. In this connection the missionary method followed by Gregory Thaumaturgus (to which we have already referred on p. 315) is thoroughly characteristic ; by consenting to anything, by not merely tolerating but actually promoting a certain syncretism, it achieved, so far as the number of converts was concerned, a most brilliant success. In the following Book (Chap. III., sect. III. 9B.) detailed information will be given upon this point.

---

further, the *Acta Jacobi et Mariani* (Ruinart, p. 273), where the mother of Marianus exults in her son's death as a martyr.

[1] As, *e.g.*, in the case of Augustine's home ; cp. his *Confess.*, i. 11 (17): " Iam [as a boy] credebam et mater et omnis domus, nisi pater solus, qui tamen non evicit in me ius maternae pietatis, quominus in Christum crederem " (" Already I believed, as did my mother and the whole household except my father ; yet he did not prevail over the power of my mother's piety to prevent me believing in Christ "). Augustine's father is described as indifferent, weak, and quite superficial.

JESUS called those who gathered round him "disciples" (μαθηταί); he called himself the "teacher"[1] (this is historically certain), while those whom he had gathered addressed him as teacher,[2] and described themselves as disciples (just as the adherents of John the Baptist were also termed disciples of John). From this it follows that the relation of Jesus to his disciples during his lifetime was determined, not by the conception of Messiah, but by that of teacher. As yet the Messianic dignity of Jesus —only to be revealed at his return—remained a mystery of faith still dimly grasped. Jesus himself did not claim it openly until his entry into Jerusalem.

After the resurrection his disciples witnessed publicly and confidently to the fact that Jesus was the Messiah, but they still continued to call themselves "disciples"—which proves how tenacious names are when once they have been affixed. The twelve confidants of Jesus were called "the twelve disciples" (or, "the twelve").[3] From Acts (cp. i., vi., ix., xi., xiii.–xvi., xviii., xxi.) we learn that although, strictly speaking, "disciples"

---

[1] The saying addressed to the disciples in Matt. xxiii. 8 (ὑμεῖς μὴ κληθῆτε ῥαββεί· εἷς γάρ ἐστιν ὑμῶν ὁ διδάσκαλος, πάντες δὲ ὑμεῖς ἀδελφοί ἐστε) is very noticeable. One would expect μαθηταί instead of ἀδελφοί here; but the latter is quite appropriate, for Jesus is seeking to emphasize the equality of all his disciples and their obligation to love one another. It deserves notice, however, that the apostles were not termed "teachers," or at least very rarely, with the exception of Paul.

[2] Parallel to this is the term ἐπιστάτης, which occurs more than once in Luke.

[3] Οἱ μαθηταί is not a term exclusively reserved for the twelve in the primitive age. All Christians were called by this name. The term ἡ μαθήτρια also occurs (cp. Acts ix. 36, and Gosp. Pet. 50).

had ceased to be applicable, it was retained by Christians for one or two decades as a designation of themselves, especially by the Christians of Palestine.[1] Paul never employed it, however, and gradually, one observes, the name of οἱ μαθηταί (with the addition of τοῦ κυρίου) came to be exclusively applied to *personal* disciples of Jesus, *i.e.*, in the first instance to the twelve, and thereafter to others also,[2] as in Papias, Irenæus, etc. In this way it became a title of honour for those who had themselves seen the Lord (and also for Palestinian Christians of the primitive age in general?), and who could therefore serve as evidence against heretics who subjected the person of Jesus to a docetic decomposition. Confessors and martyrs during the second and third centuries were also honoured with this high title of "disciples of the Lord." They too became, that is to say, *personal* disciples of the Lord. Inasmuch as they attached themselves to him by their confession and he to them (Matt. x. 32), they were promoted to the same rank as the primitive personal disciples of Jesus; they were as near the Lord in glory as were the latter to him during his earthly sojourn.[3]

[1] In Acts xxi. 16 a certain Mnason is called ἀρχαῖος μαθητής, which implies perhaps that he is to be regarded as a personal disciple of Jesus, and at any rate that he was a disciple of the first generation. One also notes that, according to the source employed by Epiphanius (*Hær.*, xxix. 7), μαθηταί was the name of the Christians who left Jerusalem for Pella. I should not admit that Luke is following an unjustifiable archaism in using the term μαθηταί so frequently in Acts.

[2] Is not a restriction of the idea voiced as early as Matt. x. 42 (ὃς ἂν ποτίσῃ ἕνα τῶν μικρῶν τούτων ποτήριον ψυχροῦ μόνον εἰς ὄνομα μαθητοῦ)?

[3] During the period subsequent to Acts it is no longer possible, so far as I know, to prove the use of μαθηταί (without the addition of τοῦ κυρίου or Χριστοῦ) as a term used by all adherents of Jesus to designate themselves; that is, if we leave out of account, of course, all passages —and they are not altogether infrequent—in which the word is not technical. Even with the addition of τοῦ κυρίου, the term ceases to be a title for Christians in general by the second century.—One must not let oneself be misled by late apochryphal books, nor by the apologists of the second century. The latter often describe Christ as their teacher, and themselves (or Christians generally) as disciples, but this has no connection, or at best an extremely loose connection, with the primitive terminology. It is moulded, for apologetic reasons, upon the terminology of the philosophic schools, just as the apologists chose to talk about "dogmas" of the Christian teaching, and "theology" (see my *Dogmensgeschichte*, I.[(3)] pp. 482 f.; Eng. trans., ii. 176 f.). As everyone is aware, the apologists knew perfectly well that, strictly speaking, Christ was not a teacher, but rather lawgiver (νομοθέτης), law (νόμος), Logos (λόγος), Saviour (σωτήρ), and judge (κριτής),

The term "disciples" fell into disuse, because it no longer expressed the relationship in which Christians now found themselves placed. It meant at once too little and too much. Consequently other terms arose, although these did not in every instance become technical.

The Jews, in the first instance, gave their renegade compatriots special names of their own, in particular "Nazarenes," "Galileans," and perhaps also "Poor" (though it is probably quite correct to take this as a self-designation of Jewish Christians, since "Ebionim" in the Old Testament is a term of respect). But these titles really did not prevail except in small circles. "Nazarenes" alone enjoyed and for long retained a somewhat extensive circulation.[1]

so that an expression like κυριακὴ διδασκαλία, or "the Lord's instructions" (apologists and Clem., *Strom.*, VI. xv. 124, VI. xviii. 165, VII. x. 57, VII. xv. 90, VII. xviii. 165), is not to be adduced as a proof that the apologists considered Jesus to be really their teacher. Rather more weight would attach to διδαχὴ κυρίου (the title of the well-known early catechism), and passages like 1 Clem. xiii. 1 (τῶν λόγων τοῦ κυρίου Ἰησοῦ οὓς ἐλάλησεν διδάσκων=the Word of the Lord Jesus which he spoke *when teaching*); Polyc. 2 (μνημονεύοντες ὧν εἶπεν ὁ κύριος διδάσκων=remembering what the Lord said *as he taught*); Ptolem., *ad Flor.* v. (ἡ διδασκαλία τοῦ σωτῆρος); and *Apost. Constit.*, p. 25 (*Texte u. Unters.*, ii., part 5—προορῶντας τοὺς λόγους τοῦ διδασκάλου ἡμῶν=the words of our *teacher*); p. 28 (ὅτε ᾔτησεν ὁ διδάσκαλος τὸν ἄρτον=when the *teacher* asked for bread); p. 30 (προέλεγεν ὅτε ἐδίδασκεν=he foretold when he *taught*). But, apropos of these passages, we have to recollect that the *Apostolic Constitutions* is a work of fiction, which makes the apostles its spokesmen (thus it is that Jesus is termed ὁ διδάσκαλος in the original document underlying the Constitutions, *i.e.*, the disciples call him by this name in the fabricated document).— There are numerous passages to prove that martyrs and confessors were those, and those alone, to whom the predicate of "disciples of Jesus" was attached already, in the present age, since it was they who actually followed and imitated Jesus. Compare, *e.g.*, Ignat., *ad Ephes.* i. (ἐλπίζω ἐπιτυχεῖν ἐν Ῥώμῃ θηριομαχῆσαι, ἵνα ἐπιτυχεῖν δυνηθῶ μαθητὴς εἶναι=my hope is to succeed in fighting with beasts at Rome, so that I may succeed in being a disciple); *ad Rom.* iv. (τότε ἔσομαι μαθητὴς ἀληθὴς τοῦ Χριστοῦ, ὅτε οὐδὲ τὸ σῶμά μου ὁ κόσμος ὄψεται =then shall I be a true disciple of Christ, when the world no longer sees my body; *ad Rom.* v. (ἐν τοῖς ἀδικήμασιν αὐτῶν μᾶλλον μαθητεύομαι=through their misdeeds I became more a disciple than ever); *Mart. Polyc.* xvii. (τὸν υἱὸν τοῦ θεοῦ προσκυνοῦμεν, τοὺς δὲ μάρτυρας ὡς μαθητὰς καὶ μιμητὰς τοῦ κυρίου ἀγαπῶμεν =we worship the Son of God, and love the martyrs as disciples and imitators of the Lord). When Novatian founded his puritan church, he seems to have tried to resuscitate the idea of every Christian being a disciple and imitator of Christ.

[1] The first disciples of Jesus were called Galileans (cp. Acts i. 11, ii. 7), which primarily was a geographical term to denote their origin, but was also

The Christians called themselves " God's people," " Israel in spirit ($\kappa\alpha\tau\grave{\alpha}$ $\pi\nu\epsilon\hat{v}\mu\alpha$)," " the seed of Abraham," " the chosen people," " the twelve tribes," " the elect,"," the servants of God,"

intended to heap scorn on the disciples as semi-pagans. The name rarely became a technical term, however. Epictetus once employed it for Christians (Arrian, *Diss.*, IV. vii. 6). Then Julian resurrected it (Greg. Naz., *Orat.* iv. : καινοτομεῖ ὁ ʼIουλιανὸς περὶ τὴν προσηγορίαν, Γαλιλαίους ἀντὶ Χριστιανῶν ὀνομάσας τε καὶ καλεῖσθαι νομοθετήσας . . . . ὄνομα [Γαλιλαῖοι] τῶν οὐκ εἰωθότων) and employed it as a term of abuse, although in this as in other points he was only following in the footsteps of Maximinus Daza, or of his officer Theoteknus, an opponent of Christianity (if this Theoteknus is to be identified with Daza's officer), who (according to the *Acta Theodoti Ancyrani*, c. xxxi.) dubbed Theodotus προστάτης τῶν Γαλιλαίων, or "the ringleader of the Galileans." These *Acta*, however, are subsequent to Julian. We may assume that the Christians were already called " Galileans " in the anti-Christian writings which Daza caused to be circulated. The *Philopatris* of pseudo-Lucian, where "Galileans" also occurs, has nothing whatever to do with our present purpose ; it is merely a late Byzantine forgery. With the description of Christians as " Galileans," however, we may compare the title of "Phrygians" given to the Montanists.—The name " Ebionites" (or poor) is not quite obvious. Possibly the Christian believers got this name from their Jewish opponents simply because they *were* poor, and accepted the designation. More probably, however, the Palestinian Christians called themselves by this name on the basis of the Old Testament. Recently, Hilgenfeld has followed the church-fathers, Tertullian, Epiphanius (*Hær.*, xxx. 18), etc., in holding that the Ebionites must be traced back to a certain Ebion who founded the sect ; Dalman also advocates this derivation. Technically, the Christians were never described as " the poor " throughout the empire ; the passage in Minuc., *Octav.* xxxvi., is not evidence enough to establish such a theory.—The term "Nazarenes " or "Nazoreans " (a Jewish title for all Jewish Christians, according to Jerome, *Ep.* cxii. 13, and a common Persian and Mohammedan title for Christians in general) occurs first of all in Acts xxiv. 5, where Paul is described by Tertullian the orator as πρωτοστάτης τῆς τῶν Ναζωραίων αἱρέσεως. As Jesus himself is called ὁ Ναζωραῖος in the gospels, there seems to be no doubt that his adherents were so named by their opponents ; it is surprising, though not unexampled. The very designation of Jesus as ὁ Ναζωραῖος is admittedly a problem. Did the title come really from Ναζαρέτ (Ναζαρά) the town ? Furthermore, Matt. ii. 23 presents a real difficulty. And finally, Epiphanius knows a pre-Christian sect of Jewish Nazarenes (*Hær.* xviii. ; their pre-Christian origin is repeated in ch. xxix. 6) in Galaaditis, Basanitis, and other trans-Jordanic districts. They had distinctive traits of their own, and Epiphanius (*Hær.* xxix.) distinguishes them from the Jewish Christian sect of the same name as well as from the Nasireans (cp. *Hær.*, xxix. 5), observing (between xx. and xxi., at the conclusion of his first book) that all Christians were at first called Nazoreans by the Jews. Epiphanius concludes by informing us that before Christians got their name at Antioch, they were for a short while called " Jessæans," which he connects with the Therapeutæ of Philo. Epiphanius is known to have fallen into the greatest confusion over the primitive sects, as is plain from this very passage. We might therefore pass by his pre-Christian Nazarenes without more ado, were it not for the difficulty connected with ὁ Ναζωραῖος as a title of Jesus (and " Nazarenes " as a title for his

"believers," "saints," "brethren," and the church of God."[1] Of these names the first seven (and others of a similar character) never became technical terms taken singly, but, so to speak, collectively. They show how the new community felt itself to be heir to all the promises and privileges of the Jewish nation. At the same time, "the elect"[2] and "the servants of God"[3] came very near being technical expressions.

From the usage and vocabulary of Paul, Acts, and later writings,[4] it follows that "believers" (πιστοί) was a technical

adherents). This has long been felt by scholars, and W. B. Smith, in a lecture at St. Louis (reprinted in *The Monist*, Jan. 1905, pp. 25-45), has recently tried to clear up the problem by means of a daring hypothesis. He conjectures that Jesus had nothing to do with Nazareth, in fact that this town was simply invented and maintained by Christians, on the basis of a wrong interpretation of Ναζωραῖος. ʿΟ Ναζωραῖος is to be understood as a title equivalent to "Nazar-ja" (God is guardian), in the sense of ὁ σωτήρ=Jesus, etc. This is not the place to examine the hypothesis; it will be a welcome find for the "historical religion" school. An unsolved problem undoubtedly there is; but probably, despite Epiphanius and Smith, the traditional explanation may answer all purposes, the more so as the pre-Christian Nazarenes had nothing that reminds us of the early Christians. Epiphanius says that they were Jews, lived like Jews (with circumcision, the sabbath, festivals, rejecting fate and astronomy), acknowledged the fathers from Adam to Moses (Joshua), but rejected the Pentateuch (!!). Moses, they held, did receive a law, but not the law as known to the Jews. They observed the law apart from all its sacrificial injunctions, and ate no flesh, holding that the books of Moses had been falsified. Such is the extent of Epiphanius' knowledge. Are we really to believe that there was a pre-Christian Jewish sect across the Jordan, called Nazarenes, who rejected sacrifice and the eating of flesh? And, supposing this were credible, what could be the connection between them and Jesus, since their sole characteristic, noted by Epiphanius, viz., the rejection of sacrifice and flesh, does not apply to Jesus and the primitive Christians? Is it not more likely that Epiphanius, who simply says the "report" of them had reached him, was wrong in giving the name of Nazarenes to gnostic Jewish Christians, about whom he was imperfectly informed, or to some pre-Christian Jewish sect which lived across the Jordan? Or is there some confusion here between Nazirites and Nazarenes?

[1] So far as I know, no title was ever derived from the name of "Jesus" in the primitive days of Christianity.—On the question whether Christians adopted the name of "Friends" as a technical title, see the first Excursus at the close of this chapter.

[2] Cp. *Minuc. Felix*, xi. "Elect" is opposed to οἱ πολλοί. Hence the latter is applied by Papias to false Christians (Eus., *H.E.*, iii. 39), and by Heracleon the gnostic, on the other hand, to ordinary Christians (Clem., *Strom.* IV. ix. 73).

[3] Cp. the New Testament, and especially the "Shepherd" of Hermas.

[4] Von Wilamowitz-Moellendorff is perhaps right in adducing also *Min. Felix*, xiv., where Cæcilius calls Octavius "pistorum praecipuus et postremus philosophus" ("chief of believers and lowest of philosophers"). "Pistores" here does not mean

term. In assuming the name of "believers" (which originated, we may conjecture, on the soil of Gentile Christianity), Christians felt that the decisive and cardinal thing in their religion was the message which had made them what they were, a message which was nothing else than the preaching of the *one* God, of his son Jesus Christ, and of the life to come.

The three characteristic titles, however, are those of "saints," "brethren," and "the church of God," all of which hang together. The abandonment of the term "disciples" for these self-chosen titles[1] marks the most significant advance made by those who believed in Jesus (cp. Weizsäcker, *op. cit.*, pp. 36 f. ; Eng. trans., i. pp. 43 f.). They took the name of "saints," because they were sanctified by God and for God through the holy Spirit sent by Jesus, and because they were conscious of being truly holy and partakers in the future glory despite all the sins that

---

"millers," but is equivalent to πιστῶν. The pagan in Macarius Magnes (III. xvii.) also calls Christians ἡ τῶν πιστῶν φρατρία. From Celsus also one may conclude that the term πιστοί was technical (Orig., *c. Cels.*, I. ix.). The pagans employed it as an opprobrious name for their opponents, though the Christians wore it as a name of honour ; they were people of mere "belief" instead of people of intelligence and knowledge, *i.e.*, people who were not only credulous but also believed what was absurd (see Lucian's verdict on the Christians in *Proteus Peregrinus*).—In Noricum an inscription has been found, dating from the fourth century (*C.I.L.*, vol. iii. Supplem. Pars Poster., No. 13,529), which describes a woman as "Christiana fidelis," *i.e.*, probably as a baptized Christian. "Fidelis" in the Canon of Elvira means baptized Christian, and "Christianus" means catechumen. The name of "Pistus" was afterwards a favourite name among Christians : two bishops of this name were at the Council of Nicæa. The opposite of "fidelis" was "paganus" (see below).

[1] They are the usual expressions in Paul, but he was by no means the first to employ them ; on the contrary, he must have taken them over from the Jewish Christian communities in Palestine. At the same time they acquired a deeper content in his teaching. In my opinion, it is impossible to maintain the view (which some would derive from the New Testament) that the Christians at Jerusalem were called "the saints," κατ' ἐξοχήν, and it is equally erroneous to conjecture that the Christianity of the apostolic and post-apostolic ages embraced a special and inner circle of people to whom the title of "saints" was exclusively applied. This cannot be made out, either from I Tim. v. 10, or from Heb. xiii. 24, or from Did. iv. 2, or from any other passage, although there was at a very early period a circle of ascetics, *i.e.*, of Christians who, in this sense, were specially "holy." The expression "the holy apostles" in Eph. iii. 5 is extremely surprising ; I do not think it likely that Paul used such a phrase.—The earliest attribute of the word "church," be it noted, was "holy"; cp. the collection of passages in Hahn-Harnack's *Bibliothek der Symbole* [3], p. 388, and also the expressions "holy people" (ἔθνος ἅγιον, λαὸς ἅγιος), "holy priesthood."

daily clung to them.[1] It remains the technical term applied
by Christians to one another till after the middle of the second
century (cp. Clem. Rom., Hermas, the Didachê, etc.); thereafter
it gradually disappears,[2] as Christians had no longer the courage
to call themselves " saints," after all that had happened. Besides, what really distinguished Christians from one another by
this time was the difference between the clergy and the laity (or
the leaders and the led), so that the name " saints " became
quite obliterated; it was only recalled in hard times of persecution. In its place, " holy orders " arose (martyrs, confessors,
ascetics, and finally—during the third century—the bishops),
while " holy media " (sacraments), whose fitful influence covered
Christians who were personally unholy, assumed still greater
prominence than in the first century. People were no longer
conscious of being personally holy,[3] but then they had holy
martyrs, holy ascetics, holy priests, holy ordinances, holy
writings, and a holy doctrine.

Closely bound up with the name of " saints " was that of
" brethren " (and " sisters "), the former denoting the Christians'
relationship to God and to the future life (or βασιλεία τοῦ θεοῦ,
the kingdom of God), the latter the new relationship in which
they felt themselves placed towards their fellow-men, and, above
all, towards their fellow-believers (cp. also the not infrequent
title of " brethren in the Lord "). After Paul, this title became
so common that the pagans soon grew familiar with it, ridicul-
ing and besmirching it, but unable, for all that, to evade the
impression which it made. For the term did correspond to the
conduct of Christians.[4] They termed themselves a brotherhood

---

[1] The actual and sensible guarantee of holiness lay in the holy media, the
"charismata," and the power of expelling demons. The latter possessed not
merely a real but a personal character of their own. For the former, see 1 Cor.
vii. 14: ἡγίασται ὁ ἀνὴρ ὁ ἄπιστος ἐν τῇ γυναικί, καὶ ἡγίασται ἡ γυνὴ ἡ ἄπιστος
ἐν τῷ ἀδελφῷ· ἐπεὶ ἄρα τὰ τέκνα ὑμῶν ἀκάθαρτά ἐστιν, νῦν δὲ ἅγιά ἐστιν.

[2] But Gregory Thaumaturgus still calls Christians in general "the saints," in the
seventh of his canons.

[3] The church formed by Novatian in the middle of the third century called itself
"the pure" (καθαροί), but we cannot tell whether this title was an original formation or the resuscitation of an older name. I do not enter into the question of
the names taken by separate Christian sects and circles (such as the Gnostics, the
Spiritualists, etc.).

[4] See the opinions of pagans quoted by the apologists, especially Tertull., Apol.

($\dot{a}\delta\epsilon\lambda\phi\acute{o}\tau\eta s$; cp. 1 Pet. ii. 17, v. 9, etc.) as well as brethren ($\dot{a}\delta\epsilon\lambda\phi o\acute{\iota}$), and to realize how fixed and frequent was the title, to realize how truly it answered to their life and conduct,[1] one has only to study, not merely the New Testament writings (where Jesus himself employed it and laid great emphasis upon it[2]), but Clemens Romanus, the Didachê, and the writings of the apologists.[3] Yet even the name of "the brethren," though it outlived that of "the saints," lapsed after the close[4] of the third century; or rather, it was only ecclesiastics who really continued to call each other "brethren,"[5] and when a priest gave the title of "brother" to a layman, it denoted a special mark of honour.[6] "Brethren" ("fratres") survived only in

---

xxxix., and Minuc., *Octav.*, ix., xxxi., with Lucian's *Prot. Peregrinus.* Tertullian avers that pagans were amazed at the brotherliness of Christians: "See how they love one another!"—In pagan guilds the name of "brother" is also found, but— so far as I am aware—it is not common. From Acts xxii. 5, xxviii. 21, we must infer that the Jews also called each other "brethren," but the title cannot have had the significance for them that it possessed for Christians. Furthermore, as Jewish teachers call their pupils "children" (or "sons" and "daughters"), and are called by them in turn "father," these appellations also occur very frequently in the relationship between the Christian apostles and teachers and their pupils (cp. the numerous passages in Paul, Barnabas, etc.).

[1] Details on this point, as well as on the import of this fact for the Christian mission, in Book II. Chap. III.

[2] Cp. Matt. xxiii. 8 (see above, p. 399), and xii. 48, where Jesus says of the disciples, ἰδοὺ ἡ μητήρ μου καὶ οἱ ἀδελφοί μου. Thus they are not merely brethren, but *his* brethren. This was familiar to Paul (cp. Rom. viii. 29, πρωτότοκος ἐν πολλοῖς ἀδελφοῖς), but afterwards it became rare, though Tertullian does call the flesh "the sister of Christ" (*de Resurr.* ix., cp. *de Carne*, vii.).

[3] Apologists of a Stoic cast, like Tertullian (*Apol.* xxxix.), did not confine the name of "brethren" to their fellow-believers, but extended it to all men: "Fratres etiam vestri sumus, iure naturae matris unius" ("We are your brethren also in virtue of our common mother Nature").

[4] It still occurs, though rarely, in the third century; cp., *e.g.*, Hippolytus in the *Philosophumena*, and the *Acta Pionii*, ix. Theoretically, of course, the name still survived for a considerable time; cp., *e.g.*, Lactant., *Div. Inst.*, v. 15: "Nec alia causa est cur nobis invicem fratrum nomen impertiamus, nisi quia pares esse nos credimus" [p. 168]; August., *Ep.* xxiii. 1: "Non te latet praeceptum esse nobis divinitus, ut etiam eis qui negant se fratres nostros esse dicamus, fratres nostri estis."

[5] By the third century, however, they had also begun to style each other "dominus."

[6] Eusebius describes, with great delight, how the thrice-blessed emperor addressed the bishops and Christian people, in his numerous writings, as ἀδελφοὶ καὶ συνθεράποντες (*Vita Const.*, iii. 24).

sermons, but confessors were at liberty to address ecclesiastics and even bishops by this title (cp. Cypr., *Ep.* liii.).[1]

Since Christians in the apostolic age felt themselves to be "saints" and "brethren," and, in this sense, to be the true Israel and at the same time God's new creation,[2] they required a solemn title to bring out their complete and divinely appointed character and unity. As "brotherhood" (ἀδελφότης, see above) was too one-sided, the name they chose was that of "church" or "the church of God" (ἐκκλησία, ἐκκλησία τοῦ θεοῦ). This was a masterly stroke. It was the work,[3] not of Paul, nor even of Jesus, but of the Palestinian communities, which must have described themselves as קָהָל. Originally, it was beyond question a collective term;[4] it was the most solemn expression of the Jews for their worship[5] as a collective body, and as such it was taken over by the Christians. But ere long it was applied to the individual communities, and then again to the general meeting for worship. Thanks to this many-sided usage, together with its religious colouring ("the church called by God") and the possibilities of personification which it offered, the conception and the term alike rapidly came to the front.[6]

[1] The gradual restriction of "brethren" to the clergy and the confessors is the surest index of the growing organization and privileges of the churches.

[2] On the titles of "a new people" and "a third race," see Book II. Chap. VI.VII

[3] Paul evidently found it in circulation ; the Christian communities in Jerusalem and Judea already styled themselves ἐκκλησίαι (Gal. i. 22). Jesus did not coin the term ; for it is only put into his lips in Matt. xvi. 18 and xviii. 17, both of which passages are more than suspect from a critical standpoint (see Holtzmann, *ad loc.*) ; moreover, all we know of his preaching well-nigh excludes the possibility that he entertained any idea of creating a special ἐκκλησία (so Matt. xvi. 18), or that he ever had in view the existence of a number of ἐκκλησίαι (so Matt. xviii. 17).

[4] This may be inferred from the Pauline usage of the term itself, apart from the fact that the particular application of all such terms is invariably later than their general meaning. In Acts xii. 1, Christians are first described as οἱ ἀπὸ τῆς ἐκκλησίας.

[5] קָהָל (usually rendered ἐκκλησία in LXX.) denotes the community in relatïɔn to God, and consequently is more sacred' than the profaner עֵדָה (regularly translated by συναγωγή in the LXX.). The acceptance of ἐκκλησία is thus intelligible for the same reason as that of "Israel," "seed of Abraham," etc. Among the Jews, ἐκκλησία lagged far behind συναγωγή in practical use, and this was all in favour of the Christians and their adoption of the term.

[6] Connected with the term ἐκκλησία is the term ὁ λαός, which frequently occurs as a contrast to τὰ ἔθνη. It also has, of course, · Old Testament associations of its own.

Its acquisition rendered the capture of the term "synagogue"[1] a superfluity, and, once the inner cleavage had taken place, the very neglect of the latter title served to distinguish Christians sharply from Judaism and its religious gatherings even in terminology. From the outset, the Gentile Christians learned to think of the new religion as a "church" and as "churches." This did not originally involve an element of authority, but such an element lies hidden from the first in any spiritual magnitude which puts itself forward as at once an ideal and an actual fellowship of men. It possesses regulations and traditions of its own, special functions and forms of organization, and these become authoritative; withal, it supports the individual and at the same time guarantees to him the content of its testimony. Thus, as early as 1 Tim. iii. 15 we read: οἶκος θεοῦ, ἥτις ἐστὶν ἐκκλησία θεοῦ ζῶντος, στῦλος καὶ ἑδραίωμα τῆς ἀληθείας. "Ecclesia mater" frequently occurs in the literature of the second century. Most important of all, however, was the fact that ἐκκλησία was conceived of, in the first instance, not simply as an earthly but as a heavenly and transcendental entity.[2] He who belonged to the ἐκκλησία ceased to have the rights of a citizen on earth;[3] instead of these he acquired an assured citizenship in heaven. This transcendental meaning of the term still retained

[1] On the employment of this term by Christians, see my note on Herm., Mand. xi. It was not nervously eschewed, but it never became technical, except in one or two cases. On the other hand, it is said of the Jewish Christians in Epiph., Hær., xxx. 18, "They have presbyters and heads of synagogues. They call their church a synagogue and not a church; they are proud of no name but Christ's" (πρεσβυτέρους οὗτοι ἔχουσι καὶ ἀρχισυναγώγους· συναγωγὴν δὲ οὗτοι καλοῦσι τὴν ἑαυτῶν ἐκκλησίαν καὶ οὐχὶ ἐκκλησίαν· τῷ Χριστῷ δὲ ὀνόματι μόνον σεμνύνονται). Still, one may doubt if the Jewish Christians really forswore the name קהל (ἐκκλησία); that they called their gatherings and places of meeting συναγωγαί, may be admitted.

[2] The ecclesia is in heaven, created before the world, the Eve of the heavenly Adam, the Bride of Christ, and in a certain sense Christ himself. These Pauline ideas were never lost sight of. In Hermas, in Papias, in Second Clement, in Clement of Alexandria, etc., they recur. Tertullian writes (de Pænit. x.): "In uno et altero Christus est, ecclesia vero Christus. ergo cum te ad fratrum genua protendis, Christum contrectas, Christum exoras" ("In a company of one or two Christ is, but the Church is Christ. Hence, when you throw yourself at your brother's knee, you touch Christ with your embrace, you address your entreaties to Christ").

[3] The self-designation of Christians as "strangers and sojourners" became almost technical in the first century (cp. the epistles of Paul, 1 Peter, and

vigour and vitality during the second century, but in the course of the third it dropped more and more into the rear.[1]

During the course of the second century the term ἐκκλησία acquired the attribute of " catholic " (in addition to that of " holy "). This predicate does not contain anything which implies a secularisation of the church, for " catholic " originally meant Christendom as a whole in contrast to individual churches (ἐκκλησία καθολική = πᾶσα ἡ ἐκκλησία). The conception of " all the churches " is thus identical with that of " the church in general." But a certain dogmatic element did exist from the very outset in the conception of the general church, as the idea was that this church had been diffused by the apostles over all the earth. Hence it was believed that only what existed everywhere throughout the church could be true, and at the same time absolutely true, so that the conceptions of "all Christendom," " Christianity spread over all the earth," and " the true church," came to be regarded at a pretty early period as identical. In this way the term " catholic " acquired a pregnant meaning, and one which in the end was both dogmatic and political. As this was not innate but an innovation, it is not unsuitable to speak of pre-catholic and catholic Christianity. The term " catholic church " occurs first of all in Ignatius (*Smyrn.*, viii. 2 : ὅπου ἄν φανῇ ὁ ἐπίσκοπος, ἐκεῖ τὸ πλῆθος ἔστω· ὥσπερ ὅπου ἄν ᾖ Χριστὸς Ἰησοῦς, ἐκεῖ ἡ καθολικὴ ἐκκλησία), who writes : " Wherever the bishop appears, there let the people be ; just as wherever Christ Jesus is, there is the catholic church." Here, however, the words do not yet denote a new conception of the church, in which it is represented as an empirical and authoritative society. In *Mart. Polyc. Inscr.*, xvi. 2, xix. 2, the word is probably an interpolation ("catholic" being here equivalent to " orthodox": ἡ ἐν Σμύρνῃ καθολικὴ ἐκκλησία). From Iren., iii. 15. 2 (" Valentiniani eos qui sunt ab ecclesia ' communes ' et ' ecclesiasticos ' dicunt "= " The Valentinians called those who

Hebrews), while παροικία (With παροικεῖν=to sojourn) became actually a technical term for the individual community in the world (cp. also Herm., *Simil. I.*, on this).

[1] Till far down into the third century (cp. the usage of Cyprian) the word " secta " was employed by Christians quite ingenuously to denote their fellowship. It was not technical, of course, but a wholly neutral term.

belong to the Church by the name of 'communes' and · ιννν. in astici'") it follows that the orthodox Christians were called "catholics" and "ecclesiastics" at the period of the Valentinian heresy.[1] Irenæus himself does not employ the term; but the thing is there (cp. i. 10. 2; ii. 9. 1, etc.; similarly Serapion in Euseb., *H.E.*, v. 19, πᾶσα ἡ ἐν κόσμῳ ἀδελφότης). After the *Mart. Polyc.* the term "catholic," as a description of the orthodox and visible church, occurs in the Muratorian fragment (where "catholica" stands without "ecclesia" at all, as is frequently the case in later years throughout the West), in an anonymous anti-Montanist writer (Eus., *H.E.*, v 16. 9), in Tertullian (*e.g.*, *de Præscript.*, xxvi., xxx.; *adv. Marc.*, iv. 4, iii. 22), in Clem. Alex (*Strom.*, vii. 17, 106 f.), in Hippolytus (*Philos.*, ix. 12), in *Mart. Pionii* (2. 9. 13. 19), in Pope Cornelius (Cypr., *Epist.* xlix. 2), and in Cyprian. The expression "catholica traditio" occurs in Tertullian (*de Monog.* ii.), "fides catholica" in Cyprian (*Ep.* xxv.), κανών καθολικός in *Mart. Polyc.* (Mosq. *ad fin.*), and Cyprian (*Ep.* lxx. 1), and "catholica fides et religio" in *Mart. Pionii* (18). Elsewhere the word appears in different connections throughout the early Christian literature. In the Western symbols the addition of "catholica" crept in at a comparatively late period, *i.e.*, not before the third century. In the early Roman symbol it does not occur.

We now come to the name "Christians," which became the cardinal title of the faith. The Roman authorities certainly employed it from the days of Trajan downwards (cp. Pliny and the rescripts, the "cognitiones de Christianis"), and probably even forty or fifty years earlier (1 Pet. iv. 16; Tacitus), whilst it was by this name that the adherents of the new religion were known among the common people (Tacitus; cp. also the well-known passage in Suetonius).

---

[1] Ἐκκλησιαστικοί, however, was also a term for orthodox Christians as opposed to heretics during the third century. This is plain from the writings of Origen; cp. Hom. *in Luc.* XVI., vol. v. p. 143 ("ego quia opto esse ecclesiasticus et non ab haeresiarcha aliquo, sed a Christi vocabulo nuncupari"), Hom. *in Jesaiam* VII., vol. xiii. p. 291, Hom. *in Ezech.* II. 2, vol. xiv. p. 34 ("dicor ecclesiasticus"), Hom. *in Ezech.* III. 4, vol. xiv. p. 47 ("ecclesiastici," as opposed to Valentinians and the followers of Basilides), Hom. *in Ezech.* VI. 8, vol. xiv. p. 90 (cp. 120), etc.

A word in closing on the well-known passage from Tacitus (*Annal.*, xv. 44). It is certain that the persecution mentioned here was really a persecution of Christians (and not of Jews), the only doubtful point being whether the use of " Christiani" ("quos per flagitia invisos vulgus Christianos appellabat") is not a *hysteron proteron.* Yet even this doubt seems to me unjustified. If Christians were called by this name in Antioch about 40–45 A.D., there is no obvious reason why the name should not have been known in Rome by 64 A.D., even although the Christians did not spread it themselves, but were only followed by it as by their shadow. Nor does Tacitus (or his source) aver that the name was used by Christians for their own party : he says the very opposite ; it was the people who thus described them. Hitherto, however, the statement of Tacitus has appeared rather unintelligible, for he begins by ascribing the appellation of " Christians" to the common people, and then goes on to relate that the "autor nominis," or author of the name, was Christ, in which case the common people did a very obvious and natural thing when they called Christ's followers " Christians." Why, then, does Tacitus single out the appellation of " Christian." as a popular epithet? This is an enigma which I once proposed to solve by supposing that the populace gave the title to Christians in an obscene or opprobrious sense. I bethought myself of " crista," or of the term " panchristarii," which (so far as I know) occurs only once in Arnobius, ii. 38 : " Quid fullones, lanarios, phrygiones, cocos, panchristarios, muliones, lenones, lanios, meretrices (What of the fullers, woolworkers, embroiderers, cooks, confectioners, muleteers, pimps, butchers, prostitutes) ?". Tacitus, we might conjecture, meant to suggest this meaning, while at the same time he explained the real origin of the term in question. But this hypothesis was unstable, and in my judgment the enigma has now been solved by means of a fresh collation of the Tacitus MS. (see G. Andresen, *Wochenschr. f. klass. Philologie*, 1902, No. 28, col. 780 f.), which shows, as I am convinced from the facsimile, that the original reading was " Chrestianos," and that this was subse-

its adherents from its master? Are not philosophers called after the founder of their philosophies—Platonists, Epicureans, and Pythagoreans ?")

quently corrected (though "Christus" and not "Chrestus" is the term employed *ad loc.*). This clears up the whole matter. The populace, as Tacitus says, called this sect "Chrestiani," while he himself is better informed (like Pliny, who also writes "Christian"), and silently corrects the mistake in the spelling of the names, by accurately designating its author (autor nominis) as "Christus." Blass had anticipated this solution by a conjecture of his own in the passage under discussion, and the event has proved that he was correct. The only point which remains to be noticed is the surprising tense of "appellabat." Why did not Tacitus write "appellat," we may ask? Was it because he wished to indicate that everyone nowadays was well aware of the origin of the name?[1]

One name still falls to be considered, a name which of course never became really technical, but was (so to speak) semi-technical; I mean that of στρατιώτης Χριστοῦ (miles Christi, a soldier of Christ).[2] With Paul this metaphor had already become so common that it was employed in the most diverse ways; compare the great descriptions in 2 Cor. x. 3–6 (στρατευόμεθα—τὰ ὅπλα τῆς στρατείας—πρὸς καθαίρεσιν ὀχυρωμάτων—λογισμοὺς καθαιροῦντες—αἰχμαλωτίζοντες), and the elaborate sketch in Ephes. vi. 10–18, with 1 Thess. v. 8 and 1 Cor. ix. 7, xi. 8; note also how Paul describes his fellow-prisoners as "fellow-captives" (Rom. xvi. 7; Col. iv. 10; Philemon 23), and his fellow-workers as "fellow-soldiers" (Phil. ii. 25; Philemon 2). We come across the same figure again in the pastoral epistles (1 Tim. i. 18: ἵνα στρατεύῃ τὴν καλὴν στρατείαν; 2 Tim. ii. 3 f.: συνκακοπάθησον ὡς καλὸς στρατιώτης Ἰ· Χ. οὐδεὶς στρατευόμενος ἐμπλέκεται ταῖς τοῦ

---

[1] Lietzmann (*Gött. Gel. Anzeig.*, No. 6, 1905, p. 488), thinks that this interpretation is too ingenious. "Tacitus simply means to say that Nero punished the *so-called* Christians 'qui per flagitia invisi erant,' but, in his usual style, he links this to another clause, so that the tense of the 'erant' is taken over into an inappropriate connection with the 'appellabat.' Whereupon follows, quite appropriately, an historical remark on the origin and nature of the sect in question." But are we to suppose that the collocation of this "inappropriate" tense with the change from Christiani to Christus is accidental?

[2] Since the first edition of the present work appeared, I have treated this subject at greater length in my little book upon *Militia Christi: the Christian Religion and the Military Profession during the First Three Centuries* (1905).

βίου πραγματείαις, ἵνα τῷ στρατολογήσαντι ἀρέσῃ. ἐὰν δὲ
ἀθλήσῃ τις, οὐ στεφανοῦται ἐὰν μὴ νομίμως ἀθλήσῃ; 2 Tim.
iii. 6: αἰχμαλωτίζοντες γυναικάρια). Two military principles
were held as fixed, even within the first century, for apostles
and missionaries. (1) They had the right to be supported by
others (their converts or churches). (2) They must not engage
in civil pursuits. Thereafter the figure never lost currency,[1]
becoming so naturalized,[2] among the Latins especially (as a
title for the martyrs pre-eminently, but also for Christians in
general), that "soldiers of Christ" (milites Christi) almost
became a technical term with them for Christians; cp. the
writings of Tertullian, and particularly the correspondence of
Cyprian—where hardly one letter fails to describe Christians
as "soldiers of God" (milites dei), or "soldiers of Christ"
(milites Christi), and where Christ is also called the "imperator"
of Christians.[3] The preference shown for this figure by

[1] Cp., e.g., Ignat., ad Polyc. vi. (a passage in which the technical Latinisms
are also very remarkable): ἀρέσκετε ᾧ στρατεύεσθε, ἀφ' οὗ καὶ τὰ ὀψώνια κομίσεσθε·
μήτις ὑμῶν δεσέρτωρ εὑρεθῇ. τὸ βάπτισμα ὑμῶν μενέτω ὡς ὅπλα, ἡ πίστις ὡς
περικεφαλαία, ἡ ἀγάπη ὡς δόρυ, ἡ ὑπομονὴ ὡς πανοπλία· τὰ δεπόσιτα ὑμῶν τὰ
ἔργα ὑμῶν, ἵνα τὰ ἀκκεπτα ὑμῶν ἄξια κομίσησθε ("Please him for Whom ye fight,
and from Whom ye shall receive your pay. Let none of you be found a deserter.
Let your baptism abide as your shield, your faith as a helmet, your love as a
spear, your patience as a panoply. Let your actions be your deposit, that ye
may receive your due assets"); cp. also ad Smyrn. i. (ἵνα ἄρῃ σύσσημον εἰς τοὺς
αἰῶνας, "that he might raise an ensign to all eternity").

[2] Clemens Romanus's work is extremely characteristic in this light, even by
the end of the first century. He not only employs military figures (e.g., xxi.:
μὴ λιποτακτεῖν ἡμᾶς ἀπὸ τοῦ θελήματος αὐτοῦ=we are not to be deserters from
his will; cp. xxviii.: τῶν αὐτομολούντων ἀπ' αὐτοῦ=running away from him),
but (xxxvii.) presents the Roman military service as a model and type for
Christians: στρατευσώμεθα οὖν, ἄνδρες ἀδελφοί, μετὰ πάσης ἐκτενείας ἐν τοῖς
ἀμώμοις προστάγμασιν αὐτοῦ· κατανοήσωμεν τοὺς στρατευομένους τοῖς ἡγουμένοις
ἡμῶν· πῶς εὐτάκτως, πῶς εὐείκτως, πῶς ὑποτεταγμένως ἐπιτελοῦσιν τὰ διατασ-
σόμενα· οὐ πάντες εἰσὶν ἔπαρχοι οὐδὲ χιλίαρχοι οὐδὲ ἑκατόνταρχοι οὐδὲ πεντακόν-
ταρχοι οὐδὲ τὸ καθεξῆς, ἀλλ' ἕκαστος ἐν τῷ ἰδίῳ τάγματι τὰ ἐπιτασσόμενα ὑπὸ
τοῦ βασιλέως καὶ τῶν ἡγουμένων ἐπιτελεῖ ("Let us then enlist, brethren, in his
flawless ordinances with entire earnestness. Let us mark those who enlist under
our commanders, how orderly, how readily, how obediently, they carry out their
injunctions; all of them are not prefects or captains over a hundred men, or over
fifty, or so forth, but every man in his proper rank carries out the orders of the
king and the commanders").

[3] Cp. Ep. xv. 1 (to the martyrs and confessors): "Nam cum omnes milites
Christi custodire oportet praecepta imperatoris sui [so Lact., Instit., vi. 8 and
vii. 27], tunc vos magis praeceptis eius obtemperare plus convenit" ("For while

Christians of the West, and their incorporation of it in definite representations, may be explained by their more aggressive and at the same time thoroughly practical temper. The currency lent to the figure was reinforced by the fact that "sacramentum" in the West (*i.e.*, any μυστήριον or mystery, and also anything sacred) was an extremely common term, while baptism in particular, or the solemn vow taken at baptism, was also designated a "sacramentum." Being a military term (=the military oath), it made all Western Christians feel that they must be soldiers of Christ, owing to their sacrament, and the probability is, as has been recently shown (by Zahn, *Neue kirchl. Zeitschrift,* 1899, pp. 28 f.), that this usage explains the description of the pagans as "pagani." It can be demonstrated that the latter term was already in use (during the early years of Valentinian I.; cp. Theodos., *Cod.* xvi. 2. 18) long before the development of Christianity had gone so far as to enable all non-Christians to be termed "villagers"; hence the title must rather be taken in the sense of "civilians" (for which there is outside evidence) as opposed to "milites" or soldiers. Non-Christians are people who have not taken the oath of service to God or Christ, and who consequently have no part in the sacrament ("Sacramentum ignorantes," Lactant.)! They are mere "pagani."[1]

it behoves all the soldiers of Christ to observe the instructions of their commander, it is the more fitting that you should obey his instructions"). The expression "camp of Christ" (castra Christi) is particularly common in Cyprian; cp. also *Ep.* liv. 1 for the expression "unitas sacramenti" in connection with the military figure. Cp. pseudo-Augustine (Aug., *Opp.* v., App. p. 150): "Milites Christi sumus et stipendium ab ipso donativumque percepimus" ("We are Christ's soldiers, and from him we have received our pay and presents").—I need not say that the Christian's warfare was invariably figurative in primitive Christianity (in sharp contrast to Islam). It was left to Tertullian, in his *Apology*, to play with the idea that Christians might conceivably take up arms in certain circumstances against the Romans, like the Parthians and Marcomanni; yet even he merely toyed with the idea, for he knew perfectly well, as indeed he expressly declares, that Christians were not allowed to kill (occidere), but only to let themselves be killed (occidi).

[1] For the interpretation of paganus as "pagan" we cannot appeal to Tertull., *de Corona*, xi. (perpetiendum pro deo, quod aeque fides pagana condixit=for God we must endure what even civic loyalty has also borne; apud Jesum tam miles est paganus fidelis, quam paganus est miles fidelis=with Jesus the faithful citizen is a soldier, just as the faithful soldier is a citizen; cp. *de Pallio*, iv.), for "fides

Pagans in part caught up the names of Christians as they

pagana" here means, not pagan faith or loyalty (as one might suppose), but the duty of faith in those who do not belong to the military profession, *i.e.*, in those who are civilians. The subsequent discussion makes this clear, and it also shows that "paganus" was commonly used to mean "civilian." In fact, this connotation can be proved from seven passages in Tacitus. It passed from the military language into that of ordinary people in the course of the first two centuries. The ordinary interpretation of the term (=villagers) rests on the authority of Ulphilas (so still, Schubert, *Lehrbuch d. Kirchengeschichte*, I. p. 477), who has similarly coined the term "heathen" (from pagus), and also on the later Latin church-fathers, who explain "pagani" as "villagers" (cp., *e.g.*, Orosius, *adv. Paganes*, præf. c. 9: "Pagani alieni a civitate dei ex locorum agrestium conpitis et pagis pagani vocantur"). Wilh. Schulze, however (cp. *Berliner Akad. Sitzungsberichte*, 1905, July 6), holds that the term "heathen" in Orosius has nothing to do with "heathen," but is a loan-word (ἔθνος), which was pronounced also ἔθνος, as the Coptic and Armenian transliteration shows. Even were this derivation shown to be incorrect, neither Ulphilas nor any of the later Latin fathers could fix the original meaning of "paganus." None of them knew its original sense. About 300 A.D.—to leave out the inscription in *C.I.L.*, x. 2, 7112— the non-Christian religions could not as yet be designated as "peasant" or "rural" religions. All doubts would have been set at rest if the address of Commodian's so-called *Carmen Apologeticum* had run "adversus paganes" (as Gennadius, *de Vir. Inlust.* 15, suggests), but unfortunately the only extant manuscript lacks any title.—The military figure originated (prior to the inferences drawn from the term "sacramentum" in the West) in the great struggle which every Christian had to wage against Satan and the demons (Eph. vi. 12: οὐκ ἔστιν ἡμῖν ἡ πάλη πρὸς αἷμα καὶ σάρκα, ἀλλὰ πρὸς τὰς ἀρχάς, πρὸς τὰς ἐξουσίας, πρὸς τοὺς κοσμοκράτορας τοῦ σκότους τούτου, πρὸς τὰ πνευματικὰ τῆς πονηρίας ἐν τοῖς ἐπουρανίοις). Once the state assumed a hostile attitude towards Christians, the figure of the military calling and conflict naturally arose also in this connection. God looks down, says Cyprian (*Ep.* lxxvi. 4), upon his troops: "Gazing down on us amid the conflict of his Name, he approves those who are willing, aids the fighters, crowns the conquerors," etc. ("In congressione nominis sui desuper spectans volentes conprobat, adiuvat dimicantes, vincentes coronat," etc.). Nor are detailed descriptions of the military figure awanting ; cp., *e.g.*, the seventy-seventh letter addressed to Cyprian (ch. ii.): "Tu tuba canens dei milites, caelestibus armis instructos, ad congressionis proelium excitasti et in acie prima, spiritali gladio diabolum interfecisti, agmina quoque fratrum hinc et inde verbis tuis composuisti, ut invidiae inimico undique tenderentur et cadavera ipsius publici hostis et nervi concisi calcarentur" ("As a sounding trumpet, thou hast roused the soldiers of God, equipped with heavenly armour, for the shock of battle, and in the forefront thou hast slain the devil with the sword of the Spirit ; on this side and on that thou hast marshalled the lines of the brethren by thy words, so that snares might be laid in all directions for the foe, the sinews of the common enemy be severed, and carcases trodden under foot"). The African Acts of the Martyrs are full of military expressions and metaphors ; see, *e.g.*, the *Acta Saturnini et Dativi*, xv. (Ruinart, *Acta Mart.*, p. 420). It is impossible to prove, as it is inherently unlikely, that the "milites" of Mithra exercised any influence upon the Christian conceptions of Christianity as a conflict. These "milites" of Mithra were simply one of the seven stages of Mithraism, and we must never regard as direct borrowings from a pagan cult ideas which were

27

heard them on the latter's lips,[1] but of course they used most commonly the title which they had coined themselves, viz., that of "Christians." Alongside of this we find nicknames and sobriquets like "Galileans," "ass-worshippers" (Tert., *Apol.* xvi., cp. *Minut.*), "magicians" (*Acta Theclæ*, Tertull.), "Third race," "filth" (*copria*, cp. Commod., *Carm. Apolog.* 612, Lact., v. 1. 27), "sarmenticii" and "semi-axii" (stake-bound, faggot-circled ; Tert., *Apol.* i.).[2]

Closely bound up with the "names" of Christians is the discussion of the question whether individual Christians got new names as Christians, or how Christians stood with regard to ordinary pagan names during the first three centuries. The answer to this will be found in the second Excursus appended to the present chapter.

spread all over the church at a primitive period of its existence. On the other hand, it is likely that Christians in the Roman army desired the same treatment and consideration which was enjoyed by adherents of Mithra in the same position. Hence the action of the soldier described by Tertullian in the *de Corona.*—The above-mentioned essay of Schulze is now printed in the *Sitzungsberichte d. Preuss. Akad. d. Wiss.*, 1905, pp. 726 f., 747 f. ("Greek Loan-Words in Gothic"). He acknowledges (i.) that "pagani" cannot have been adopted by Christians in order to describe "pagans" as people dwelling in the country ; (ii.) he proves carefully and conclusively that the term "heathen" in Ulphilas has nothing to do with heathen, but is a loan-word ($\xi\theta\nu o\varsigma$). Non-Christians were originally called "pagani" as "sacramentum ignorantes" (Lactant., v. 1), or because they were "far from the city of God" ("longe sunt a civitate dei," Cassiod., *in Cant.*, vii. 11 ; cp. Schulze, p. 751). Attention has also been called of late to several inscriptions with the word "paganicum" (cp. *Compt. rendus de l'acad. des Inscr. et Belles Lett.*, 1905, May-June, pp. 296 f.). The scope and the meaning of the word are rather obscure ("une sorte de chapelle rurale"? A building in the country devoted to public purposes? Or has the reference to the country even here become obliterated ?).

[1] Celsus, for instance, speaks of the church as "the great church" (to distinguish it from the smaller Christian sects).

[2] Terms drawn derisively from the methods of death inflicted upon Christians.

EXCURSUS I

"FRIENDS" (οἱ φίλοι).

THE name φίλοι (οἰκεῖοι) τοῦ θεοῦ ("amici dei," "cari deo") was frequently used as a self-designation by Christians, though it was not strictly a technical term. It went back [1] to the predicate of Abraham, who was called "the Friend of God" in Jewish tradition. It signified that every individual Christian stood in the same relation to God as Abraham [2] had done. According to two passages in the gospels,[3] Jesus called his

[1] Cp. Jas. ii. 23 with the editors' notes. The prophets occasionally shared this title, cp. Hippolyt., *Philos.*, x. 33: δίκαιοι ἄνδρες γεγένηνται φίλοι θεοῦ· οὗτοι προφῆται κέκληνται ("Just men have become friends of God, and these are named prophets"). Justin gives the name of Χριστοῦ φίλοι ("Christ's friends") to the prophets who wrote the Old Testament (*Dial.* viii.). John the Baptist is φίλος Ἰησοῦ (John iii. 29). Cp. Eus., *Demonstr.*, i. 5.

[2] Later, of course, it was applied pre-eminently to martyrs and confessors :— Ephes. ii. 19: οὐκέτι ἐστὲ ξένοι καὶ πάροικοι, ἀλλ' ἐστὲ συμπολῖται τῶν ἁγίων καὶ οἰκεῖοι τοῦ θεοῦ; Valentinus (in Clem., *Strom.*, vi. 6. 52): λαὸς ὁ ἠγαπημένου, ὁ φιλούμενος καὶ φιλῶν αὐτόν; Clem., *Protrept.*, xii. 122: εἰ κοινὰ τὰ φίλων, θεοφιλὴς δὲ ὁ ἄνθρωπος τῷ θεῷ—καὶ γὰρ οὖν φίλος μεσιτεύοντος τοῦ λόγου—γίνεται δὴ οὖν τὰ πάντα τοῦ ἀνθρώπου, ὅτι τὰ πάντα τοῦ θεοῦ, καὶ κοινὰ ἀμφοῖν τοῖν φιλοῖν τὰ πάντα, τοῦ φεοῦ καὶ τοῦ ἀνθρώπου; *Pædag.*, i. 3: φίλος ὁ ἄνθρωπος τῷ θεῷ (for the sake of the way in which he was created; so that all human beings are friends of God); Origen, *de Princ.*, I. 6. 4: "amici dei"; Tertullian, *de Pœnit.* ix. (the martyrs, "cari dei"); Cyprian, *ad Demetr.* xii. (" cari deo "), and pseudo-Clem., *Recogn.*, i. 24: "Ex prima voluntate iterum voluntas; post haec mundus; ex mundo tempus; ex hoc hominum multitudo; ex multitudine electio amicorum, ex quorum unanimitate pacificum construitur dei regnum"; pseudo-Cypr., *de Sing. Cler.* 27: "amici dei."

[3] Luke xii. 4: λέγω ὑμῖν, τοῖς φίλοις μου; John xv. 13 f.: ὑμεῖς φίλοι μού ἐστε, ἐὰν ποιῆτε ἃ ἐντέλλομαι ὑμῖν. οὐκέτι λέγω ὑμᾶς δούλους . . . . ὑμᾶς δὲ εἴρηκα φίλους, ὅτι πάντα ἃ ἤκουσα παρὰ τοῦ πατρός μου ἐγνώρισα ὑμῖν. Hence the disciples are γνώριμοι of Jesus (Clem., *Paed.*, i. 5, beginning; Iren., iv. 13. 4: "In eo quod amicos dicit suos discipulos, manifeste ostendit se esse verbum Dei, quem et Abraham . . . . sequens amicus factus est dei . . . . quoniam amicitia

disciples his "friends." But in after-years this title (or that of οἱ γνώριμοι) was rarely used.

The term οἱ φίλοι is to be distinguished from that of φίλοι τοῦ θεοῦ (χριστοῦ). Did Christians also call each other "friends"? We know the significance which came to attach to friendship in the schools of Greek philosophy. No one ever spoke more nobly and warmly of friendship than Aristotle. Never was it more vividly realized than in the schools of the Pythagoreans and the Epicureans. If the former went the length of a community of goods, the Samian sage outstripped them with his counsel, "Put not your property into a common holding, for that implies a mutual distrust. And if people distrust each other, they cannot be friends" (μὴ κατατίθεοθαι τὰς οὐσίας εἰς τὸ κοινὸν · ἀπιστούντων γὰρ τὸ τοιοῦτον · εἰ δ' ἀπίστων, οὐδὲ φίλων). The intercourse of Socrates with his scholars—scholars who were at the same time his friends—furnished a moving picture of friendship. Men could not forget how he lived with them, how he laboured for them and was open to them up to the very hour of his death, and how everything he taught them came home to them as a friend's counsel. The Stoic ethic, based on the absence of any wants in the perfect wise man, certainly left no room for friendship, but (as is often the case) the Stoic broke through the theory of his school at this point, and Seneca was not the only Stoic moralist who glorified friendship and showed how it was a moral necessity to life. No wonder that the Epicureans, like the Pythagoreans before them, simply called themselves "friends." It formed at once the simplest and the deepest expression for that inner bond of life into which men found themselves transplanted when they entered the fellowship of the school. No matter whether it was the common reverence felt for the master, or the community of sentiment and aspiration among the members, or the mutual aid owed by each individual to his

---

dei συγχωρητική ἐστι τῆς ἀθανασίας τοῖς ἐπιλαβοῦσιν αὐτήν "). Perhaps the words quoted by Clement (*Quis Dives*, xxxiii.: δώσω οὐ μόνον τοῖς φίλοις, ἀλλὰ καὶ τοῖς φίλοις τῶν φίλων) are an apocryphal saying of Jesus, but their origin is uncertain (cp. Jülicher in *Theol. Lit. Zeitung*, 1894, No. 1). An inscription has been found in Isaura Nova with the legend φίλτατος ὁ μακάριος ὁ θεοῦ φίλος (cp. A. M. Ramsay in *Journal of Hellenic Studies*, xxiv., 1904, p. 264, "The Early Christian Art of Isaura Nova ").

fellows—the relationship in every case was covered by the term of " the friends."

We should expect to find that Christians also called' themselves " the friends." But there is hardly any passage bearing this out. In one of the " we " sections in Acts (xxvii. 3) we read that Paul the prisoner was permitted πρὸς τοὺς φίλους πορευθέντι ἐπιμελείας τυχεῖν. Probably οἱ φίλοι here means not special friends of the apostle, but Christians in general (who elsewhere are always called in Acts οἱ ἀδελφοί). But this is the only passage in the primitive literature which can be adduced. Luke, with his classical culture, has permitted himself this once to use the classical designation. In 3 John 15 (ἀσπάζονται σε οἱ φίλοι· ἀσπάζου τοὺς φίλους κατ' ὄνομα) it is most likely that special friends are meant, not all the Christians at Ephesus and at the place where the letter is composed. Evidently the natural term οἱ φίλοι did not gain currency in the catholic church, owing to the fact that οἱ ἀδελφοί (cp. above, pp. 405 f.) was preferred as being still more inward and warm. In gnostic circles, on the other hand, which arose subsequently under the influence of Greek philosophy, οἱ φίλοι seems to have been used during the second century. Thus Valentinus wrote a homily περὶ φίλων (cp. Clem., Strom., vi. 6. 52); Epiphanius, the son of Carpocrates, founded a Christian communistic guild after the model of the Pythagoreans, and perhaps also after the model of the Epicurean school and its organization (Clem., Strom., iii. 5–9); while the Abercius-inscription, which is probably gnostic, tells how faith furnished the fish as food for (τοῖς) φίλοις. Clement of Alexandria would have had no objection to describe the true gnostic circle as " friends." It is he who preserves the fine saying (Quis Dives, xxxii.): " The Lord did not say [in Luke xvi. 9] give, or provide, or benefit, or aid, but make a friend. And friendship springs, not from a single act of giving, but from invariable relief vouchsafed and from long intercourse" (οὐ μὴ οὐδ' εἶπεν ὁ κύριος, Δος, ἢ Παράσχες, ἢ 'Ευεργέτησον, ἢ Βοήθησον· φίλον δὲ ποιῆσαι· ὁ δὲ φίλος οὐκ ἐκ μίας δόσεως γίνεται, ἀλλ' ἐξ ὅλης ἀναπαύσεως καὶ συνουσίας μακρᾶς).

EXCURSUS II

CHRISTIAN NAMES

DOES the use of Christian names taken from the Bible go back to the first three centuries? In answering this question, we come upon several instructive data.

Upon consulting the earliest synodical Acts in our possession, those of the North African synod in 256 A.D. (preserved in Cyprian's works), we find that while the names of the eighty-seven bishops who voted there are for the most part Latin, though a considerable number are Greek, not one Old Testament name occurs. Only two are from the New Testament, viz., Peter (No. 72) and Paul (No. 47). Thus, by the middle of the third century pagan names were still employed quite freely throughout Northern Africa, and the necessity of employing Christian names had hardly as yet arisen. The same holds true of all the other regions of Christendom. As inscriptions and writings testify, Christians in East and West alike made an exclusive or almost exclusive use of the old pagan names in their environment till after the middle of the third century, employing, indeed, very often names from pagan mythology and soothsaying. We find Christians called Apollinaris, Apollonius, Heraclius, Saturninus, Mercurius, Bacchylus, Bacchylides, Serapion, Satyrus, Aphrodisius, Dionysius, Hermas, Origen, etc., besides Faustus, Felix, and Felicissimus. "The martyrs perished because they declined to sacrifice to the gods whose names they bore"!

Now this is remarkable! Here was the primitive church exterminating every vestige of polytheism in her midst, tabooing pagan mythology as devilish, living with the great personalities of the Bible and upon their words, and yet freely employing the pagan names which had been hitherto in vogue! The problem becomes even harder when one recollects that the Bible itself contains examples of fresh names being given,[1] that surnames and alterations of a name were of frequent occurrence in the Roman empire (the practice, in fact, being legalized by the emperor Caracalla in 212 for all free men), and that a man's name in antiquity was by no means regarded by most people as a matter of indifference.

We may be inclined to seek various reasons for this indifference displayed by the primitive Christians towards names. We may point to the fact that a whole series of pagan names must have been rendered sacred from the outset by the mere fact of distinguished Christians having borne them. We may further recollect how soon Christians got the length of strenuously asserting that there was nothing in a name. Why, from the days of Trajan onwards they were condemned on account of the mere name of " Christian " without anyone thinking it necessary to inquire if they had actually committed any crime! On the other hand, Justin, Athenagoras, and Tertullian, as apologists of Christianity, emphasize the fact that the name is a hollow vessel, that there can be no rational " charge brought against words,"—" except, of course," adds Tertullian, " when a name sounds barbarian or ill-omened, or when it contains some insult or impropriety!" " Ill-omened"! But had " dæmonic" names like Saturninus, Serapion, and Apollonius no evil connotation upon the lips of Christians, and did not Christians, again, attach a healing virtue to the very language of certain formulas (e.g., the utterance of the name of Jesus in exorcisms), just as the heathen did? No; surely this does not serve to explain the indifference felt by Christians towards mythological titles. But if not, then how are we to explain it ?

Hardly any other answer can be given to the question than this, that the general custom of the world in which people were living proved stronger than any reflections of their own. At

---

[1] Thus in the gospels we read of Jesus calling Simon " Kephas " and the sons of Zebedee " Boanerges." In Acts iv. 36 we are told that the Apostles named a man called Joseph " Barnabas" (Saulus Paulus does not come under this class).

all times, new names have encountered a powerful resistance in the plea, "There is none of thy kindred that is called by this name" (Luke i. 61). The result was that people retained the old names, just as they had to endorse or to endure much that was of the world, so long as they were in the world. It was not worth while to alter the name which one found oneself bearing. Why, everyone, be he called Apollonius or Serapion, had already got a second, distinctive, and abiding name in baptism, the name of "Christian." Each individual believer bore that as a proper name. In the Acts of Carpus (during the reign of Marcus Aurelius) the magistrate asked the accused, "What is thy name?" The answer was, "My first and foremost name is that of 'Christian'; but if thou demandest my wordly name as well, I am called 'Carpus.'" The "worldly" name was kept up, but it did not count, so to speak, as the real name. In the account of the martyrs at Lyons, Sanctus the Christian is said to have withheld his proper name from the magistrate, contenting himself with the one reply, "I am a Christian!"[1]

This one name satisfied people till about the middle of the third century; along with it they were content to bear the ordinary names of this world "as though they bore them not." Even surnames with a Christian meaning are extremely rare. It is the exception, not the rule, to find a man like bishop Ignatius calling himself by the additional Christian title of Theophorus at the opening of the second century.[2] The change first came a little before the middle of the third century. And

---

[1] Similarly Eusebius (*Mart. Pal.*, p. 82, ed. Violet): "The confessors, when asked by the judge where they came from, forbore to speak of their home on earth, but gave their true heavenly home, saying, We belong to the Jerusalem which is above" (cp. also, in *Eugipii epist. ad Pascasium*, 9, how St Severin describes his origin). Augustine also is evidence for the use of "Christianus" as a proper name. Looking back on his childhood (though he was not baptized till he was a man), he writes: "In ecclesia mihi nomen Christi infanti est inditum" (*Confess.*, vi. 4. 5).

[2] Other surnames (which were not Christian) also occur among Christians; cp. Tertull., *ad Scapulam*, iv. : "Proculus Christianus, qui Torpacion cognominabatur." Similar cases were not unusual at that time. The Christian soldier Tarachus (*Acta Tarachi* in Ruinart's *Acta Martyr.*, Ratisbon 1859, p. 452) says: "My parents called me Tarachus, and when I became a soldier I was called Victor" ("a parenti-

the surprising thing is that the change, for which the way had been slowly paved, came, not in an epoch of religious elevation, but rather in the very period during which the church was coming to terms with the world on a larger scale than she had previously done. In the days when Christians bore pagan names and nothing more, the dividing line between Christianity and the world was drawn much more sharply than in the days when they began to call themselves Peter and Paul! As so often is the case, the forms made their appearance just when the spirit was undermined. The principle of "nomen est omen" was not violated. It remained extraordinarily significant. For the name indicates that one has to take certain measures in order to keep hold of something that is in danger of disappearing.

In many cases people may not have been conscious of this. On the contrary, three reasons were operative. One of these I have already mentioned, viz., the frequent occurrence throughout the empire (even among pagans) of alteration in a name, and also of surnames being added, after the edict of Caracalla (in 212 A.D.). The second lay in the practice of infant baptism, which was now becoming quite current. As a name was conferred upon the child at this solemn act, it naturally seemed good to choose a specifically Christian name. Thirdly and lastly, and—we may add—chiefly, the more the church entered the world, the more the world also entered the church. And with the world there entered more and more of the old pagan superstition that "nomen est omen," the dread felt for words, and, moreover, the old propensity for securing deliverers, angels,

---

bus dicor Tarachus, et cum militarem nominatus sum Victor"). Cyprian (according to Jerome, de Vir. Illustr. xlviii.) called himself Cæcilius after the priest who was the means of his conversion; besides that he bore the surname of Thascius, so that his full name ran, "Cæcilius Cyprianus qui et Thascius" (Ep. lxii., an epistle which is written to a Christian called "Florentius qui et Puppianus"). Cumont (Les Inscr. chrét. de l'Asie mineure, p. 22) has collected a series of examples from the inscriptions, some of which are undoubtedly Christian: Γέρων ὁ καὶ Κυριακός, Ἄτταλος ἐπίκλην Ἡσαΐας, Optatina Resticia Pascasia, M. Cæcilius Saturninus qui et Eusebius, Valentina ancilla quae et Stephana, Ascia vel Maria. Of the forty martyrs of Sebaste two bear double names of this kind, viz., Λεόντιος ὁ καὶ Θεόκτιστος Βικράτιος ὁ καὶ Βιβιανός. In The Martyrdom of St Conon we find a Ναόδωρος ὁ καὶ Ἀπελλῆς. The martyr Achatius says, "I am called Agathos-angelus" ("vocor Agathos-angelus").

and spiritual heroes upon one's side, together with the " pious " belief that one inclined a saint to be one's protector and patron by taking his name. Such a form of superstition has never been quite-absent from Christianity, for even the primitive Christians were not merely Christians but also Jews, Syrians, Asiatics, Greeks, or Romans. But then it was controlled by other moods or movements of the Spirit. During the third century, how-ever, the local strain again rose to the surface. People no longer called their children Bacchylus or Arphrodisius with the same readiness, it is true. *But they began to call themselves Peter and Paul in the same sense as the pagans called their children Dionysius and Serapion.*

The process of displacing mythological by Christian names was carried out very slowly. It was never quite completed, for not a few of the former gradually became Christian, thanks to some glorious characters who had borne them ; in this way, they entirely lost their original meaning. One or two items from the history of this process may be adduced at this point in our discussion.

At the very time when we find only two biblical names (those of Peter and Paul) in a list of eighty-seven episcopal names, bishop Dionysius of Alexandria writes that Christians prefer to call their children Peter and Paul.[1] It was then also that Christian changes [2] of name began to be common. It is noted (in Eus., *H.E.*, vi. 30) that Gregory Thaumaturgus exchanged the name of Theodore for Gregory, but this instance is not quite clear.[3] We are told that a certain Sabina, during the

---

[1] In Eus., *H.E.*, vii. 25. 14: ὥσπερ καὶ ὁ Παῦλος πολὺς καὶ δὴ καὶ ὁ Πέτρος ἐν τοῖς τῶν πιστῶν παισὶν ὀνομάζεται (" Even as the children of the faithful are often called after Paul and also after Peter "). This is corroborated by an inscription from the third century (de Rossi, in *Bullett. di archæol. crist.*, 1867, p. 6): DM M . ANNEO . PAVLO . PETRO . M . ANNEVS . PAVLVS : FILIO . CARISSIMO. The inscription is additionally interesting on account of the fact that Seneca came from this *gens*.

[2] It has been asserted that Pomponia Græcina retained or assumed the name of Lucina as a Christian (de Rossi, *Roma Sotterr.*, I. p. 319, II. pp. 362, etc.), but this is extremely doubtful.—Changes of name were common among the Jews as well as in the Diaspora (see *C.I.G.*, vol. iv. No. 9905 : " Beturia Paula—que bixit ann. LXXXVI. meses VI.·proselyta ann. XVI. nomine Sara mater synagogarum Campi et Bolumni ").

[3] Did he call himself Gregory as an " awakened " man ?

reign of Decius (in 250 A.D.) called herself Theodota when she was asked at her trial what was her name.[1] In the Acta of a certain martyr called Balsamus (311 A.D.), the accused cries : " According to my paternal name I am Balsamus, but according to the spiritual name which I received at baptism, I am Peter."[2] Interesting, too, is the account given by Eusebius (*Mart. Pal.*, xi. 7 f.) of five Egyptian Christians who were martyred during the Diocletian persecution. They all bore Egyptian names. But when the first of them was questioned by the magistrate, he replied not with his own name but with that of an Old Testament prophet. Whereupon Eusebius observes, " This was because they had assumed such names instead of the names given them by their parents, names probably derived from idols ; so that one could hear them calling themselves Elijih,[3] Jeremiah, Isaiah, Samuel, and Daniel, thus giving themselves out to be Jews in the spiritual sense, even the true and genuine Israel of God, not merely by their deeds, but by the names they bore."

Obviously, the ruling idea here is not yet that of patron saints ; the prophets are selected as models, not as patrons. Even the change of name itself is still a novelty. This is borne out by the festal epistles of Athanasius in the fourth century, which contain an extraordinary number of Christian names, almost all of which are the familiar pagan names (Greek or Egyptian). Biblical names are still infrequent, although in one passage, writing of a certain Gelous Hierakammon, Athanasius does remark that " out of shame he took the name of Eulogius in addition to his own name."[4]

It is very remarkable that down to the middle of the fourth century Peter and Paul are about the only New Testament names to be met with, while Old Testament names again are so rare that the above case of the five Egyptians who had assumed prophetic names must be considered an exception to the rule.

---

[1] Cp. *Acta Pionii*, ix. ; this instance, however, is hardly relevant to our purpose, as Pionius instructed Sabina to call herself Theodota, in order to prevent herself from being identified.

[2] Three martyrs at Lampsacus are called Peter, Paul, and Andrew (cp. Ruinart's *Acta Martyr.*, 1850, pp. 205 f.).

[3] See *Mart. Pal.*, x. 1, for a martyr of this name.

[4] *Festal Epistles*, ed. by Larsow (p. 80).

Even the name of John, so far as I know, only began to appear within the fourth century, and that slowly. On the other hand, we must not here adduce a passage from Dionysius of Alexandria, which has been already under review. He certainly writes: " In my opinion, many persons [in the apostolic] had the same name as John, for out of love for him, admiring and emulating him, and desirous of being loved by the Lord even as he was, many assumed the same surname, just as many of the children of the faithful are also called Peter and Paul." But what Dionysius says here about the name of John is simply a conjecture with regard to the apostolic age, while indirectly, though plainly enough, he testifies that Christians in his own day were called Peter and Paul, but not John.[1] This preference assigned to the name of the two apostolic leaders throughout the East and West alike is significant,[2] and it is endorsed by a passage from Eustathius, the bishop of Antioch, who was a contemporary of Athanasius. " Many Jews," he writes, " call themselves after the patriarchs and prophets, and yet are guilty of wickedness. Many [Christian] Greeks call themselves Peter and Paul, and yet behave in a most disgraceful fashion." Evidently the Old Testament names were left as a rule to the Jews, while Peter and Paul continue apparently to be the only New Testament names which are actually in use. This state of matters lasted till the second half of the fourth century.[3] As the saints, prophets,

[1] No older evidence is available. It is no proof to the contrary of what we have said, that the father of the Roman bishop Anicetus is said to have been called "John"; for, apart from the untrustworthiness of the notice (in the *Liber Pontif.*), he must have been a Syrian, and certainly he was not called after the apostle. According to the *Acta Johannis* (Prochorus), Basilius and Charis called the child given them by means of John, after the apostle's name, but these Acts belong to the post-Constantine age.

[2] It is not certain that where "Paul" is found as a Christian name it must be referred to the great apostle. But "Paul" was rather more common than "Peter" even yet. We find it first of all as the name of a gnostic Christian of Antioch, who stayed with young Origen at the house of a wealthy lady in Alexandria (Eus., *H.E.*, vi. 2. 14). Then there is Paul of Samosata, and the martyr Paul (*Mart. Pal.*, p. 65), besides another martyr of the same name at Jamnia (*op. cit.*, p. 86).

[3] The bishops who attended the council of Nicæa got their names between 250 and 290. Of the 237 names which have come down to us, six-sevenths are common pagan names; there are even some like Aphrodisius, Orion, etc. About 18 names are "pious," but neutral as regards any distinctively Christian value,

patriarchs, angels, etc., henceforth took the place of the dethroned gods of paganism, and as the stories of these gods were transformed into stories of the saints, the supersession of mythological names now commenced in real earnest.[1] Now, for the first time, do we often light upon names like John, James, Andrew, Simon, and Mary, besides—though much more rarely in the West—names from the Old Testament. At the close of the fourth century, Chrysostom, *e.g.* (cp. Hom. 52, *in Matth.*

e.g., Eusebius (five times), Hosius, Theodorus, Theodotus, Diodorus, Theophilus ; of these, however, Pistus (twice, both times from the Balkan peninsula) may be regarded with a certain probability as Christian. The other 19 names show Paul six times (Palestine, Cœle-Syria, proconsular Asia, Phrygia, Isauria, and Cappadocia), Peter four times (Palestine twice, Cœle-Syria, Egypt : it is interesting to notice the absence of Asia), Mark three times (Lydia, Calabria, Achaia—but it is extremely questionable, at least, if the name was taken from the evangelist), John once (Persia) and James once (Nisibis),—though in both cases it is doubtful if the apostles were taken as the originals, since Jewish names would be common in the far East,—Moses once (in Cilicia, perhaps a Jew by birth), Stephen twice (Cappadocia and Isauria—very doubtful if any reference to the biblical Stephen), and Polycarp once (Pisidia). It is quite possible that the last-named may have been called after the great bishop of Smyrna, but there was also a Polycarp among the 87 bishops of the Synod of Carthage. As for the Old Testament names, the earliest instances, which are still very rare (in the second half of the third century), are almost all from Egypt. A list may be appended here, at Lietzmann's suggestion. Hilary, in the extant fragments of his collection of documents relating to the Roman controversy (II. and III.), gives 134 episcopal names for the council of Sardica (61 orthodox and 73 semi-Arian), while Athanasius gives 284 orthodox names for the same synod (*Apol. c. Arian.* 50), though he has unfortunately omitted the episcopal sees All these bishops must have got their names between 270 and 310 A.D. Among Hilary's 134, there is a Moses, an Isaac, a Jonah (?), and a Paul (the Moses in Thessalian Thebes, the Isaac in Luetum [=Λουειθά, Arab. Petr. ?]). *All the rest bear current and in part purely pagan names* (the latter may have been quite probably Jews by birth). As for the 284 names of Athanasius, the same holds true of 270. The other 14 (*i.e.*, only 5 per cent.) include Paul (five times), Peter (once), Andrew (once ; in Egypt, possibly after the apostle), Elijah (three times, in Egypt), Isaiah, Isaac, Joseph, Jonah (just once)—all in Egypt, except Jonah. This confirms what we have just said. The pagan names have remained untouched. Only " Paul " and " Peter " (to a slight extent) have slipped in. The Old Testament names are still confined to Egypt, and even there they are not yet common.

[1] The thirtieth of the Arabic canons of Nicæa is unauthentic and late : " Fideles nomina gentilium filiis suis non imponant ; sed potius omnis natio Christianorum suis nominibus utatur, ut gentiles suis utuntur, imponanturque nomina Christianorum secundum scripturam in baptismo " (" Let not the faithful give pagan names to their children. Rather let the whole Christian people use its own names, as pagans use theirs, giving children at baptism the names of Christians according to the Scripture ").

Migne, vol. lx. 365), exhorts the believers to call their children after the saints, so that the saints may serve them as examples of virtue. But in giving this counsel he does not mention its most powerful motive, a motive disclosed by Theodoret, bishop of Cyprus in Syria, thirty years afterwards. It is this : that people are to give their children the names of saints and martyrs, in order to win them the protection and patronage of these heroes.[1] Then and thereafter this was the object which determined the choice of names. The result was a selection of names varying with the different countries and provinces; for the calendar of the provincial saints and the names of famous local bishops who were dead were taken into account together with the Bible. As early as the close of the fourth century, *e.g.*, people in Antioch liked to call their children after the great bishop Meletius. Withal, haphazard and freedom of choice always played some part in the choice of a name, nor was it every ear that could grow accustomed to the sound of barbarian Semitic names. As has been observed already, the Western church was very backward in adopting Old Testament names, and this continued till the days of Calvinism.

---

[1] *Græc. affect. curat.*, viii. p. 923, ed. Schulze.

CHRISTIAN preaching aimed at winning souls and bringing individuals to God, "that the number of the elect might be made up," but from the very outset it worked through a community and proposed to itself the aim of uniting all who believed in Christ. Primarily, this union was one which consisted of the disciples of Jesus. But, as we have already seen, these disciples were conscious of being *the true Israel* and *the ecclesia of God.* Such they held themselves to be. Hence they appropriated to themselves the form and well-knit frame of Judaism, spiritualizing it and strengthening it, so that by one stroke (we may say) they secured a firm and exclusive organization.

But while this organization, embracing all Christians on earth, rested in the first instance solely upon religious ideas, as a purely ideal conception it would hardly have remained effective for any length of time, had it not been allied to *local organization.* Christianity, at the initiative of the original apostles and the brethren of Jesus, began by borrowing this as well from Judaism, *i.e.,* from the synagogue. Throughout the Diaspora the Christian communities developed at first out of the synagogues with their proselytes or adherents. *Designed to be essentially a brotherhood, and springing out of the synagogue, the Christian society developed a local organization which was of double strength,* superior to anything achieved by the societies

---

[1] Cp. on this Von Dobschütz's *Die urchristlichen Gemeinden* (1902) [translated in this library under the title of *Christian Life in the Primitive Church*].

of Judaism.[1] One extremely advantageous fact about these local organizations in their significance for Christianity may be added. It was this: every community was at once a unit, complete in itself; but it was also a reproduction of the collective church of God, and it had to recognize and manifest itself as such.[2]

Such a religious and social organization, destitute of any political or national basis and yet embracing the entire private life, was a novel and unheard-of thing upon the soil of Greek and Roman life, where religious and social organizations only existed as a rule in quite a rudimentary form, and where they lacked any religious control of life as a whole. All that people could think of in this connection was one or two schools of philosophy, whose common life was also a religious life. But here was a society which united fellow-believers, who were resident in any city, in the closest of ties, presupposing a relationship which was assumed as a matter of course to last through life itself, furnishing its members not only with holy unction administered once and for all or from time to time, but with a daily bond which provided them with spiritual benefits

[1] We cannot discuss the influence which the Greek and Roman guilds may have exercised upon Christianity. In any case, it can only have affected certain *forms*, not the essential fact itself or its fixity.

[2] We do not know how this remarkable conviction arose, but it lies perfectly plain upon the surface of the apostolic and post-apostolic ages. It did not originate in Judaism, since—to my knowledge—the individual Jewish synagogue did not look upon itself in this light. Nor did the conception spring up at a single stroke. Even in Paul two contradictory conceptions still lie unexplained together : while, on the one hand, he regards each community, so to speak, as a "church of God," sovereign, independent, and responsible for itself, on the other hand his churches are at the same time his own creations, which consequently remain under his control and training, and are in fact even threatened by him with the rod. He is their father and their schoolmaster. Here the apostolic authority, and, what is more, the general and special authority, of the apostle as the founder of a church invade and delimit the authority of the individual community, since the latter has to respect and follow the rules laid down and enforced by the apostle throughout all his churches. This he had the right to expect. But, as we see from the epistles to the Corinthians, especially from the second, conflicts were inevitable. Then again in 3 John we have an important source of information, for here the head of a local church is openly rebelling and asserting his independence, against the control of an apostle who attempts to rule the church by means of delegates. When Ignatius reached Asia not long afterwards, the idea of the sovereignty of the individual church had triumphed.

and imposed duties on them, assembling them at first daily and then weekly, shutting them off from other people, uniting them in a guild of worship, a friendly society, and an order with a definite line of life in view, besides teaching them to consider themselves as the community of God.

Neophytes, of course, had to get accustomed or to be trained at first to a society of this kind. It ran counter to all the requirements exacted by any other cultus or holy rite from its devotees, however much the existing guild-life may have paved the way for it along several lines. That its object should be the *common edification of the members*, that the community was therefore to resemble a single body with many members, that every member was to be subordinate to the whole body, that one member was to suffer and rejoice with another, that Jesus Christ did not call individuals apart but built them up into a society in which the individual got his place—all these were lessons which had to be learnt. Paul's epistles prove how vigorously and unweariedly he taught them, and it is perhaps the weightiest feature both in Christianity and in the work of Paul that, so far from being overpowered, the impulse towards association was most powerfully intensified by the individualism which here attained its zenith. (For to what higher form can individualism rise than that reached by means of the dominant counsel, " Save thy soul "?) Brotherly love constituted the lever; it was also the entrance into that most wealthy inheritance, the inheritance of the firmly organized church of Judaism. In addition to this there was also the wonderfully practical idea, to which allusion has already been made, of setting the collective church (as an ideal fellowship) and the individual community in such a relationship that whatever was true of the one could be predicated also of the other, the church of Corinth or of Ephesus, *e.g.*, being *the* church of God. Quite apart from the content of these social formations, no statesman or politician can hesitate to admire and applaud the solution which was thus devised for one of the most serious problems of any large organization, viz., how to maintain intact the complete autonomy of the local communities and at the same time to knit them into a general nexus, possessed of strength and unity, which should embrace all the empire and gradually develop also into a collective organization.

What a sense of stability a creation of this kind must have given the individual! What powers of attraction it must have exercised, as soon as its objects came to be understood! It was this, and not any evangelist, which proved to be the most effective missionary. In fact, we may take it for granted that the mere existence and persistent activity of the individual Christian communities did more than anything else to bring about the extension of the Christian religion.[1]

Hence also the injunction, repeated over and again, " Let us not forsake the assembling of ourselves together,"—" as some do," adds the epistle to the Hebrews (x. 25). At first and indeed always there were naturally some people who imagined that one could secure the holy contents and blessings of

---

[1] We possess no detailed account of the origin of any Christian community, for the narrative of Acts is extremely summary, and the epistles of Paul presuppose the existence of the various churches. Acts, indeed, is not interested in the local churches. It is only converted brethren that come within its ken ; its pages reflect but the onward rush of the Christian mission, till that mission is merged in the legal proceedings against Paul. The apocryphal Acts are of hardly any use. But from I Thessalonians, I Corinthians, and Acts we can infer one or two traits. Thus, while Paul invariably attaches himself to Jews, where such were to be found, and preaches in the synagogues, the actual result is that the small communities which thus arose are drawn mainly from "God-fearing" pagans, and upon the whole from pagans in general, not from Jews. Those who were first converted naturally stand in an important relation to the organization of the churches (Clem. Rom. xlii.: οἱ ἀπόστολοι κατὰ χώρας καὶ πόλεις κηρύσσοντες . . . . καθίστανον τὰς ἀπαρχὰς αὐτῶν, δοκιμάσαντες τῷ πνεύματι, εἰς ἐπισκόπους καὶ διακόνους τῶν μελλόντων πιστεύειν = Preaching throughout the country districts and cities, the apostles . . . . appointed those who were their firstfruits, after proving them by the Spirit, to be bishops and deacons for those who were to believe) ; as we learn from I Thess. v. 12 f. and Phil. i. I, a sort of local superintendence at once arose in some of the communities. But what holds true of the Macedonian churches is by no means true of all the churches, at least during the initial period, for it is obvious that in Galatia and at Corinth no organization whatever existed for a decade, or even longer. The brethren submitted to a control of "the Spirit." In Acts xiv. 23 (χειροτονήσαντες αὐτοῖς κατ᾽ ἐκκλησίαν πρεσβυτέρους) the allusion may be accurate as regards one or two communities (cp. also Clem. Rom. xliv.), but it is an extremely questionable statement if it is held to imply that the apostles regularly appointed officials in every locality, and that these were in all cases "presbyters." Acts only mentions church-officers at Jerusalem (xv. 4) and Ephesus (xx. 28, presbyters who are invested with episcopal powers).

Christianity as one did those of Isis or the Magna Mater, and then withdraw. Or, in cases where people were not so short-sighted, levity, laziness, or weariness were often enough to detach a person from the society. A vainglorious sense of superiority and of being able to dispense with the spiritual aid of the society, was also the means of inducing many to withdraw from fellowship and from the common worship. Many, too, were actuated by fear of the authorities; they shunned attendance at public worship, to avoid being recognized as Christians.[1]

"Seek what is of common profit to all," says Clement of Rome (c. xlviii.). "Keep not apart by yourselves in secret," says Barnabas (iv. 10), "as if you were already justified, but meet together and confer upon the common weal." Similar passages are often to be met with.[2] The worship on Sunday is of course obligatory, but even at other times the brethren are expected to meet as often as possible. "Thou shalt seek out every day the company of the saints, to be refreshed by their words" (Did., iv. 2). "We are constantly in touch with one another," says Justin, after describing the Sunday worship (Apol., I. lxvii.), in order to show that this is not the only place of fellowship. Ignatius,[3] too, advocates over and over again more frequent meetings of the church; in fact, his letters are written primarily for the purpose of binding the individual member as closely as possible to the community and thus

---

[1] Cp. Tertullian, de Fuga, iii. : "Timide conveniunt in ecclesiam : dicitis enim, quoniam incondite convenimus et simul convenimus et complures concurrimus in ecclesiam, quaerimur a nationibus et timemus, ne turbentur nationes" ("They gather to church with trembling. For, you say, since we assemble in disorder, simultaneously, and in great numbers, the heathen make inquiries, and we are afraid of stirring them up against us").

[2] Herm., Simil., IX. xx. : οὗτοι οἱ ἐν πολλοῖς καὶ ποικίλαις πραγματείαις ἐμπεφυρμένοι οὐ κολλῶνται τοῖς δούλοις τοῦ θεοῦ, ἀλλ' ἀποπλανῶνται ("These, being involved in many different kinds of occupations, do not cleave to the servants of God, but go astray"); IX. xxvi. : γενόμενοι ἐρημώδεις, μὴ κολλώμενοι τοῖς δούλοις τοῦ θεοῦ, ἀλλὰ μονάζοντες ἀπολλύουσι τὰς ἑαυτῶν ψυχάς ("Having become barren, they cleave not to the servants of God, but keep apart and so lose their own souls").

[3] Cp. Ephes. xiii. : σπουδάζετε πυκνότερον συνέρχεσθαι εἰς εὐχαριστίαν θεοῦ ("Endeavour to meet more frequently for the praise of God"); Polyc. iv. : πυκνότερον συναγωγαὶ γινέσθωσαν ("Let meetings be held more frequently"); cp. also Magn. iv.

securing him against error, temptation, and apostasy. The means to this end is an increased significance attaching to the church. In the church alone all blessings are to be had, in its ordinances and organizations. It is only the church firmly equipped with bishop, presbyters, and deacons, with common worship and with sacraments, which is the creation of God.[1] Consequently, beyond its pale nothing divine is to be found, there is nothing save error and sin; all clandestine meetings for worship are also to be eschewed, and no teacher who starts up from outside is to get a hearing unless he is certificated by the church. The absolute subordination of Christians to the local community has never been more peremptorily demanded, the position of the local community itself has never been more eloquently laid down, than in these primitive documents. Their eager admonitions reveal the seriousness of the peril

[1] The common worship, with its centre in the celebration of the Supper, is the cardinal point. No other cultus could point to such a ceremony, with its sublimity and unction, its brotherly feeling and many-sidedness. Here every experience, every spiritual need, found nourishment. The collocation of prayer, praise, preaching, and the reading of the Word was modelled upon the worship of the synagogue, and must already have made a deep impression upon pagans; but with the addition of the feast of the Lord's supper, an observance was introduced which, for all its simplicity, was capable of being regarded, as it actually was regarded, from the most diverse standpoints. It was a mysterious, divine gift of knowledge and of life; it was a thanksgiving, a sacrifice, a representation of the death of Christ, a love-feast of the brotherhood, a support for the hungry and distressed. No single observance could well be more than that, and it preserved this character for long, even after it had passed wholly into the region of the mysterious. The members of the church took home portions of the consecrated bread, and consumed them during the week. I have already (pp. 150 f.) discussed the question how far the communities in their worship were also unions for charitable support, and how influential must have been their efforts in this direction.—A whole series of testimonies, from Pliny to Arnobius (iv. 36), proves that the preaching to which people listened every Sunday bore primarily on the inculcation of morality: "In conventiculis summus oratur deus, pax cunctis et venia postulatur magistratibus exercitibus regibus familiaribus inimicis, adhuc vitam degentibus et resolutis corporum vinctione, in quibus aliud auditur nihil nisi quod humanos faciat, nisi quod mites, verecundos, pudicos, castos, familiaris communicatores rei et cum omnibus vobis solidae germanitatis necessitudine copulatos." ("At our meetings prayers are offered to Almighty God, peace and pardon are asked for all in authority, for soldiers, kings, friends, enemies, those still in life, and those freed from the bondage of the flesh; at these gatherings nothing is said except what makes people humane, gentle, modest, virtuous, chaste, generous in dealing with their substance, and closely knit to all of you within the bonds of brotherhood").

which threatened the individual Christian who should even in the slightest degree emancipate himself from the community; thereby he would fall a prey to the "errorists," or slip over into paganism. At this point even the heroes of the church were threatened by a peril, which is singled out also for notice. As men who had a special connection with Christ, and who were quite aware of this connection, they could not well be subject to orders from the churches; but it was recognized even at this early period that if they became "inflated" with pride and held aloof from the fellowship of the church, they might easily come to grief. Thus, when the haughty martyrs of Carthage and Rome, both during and after the Decian persecution, started cross-currents in the churches and began to uplift themselves against the officials, the great bishops finally resolved to reduce them under the laws common to the whole church.

While the individual Christian had a position of his own within the organization of the church, he thereby lost, however, a part of his autonomy along with his fellows. The so-called Montanist controversy was in the last resort not merely a struggle to secure a stricter mode of life as against a laxer, but also the struggle of a more independent religious attitude and activity as against one which was prescribed and uniform. The outstanding personalities, the individuality of certain people, had to suffer in order that the majority might not become unmanageable or apostates. Such has always been the case in human history. It is inevitable. Only after the Montanist conflict did the church, as individual and collective, attain the climax of its development; henceforth it became an object of desire, coveted by everyone who was on the look-out for power, inasmuch as it had extraordinary forces at its disposal. It now bound the individual closely to itself; it held him, bridled him, and dominated his religious life in all directions. Yet it was not long before the monastic movement originated, a movement which, while it recognized the church in theory (doubt upon this point being no longer possible), set it aside in actual practice.

The progress of the development of the juridical organization from the firmly organized local church [1] to the provincial church,[2] from that again to the larger league of churches, a league which realized itself in synods covering many provinces, and finally from that league to the collective church, which of course was never quite realized as an organization, though it was always present in idea—this development also contributed to the strengthening of the Christian self-consciousness and missionary activity.[3] It was indeed a matter of great moment to be able to proclaim that this church not only embraced humanity in its religious conceptions, but also presented itself to the eye as an immense single league stretching from one side of the empire to another, and, in fact, stretching beyond even these imperial boundaries. This church arose through the co-operation of the Christian ideal with the empire, and thus every great force which operated in this sphere had also its part to play in the building up of the church, viz., the universal Christian idea of a bond of humanity (which, at root, of course, meant no more than a bond between the scattered elect throughout mankind), the Jewish church, and the Roman empire. The last named, as has been rightly pointed out, became bankrupt over the church ;[4] and the same might be said of the Jewish church, whose powers of attraction ceased for a large circle of people so soon as the Christian church had developed, the latter taking them over into its own life.[5] Whether the Christian communities were as free creations as they were in the first century, whether they set

---

[1] Christians described themselves at the outset as παροικοῦντες ("sojourners"; cp. p. 252) ; the church was technically "the church sojourning in the city" (ἡ ἐκκλησία ἡ παροικοῦσα τὴν πόλιν), but it rapidly became well defined, nor did it by any means stand out as a structure destined to crumble away.

[2] How far this ascent, when viewed from other premises which are equally real, corresponded to a descent, may be seen from the first Excursus to this chapter.

[3] Tert., de Præscript. xx. : "Sic omnes [sc. ecclesiae] primae et omnes apostolicae, dum una omnes, probant unitatem communicatio pacis et appellatio fraternitatis et contesseratio hospitalis, quae iura non alio natio regit quam eiusdem sacramenti una traditio" ("Thus all are primitive and all apostolic, since they are all alike certified by their union in the communion of peace, the title of brotherhood, and the interchange of hospitable friendship — rights whose only rule is the one tradition of the same mystery in all").

[4] It revived, however, in the Western church.

[5] Ever since the fall of the temple, however, the Jewish church had consciously and voluntarily withdrawn into itself more and more, and abjured the Greek spirit.

up external ordinances as definite and a union as comprehensive as was the case in the third century—in either case these communities exerted a magnetic force on thousands, and thus proved of extraordinary service to the Christian mission.

Within the church-organization the most weighty and significant creation was that of the monarchical episcopate.[1] It was the bishops, properly speaking, who held together the individual members of the churches; their rise marked the close of the period during which charismata and offices were in a state of mutual flux, the individual relying only upon God, himself, and spiritually endowed brethren. After the close of the second century bishops were the teachers, high priests, and judges of the church. Ignatius already had compared their position in the individual church to that of God in the church collective. But this analogy soon gave way to the *formal* quality which they acquired, first in Rome and the West, after the gnostic controversy. In virtue of this quality, they were regarded as representatives of the apostolic office. According to Cyprian, they were "judices vice Christi" (judges in Christ's room); and Origen, in spite of his unfortunate experience with bishops, had already written that "if kings are so called from reigning, then all who rule the churches of God deserve to be called kings" ("si reges a regendo dicuntur, omnes utique, qui ecclesias dei regunt, reges merito appellabuntur," Hom. xii. 2 *in Num.*, vol. x. p. 133, Lomm.). On their conduct the churches depended almost entirely for weal or woe. As the office grew to maturity, it seemed like an original creation; but this was simply because it drew to itself from all quarters both the powers and the forms of life.

The extent to which the episcopate, along with the other clerical offices which it controlled, formed the backbone of the church,[2] is shown by the fierce war waged against it by the

---

[1] I leave out of account here all the preliminary steps. It was with the monarchical episcopate that this office first became a power in Christendom, and it does not fall within the scope of the present sketch to investigate the initial stages—a task of some difficulty, owing to the fragmentary nature of the sources and the varieties of the original organization throughout the different churches.

[2] Naturally, it came more and more to mean a position which was well-pleasing to God and specially dear to him; this is implied already in the term "priest,"

state during the third century (Maximinus Thrax, Decius, Valerian, Diocletian, Daza, Licinius), as well as from many isolated facts. In the reign of Marcus Aurelius, Dionysius of Corinth tells the church of Athens (Eus., *H.E.*, iv. 23) that while it had well-nigh fallen from the faith after the death of its martyred bishop Publius, its new bishop Quadratus had reorganized it and filled it with fresh zeal for the faith. In *de Fuga*, xi. Tertullian says that when the shepherds are poor creatures the flock is a prey to wild beasts, " as is never more the case than when the clergy desert the church in a persecution " ("quod nunquam magis fit quam cum in persecutione destituitur a clero "). Cyprian (*Ep.* lv. 11) tells how in the persecution bishop Trophimus had lapsed along with a large section of the church, and had offered sacrifice; but on his return and penitence, the rest followed him, " qui omnes regressuri ad ecclesiam non essent, nisi cum Trofimo comitante venissent " ("none of whom would have returned to the church, had they not had the companionship of Trophimus "). When Cyprian lingered in retreat during the persecution of Decius, the whole community threatened to lapse. Hence one can easily see the significance of the bishop for the church; with him it fell, with him it stood,[1] and in these days a vacancy or interregnum meant a serious crisis for any church. Without being properly a missionary,

which became current after the close of the second century. Along with the higher class of heroic figures (ascetics, virgins, confessors), the church also possessed a second upper class of clerics, as was well known to pagans in the third century. Thus the pagan in Macarius Magnes (III. xvii.) writes, apropos of Matt. xvii. 20, xxi. 21 ("Have faith as a grain of mustard-seed"): "He who has not so much faith as this is certainly unworthy of being reckoned among the brotherhood of the faithful; so that the majority of Christians, it follows, are not to be counted among the faithful, and in fact even among the bishops and presbyters there is not one who deserves this name."

[1] This is the language also of the heathen judge to bishop Achatius: "a shield and succourer of the region of Antioch" ("scutum quoddam ac refugium Antiochiae regionis"; Ruinart, *Acta Mart.*, Ratish., 1859, p. 201): "Veniet tecum [*i.e.*, if you return to the old gods] omnis populus, ex tuo pendet arbitirio" ("All the people will accompany you, for they hang on your decision "). The bishop answers of course: "Illi omnes non meo nutu, sed dei praecepto reguntur; audiant me itaque, si iusta persuadeam, sin vero perversa et nocitura, contemnant" ("They are ruled, not by my beck and call, but all of them by God's counsel; wherefore let them hearken to me, if I persuade them to what is right; but despise me, if I counsel what is perverse and mischievous."—Hermas (*Sim.*, IX. xxxi.) says of the

the bishop exercised a missionary function.[1] In particular, he preserved individuals from relapsing into paganism, while any bishop who really filled his post was the means of winning over many fresh adherents. We have instances of this, e.g., in the case of Cyprian or of Gregory Thaumaturgus. The episcopal dignity was at once heightened and counterbalanced by the institution of the synods which arose in Greece and Asia (modelled possibly upon the federal diets),[2] and eventually were adopted by a large number of provinces after the opening of the third century. On the one hand, this association of the bishops entirely took away the rights of the laity, who found before very long that it was no use now to leave their native church in order to settle down in another. Yet a synod, on the other hand, imposed restraints upon the arbitrary action of a bishop, by setting itself up as an ecclesiastical "forum publicum" to which he was responsible. The correspondence of Cyprian presents several examples of individual bishops being thus arraigned by synods for arbitrary or evil conduct. Before very long too (possibly from the very outset) the synod, this "representatio totius nominis Christiani," appeared to be a specially trustworthy organ of the holy Spirit. The synods which expanded in the course of the third century from provincial synods to larger councils, and which would seem to have anticipated Diocletian's redistribution of the empire in the East, naturally gave an extraordinary impetus to the prestige and authority of the church, and thereby heightened its powers

shepherds : "Sin aliqua e pecoribus dissipata invenerit dominus, vae crit pastoribus. quod si ipsi pastores dissipati reperti fuerint, quid respondebunt pro pecoribus his? numquid dicunt, a pecore se vexatos? non credetur illis. incredibilis enim res est, pastorem pati posse a pecore " ("But if the master finds any of the sheep scattered, woe to the shepherds. For if the shepherds themselves be found scattered, how will they answer for these sheep? Will they say that they were themselves worried by the flock? Then they will not be believed, for it is absurd that a shepherd should be injured by his sheep ").

[1] For a distinguished missionary or teacher who had founded a church becoming its bishop, cp. Origen, Hom. xi. 4 *in Num.* [as printed above, p. 351].

[2] Cp. (trans. below, under " Asia Minor," § 9, in Book IV. Chap. III.) Tertull., *de Jejunio*, xiii. : "Aguntur per Graecias (for the plural, cp. Eus., *Vita Const.*, iii. 19) illa certis in locis concilia ex universis ecclesiis, per quae et altiora quaeque in commune tractantur et ipsa repraesentatio totius nominis Christiani magna veneratione celebratur."

of attraction. Yet the entire synodal system really flourished in the East alone (and to some extent in Africa). In the West it no more blossomed than did the system of metropolitans, a fact which was of vital moment to the position of Rome and of the Roman bishop.[1]

One other problem has finally to be considered at this point, a problem which is of great importance for the statistics of the church. It is this: how strong was the tendency to create independent forms within the Christian communities, *i.e.*, to form complete *episcopal* communities? Does the number of communities which were episcopally organized actually denote the number of the communities in general, or were there, either as a rule or in a large number of provinces, any considerable number of communities which possessed no bishops of their own, but had only presbyters or deacons, and depended upon an outside bishop? The following Excursus[2] is devoted to the answering of this important question. Its aim is to show that the creation of complete episcopal communities was the general rule in most provinces (excluding Egypt) down to the middle of the third century, however small might be the number of Christians in any locality, and however insignificant might be the locality itself.

As important, if not even more important, was the tendency, which was in operation from the very first, to have all the Christians in a given locality united in a single community. As

[1] I do not enter here into the development of the constituti·n in detail, although by its close relation to the divisions of the empire it has many vital points of contact with the history of the Christian mission (see Lübeck, *Reichseinteilung und kirchliche Hierarchie des Orients bis zum Ausgang des 4 Jahrhunderts*, 1901). I simply note that the ever-increasing dependence of the Eastern church upon the redistributed empire (a redistribution which conformed to national boundaries) imperilled by degrees the unity of the Church and the universalism of Christianity. The church began by showing harmony and vigour in this sphere of action, but centrifugal influences soon commenced to play upon her, influences which are perceptible as early as the Paschal controversy of 190 A.D. between Rome and Asia, which are vital by the time of the controversy over the baptism of heretics, and which finally appear as disintegrating forces in the fourth and fifth centuries. In the West the Roman bishop knew how to restrain them admirably, evincing both tenacity and clearness of purpose.

[2] Read before the Royal Prussian Academy of Science, on 28th Nov. 1901 (pp. 1186 f.).

the Pauline epistles prove, house-churches were tolerated at the outset (we do not know how long),[1] but obviously their position was (originally or very soon afterwards) that of members belonging to the local community as a whole. This original relationship is, of course, as obscure to us as is the evaporation of such churches. Conflicts there must have been at first, and even attempts to set up a number of independent Christian θίασοι in a city; the "schisms" at Corinth, combated by Paul, would seem to point in this direction. Nor is it quite certain whether, even after the formation of the monarchical episcopate, there were not cases here and there of two or more episcopal communities existing in a single city. But even if this obtained in certain cases, their number must have been very small; nor do these avail to alter the general stamp of the Christian organization throughout its various branches, i.e., the general constitution according to which every locality where Christians were to be found had its own independent community, and only one community.[2] This organization, with its simplicity and naturalness, proved itself extraordinarily strong. No doubt, the community was soon obliged to direct the full force of its

---

[1] We cannot determine how long they lasted, but after the New Testament we hear next to nothing of them—which, by the way, is an argument against all attempts to relegate the Pauline epistles to the second century. For the house-churches, see the relevant sections in Weizsäcke's *History of the Apostolic Age.* Hebrews is most probably addressed to a special community in Rome. Schiele has recently tried to prove, for reasons that deserve notice, that the community in question was developed from the Συναγωγὴ τῶν Ἑβραίων, for which there is inscriptional evidence at Rome (*American Journal of Theology*, 1905, pp. 290 f.), and I have tried to connect the epistle with Prisca and Aquila (*Zeits. für die neutest. Wiss.*, i., 1900, pp. 16 f.). The one theory does not exclude the other.

[2] The relation of the Christian διδασκαλεία to the local church (cp. above, p. 356) is wrapt in obscurity. We know of Justin's school, of Tatian's, Rhodon's, Theodotus's, Praxeas's, Epigonus's, and Cleomenes's in Rome, of the transition of the Thedotian school into a church (the most interesting case of the kind known to us), of catechetical schools in Alexandria, of Hippolytus scorning the Christians in Rome who adhered to Callistus, i.e., the majority of the church (or a school), of the various gnostic schools, of Lucian's school at Antioch side by side with the church, etc. But this does not amount to a clear view of the situation, for we learn very little apart from the fact that such schools existed. Anyone might essay to prove that by the second half of the second century there was a general danger of the church being dissipated into nothing but schools. Anyone else might undertake to prove that even ordinary Christianity here and there deliberately assumed the character of a philosophic school in order to secure freedom and

anti-pagan exclusiveness against such brethren of its own number as refused submission to the church upon any pretext whatsoever. *The sad passion for heresy-hunting, which prevailed among Christians as early as the second century, was not only a result of their fanatical devotion to true doctrine, but quite as much an outcome of their rigid organization and of the exalted predicates of honour which they applied to themselves as "the church of God."* Here the reverse of the medal is to be seen. The community's valuation of itself, its claim to represent the ἐκκλησία τοῦ θεοῦ ("the church of God" or "the catholic church" in Corinth, Ephesus, etc.) prevented it ultimately from recognizing or tolerating any Christianity whatever outside its own boundaries.[1]

safeguard its interests against the state and a hostile society (as was the case, we cannot doubt, with some circles; cp. above, p. 364). Both attempts would bring in useful material, but neither would succeed in proving its thesis. So much is certain, however, that, during the second century and perhaps here and there throughout the third as well, the "schools" spelt a certain danger for the unity of the episcopal organization of the churches, and that the episcopal church had succeeded, by the opening of the third century, in rejecting the main dangers of the situation. The materials are scanty, but the question deserves investigation by itself.

[1] Celsus had already laid sharp stress on heresy-hunting and the passion with which Christians fought one another: βλασφημοῦσιν εἰς ἀλλήλους οὗτοι πάνδεινα ῥητὰ καὶ ἄρρητα, καὶ οὐκ ἂν εἴξαιεν οὐδὲ καθ' ὁτιοῦν εἰς ὁμόνοιαν πάντη ἀλλήλους ἀποστυγοῦντες (V. lxiii.: "These people utter all sorts of blasphemy, mentionable and unmentionable, against one another, nor will they give way in the smallest point for the sake of concord, hating each other with a perfect hatred ").

EXCURSUS I

ECCLESIASTICAL ORGANIZATION AND THE EPISCOPATE (IN THE
PROVINCES, THE CITIES, AND THE VILLAGES), FROM PIUS
TO CONSTANTINE.

" In 1 Tim. iii. (where only bishops and deacons are mentioned)
the apostle Paul has not forgotten the presbyters, for at first the
same officials bore the name of 'presbyter' as well as that of
'bishop.' . . . . Those who had the power of ordination and are
now called 'bishops' were not appointed to a *single* church but
to a whole province, and bore the name of 'apostles.' Thus
St Paul set Timothy over all Asia, and Titus over Crete. And
plainly he also appointed other individuals to other provinces in
the same way, each of whom was to take charge of a whole
province, making circuits through all the churches, ordaining
clergy for ecclesiastical work wherever it was necessary, solving
any difficult questions which had arisen among them, setting
them right by means of addresses on doctrine, treating sore sins
in a salutary fashion, and in general discharging all the duties
of a *superintendent*—all the towns, meanwhile, possessing the
presbyters of whom I have spoken, men who ruled their respective
churches. Thus in that early age there existed those who are
now called bishops, but who were then called apostles, discharging functions for a whole province which those who are nowadays
ordained to the episcopate discharge for a single city and a
single district. Such was the organization of the church in
those days. But when the faith became widely spread, filling
not merely towns, but also country districts with believers,[1]

---

[1] Gk.: μέγισται δὲ οὐ πόλεις μόνον ἀλλὰ καὶ χῶραι τῶν πεπιστευκότων ἦσαν ;
Lat. version = repletae autem sunt non modo civitates credentium, sed regiones.
Read μεσταί therefore instead of μέγισται.

then, as the blessed apostles were now dead, came those who took charge of the whole [province]. They were not equal to their predecessors, however, nor could they certify themselves, as did the earlier leaders, by means of miracles, while in many other respects they showed their inferiority. Deeming it therefore a burden to assume the title of 'apostles,' they distributed the other titles [which had hitherto been synonymous], leaving that of 'presbyters' to the presbyters, and assigning that of 'bishops' to those who possessed the right of ordination, and who were consequently entrusted with leadership over all the church. These formed the majority, owing, in the first instance, to the necessity of the case, but subsequently also, on account of the generous spirit shown by those who arranged the ordinations.[1] For at the outset there were but two, or at most three, bishops usually in a province—a state of matters which prevailed in most of the Western provinces until quite recently, and which may still be found in several, even at the present day. As time went on, however, bishops were ordained not merely in towns, but also in small districts, where there was really no need of anyone being yet invested with the episcopal office."

So Theodore of Mopsuestia in his commentary upon First Timothy.[2] The assertion that "bishop" and "presbyter" were identical in primitive ages occurs frequently about the year 400, but Theodore's statements in general are, to the best of my knowledge, unique; they represent an attempt to depict the primitive organization of the church, and to explain the most important revolution which had taken place in the history of the church's constitution. Theodore's idea is, in brief, as follows. From the outset, he remarks—*i.e.* in the apostolic age, or by original apostolic institution—there was *a monarchical office* in the churches, *to which pertained the right of ordination.* This

---

[1] Gk.: διὰ μὲν τὴν χρείαν τὸ πρῶτον, ὕστερον δὲ καὶ ὑπὸ φιλοτιμίας τῶν ποιούντων ; Ambition, it might be conjectured, would be mentioned as the motive at work, but in that case τῶν ποιούντων would require to be away. Φιλοτιμία therefore must mean "liberal spirit," and this is the interpretation given in the Latin version : "Postea vero et illis adiecti sunt alii liberalitate eorum qui ordinationes faciebant." Dr Bischoff, however, proposes παροικούντων for ποιούντων.

[2] See Swete's *Theodori episcopi Mopsuesteni in epp. b. Pauli commentarii*, vol. ii. (1882), pp. 121 f.

office was one *belonging to the provincial churches* (each province possessing a single superintendent), and its title was that of "apostle." Individual communities, again, were governed by bishops (presbyters) and deacons. Once the apostles [1] (*i.e.* the original apostles) had died, however, a revolution took place. The motives assigned for this by Theodore are twofold: in the first place, the spread of the Christian religion, and in the second place, the weakness felt by the second generation of the apostles themselves. The latter therefore resolved (i.) to abjure and thus abolish [2] the name of "apostle," and (ii.) to distribute the monarchical power, *i.e.*, the right of ordination, among several persons throughout a province. Hence the circumstance of two or three bishops existing in the same province—the term "bishop" being now employed in the sense of monarchical authority. That state of matters was the rule until quite recently in most of the Western provinces, and it still survives in several of them. In the East, however, it has not lasted. Partly owing to the requirements of the case (*i.e.*, the increase of Christianity throughout the provinces), partly owing to the "liberality" of the apostles,[3] the number of the bishops has multiplied, so that not only towns, but even villages, have come to possess bishops, although there was no real need for such appointments.

We must in the first instance credit Theodore with being sensible of the fact that the organization of the primitive churches was originally on the broadest scale, and *only came down by degrees* (to the local communities). Such was indeed the case. The whole was prior to the part. That is, the

---

[1], This is the first point of obscurity in Theodore's narrative. "The blessed apostles" are not all the men whom he has first mentioned as "apostles," but either the apostles in the narrowest sense of the term, or else these taken together with men like Timothy and Titus.

[2] This has to be supplied by the reader (which is the second obscure point); the text has merely βαρὺ νομίσαντες τὴν τῶν ἀποστόλων ἔχειν προσηγορίαν. Theodore says nothing about what became of them after they gave up their name and rights.

[3] This is the third point of obscurity in Theodore's statement. By φιλοτιμία τῶν ποιούντων it seems necessary to understand the generosity of the retiring "apostles," and yet the process went on—according to Theodore himself—even after these apostles had long left the scene.

organization effected by the apostles was in the first place universal; its scope was the provinces of the church. It is Judæa, Samaria, Syria, Cilicia, Galatia, Asia, Macedonia, etc., that are present to the minds of the apostles, and figure in their writings. Just as, in the missions of the present day, outside sects capture " Brandenburg," " Saxony," and " Bavaria " by getting a firm foothold in Berlin, Dresden, München, and one or two important cities; just as they forthwith embrace the whole province in their thoughts and in some of the measures which they adopt, so was it then. Secondly, Theodore's observation upon the extension of the term "apostle" is in itself quite accurate. But it is just at this point, of course, that our doubts begin. It is inherently improbable that the apostles, *i.e.*, the twelve together with Paul, appointed the other "apostles" (in the wider sense of the word) collectively; besides, it is contradicted by positive evidence to the contrary,[1] and Theodore's statement of it may be very simply explained as due to the preconceived opinion that everything must ultimately run back to the apostles' institution. Further, the idea of each province having an apostle-bishop set over it is a conjecture which is based on no real evidence, and is contradicted by all that we know of the universal ecclesiastical nature of the apostolic office. Finally, we cannot check the statement which would bind up the right of ordination exclusively with the office of the apostle-bishop. In all these respects Theodore seems to have introduced into his sketch of the primitive churches' organization features which were simply current in his own day, as well as hazardous hypotheses. Moreover, we can still show how slender are the grounds on which his conjectures rest. Unless I am mistaken, he has nothing at his disposal in the shape of materials beyond the traditional idea, drawn from the pastoral epistles, of the position occupied by Timothy and Titus in the church, as well as the ecclesiastical notices and legends of the work of John in Asia.[2] All this he has generalized, evolving therefrom the

---

[1] Compare the remarks of Paul and the Didachê upon apostles, prophets, and teachers. The apostles are appointed by God or "the Spirit."

[2] It is even probable that he has particularly in mind, along with Tit. i. 5 f. and 1 Tim. iii. 1 f., the well-known passage in Clem. Alex., *Quis Dives Salvetur* (cp. Eus., *H.E.*, III. xxiii.), since his delineation of the tasks pertaining to the

conception of a general appointment of "apostles" who are equivalent to "provincial bishops."[1] "Apostles" are equivalent to "provincial bishops"; such is Theodore's conception, and the conception is a fantasy. Whether it contains any kernel of historical truth, we shall see later on. Meantime we must, in the first instance, follow up Theodore's statements a little further.

He is right in recognizing that any survey of the origin of the church's organization must be based upon the apostles and their missionary labours. We may add, the organization which arose during the mission and in consequence of the mission, would attempt to maintain itself even after local authorities and institutions had been called into being which asserted rights of their own. But the distinctive trait in Theodore's conception consists in the fact that *he knows absolutely nothing of any originally constituted rights appertaining to local authorities.* He has no eyes for all that the New Testament and the primitive Christian writings, as a whole, contain upon this point; for even here, on his view, everything must have flowed from some apostolic injunction or concession—*i.e.*, from above to below. He adduces, no doubt, the "weakness" of the "apostles" in the second generation— which is quite a remarkable statement, based on the cessation of miraculous gifts.[2] But it was in virtue of their own resolve that the apostles withdrew from the scene, distributing their

apostle-bishop coincides substantially with what is narrated of the work of John in that passage (§ 6 : ὅπου μὲν ἐπισκόπους καταστήσων, ὅπου δὲ ὅλας ἐκκλησίας ἁρμόσων, ὅπου δὲ κλήρῳ ἕνα γέ τινα κληρώσων τῶν ὑπὸ τοῦ πνεύματος σημαινομένων = "Appointing bishops in some quarters, arranging the affairs of whole churches in other quarters, and elsewhere selecting for the ministry some one of those indicated by the Spirit"; cp. also the description of how John dealt with a difficult case).

[1] *Clem. Rom.* xl. f. cannot have been present to his mind, for his remarkable and ingenious idea of the identity of "apostles" and "provincial bishops" would have been shattered by a passage in which it is quite explicitly asserted that the apostles κατὰ χώρας καὶ πόλεις κηρύσσοντες καὶ τοὺς ὑπακούοντας τῇ βουλήσει τοῦ θεοῦ βαπτίζοντες καθίστανον τὰς ἀπαρχὰς αὐτῶν, δοκιμάσαντες τῷ πνεύματι, εἰς ἐπισκόπους καὶ διακόνους τῶν μελλόντων πιστεύειν (see above, p. 434), while xlii. describes a succession, not of apostles one after another, but of bishops.

[2] It seems inevitable that we should take Theodore as holding that the cessation of the miraculous power hitherto wielded by the apostles was a divine indication that they were now to efface themselves.—It was a widely spread conviction (see Origen in several passages, which Theodore read with care) that the apostolic

power to other people; for *only there could the local church's authority originate*! Such is his theory; it is extremely ingenious, and dominated throughout by a magical conception of the apostolate. The local church-authority (or the monarchical and supreme episcopate) within the individual community owed its origin to the "apostolic" provincial authority, by means of a conveyance of power. During the lifetime of the apostles it was quite in a dependent position. Even after their departure, the supreme episcopal authority did not emerge at once within each complete community. On the contrary, says Theodore, it was only two or three towns in every province which at the outset possessed a bishop of their own (*i.e.*, in the new sense of the term "bishop"). Not until a later date, and even then only by degrees, were other towns and even villages added to these original towns, while in the majority of provinces throughout the West the old state of matters prevailed, says Theodore, till quite recently. In some provinces it prevails at present.[1]

This theory about the origin of the local monarchical episcopate baffles all discussion.[2] We may say without any hesitation that Theodore had no authentic foundation for it whatever. Even when he might seem to be setting up at least the semblance of historic trustworthiness for his identification of "apostles" with "provincial bishops," by his reference to Timothy, Titus, and John, the testimony breaks down entirely. We are forced to ask, Who were these retiring apostles? What sources have we for our knowledge of their resignation? How do we learn of this conveyance of authority which they are declared to have executed? These questions, we may say quite plainly,

---

power of working miracles ceased at some particular moment in their history. The power of working miracles and the apostles' power of working miracles are not, however, identical.

[1] Theodore seems to regard this original state of matters as the ideal. At any rate, he expresses his dislike for the village-episcopacy.

[2] All the more so that Theodore goes into the question of how the individual community was ruled *at first* (whether by some local council or by a single presbyter-bishop). He says nothing, either, of the way in which the monarchical principle was reached in the individual community. We seem shut up to the conjecture that in his view the individual communities were ruled by councils for several generations.

Theodore ought to have felt in duty bound to answer; for in what sources can we read anything of the matter? It was not without reason that Theodore veiled even the exact time at which this great renunciation took effect. We can only suppose that it was conceived to have occurred about the year 100 A.D.[1]

At the same time there is no reason to cast aside the statements of Theodore *in toto*. They start a whole set of questions to which historians have not paid sufficient attention, questions relating to the position of bishops in the local church, territorial or provincial bishops (if such there were), and metropolitans. To state the problem more exactly: Were there territorial (or provincial) bishops in the primitive period? And was the territorial bishop perhaps older than the bishop of the local church? Furthermore, did the two disparate systems of organization denoted by these offices happen to rise simultaneously, coming to terms with each other only at a later period? Finally, was the metropolitan office, which is not visible till the second half of the second century, originally an older creation? Can it have been merely the sequel of an earlier monarchical office which prevailed in the ecclesiastical provinces? These questions are of vital moment to the history of the extension of Christianity, and in fact to the statistics of primitive Christianity; for, supposing that it was the custom in many provinces to be content with one or two or three bishoprics for several generations, it would be impossible to conclude from the small number of bishoprics in certain provinces that Christianity was only scantily represented in these districts. The investigation of this question is all the more pressing, as Duchesne has recently (*Fastes épiscopaux de l'ancienne Gaule*, i., 1894, pp. 36 f.) gone into it, referring—although with caution—to the statements of Theodore, and deducing far-reaching conclusions with regard to the organization of the churches in Gaul. We shall require, in the first instance,

---

[1] Theodore adduces but one "proof" for his assertion that originally there were only two or three bishoprics in every province. He refers to the situation in the West as this had existed up till recently, and as it still existed in some quarters. But the question is whether he has correctly understood the circumstances of the case, and whether these circumstances can really be linked on to what is alleged to have taken place about the year 100.

to make ourselves familiar with his propositions [1] (pp. 1–59). I give the main conclusion in his own words.

P. 32 : " Dans les pays situés à quelque distance de la Mediterranée et de la basse vallée du Rhône, il ne s'est fondé aucune église (Lyon exceptée) avant le milieu du IIIe siècle environ."

Pp. 38 f. : " Il en résulte que, dans l'ancienne Gaule celtique, avec ses grandes subdivisions en Belgique, Lyonnaise, Aquitaine et Germanie, une seule église existait au IIe siècle, celle de Lyon . . . . ce que nos documents nous apprennent, c'est que l'église de Lyon était, en dehors de la Narbonnaise, non la première, mais la seule. *Tous les chrétiens épars depuis le Rhin jusqu' aux Pyrénées* [2] *ne formaient qu'une seule communauté ; ils reconnaissaient un chef unique, l'évêque de Lyon.*"

P. 59 : " Avant la fin du IIIe siècle—sauf toujours la région du bas Rhône et de la Méditerranée—peu d'évêchés en Gaule et cela seulement dans les villes les plus importantes. A l'origine, au premier siècle chrétien pour notre pays (150–250), une seule église, celle de Lyon, réunissant dans un même cercle d'action et de direction tous les groupes chrétiens épars dans les diverses provinces de la Celtique."

Duchesne reaches this conclusion by means of the following observations :—

1. No reliable evidence for a single Gallic bishopric, apart from that of Lyons, goes back beyond the middle of the third century.[3] Nor do the episcopal lists, so far as they are relevant in this connection, take us any farther back. Verus of Vienne, *e.g.*, who was present at the council of Arles in 314 A.D., is counted as the fourth bishop in these lists ; which implies that the bishopric of Vienne could hardly have been founded before ± 250 A.D.

---

[1] Duchesne, be it observed, only draws these conclusions for Gaul, nor has he yet said his last word upon the other provinces. I have reason to believe that his verdict and my own are not very different ; hence in what follows I am attacking, not himself, but conclusions which may be drawn from his statements.

[2] The mention of the Pyrenees shows that Duchesne includes Aquitania and the extreme S.W. of France in the province of which Lyons is said to have formed the only bishopric.

[3] Arles alone was certainly in existence before 250 A.D., as the correspondence of Cyprian proves. But Arles lay in the provincia Narbonensis, which is excluded from our present purview.

2. The heading of the well-known epistle from Vienne and Lyons (Eus., *H.E.*, v. 1) runs thus : οἱ ἐν Βιέννῃ καὶ Λουγδούνῳ τῆς Γαλλίας παροικοῦντες δοῦλοι Χριστοῦ ("the servants of Christ sojourning at Vienne and Lyons"). This heading resembles others, such as ἡ ἐκκλησία τοῦ θεοῦ ἡ παροικοῦσα Ῥώμην, or Κόρινθον, Φιλίππους, Σμύρναν, etc. ("the church of God sojourning at Rome, Corinth, Philippi, Smyrna," etc.), and consequently represents both churches as a unity—at least upon that reading of the words which first suggests itself.[1]

3. In this epistle "Sanctus, deacon from Vienne, is mentioned —a phrase which would hardly be intelligible if it alluded to one of the deacons of the bishop of Vienne, but which is perfectly natural if Sanctus was the deacon who managed the inchoate church of Vienne, as a delegate of the Lyons bishop. In that event Vienne had no bishop of its own.

4. Irenæus in his great work speaks of *churches* in Germany and also among the Iberians, the Celts, and the Libyans. Now it is a well-established fact that there were no organized churches, when he wrote, in Germany (*i.e.*, in the military province, for free Germany is out of the question). When Irenæus speaks of *churches*, he must therefore mean churches which were not episcopal churches.[2]

5. Theodore testifies that till quite recently there had been only two or three bishops in the majority of the Western provinces, and that this state of matters still lasted in one or two of them. Now, as a large number of bishoprics can be shown to have existed in southern and middle Italy, as well as in Africa, we are thrown back upon the other countries of the West. Strictly speaking, it is true, Theodore's evidence only covers his own period ; but it fits in admirably with our first four arguments, and it is in itself quite natural, that bishoprics were less numerous in the earlier than in the later period.

---

[1] Certainly this argument is advanced with some caution (p. 40) : "Cette formule semble plutôt désigner un groupe ecclésiastique que deux groupes ayant chacun son organization distincte : en tout cas, elle n'offre rien de contraire à l'indistinction des deux églises."

[2] It is in this way, I believe, that Duchesne's line of argument must be taken (pp. 40 f.). But its trend is not quite clear to my mind.

6. Eusebius mentions a letter from " the parishes in Gaul over which Irenæus presided" (τῶν κατὰ Γαλλίαν παροικιῶν ἃς Εἰρηναῖος ἐπεσκόπει, *H.E.*, v. 23). Now although παροικία usually means the diocese of a bishop, in which sense Eusebius actually employs it in this very chapter, we must nevertheless attach another meaning to it here. " Le verbe ἐπισκοπεῖν ne saurait s'entendre d'une simple présidence comme serait celle d'un métropolitain à la tête de son concile. Cette dernière situation est visée dans le même passage d'Eusèbe ; en parlant de l'évêque Théophile, qui présida celui du Pont, il se sert de l'expression προὐτέτακτο." In the present instance, then, παροικίαι denote " groupes détachés, dispersés, d'une même grande église "—" plusieurs groupes de chrétiens, épars sur divers points du territoire, un seul centre ecclésiastique, un seul évêque, celui de Lyon."

7. Analogous phenomena (*i.e.*, the existence of only one bishop at first and for some time to come) occur also in other large provinces, but the proof of this would lead us too far afield.[1] Duchesne contents himself with adducing a single instance which is especially decisive. The anonymous anti-Montanist who wrote in 192–193 A.D. (Eus., *H.E.*, v. 16) relates how on reaching Ancyra in Galatia he found the Pontic church (τὴν κατὰ Πόντον ἐκκλησίαν) absorbed and carried away by the new prophecy. Now Ancyra does not lie in Pontus, and—" ce n'est pas des nouvelles de l'église du Pont qu'il a eues à Ancyre, c'est l'église elle-même, l'église du Pont, qu'il y a rencontrée." Hence it follows in all likelihood[2] that the church of Pontus had still its " chef-lieu" in Ancyra during the reign of Septimius Severus (*c.* 200 A.D.).[3]

8. The extreme slowness with which bishoprics increased in

---

[1] P. 42 : " D'autres églises que celle de Lyon ont eu d'abord un cercle de rayonnement très étendu et ne se sont en quelque sorte subdivisées qu'après une indivision d'assez longue durée. Je ne veux pas entrer ici dans l'histoire de l'évangélization de l'empire romain : cela m'entraînerait beaucoup trop loin. Il me serait facile de trouver en Syrie, en Égypte et ailleurs des termes de comparaison assez intéressants. Je les néglige pour me borner à un seul exemple," etc.

[2] Duchesne also mentions the allusions to Christians in Pontus which we find in Gregory Thaumaturgus.

[3] This is the period, therefore, in which Duchesne places the anonymous anti-Montanist. In my opinion, it is rather too late.

Gaul is further corroborated by the council of Arles (314 A.D.), at which four provinces (la Germaine I., la Séquanaise, les Grées et Pennines, les Alpes Maritimes) were unrepresented. It may be assumed that as yet they contained no autonomous churches whatever.[1]

Before examining these arguments in favour of the hypothesis that episcopal churches were in existence, which covered wide regions and a number of cities, and in fact several provinces together, let me add a further series of statements which appear also to tell in favour of it.

(1) Paul writes . . . . τῇ ἐκκλησίᾳ τοῦ θεοῦ τῇ οὔσῃ ἐν Κορίνθῳ σὺν τοῖς ἁγίοις πᾶσιν τοῖς οὖσιν ἐν ὅλῃ τῇ Ἀχαΐᾳ (2 Cor. i. 1).

(2) In the Ignatian epistles (c. 115 A.D.) not only is Antioch called ἡ ἐν Συρίᾳ ἐκκλησία (" the church in Syria," Rom. ix., Magn. xiv., Trall. xiii.) absolutely, but Ignatius even describes himself as " the bishop of Syria " (ὁ ἐπίσκοπος Συρίας, Rom. ii.).

(3) Dionysius of Corinth writes a letter " to the church sojourning at Gortyna, with the rest of the churches in Crete, commending Philip their bishop " (τῇ ἐκκλησίᾳ τῇ παροικούσῃ Γορτύναν ἅμα ταῖς λοιπαῖς κατὰ Κρήτην, Φίλιππον ἐπίσκοπον αὐτῶν ἀποδεχόμενος.—Eus., H.E., iv. 23. 5).

(4) The same author (op. cit., iv. 23. 6) writes a letter " to the church sojourning in Amastris, together with those in Pontus, in which he alludes to Bacchylides and Elpistus as having incited him to write . . . . and mentions their bishop Palmas by name " (τῇ ἐκκλησίᾳ τῇ παροικούσῃ Ἄμαστριν ἅμα ταῖς κατὰ Πόντον, Βακχυλίδου μὲν καὶ Ἐλπίστου ὡσὰν αὐτὸν ἐπὶ τὸ γράψαι προτρεψάντων μεμνημένος . . . . ἐπίσκοπον αὐτῶν ὀνόματι Πάλμαν ὑποσημαίνων).

---

[1] A counter-argument is noticed by Duchesne. In Cypr., Ep. lxviii., we are told that Faustinus, the bishop of Lyons, wrote to Stephen the pope (c. 254 A.D.), not only in his own name but in that of ." the rest of my fellow-bishops who hold office in the same province" ("ceteri coepiscopi nostri in eadem provincia constituti "). Duchesne admits that the earliest of the bishoprics (next to that of Lyons) may have been already in existence throughout the provincia Lugdunensis, but he considers that it is more natural to think of bishops on the lower Rhone and on the Mediterrànean, i.e., in the provincia Narbonesis, which had had bishops for a long while.

(5) In Eus., *H.E.*, iii. 4. 6, we read that "Timothy is stated indeed to have been the first to obtain the episcopate of the parish in Ephesus, just as Titus did over the churches in Crete" (Τιμόθεός γε μὴν τῆς ἐν Ἐφέσῳ παροικίας ἱστορεῖται πρῶτος τὴν ἐπισκοπὴν εἰληχέναι, ὡς καὶ Τίτος τῶν ἐπὶ Κρήτης ἐκκλησιῶν).

(6) "In the name of the brethren in Gaul over whom he presided, Irenæus sent despatches," etc. (ὁ Εἰρηναῖος ἐκ προσώπου ὧν ἡγεῖτο κατὰ τὴν Γαλλίαν ἀδελφῶν ἐπιστείλας, Eus., *H.E.*, v. 24. 11); cp. vi. 46: Διονύσιος τοῖς κατὰ Ἀρμενίαν ἀδελφοῖς ἐπιστέλλει, ὧν ἐπεσκόπευε Μερουζάνης ("Dionysius despatched a letter to the brethren in Armenia over whom Merozanes presided").

(7) "Demetrius had just then obtained the episcopate over the parishes in Egypt, in succession to Julian" (τῶν δὲ ἐν Αἰγύπτῳ παροικιῶν τὴν ἐπισκοπὴν νεωστὶ τότε μετὰ Ἰουλιανοῦ Δημήτριος ὑπειλήφει—Eus., *H.E.*, vi. 2. 2).

(8) "Xystus . . . . was over the church of Rome, Demetrianus . . . . over that of Antioch, Firmilianus over Cæsarea in Cappadocia, and besides these Gregory and his brother Athenodorus over *the churches in Pontus*" (τῆς μὲν Ῥωμαίων ἐκκλησίας . . . . Ξύστος, τῆς δὲ ἐπ᾽ Ἀντιοχείας . . . . Δημητριανός, Φιρμιλιανὸς δὲ Καισαρείας τῆς Καππαδοκῶν, καὶ ἐπὶ τούτοις τῶν κατὰ Πόντον ἐκκλησιῶν Γρηγόριος καὶ ὁ τούτου ἀδελφὸς Ἀθηνόδωρος.—Eus., *H.E.*, vii. 14).

(9) "Firmilianus was bishop of Cæsarea in Cappadocia, Gregory and his brother Athenodorus were pastors of *the parishes in Pontus*, and besides these Helenus of the parish in Tarsus, with Nicomas of Iconium," etc. (Φιρμιλιανὸς μὲν τῆς Καππαδοκῶν Καισαρείας ἐπίσκοπος ἦν, Γρηγόριος δὲ καὶ Ἀθηνόδωρος ἀδελφοὶ τῶν κατὰ Πόντον παροικιῶν ποιμένες, καὶ ἐπὶ τούτοις Ἕλενος τῆς ἐν Ταρσῷ παροικίας, καὶ Νικομᾶς τῆς ἐν Ἰκονίῳ, etc.—Eus., *H.E.*, vii. 28).

(10) "Meletius, bishop of the churches in Pontus" (Μελέτιος τῶν κατὰ Πόντον ἐκκλησιῶν ἐπίσκοπος.—Eus., *H.E.*, vii. 32. 26).

(11) "Basilides, bishop of the parishes in Pentapolis" (Βασιλείδης ὁ κατὰ τὴν Πενεάπολιν παροικῶν ἐπίσκοπος.—Eus., *H.E.*, vii. 26. 3).

(12) Signatures to council of Nicæa (ed. Gelzer et socii):

" Calabria—Marcus of Calabria ; Dardania—Dacus of Mace-
donia ; Thessaly—Claudianus of Thessaly and Cleonicus of
Thebes ; Pannonia—Domnus of Pannonia; Gothia—Theophilus
of Gothia ; Bosporus — Cadmus of Bosporus (Καλαβρίας·
Μάρκος Κ. — Δαρδανίας· Δάκος Μακεδονίας. — Θεσσαλίας·
Κλαυδιανὸς Θ., Κλέονικος Θηβῶν.—Παννονίας· Δόμνος Π.—
Γοτθίας· Θεόφιλος Γ.—Βοσπόρου· Κάδμος Β.).

(13) *Apost. Constit.*, vii. 46 : Κρήσκης τῶν κατὰ Γαλατίαν
ἐκκλησιῶν, ᾽Ακύλας δέ καὶ Νικήτης τῶν κατὰ ᾽Ασίαν παροικιῶν
(" Crescens over the churches in Galatia, Aquila and Nicetes
over the parishes in Asia ").[1]

(14) Sozomen (vii. 19) declares that the Scythians had only
a single bishop, although their country contained many towns
(cp. also Theodoret, *H.E.*, iv. 31, where Bretanio is called the
high priest of all the towns in Scythia).

On 1. I note that Duchesne's first argument is an argument
from silence. Besides, it must be added that we have no
writings in which any direct notice of the early Gothic bishoprics
could be expected, so that the argument from silence hardly
seems worthy of being taken into account in this connection.
The one absolutely reliable piece of evidence (Cypr., *Ep.* lxviii.)[2]
for the history of the Gothic church, which reaches us from
the middle of the third century, is certainly touched upon by
Duchesne, but he has not done it full justice. This letter of
Cyprian to the Roman bishop Stephen, which aims at persuading
the latter to depose Marcian, the bishop of Arles, who held to
Novatian's ideas, opens with the words : " Faustinus, our
colleague, residing at Lyons, has repeatedly sent me information
which I know you also have received both from him and also from
the rest of our fellow-bishops established in the same province "
(" Faustinus collega noster Lugduni consistens semel adque
iterum mihi scripsit significans ea quae etiam vobis scio utique
nuntiata tam ab eo quam a ceteris coepiscopis nostris in eadem

---

[1] Merely for the sake of completeness let me add that the *Liber Praedestinatus*
mentions " Diodorus episc. Cretensis" (xii.), " Dioscurus Cretensis episc." (xx.),
"Craton episc. Syrorum " (xxxiii.), " Aphrodisius Hellesponti episc." (xlvii.),
" Basilius episc. Cappadociae" (xlviii.), "Zeno Syrorum episc." (l.), and
" Theodotus Cyprius episc." (lvi.).

[2] See page 455.

provincia constitutis "). It is extremely unlikely that by " eadem provincia" here we are meant to understand the provincia Narbonensis. For, in the first place, Lyons did not lie in that province; in the second place, had the bishops of Narbonensis been themselves opponents of Marcian and desirous of getting rid of him, Cyprian's letter would have been couched in different terms, and it would hardly have been necessary for the three great Western bishops of Lyons, Carthage, and Rome to have intervened; thirdly, Cyprian writes in ch. ii. (" Quapropter facere te oportet plenissimas litteras ad coepiscopos nostros in . Gallia constitutos, ne ultra Marcianum pervicacem et superbum . . . . collegio nostro insultare patiantur "): " Wherefore it behoves you to write at great length to our fellow-bishops established in Gaul, not to tolerate any longer the wanton and insolent insults heaped by Marcian . . . . upon our assembly "; and in ch. iii. (" Dirigantur in provinciam et ad plebem Arelate consistentem a te litterae quibus abstento Marciano alius in loco eius substituatur "): " Let letters be sent by you to the province and to the people residing at Arles, to remove Marcian, and put another person in his place." Obviously, then, it is a question here of two (or three) letters, i.e., of one addressed to the bishops of Gaul, and of a second (or even a third) addressed not only to the " plebs Arelate consistens," but also to the " provincia" (which can only mean the provincia Narbonensis, in which Arles lay). It follows from this that the " coepiscopi nostri in Gallia constituti " (ii.) are hardly to be identified with the bishops of Narbonensis, which leads to the further conclusion that these " coepiscopi " are the bishops of the provincia Lugdunensis—a conclusion which in itself appears to be the most natural and obvious explanation of the passage. *The provincia Lugdunensis thus had several bishops in the days of Cyprian, who were already gathered into one Synod,*[1] *and corresponded with Rome.* We cannot make out from this passage how old these bishoprics were, but it is at any rate unlikely that all of them had just been founded. In this connection Duchesne also refers to the fact that bishop Verus of Vienne, who was present at the council

---

[1] This must be the meaning of Cyprian's phrase, "tam a Faustino quam a ceteris coepiscopis nostris in eadem provincia constitutis."

of Arles in 314, is counted in one ancient list as the fourth
bishop of Vienne; which makes the origin of the local bishopric
fall hardly earlier than ± 250 A.D.   But the list is not ancient.
Besides, it is a questionable authority.   And, even granting
that it were reliable, it is quite arbitrary to assume a mean term
of eighteen years as the duration of an individual episcopate;
while, even supposing that such a calculation were accurate,
it would simply follow that Vienne (although situated in
the provincia Narbonensis, where even Duchesne admits that
bishoprics had been founded in earlier days) did not receive her
bishopric till later.   No inference could be drawn from this
regarding the town of Lyons.

On 2.   Duchesne holds that the heading of the letter (in
Eus., *H.E.*, v. 1: οἱ ἐν Βιέννῃ καὶ Λουγδούνῳ τῆς Γαλλίας
παροικοῦντες δοῦλοι τοῦ Χριστοῦ) seems to describe the
Christians of Vienne and Lyons as if they were a single church.
But if such were the case, one would expect Lyons to be put
first, since it was Lyons and not Vienne which had a bishop.
Besides, the letter does not speak of ἐκκλησίαι or ἐκκλησία but
of δοῦλοι Χριστοῦ, just as the address of the letter mentions
"the brethren in Asia and Phrygia" (οἱ κατὰ τὴν Ἀσίαν καὶ
Φρυγίαν ἀδελφοί) and not "churches" at all.   Hence nothing
at all can be gathered from this passage regarding the organization of the local Christians.   Though Vienne and Lyons belonged
to different provinces, they lay very close together; and as the
same calamity had befallen the Christians of both places, one
can quite understand how they write a letter in common on
that subject.

On 3.   "Their whole fury was aroused exceedingly against
Sanctus the deacon from Vienne" (ἐνέσκηψεν ἡ ὀργὴ πᾶσα εἰς
Σάγκτον τὸν[1] διάκονον ἀπὸ Βιέννης).   It is possible to take this,
with Duchesne, as referring to a certain Sanctus who managed
the inchoate church of Vienne as a delegate of the Lyons bishop.
But the explanation is far from certain.   This sense of ἀπό is
unusual (though not intolerable),[2] and the words may quite well

---

[1] So, rightly, Schwartz.

[2] Cp. Eus., *H.E.*, v. 19: Αἴλιος Πούπλιος Ἰούλιος ἀπὸ Δεβελτοῦ κολωνείας τῆς
Θρᾴκης ἐπίσκοπος ("Aelius Publius Julius, bishop of Debeltum, a colony of

be rendered, "the deacon who came from Vienne" [sc. belonging to the church of Lyons].[1]   But even supposing that Sanctus was described here as the deacon of Vienne, it seems to me hasty and precarious to infer, with Duchesne, that Vienne had only a single deacon and no bishop (not even a presbyter) at all. Surely this is to build too much upon the article before διάκονον. Of course, it may be so; we shall come back to this passage later on.   Meantime, suffice it to say that the explicit description of Pothinus in the letter as "entrusted with the bishopric *of Lyons*" (τὴν διακονίαν τῆς ἐπισκοπῆς τῆς ἐν Λουγδούνῳ πεπιστευμένος), instead of as "*our* bishop" or even "*the* bishop," does not tell in favour of the hypothesis that Lyons alone, and not Vienne, had a bishop at that period.

On 4.   The passage from Iren., i. 10. 2 (καὶ οὔτε αἱ ἐν Γερμανίαις ἱδρυμέναι ἐκκλησίαι ἄλλως πεπιστεύκασιν ἢ ἄλλως παραδιδόασιν, οὔτε ἐν ταῖς Ἰβηρίαις, οὔτε ἐν Κελτοῖς, οὔτε κατὰ τὰς ἀνατολὰς οὔτε ἐν Αἰγύπτῳ, οὔτε ἐν Λιβύῃ οὔτε αἱ κατὰ μέσα τοῦ κόσμου ἱδρυμέναι = Nor did the churches planted in Germany hold any different faith or tradition, any more than do those in Iberia or in Gaul or in the East or in Egypt or in Libya or in the central region of the world) remains neutral if we read it and interpret it very sceptically.   The language affords no clue to the way in which the churches in Germany and among the Celts were organized.   But the most obvious interpretation is that these "churches" were just as entire and complete in themselves as the churches of the East, of Egypt, of Libya, and of all Europe, which are mentioned with them on the same level.   At any rate, nothing can be inferred from this passage in support of Duchesne's opinion.   It is a pure "petitio principii" to hold that complete churches could not have existed in Germany.

Thrace").   The parallel, of course, is not decisive, as Julius was at a gathering in Phrygia when he penned these words.

[1] Cp. what immediately follows—"against Attalus a native of Pergamum" (εἰς Ἄτταλον Περγαμηνὸν τῷ γένει), and also § 49 (Ἀλέξανδρός τις, Φρὺξ μὲν τὸ γένος, ἰατρὸς δὲ τὴν ἐπιστήμην = a certain Alexander, of Phrygian extraction, and a physician by profession).   Neumann, in his *Röm. Staat und die allgem. Kirche*, i. (1890), p. 30, writes thus: "As Sanctus, the deacon of Vienna, appears before the tribunal of the legate of Lyons, he must have been arrested in Lyons."

On 5.   No weight attaches to Theodore's evidence regarding the primitive age.   Yet even he presupposes that after the exit of the "apostles" (= provincial bishops) each separate province had two or three bishops of its own, while Duchesne would prove that the three Gauls had merely one bishop between them for about a hundred years.

On 6.   At first sight, this argument seems to be particularly conclusive, but on a closer examination it proves untenable, and in fact turns round in exactly an opposite direction.   The expression τῶν κατὰ . . . . ἐπεσκόπει cannot, we are told, be understood to mean episcopal dioceses over which Irenæus presided as metropolitan; it merely denotes scattered groups of Christians (though in the immediate context ἡ παροικία does mean an episcopal diocese), as ἐπισκοπεῖν need only imply direct episcopal functions.   Yet in *H.E.*, vii. 26. 3, Eusebius describes Basilides as ὁ κατὰ τὴν Πεντάπολιν παροικιῶν ἐπίσκοπος (see (11)), and Meletius (*H.E.*, vii. 32. 26; cp. (10)) as τῶν κατὰ Πόντον ἐκκλησιῶν ἐπίσκοπος, and it is quite certain—even on the testimony of Eusebius himself—that there were several bishoprics at that period in Pentapolis and Pontus.[1]   Ἐπίσκοπος *παροικιῶν, therefore, denotes in this connection the position of metropolitan,*[2] and it is in this sense that παροικίας ἐπισκοπεῖν must also be understood with reference to Irenæus.   The latter, Eusebius meant, was metropolitan of the episcopal dioceses in Gaul.   So far from proving, then, that about 100 A.D. there was only one bishop in Gaul, *our passage proves the existence of several bishops.*[3]

[1] In this very chapter Eusebius mentions the bishopric of Berenicê in Pentapolis.

[2] On Eus., *H.E.*, vi. 2. 2, see below (P. 462).

[3] Thus the expression used by Eusebius in *H.E.*, v. 24. 11 (ὁ Εἰρηναῖος ἐκ προσώπου ὧν ἡγεῖτο κατὰ τὴν Γαλλίαν ἀδελφῶν ἐπιστείλας—cp. (6)) is also to be understood as a reference to the metropolitan rank of Irenæus, since it is employed as a simple equivalent for the above expression in v. 23.   Probst (*Kirchliche Disziplin in den drei ersten christlichen Jahrhunderten*, p. 97) and some other scholars even go the length of including Gallic *bishops* among the ἀδελφοί, an interpretation which is not necessary, although it is possible, and rests on one strong piece of evidence in the "parishes" of v. 23.—The outcome of both passages relating to Irenæus and Gaul is that it is impossible to ascertain whether the Meruzanes mentioned in *H.E.* vi. 46 as the bishop of the Armenian brethren was the sole local bishop at that period or the metropolitan.   See on (6).

On 7. This argument is quite untenable. The church of Pontus, we are told, had its episcopal headquarters in the Galatian Ancyra about 200 A.D.! But about 190 A.D. it already had a metropolitan of its own, for Eusebius mentions a writing sent during the Paschal controversy by "the bishops of Pontus over whom Palmas, as their senior, presided" (τῶν κατὰ Πόντον ἐπισκόπων, ὧν Πάλμας ὡς ἀρχαιότατος προυτέτακτο, H.E., v. 23). How Duchesne could overlook this passage is all the more surprising, inasmuch as a little above he quotes from this very chapter. Besides, this Palmas, as we may learn from Dionysius of Corinth (in Eus., H.E., iv. 23. 6; see below, p. 463), seems to have stayed not in Ancyra but in Amastris. Further-more, in the passage in question τόπον (so Schwartz) must be read[1] instead of Πόντον, despite the Syriac version. Πόντον is meaningless here, even if the territorial bishop of Pontus resided at that time in Ancyra. Thus it is not in Pontus, but in Phrygia and Gaul, that we hear of Montanist agitations, and, moreover, one could not possibly have got acquainted with the church of Pontus in Ancyra, even if the latter place had been the residence of that church's head. Can one get acquainted in Alexandria nowadays with the church of Abyssinia?

On 8. Duchesne's final argument proves nothing, because it is uncertain whether the four recent provinces mentioned here had still no bishops by 314 A.D. Nothing can be based on the fact that they were not represented at Arles, for the representa-tion of churches at the great synods was always an extremely haphazard affair. But even supposing that these provinces were still without bishops of their own, this proves nothing with regard to Lyons.

I have added to Duchesne's reasons fourteen other passages which appear to favour his hypothesis. Three of these (6), (10), (11) have been already noticed under 6., and our conclusion was that they were silent upon provincial bishops, being concerned

---

[1] Προσφάτως γενόμενος ἐν 'Αγκύρᾳ τῆς Γαλατίας καὶ καταλαβὼν τὴν κατὰ τόπον (not Πόντον) ἐκκλησίαν ὑπὸ τῆς νέας ταύτης . . . . ψευδοπροφητείας διατεθρυλη-μένην ("When I was recently at Ancyra in Galatia, I found the local church quite upset by this novel form . . . . of false prophecy"). Κατὰ Πόντον is in one other passage of Eusebius a mistake for κατὰ πάντα τόπον (iv. 15. 2).

rather with metropolitans. It remains for us to review briefly the other eleven.

We must not infer from 2 Cor. i. 1 that, when Paul wrote this epistle, all the Christians of Achaia belonged to the church of Corinth. In Rom. xvi. 1 f. Paul mentions a certain Phœbê, διάκονος τῆς ἐκκλησίας τῆς ἐν Κεγχρεαῖς, speaking highly of her as having been a προστάτις πολλῶν καὶ ἐμοῦ αὐτοῦ, so that, while many Christians scattered throughout Achaia may have also belonged to the church at Corinth at that period, there was nevertheless a church at Cenchreæ besides, which we have no reason to suppose was not independent.

Ignatius's description of himself as " bishop of Syria," and his description of the church of Antioch as ἡ ἐν Συρίᾳ ἐκκλησία, appear to prove decisively that there was only one bishop then in Syria, viz., at Antioch (2). Yet in ad Phil. x. we read how some of the neighbouring churches sent bishops, others presbyters and deacons, to Antioch (ὡς καὶ αἱ ἔγγιστα ἐκκλησίαι ἔπεμψαν ἐπισκόπους, αἱ δὲ πρεσβυτέρους καὶ διοκόνους), which shows that there were bishoprics[1] in Syria, and indeed in the immediate vicinity of Antioch, c. 115 A.D. The bishop of Antioch called himself "bishop of Syria" on account of his metropolitan position.

From Eus., H.E., iv. 23. 5–6, it would appear that there was only a single bishop (3), (4), in Crete and in Pontus c. 170 A.D., inasmuch as Dionysius of Corinth designates Philip as bishop of Gortyna and the rest of the churches in Crete, and Palmas bishop of Amastris and the churches of Pontus. But whether the expression be attributed to Dionysius himself, or ascribed, as is more likely, to Eusebius, the fact remains that the same collection of the letters of Dionysius contained one to the church of Cnossus in Crete, or to its bishop Pinytus (loc cit., § 7), while, as we have already seen (on 7), Palmas was not the sole bishop in Pontus. Philip and Palmas were therefore not provincial bishops but metropolitans, with other bishops at their side.

[1] Some of the bishoprics adjoining Antioch, of which Eusebius speaks in H.E., vii. 30. 10 (ἐπίσκοποι τῶν ὁμόρων ἀγρῶν τε καὶ πόλεων), were therefore in existence by c. 115 A.D.—It seems to me impossible that Philadelphia is referred to in the expression αἱ ἔγγιστα ἐκκλησίαι in Phil. x. (" the nearest churches "). Even Lightfoot refers it to Syria. To be quite accurate he ought to have said, " to the church in Antioch," as that church is mentioned just above.

The statement of Eusebius (5) that Titus was bishop of the Cretan churches is an erroneous inference from Titus i. 5; it is destitute of historical value.

According to the habitual terminology of Eusebius (7), τῶν δὲ ἐν Αἰγύπτῳ παροικιῶν τὴν ἐπισκοπὴν τότε Δημήτριος ὑπειλήφει describes Demetrius as a metropolitan, not as a provincial bishop (see above, on (6)). Other evidence, discussed by Lightfoot (in his *Commentary on Philippians*, 3rd ed., pp. 228 f.), would seem to render it probable that Demetrius was really the only bishop (in the monarchical sense) in Egypt in 188–189 A.D.; but this fact is no proof whatever that the Alexandrian bishop was a "provincial" bishop, for it does not preclude the possibility that, while Demetrius was the first monarchical bishop in Alexandria itself, Egypt in general did not contain any churches up till then except those which were superintended by presbyters or deacons. The whole circumstances of the situation are of course extremely obscure. Nevertheless, it does look as if Demetrius and his successor Heraclas were the first bishops (in the proper sense of the term), and as if they ordained similar bishops (Demetrius ordained three, and Heraclas twenty) for Egypt. It is perfectly possible, no doubt, but at the same time it is incapable of proof, that the Egyptian churches were in a dependent position towards the Alexandrian church at a time when Alexandria itself had as yet no bishop of its own.

In both of the passages (8) and (9) where Gregory and Athenodorus are described as *bishops of the Pontic church*, the dual number shows that we have to do neither with provincial nor with metropolitan bishops. Eusebius is expressing himself vaguely, perhaps because he did not know the bishoprics of the two men.

In Eus., *H.E.*, viii. 13. 4–5, two bishops who happen to bear the same name ("Silvanus") are described as bishops of the churches "round Emesa," or round "Gaza" (12). There can be no question of provincial bishops here, however, as we know that these districts contained a large number of bishoprics. The position of matters can be understood from the history of Emesa and Gaza, both of which long remained pagan towns;

we are told that they would not tolerate a Christian bishop. Bishops, therefore, were unable to reside in either place. But as the groups of Christian villages in the vicinity had bishops for themselves (so essential did the episcopal organization seem to Eastern Christians), there were probably bishops *in partibus infidelium* for Emesa and Gaza, although otherwise they were territorial bishops, over quite a limited range of territory.

As regards provincial bishops, it seems possible to cite the signatures to the council of Nicæa (13), viz., the five instances in which the name of the province accompanies that of the bishop. These are Calabria, Thessaly, Pannonia, Gothia, and the Bosphorus.[1] But in the case of Thessaly, bishop Claudianus of Thessaly is accompanied by bishop Cleonicus of Thebes, so that the former was not a provincial bishop but a metropolitan. Besides, it is quite certain that Calabria and Pannonia had more than one bishop in 325 A.D., although only the metropolitans of these provinces were present at Nicæa (as indeed was also the case with Africa, whose metropolitan alone was in attendance). Thus only Gothia and the Bosphorus are left. But as these lay outside the Roman empire, and as quite a unique set of conditions prevailed throughout these regions, the local situation there cannot form any standard for estimating the organization of churches inside the empire. The bishops above mentioned may have been the only bishops there.

No value whatever attaches to the statements of the *Apost. Constit.* (14) and of the *Liber Predestinatus*. The former are based, so far as regards the first half of them, upon an arbitrary deduction from 2 Tim. iv. 10, while their second half is utterly futile, since several Asiatic city bishoprics are mentioned in the context. The latter statement is a description of *metropolitans* (*i.e.*, so far as any idea whatever can be ascribed to the forger), as is proved abundantly by the entry, " Basilius, bishop of Cappadocia." Finally, the communication of Sozomen (15), which he himself describes as a curiosity, refers to a barbarian country.

---

[1] The signature Δαρδανίας · Δάκος Μακεδονίας is obscure, and must therefore be set aside.

The result is, therefore, that the alleged evidence for the hypothesis of provincial bishops instead of local (city) bishops and metropolitans throughout the empire, yields no proof at all. Out of all the material which we have examined, nothing is left to support this conjecture. The sole outcome of it is the unimportant possibility that in 178 A.D. (and even till about the middle of the third century), Vienne had no independent bishop of its own. Even this conjecture, as has been shown, is far from necessary, while it is opposed by the definite testimony of Eusebius, who knew of a letter from the parishes of Gaul *c.* 190 A.D.[1] And even supposing it were to the point, we should have to suppose that the Christians in Vienne were numbered, not by hundreds, but merely by dozens, about the year 178, *i.e.*, some decades later still.

It is certain (cp. pp. 432 f.) that an internal tension prevailed between two forms of organization during the first two generations of the Christian propaganda. These forms were (I) the church as a missionary church, created by a missionary or apostle, whose work it remained; and (2) the church as a local church, complete in itself, forming thus an image and expression of the church in heaven. As the creation of an apostolic missionary, the church was responsible to its founder, dependent

---

[1] If there were several (episcopal) parishes in Gaul *c.* 190 A.D., Vienne would also form one such parish. The hypothesis that a number of bishoprics existed in middle and northern Gaul in the days of Irenæus is confirmed by the fact that Irenæus (in a passage i. 10, to which I shall return) speaks, not of Christians in Germany, but of "*the churches founded in Germany.*" Would he have spoken of them if these churches had not had any bishops? While, if they did possess bishops of their own,—and according to iii. 3. 1, the episcopal succession reaching back to the apostles could be traced in *every individual church*,—then how should there have been still no bishops in middle and northern Gaul?

The passage iii. 3. 1 runs thus: "Traditionem apostolorum in toto mundo manifestatam, in omni ecclesia adest perspicere omnibus qui vera velint videre, et habemus annumerare eos qui ab apostolis instituti sunt episcopi in ecclesiis et successiones eorum usque ad nos. . . . . Sed quoniam valde longum est, in hoc tali volumine omnium ecclesiarum enumerare successiones," etc. ("All who desire to see facts can clearly see the tradition of the apostles, which is manifest all over the world, *in every church* ; we are also able to enumerate those whom the apostles appointed as bishops in the churches, as well as to recount their line of succession down to our own day. . . . . Since, however, in a volume of this kind it would take up great space to enumerate the various lines of succession throughout all the churches," etc.).

upon him, and obliged to maintain the principles which he invariably laid down in the course of his activity as a founder of various churches. As a compact local church, again, it was responsible for itself, with no one over it save the Lord in heaven. Through the person of its earthly founder, it stood in a real relationship to the other churches which he had founded. But as a local church it stood by itself, and any connection with other churches was quite a voluntary matter.

That the founders themselves desired the churches to be independent, is perfectly clear in the case of Paul, and we have no reason to believe that other founders of churches took another view (cp. the Roman church). No doubt they still continued to give pedagogic counsels to the churches, and in fact to act as guardians to them. But this was exceptional; it was not the rule. The Spirit moved them to such action, and their apostolic authority justified them in it, while the unfinished state of the communities seemed to demand it.[1] And in the primitive decision upon the length of time that an apostle could remain in a community, as in similar cases, the communities secured, *ipso facto*, a means of self-protection within their own jurisdiction. Probably the perfected organization of the Jerusalem church became, *mutatis mutandis*, a pattern for all and sundry: Christian communities were not "churches of Paul" or "of Peter" (ἐκκλησίαι Παύλου, Πέτρου); each was a "church of God" (ἐκκλησία τοῦ θεοῦ).

The third epistle of John affords one clear proof that conflicts did occur between the community and its local management upon the one hand and the "apostles" on the other. This same John (or, in the view of many critics, a different person) does not impart his counsels to the Asiatic communities directly. He makes the "Spirit" utter them. He proclaims, not his own coming with a view to punish them, but the coming of the Lord as their judge. But we need not enter more particularly into these circumstances and conditions. The point is that the apostolic authority soon faded; nor was it transmuted as a

---

[1] What they did, the churches also did themselves in certain circumstances. Thus, the Roman church exhorted, and in fact acted as guardian to, the Corinthian church in one sore crisis (*c.* 96 A.D.).

whole, for all that passed over to the monarchical episcopate was but a limited portion of its contents.

The apostolic authority and praxis meant a certain union of several communities in a single group. When it vanished, this association also disappeared. But another kind of tie was now provided for the communities of a single province by their provincial association, and proofs of this are given by the Pauline epistles and the Apocalypse of John. The epistle to the Galatians, addressed to all the Christian communities of Galatia, falls to be considered in this aspect, and much more besides. Paul's range of missionary activity was regulated by the provinces ; Asia, Macedonia, Achaia, etc., were ever in his mind's eye. He prosecutes the great work of his collection by massing together the communities of a single province, and the so-called epistle " to the Ephesians " is addressed, as many scholars opine, to a large number of the Asiatic communities. John writes to the churches of Asia.[1] Even at an earlier period a letter had been sent (Acts xv.) from Jerusalem to the churches of Syria and Cilicia.[2] The communities of Judæa were so closely bound up with that of Jerusalem, as to give rise to the hypothesis (Zahn, *Forschungen*, vi. p. 300) that the ancient episcopal list of Jerusalem, which contains a surprising number of names, is a conflate list of the Jerusalem bishops and of those from the other Christian communities in Palestine. Between the apostolic age and *c.* 180 A.D., when we first get evidence of provincial church synods, similar proofs of union among the provincial churches are not infrequent. Ignatius is concerned, not only for the church of Antioch, but for that of Syria ; Dionysius of Corinth writes to the communities of Crete and to those in Pontus ; the brethren of Lyons write to those in Asia and Phrygia ; the Egyptian communities form a sphere complete in itself, and the churches of Asia present themselves to more than Irenæus as a unity.

Not in all cases did a definite town, such as the capital,

[1] By addressing himself also to the church at Laodicea, he passes on into the neighbouring district of Phrygia. But the other six churches are all Asiatic.

[2] The collocation of Christians from several large provinces in 1 Peter is remarkable. But as the address of this letter has been possibly drawn up artificially, I do not take it here into account.

become the headquarters which dominated the ecclesiastical province. No doubt Jerusalem (while it lasted), Antioch,[1] Corinth,[2] Rome, Carthage, and Alexandria formed not merely the centres of their respective provinces, but in part extended their sway still more widely, both in virtue of their importance as large cities, and also on account of the energetic Christianity which they displayed.[3] Yet Ephesus, for example, did not become for a long while the ecclesiastical metropolis of Asia in the full sense of the term ; Smyrna and other cities competed with it for this honour.[4] In Palestine, Aelia (Jerusalem) and Cæsarea stood side by side. Certain provinces, like Galatia and extensive districts of Cappadocia, had no outstanding towns

---

[1] Cp. the very significant address in Acts xv. 23 : οἱ ἀπόστολοι καὶ οἱ πρεσβύτεροι ἀδελφοὶ τοῖς κατὰ τὴν Ἀντιόχειαν καὶ Συρίαν καὶ Κιλικίαν ἀδελφοῖς. For our present purpose, it does not matter whether the letter is genuine or not.

[2] According to the extract from the correspondence of Dionysius of Corinth, given by Eusebius (*H.E.*, IV. 23), the bishop of Corinth seems to have stood in a different relation to the churches of Lacedæmon and Athens from that in which he stood towards communities lying outside Greece.

[3] This requires no proof, as regards Rome. But the church of Jerusalem also pushed far beyond Palestine ; it gave Paul serious trouble in the Diaspora, and tried even to balk his plans. In the third century bishop Firmilian set up the "observationes" of the Gentile Christian church at Jerusalem against those of Rome, thereby attributing to the former a certain prestige outside Palestine for the church at large. The bishop of Antioch, again, reached as far as Cilicia, Mesopotamia, and Persia ; the bishop of Carthage as far as Mauretania ; the bishop of Alexandria as far as Pentapolis. Cp. the second canon of the Council of Constantinople (381), which prohibits a bishop or metropolitan from invading another diocese, but at the same time expressly makes an exception of "barbarian" districts, on the ground of ancient use and wont (τὰς δὲ ἐν τοῖς βαρβαρικοῖς ἔθνεσιν τοῦ θεοῦ ἐκκλησίας οἰκονομεῖσθαι χρὴ κατὰ τὴν κρατήσασαν συνήθειαν τῶν πατέρων.—The sphere of Alexandria's influence, however, several times embraced Palestine and Syria, even prior to Athanasius, Cyril, and Dioscorus. It is very remarkable, *e.g.*, that no fewer than three Alexandrians— Eusebius, Anatolius, and Gregory—occupied the see of Laodicea (Syr.) at the close of the third and the beginning of the fourth centuries (Eus., *H.E.*, vii. 32 ; Philostorgius, viii. 17). There was already a sort of prescriptive right which afterwards passed into the division of the patriarchate. Thus, in the intercourse of the churches the Roman bishop already represented all the West (including Illyria afterwards) ; while the bishop of Antioch, as well as the bishop of Alexandria, seem to have had the prescriptive privilege of attending to the entire East. Apart from this privilege, however, the spheres of Alexandria (South) and Antioch (Middle and North) respectively were delimited. Cæsarea (Cappadocia) and Ephesus now attained positions of some independence.

[4] All this was connected, of course, with the political organization of Asia.

at all, and when we are told that in the provinces of Pontus, Numidia, and Spain the *oldest* bishop always presided at the episcopal meetings, the inference is that no single city could have enjoyed a position of superiority to the others from the ecclesiastical standpoint.

But the question now arises, whether the "metropolitans," [1] who had been long in existence before they were recognized by the law of the church or attained their rights and authority, in any way repressed the tendency towards the increase of independent communities within a province; and further, whether, in the interests of their own power, the bishops also made any attempt to retard the organization of new *independent* communities under episcopal government. In itself, such a course of action would not be surprising. For wherever authority and rights develop, ambition and the love of power invariably are unchained.

In order to solve this problem, we must first of all premise that the tendency of early Christianity to form complete, independent communities, *under episcopal government*, was extremely strong. [2]

---

[1] A learned treatise in Russian has just been published on the metropolitans by P. Giduljanow (*Die Metropoliten in den ersten drei Jahrhunderten des Christentums*, Moscow, 1905), which also contains ample material for ecclesiastical geography, besides a coloured map of "The Eastern Half of the Roman Empire during the First Three Christian Centuries." Special reference is made to the ecclesiastical arrangements and spheres in their relation to the political framework.

[2] As Ignatius cannot conceive of a community existing at all without a bishop, so Cyprian also judges that a bishop is absolutely necessary to every community; without him its very being appears to break up (see especially *Ep.* lxvi. 5). The tendencies voiced by Ignatius in his epistles led to every Christian community in a locality, however small it might be, securing a bishop, and we have every reason to suppose that the practice which already obtained in Syria and Asia corresponded to these tendencies. From the outset we observe that local churches spring into life on all sides, as opposed to uncertain transient unions, and while Christians might and did group themselves in other forms (*e.g.*, mere guilds of worship and schools of thought), these were invariably attacked and suppressed. Neighbouring cities, like Laodicea, Colossê, and Hierapolis, had churches of their own from the very first. So had the seaport of Corinth, as early as the days of Paul, while the localities closely "adjacent to" Antioch (Syr.) had churches of their own in Trajan's reign (Ignat., *ad Phil.* x.), and not long afterwards we have evidence of village churches also. Then, as soon as we hear of the monarchical episcopate, it is in relation to small communities. The localities which lay near Antioch had their own bishops, and two decades afterwards we find a bishop quartered in the Phrygian village of Comana (Eus., *H.E.*, v. 16). The Nicene

Furthermore, I do not know of a single case, from the first three centuries, which would suggest any tendency, either upon the part of metropolitans or of bishops, to curb the independent organization of the churches. Not till after the opening of the fourth century does the conflict against the chor-episcopate[1] commence; at least there are no traces of it, so far as I know, previous to that period. Then it is also that—according to our sources—the bishops begin their attempt to prohibit the erection of bishoprics in the villages, as well as to secure the discontinuance of bishoprics in small neighbouring townships —all with the view of increasing their own dioceses.[2]

Furthermore, we have not merely an "argumentum e silentio" before us here. On the contrary, after surveying (as we shall do in Book IV.) the Christian churches which can be traced *circa* 325 A.D., we see that it is quite impossible for any tendency to have prevailed throughout the large majority of the Roman provinces which checked the formation of bishoprics, inasmuch as almost all the churches in question can be proved to have been episcopal. We conclude, then, that *wherever communities,*

Council was attended by village bishops from Syria, Cilicia, Cappadocia, Bithynia, and Isauria, who had the same rights as the town bishops. In the so-called *Apostolic Constitutions* (middle of second century) we read : "If the number of men be small, and twelve persons cannot be found at one place, who are entitled to elect a bishop, let application be made to any of the nearest churches which is well established, so that three chosen men may be sent who shall carefully ascertain who is worthy," etc. Which assumes that even in such cases a complete or episcopal church is the outcome. We must therefore assume that it was the rule in some at least, and probably in many, of the provinces to give every community a bishop. Thus the number of the local churches or communities would practically be equivalent to the number of bishoprics.

[1] Cp. Gillmann, *Das Institut der Chorbischöpe im Orient* (1903). The names of these clergy are χωρεπίσκοποι, ἐπίσκοποι τῶν ἀγρῶν (ἐν ταῖς κώμαις ἢ ταῖς χώραις), συλλειτουργοί [*i.e.*, of the town bishops]. Originally, as the name ἐπίσκοποι shows, they stood alongside of the town bishops ; but as a real distinction was drawn from the outset between the bishop of a provincial capital and the bishops of other towns, so a country bishop always was inferior to his colleagues in the towns, and indeed often occupied a position of real dependence on them (cp. Gillmann, pp. 30 f.).

[2] The chor-episcopi were first of all de-classed by their very name ; then they were deprived of certain rights retained by the town bishops, including especially the right of ordination. Finally, they were suppressed. The main stages of this struggle throughout the East are seen in the following series of decisions. Canon xiii. of the Council of Ancyra (314 A.D.): χωρεπισκόπους μὴ ἐξεῖναι πρεσβυτέρους ἢ διακόνους χειροτονεῖν ("Chor-episcopi are not allowed to elect

episcopally governed, were scanty, Christians were also scanty upon the whole; while, if a town had no bishop at all, the number of local Christians was insignificant. Certainly during the course of the Christian mission, in several cases, whole decades passed without more than one bishop in a province or in an extensive tract of country. We might also conjecture, *a priori*, that wherever a district was uncultivated or destitute of towns —as on the confines of the empire and beyond them—years passed without a single bishop being appointed, the scattered local Christians being superintended by the bishop of the nearest town, which was perhaps far away. It is quite credible that, even after a fully equipped hierarchy had been set up in such an outlying district, this bishop should have retained certain rights of supervision—for it is a question here, not simply of personal desire for power, but of rights which had been already acquired. Still, it is well-nigh impossible for us nowadays to gain any clear insight into circumstances of this kind, since after the second century all such cases were treated

presbyters or deacons"). Canon xiii. of the Council of Neo-Cæsarea : οἱ χωρεπίσ-κοποι εἰσι μὲν εἰς τύπον τῶν ἑβδομήκοντα· ὡς δὲ συλλειτουργοὶ διὰ τὴν σπουδὴν τὴν εἰς τοὺς πτωχοὺς προσφέρουσι τιμώμενοι ("The chor-episcopi are indeed on the pattern of the Seventy, and they are to have the honour of making the oblation, as felloW - labourers, on account of their devotion to the poor"). Canon viii. of the Council of Antioch (341 A.D.): "Country priests are not to issue letters of peace [*i.e.*, certificates] ; they are only to forWard letters to the neighbouring bishop. Blameless chor-episcopi, hoWever, can grant letters of peace." *Ibid.*, canon x.: "Even if bishops in villages and country districts, the so-called chor-episcopi, have been consecrated as bishops, they must recognize the limits of their position. Let them govern the churches under their sWay and be content with this charge and care, appointing lectors and sub-deacons and exorcists ; let them be satisfied With expediting such business, but never dare to ordain priest or deacon Without the bishop of the toWn to Whom the rural bishop and the district itself belong. Should anyone dare to contravene these orders, he shall be deprived of the position Which he now holds. A rural bishop shall be appointed by the bishop of the toWn to which he belongs" (cp. on this, Gillmann, pp. 90 f.). Canon vi. of the Council of Sardica (343 A.D.): "Licentia vero danda non est ordinandi episcopum aut in vico aliquo aut in modica civitate, cui sufficit unus presbyter, quia non est necesse ibi episcopum fieri, ne vilescat nomen episcopi et auctoritas. non debent illi ex alia provincia invitati facere episcopum, nisi aut in his civitatibus, quae epis-copos habuerunt, aut si qua talis aut tam populosa est civitas, quae mereatur habere episcopum" (the contemporary Greek version does not correspond to the original ; its closing part runs thus : ἀλλ' οἱ τῆς ἐπαρχίας ἐπίσκοποι ἐν ταύταις ταῖς πόλεσι καθιστᾶν ἐπισκόπους ὀφείλουσιν, ἔνθα καὶ πρότερον ἐτύγχανον γεγονότες

and recorded from the standpoint of a dogmatic theory of ecclesiastical polity—the theory that the right of ordination was a monopoly of the original apostles, and consequently that all bishoprics were to be traced back, either directly to them, or to men whom they had themselves appointed. The actual facts of the great mission promoted by Antioch (as far as Persia, eastwards), Alexandria (into the Thebais, Libya, Pentapolis, and eventually Ethiopia), and Rome seemed to corroborate this theory. The authenticated instances from ancient history (for we have no detailed knowledge of the Bosphorus or of Gothia) permit us to infer, e.g., that the power of ordination possessed by the bishop of Alexandria extended over four provinces. Still, as has been remarked already, the original local conditions remain obscure. It is relevant also at this point to notice the tradition, possibly an authentic one, that the first bishop of Edessa was consecrated by the bishop of Antioch (*Doctr. Addæi*, p. 50), and that the Persian church was for a long while dependent upon the

ἐπίσκοποι· εἰ δὲ εὑρίσκοιτο οὕτω πληθύνουσά τις ἐν πολλῷ ἀριθμῷ λαοῦ πόλις, ὡς ἀξίαν αὐτὴν καὶ ἐπισκοπῆς νομίζεσθαι, λαμβανέτω). " It is absolutely forbidden to ordain a bishop in any village or small town for which a single presbyter is sufficient—for it is needless to ordain bishops there—lest the name and authority of bishops be lowered. Bishops called in from another province ought not to appoint any bishop except in those cities where there were bishops previously ; or if any city contains a population large enough to merit a see, then let one be founded there." Canon lvii. of the Council of Laodicea : "In villages and country districts no bishops shall be appointed, but only visitors (περιοδευταί), nor shall those already appointed act without the consent of the city bishop." By the opening of the fifth century this process had gone to such a length that Sozomen (*H.E.*, vii. 19) notes, as a curiosity, that "there are cases where in other nations bishops do the work of priests in villages, as I myself have seen in Arabia and Cyprus and in Phrygia among the Novatians and Montanists" (ἐν ἄλλοις ἔθνεσίν ἐστιν ὅπη καὶ ἐν κώμαις ἐπίσκοποι ἱεροῦνται, ὡς παρὰ 'Αραβίοις καὶ Κύπροις ἔγνων καὶ παρὰ τοῖς ἐν Φρυγίαις Ναυατιανοῖς καὶ Μοντανισταῖς. (According to Theodore of Mopsuestia—see Swete's cd., vol. ii. p. 44—this was still in force about the year 400 in the district which he supervised, much to his disgust). In Northern Africa, upon the other hand, no action was taken against the smaller bishops. Augustine himself (*Ep.* cclxi.) erected a new bishopric within his own diocese, whilst even after the year 400 it is plain that the number of bishoprics in Northern Africa went on multiplying. We may take it that in provinces where the village bishoprics were numerous (*i.e.*, in the majority of the provinces of Asia Minor, besides Syria and Cyprus), the total number of bishoprics did not materially increase after 325 A.D. Probably, indeed, it even diminished.

church of Antioch, from which it drew its metropolitans.[1] When this was in force, the imperial church had already firmly embraced the theory that episcopal ordination could only be perpetuated within the apostolic succession.

There are also instances, of course, in which, during the third century (for, apart from Egypt, no sure proofs can be adduced at an earlier period), Christian communities arose in country districts which were superintended by presbyters or even by deacons alone, instead of by a bishop. Such cases, however, are by no means numerous.[2] They are infrequent till in and after the age of Diocletian.[3] Previous to that period, so far as I know, there was but one large district in which presbyterial organization was indeed the rule, viz., Egypt. Yet, as has been already observed, the circumstances of Egypt are extremely obscure. It is highly probable that for a considerable length of time there were no monarchical bishops at all in that country, the separate churches being grouped canton-wise and super-intended by presbyters. Gradually the episcopal organization extended itself during the course of the third century, yet even in the fourth century there were still large village churches which had no bishop. We must, however, be on our guard

---

[1] Hoffmann, *Auszüge aus syrischen Akten persischer Märtyrer* (1880), p. 46 ; and Uhlemann, *Zeitschrift f. d. hist. Theol.* (1861), p. 15. But the primitive history of Christianity in Persia lies wrapt in obscurity or buried in legend.

[2] No case is known, so far as I am aware, during the pre-Constantine period in Northern Africa. One might infer, from epistles i. and lviii. of Cyprian, that there were no bishops at Furni and Thibaris, but from *Sentent. Episcop.* (59 and 37) it is evident that even these churches were ruled by one bishop. Probably the see was vacant when Cyprian wrote epistle i. ; but this hypothesis is needless so far as regards epistle lviii. The reference to Cypr., *Ep.* lxviii. 5, is extremely insecure. It is unlikely that even in Middle and Lower Italy churches existed without bishops during the third century. We must not use *cpp.* 4 and 7 of the letter written by Firmilian of Iconium (Cypr., *Ep.* lxxv.) as an argument in favour of churches without bishops, surprising as is the expression "seniores et praepositi" or "praesident maiores natu." There was such a church at the village of Malus near Ancyra (see *Acta Mart. Theodot.*, 11. 12), but the evidence is almost worthless, as the *Acta* in question are not contemporary.

[3] We must not, of course, include cases in which presbyters, or presbyters and deacons, ruled a community during an episcopal vacancy. Even though they employed language which can only be described as episcopal (cp. the eighth document of the Roman clergy among Cyprian's letters), they were simply regents ; see *Ep.* xxx. 8, "We thought that no new step should be taken before a bishop was appointed" (ante constitutionem episcopi nihil innovandum putavimus).

against drawing conclusions from Egypt and applying them to any of the other Roman provinces. It has been inferred, from the subscriptions to the Acts of the synod of Elvira, that some Spanish towns, which were merely represented by presbyters at the synod, did not possess any bishops of their own. This may be so, but the very Acts of the synod clearly show how precarious is the inference; for, while many presbyters subscribed these Acts, it can be proved that in almost every case the town churches which they represented did possess a bishop. The latter was prevented from being present at the synod, and, like the Roman bishop, he had himself represented by a presbyter or deputation of the clergy. Nevertheless it is indisputable, on the ground of the sixty-seventh canon of Elvira ("si quis diaconus regens plebem sine episcopo vel presbytero," etc.), that there were churches in Spain which had not a bishop or even a presbyter, although we know as little about the number of such churches as about the conditions which prevented the appointment of a bishop or presbyter. In any case, the management of a church by a deacon must have always been the exception (mainly an emergency measure in the days of persecution), since it was unlawful for him to perform the holy sacrifice (see the fifteenth canon of Arles). It is impossible to decide whether the ἐπιχώριοι πρεσβύτεροι mentioned in the thirteenth canon of Neo-Cæsarea mean independent presbyters in country churches, or presbyters who had a chor-episcopus over them. Possibly the latter is the true interpretation, since we must assume a specially vigorous development of the chor-episcopate in the neighbouring country of Cappadocia, which sent no fewer than five chor-episcopi to the council of Nicæa. On the other hand, it follows from the Testament of the Forty Martyrs of Sebaste that there were churches in the adjoining district of Armenia which were ruled by a presbyter, and in which no chor-episcopate seems to have existed (cp. Gillmann, p. 36). Armenia, however, was a frontier province, and we cannot transfer its peculiar circumstances en masse to the provinces of Pontus and Cappadocia. The "priests in the country," mentioned in the eighth canon of Antioch (341 A.D.), are certainly priests who had supreme authority in their local spheres; but the synod of Antioch was held in the post-Constantine period, and the circumstances of 341 A.D. do not furnish any absolute rule for those of an earlier age. It is natural to suppose that the contemporary organization of the cantons in Gaul,[1] which hindered the development of towns, proved also an obstacle to the thorough organization of the episcopal system ; hence one might conjecture that imperfectly organized churches were numerous in that country (as in England). But on this point we know absolutely nothing. Besides, even in the second century there was a not inconsiderable number of towns in Gaul where the local conditions were substantially the same as those which prevailed in the other Roman towns.[2]

It is impossible, therefore, to prove that for whole decades there were territorial or provincial bishops who ruled over a number of dependent Christian churches in the towns; we must rather assume that if bishops actually did wield episcopal rights in a number of towns, it was in towns where only an infinitesimal number of Christians resided within the walls. Anyone who asserts the contrary with regard to some provinces cannot be refuted. I admit that. But the burden of proof rests with him. The assertion, for example, that Autun, Rheims, Paris, etc., had a fairly large number of Christians by the year 240 or thereabouts, while the local Christian churches had no bishop, cannot be proved incorrect, in the strict sense of the term. We have no materials for such a proof. But all analogy favours the conclusion: if the Christians in Autun, Rheims, Paris, etc., were so numerous *circa* 240 A.D., then they had bishops; if they had no bishops, then they were few and far between. In my opinion, we may put it thus: (1) It is

---

[1] See Mommsen's *Röm. Gesch.*, v. 81 f. [Eng. trans., i. 92 f.], and also Marquardt's *Röm. Staatsverwaltung*, i. 7 f.

[2] Two systems prevailed in the civil government, as regards the country districts ; the latter were either placed under the jurisdiction of a neighbouring town or assigned magistrates of their own (see Hatch-Harnack, *Gesellschaftsverfassung der christlichen Kirchen*, p. 202). The latter corresponded to the chor-episcopate, the former to the direct episcopal jurisdiction and administration of the town bishop. The blending of the two systems, with more or less independent country presbyters and reserved rights on the part of the bishop, was the latest development. Its earliest stage falls within the second half of the third century. A number of small localities were often united into a commune, whose centre was called μητροκωμία.

quite possible, indeed it is extremely likely (cp. the evidence of Cyprian), that before the middle of the third century there were already some other episcopal churches in Gaul, even apart from the " province "; (2) if Lyons was really the sole episcopal church of the country, then there was only an infinitesimal number of Christians in Gaul outside that city.

We come back now to one of Theodore's remarks. " At the outset," he wrote, " there were but two or three bishops, as a rule, in a province—a state of matters which prevailed in most of the Western provinces till quite recently, and which may still be found in several, even at the present day." This is a statement which yields us no information whatever. Theodore did not know any more than we moderns know about the state of matters " at the outset." The assertion that there were not more than two or three bishops in the *majority* of the Western provinces " till quite recently," is positively erroneous, and it only proves how small was Theodore's historical knowledge of the Western churches; finally, while the information that several Western provinces even yet had no more than two or three bishops, is accurate, it is irrelevant, since we know, even apart from Theodore's testimony, that the number of bishoprics in the Roman provinces adjoining the large northern frontier of the empire, as well as in England, was but small. But this scantiness of contemporary bishoprics did not denote an earlier (and subsequently suspended) phase of the church's organization tenaciously maintaining itself. What it denoted was a result of the local conditions of the population and also the rarity of Christians in those districts. So far, of course, these local circumstances resembled those in which Christianity subsisted from the very outset over all the empire, when the Christians— and the Romans—of the region lived still in the Diaspora.

At this point we might conclude by saying that the striking historical paragraph of Theodore does not cast a single ray of truth upon the real position of affairs. But in the course of our study we have over and again touched upon the special position of the metropolitan, or leading bishop of the province.[1]

---

[1] Augustine once (*Ep.* xxii. 4) remarks of the Carthaginian church in relation to the churches of the province : " Si ab una ecclesia inchoanda est medicina [*i.e.*,

It is perfectly clear, from a number of passages, that the metropolitan was frequently described in the time of Eusebius simply as "the bishop of the province." The leading bishop was thus described even as early as Dionysius of Corinth or Ignatius himself. With regard to the history of the extension of Christianity—in so far as we are concerned to determine the volume of tendency making for the formation of independent churches—the bearing of this fact is really neutral. But it is not neutral with regard to our conception of the course taken by *the history of ecclesiastical organization.* Unluckily our sources here fail us for the most part. The uncertain glimpses they afford do not permit us to obtain any really historical idea of the situation, or even to reconstruct any course of development along this line. How old is the metropolitan? Is his position connected with a power of ordination which originally passed from one man to another in the province? Does the origin of the metropolitan's authority go back to a time when the apostles still survived? Was there any connection between them? And are we to distinguish between one bishop and another, so that in earlier age there would be bishops who did not ordain, or who were merely the vicars of a head bishop?[1] To all these questions we are probably to return a negative answer *in general*, though an affirmative may perhaps be true in one or two cases. Certainty we cannot reach. At least, in spite of repeated efforts, I have not myself succeeded in gaining any sure footing. Frequently the *facts* of the situation may have operated quite as strongly as the rights of the case; *i.e.*, an

the suppression of an abuse], sicut videtur audaciae mutare conari quod Carthaginiensis ecclesia tenet, sic magnae impudentiae est velle servare quod Carthaginiensis ecclesia correxit." This would represent a widely spread opinion, held long before the fourth century, with regard to the authority of the metropolitan church.

[1] We are led to put this question by learning that injunctions were laid down in the fourth century, which delimited the ordination rights of the chor-episcopi (see above, p. 471). Does this restriction go back to an earlier age? Hardly to one much earlier, though Gillmann (p. 121) is right in holding that the decisions of Ancyra and Neo-Cæsarea did not come with the abruptness of a pistol-shot; they codified what had previously been the partial practice of wide circles in the church. We must therefore look back as far as the period beginning with the edict of Gallienus. But we know nothing as to whether the country bishop was in any respect subordinate to the city bishop from the first (especially in the matter of ordination). *A priori*, it is unlikely that he was.

individual bishop may have exercised rights at first, and for a considerable period, without possessing any title thereto, but simply as the outcome of a strong position held either on personal grounds or on account of the civic repute and splendour of his town churches.[1] The state provincial organization and administration, with the importance which it lent to individual towns, may have also begun here and there to affect the powers of individual bishops in individual provinces by way of aggrandizement.[2] But all this pertains, probably, to the sphere of those elements in the situation which we may term "irrational," elements which do not admit of generalization or of any particular application to ecclesiastical rights and powers within the primitive age. No evidence for the definition of the metropolitan's *right of jurisdiction* can be found earlier than the age in which the synodal organization had defined itself, and the presupposition of such a right lay in the sturdy independence, the substantial equality, and the closely knit union of all the bishops in any given province. All the "preliminary stages" lie enveloped in mist. And the scanty rays which struggle through may readily prove deceptive will-o'-the-wisps.

These investigations into the problems connected with the history of the extension of Christianity lead to the following result, viz., that the *number* of bishoprics in the individual provinces of the Roman empire affords a criterion, which is essentially reliable, for estimating the strength of the Christian

---

[1] One recollects at this point, *e.g.*, the second epistle of Cyprian, mentioned already on pp. 175, which tells how the Carthaginian church was prepared to undertake the support of an erstwhile teacher of the dramatic art, if his own church was not in a position to do so. It is clear that the Carthaginian church or bishop would acquire a superior position amid the sister provincial churches, if cases of this kind occurred again and again. Compare also the sixty-second epistle, in which the Carthaginian church not only subscribes 100,000 sesterces towards the emancipation of Christians in Africa who had been carried off captives by the barbarians, but also expresses herself ready to send still more in case of need [cp. pp. 175 f., 301]. It is well known that the repute of the Roman church and its bishops was increased by such donations, which were bestowed frequently even on remote churches.

[2] The instructive investigations of Lübeck ("Reichseinteilung und kirchliche Hierarchie des Orients," in *Kirchengeschichtliche Studien*, herausgeg. von Knöpfler, Schrörs, und Sdralek, Bd. v. Heft 4, 1901) afford many suggestions on this point,

movement. The one exception is Egypt. Apart from that province, we may say that Christian communities, not episcopally organized, were quite infrequent throughout the East and the West alike during the years that elapsed between Antoninus Pius and Constantine.[1] Not only small towns, but villages also had bishops. Cyprian was practically right when he wrote to Antonian (*Ep.* lv. 24) : " Iam pridem per omnes provincias et per

---

[1] Previous to the middle of the third century I do not know of a single case (leaving out Egypt). All the evidence that has been gathered from the older period simply shows that there were Christians in the country, or that country people here and there came in to worship in the towns ; evidently they had no place of worship at home, and consequently no presbyters. Furthermore, the original character of the presbyter's office, a character which can be traced down into the third century, excludes any differentiation among the individual, independent presbyters, each of whom was a presbyter as being the member of a college and nothing more (cp. also Hatch-Harnack, *Gesellschaft. der christlichen Kirchen*, pp. 76 f., 200 f. ; the right of presbyters to baptize was originally a transmitted right and nothing more. Hatch refers the rise of parishes also to a later time). I should conjecture that the organization of presbyterial village churches began first of all when the town congregation in the largest towns had been divided into presbyters' and deacons' districts, and when the individual presbyters had thus become relatively independent. In Rome this distribution emerged rather later than the middle of the third century, and originally it sprang from the division into civic quarters (not the synagogue). The necessity of having clergy appointed for the country, even where there were no bishops, emerged further throughout the East wherever a martyr's grave or even a churchyard had to be looked after (cp. the Testament of the Forty Martyrs of Sebaste). Again, we know from the history of Gregory Thaumaturgus and other sources (cp. the *Acta Theodoti Ancyr.*) that after the middle of the third century the great movement had begun which sought to appropriate and consecrate as Christian the sacred sites and cults of paganism throughout the country, as well as to build shrines for the relics of the saints. In these cases also a presbyter, or at least a deacon, was required, in order to take care of the sanctuary. Finally, the severe persecutions of Decius, Valerian, Diocletian, and Maximinus Daza drove thousands of Christians to take refuge in the country ; the last-named emperor, moreover, deliberately endeavoured to eject Christians from the towns, and condemned thousands to hard labour in the mines throughout the country. We know, thanks to the information of Dionysius of Alexandria and Eusebius, that in such cases communities sprang up in the country districts for the purpose of worship ; naturally these were without a bishop, unless one happened to be among their number. It may be supposed that all these circumstances combined to mature the organization of presbyterial communities, an organization which subsequently, under the countenance of the town bishops, entered upon a victorious course of rivalry with the old chor-episcopate. Frequently, however, in the country the nucleus lay, not in the community, but in the sacred sites—and such were in existence even before the adoption and consecration of pagan ones, in the shape of martyrs' graves and churchyards. These considerations lead me to side with Thomassin in the controversy between

urbes singulas ordinati sunt episcopi" ("Bishops have been for long ordained throughout all the provinces and in each city ").[1] And what was unique in the age of Sozomen (*H.E.*, vii. 19), viz., that only one bishop ruled in Scythia, though it had many towns[2]—this would also have been unique a century and a half earlier.

In conclusion, it must be remembered that the whole of this investigation relates solely to the age between Pius and Constantine, not to the primitive period during which the monarchical episcopate first began to develop. During this period—which lasted in certain provinces till Domitian and Trajan, and in many others still longer—a collegiate government of the individual church, by means of bishops and deacons (or by means of a college of presbyters, bishops, and deacons), was normal. How this passed over into the other (*i.e.*, the monarchic control) we need not ask in this connection. But the hypothesis that wherever communities which are not

that critic and Binterim : the "country parish" did not begin its slow process of development till after about 250 A.D. On the other hand, I disagree with Thomassin in thinking that the "country episcopate" is the older of the two. It can be traced back unmistakably in Phrygia to the beginning of the Montanist controversy. For the origin of the "country parishes," cp. the recent keen investigations by Stutz and his pupil (Stutz, *Gesch. des kirchl. Benefizialwesens I.*, 1895 ; Schäfer, *Pfarrkirche und Stift im deutschen Mittelalter*, 1903 ; and Stutz's review, in *Gött. Gel. Anz.*, 1904, No. 1, pp. 1–86, of Imbart de la Tour's *Les paroisses rurales du 4e au 11e siècle*, 1900). Although these studies do not touch the pre-Constantine period, they need to be collated by anyone who desires to elucidate the history of the primitive organization of the church.

[1] With this reservation, that in certain provinces the tendency to form independent communities proceeded more briskly than in others. This, however, is purely a matter of conjecture ; it cannot be strictly proved. The episcopal churches of the third century were most numerous in North Africa, Palestine, Syria, Asia, and Phrygia ; and this tells heavily in support of the view that the Christians of these provinces were also most numerous. Africa is the one country where I should conjecture that special circumstances led to a rapid increase of independent, *i.e.*, of episcopal communities ; but what those circumstances were, no one can tell.

[2] When Sozomen continues : ἐν ἄλλοις δὲ ἔθνεσιν ἐστὶν ὅπη καὶ ἐν κώμαις ἐπίσκοποι ἱεροῦνται, ὡς παρὰ 'Αραβίοις καὶ Κυπρίοις ἔγνων καὶ παρὰ τοῖς ἐν Φρυγίαις Ναυατιανοῖς καὶ Μοντανισταῖς [cp. above, p. 473], we see that village bishops no longer existed in most of the provinces when he wrote (*c.* 430 A.D.). That they had been common at an earlier period is shown by the mere fact of their survival among the Phrygian adherents of Novatian and Montanus, since these sects held fast to ancient institutions.

episcopally organized are to be found throughout the third century, they are to be considered as having retained the primitive organization—this hypothesis, I repeat, is not merely incapable of proof, but incorrect. Such non-episcopal village churches are plainly *recent* churches, which are managed, not by a college of presbyters, but by one or two presbyters. They are "country parishes" whose official "presbyters" have nothing in common with the members of the primitive college of presbyters except the name. Here I would again recall how Egypt forms the exception to the rule, inasmuch as large Christian churches throughout Egypt still continue to be governed by the collegiate system down to the middle of the third century. Nothing prevents us, in this connection, from supposing that these churches did hold tenaciously to the primitive form of ecclesiastical organization. Yet alongside of the presbyters in Egypt, even διδάσκαλοι would seem also to have had some share in the administration of the churches (Dionys. Alex., in Eus., *H.E.*, vii. 24).

EXCURSUS II

THE CATHOLIC CONFEDERATION AND THE MISSION

BEFORE general synods and patriarchs arose within the church, prior even to the complete development of the metropolitan system, there was a catholic confederation which embraced the majority of the Christian churches in the East and the West alike. It came into being during the gnostic controversies; it assumed a relatively final shape during the Montanist controversy; and its headquarters were at Rome. The federation had no written constitution. It did not possess one iota of common statutes. Nevertheless, it was a fact. Its common denominator consisted of the apostles' creed, the apostolic canon, and belief in the apostolical succession of the episcopate. Indeed, long before these were generally recognized as the common property of the churches, the maintenance of this body of doctrine constituted a certain unity by itself. Externally, this unity manifested itself in inter-communion, the brotherly welcome extended to travellers and wanderers, the orderly notification of any changes in ecclesiastical offices, and also the representation of churches at synods beyond the bounds of their own provinces and the forwarding of contributions. What was at first done spontaneously—and as a result of this, in many cases, both arbitrarily and uselessly—became a matter of regular prescriptive right, carried out along fixed lines of its own.

The fact of this catholic federation was of very great moment to the spread of the church. The Christian was at home everywhere, and he could feel himself at home, thanks to this inter-communion. He was protected and controlled wherever he went. The church introduced, as it were, a new franchise among her members. In the very era when Caracalla bestowed Roman citizenship upon the provincials—a concession which amounted to very little, and which failed to achieve its ends—the catholic citizenship became a significant reality.

EXCURSUS III

FROM the close of the first century the Roman church was in a position of practical primacy over Christendom. It had gained this position as the church of the metropolis, as the church of Peter and Paul, as the community which had done most for the catholicizing and unification of the churches, and above all as the church which was not only vigilant and alert but ready [1] to aid any poor or suffering church throughout the empire with gifts. [2] The question now rises, Was this church not also specially active in the Christian mission, either from the first or at certain epochs of the pre-Constantine period? Our answer must be in the negative. Any relevant evidence on this point plainly belongs to legends with a deliberate purpose and of late origin. All the stories about Peter founding churches in Western and Northern Europe (by means of delegates and subordinates) are pure fables. Equally fabulous is the mass of similar legends about the early Roman bishops, e.g., the legend of Eleutherus and Britain. The sole residuum of truth is the tradition, underlying the above-mentioned legend, that Rome and Edessa were in touch about 200 A.D. This fragment of information is isolated, but, so far as I can see, it is trustworthy. We must not infer from it, however, that any deliberate missionary movement had been undertaken by Rome. The Christianizing

---

[1] Evidence is forthcoming from the second and the third centuries, for Corinth, Arabia, Cappadocia, and Mesopotamia (cp. above, pp. 157, 185, 376 ; and below, Book IV.). In a still larger number of cases Rome intervened with her advice and opinion.

[2] A considerable amount of the relevant material is collected in my *History of Dogma*, I.[3] pp. 455 f. (Eng. trans., vol. ii. pp. 149-168), under the title of "Catholic and Roman."

of Edessa was a spontaneous result. Abgar the king may indeed have spoken to the local bishop when he was at Rome, and a letter which purports to be from Eleutherus to Abgar might also be historical. The Roman bishop may perhaps have had some influence in the catholicizing of Edessa and the bishops of Osrhoene. But a missionary movement in any sense of the term is out of the question. Furthermore, if Rome had undertaken any organized mission to Northern Africa (or Spain, or Gaul, or Upper Italy) we would have found echoes of it, at least in Northern Africa. Yet in the latter country, when Tertullian lived, people only knew that while the Roman church had an apostolic origin, their own had not; consequently the " auctoritas " of the former church must be recognized. Possibly this contains a reminiscence of the fact that Christianity reached Carthage by way of Rome, but even this is not quite certain. Unknown sowers sowed the first seed of the Word in Carthage also; they were commissioned not by man but by God. By the second century their very names had perished from men's memory.

The Roman church must not be charged with dereliction of duty on this score. During the first centuries there is no evidence whatever for organized missions by individual churches ; such were not on the horizon. But it was a cardinal duty to "strengthen the brethren," and this duty Rome amply discharged.

CHAPTER V

COUNTER-MOVEMENTS

1

Wᴇ have already discussed (pp. 57 f.) the first systematic
opposition offered to Christianity and its progress, viz., the))
Jewish counter-mission initiated from Jerusalem. This expired
with the fall of Jerusalem, or rather, as it would seem, not
earlier than the reign of Hadrian. Yet its influence continued
to operate for long throughout the empire, in the shape of
malicious charges levelled by the Jews against the Christians.
The synagogues, together with individual Jews, carried on the
struggle against Christianity by acts of hostility and by inciting
hostility.[1]

We cannot depict in detail the counter-movements on the
part of the state, as these appear in its persecutions of the

---

[1] Cp. the martyrdom of Polycarp or of Pionius. In the *Martyr. Cononis* the
magistrate says to the accused: τί πλανᾶσθε, ἄνθρωπον θεὸν λέγοντες, καὶ τοῦτον
βιοθανῆ; ὡς ἔμαθον παρὰ ’Ιουδαίων ἀκριβῶς, καὶ τί τὸ γένος αὐτοῦ καὶ ὅσα ἐνεδείξατο
τῷ ἔθνει αὐτῶν καὶ πῶς ἀπέθανεν σταυρωθείς· προκομίσαντες γὰρ αὐτοῦ τὰ
ὑπομνήματα [? ?] ἐπανέγνωσάν μοι (von Gebhardt's *Acta Mart. Selecta*, p. 131):
"Why do ye err, calling a man God, and that too a man who died a violent death?
For so have I learnt accurately from the Jews, both as to his race and his manifestation to their nation and his death by crucifixion. They brought forward his
memoirs and read them out to me." In his polemical treatise, Celsus makes a
Jew come forward against the Christians—and this reflected the actual state of
matters. Any pagans who wished to examine Christianity closely and critically,
had first of all to get information from the Jews. On the other hand, as has
been already shown (pp. 66 f.), the Christians did not fail to condemn the Jews
most severely. The instance narrated by Hippolytus (*Philos*, ix. 12) apropos of
the Roman Christian Callistus, is certainly remarkable, but none the less symp-
tomatic. In order to secure a genuine martyrdom, Callistus posted himself on
Sabbath at a synagogue and derided the Jews.

church.[1] All that need be done here is to bring out some of the leading points, with particular reference to the significance, both negative and positive, which the persecutions possessed for the Christian mission.

Once Christianity presented itself in the eyes of the law and the authorities as a religion distinct from that of Judaism, its character as a *religio illicita* was assured. No express decree was needed to make this plain. In fact, the "non licet" was rather the presupposition underlying all the imperial rescripts against Christianity. After the Neronic persecution, which was probably[2] instigated by the Jews (see above, p. 58), though it neither extended beyond Rome nor involved further consequences, Trajan enacted that provincial governors were to use their own discretion, repressing any given case,[3] but declining to ferret Christians out.[4] Execution was their fate if, when suspected of *lèse-majesté* as well as of sacrilege,[5] they stubbornly refused to sacrifice before the images of the gods of the emperor, thereby avowing themselves guilty of the former crime. *On the cultus of the Cæsars, and on this point alone, the state and the church came into collision.*[6] The apologists are really incorrect in asserting that the Name itself ("nomen ipsum") was visited with death. At least, the statement only becomes correct when

---

[1] See Neumann's *Der römische Staat und die allg. Kirche*, i. 1890 ; Mommsen, "Der Religionsfrevel nach röm. Recht" (in the *Hist. Zeitschr.*, vol. lxiv. [N.S. vol. xxviii.], part 3, pp. 389–429; Harnack on "Christenverfolgung" in the *Prot. Real-Encykl.* III.[(3)] ; Weiss, *Christenverfolgungen* (1899) ; and Linsenmayer's *Die Bekämpfung des Christentums durch den röm. Staat* (1905).

[2] Without this hypothesis it is scarcely possible, in my opinion, to understand the persecution. Cp. my essay in *Texte u. Unters.*, xxviii. 2 (1905).

[3] Trajan approves Pliny's procedure in executing Christians who, upon being charged before him, persistently refused to sacrifice. But he adds, "nothing can be laid down as a general principle, to serve as a fixed rule of procedure" (" in universum aliquid quod quasi certam formam habeat constitui non potest ").

[4] This did not, of course, exclude criminal procedure in certain cases at the discretion of the governor. Even during the second century special regulations were enacted for the treatment of Christians. For a true appreciation of the repressive and the criminal procedure, cp. Augar in *Texte u. Unters.*, xxviii. 4 (1905).

[5] "Atheism" ; cp. my essay in *Texte u. Unters.* (*ibid.*).

[6] Tert., *Apol.* x. : "Sacrilegii et majestatis rei convenimur, summa haec causa, immo tota est " (" We are arraigned for sacrilege and treason ; that is the head and front, nay, the sum total of our offence"). But the "sacrilegium" was hardly to be distinguished practically from "majestas."

we add the corollary that this judicial principle was adopted simply because the authorities found that no true adherent of this sect would ever offer sacrifice.[1] He was therefore an atheist and an enemy of the state.

Down to the closing year of the reign of Marcus Aurelius, the imperial rescripts with which we are acquainted were designed, not to protect the Christians, but to safeguard the administration of justice and the police against the encroachments of an anti-Christian mob,[2] as well as against the excesses of local councils who desired to evince their loyalty in a cheap fashion by taking measures against Christians. Anonymous accusations had been already prohibited by Trajan. Hadrian had rejected the attempts of the Asiatic diet, by means of popular petitions, to press governors into severe measures against the Christians. Pius in a number of rescripts interdicted all "novelties" in procedure; beyond the injunctions that Christians were not to be sought out ("quaerendi non sunt"), and that those who abjured their faith were to go scot-free, no step was to be taken. During this period, accusations preferred by private individuals came to be more and more restricted, both in criminal procedure as a whole, and in trials for treason. Even public opinion[3] was becoming more and more adverse to them. And all this told in favour of Christianity. Most governors or magistrates recognized that there was no occasion for them to interfere with Christians; convinced of their real harmlessness, they let them go their own way. Naturally, the higher any person stood in public life, the greater risk he ran

[1] Pliny (*Ep.* xcvi. 5): "Quorum nihil posse cogi dicuntur qui sunt re vera Christiani" ("Things which no real Christian, it is said, can be made to do").

[2] Observe that society and the populace down to about Caracalla's reign (and during that reign) were keenly opposed to Christianity; the state had actually to curb their zeal. Thereafter, the fanaticism of the rabble and the aversion of a section of society steadily declined. People likely began to get accustomed to the fact of the new religion's existence. Tertullian (*Scorp.* i.) says that the "ethnici de melioribus" (the better sort of pagans) asked: "Siccine tractari sectam nemini molestam? perire homines sine causa?" ("Is a harmless sect to be treated thus? Are men to die for no reason?"). This meant that Roman emperors and governors of pagan disposition had to redouble their vigilance.

[3] Tertullian does declare (*Apol.* ii.) that "every man is a soldier against traitors and public enemies" ("in reos majestatis et publicos hostes omnis homo miles est"), but he is referring to open criminals, not to suspected persons.

of coming into collision with the authorities on the score of his
Christian faith. Only on the lowest level of society, in fact,.
did this danger become at all equally grave, since life was not
really of very much account to people of that class. People
belonging to the middle classes, again, were left unmolested
upon the whole; that is, unless any conspiracy succeeded in
haling them before a magistrate. Down to the middle of the
third century, this large middle class furnished but a very small
number of martyrs. Irenæus writes (about 185 A.D.; see above,
p. 369): " Mundus pacem habet per Romanos, et nos [Christiani]
sine timore in via ambulamus et navigamus quocumque voluerimus." Soldiers, again, were promptly detected whenever they
made any use of their Christian faith in public. So were all
Christians who belonged to the numerous domains of the
emperors.

Apart from the keen anti-Christian temper of a few proconsuls and the stricter surveillance of the city-prefects, this
continued to be the prevailing attitude of the state down to
the days of Decius, i.e., to the year 249. During this long
interval, however, three attempts at a more stringent policy
were made. " Attempts " is the only term we can use in this
connection, for all three lost their effect comparatively soon.
Marcus Aurelius impressed upon magistrates and governors the
duty of looking more strictly after extravagances in religion,
including those of Christianity. The results of this rescript
appear in the persecution of 176–180 A.D.; but when
Commodus came to the throne, the edict fell into abeyance.
Then, in 202 A.D., Septimius Severus forbade conversions to
Christianity, which of course involved orders to keep a stricter
watch on Christians in general. As the persecutions of the
neophytes and catechumens in 202–203 attest, the rescript was
not issued idly; yet before long it too was relaxed. Finally,
Maximinus Thrax ordered the clergy to be executed, which
implied the duty of hunting them out—in itself a fundamental
innovation in the imperial policy. Outside Rome, however, it
is unlikely that this order was put into practice, save in a few
provinces, although we do not know what were the obstacles
to its enforcement. Down to the days of Maximinus Thrax

the clergy do not appear to have attracted much more notice than the laity, and the edict of Maximinus did not strike many of them down. Still, it was significant. Plainly, the state had now become alive to the influential position occupied by the Christian clergy.

These attempts at severity were of brief duration. But the comparative favour shown to Christianity, upon the other hand, by Commodus, Alexander Severus, and Philip the Arabian led to a steady improvement in the prospects of Christianity with the passage of every decade.

Viewed externally, then, the persecutions up to the middle of the third century were not so grave as is commonly represented. Origen expressly states that the number of the martyrs during this period was small; they could easily be counted.[1] A glance at Carthage and Northern Africa (as seen in the writings of Tertullian) bears out this observation. Up till 180 A.D. there were no local martyrs at all; up to the time of Tertullian's death there were hardly more than a couple of dozen, even when Numidia and Mauretania are included in the survey. And these were always people whom the authorities simply made an example of. Yet it would be a grave error to imagine that the position of Christians was quite tolerable. No doubt they were able, as a matter of fact, to settle down within the empire, but the sword of Damocles hung over every Christian's neck, and at any given moment he was sorely tempted to deny

---

[1] Cp. c. Cels. III. viii. It is also significant that he expressly declares the last days would be heralded by general persecutions, whereas hitherto there had been only partial persecutions: "Nunquam quidem consenserunt omnes gentes adversus Christianos; cum autem contigerint quae Christus praedixit, tunc quasi succendendi sunt omnes a quibusdam gentilibus incipientibus Christianos culpare, ut tunc fiant *persecutiones iam non ex parte sicut ante*, sed generaliter ubique adversus populum dei" (Comment. Ser. *in Matt.* xxxix., vol. iv. p. 270, ed. Lommatzsch)="Never, indeed, have all nations combined against Christians. But when the events predicted by Christ come to pass, then all must be as it were inflamed by some of the heathen who begin to charge Christians, so that perse-cutions then occur universally against all God's people, instead of here and there, as hitherto has been the case" (cp. also p. 271). Not to exaggerate Origen's remark about the small number of the martyrs, cp. Iren. iv. 33. 9: "Ecclesia omni in loco multitudinem martyrum in omni tempore praemittit ad patrem" ("The church in every place and at all times sends on a multitude of martyrs before her to the Father").

his faith, since denial meant freedom from all molestation. The Christian apologists complained most of the latter evil, and their complaint was just. The premium set by the state upon denial of one's faith was proof positive, to their mind, that the administration of justice was controlled by demonic influence.

Despite the small number of martyrs, we are not to underrate the courage requisite for becoming a Christian and behaving as a Christian. We are specially bound to extol the staunch adherence of the martyrs to their principles. By the word or the deed of a moment, they might have secured exemption from their punishment, but they preferred death to a base immunity.[1]

The illicit nature of Christianity unquestionably constituted a serious impediment to its propaganda, and it is difficult to say whether the attractiveness of all forbidden objects and the heroic bearing of the martyrs compensated for this drawback. It is an obstacle which the Christians themselves rarely mention; they dwell all the more upon the growth which accrued to them ever and anon from the martyrdoms.[2] All over, indeed, history

---

[1] Martyrs and confessors, of course, were extravagantly honoured in the churches, and the prospect of "eternal" glory might allure several (Marcus Aurelius condemns the readiness of Christians for martyrdom as pure fanaticism and vainglory; cp. also Lucian's *Proteus Peregrinas*). The confessors were assigned a special relationship to Christ. As they had attached themselves to him, so he had thereby attached himself to them. They were already accepted, already saved; Christ gave utterance through their lips henceforth. Furthermore, they had a claim to be admitted into the ranks of the clergy (oldest passage on this in Tertullian, *de Fuga*, xi.); and on important ecclesiastical occasions, especially on all matters relating to penitence, their decision had to be accepted (cp., *e.g.*, Tert., *ad Mart.* i., where they restore the excommunicated). It was not easy to differ from them. The blood shed by martyrs was held to possess an expiatory value like the blood of Christ (cp., *e.g.*, Origen, Hom. xxiv. 1 *in Num.* vol. x. p. 293, Hom. vii. 2. *in Judic.* vol. xi. p. 267). Even in Tertullian's day there were hymns to the martyrs (cp. *de Scorp.* vii: "cantatur et exitus martyrum"). On the other hand, we must not forget how the Christians themselves depreciated martyrdom when the martyrs did not belong to their own party in the church. How the opponents of the Montanists scoffed and sneered at the Montanist confessors! And how meanly Tertullian speaks (*e.g.*, in *de Ieiun.* xii.), towards the end of his life, about the catholic martyrs! Think of Tertullian on Praxeas the confessor, of Hippolytus on Callistus the confessor, of Cyprian on martyrs who were disagreeable to him! And sneers were not all. They spoke of vainglory in this connection, just as Marcus Aurelius did.

[2] Cp., *e.g.*, Justin, *Apol.* ii. 12 (where he admits that the Christian martyrdoms helped to convert him), *Dial.* cx.; Tert., *Apol.* l.; Lact., *Inst.*, v. 19; and August., *Epist.* iii.

shows us that it is the "religio pressa" which invariably waxes strong and large.   Persecution serves as an excellent means of promoting expansion.[1]

From the standpoint of morals, the position of living under a sword which fell but rarely, constituted a serious peril. Christians could go on feeling that they were a persecuted flock.   Yet as a rule they were nothing of the kind.   Theoretically, they could credit themselves with all the virtues of heroism, and yet these were seldom put to the proof.   They could represent themselves as raised above the world, and yet they were constantly bending before it.   As the early Christian literature shows, this unhealthy state of matters led to undesirable consequences.[2]

[1] Reference must be made, however, to the fact that even among Christians there were certain circles which eschewed open confession and martyrdom for good reasons.   Clement of Alexandria and Tertullian (*Scorp.* i.) mention the Valentinians and some other gnostics in this connection.   But obviously there were some in the church who shared this view.   "Nesciunt simplices animae," they held, "quid quomodo scriptum sit, ubi et quando et coram quibus confitendum, nisi quod nec simplicitas ista, sed vanitas, immo dementia pro deo mori, ut qui me salvum faciat.   sic is occidet, qui salvum facere debebit ?   semel Christus pro nobis obiit, semel occisus est, ne occideremur.   si vicem repetit, num et ille salutem de mea nece expectat ?   an deus hominum sanguinem flagitat, maxime si taurorum et hircorum recusat ?   certe peccatoris paenitentiam mavult quam mortem " (" The simple souls do not know what is written, or the meaning of what is written, about where and when and before whom we must make confession ; all they know is that to die for God, who preserves me, is not simple artlessness but folly and madness !   Shall he slay me, who ought to preserve me ?   Christ died once for us, was killed once, that we should not die.   If he requires this in return, does he look for salvation from my death ?   Or does God, who refuses the blood of bulls and goats, demand the blood of men ?   Assuredly he would rather have the sinner repent than die.")   They also said (ch. xv.) that the word of Jesus about confessing him does not apply to a human tribunal but to that of the heavenly ones (æons) through whose sphere the soul rises up after death (" Non in terris confitendum apud homines, minus vero, ne deus humanum sanguinem sitiat nec Christus vicem passionis, quasi et ipse de ea salutem consecuturus, exposcat ").

[2] This does not even take into account the clandestine arrangements made with local authorities, or the intrigues and corruption that went on.   From Tertullian's treatise *de Fuga* we learn that Christian churches in Africa frequently paid moneys to the local funds—*i.e.*, of course, to the local authorities—to ensure that their members were left unmolested.   The authorities themselves often advised this. Cp. Tert., *Apol.* xxvii. : " Datis consilium, quo vobis abutamur " (" You advise us to take unfair advantage of you ") ; and *ad Scap.* iv. : " Cincius Severus [the proconsul] Thysdri ipse dedit remedium, quomodo responderent Christiani, ut dimitti possent " (" Cincius Severus himself pointed out the remedy at Thysdrus, showing how Christians should answer so as to get acquitted ").

The development went on apace between 259 and 303. From the days when Gallienus ruled alone, Gallienus who restored to Christianity the very lands and churches which Valerian had confiscated, down to the nineteenth year of Diocletian, Christians enjoyed a halcyon immunity which was almost equivalent to a manifesto of toleration.[1] Aurelian's attempt at repression never got further than a beginning, and no one followed it up; the emperor and his officials, like Diocletian the reformer subsequently, had other business to attend to. It was during this period that the great expansion of the Christian religion took place. For a considerable period Christians had held property and estates (in the name, I presume, of men of straw); now they could come before the public fearlessly,[2] as if they were a recognized body.[3]

Between 249 and 258, however, two chief and severe persecutions of Christians took place, those under Decius and Valerian, while the last and fiercest began in February of 303. The former lasted only for a year, but they sufficed to spread fearful havoc among the churches. The number of the apostates was much larger, very much larger indeed, than the number of the martyrs. The rescript of Decius, a brutal stroke which was quite unworthy of any statesman, compelled at one blow all Christians, including even women and children, to return to their old religion or else forfeit their lives. Valerian's rescripts were the work of a statesman. They dealt merely with the clergy, with people of good position, and with members of the court; all other Christians were let alone, provided that they refrained from worship. Their lands and churches were,

[1] From the fragments of Porphyry's polemical treatise, and indeed from his writings as a whole, we see how Christians were recognized (in contemporary society) as a well-known party which had no longer to fear any violence.

[2] We do not know under what title they came forward.

[3] Cp. the pagan (Porphyry) in Macar. Magnes., iv. 21 : οἱ Χριστιανοὶ μιμούμενοι τὰς κατασκευὰς τῶν ναῶν μεγίστους οἴκους οἰκοδομοῦσιν ("The Christians erect large buildings, in imitation of the temple-fabrics"). So previously Cæcilius, Minuc. ix.: "Per universum orbem sacraria ista taeterrima impiae coitionis adolescunt" ("All over the world the utterly foul rites of that impious union are flourishing apace"). For details on church-building, see below.—The epithet of Χριστιανός occurs quite openly for the first time, so far as I am aware, in the year 279 upon a tomb in Asia Minor (see Cumont, Les Inscr. chrét. de l'Asie mineure, p. 11).

however, confiscated.[1] The tragic fate of both emperors ("mortes persecutorum!") put a stop to their persecutions. Both had essayed the extirpation of the Christian church, the one by the shortest possible means, the other by more indirect methods.[2] But in both cases the repair of the church was effected promptly and smoothly, while the wide gaps in its membership were soon filled up again, once the rule was laid down that even apostates could be reinstated.

The most severe and prolonged of all the persecutions was the last, the so-called persecution under Diocletian. It lasted longest and raged most fiercely in the east and south-east throughout the domain of Maximinus Daza; it burned with equal fierceness, but for a shorter period, throughout the jurisdiction of Galerius; while over the domain of Maximianus and his successors its vigour was less marked, though it was still very grievous. Throughout the West it came to little. It began with imperial rescripts, modelled upon the statesman-like edict of Valerian, but even surpassing it in adroitness. Presently, however, these degenerated into quite a different form, which, although covered by the previous edicts of Decius, outdid them in pitiless ferocity throughout the East. Daza alone had recourse to preventive measures of a positive character. He had Acts of Pilate fabricated and circulated in all directions (especially throughout schools), which were drawn up in order to misrepresent Jesus;[3] on the strength of confessions extorted

---

[1] The state never attacked the religion of private individuals. All it waged war upon was the refusal to perform the ceremonies of the cultus. Cp. the pregnant statement of the *Acta Cypriani*, i.: "Sacratissimi imperatores praeceperunt, eos qui Romanam religionem non colunt, debere Romanas caerimonias recognoscere" ("The most sacred Roman emperors enjoined that those who did not adhere to the Roman religion should recognize the Roman rites"). It was on principle therefore that Valerian and Diocletian attempted to stamp out Christian worship.

[2] Obviously, they saw that the procedure hitherto adopted was absurd, and that it had failed to harm the church. They rightly judged that Christians must be exterminated, if they were not to be let alone. "They must be sought out and punished" ("Quaerendi et puniendi sunt").

[3] "Even the school teachers were to lecture on these zealously to their pupils, instead of upon the usual scholastic subjects; they were also to see that they were learnt by heart.' "Children at school repeated the names of Jesus and of Pilate every day, and also recited the Acts of Pilate, which were composed in order to deride us."

from Christians, he revived the old, abominable charges brought against them, and had these published far and wide in every city by the authorities (Eus., *H.E.*, i. 9; ix. 5. 7); he got a high official of the state to compose a polemical treatise against Christianity;[1] he invited cities to bring before him anti-Christian petitions;[2] finally—and this was the keenest stroke of all—he attempted to revive and reorganize all the cults, headed of course by that of the Cæsars, upon the basis of the new classification of the provinces, in order to render them a stronger and more attractive counterpoise to Christianity.[3] " He ordered temples to be built in every city, and enacted the careful restoration of such as had collapsed through age; he also established idolatrous priests in all districts and towns, placing a high priest over them in every province, some official who had distinguished himself in some line of public service. This man was also furnished with a military guard of honour." Eus., *H.E.*, viii. 14; see ix. 4: " Idolatrous priests were now appointed in every town, and Maximinus further appointed high priests himself. For the latter position he chose men of distinction in public life, who had gained high credit in all the offices they had filled. They showed great zeal, too, for the worship of those gods." Ever since the close of the second century the synodal organization of the church, with its metropolitans, had been moulded on the provincial diets of the empire—*i.e.*, the latter formed the pattern of the former. But so much more thoroughly had it been worked out, that now, after the lapse of a century, the state attempted itself to copy this synodal organization with its priesthood so firmly centralized and so distinguished for moral character. Perhaps this was the greatest, at any rate it was the most conspicuous, triumph of the church prior to Constantine.

The extent of the apostasy which immediately ensued is

---

[1] The emperor himself is probably concealed behind Hierocles.

[2] The cities were subservient to this command; cp. the inscription of Arycanda and Eus., *H.E.*, ix. 7.

[3] Julian simply copied him in all these measures. The moving spirit of the whole policy was Theoteknus (Eus., *H.E.*, ix. 2 f.), for we cannot attribute it to an emperor who was himself a barbarian and abandoned to the most debased forms of excess.

unknown, but it must have been extremely large. When Constantine conquered Maxentius, however, and when Daza succumbed before Constantine and Licinius, as did Licinius in the end before Constantine, the persecution was over.[1] During its closing years the churches had everywhere recovered from their initial panic; both inwardly and outwardly they had gained in strength. Thus when Constantine stretched out his royal hand, he found a church which was not prostrate and despondent but well-knit, with a priesthood which the persecution had only served to purify. He had not to raise the church from the dust, otherwise that politician would have hardly stirred a finger : on the contrary, the church confronted him, bleeding from many a wound, but unbent and vigorous. All the counteractive measures of the state had proved of no avail; besides, of course, these were no longer supported by public opinion at the opening of the fourth century, as they had been during the second. Then, the state had to curb the fanaticism of public feeling against the Christians ; now, few were to be found who countenanced hard measures of the state against the church. Gallienus himself had, on his deathbed, to revoke the edicts of persecution, and his rescript, which was unkindly phrased (Eus., *H.E.*, viii. 17), was ultimately replaced by Constantine's great and gracious decree of toleration (Eus., *H.E.*, x. 5 ; Lact., *de Mort.* xlviii.).

2

Several examples have been already given (in Book II., Chapters IV. and VI.) of the way in which Christians were thought of by Greek and Roman society and by the common people during the second century.[2] Opinions of a more friendly nature were not common. No doubt, remarks like these were

---

[1] Licinius was driven in the end to become a persecutor of the Christians, by his opposition to Constantine (cp. the conclusion of Eusebius's Church History and his *Vita Const.*, i. *ad fin.*, ii. *ad init.*). Among his laws, that bearing upon the management of prisons (to which allusion has been made already ; cp. p. 164) deserves notice (cp. Eus., *H.E.*, x. 8), as do the rescripts against the mutual intercourse of bishops, the holding of synods, the promiscuous attendance of men and women at worship, and the instruction of women by the bishops (*Vita Const.*, i. 51. 53).

[2] A complete survey is given in my *Gesch. der altchristl. Litt.*, i. pp. 865 f.

to be heard: "Gaius Seius is a capital fellow. Only, he's a
Christian!"—"I'm astonished that Lucius Titius, for all his
knowledge, has suddenly turned Christian" (Tert., *Apol.* iii.).—
"So-and-so thinks of life and of God just as we do, but
he mingles Greek ideas with foreign fables" (Eus., *H.E.*,
vi. 19).[1] They were reproached with being inconceivably
credulous and absolutely devoid of judgment, with being
detestably idle ("contemptissma inertia") and useless for
practical affairs ("infructuositas in negotiis").[2] These, however,
were the least serious charges brought against them. The
general opinion was that Christian doctrine and ethics, with
their absurdities and pretensions,[3] were unworthy of any
one who was free and cultured (so Porphyry especially).[4]

---

[1] This is Porphyry's opinion of Origen. It deserves to be quoted in full, for its
unique character. "Some Christians, ... instead of abandoning the Jewish
scriptures, have addressed themselves to the task of explaining them. These
explanations are neither coherent and consistent, nor do they harmonize with the
text ; instead of furnishing us with a defence of these foreign sects they rather give
us praise and approbation of their doctrines. They produce expositions which
boast of what Moses says unambiguously, as if it were obscure and intricate, and
attach thereto divine influence as to oracles full of hidden mysteries. . . . .
This sort of absurdity can be seen in the case of a man whom I met in my youth
[at Cæsarea], and who at that time was very famous, as he still is by his writings.
I mean Origen, whose fame is widely spread among the teachers of these doctrines.
He was a pupil of Ammonius, the greatest philosopher of our day, and—so far as
knowledge was concerned—he had gained much from the instruction of his
teacher. But in the right conduct of life he went directly against Ammonius. . . . .
Educated as a Greek among Greeks, he diverged to barbarous impudence. To this
he devoted himself and his attainments ; for while he lived outwardly like a
Christian, in this irregular fashion, he was a Greek in his conception of life and of
God, mixing Greek ideas with foreign fables. Plato was his constant companion.
He had also the works of Numenius, Cronius, Apollophanes, Longinus, Moderatus,
Nikomachus, and the most eminent Pythagoreans constantly in his hands. He
also used the writings of the Stoic Chæremon and of Cornutus. Thence he derived
the allegorical method of exegesis common in the Greek mysteries, and applied it
to the Jewish scriptures."

[2] Cp. the charge brought against the consul, T. Flavius Clemens (in Suetonius).
Tert., *Apol.* xlii. : "Infructuosi in negotiis dicimur." What Tertullian makes
the cloak say (*de Pallio*, v. ; cp. above, p. 306) is to be understood as a Christian's
utterance. The heathen retorted that this was "ignavia."

[3] Cp. Tert., *de Scorp.* vii. : "funesta religio, lugubres ritus, ara rogus, pollinctor
sacerdos" (the deadly religion, the mournful ceremonies, the altar-pyre, and the
undertaker-priest).

[4] No one takes the trouble, the apologists complain, to find out what Christianity really is (Tert., *Apol.* i.f.) ; even a pagan thinker would be condemned forth-

The majority, educated and uneducated alike, were still more hostile in the second century. In the foreground of their calumnies stood the two charges of Œdipodean incest and Thyestean banquets, together with that of foreign, outlandish customs, and also of high treason. Moreover, there were clouds of other accusations in the air. Christians,[1] it was reported, were magicians and atheists; they worshipped a god with an ass's head, and adored the cross, the sun, or the genitalia of their priests (Tert., *Apol.* xvi., and the parallels in Minucius).[2] It was firmly believed that they were magicians, that they had control over wind and weather, that they commanded plagues and famines, and had influence over the sacrifices.[3] "Christians to the lions"—this was the cry of

with if he propounded ideas which agree with those of Christianity. Cp. Tert., *de Testim.* i. " Ne suis quidem magistris alias probatissimis atque lectissimis fidem inclinavit humana de incredulitate duritia, sicubi in argumenta Christianae defensionis impingunt. tunc vani poetae . . . . tunc philosophi duri, cum veritates fores pulsant. hactenus sapiens et prudens habebitur qui prope Christianum pronuntiaverit, cum, si quid prudentiae aut sapientiae affectaverit seu caerimonias despuens seu saeculum revincens pro Christiano denotetur " [" The hardness of the human heart in its unbelief prevents them even from crediting their own teachers (who otherwise are highly approved and most excellent), whenever they touch upon any arguments which favour Christianity. Then are the poets vain, ... then are the philosophers senseless, when they knock at the gates of truth. Anyone who goes the length of almost proclaiming Christian ideas will be held to be wise and sagacious so far ; he will be branded as a Christian if he affect wisdom and knowledge in order to scoff at their rites or to expose the age "). Christian writings were not read. " Tanto abest ut nostris literis annuant homines, *ad quas nemo venit nisi iam Christianus*" (Tert., *loc. cit.*: "Far less do men assent to our writings ; nay, none comes to them unless he is a Christian already ").

[1] Christ himself was held to be a magician ; cp. evidence on this point from Justin to Commodian.

[2] It is not difficult to trace the origin of these calumnies. The ass's head came, as Tertullian himself was aware, from the *Histories* of Tacitus, and referred originally to the Jews. They were doubtless worshippers of the sun, because they turned to the east in prayer. The third libel was of course based upon the attitude assumed at confession.

[3] Emphasis was often laid also upon the empty and terrible chimeras circulated by Christians (*Minuc.* v.). Origen (Comment. Ser. *in Matth.* xxxix., vol. iv. p. 270, Lomm.): "Scimus et apud nos terrae motum factum in locis quibusdam et factas fuisse quasdam ruinas, ita ut, qui erant impii extra fidem, causam terrae motus dicerent Christianos, propter quod et persecutiones passae sunt ecclesiae et incensae sunt ; non solum autem illi, sed et qui videbantur prudentes, talia in publico dicerent quia propter Christianos fiunt gravissimi terrae motus " ("We know, too, that there have been earthquakes in our midst,

the mob.[1] And even when people were less rash and cruel, they could not get over the fact that it seemed mere pride and madness to abandon the religion of one's ancestors.[2] Treatises against Christianity were not common in the second or even in the third century, but there may have been controversial debates. A Cynic philosopher named Crescens attacked Justin in public, though he seems to have done no more than echo the popular charges against Christianity. Fronto's attack moved almost entirely upon the same level, if it be the case that his arguments have been borrowed in part by the pagan Cæcilius in Minucius Felix. Lucian merely trifled with the question of Christianity. He was no more than a reckless, though an acute, journalist. The orator Aristides, again, wrote upon Christianity with ardent contempt,[3] while the treatise of

With several ruinous results, so that the impious unbelievers declared that Christians were to blame for the earthquakes. Hence the churches have suffered persecutions and been burnt. And not only such people, but others who seemed really sensible gave open expression to the opinion that Christians are the cause of the fearful earthquakes"). Similar allusions often occur in Tertullian. The fear of Christians influencing the sacrifices played some part in the initial persecution of Diocletian.

[1] "Christianos ad leones !" Tertullian recalls this fearful shout no fewer than four times (*Apol.* xl., *de Spectac.* xxvii., *de Exhort.* xii., *de Resurr.* xxiii.).

[2] Cp. Clem. Alex., *Protrept.*, x. 89: ἀλλ' ἐκ πατέρων, φατέ, παραδεδομένον ἡμῖν ἔθος ἀνατρέπειν οὐκ εὔλογον ("But, you say, it is discreditable to overturn the custom handed down to us from our fathers"). The author of the pseudo-Justin *Cohort. ad Græcos* goes into this argument with particular thoroughness (cp. i., xiv., xxxv.–xxxvi.).

[3] *Orat.* xlvi. He defends "the Greek nationality against the Christian and philosophic cosmopolitanism." To him, Christians are despisers of Hellenism (cp. Bernays, *Ges. Abhandl.*, ii. p. 364). How a man like Tatian must have irritated him ! Neumann (*Der röm. Staat u. die allgem. Kirche*, p. 36) thus recapitulates the charge of Aristides (though Lightfoot, in his *Ignatius*, vol. i. p. 517, thinks that it is the Cynics who are pilloried): "People who themselves are simply of no account venture to slander a Demosthenes, while solecisms at least, if nothing more, are to be found in every one of their own words. Despicable creatures themselves, they despise others; they pride themselves on their virtues, but never practise them ; they preach self-control, and are lustful. Community of interests is their name for robbery, philosophy for ill-will, and poverty for an indifference to the good things of life. Moreover, they degrade themselves by their avarice. Impudence is dubbed freedom by them, malicious talk becomes openness forsooth, the acceptance of charity is humanity. Like the godless folk in Palestine, they combine servility with sauciness. They have severed themselves deliberately from the Greeks, or rather from all that is good in the world. Incapable of co-operating for any useful end whatsoever, they yet are masters of the art

Hierocles, which is no longer extant, is described by Eusebius as extremely trivial. Celsus and Porphyry alone remain, of Christianity's opponents.[1] Only two men; but they were a host in themselves.

They resembled one another in the seriousness with which they undertook their task, in the pains they spent on it, in the loftiness of their designs, and in their literary skill. The great difference between them lay in their religious standpoint. Celsus's interest centres at bottom in the Roman empire.[2] He is a religious man because the empire needs religion, and also because every educated man is responsible for its religion. It is hard to say what his own conception of the world amounts to. But for all the hues it assumes, it is never coloured like that of Cicero or of Seneca. For Celsus is an agnostic above all things,[3]

of undermining a household and setting its members by the ears. Not a word, not an idea, not a deed of theirs has ever borne fruit. They take no part in organizing festivals, nor do they pay honour to the gods. They occupy no seats on civic councils, they never comfort the sad, they never reconcile those who are at variance, they do nothing for the advancement of the young, or indeed of anybody. They take no thought for style, but creep into a corner and talk stupidly. They are venturing already on the cream of Greece and calling themselves 'philosophers'! As if changing the name meant anything! As if that could of itself turn a Thersites into a Hyacinthus or a Narcissus!"

[1] Lactantius professes to know that "plurimi et multi" wrote in Greek and Latin against the Christians in Diocletian's reign (*Instit.*, v. 4), but even he adduces only one anonymous writer besides Hierocles. Occasionally a single *littérateur* who was hostile to Christianity stirred up a local persecution, as, *e.g.*, was probably the case with Crescens the Cynic philosopher at Rome. Even before the edict of Decius a persecution had broken out in Alexandria, of which Dionysius (in Eus., *H.E.*, vi. 41. 1) writes as follows: οὐκ ἀπὸ τοῦ βασιλικοῦ προστάγματος ὁ διωγμὸς παρ' ἡμῖν ἤρξατο, ἀλλὰ γὰρ ὅλον ἐνιαυτὸν προύλαβε, καὶ φθάσας ὁ κακῶν τῇ πόλει ταύτῃ μάντις καὶ ποιητής, ὅστις ἐκεῖνος ἦν, ἐκίνησε καὶ παρώρμησε καθ' ἡμῶν τὰ πλήθη τῶν ἐθνῶν, εἰς τὴν ἐπιχώριον αὐτοὺς δεισιδαιμονίαν ἀναρριπίσας ("Our persecution did not begin with the imperial decree, but preceded that decree by a whole year. The prophet and framer of evil for this city, whoever he was, previously stirred up and aroused against us the pagan multitude, reviving in them the superstition of their country").

[2] We can only surmise about his personality and circumstances. He represented the noble, patriotic, and intelligent bureaucracy of Rome, about which we know so little otherwise.

[3] The same sort of attitude is adopted by the pagan Cæcilius (in *Min. Felix*, v. f.), a sceptic who approves of religion in general, but who entertains grave doubts about a universal providence. "Amid all this uncertainty, your best and noblest course is to accept the teaching of your forebears, to honour the religious customs which have been handed down to you, and humbly to adore the deities

so that he appreciates the relative validity of idealism apart from any stiffening of Stoicism, just as he appreciates the relative validity of every national religion, and even of mythology itself. Porphyry,[1] on the other hand, is a thinker pure and simple, as well as a distinguished critic. And he is not merely a religious philosopher of the Platonic school, but a man of deeply religious temperament, for whom all thought tends to pass into the knowledge of God, and in that knowledge to gain its goal.

Our first impression is that Celsus has not a single good word to say for Christianity. He re-occupies the position taken by its opponents in the second century; only, he is too fair and noble an adversary to repeat their abominable charges. To him Christianity, this bastard progeny of Judaism [2]—itself the basest of all national religions—appears to have been nothing but an absurd and sorry tragedy from its birth down to his own day. He is perfectly aware of the internal differences between Christians, and he is familiar with the various stages of development in the history of their religion. These are cleverly employed in order to heighten the impression of its instability. He plays off the sects against the catholic church, the primitive age against the present, Christ against the apostles, the various revisions of the Bible against the trustworthiness of the text, and so forth, although, of course, he admits that the whole thing was quite as bad at first as it is at present. Even Christ is not exempted from this criticism. What is valuable in his teaching was borrowed from the philosophers; the rest, *i.e.*, whatever is characteristic of himself, is error and deception, so much futile

---

whom your fathers taught you not to know but, first and foremost, to fear." Chap. vii. then runs in quite a pious current.

[1] Born at Tyre. His original name was Malchus, so that he was a Semite (for Malchus as a Christian name in the vicinity of Cæsarea (Pal.) during Valerian's reign, cp. Eus., *H.E.*, vii. 12).

[2] Like Porphyry and Julian at a later period, however, Celsus lets Judaism alone, because it was a national religion. Apropos of an oracle of Apollo against the Christians, Porphyry observes : " In his quidem irremediabile sententiae Christianorum manifestavit Apollo, quoniam Judaei suscipiunt deum magis quam isti" (" In these verses Apollo exposed the incurable corruption of Christians, since it is the Jews, said he, more than the Christians, who recognize God "), Aug., *de Civit. Dei*, xix. 26.

mythology. In the hands of those deceived deceivers, the apostles, this was still further exaggerated ; faith in the resurrection rests upon nothing better than the evidence of a deranged woman, and from that day to this the mad folly has gone on increasing and exercising its power—for the assertion, which is flung out at one place, that it would speedily be swept out of existence, is retracted on a later page. Christianity, in short, is an anthropomorphic myth of the very worst type. Christian belief in providence is a shameless insult to the Deity—a chorus of frogs, forsooth, squatting in a bog and croaking, " For our sakes was the world created " !

But there is another side to all this. The criticism of Celsus brings out some elements of truth which deserve to be considered ; and further, wherever the critic bethinks himself of religion, he betrays throughout his volume an undercurrent of feeling which is far from being consonant with his fierce verdict. For although he shuts his eyes to it, apparently unwilling to admit that Christianity could be, and had already been, stated reasonably, he cannot get round that fact ; indeed—unless we are quite deceived—he has no intention whatever of concealing it from the penetrating reader. Since there has really to be such a thing as religion, since it is really a necessity, the agnosticism of Celsus leads him to make a concession which does not differ materially from the Christian conception of God. He cannot take objection to much in the ethical counsels of Jesus—his censure of them as a plagiarism being simply the result of perplexity. And when Christians assert that the Logos is the Son of God, what can Celsus do but express his own agreement with this dictum ? Finally, the whole book culminates in a warm patriotic appeal to Christians not to withdraw from the common *régime*, but to lend their aid in order to enable the emperor to maintain the vigour of the empire with all its ideal benefits.[1] Law and piety must be upheld against their inward and external foes ! Surely we can read between

---

[1] In several of the proceedings against Christians the magistrate expresses his concern lest the exclusiveness of Christians excite anarchy ; cp., *e.g.*, the *Acta Fructuosi Tarrac.* ii. : " Qui audiuntur, qui timentur, qui adorantur, si dii non coluntur nec imperatorum vultus adorantur ? "

the lines. Claim no special position for yourselves, says Celsus, in effect, to Christians! Don't rank yourselves on the same level as the empire! On these terms we are willing to tolerate you and your religion. At bottom, in fact, the "True Word" of Celsus is nothing more than a political pamphlet, a thinly disguised overture for peace.[1]

A hundred years later, when Porphyry wrote against the Christians, a great change had come over the situation. Christianity had become a power. It had taken a Greek shape, but "the foreign myths" were still retained, of course, while in most cases at least it had preserved its sharp distinction between the creator and the creation, or between God and nature, as well as its doctrine of the incarnation and its paradoxical assertions of an end for the world and of the resurrection. This was where Porphyry struck in, that great philosopher of the ancient world. He was a pupil of Plotinus and Longinus. For years he had been engaged in keen controversy at Rome with teachers of the church and gnostics, realizing to the full that the matter at stake was God himself and the treasure possessed by mankind, viz., rational religious truth. Porphyry knew nothing of political ideals. The empire had indeed ceased to fill many people with enthusiasm. Its restorer had not yet arrived upon the scene, and religious philosophy was living meanwhile in a State which it wished to begin and rebuild. Porphyry himself retired to Sicily, where he wrote his fifteen books "Against the Christians." This work, which was "answered" by four leading teachers of the church (Methodius, Eusebius, Apollinarius, and Philostorgius), perished, together with his other polemical treatises, owing to the victory of the church and by order of the emperor. All that we possess is a number of fragments, of which the most numerous and important occur in Macarius Magnes. For I have no doubt whatever that Porphyry is the pagan philosopher in that author's "Apocriticus."[2]

---

[1] Cæcilius, too, was in the last resort a politician and a patriot, since he defended the old religion by asserting that "by means of it Rome has won the World" (*Min. Felix*, vi.).

[2] At best we must leave it an open question whether a plagiarism has been perpetrated upon Porphyry.

This work of Porphyry is perhaps the most ample and thoroughgoing treatise which has ever been written against Christianity. It earned for its author the titles of πάντων δυσμενέστατος καὶ πολεμώτατος ("most malicious and hostile of all"), "hostis dei, veritatis inimicus, sceleratarum artium magister" (God's enemy, a foe to truth, a master of accursed arts), and so forth.[1] But, although our estimate can only be based on fragments, it is not too much to say that the controversy between the philosophy of religion and Christianity lies to-day in the very position in which Porphyry placed it. Even at this time of day Porphyry remains unanswered. Really he is unanswerable, unless one is prepared first of all to agree with him and proceed accordingly to reduce Christianity to its quintessence. In the majority of his positive statements he was correct, while in his negative criticism of what represented itself in the third century to be Christian doctrine, he was certainly as often right as wrong. In matters of detail he betrays a good deal of ignorance, and he forgets standards of criticism which elsewhere he has at his command.

The weight which thus attaches to his work is due to the fact that it was based upon a series of very thoroughgoing studies of the Bible, and that it was undertaken from the religious standpoint. Moreover, it must be conceded that the author's aim was neither to be impressive nor to persuade or take the reader by surprise, but to give a serious and accurate refutation of Christianity. He wrought in the bitter sweat of his brow—this idealist, who was convinced that whatever was refuted would collapse. Accordingly, he confined his attention to what he deemed the cardinal points of the controversy. These four points were as follows:—He desired to demolish the myths of Christianity, i.e., to prove that, in so far as they

---

[1] Augustine, however, called him "the noble philosopher, the great philosopher of the Gentiles, the most learned of philosophers, although the keenest foe to Christians" ("philosophus nobilis, magnus gentilium philosophus, doctissimus philosophorum, quamvis Christianorum acerrimus inimicus," de Civit. Dei, xix. 22). Compare the adjectives showered on him by Jerome: "Fool, impious, blasphemer, mad, shameless, a sycophant, a calumniator of the church, a mad dog attacking Christ" ("Stultus, impius, blasphemus, vesanus, impudens, sycophantes, calumniator ecclesiae, rabidus adversus Christum canis").

were derived from the Old and New Testaments, they were
historically untenable, since these sources were themselves
turbid and full of contradictions. He did not reject the Bible
in toto as a volume of lies. On the contrary, he valued a great
deal of it as both true and divine. Nor did he identify the
Christ of the gospels with the historical Christ.[1] For the
latter he entertained a deep regard, which rose to the pitch of a
religion. But with relentless powers of criticism he showed in
scores of cases that if certain traits in the gospels were held to
be historical, they could not possibly be genuine, and that they
blurred and distorted the figure of Christ. He dealt similarly
with the ample materials which the church put together
from the Old Testament as "prophecies of Christ." But the
most interesting part of his criticism is unquestionably that
passed upon Paul. If there are any lingering doubts in the
mind as to whether the apostle should be credited, in the last
instance, to Jewish instead of to Hellenistic Christianity, these
doubts may be laid to rest by a study of Porphyry. This

---

[1] It is only in a modified sense, therefore, that he can be described as an
"opponent" of Christianity. As Wendland very truly puts it, in his *Christentum
u. Hellenismus* (1902), p. 12, "The fine remarks of Porphyry in the third book
of his περὶ τῆς ἐκ λογίων φιλοσοφίας (pp. 180 f., Wolff), remarks to which theologians have not paid attention, show how from the side of Neoplatonism also
attempts were made to bring about a mutual understanding and reconciliation."
"Praeter opinionem," says Porphyry (cp. August., *de Civit. Dei*, xix. 23), "profecto quibusdam videatur esse quod dicturi sumus. Christum enim dii piissimum
pronuntiaverunt et immortalem factum et cum bona praedicatione eius meminerunt,
Christianos vero pollutos et contaminatos et errore implicatos esse dicunt"
("What I am going to say may indeed appear extraordinary to some people.
The gods have declared Christ to have been most pious ; he has become immortal,
and by them his memory is cherished. Whereas the Christians are a polluted sect,
contaminated and enmeshed in error "). Origen (*Cels.*, I. xv., IV. li.) tells how
Numenius, the Pythagorean philosopher, quoted the Jewish scriptures with deep
respect, interpreting them allegorically (*Clem. Alex.*, *Strom.*, i. 22. 150, indeed
ascribes to him the well-known saying that Plato is simply Moses Atticizing—
τί γάρ ἐστι Πλάτων ἢ Μωυσῆς ἀττικίζων ; cp. also Hesych. Miles. in Müller's
Fragm. Hist. Gr., iv. 171, and Suidas, s. v. "Νουμήνιος," with the more cautious
remarks of Eusebius in his *Præp.*, xi. 9. 8-18, 25). Amelius the Platonist, a contemporary of Origen, quoted the gospel of John with respect (Eus., *Præp.*, xi.
19. 1) ; cp. August., *de Civit. Dei*, x. 29: "Initium evangelii secundum Johannem
quidam Platonicus aureis litteris conscribendum et per omnes ecclesias in locis
eminentissimis proponendum esse dicebat " ("A certain Platonist used to say that
the opening of John's gospel should be inscribed in golden letters and set up in
the most prominent places of every church ").

critic, a Hellenist of the first water, feels keener antipathy to Paul than to any other Christian. Paul's dialectic is totally unintelligible to him, and he therefore deems it both sophistical and deceitful. Paul's proofs resolve themselves for him into flat contradictions, whilst in the apostle's personal testimonies he sees merely an unstable, rude, and insincere rhetorician, who is a foe to all noble and liberal culture. It is from the hostile criticism of Porphyry that we learn for the first time what highly cultured Greeks found so obnoxious in the idiosyncrasies of Paul. In matters of detail he pointed to much that was really offensive; but although the offence in Paul almost always vanishes so soon as the critic adopts a different standpoint, Porphyry never lighted upon that standpoint.[1]

Negative criticism upon the historical character of the Christian religion, however, merely paved the way for Porphyry's full critical onset upon the three doctrines of the faith which he regarded as its most heinous errors. The first of these was the Christian doctrine of creation, which separated the world from God, maintained its origin within time, and excluded any reverent, religious view of the universe as a whole. In rejecting this he also rejected the doctrine of the world's overthrow as alike irrational and irreligious; the one was involved in the other. He then directed his fire against the doctrine of the Incarnation, arguing that the Christians made a false separation (by their doctrine of a creation in time) and

---

[1] The apostle Paul began to engage the attention of pagans as well. This comes out, *e.g.*, in the cross-examinations of the Egyptian governor Culcianus (shortly after 303 A.D.), as is confirmed by the two discussions between him and Phileas and Dioscorus (cp. Quentin, " Passio S. Dioscuri " in *Anal. Boll.*, vol. xxv., 1905, pp. 321 f.), discussions which otherwise are quite independent of each other. In the latter Culcianus asks, " Was Paul a god ? " In the former he asks, " He did not immolate himself ? " Further, " Paul was not a persecutor ? " " Paul was not an uneducated person ? He was not a Syrian ? He did not dispute in Syriac ? " (To which Phileas replies, " He was a Hebrew ; he disputed in Greek, and held wisdom to be the chief thing.") Finally, " Perhaps you are going to claim that he excelled Plato ? " I know of nothing like this in other cross-examinations, and I can only conjecture, with Quentin, that it is an authentic trait. At that period, about the beginning of the Diocletian persecution, the Scriptures were ordered to be given up. The very fact of this order shows that the state had come to recognize their importance, and this in turn presupposes, as it promoted, a certain acquaintance with their contents.

a false union (by their doctrine of the incarnation) between God and the world. Finally, there was the opposition he offered to the Christian doctrine of the resurrection.

On these points Porphyry was inexorable, warring against Christianity as against the worst of mankind's foes; *but in every other respect he was quite at one with the Christian philosophy of religion, and was perfectly conscious of this unity.* And in his day the Christian philosophy of religion was no longer entirely inexorable on the points just mentioned; it made great efforts to tone down its positions for the benefit of Neoplatonism, as well as to vindicate its scientific (and therefore its genuinely Hellenic) character.

How close [1] the opposing forces already stood to one another! Indeed, towards the end of his life Porphyry seems to have laid greater emphasis upon the points which he held in common with the speculations of Christianity; [2] the letter he addressed to his wife Marcella might almost have been written by a Christian. [3]

In the work of Porphyry Hellenism wrote its testament with regard to Christianity—for Julian's polemical treatise savoured

---

[1] This is particularly clear from the Neoplatonic works which were translated into Latin, and which came into the possession of Augustine (*Confess.*, vii. 9). He owed a great deal to them, although he naturally conceals part of his debt. He admits frankly that the ideas of John i. 1–5, 9, 10, 13, 16, and Phil. ii. 6, were contained in these volumes.

[2] The magical, thaumaturgic element which Porphyry, for all his clear, scientific intellect, held in honour, was probably allowed to fall into the background while he attacked the Christians. But his Christian opponents took note of it. Here, indeed, was one point on which *they* were the more enlightened of the two parties, so far as they were not already engulfed themselves in the cult of relics and bones. The characterization of Porphyry which Augustine gives in the *de Civit. Dei* (x. 9) is admirable: "Nam et Porphyrius quandam quasi purgationem animae per theurgian, cunctanter tamen et pudibunda quodam modo disputatione, promittit, reversionem vero ad deum hanc artem praestare cuiquam negat, ut videas eum inter vitium sacrilegae curiositatis et philosophiae professionem sententiis alternantibus fluctuare" ("For even Porphyry holds out the prospect of some kind of purgation of the soul by aid of theurgy; though he does so with some hesitation and shame, denying that this art can secure for anyone a return to God. Thus you can detect his judgment vacillating between the profession of philosophy and an art which he feels to be both sacrilegious and presumptuous").

[3] The Christian charm of the letter comes from the pagan basis of the Sextus sayings which are preserved in the Christian recension; cp. my *Chronologie*, ii. 2. pp. 190 f.

more of a retrograde movement. The church managed to get the testament ignored and invalidated, but not until she had four times answered its contentions. It is an irreparable loss that these replies have not come down to us, though it is hardly a loss so far as their authors are concerned.

We have no information regarding the effect produced by the work, beyond what may be gathered from the horror displayed by the fathers of the church. Yet even a literary work of superior excellence could hardly have won the day. The religion of the church had become a world-religion by the time that Porphyry wrote, and no professor can wage war successfully against such religions, unless his hand grasps the sword of the reformer as well as the author's pen.

The daily intercourse of Christians and pagans is not to be estimated, even in Tertullian's age, from the evidence supplied by episodes of persecution. It is unnecessary to read between the lines of his ascetic treatises, for numerous passages show, involuntarily but unmistakably, that as a rule everything went on smoothly in their mutual relationships. People lived together, bought and sold, entertained each other, and even intermarried. In later days it was certainly not easy to distinguish absolutely between a Christian and a non-Christian in daily life. Many a Christian belonged to "society" (see Book IV. Chap. II.), and the number of those who took umbrage at the faith steadily diminished. Julius Africanus was the friend of Alexander Severus and Abgar. Hippolytus corresponded with the empress. Origen had a position in the world of scholarship, where he enjoyed great repute. Paul of Samosata, who was a bishop, formed an influential and familar figure in the city of Antioch. The leading citizens of Carthage—who do not seem to have been Christians—were friends of Cyprian, according to the latter's biography (ch. xiv.), and even when he lay in prison they were true to him. "Meantime a large number of eminent people assembled, people, too, of high rank and good family as well as of excellent position in this world. All of these, for the sake of their old friendship with Cyprian, advised him to beat a retreat. And to make their advice substantial, they further offered him places to which he might retire " (" Conveniebant interim plures egregii et clarissimi ordinis et sanguinis, sed et saeculi nobilitate generosi, qui propter amicitiam eius antiquam secessum subinde suaderent, et ne parum esset nuda suadela, etiam loca in quae secederet offerebant "). Arnobius, Lactantius, and several others were philosophers and teachers of repute. Yet all this cannot obscure the fact that, even by the opening of the fourth century, Christianity still found *the learning of the ancient world*, so far as that survived, in opposition to itself. One swallow does not make a summer. One Origen, for all his following, could not avail to change the real posture of affairs. Origen's Christianity was passed over as an idiosyncrasy ; it commended itself to but a small section of contemporary scholars ; and while people learned criticism, erudition, and philosophy from him, they shut their eyes to his religion. Nor were matters otherwise till the middle of the fourth century. Learning continued to be " pagan." It was the great theologians of Cappadocia and, to a more limited extent, those of Antioch (though the latter, judged by modern standards, were more scientific than the former), who were the first to inaugurate a change in this respect, albeit within well-defined limits. They were followed in this by Augustine. Throughout the East, ancient learning really never came to terms at all with Christianity, not even by the opening of the fifth century ; but, on the other hand, it was too weak to be capable of maintaining itself side by side with the church in her position of privilege, and consequently it perished by degrees. By the time that it died, however, Christianity had secured possession of a segment, which was by no means inconsiderable, of the circle of human learning.

Conclusion

Hergenröther (*Handbuch der allgem. Kirchengesch.*, i. pp. 109 f.) has drawn up, with care and judgment, a note of twenty causes for the expansion of Christianity, together with as many causes which must have operated against it. The survey is not without value, but it does not clear up the problem. If the missionary preaching of Christianity in word and deed embraced all that we have attempted to state in Book II., and if it was allied to forces such as those which have come under our notice in Book III., then it is hardly possible to name the collective reasons for the success, or for the retardation, of the movement. Still less can one think of grading them, or of determining their relative importance one by one. Finally, one has always to recollect not only the variety of human aptitudes and needs and culture, but also the development which the missionary preaching of Christianity itself passed through, between the initial stage and the close of the third century.

Reflecting more closely upon this last-named consideration, one realizes that the question here has not been correctly put, and also that it does not admit of any simple, single answer. At the opening of the mission we have Paul and some anonymous apostles. They preach the unity of God and the near advent of judgment, bringing tidings to mankind of Jesus Christ, who had recently been crucified, as the Son of God, the Judge, the Saviour. Almost every statement here seems paradoxical and upsetting. Towards the close of our epoch, there was probably hardly one regular missionary at work. The scene was occupied by a powerful church with an impressive cultus of its own, with priests, and with sacraments, embracing a system of doctrine and a philosophy of religion which were capable of competing on successful terms with any of their rivals. *This church exerted a missionary influence in virtue of her very existence, inasmuch as she came forward to represent the consummation of all previous movements in the history of religion. And to this church the human race round the basin of the Mediterranean belonged without exception, about the year 300, in so far as the religion, morals, and higher attainments of these nations were of any consequence.* The paradoxical, the staggering elements in Christianity were still there. Only, they were set in a broad frame of what was familiar and desirable and " natural"; they were clothed in a vesture of mysteries which made people either glad to welcome any strange, astonishing item in the religion, or at least able to put up with it.[1]

---

[1] Alongside of the church in its developed form, one man may perhaps be mentioned who did more than all the rest put together for the mission of Christi-

Thus, in the first instance at any rate, our question must not run, "How did Christianity win over so many Greeks and Romans as to become ultimately the strongest religion in point of numbers?" The proper form of our query must be, "How did Christianity express itself, so as *inevitably* to become the religion for the world, tending more and more to displace other religions, and drawing men to itself as to a magnet?" For an answer to this question we must look partly to the history of Christian dogma and of the Christian cultus. For the problem does not lie solely within the bounds of the history of Christian missions, and although we have kept it in view throughout the present work, it is impossible within these pages to treat it exhaustively.

One must first of all answer this question by getting some idea of *the particular shape* assumed by Christianity as a missionary force about the year 50, the year 100, the year 150, the year 200, the year 250, and the year 300 respectively, before we can think of raising the further question as to what forces may have been dominant in the Christian propaganda at any one of these six epochs. Neither, of course, must we overlook the difference between the state of matters in the East and in the West, as well as in several groups of provinces. And even were one to fulfil all these preliminary conditions, one could not proceed to refer to definite passages as authoritative for a solution of the problem. All over, one has to deal with considerations which are of a purely general character. I must leave it to others to exhibit these considerations— with the caveat that it is easy to disguise the inevitable uncertainties that meet us in this field by means of the pedantry which falls back on rubrical headings. The results of any survey will be trustworthy only in so far as they amount to such commonplaces as, *e.g.*, that the distinctively religious element was a stronger factor in the mission at the outset than at a later period, that a similar remark applies to the charitable

anity among the learned classes, not only during his lifetime, but still more after his death. I mean Origen. He was the "Synzygus" of the Eastern church in the third century. The abiding influence of the man may be gathered, two centuries after he died, from the pages of Socrates the church historian. He domiciled the religion of the church in Hellenism (for thinkers and cultured people), so far as such a domicile was possible.

and economic element in Christianity, that the conflict with polytheism attracted some people and offended others, that the same may be said of the rigid morality, and so forth.

From the very outset Christianity came forward with a spirit of *universalism*, by dint of which it laid hold of *the entire life of man* in all its functions, throughout its heights and depths, in all its feelings, thoughts, and actions. This guaranteed its triumph. In and with its universalism, it also declared that the Jesus whom it preached was the *Logos*. To him it referred everything that could possibly be deemed of human value, and from him it carefully excluded whatever belonged to the purely natural sphere. From the very first it embraced humanity and the world, despite the small number of the elect whom it contemplated. Hence it was that those very powers of attraction, by means of which it was enabled at once to absorb and to subordinate the whole of Hellenism, had a new light thrown upon them. They appeared almost in the light of a necessary feature in that age. Sin and foulness it put far from itself. But otherwise it built itself up by the aid of any element whatsoever that was still capable of vitality (above all, by means of a powerful organization). Such elements it crushed as rivals and conserved as materials of its own life. It could do so for one reason—a reason which no one voiced, and of which no one was conscious, yet which every truly pious member of the church expressed in his own life. The reason was, that Christianity, viewed in its essence, was something simple, something which could blend with coefficients of the most diverse nature, something which, in fact, sought out all such coefficients. For Christianity, in its simplest terms, meant God as the Father, the Judge and the Redeemer of men, revealed in and through Jesus Christ.

And was not this religion bound to conquer? *Alongside of* other religions it could not hold its own for any length of time; still less could it succumb. Yes, victory was inevitable. It had to prevail. All the motives which operated in its extension are as nothing when taken one by one, in face of the propaganda which it exercised by means of its own development from Paul to Origen, a development which maintained withal an exclusive attitude towards polytheism and idolatry of every kind.

ADDENDA TO VOLUME I

P. 57, note 2, add: "We cannot at this point enter into the very complicated question of Paul's reputation in the Gentile church. The highest estimate of him prevailed among the Marcionites. Origen, after declaring that they held that Paul sat on Christ's right hand in heaven, with Marcion on his left, adds: 'Porro alii legentes: Mittam vobis advocatum spiritum veritatis, volunt intellegere apostolum Paulum' (Hom. xxv. *in Lucam*, vol. v. pp. 181 f., ed. Lomm.). Even were these people supposed to belong to the Catholic church—which I think unlikely—this conception would not be characteristic of the great church. It would be rather abnormal."

P. 57, line 5 from top, add the following note: "The persecution of king Herod now began. It was directed against the twelve (Acts xii.). He made an example of James the son of Zebedee, whom he caused to be executed (why, we do not know). Then he had Peter put in prison, and, although the latter escaped death, he had to leave Jerusalem. This took place in the twelfth year after the death of Christ. Thereafter only individual apostles are to be found at Jerusalem. Peter was again there at the Apostolic Council (so called). Paul makes his agreement not with the eleven, however, but simply with Peter, James the Lord's brother, and John. Where were the rest? Were they no longer in Jerusalem? or did they not count on such an occasion?"

PRINTED BY
NEILL AND COMPANY, LIMITED,
EDINBURGH.